THE INTERNATIONAL DIRECTORY OF

CIVIL AIRCRAFT

2003/2004

by Gerard Frawley

Contents

Published by Aerospace Publications Pty Ltd (ACN: 001 570 458) PO Box 1777, Fyshwick ACT 2609, Australia.
Phone (02) 6280 0111, fax (02) 6280 0007, website address www.ausaviation.com.au – publishers of monthly
Australian Aviation magazine.

ISBN 1 875671 58 7

Front cover: (top left) A340-600 [Paul Merritt]; (top right) Bombardier CRJ700 [Bombardier]; (bottom left) Eurocopter EC 130 [Eurocopter]; (bottom right) Pilatus PC-12 [Paul Merritt]. Back cover (clockwise from top left): MD-11 [Swiss]; Antonov An-225 [Paul Merritt]; Bell/Agusta AB139 [Paul Merritt]; ERJ 145 [Embraer]; Douglas DC-3; Mooney Ovation [Mooney].

Photographers' websites:
Paul Sadler - www.southernskyphoto.com.au
Paul Merritt - www.aviationexposure.com
Sebastian Zacharias - www.aviaarchive.com
Toni Marimon - http://fly.to/pmi
Lars Wahlstrom - www.imcat.com
Alvaro Romero - http://geocities.com/alvaror.geo/
Jonathan Derden - www.av8rphotos.com
Don Boyd - www.sunbirdphotos.com

Introduction

This is the fifth edition of the *International Directory of Civil Aircraft*. Thank you for purchasing it, I hope you find it of value.

Like its predecessors, this edition aims to present a comprehensive reference on almost every single civil aircraft (excluding kitplanes, ultralights and very light aircraft) in use or under development around the world. All told this volume includes 394 aircraft entries, including more than a dozen new types.

The new aircraft entries range from the Cessna Citation Mustang to the Sukhoi S-80. A small number of entries in the previous edition have been deleted, due to program cancellations or retirements from service (including the Bristol Freighter, Shorts Belfast and the cancelled 747X). Of those entries carried over, almost every one has been changed and revised, many quite significantly. In particular aircraft in production evolve over time with improvements made and new subvariants released, and this book details all these changes and is up to date as at late December 2002. Most of the photographs are new.

The aircraft are presented alphabetically by manufacturer and then either by model number, chronologically, or by family types. In some cases aircraft may appear out of strict model number order to allow variants of the same basic family to appear on the same and/or facing pages, allowing easy comparisons of related models.

Aircraft manufacturer mergers and rationalisations means there is the potential for confusion about under which manufacturer's name and some aircraft entries should appear. The general rule here is if the aircraft is *currently in production* it is listed under the name of its manufacturer (ie Boeing 717 and not McDonnell Douglas MD-95), if the aircraft is out of production, it is listed under the manufacturer's name with which it is most closely related (ie McDonnell Douglas MD-80). If you are unsure where an aircraft appears, try the comprehensive index at the back of the book.

A fully revised and updated *International Directory of Civil Aircraft* is released every two years, with the replacement for this book due to appear in early 2005. In the meantime the next edition of the companion *International Directory of Military Aircraft* is due for release in early 2004. Between them the military and civil aircraft directories provide an unparalleled, affordable reference source on over 700 civil and military aircraft.

Finally, thanks to those that helped with this book, which, with its more than 200,000 words of text and 400 or so photographs, is no small task. Several photographers deserve thanks, including Rob Finlayson, Keith Gaskell, Sebastian Zacharias, Toni Marimon, Peter Vercruijsse, Bill Lines, Paul Merritt and Paul Sadler. *Propliner* magazine's Tony Merton Jones allowed me to pick his brains on the status of a number of older airliners/freighters. Numerous aircraft manufacturer reps responded to requests for information. Publisher Jim Thorn also leant his hand to proofreading, while Lee-Ann Sim was invaluable with her production work. Finally, thanks to an ever patient Kerrie for her support.

Gerard Frawley
Canberra, January 2003.

Civil Aviation in Review

September 11 2001. Two hijacked airliners plunge into New York's World Trade Center Twin Towers, a third into the Pentagon in Washington, and a fourth into a Pennsylvania field. The Twin Towers collapse. Three thousand innocent people are killed. And the US airline and aerospace industry begins to haemorrhage.

The scars of the world's most spectacular act of terrorism are taking a long time to heal. Leaving aside the vast human tragedy of these events, the economic damage caused to the aerospace industry in the US in particular is immense in scale, and their effects will take some years to play out.

Even before September 11, America's airlines were beginning to hurt, a reflection of a softening economy. September 11's *Wall Street Journal* predicted that US airlines would lose $US2.5bn in 2001. Sadly, following the impact of the terror attacks, *individual airlines* would soon post losses of that size.

The immediate impact of the terror attacks was a total shutdown of the US air transport system. Thousands of flights across North America were instructed to land immediately. For days no commercial or civil aircraft flew in the US, and the air transport system came to an almost instant halt.

Within a week flights were allowed to resume, but normalcy did not. US Air Force fighters patrolled major cities and landmarks to shoot down any new hijacked airliners. Armed soldiers patrolled airports. The flying public stayed away from flying in droves. The US President and Congress approved a $US15bn bailout package for US airlines. Plans for increased aircraft security and sky marshals were drawn up.

US airlines drastically cut capacity and flight frequencies, announcing wholesale retirements of aircraft fleet types. Passengers were put off flying by the fear of more terror attacks and an increased 'hassle factor', mainly longer check-in times due to increased security measures.

Through 2002 there was no recovery in traffic in the United States, but that nation's general economic malaise has not helped, and in the US airlines have been swimming in a sea of red ink. Consequently there have been two high profile bankruptcy filings – US Airways and United Airlines, which fly on under Chapter 11 protection from creditors – and continued restructuring across the industry.

What affects the airlines obviously affects the companies that build their airliners. In the aftermath of September 11 the desert airports of Marana, Mojave and Victorville in the US began to fill with ageing 737-200s, 727s and Fokker 100s as airlines cut back whole fleets. Even some brand new airliners were delivered straight into storage in the desert to await better times.

At one stage something like 10% of the world's airline fleet was sitting idle in the US deserts. In this environment few airlines were in a buying mood, impacting manufacturers Boeing, Airbus, Bombardier and Embraer.

The downturn has hit Boeing the hardest. It has laid off over 30,000 employees involved in airliner production, and cut production rates. Airbus has been less affected, its production rates were lower to begin with, despite a larger order backlog, and fewer of its customers were from the US, so it was not as hurt by cancellations and the orders drought from US airlines.

Boeing delivered around 520 jetliners in 2001, in 2002 this figure was due to fall to around 380 (with a consequent 20% drop in revenues). Before September 11 Boeing had planned to cut production rates in 2002, but not to that extent. In 2003 Boeing plans to deliver just 275 airliners (taking it back to mid 1990s rates – the peak year so far was 620 deliveries in 1999).

In comparison, Airbus plans to deliver around 300 jetliners in 2002 and 2003 – its peak year was 2001, with 311 deliveries.

Despite the gloom, orders for 2002 weren't too bad. Through to late December Boeing had booked 220 firm

Desert birds. Over 120 jetliners in storage at Mojave, California, in late 2002, most of them arriving following the September 11 accelerated downturn. This photo is dominated by retired US Airways 737s and Fokker 100s. US Airways retired its Fokker 100 fleet and shutdown its Metrojet subsidiary (the red 737s) post September 11, and the airline entered Chapter 11 bankruptcy protection in August 2002. (Howard Geary)

orders, which after 46 cancellations gave it a net order total of 174 for the year. Similarly Airbus had announced 177 firm orders and 19 cancellations. Between them the two manufacturers have booked around 330 net orders for 2002. Not too bad for what should prove to be one of the bottom years of the current trough.

Undoubtedly though it has been a buyers market since September 11. A few financially strong airlines such as Qantas and Ryanair moved quickly to secure new aircraft at what likely would have been close to distressed seller prices.

Sadly though Qantas and Ryanair were exceptions to the trend. In the post September 11 aided downturn, not just US airlines have been in distress. In Europe flag carriers Sabena and Swissair collapsed, while others which had a high exposure to trans Atlantic routes, such as British Airways, have also been hurt. In Australia Ansett collapsed and was shutdown completely, although its fate had little to do with September 11.

But it is hard to match the scale of the financial losses

of the major US carriers. For the 12 months to the end of September 2002, for example, American Airlines lost a staggering $US2.98bn. For the first nine months of 2002, US Airways (which entered Chapter 11 bankruptcy protection in August 2002) lost $US850m.

In North America and Europe in particular, the full service carriers don't just have to contend with a traffic downturn, but also the ever expanding low cost carriers, such as Southwest, Ryanair and easyJet. The growth of these airlines, and their compatriots jetBlue, Westjet and AirTran, are fuelling demand for single aisle airliners, keeping the 737 and A320 production lines ticking over.

Lower down the size scale, the regional jet manufacturers have not been immune to the airline industry downturn. The hot selling 50 seat jets – Bombardier's CRJ200 and Embraer's ERJ 145, continue to sell reasonably well. Interestingly, in the US, which most 50 seat jets call home, regional affiliates of the major carriers have been faring fairly well. The majors have been using their affiliates with their small jets to operate routes that post September 11 are marginal and can no longer sustain larger jets.

But the regional manufacturers' attempts to replicate the success of the 50 seat class further up the size range has not been so successful. Bombardier's CRJ700 70 seat stretch of the CRJ200 has sold well (with almost 200 orders), but other larger regional jets have failed to gain much traction in the market.

The 90 seat CRJ900 development of the CRJ700 for example has only attracted 30 firm orders. Embraer's Embraer 170, 175, 190 and 195 family of 70-110 seaters has booked about 110 sales, probably less than the Brazilian manufacturer would have.

However Embraer effectively has this market to itself with the financial collapse of Fairchild Dornier and BAE System's decision to drop its RJX upgrade of the Avro RJ (bringing down the curtain on the last all British airliner program). Despite an apparently healthy order book for its regional jet lines, Fairchild Dornier was placed into the hands of an administrator shortly after its 728 prototype rolled out in March 2002. In the dying days of 2002 it looked likely that the company would be liquidated and the 728/928 and 328JET programs terminated.

The Avro RJX and Fairchild Dornier 728/928 programs aren't alone in their fates however. Boeing has terminated three proposed aircraft programs in recent times.

On March 29 2001 Boeing announced it was cancelling work on its 747X and Longer Range 767-400 programs, and stunned the world by instead taking the covers off its daring 'Sonic Cruiser' concept.

The Sonic Cruiser would have cruised at Mach 0.98, carrying around 250 passengers over very long ranges at economics comparable to the 767-300. Its high speed cruise promised to reduce trip times on long range flights by around 15% compared to conventional long range airliners. Its futuristic configuration included twin vertical fins, canards mounted on the forward fuselage, a 'gloved' delta wing and rear mounted engines.

When the Sonic Cruiser was revealed Boeing critics suggested it was a PR exercise to mask the cancellation of the 747X and distract attention from the just launched A380. Boeing did appear quite serious in developing the Sonic Cruiser, expending considerable energy refining the concept and work-shopping it with airlines. However towards the second half of 2002 Boeing began hinting that the Sonic Cruiser may be cancelled or at least postponed for some years, before finally pulling the plug on December 20.

Ultimately it seems airlines were just not prepared to charge their customers a premium for high speed travel.

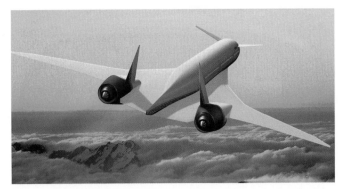

Flying into the sunset – Boeing dropped its technologically promising Sonic Cruiser in the dying days of 2002. Instead it will develop a conventional 250 seater.

Instead, in the post September 11 downturn with high fuel costs, most airlines were interested in generating new efficiencies.

In the Sonic Cruiser's place Boeing, with the encouragement of the airlines it had spoken to about the Sonic Cruiser, will develop a new 'super efficient' airliner. This would effectively be a 767 replacement incorporating advanced technologies and techniques that would have been employed on the Sonic Cruiser.

Boeing has also suspended work on the re-engined, higher gross weight Longer Range 767-400, which attracted little sales interest, and has also delayed development of the ultra long range 777-200LR, with deliveries not likely until 2006.

On the positive ledger for Boeing, the company rolled out its 777-300ER in November 2002. This increased weight development of the 777-300 flies about 2800km (1500nm) further than the basic aircraft.

Across the Atlantic at Airbus, the European manufacturer has had a busy but much more stable time in recent years.

Airbus is hard at work bringing its 555 seat A380 to reality. First flight is planned for early 2005 and service entry in the first quarter of 2006 (with Singapore Airlines). By late 2002 over 90% of equipment suppliers had been selected for the A380, and more than 3000 engineers were working on the project. Detailed design was finalised in late 2001 and first metal cut on A380 components took place in January 2002. In early 2002 Airbus began construction work on its enormous A380 final assembly plant at Toulouse.

Airports too are investing in preparations for the A380's service entry. For example New York's John F

Boeing rolled out the 777-300ER in November 2002, a bright spot in an up and down year for the manufacturer. (Boeing)

Cirrus Design is leading the way for light aircraft design. This is the new all glass instrument panel it has developed for the SR22. (Cirrus)

Kennedy Airport is spending $US100m making sure it can handle the big jet – a big sum, but only 2% of the airport's 10 year masterplan for capital spending.

Airbus' next biggest aircraft, the A340-600, entered service in 2002, while its ultra long range A340-500 should follow in early 2003.

Airbus' recent problem child has been the 100 seat class A318, a shortened development of the A319. The A318's problem has been development problems with its new Pratt & Whitney PW6000 powerplant. Instead the CFM56 has become the lead engine on the program, and the A318 is now due to enter service in July 2003, about seven months late.

Another promising program that is running late, but will come to fruition in 2003, is the SMA SR 305 diesel engine for general aviation applications. Deliveries of production light aircraft powered by the SMA should enter service in 2003, with EADS Socata and Cirrus leading the charge with their MS 200 and SR21tdi high performance light singles.

Jet fuel burning diesel engines seem to be sparking something of a mini revolution in GA, particularly in Europe where avgas is particularly expensive. A new generation of jet fuel burning diesel engines led by the SR and the Thielert Centurion 1.7 promise reduced fuel consumption and better performance and maintainability, while burning cheaper fuel to begin with. Both these powerplants will also have single level power control, combining throttle, mixture and pitch in the one control.

Other technological advances are finally filtering through to GA aircraft. A number of conventional avgas burning powerplants are also being fitted with FADEC which electronically controls all throttle, fuel mixture and propeller pitch settings, allowing single lever control and more efficiency and ensuring optimum fuel efficiency. Even the humble two seat Liberty XL-2 will be so-equipped.

Advances in avionics are also putting glass cockpits in GA aircraft. In mid 2003 Cirrus Design announced it was introducing an optional primary flight display to its very popular SR22 high performance light single, resulting in the first production piston powered light aircraft with a full glass cockpit.

The SR22's large 26cm (10.4in) primary flight display features an enhanced ADI and enhanced HSI, together with altitude, speed and vertical speed information. It is mounted alongside the existing multifunction display, which can present map, checklist and engine information.

And GA aircraft buyers are responding to such new technology improvements. At a time when overall light aircraft sales are falling (in line with the same economic downturn that is affecting the airlines), Cirrus was one of the few light aircraft manufacturers that actually increased production in 2002. Cessna and Piper, mean-

while, building essentially updated variants of 1960s designs, have slowed production. Cirrus delivered 119 SR20s and SR22s in the third quarter of 2002, compared to 43 a year earlier.

In all, US manufacturers were due to deliver 2150 GA aircraft (including business jets) in 2002, about the same as 1998 and 650 fewer aircraft than in 2000.

Not only are Cessna and Piper cutting back on production, so too are business jet manufacturers. In 2002 Canada's Bombardier announced it was suspending production of its business jet lines for four months (it also temporarily halted Dash 8 production for six to eight weeks). Dassault announced production of its Falcon line will drop from 72 in 2002 to 60 in 2003.

Another bright spot in GA is the entry level business jet category. In late 2002 Cessna launched the new Citation Mustang six seat jet, and before the end of the year over 300 had been sold.

Others are trying to get in on the entry level jet market. Eclipse Aviation has been developing its six seat Eclipse 500, which promised to be considerably cheaper than the Mustang and attracted a lot of sales interest. But at the very least this program will be delayed as Eclipse terminated its agreement with engine manufacturer Williams International, and at late 2002 was looking for a new engine supplier.

Another six seat light jet will be the Adams Aircraft A700 development of the A500 push-pull piston twin.

In other GA news, high performance single manufacturer Mooney survived bankruptcy after being taken over by AASI, the company which was developing the twin turboprop Jetcruzer. AASI resumed Mooney production (under the Mooney banner) in mid 2002, but decided to drop its long running Jetcruzer project.

One apparent recent GA casualty is the Ilyushin Il-103. Production appears to have stopped of this promising Russian designed four seater. A couple of other high profile Ilyushin programs have been axed since our last Directory, including the westernised and stretched Il-96-300 and, it seems, the stretched Il-76MF.

Russian aircraft production continues at just a trickle – just 14 commercial aircraft were built in 2001.

While Russia's aviation industry struggles to pick itself up off the mat, neighbouring China is working hard to develop its aerospace sector. In early December 2002 Embraer signed an agreement with AVIC II (China Aviation Industry Corp II) which will see the highly successful ERJ 145 family built under licence in China in partnership with Harbin by the Harbin Embraer Aircraft Industry Company. Deliveries are due from December 2003.

So as the world prepares to celebrate the centenary of powered flight in December 2003, the civil aerospace industry is enduring its ups and downs. But there's no doubt that the Wright brothers would be highly impressed with the size and the magnitude of the achievements of the industry they gave birth to.

Made in China? Brazil's most famous aircraft export, the ERJ 145 family of regional jets, is to be built under licence in China. (Embraer)

CIVIL AIRCRAFT

Adam Aircraft A500 & A700

Country of origin: United States of America

Type: A500 – Six seat piston twin. A700 – Six seat light jet.

Powerplant: A500 – Two 260kW (350hp) Teledyne Continental TSIO-550E turbocharged FADEC equipped flat six piston engines driving three blade constant speed Hartzell propellers. A700 – Two 5.3kN (1200lb) Williams International FJ33 turbofans.

Performance: A500 – Max speed 463km/h (250kt), max cruising speed at 75% power 223kt (413km/h), economical cruising speed at 60% power 200kt (370km/h). Initial rate of climb 1800ft/min. Max operating altitude 25,000ft. Range at max cruising speed 1890km (1020nm), at economical cruising speed 2130km (1150nm). A700 – Max cruising speed 630km/h (340kt). Range with IFR reserves at max cruising speed (1100nm).

Weights: A500 – Max takeoff 2860kg (6300lb). Useful load 953kg (2100lb). A700 – Weights not published at late 2002.

Dimensions: A500 – Wing span 13.4m (44.0ft), length 11.2m (36.7ft), height 2.9m (9.5ft). A700 – Wing span 13.4m (44.0ft), length 12.4m (40.75ft), height 2.93m (9.6ft).

Capacity: Standard seating for six, with club four seating behind pilot and passenger.

Production: First A500 deliveries 2003, A700 deliveries 2004.

History: Denver, Colorado based Adam Aircraft is developing two all new carbonfibre construction six place light aircraft, the twin piston A500 and the jet powered A700.

Adam Aircraft Industries was founded by CEO George F 'Rick' Adam and president John Knudsen in 1998. Its first product is the piston twin A500 designed by Burt Rutan, whose Scaled Composites design company began work on the project in September 1999. The Scaled Composites proof of concept aircraft, the M-309, first flew from Mojave, California, on March 21 2000. The first Adam built production conforming A500 prototype first flew on July 11 2002. Three Adam built A500 development aircraft will be used for flight testing, with FAA certification planned for the first half of 2003.

The 'centreline thrust' A500 features pusher and tractor engines, which eliminate engine out asymmetric handling problems normally experienced when one of a twin's engines fails. It also features a high aspect ratio wing, twin boom tail configuration and retractable undercarriage. The airframe is made entirely of carbonfibre.

The A500's twin turbocharged 260kW (350hp) TSIO-550s feature FADEC allowing single lever engine controls. Sidestick controllers replace conventional yokes or sticks, while standard avionics includes a dual Garmin GNS 530 comms/nav system and S-TEC 55x autopilot, plus conventional round dial instruments. An annunciator panel is fitted below the glare shield.

In October 2002 Adam Aircraft announced it was developing the A700 twin jet development of the A500. The A700 will share 80% parts commonality with the A500, but will be powered by two 5.3kN (1200lb) Williams International FJ33 turbofans mounted at the rear of a stretched fuselage. It will also feature a glass cockpit as standard. First flight is planned for the second half of 2003, with deliveries from late 2004.

Photo: The prototype A500 on its first flight. (Adam Aircraft)

Aermacchi SF.260

Country of origin: Italy

Type: Two seat trainer and high performance light aircraft

Powerplant: SF.260A & C – One 195kW (260hp) Lycoming O-540-E4A5 flat six piston engine driving a two blade constant speed propeller.

Performance: SF.260A – Max cruising speed 345km/h (186kt). Initial rate of climb 1770ft/min. Service ceiling 21,370ft. Range with max fuel 2050km (1107nm). SF.260C – Max speed 347km/h (187kt), max cruising speed 330km/h (178kt). Initial rate of climb 1790ft/min. Service ceiling 19,000ft. Max range 1490km (805nm).

Weights: SF.260A – Empty 700kg (1543lb), max takeoff (aerobatic) 1000kg (2205lb), max takeoff (utility) 1102kg (2430lb).

Dimensions: SF.260A – Wing span over tip tanks 8.40m (27ft 7in), length 7.02m (23ft 0in), height 2.60m (8ft 6in). Wing area 10.1m² (108.5sq ft). SF.260C – Wing span 8.35m (27ft 5in), length 7.10m (23ft 4in), height 2.41m (7ft 11in). Wing area 10.1m² (108.7sq ft).

Capacity: Seating for two side by side, plus rear seat capable of seating one adult or two small children.

Production: Over 850 SF.260s have been built (750 by SIAI-Marchetti) of which approximately 170 built for civil customers.

History: The nimble SIAI-Marchetti SF.260 has sold in modest numbers to civil operators worldwide but is popular as a basic military trainer.

Italian aircraft designer Stelio Frati (who was responsible for a number of light aircraft designs) penned the SF.260 in the early 1960s. Aviamilano built a 185kW (250hp) Lycoming O-540 powered prototype as the F.250, however until its takeover by Aermacchi in 1997 SIAI-Marchetti undertook all production (initially under licence, before later assuming full responsibility for the program) of the aircraft as the 195kW (260hp) O-540 powered SF.260. The second SF.260 to fly was the first built by SIAI-Marchetti and the first with the more powerful version of the O-540. This second prototype first flew in 1966.

The initial civil production model was the SF.260A, and a number were sold in the USA as the Waco Meteor. In 1974 production switched to the SF.260B with improvements first developed for the military SF.260M, including a stronger undercarriage, a redesigned wing leading edge and a taller fin. The B was soon followed by the further improved SF.260C, with increased span wing.

While the SF.260 has been further developed into E and F forms these have been sold to military operators only. The 260kW (350shp) Allison (now Rolls-Royce) 250-B17D turboprop powered SF.260TP meanwhile has been built since the early 1980s, but it too has been sold only to military customers. Nevertheless Italian civil certification was awarded in October 1993, opening the door to possible civil sales.

In 1997 Aermacchi took over SIAI-Marchetti, with low rate production continuing against military orders.

In civil use the SF.260 is now regarded as something of a classic thoroughbred. Its clean lines, retractable undercarriage and relatively powerful engine guarantee spirited performance.

Photo: An SF.260A. (Keith Myers)

Aero Boero 95, 115, 150 & 180

Country of origin: Argentina

Type: Family of three and four seat light aircraft

Powerplant: AB 95 Standard – One 70kW (95hp) Continental C-90-8F flat four driving a two blade fixed pitch prop. AB 115 Trainer – One 85kW (115hp) Textron Lycoming O-235-C2A. AB 180 RVR – One 135kW (180hp) Textron Lycoming O-360-A1A driving a two blade fixed pitch Sensenich or constant speed Hartzell prop.

Performance: AB 95 – Max speed 204km/h (110kt), cruising speed 170km/h (92kt), long range cruising speed 159km/h (86kt). Range at long range cruising speed 959km (518nm). AB 115 Trainer – Max cruising speed 169km/h (91kt). Initial rate of climb 669ft/min. Range with max fuel 1230km (664nm). AB 180 RVR – Max speed 225km/h (122kt), max cruising speed 201km/h (108kt). Initial rate of climb 1025ft/min. Range with max fuel 1180km (636nm).

Weights: AB 95 – Empty 400kg (882lb), loaded 700kg (1543lb). AB 115 Trainer – Empty 556kg (1226lb), max takeoff 802kg (1768lb). AB 180 RVR – Empty 602kg (1327lb), max takeoff 890kg (1962lb).

Dimensions: AB 95 – Wing span 10.42m (34ft 2in), length 6.91m (22ft 8in), height 2.19m (7ft 2in). AB 115 Trainer & AB 180 RVR – Wing span 10.78m (35ft 5in), length 7.08m (23ft 3in), height 2.05m (6ft 9in). Wing area 17.4m² (187.4sq ft).

Capacity: Accommodation for one pilot and two passengers, or three/four passengers in initial AB 180 model. Ag aircraft fitted with ventral tank pod (for approx 270 litres/60Imp gal/71US gal).

Production: Approx 600 of all variants built, including over 300 out of a Brazilian government order for 450.

History: Development from the basic AB 95 (which first flew in 1959) spawned one of the largest families of GA types developed in South America.

Versions of the AB 95 include the AB 95 Standard, the AB 95 De Lujo with a 75kW (100hp) Continental O-200-A engine; the AB 95 A Fumigador ag aircraft with the O-200-A engine and fitted for crop dusting or spraying; the AB 115 BS air ambulance fitted with a stretcher, the more powerful AB 95 B; and the AB 95/115 with a more streamlined engine cowling housing a 85kW (115hp) O-235 engine and main wheel fairings.

From the AB 95/115 Aero Boero developed the AB 115 with increased wing span, greater fin sweepback and longer range, and the AB 115 Trainer. Brazil ordered 450 Trainers in the late 1980s for its aero clubs. Over 300 of these were delivered to Brazil, with over 400 built in total.

The AB 180 first flew in the late 1960s and was offered in three and four seat versions with differing wingspans and a more powerful engine than those featured on the earlier AB 95 and AB 115. Developments included the AB 180 RV with greater range, reprofiled fuselage and sweptback fin; the glider tug AB 180 RVR; the high altitude AB 180 Condor with optional engine turbocharger; AB 180 Ag agricultural aircraft and the two seat AB 180 PSA preselection aircraft for student pilot flight screening. A biplane AB 180 SP was also developed. The AB 150 RV and AB 150 Ag have less powerful 110kW (150hp) O-320s compared with their corresponding AB 180 models.

Photo: An Aero Boero. (Santiago Rivas)

Aeronca 7 Champion & 11 Chief

Country of origin: United States of America

Type: Two seat light aircraft

Powerplant: 7AC – One 48kW (65hp) Continental A65-8 flat four piston engine driving a two blade fixed pitch propeller. 11BC – One 63kW (85hp) Continental C85-85F.

Performance: 7AC – Max speed 208km/h (112kt), cruising speed 183km/h (99kt). Service ceiling 12,400ft. Range 740km (400nm). 11 – Max speed 169km/h (91kt), cruising speed 153km/h (83kt). Service ceiling 10,800ft. Range 532km (287nm).

Weights: 7AC – Empty 336kg (740lb), max takeoff 553kg (1220lb). 11 – Empty 329kg (725lb), loaded 567kg (1250lb).

Dimensions: 7AC – Wing span 10.73m (35ft 2in), length 6.65m (21ft 6in), height 2.13m (7ft 0in). Wing area 15.8m² (170sq ft). 11 – Wing span 11.00m (36ft 1in), length 6.35m (20ft 10in), height 2.08m (6ft 10in). Wing area 16.3m² (175.5sq ft).

Capacity: 7 – Pilot and passenger in tandem. 11 – Pilot and passenger side by side.

Production: Approx 10,000 Aeronca Champions (including L-16s and 7200 7ACs) and 1750 Chiefs built between 1946 and 1951.

History: The Aeronca Champion was a highly popular light aircraft in the USA in the immediate postwar period, with over 10,000 built.

The Champion was based on the prewar Model K Scout, with which it shares a similar configuration, but with tandem instead of side by side seating and a reduced span but increased chord flap-less wing.

The first production version of the Champion was the 7AC, with succeeding versions similar except for the powerplant fitted. These versions were the 7BC with a 63kW (85hp) Continental C85-12 or O-190-1 (and built in large numbers for the US Army as the L-16 liaison platform); the 7CC with a Continental C90-12F; the 7DC with a Continental C85; and the 7EC with a 67kW (90hp) Continental C90.

Aeronca sold the production rights of the Champion to the Champion Aircraft Corporation in 1951. Champion Aircraft dropped production of its namesake that year and instead developed the 7EC Traveller (which first flew in 1955), 7FC tricycle undercarriage Tri-Traveller and the 110kW (150hp) Lycoming O-320 powered Model 7GCB Challenger, with increased span wing with flaps. The Challenger formed the basis for the Citabria and subsequent Decathlon and Scout, which are described under American Champion.

In September 1970 Bellanca acquired the assets of the Champion Aircraft Company and elected to return the Champion to production as the 7ACA Champ. Based on the 7AC, changes included a 45kW (60hp) Franklin 2A-120-B engine in place of the by then out of production Continental, cantilever spring steel main landing gear and modernised interior. Small numbers were built in the early 1970s.

Meanwhile the Aeronca Chief was introduced in 1946. Compared to the Champion it featured a wider cabin for side by side seating. Versions of the Chief (initial production was of the 11AC) were the Scout pilot trainer; 11BC with a dorsal fin and more powerful 63kW (85hp) Continental engine; and 11CC Super Chief with the Continental C85 with improvements to the fuselage giving greater interior space. A further development was the 15AC four seater.

Photo: An Aeronca 11AC Chief. (Lance Higgerson)

Aerospatiale/BAC Concorde

Countries of origin: France and United Kingdom

Type: Medium range supersonic airliner

Powerplants: Four 170.2kN (38,050lb) Rolls-Royce SNECMA Olympus 593 Mk 610 afterburning turbojets.

Performance: Max cruising speed at 51,300ft Mach 2.04, or 2179km/h (1176kt), typical supersonic cruise speed Mach 2.02. Service ceiling 60,000ft. Range with max fuel, reserves and 8845kg (19,500lb) payload 6580km (3550nm).

Weights: Operating empty 78,700kg (173,500lb), max takeoff 185,065kg (408,000lb). Max payload 12,700kg (28,000lb).

Dimensions: Wing span 25.56m (83ft 10in), length 62.17m (203ft 9in), height 11.40m (37ft 5in). Wing area 358.3m² (3856sq ft).

Capacity: Two pilots and flight engineer on the flightdeck. Accommodation for 128 passengers at four abreast with 86cm (34in) pitch in main cabin. Max seating for 144 at 81cm (32in) pitch.

Production: Two prototypes (001 & 002), two preproduction aircraft (01 & 02) and 16 production aircraft. Total 20.

History: The magestic Concorde remains the only supersonic airliner to have seen regular, scheduled service.

An engineering masterpiece but commercial failure, the Concorde was the result of a collaborative venture between the aviation industries of Britain and France. It dates back to design work for a supersonic airliner carried out by Sud Aviation and Bristol, whose respective Super Caravelle and Bristol 233 designs were remarkably similar in configuration to each other. The forecast high development costs of any SST program and the similarities in the designs led to a 1962 government agreement between France and Britain which resulted in the British Aircraft Corporation (into which Bristol had been merged) and Sud-Aviation (which became a part of Aerospatiale in 1970) joining to design and develop such an aircraft.

Concorde evolved to be a relatively long range aircraft (for the period) capable of flying trans Atlantic sectors. Design features include a highly complex delta wing featuring cambering and ogival leading edges, with pairs of afterburning engines mounted in pods under the wing undersurface. Concorde's fuel system was designed to trim the aircraft longitudinally by transferring fuel between tanks to offset the change in the centre of pressure as the aircraft accelerates and decelerates. The variable geometry nose is lowered while taxying, on takeoff and landing to improve the flightcrew's visibility, and Concorde was the first airliner to feature fly-by-wire.

The Concorde first flew on March 2 1969 but did not enter airline service until January 1976. Although a sales failure, Concorde proved very popular in service with its high flying clientele, plying the North Atlantic and often used on charter flights.

Sadly on July 25 2000 an Air France Concorde crashed shortly after takeoff from Paris' Charles de Gualle airport, killing 113, when debris from a tyre blowout punctured the fuel tanks. As a result British Airways' seven and Air France's four surviving aircraft were grounded. Following the incorporation of modifications including Kevlar-rubber fuel tank liners and new tyres, Concorde's airworthiness certificate was restored in September 2001.

Photo: Four British Airways Concordes. (British Airways)

Aerospatiale (Sud) Alouette II & Lama

Country of origin: France

Type: Light utility helicopters

Powerplant: SA 313B Alouette II – One 270kW (360shp) Turbomeca Artouste IIC6 turboshaft driving a three blade main rotor and two blade tail rotor. SA 315B Lama – One 650kW (870shp) Turbomeca Artouste IIIB turboshaft, derated to 410kW (550shp).

Performance: SA 313B – Max speed 185km/h (100kt), max cruising speed 165km/h (90kt). Initial rate of climb 825ft/min. Hovering ceiling in ground effect 5400ft. Range with max fuel 300km (162nm), range with max payload 100km (54nm). SA 315B – Max cruising speed 192km/h (103kt). Max initial rate of climb 1080ft/min. Hovering ceiling in ground effect 16,565ft, out of ground effect 15,090ft. Range with max fuel 515km (278nm).

Weights: SA 313B – Empty 895kg (1973lb), max takeoff 1600kg (3527lb). SA 315B – Empty 1020kg (2250lb), max takeoff 1950kg (4300lb), or 2300kg (5070lb) with external sling load.

Dimensions: SA 313B – Main rotor diameter 10.20m (33ft 5in), fuselage length 9.70m (31ft 10in), height 2.75m (9ft 0in). SA 315B – Main rotor diameter 11.02m (36ft 2in), length overall 12.92m (42ft 5in), fuselage length 10.26m (33ft 8in), height overall 3.09m (10ft 2in). Main rotor disc area 95.4m² (1026.7sq ft).

Capacity: Typical seating for five. Lama can lift a 1135kg (2500lb) external sling load.

Production: 1303 Alouette IIs, including 360 SA 318Cs, were built for military and commercial customers. Sud/Aerospatiale built 407 Lamas, while seven were built in Brazil and more than 245 in India as the HAL Cheetah.

History: Among the first turbine powered helicopters in the world, the Alouette II and Lama remain in service in fairly large numbers.

For a time the most successful western European helicopter in terms of numbers built, the Alouette II was based on the original Sud-Est Alouette SA 3120 which first flew on March 12 1955. Two prototypes were built and these were powered by Salmson 9 piston engines.

Production deliveries of the turbine powered SE 313B Alouette II occurred from 1957, the first machines bound for the French military. Civil certification was awarded on January 14 1958, although most SA/SE 313B production was for military customers.

The Alouette II was soon followed by a more powerful Turbomeca Astazou powered development, the SA 318C Alouette II Astazou, which first flew on January 31 1961. Power was supplied by a 395kW (530shp) Astazou IIA derated to 270kW (360shp), which increased the type's maximum speed and maximum takeoff weight, but otherwise the Alouette II and Alouette II Astazou were similar.

The SA 315B Lama was initially developed for the Indian Army as a utility helicopter with improved hot and high performance. Called Cheetah in Indian service, the Lama mated the Alouette II's airframe with the larger Alouette III's dynamic components including Artouste IIIB engine. The Lama's first flight was on March 17 1969.

Aerospatiale built 407 through to 1989, while HAL in India has built small numbers since the mid 1990s.

Photo: A Helicopters (NZ) SA 315B Lama. (Peter Clark)

Aerospatiale (Sud) Alouette III

Country of origin: France

Type: Light utility helicopter

Powerplant: SA 316C – One 450kW (600shp) derated Turbomeca Artouste IIID turboshaft driving a three blade main rotor and three blade tail rotor. SA 319 – One 450kW (600shp) derated Turbomeca Astazou XIV turboshaft.

Performance: SA 316C – Max speed 220km/h (118kt), max cruising speed 195km/h (105kt). Initial rate of climb 885ft/min. Hovering ceiling in ground effect 7380ft/min. Range with max fuel 540km (290nm). SA 319B – Max cruising speed 197km/h (106kt). Initial rate of climb 885ft/min. Hovering ceiling in ground effect 10,170ft, out of ground effect 5575ft. Range with six passengers 605km (327nm).

Weights: SA 316C – Empty 1134kg (2500lb), max takeoff 2250kg (4960lb). SA 319B – Empty 1140kg (2513lb), max takeoff 2250kg (4960lb).

Dimensions: SA 316/319 – Main rotor diameter 11.02m (36ft 2in), length overall 12.54m (42ft 2in), fuselage length 10.03m (32ft 11in), height 3.00m (9ft 10in). Main rotor disc area 95.4m^2 (1026.7sq ft)

Capacity: Typical seating for seven, with two passengers and pilot on front bench seat and four on rear bench seat. In aerial ambulance configuration accommodates pilot, two medical attendants and two stretcher patients.

Production: Approximately 1500 Alouette IIIs were built in France, plus production in India (330+), Romania (200) and Switzerland, most for military customers, but some are in civil use.

History: The Alouette III is an enlarged development of the Alouette II series, and until the mid 1980s was Aerospatiale's most successful helicopter in terms of numbers built (surpassed by the Ecureuil).

Like the Alouette II, the Alouette III traces its development back to the Sud-Est SE 3101 Alouette piston powered prototypes, the first of which first flew on July 31 1951. The Alouette III first flew as the SE 3160 on February 28 1959. Compared with the Alouette II, the III is larger and seats seven, but in its initial SA 316A form was powered by the Turbomeca Artouste turboshaft.

The SE 3160 Alouette III remained in production for almost a decade until 1969, when it was replaced by the improved SA 316B with strengthened transmission and a greater max takeoff weight. The SA 316C, with higher rated engine, replaced the SA 316B in production from early 1972.

The SA 319 Alouette III Astazou is a development of the SA 316 powered by a derated 450kW (600shp) Turbomeca Astazou XIV turboshaft, yielding better hot and high performance and improved fuel economy. The SA 319 entered production in 1971 (Sud Aviation had become part of Aerospatiale on January 1 1970).

The SA 319 and SA 316C remained in production side by side through the 1970s and into the early 1980s. HAL of India has licence built more than 300 Alouette IIIs as the Chetak, mainly for that country's military, but also for government and civil customers. ICA of Brasov in Romania licence built SA 316Bs as IAR 316Bs.

Like the Alouette II, the III has been used in a wide range of utility roles, and many armed military variants have been built.

Photo: The Alouette III. (via Tony Arbon)

Aerospatiale SA 330 Puma

Country of origin: France

Type: Twin engine medium lift helicopter

Powerplants: SA 330J – Two 1175kW (1575shp) Turbomeca Turmo IVC turboshafts driving a four blade main rotor and five blade tail rotor. SA 330G/F – Two 1070kW (1435shp) Turbomeca Turmo IIIC4s.

Performance: SA 330J – Max speed 262km/h (141kt), max cruising speed at sea level 257km/h (139kt). Hovering ceiling in ground effect 7315ft. Initial rate of climb 1400ft/min. Max range with standard fuel 550km (297nm).

Weights: Empty 3766kg (8305lb), max takeoff 7500kg (16,535lb) with sling load, standard max takeoff 7400kg (16,315lb).

Dimensions: Rotor diameter 15.08m (49ft 6in), length overall rotors turning 18.15m (59ft 6in), fuselage length 14.06m (46ft 2in), height 5.14m (16ft 11in). Main rotor disc area 177.0m^2 (1905sq ft).

Capacity: Crew of one or two pilots on flightdeck, plus jumpseat. Passenger configurations in main cabin range from 8, 10 or 12 seat executive layouts, or for 17 to 20 passengers in an airline arrangement. A 3200kg (7055lb) external sling load can be carried.

Production: 696 Pumas of different versions, including military, had been sold, when Aerospatiale production ceased in 1987. Limited production in Romania by IAR continued into the 1990s, largely for that country's military. IAR has built over 160 as the IAR-330L.

History: The Aerospatiale Puma is perhaps the most successful European built medium lift helicopter, and while the majority of Pumas have been sold to military customers (largely for use as troop transports), a significant number are in commercial use.

The Puma was first designed to meet a French army requirement for a medium lift helicopter capable of operating in all weather conditions. The first of two SA 330 prototypes first flew on April 15 1965, with the first production aircraft flying in September 1968. A 1967 decision by Britain's Royal Air Force to order the Puma as its new tactical helicopter transport resulted in substantial Westland participation in the helicopter's design and construction.

Early versions of the Puma were for military customers, including the SA 330B, C, E and H. The initial civil models were the Turmo IIIC powered SA 330F passenger and SA 330G freight versions, which became the first helicopters certificated for single pilot IFR operations in A and B conditions.

The SA 330J is the definitive civil Puma, and compared to the earlier F and G has composite main rotors and an increased maximum takeoff weight. The weather radar equipped J also became the first helicopter certificated for all weather operations including flight in icing conditions, awarded in April 1978.

IPTN of Indonesia assembled a small number of SA 330s before switching to the Super Puma. After Aerospatiale ceased production in 1987, the sole production source for the Puma became IAR of Romania.

The stretched AS 332 Super Puma development is described separately under Eurocopter.

Photo: The US Navy contracts civil SA 330 Pumas to perform vertical replenishment tasks for its Military Sealift Command. Pictured is an SA 330J. (James Vidrine, USN)

Aerospatiale SA 341/342 Gazelle

Country of origin: France

Type: Utility helicopter

Powerplant: SA 341G – One 440kW (590shp) max continuous Turbomeca Astazou XIV turboshaft driving a three blade main rotor and Fenestron shrouded tail rotor.

Performance: SA 341G – Max cruising speed at S/L 264km/h (142kt), econ cruising speed at S/L 233km/h (126kt). Initial rate of climb 1770ft/min. Service ceiling 16,400ft. Hovering ceiling out of ground effect 6560ft. Range at S/L with max fuel 670km (361nm), range with a 500kg (1102lb) payload 360km (194nm).

Weights: SA 341G – Empty equipped 917kg (2022lb), max takeoff 1800kg (3970lb).

Dimensions: Main rotor diameter 10.50m (34ft 6in), length overall 11.97m (39ft 4in), fuselage length 9.53m (31ft 3in), height overall 3.15m (10ft 3in). Main rotor disc area 86.5m² (931sq ft).

Capacity: Maximum seating for five including pilot. Rear seat can be folded down to accommodate freight.

Production: 1255 Gazelles built in France, although the large majority of these were for military service. Further production took place in the UK with Westland, and the former Yugoslavia.

History: The Gazelle was the first helicopter to introduce Aerospatiale's (and now Eurocopter's) trademark Fenestron shrouded tail rotor system.

While civil Gazelles are not too common, some are in service as personal or corporate transports. However the Gazelle remains in widespread military service worldwide, and a large number of military variants have been developed.

The Gazelle was designed as a replacement for the popular Alouette II series. Design features included the Alouette II Astazou's powerplant and transmission system, and most noticeably the Fenestron tail rotor, where the tail rotor is housed within the vertical tail.

The prototype SA 340 Gazelle, powered by an Astazou III, first flew on April 7 1967. The Astazou III also powered the subsequent production model, the SA 341, which first flew on August 16 1971.

Like the larger Puma, the Gazelle was the subject of a 1967 agreement that saw it jointly built by Westland in the UK and Aerospatiale in France.

The civil production Gazelle model is the SA 341G, and is powered by the Astazou IIIA. The SA 341G was the first helicopter certificated to be flown by a single pilot under Cat I weather conditions. This was achieved in January 1975 (and was subsequently upgraded to Cat II). The Stretched Gazelle variant of the SA 341G features a slightly modified rear cabin allowing an extra 20cm (8in) of rear legroom.

The improved SA 342 features a more powerful Astazou XIV and refined Fenestron design, giving the civil SA 342J a 100kg (220lb) increase in payload. The SA 342 became available from 1977.

The helicopter subsidiaries of Deutsche Aerospace and Aerospatiale merged to form Eurocopter in 1992, and continued low rate production for military customers through to the mid 1990s.

Photo: A British registered SA 341G Gazelle. (Lee Archer)

Aerospatiale SA 360 & SA 365 Dauphin

Country of origin: France

Type: Mid size utility helicopters

Powerplant: SA 360 – One 785kW (1050shp) Turbomeca Astazou XVIIIA turboshaft driving a four blade main rotor and Fenestron shrouded tail rotor. SA 365C – Two 505kW (680shp) Turbomeca Arriel turboshafts driving a four blade main rotor and 11 blade Fenestron shrouded tail rotor.

Performance: SA 360 – Cruising speed at S/L 275km/h (148kt), economical cruising speed 245km/h (132kt). Initial rate of climb 1770ft/min. Hovering ceiling in ground effect 7380ft. Range at S/L with max fuel 680km (367nm). SA 365C – Cruising speed 255km/h (137kt). Initial rate of climb 1970ft/min. Hovering ceiling in ground effect 11,710ft, out of ground effect 9315ft. Range at econ cruising speed 465km (251nm).

Weights: SA 360 – Basic operating 1637kg (3609lb), max takeoff 3000kg (6613lb). SA 365C – Empty 1876kg (4136lb), max takeoff 3400kg (7495lb).

Dimensions: SA 360/361 – Main rotor diameter 11.50m (37ft 9in), fuselage length 10.98m (36ft 0in), height 3.50m (11ft 6in). SA 365C – Same except main rotor diameter 11.68m (38ft 4in), length overall 13.32m (43ft 9in).

Capacity: Standard accommodation for 10, including one pilot, in three seat rows, with pilot and one passenger in front row, four passengers in centre row and four passengers in rear row. Max seating for 14. Executive configurations can seat four to six passengers. Air ambulance configuration accommodates up to four stretcher patients and a medical attendant.

Production: Approx 40 SA 360s and 50 SA 365Cs built.

History: The single engine SA 360 Dauphin and twin SA 365C Dauphin 2 were developed as replacements for the Alouette III.

The prototype SA 360 first flew on June 2 1972 and was powered by a 730kW (980shp) Turbomeca Astazou XVI turboshaft. After 180 development flights a more powerful 785kW (1050shp) Astazou XVIIIA was substituted, and weights were fitted to the rotor tips to reduce vibration and eliminate ground resonance. The first prototype flew in this new configuration on May 4 1973, following a second prototype built to the new standard which had flown for the first time that January. The first production aircraft, designated the SA 360C, flew in April 1975.

The SA 361 is a more powerful variant with improved hot and high performance and a greater payload capability. Deliveries of the SA 361 began in the second half of 1978. A military variant of the SA 361, the SA 361F, was offered fitted with up to eight HOT anti tank missiles, but was not ordered into production.

The twin engine SA 365C Dauphin 2 meanwhile was announced in early 1973. First flight was on January 24 1975. Compared with the SA 360 it features twin Arriel turboshafts and a new engine fairing, a Starflex main rotor hub and a higher max takeoff weight. Production deliveries began in December 1978.

SA 360 and SA 365 production ceased in 1981 in preference for the much improved AS 356N, described under Eurocopter.

Photo: An SA 365C with skid undercarriage. (Jim Thorn)

Aerospatiale N 262, Fregate & Mohawk

Country of origin: France

Type: Short range turboprop commuter airliner

Powerplants: 262 Fregate – Two 843kW (1130shp) Turbomeca Bastan VIIC turboprops driving three blade variable pitch Ratier-Figeac FH.146 propellers. Mohawk 298 – Two 880kW (1180shp) Pratt & Whitney Canada PT6A-45 turboprops driving five blade variable pitch Hamilton Standard props.

Performance: Fregate – Max level speed 418km/h (225kt) at 20,000ft, economical cruising speed 408km/h (220kt). Max range with full fuel and no reserves 2400km (1295nm), range with 26 pax and reserves 1020km (550nm). Mohawk – Max speed 385km/h (208kt), economical cruising speed 375km/h (203kt). Max range with full fuel and no reserves 2132km (1151nm).

Weights: Fregate – Basic empty 6200kg (13,668lb), max takeoff 10,800kg (23,810lb). Mohawk – Empty 7030kg (15,498lb), max takeoff 10,600kg (23,370lb).

Dimensions: Fregate & Mohawk – Wing span 22.60m (74ft 2in), length 19.28m (63ft 3in), height 6.21m (20ft 4in). Wing area 55.0m² (592sq ft).

Capacity: Flightcrew of two and max seating for 29 passengers at three abreast. Standard seating layout for 26 passengers.

Production: 110 of all variants of the 262 (including the 298 and miscellaneous military orders) built. 10 in airline service in 2002.

History: The N 262 regional airliner traces back to the Max Holste MH 260 Super Broussard, which first flew on July 29 1960.

The MH 260 was a Turbomeca Bastan turboprop powered development of the one-off MH 250 prototype. The MH 250 was powered by Pratt & Whitney Wasp radial piston engines and first flew on May 20 1959. Nord then built just 10 MH 260s (flown by Air Inter and Norway's Widerøe) before significantly redesigning the aircraft in 1961. The resulting Nord N 262, which first flew on December 24 1962, featured a revised fuselage with a circular cross section, pressurisation and more powerful engines.

Four major variants of the 262 were built: the initial production 262A with 805kW (1080shp) Bastan VIC engines; the 262B (just four built for Air Inter), and the 262C and D, later renamed the Fregate, with more powerful Bastan VII engines giving a higher cruising speed and better hot and high performance, and modified wing tips. The Fregate entered production in 1970 as the N 262 following the merger of Nord and Sud, and hence it became an Aerospatiale product.

In the mid to late 1970s US commuter airline Allegheny Airlines – through its subsidiary Mohawk Air Services – extensively upgraded its fleet of 262s, resulting in the Mohawk 298 (the designation reflected the FAA FAR Part 298 airworthiness regulation). The upgrade involved re-engining the 262s with more powerful Pratt & Whitney Canada PT6A-45 turboprops with five blade props, and fitting new avionics and a new auxiliary power unit.

The first Mohawk 298 flew on January 7 1975, while the last of nine converted was completed in 1978.

Photo: This 262 is used in Denmark for airways calibration work. (Egon Johansen)

Aerospatiale SN 601 Corvette

Country of origin: France

Type: Light corporate jet

Powerplants: Two 11.1kN (2500lb) Pratt & Whitney Canada JT15D-4 turbofans.

Performance: Max cruising speed 760km/h (410kt), economical cruising speed 566km/h (306kt). Range at max cruising speed with tip tanks and 45 minute reserves 2390km (1290nm), at economical cruising speed 2555km (1380nm). Range with 12 passengers at max cruising speed 1480km (800nm), at economical cruising speed 1555km (840nm).

Weights: Empty 3510kg (7738lb), max takeoff 6600kg (14,550lb).

Dimensions: Wing span 12.87m (42ft 3in), length 13.83m (45ft 5in), height 4.23m (13ft 11in). Wing area 22.0m² (236.8sq ft).

Capacity: Flightcrew of one or two pilots. Main cabin seating for between six and 14 passengers, depending on configuration. Galley and toilets were available optionally. Alternative configurations for ambulance, freighter, navigation aid calibration and photography missions offered.

Production: One prototype SN 600 and 39 production SN 601s built, with 30 remaining in service in 2002.

History: Although primarily a small corporate jet transport, Aerospatiale designed the Corvette to fulfil a variety or roles, including commuter airliner, aerial photography, airline pilot training, air ambulance, air taxi, express freight and navigation aid calibration work.

The Corvette was a commercial failure with just 40 built, and was Aerospatiale's only venture into the executive jet market. The 9.8kN (2200lb) JT15D-1 powered prototype SN 601 first flew on July 16 1970, but crashed on March 23 the following year after it had amassed 270 hours of test and development flying.

The subsequent production version, the SN 601, had more powerful JT15D-4 turbofans and a stretched fuselage. The first SN 601, or Corvette 100, first flew on December 20 1972. The second SN 601 Corvette (the first to full production standard) flew on March 7 1973, and a third on January 12 1974.

French civil certification for the Corvette was granted on May 28 1974. Customer deliveries, delayed by strikes at engine manufacturer Pratt & Whitney Canada (then UACL) began the following September.

Production of the Corvette continued until 1977. The initial production schedule called for 20 aircraft to be delivered in 1974 and production of six a month for 1975 and thereafter. However this proved an overly optimistic assessment of potential sales and only 40 were built (including development aircraft). Plans for a 2.08m (6ft 7in) stretched 18 seat Corvette 200 were also dropped.

Many early Corvette customers were French regional airlines (such as Air Alpes and Air Alsace), with others sold to corporate operators in Europe. Outside Europe however the type generated little sales interest in the face of very strong competition. Most of the Corvettes built remain in service today.

Photo: An SN 601 Corvette on approach to Mallorca, Spain. This example is used as a corporate jet while others were used as regional airliners, at least early in their careers. (Toni Marimon)

AgustaWestland A 109

Country of origin: Italy

Type: Light twin corporate and utility helicopter

Powerplants: A 109A Mk II – Two Allison 250-C20B turboshafts rated at 300kW (400shp) max cont, or 313kW (420shp) for takeoff, derated to 260kW (346shp) for twin engine operations. A 109E – Two 477kW (640shp) takeoff rated Pratt & Whitney Canada PW206Cs.

Performance: A 109A – Max cruising speed 285km/h (154kt), economical cruising speed 233km/h (126kt). Max initial rate of climb 2110ft/min. Range with std fuel and no res 648km (350nm). A 109E – Max cruising speed 289km/h (156kt). Max initial rate of climb 2080ft/min. Ceiling 20,000ft. Hovering ceiling out of ground effect 13,300ft. Max range 977km (528nm). Max endurance 5hr 10min.

Weights: A 109A Mk II – Empty equipped 1418kg (3126lb), max takeoff 2600kg (5732lb). A 109E – Empty 1570kg (3461lb), max takeoff 2850kg (6283lb).

Dimensions: Main rotor diameter 11.00m (36ft 1in), length with rotors turning 13.05m (42ft 10in), fuselage length 10.71m (35ft 2in), height 3.30m (10ft 10in). Main rotor disc area 95.0m² (1022.9sq ft).

Capacity: Accommodation for eight including one pilot. In medevac configuration two stretchers and two medical attendants.

Production: Approximately 730 A 109s of all variants (civil and military) had been ordered by late 2002, including over 260 Powers.

History: The AgustaWestland A 109 is a high performance light twin helicopter, widely used as a corporate transport and for EMS.

The first of four A 109 prototypes flew on August 4 1971. VFR certification was awarded on June 1 1975 (series production had already begun in 1974). First production deliveries took place in late 1976. Single pilot IFR certification was granted in January 1977.

The base A 109A was superseded by the upgraded A 109A Mk II from September 1981. Changes included an uprated transmission, redesigned tailboom and a new tail rotor driveshaft, improved rotor blade life and modern avionics. The Mk II was also available in widebody configuration with increased internal volume from bulged fuselage side panels and reshaped fuel tanks under the cabin floor. The Mk II Plus has the more powerful 250-C20R-1 engines, as does the A 109C. The 109C also has composite rotor blades.

The A 109K first flew in April 1983 and is powered by two 470kW (640shp) max continuous operation rated Turbomeca Arriel 1K1 turboshafts. The latest A 109 model is the FADEC equipped PW206C powered (477kW/640shp takeoff rated) A 109E Power, which first flew on February 8 1995 and was certificated in August 1996. Based on the A 109K2 it also features strengthened landing gear and an improved main rotor. Eight were ordered by the US Coast Guard as MH-68As. The military version is designated A 109M.

The A 109 has been offered in a number of mission specific configurations and is used widely in medevac, police and patrol roles worldwide. For the medevac mission a US firm developed the A 109 Max, with extended upward opening side doors and fairings giving greater internal volume.

Current production is of the A 109K2 and A 109 Power.

Agusta and Westland merged in 2000 to form AgustaWestland.

Photo: An A 109 Power. (AgustWestland)

AgustaWestland A 119 Koala

Country of origin: Italy

Type: Light utility helicopter

Powerplants: One 747kW (1002shp) takeoff rated, 650kW (872shp) max continuous rated Pratt & Whitney Canada PT6B-37A turboshaft driving a four blade main rotor and two blade tail rotor.

Performance: Max speed 267km/h (144kt). Service ceiling 20,000ft. Hovering ceiling out of ground effect 10,700ft, in ground effect 14,600ft. Range with auxiliary fuel 991km (535nm). Endurance 5hr 45min.

Weights: Basic empty 1430kg (3150lb), max takeoff with an internal load 2720kg (5997lb), max takeoff with a sling load 3150kg (6945lb).

Dimensions: Main rotor diameter 10.83m (35ft 6in), length overall rotors turning 13.01m (42ft 8in), fuselage length 11.07m (36ft 4in), height overall 3.50m (11ft 6in). Main rotor disc area 92.1m² (991.6sq ft).

Capacity: One pilot and passenger on flightdeck. Main cabin seats six in standard configuration. In an EMS configuration can accommodate two stretcher patients.

Production: Approx 35 sold at time of writing. Second assembly line to be established at Denel in South Africa. First delivery September 2000.

History: The 'widebody' A 119 Koala is a single engine development of the A 109 twin. It is designed for a range of utility transport missions where it makes economic sense to operate a single when the redundancy of a twin is not required.

Agusta began development work on the Koala in 1994, leading to the first prototype's maiden flight in early 1995. A second prototype flew later in that same year. Agusta originally aimed to gain certification for the A 119 in late 1996 but this was not achieved until mid 2000. Agusta said causes for the delays included strong sales demand for the A 109 Power, and that it was improving the A 119's performance in response to customer feedback.

One of the Koala's big marketing features is its large 'widebody' fuselage. Agusta says the cabin is 30% larger than those of any other current production single engine helicopter. A measure of the cabin size is that it can accommodate two stretcher patients in an EMS role, along with two medical attendants. Most other single engine helicopters typically are only equipped for a single stretcher because of a lack of space (AgustaWestland sees medical retrieval operators as prime potential Koala customers).

Access to the main cabin is via two large sliding doors, one either side of the fuselage. A baggage compartment in the rear of the fuselage is also accessible in flight.

The first prototype Koala was powered by a Turbomeca Arriel 1 turboshaft but it was subsequently re-engined with a 747kW (1002shp) takeoff rated Pratt & Whitney Canada PT6B-37, which powered the second prototype and was adopted for production aircraft. Another design feature is the Koala's composite four blade main rotor which features a titanium fully articulated maintenance free hub with elastomeric bearings and composite grips.

Photo: The A 119 Koala in flight. (AgustaWestland)

AgustaWestland EH 101

Countries of origin: Italy and United Kingdom

Type: Commuter, offshore oil rig support & utility helicopter

Powerplants: Three 1230kW (1649shp) max continuous rated General Electric CT7-6-GE-T6A turboshafts driving a five blade main rotor and four blade tail rotor.

Performance: Heliliner – Typical cruising speed 278km/h (150kt), long range cruising speed 260km/h (140kt). Service ceiling 15,000ft. Range offshore IFR equipped, standard fuel and reserves 1130km (610nm), with 30 pax, IFR equipped, fifth fuel tank and reserves 1390km (750nm). Endurance 5hr.

Weights: Heliliner – Operating empty (with IFR, offshore equipped) 9300kg (20,503lb), max takeoff 14,600kg (32,188lb).

Dimensions: Main rotor diameter 18.59m (61ft 0in), length rotors turning 22.80m (74ft 10in), fuselage length 19.53m (64ft 1in), height rotors turning 6.62m (21ft 9in). Main rotor disc area 271.5m² (2922.5sq ft).

Capacity: Flightcrew of two. Main cabin seating for 30 at four abreast and 76cm (30in) pitch. Equipped with galley and toilet.

Production: One sold to the Tokyo police. Total military orders 123.

History: AgustaWestland (formerly EH Industries) offers commercial developments of its EH 101 aimed at offshore oil rig support, airport/city centre shuttle and utility operations.

EH Industries was a collaborative venture between Westland of the UK and Agusta of Italy – which in 2000 merged to become AgustaWestland – formed to develop an anti submarine warfare helicopter for the Royal Navy and Italian navy. The partnership was formed in 1980 with both companies holding 50% each. From the outset both companies intended to develop civil and commercial models of the EH 101. Westland had design responsibility for the Heliliner, the anti submarine warfare variant was developed jointly, while Agusta headed development of military and utility transport versions with a rear loading ramp.

EH 101 full scale development began in March 1984. The first flight of an EH 101 (the Westland built PP1) was on October 9 1987, while the first civil configured EH 101, PP3, first flew on September 30 1988. The first production EH 101 (a Merlin for the Royal Navy) first flew in December 1995.

While the Royal Navy's EH 101 Merlin ASW helicopters and the Royal Air Force's Merlin HC.3 tactical transports have Rolls-Royce Turbomeca RTM322 engines, Italian and civil EH 101s have General Electric CT7 engines.

The 30 seat Heliliner variant is optimised either for offshore oil rig or airport to city centre transfers, and the rear freight door is offered as an option, while the civil utility version has the rear ramp fitted as standard. Canada's military has ordered 15 similar AW320 Cormorants for search and rescue work.

So far Tokyo's police is the only civil EH 101 customer, its single machine entered service in March 1999. In mid 2000 pre-production EH 101s PP8 and PP9 completed a 6000 hour Intensive Flight Operations Program (IFOP), the second phase of which was based in Aberdeen, UK. The program entailed flying simulated military and civil sorties to demonstrate reliability and maintainability.

Photo: Pre-production EH 101 PP8 on a North Sea oil rig.

American Champion & Bellanca series

Country or origin: United States of America

Type: Two seat utility and aerobatic light aircraft

Powerplant: 7GCBC Explorer – One 120kW (160hp) Textron Lycoming O-320-B2B flat four driving a two blade fixed pitch Sensench propeller. 8GCBC Scout – One 135kW (180hp) Lycoming O-360-C2A driving either a two blade fixed pitch or constant speed prop.

Performance: 7GCBC – Max speed 217km/h (117kt), cruising speed at 75% power 211km/h (114kt), at 65% power 198km/h (107kt). Max initial rate of climb 1345ft/min. Range at 55% power 965km (520nm). 8GCBC – Max speed 217km/h (162kt), cruising speed 209km/h (113kt). Initial rate of climb 1110ft/min. Range 725km (390nm).

Weights: 7GCBC – Empty 544kg (1200lb), max takeoff 816kg (1800lb). 8GCBC – Empty 595kg (1315lb), MTOW 975kg (2150lb).

Dimensions: 7GCBC – Wing span 10.49m (34ft 5in), length 6.92m (22ft 9in), height 2.36m (7ft 9in). Wing area 16.5m² (165sq ft). 8GCBC – Wing span 11.02m (36ft 2in), length 6.93m (22ft 9in), height 2.64m (8ft 8in). Wing area 16.7m² (180sq ft).

Capacity: Two in tandem. Scout can be fitted for crop spraying.

Production: Over 6000 of all models built. Almost 100 built in 1999.

History: The Citabria, Bellanca and Scout can trace their lineage back to the Aeronca 7 Champion (described separately).

Champion Aircraft Corporation purchased the production rights to the Aeronca 7 in 1951, and from this developed the 7EC Traveller and 7GCB Challenger. The Challenger-based Citabria first flew in May 1964. It had more glass area, a squarer tail and stressing for limited (+5g, -2g) aerobatic flight, while other features were the flapless wing and choice of 75kW (100hp) Continental O-200 or 80kW (108hp) Lycoming O-235 engines. Variants were the 110kW (150hp) O-320 powered 7GCAA and the 7GCBC with a longer span wing fitted with flaps.

Bellanca took over production of the Citabria in September 1970, renaming the 7ECA, by now then powered by an 85kW (115hp) O-235, as the Citabria; the 7GCAA the Citabria 150 and the 7GCBC the Citabria 150S. Champion initially developed the 7KCAB model, but Bellanca took this over, resulting in the fully aerobatic 8KCAB Decathlon. The ultimate Decathlon design was the 135kW (180hp) AEIO-360 powered Super Decathlon.

The Scout was designed for utility work, and appeared in 1970. The updated 8GCBC followed in 1974 with a 135kW (180hp) O-360.

Bellanca production ended in 1982, while the Champion Aircraft Company produced the range in limited numbers between 1985-86.

American Champion re-introduced all three models into production in 1990-91. American Champion currently builds the baseline 7ECA Citabria Aurora (re-introduced in 1995), the 7GCAA Citabria Adventure, the 7GCBC Citabria Explorer, 8KCAB Super Decathlon and the 8GCBC Scout (and Scout CS with constant speed propeller). These aircraft are basically similar to their earlier namesakes, save for some equipment changes and improvements, including metal spar wings (which is available for retrofit to older aircraft).

The company has also investigated returning the 7ACA Champ into production with a 60kW (80hp) Australian Jabiru engine.

Photo: An American Champion built 8GCBC Scout. (Bob Grimstead)

Airbus A300B2 & B4

Country of origin: Europe (France, Germany, Spain and UK)

Type: Medium range widebody airliner

Powerplants: A300B2/B4 – Two 227kN (51,000lb) General Electric CF6-50C or 236kN (53,000lb) Pratt & Whitney JT9D-9 turbofans.

Performance: A300B2-200 – Typical high speed cruising speed 917km/h (495kt), typical long range cruising speed 847km/h (457kt). Range with 269 passengers and reserves 3430km (1850nm). A300B4-200 – Speeds same. Range with 269 passengers and reserves 5375km (2900nm), range with max fuel 6300km (3400nm).

Weights: A300B2-200 – Operating empty 85,910kg (189,400lb), max takeoff 142,000kg (313,055lb). A300B4-200 – Operating empty 88,500kg (195,109lb), max takeoff 165,000kg (363,760lb).

Dimensions: Wing span 44.84m (147ft 1in), length 53.62m (175ft 11in), height 16.53m (54ft 3in). Wing area 260.0m² (2798.7sq ft).

Capacity: Flightcrew of two pilots and a flight engineer. Seating for between 220 and 336 single class passengers. Typical two class arrangement for 20 business and 230 economy class passengers.

Production: Total A300B2 and B4 orders 249. Approx 145 in service at late 2002, including 75 freighters.

History: The A300 is significant not only as it was world's first widebody twinjet airliner and a commercial success in its own right, but also for being the first design and foundation of the success of Airbus, now one of the world's two major jet airliner manufacturers.

Airbus Industrie was formed on December 18 1970 as a consortium with participation from the aerospace industries of France, Germany and the UK (Spain joined later) specifically to develop a twin engined 300 seat widebody 'air bus'.

Original design studies dated back to 1965, with the original 300 seat airliner concept (hence A300) over time evolving into a smaller 250 seater, the A300B. Two prototype A300B1s were built, the first of these flying from Toulouse in southern France on October 28 1972, the second on February 5 the next year. The General Electric CF6 was the only powerplant choice for initial A300s. The 2.65m (8ft 8in) longer A300B2 was the first production version. It first flew in June 1973 (the first production B2 flew in April 1974) and entered service with Air France on May 23 1974.

Subsequent versions included the B2-200 with Krueger leading edge flaps and different wheels and brakes; the B2-300 with increased weights for greater payload and multi stop capability; the B4-100, a longer range version of the B2 with Krueger flaps; and the increased max takeoff weight B4-200 which featured reinforced wings and fuselage, improved landing gear and optional rear cargo bay fuel tank. A small number of A300C convertibles were also built, these featured a main deck freight door behind the wing on the left hand side. Late in the A300B4's production life an optional two crew flightdeck was offered as the A300-200FF.

Production of the A300B4 ceased in May 1984, with manufacture switching to the improved A300-600.

The A300B4 is now popular as a freighter, with a number of companies (including Airbus) performing conversion programs, involving a forward freight door and strengthened main deck floor.

Photo: A TACA Cargo A300B4 freighter. (Rob Finlayson)

Airbus A300-600

Country of origin: Europe (France, Germany, Spain and UK)

Type: Medium range widebody airliner

Powerplants: Two 262.4kN (59,000lb) General Electric CF6-80C2A1s, or 273.6kN (61,500lb) CF6-80C2A5s, or 249kN (56,000lb) Pratt & Whitney PW4156s or 258kN (58,000lb) PW4158 turbofans.

Performance: A300-600R – Max cruising speed 897km/h (484kt), long range cruising speed 875km/h (472kt). Range at typical airline operating weight with 267 passengers with 370km (200nm) reserves and standard fuel 7505km (4050nm) with CF6s, or 7540km (4070nm) with PW4000s. A300-600 – Range at same parameters 6670km (3600nm). A300-600F – Range with max payload and reserves 4908km (2650nm).

Weights: A300-600 – Operating empty with CF6s 90,115kg (198,665lb), with PW4000s 90,065kg (198,565lb). Max takeoff 165,900kg (365,745lb). A300-600R – Operating empty 91,040kg (200,700lb) with CF6s, or 90,965kg (200,550lb) with PW4000s, max takeoff 170,500kg (375,855lb), or optionally 171,700kg (378,535lb). A300-600F – (CF6 powered) Operating empty 78,335kg (172,700lb), max takeoff 170,500kg (375,900lb).

Dimensions: Wing span 44.84m (147ft 1in), length 54.08m (177ft 5in), height 16.62m (54ft 6.5in). Wing area 260.0m² (2798.7sq ft).

Capacity: Flightcrew of two. Typical two class arrangement for 26 premium class passengers at six abreast and 240 economy class passengers at eight abreast. The A300-600 and -600R can carry 22 LD3 containers in forward and aft belly cargo holds. A300-600F total payload 55,017kg (121,290lb).

Production: 583 A300s of all models ordered by late 2002, including 334 A300-600s. Over 266 A300-600s had been delivered by late 2002, of which 252 were in service.

History: The A300-600 incorporated a number of significant improvements over the A300B4, including a two crew flightdeck and increased range.

The A300-600 introduced a two crew EFIS flightdeck with digital avionics based on that developed for the A310. Other changes included the A310's tail empennage which increased payload, small winglets (an option from 1989, standard from 1991), simplified systems, greater use of composites, Fowler flaps and increased camber on the wings, new brakes and APU, and improved payload/range through an extensive drag reducing airframe clean up and new engines. First flight was on July 8 1983, first delivery was to Saudia on March 26 1984.

The A300-600 was further developed into the longer range A300-600R, with a fuel trim tank in the tailplane and higher maximum takeoff weights. First flight was on December 9 1987, first delivery was on April 20 1988 (to American Airlines).

Convertible freight/passenger versions of all variants of the A300 have been offered, as has the all freight A300F4-600. The first new build pure freighter A300, one of 36 ordered by Federal Express, flew in December 1993. UPS is another major A300-600F customer, following its September 1998 order for 30. Most recent A300 sales have been for freighters.

Photo: A China Northern A300-600R at Beijing. (Rob Finlayson)

Airbus A300-600ST Super Transporter

Country of origin: Europe (France, Germany, Spain and UK)

Type: Oversize cargo freighter

Powerplants: Two 262.4kN (59,000lb) General Electric CF6-80C2A8 turbofans.

Performance: Max cruising speed 780km/h (421kt). Max certificated altitude 35,000ft. Range with a 40 tonne (88,105lb) payload 2778km (1500nm), range with a 26 tonne (57,268lb) payload 4630km (2500nm), range with max payload 1666km (900nm).

Weights: Empty 86,500kg (190,700lb), max payload 47,300kg (104,279lb), max takeoff 155,000kg (341,700lb).

Dimensions: Wing span 44.84m (147ft 0in), length 56.16m (184ft 3in), height 17.24m (56ft 7in). Wing area 260m² (2798.7sq ft). Internal useable length 37.70m (123ft 8in), diameter 7.40m (24ft 3in).

Capacity: The A300-600ST's internal main cabin volume is 1400m³ (49,442cu ft), and it can carry a range of oversize components, such as a fully equipped A330 or A340 wing shipset, or two A320/321 wing shipsets, or two A310 fuselage sections (front & rear).

Production: Airbus has taken delivery of five A300-600STs, the fifth delivered in 2001 is used for third party work.

History: The A300-600ST Super Transporter was designed to replace Airbus' Boeing Stratocruiser based Super Guppy transports, and are used to ferry large components such as wings and fuselage sections between Airbus' plants throughout western Europe.

Development of the A300-600ST, nicknamed Beluga and also Super Flipper, began in August 1991. The A300-600ST's tight development program – for what in many ways was effectively a new aircraft – saw the transport rolled out in June 1994, with first flight on September 13 that year. The A300-600ST then entered a 400 flight test program which culminated in mid 1995, with certification awarded that September and with delivery and entry into service with Airbus in January 1996.

All of the first four on order had been delivered by mid 1998 (allowing the Super Guppy's retirement in October 1997). A fifth Super Transporter was delivered in early 2001.

The A300-600ST is based on the A300-600 airliner, with which it shares the wing, lower fuselage, main undercarriage and cockpit. The main differences are a bulged, voluminous main deck, new forward lower fuselage, new enlarged tail with winglets and an upwards hinging main cargo door.

Program management of the A300-600ST was the responsibility of the Special Aircraft Transport Company, or SATIC, an economic interest grouping formed on a 50/50 basis by Aerospatiale and DASA (now both part of EADS) operating on behalf of Airbus. While much of the work on the aircraft was performed by the Airbus partners, other European companies were also involved in the program. The aircraft were completed by Sogerma at Toulouse.

The A300-600STs are operated for Airbus by Airbus Transport International (ATI). Apart from its Airbus work ATI increasingly also undertakes commercial third party charter work, with the fifth Super Transporter used almost exclusively for third party work. The first third party flight was on November 24 1996.

Photo: The fourth A300-600ST. (Paul Merritt)

Airbus A310

Country of origin: Europe (France, Germany, Spain and UK)

Type: Medium to long range widebody airliner

Powerplants: Initial powerplant choice of either two 213.5kN (48,000lb) Pratt & Whitney JT9D-7R4D1s or two 222.4kN (50,000lb) General Electric CF6-80A3 turbofans. Current choices of 238kN (53,500lb) CF6-80C2A2s, 262.4kN (59,000lb) CF6-80C2A8s, 231.2kN (52,000lb) PW4152s, or 249.1kN (56,000lb) PW4156s.

Performance: Max cruising speed 897km/h (484kt), long range cruising speed 850km/h (459kt). Range at typical airliner operating weight with 218 passengers and reserves 6800km (3670nm) for A310-200, 7982km (4310nm) for CF6 powered A310-300, 9580km (5170nm) for high gross weight A310-300 with CF6s.

Weights: A310-200 with CF6-80C2A2s – Operating empty 80,142kg (176,683lb), max takeoff 142,000kg (313,055lb). A310-300 with CF6-80C2A8s – Operating empty 81,205kg (179,025lb), max takeoff 150,000kg (330,695lb) standard, or higher gross weight options through to 164,000kg (361,560lb).

Dimensions: Wing span 43.89m (144ft 0in), length 46.66m (153ft 1in), height 15.80m (51ft 10in). Wing area 219.0m² (2357.3sq ft).

Capacity: Flightcrew of two. Max passenger capacity at nine abreast 280. Typical two class arrangement for 20 passengers at six abreast and 192 economy class passengers eight abreast. Cargo capacity in fore and aft underfloor compartments can hold 2.44 x 3.17m (88 x 125in) pallets or a total of up to 14 LD3 containers.

Production: Total A310 orders for 260 at late 2002, of which more than 255 had been delivered and 207 were in commercial service.

History: The A310 first began life as the A300B10, one of a number of projected developments and derivatives of Airbus' original A300B widebody twinjet airliner.

Compared with the larger A300, the A310 introduced a number of major changes. Airbus shortened the fuselage by 13 frames compared to the A300B, allowing seating for 200 to 230 passengers, and developed a new higher aspect ratio, smaller span wing. New and smaller horizontal tail surfaces, fly-by-wire outboard spoilers and a two crew EFIS flightdeck were incorporated, while the engine pylons were common to suit both engine options (GE and P&W).

The A310 program was formally launched in July 1978 and the prototype first flew on April 3 1982. Service entry was with Lufthansa in April 1983. Early production A310s did not have the small winglets that became a feature of later build A310-200s and the A310-300.

The A310-300 is a longer range development of the base A310-200, and has been in production since 1985. This version can carry a further 7000kg (15,430lb) of fuel in the tailplane.

The A310-200F freighter is available new build or as a conversion of existing aircraft and has proven quite popular (over 40 A310-200s have been converted to freighters for freight express giant FedEx). The A310-200C convertible passenger/freighter variant first entered service with Dutch operator Martinair in 1984.

Photo: A Pakistan International A310-300. Apart from the shorter fuselage, the A310 can be distinguished from the A300 by the above wing emergency exit. (Rob Finlayson)

Airbus A318

Country of origin: Europe (France, Germany, Spain and UK)

Type: 100 seat regional airliner

Powerplants: Two 97.9kN (22,000lb) Pratt & Whitney PW6122s or 106.8kN (24,000lb) PW6124s or 97.9kN (22,000lb) CFM International CFM56-5B turbofans.

Performance: PW6122 – Range with 107 pasengers at 59 tonne TO weight 2707km (1462nm), at 61.5 tonne TO weight 3630km (1960nm), at 66 tonne (145,505lb) TO weight 5222km (2820nm).

Weights: Operating empty 39,035kg (86,057lb), max takeoff 59,000kg (129,955lb) or optionally 61,500kg (135,463lb), 66,000kg (145,505lb) or 68,000kg (149,915lb).

Dimensions: Wing span 34.09m (111ft 10in), length 31.45m (103ft 2in), height 12.56m (41ft 3in). Wing area 122.6m2 (1319.7sq ft).

Capacity: Flightcrew of two. Standard seating for 107 passengers (eight premium class at four abreast and 97cm/38in pitch, 99 economy class at six abreast and 81cm/32in pitch). Single class seating for 117 at 81cm (32in) pitch at six abreast.

Production: At late 2002 Airbus held firm orders for 90 A318s.

History: The A318 is Airbus' smallest airliner and is the European manufacturer's first foray into the 100 seat market.

Airbus' initial efforts at developing a 100 seat airliner were focused on the all new AE31X program (covering the baseline 95 seat AE316 and 115-125 seat AE317) which Airbus and Alenia, as Airbus Industrie Asia, were developing in conjunction with AVIC of China and Singapore Technologies. The AE31X would have been assembled in China. However in September 1998 Airbus announced termination of the project.

Even before the cancellation of the AE31X program Airbus had been independently studying a minimum change 100 seat derivative of the A319 covered by the A319M5 designation (M5 = minus five fuselage frames). Following the AE31X's cancellation Airbus announced the commercial launch of the A319M5 as the A318 at the 1998 Farnborough Airshow. Industrial launch followed on April 26 1999 with sales commitments for 109.

Compared with the A319, the A318 is 2.4m (7ft 10in) shorter, reducing standard two class seating from 124 to 107. Powerplant choices are the all new Pratt & Whitney PW6000s or the CFM56. Other changes include a small dorsal fillet added to the tail, modified wing camber, and a reduced size cargo door (to maintain engine nacelle clearance for loading vehicles).

Otherwise the A318 retains 95% commonality with the rest of the A320 family, including the advanced flightdeck with side stick controllers and fly-by-wire flight controls allowing a pilot common type rating, and the same six abreast fuselage cross section.

A318 final assembly takes place at Hamburg, Germany, alongside the A319 and A321. The A318 is also the first airliner application for laser welding, which reduces cost and weight.

The A318 first flew with PW6000s in on January 15 2002. Performance problems with the PW6000 engine have delayed the A318's service entry from late 2002 to July 2003, with the CFM powered variant now planned to be the first to enter service.

Photo: The CFM56 powered A318 on its August 29 2002 first flight.

Airbus A319

Country of origin: Europe (France, Germany, Spain and UK)

Type: Short to medium range narrowbody airliner

Powerplants: Two 97.9kN (22,000lb) CFM International CFM56-5A4 or International Aero Engines IAE V2522-A5 turbofans, or optionally 104.5kN (23,500lb) CFM56-5A5s or V2524-A5s.

Performance: Speeds similar to A320. Range at 64 tonne (141,095lb) takeoff weight 3357km (1813nm), range at 75,500kg (166,450lb) takeoff weight with 104.5kN (23,500lb) engines 6845km (3697nm).

Weights: Operating empty 40,160kg (88,537lb) or optionally 41,203kg (90,837lb), standard max takeoff 64,000kg (141,094lb) or optionally 75,500kg (166,450lb).

Dimensions: Wing span 34.09m (111ft 10in), length 33.84m (111ft 0in), height 11.76m (38ft 7in). Wing area 122.6m² (1319.7sq ft).

Capacity: Seating for 124 passengers in a typical two class configuration (eight premium class and 116 economy class). High density single class layout can seat 142 passengers.

Production: At late 2002 total orders for the A319 stood at 742 with 484 delivered.

History: The A319 is a shortened, 124 seat class development of Airbus' highly successful single aisle A320, and competes with Boeing's Next Generation 737-700.

The A319 program was launched at the Paris Airshow in June 1993 on the strength of just six orders placed by ILFC late in 1992 and the predicted better prospects of the commercial airliner market, which were certainly realised. The first A319 airline order came from French carrier Air Inter (since merged into Air France), whose order for six was announced in February 1994. Since then Swissair (now Swiss), Air Canada, Lufthansa, Northwest, United, US Airways and British Airways are among the major customers that have ordered more than 700 A319s (all also operate A320s).

The A319 first flew on August 25 1995 from Hamburg in Germany. European JAA certification and service entry, with Swissair, took place in April 1996.

The A319 is a minimum change, shortened derivative of the highly successful A320. The major difference between the A320 and A319 is that the latter is shorter by seven fuselage frames, while in almost all other respects the A319 and A320 are identical.

The fly-by-wire A319 features Airbus' common two crew glass cockpit with sidestick controllers first introduced on the A320. There are significant crew training cost benefits and operational savings from this arrangement as the A319, A320 and A321 (and soon A318) can all be flown by pilots with the same type rating. Further, the identical cockpit means reduced training times for crews converting to the larger A330 and A340.

A319 (and A321 and A318) final assembly takes place in Hamburg. Final assembly of all other Airbus airliners, including the A320, takes place at Toulouse.

The A319 forms the basis for the new baby of the Airbus family, the A318 100 seater (described separately), and the Airbus Corporate Jetliner (also described separately).

Photo: A CFM56 powered Finnair A319. (Rob Finlayson)

Airbus A320

Country of origin: Europe (France, Germany, Spain and UK)

Type: Short to medium range airliner

Powerplants: 1998 production onwards – Two 120.1kN (27,000lb) CFM International CFM56-5B4/P or 117.9kN (26,500lb) International Aero Engines IAE V2527E-A5 turbofans.

Weights: A320-200 – Operating empty with V2527-A5s 42,482kg (93,657lb); with CFM56-5B4/Ps 42,100kg (92,815lb). Standard max takeoff for both engines 73,500kg (162,040lb) or optionally 75,500kg (166,445lb) or 77,000kg (169,755lb).

Performance: A320-200 – Max cruising speed 903km/h (487kt) at 28,000ft, econ cruising speed 840km/h (454kt) at 37,000ft. Range with 150 passengers with CFM56-5B4/Ps 4800km (2592nm), or 5185km (2800nm), or 5639km (3045nm); with V2527-A5s 4807km (2596nm) or optionally 5317km (2871nm) or 5676km (3065nm).

Dimensions: Wing span 34.09m (111ft 10in), length 37.57m (123ft 3in), height 11.76m (38ft 7in). Wing area 122.6m^2 (1319.7sq ft).

Capacity: Flightcrew of two. Main cabin can seat 179 passengers in a high density layout. Typical two class seating arrangement for 12 passengers at four abreast and 138 at six abreast. Seven LD3 based containers in fore and aft cargo holds.

Production: As of late 2002 firm orders for the A320 stood at 1623 with 1116 delivered.

History: The four member A320 family is a significant sales success and was a technological trailblazer. The 150 seat A320 is the foundation and best selling member of the family.

The A320 is perhaps best known as the first airliner to introduce a digital fly-by-wire flight control system – where control inputs from the pilot are transmitted to the flying surfaces by electronic signals rather than mechanical cables, pulleys and rods. The advantage of Airbus' fly-by-wire system, apart from a small weight saving, is that as it is computer controlled, software flight envelope protection makes it virtually impossible to exceed certain flight parameters such as G limits and the aircraft's maximum and minimum operating speeds and angle of attack limits.

Also integral to the A320 is the advanced electronic flightdeck, with six fully integrated EFIS colour displays and innovative sidestick controllers rather than conventional control columns. The A320 also employs a relatively high percentage of composite materials compared to earlier designs. Two engines are offered, the CFM56 and IAE V2500.

The A320 program was launched on March 23 1984, first flight occurred on February 22 1987, and JAA certification was awarded on February 26 1988. Launch customer Air France took delivery of its first A320 in March that year.

The initial production version was the A320-100, which was built in only small numbers for launch customers Air France and British Caledonian. The definitive A320-200 was certificated in November 1988 with increased max takeoff weight, increased fuel capacity, greater range and winglets.

The stretched A321 and shortened A319 and A318 are described separately. All four share a common pilot type rating.

Photo: A JMC Airlines A320s. (Rob Finlayson)

Airbus A321

Country of origin: Europe (France, Germany, Spain and UK)

Type: Short to medium range narrowbody airliner

Powerplants: A321-100 – Two 133.4kN (30,000lb) International Aero Engines V2530-A5s or CFM International CFM56-5B1 turbofans. CFM56-5B2s of 137.9kN (31,000lb) available as an option. A321-200 – As above or 142.3kN (32,000lb) CFM56-5B3s or 146.8kN (33,000lb) V2533-A5s.

Performance: A321-100 – Max cruising speed 903km/h (488kt), economical cruising speed 828km/h (447kt). Range with 186 passengers and reserves 4352km (2350nm) with V2530s, 4260km (2300nm) with CFM56s. A321-200 – Range 4907km (2650nm).

Weights: A321-100 – Operating empty 48,200kg (106,265lb) with V2530s, 48,085kg (106,010lb) with CFM56s. Max takeoff (with either engine option) 83,000kg (182,984lb) or 85,000kg (187,390lb). A321-200 – Operating empty 48,024kg (105,875lb) with CFM56-5B3s, 48,139kg (106,130lb) with V2533-A5s, max takeoff 89,000kg (196,210lb) or optionally 93,000kg (205,030lb).

Dimensions: Wing span 34.09m (111ft 10in), length 44.51m (146ft 0in), height 11.76m (38ft 7in). Wing area 122.6m^2 (1319.7sq ft).

Capacity: Flightcrew of two. Max seating 220 in a high density layout. Typical two class seating for 16 passengers at four abreast, and 169 passengers at six abreast.

Production: 415 A321s ordered by late 2002 with 253 delivered.

History: The 185 seat Airbus A321 is a stretch of the successful A320.

Airbus launched the A321 in November 1989 and the first development aircraft first flew on March 11 1993. European certification was awarded in December that year.

Compared with the A320 the A321's major change is the stretched fuselage, with forward and rear fuselage plugs totalling 6.93m (22ft 9in) – a front plug immediately forward of the wing of 4.27m/14ft, a rear plug directly behind the wing of 2.67m/8ft 9in.

Other changes include strengthening of the undercarriage to cope with the higher weights, more powerful engines, a simplified and revised fuel system and larger tyres for better braking. A slightly modified wing with double slotted flaps and modifications to the fly-by-wire flight controls allows the A321's handling characteristics to closely resemble the A320's. The A321 features an identical flightdeck to that on the A318, A319 and A320, and four types share the same type rating.

The basic A321-100's range is reduced compared to the A320 as fuel tankage remained unchanged. Airbus launched the longer range, heavier A321-200 in 1995, has full passenger load transcontinental US range. This is achieved through 2900 litres (766US gal/638Imp gal) greater fuel capacity with the installation of an ACT (additional centre tank), higher thrust V2533-A5 or CFM56-5B3 engines and minor structural strengthening.

The A321-200 first flew from the then Daimler Benz Aerospace's Hamburg facilities in December 1996. A321s are assembled at Hamburg, along with the A318 and A319.

Photo: An IAE V2500 powered Sichuan Airlines A321. (Rob Finlayson)

Airbus A330-200

Country of origin: Europe (France, Germany, Spain and UK)

Type: Long range widebody airliner

Powerplants: Two 300.3kN (67,500lb) General Electric CF6-80E1A4 turbofans, or 286.7kN (64,000lb) Pratt & Whitney PW4164s, or 302.5kN (68,000lb) PW4168s, or 302.5kN (68,000lb) Rolls-Royce Trent 768s or 320.2kN (72,000lb) Trent 772s.

Performance: Max cruising speed 880km/h (475kt) at 33,000ft, economical cruising speed 860km/h (464kt). Range with max passengers and reserves at 230t MTOW 11,850km (6400nm), at 217t MTOW 8890km (4800nm).

Weights: A330-200 – Operating empty 120,470kg (265,600lb) with CF6 engines, 121,070kg (266,925lb) with PW4168s, or 120,565kg (265,800lb) with Trents. Max takeoff 230,000kg (507,050lb).

Dimensions: Wing span 60.30m (197ft 10in), length 59.00m (193ft 7in), height 16.83m (55ft 2in). Wing area 363.1m² (3908.4sq ft).

Capacity: Flightcrew of two. Passenger seating arrangements for 256 in three classes or 293 in two classes.

Production: Total A330 orders stood at 426 at late 2002, of which over 243 delivered. 105 A330-200s were in service.

History: The Airbus A330-200 is a long range, shortened development of the standard A330-300.

Airbus launched development of the A330-200 in November 1995. First flight was on August 13 1997, with simultaneous European and US certification awarded on March 31 1998 with delivery to launch operator Canada 3000 the following May.

The A330-200 shares near identical systems, airframe, flightdeck and wings with the A330-300, the only major differences being the fuselage length and bigger tail. Compared with the -300 the A330-200 is 10 fuselage frames shorter, and so has an overall length of 59.00m (193ft 7in), compared with 63.70m (209ft 0in) for the standard length aircraft. This allows the A330-200 to seat 253 passengers in a three class configuration, or alternatively 293 in two classes.

The A330-200 features enlarged horizontal and vertical tail services (to compensate for the loss of moment arm with the shorter fuselage). A centre fuel tank increases fuel capacity and results in the -200's 11,850km (6400nm) range. Like the larger A330-300, the -200 is offered with a choice of three powerplants, the Rolls-Royce Trent 700, General Electric CF6-80E and Pratt & Whitney PW4000. From late 2002 A330-200s are being delivered with the improved flightdeck developed for the A330-500/600, which features larger liquid crystal displays. Airbus is also studying fitting the A330 with head-up displays.

Airbus has studied shortened versions of the A330-200 as a potential replacements for the A300. Airbus dropped the nine frame shortened A330-100 study for the eight frame shorter, 222 seat 12,970km (7000nm) range A330-500, which it publicly announced in July 2000. However the A330-500 failed to attract strong customer interest.

Another proposed A330-200 variant is the A330-200F freighter which would have a 63 tonne payload and a 7870km (4250nm) range.

Photo: A Swiss A330-200. (Swiss)

Airbus A330-300

Country of origin: Europe (France, Germany, Spain and UK)

Type: Large capacity medium to long range airliner

Powerplants: Two 300.3kN (67,500lb) General Electric CF6-80E1A4 turbofans, or 284.7kN (64,000lb) Pratt & Whitney PW4164s, or 302.5kN (68,000lb) PW4168s or Rolls-Royce Trent 768s, or 320.2kN (72,000lb) Trent 772s or 324kN (73,000lb) PW4173s.

Performance: Max cruising speed 880km/h (475kt) at 33,000ft, economical cruising speed 860km/h (464kt). Range at 230,000kg (507,050lb) max takeoff weight 10,400km (5616nm).

Weights: Operating empty 127,520kg (281,125lb) with CF6 engines, 124,855kg (275,250lb) with PW4000s, 127,615kg (281,350lb) with Trents; max takeoff 233,000kg (513,675lb).

Dimensions: Wing span 60.30m (197ft 10in), length 63.60m (208ft 8in), height 16.74m (54ft 11in). Wing area 361.6m² (3892.2sq ft).

Capacity: Flightcrew of two. Passenger seating arrangements for 295 in three classes or 335 in two class (30 premium class at 2+3+2 and 305 economy at 2+4+2). Max passengers in high density configuration 440. Front and rear underbelly cargo holds can take 32 LD3 containers or 11 pallets.

Production: Total A330 orders stood at 426 at late 2002, of which over 243 delivered. 114 A330-300s were in service.

History: The A330-300 is the largest Airbus twinjet and is closely related to the four engined long range A340-300/-200 with which it shares near identical systems, airframe, flightdeck and wings.

The A340 and A330 were launched simultaneously on June 5 1987. Although developed in parallel, the A330-300 made its first flight after the A340, on November 2 1992. It was the first aircraft to achieve simultaneous European Joint Airworthiness Authorities (JAA) and US FAA certification, on October 21 1993. Entry into service (with France's Air Inter) was in January 1994.

Differences from the A340-300/-200 aside from the number of engines are slight changes to the wing and internal systems, including fuel tankage, and the A330-300 and A340-300 share the same fuselage length. The A330 (like the A340) features a number of technologies first pioneered on the A320, including Airbus' common advanced EFIS flightdeck with sidestick controllers and fly-by-wire computerised flight control system.

Over the A330-300's life Airbus has progressively increased the airliner's max takeoff weights from the basic aircraft's 213 tonnes, to 217 tonnes, 230 tonnes and most recently in early 2001 233 tonnes, each time increasing payload range. Airbus has also looked at a 240 tonne MTOW development.

From late 2002 A330s are being delivered with the improved flightdeck developed for the A330-500/600, which features larger liquid crystal displays. Airbus is also studying fitting the A330 with head-up displays.

Airbus has studied various stretched (A330-400) and shortened (A330-100, -200 and -500) A330 variants. One stretched concept studied featured lower deck seating in place of the forward freight hold. The shortened, longer range A330-200 was launched in 1996.

Photo: An Aer Lingus A330-300. (Rob Finlayson)

Airbus A340-200 & -300

Country of origin: Europe (France, Germany, Spain and UK)

Type: Long range widebody airliners

Powerplants: A330-200/-300 – Four 145kN (32,550lb) CFM International CFM56-5C3 turbofans (initially 138.8kN/31,200lb CFM56-5Cs). A340-300E – Four 151.2kN (34,000lb) CFM56-5C4s.

Performance: A340-200 – Max cruising speed 914km/h (494kt), econ cruising speed 880km/h (475kt). Range with 263 passengers 13,805km (7450nm). A340-300 – Speeds same. Range with 295 passengers standard -300 13,334km (7200nm), -300E 13,704km (7400nm).

Weights: A340-200 – Operating empty 126,000kg (277,775lb), max takeoff 260,000kg (573,200lb). A340-300 – Operating empty 129,300kg (285,050lb), max takeoff 271,000kg (597,450lb), initially 260,000kg (573,200lb). A340-300E – Operating empty 130,200kg (287,050lb), max takeoff 275,000kg (606,275lb).

Dimensions: A340-200 – Wing span 60.30m (197ft 0in), length 59.39m (194ft 10in), height 16.74m (54ft 11in). Wing area 363.1m² (3908.4sq ft). A340-300 – Same except for length 63.70m (209ft 0in).

Capacity: Flightcrew of two. A340-200 – Typical three class arrangement for 263 passengers, or 303 in two classes. A340-300 – Typical three class accommodation for 303, or 335 in two classes. All versions are offered with underfloor passenger sleepers.

Production: A total of 262 A340-200/-300s had been ordered by late 2002, of which 203 were in service.

History: The A340-200 and -300 are the initial variants of the successful quad engined A340 family of long haul widebodies.

The A340 and closely related A330 were launched on June 5 1987. The A340-300 first flew on October 25 1991, European certification was awarded in December 1992, and service entry was in January 1993 with Lufthansa.

The A340 shares the same flightdeck including sidestick controllers and EFIS, plus fly-by-wire, basic airframe, systems, fuselage and wing with the A330 (the flightdeck is also common to the A320 series). Power is from four CFM56s, Airbus says the four engine configuration is more efficient for long range flights (as twins need more power for a given weight for engine out on takeoff performance), and quads are free from ETOPS restrictions.

The A340-300 has the same fuselage length as the A330-300, while the shortened A340-200 traded seating capacity for greater range (first flight April 1 1992). Both feature a third main undercarriage unit (with two wheels), which retracts into the fuselage. From 1996 the A340-300 gained an additional centre fuel tank, greater range and a 271,000kg (597,450lb) MTOW.

The 275,000kg (606,275lb) MTOW A340-213X (nee A340-8000) is based on the -200 but has extra fuel in three additional rear cargo hold tanks and a 15,000km (8100nm) range with 232 passengers. One was built and is now in service with Jordan's royal family.

Airbus now offers the 275,000kg (606,275lb) MTOW A340-300 Enhanced powered by the upgraded CFM56-5C Enhanced. Other features include improvements, including liquid crystal displays on the flightdeck, fly-by-wire rudder and extra crew rest facilities (developed for the A340-500/-600). Range is boosted by 370km (200nm).

Photo: A LanChile A340-300. (John Adlard)

Airbus A340-500 & -600

Country of origin: Europe (France, Germany, Spain and UK)

Type: Long range widebody airliners

Powerplants: Four 249kN (56,000lb) Rolls-Royce Trent 556 turbofans.

Performance: Typical cruising speed Mach 0.83. A340-500 – Range with 313 passengers 15,742km (8500nm). A340-600 – Range with 380 passengers 13,890km (7500nm).

Weights: A340-500 – Operating empty 170,400kg (375,665lb), max takeoff 365,000kg (804,675lb). A340-600 – Operating empty 177,000kg (390,220lb), max takeoff 365,000kg (804,675lb).

Dimensions: A340-500 – Wing span 63.70m (209ft 0in), length 67.80m (222ft 5in), height 17.80m (58ft 5in). Wing area 437.0m² (4704sq ft). A340-600 – Same except length 75.30m (247ft 1in).

Capacity: A340-500 – Flightcrew of two. Typical three class seating for 313 passengers. A340-600 Typical three class seating for 380.

Production: At late 2002 Airbus held 64 firm orders for the A340-500/-600.

History: The 16,020km (8650nm) ultra long range A340-500 and stretched 380 seat A340-600 are new variants of the Airbus A340 quad.

Compared with the A340-300 the A340-600 features a 9.07m (35ft 1in) stretch (5.87m/19ft 3in ahead of the wing and 3.20m/10ft 6in behind), allowing it to seat 372 passengers in a typical three class arrangement. This gives Airbus a true early model 747 replacement and near direct competitor to the 747-400.

The A340-500 meanwhile is stretched by only 3.19m (10ft 6in) compared with the A340-300, and so seats 313 in three classes, but has a massive range of 16,020km (8650nm), making it the longest ranging airliner in the world (at least until the 777-200LR arrives), capable for example of operating Los Angeles/Singapore nonstop.

The two new A340 models share a common wing which is based on the A330/A340's but is longer and has a tapered wingbox insert, increasing wing area and fuel capacity. Both models feature three fuselage plugs. The other change to the A340 airframe is the use of the A330-200 twin's larger fin and enlarged horizontal area stabilisers. To cope with the increased weights the centre undercarriage main gear is a four wheel bogie, rather than a two wheel unit.

Both new A340s have a high degree of commonality with the A330 and other A340 models. They will feature Airbus' common two crew flightdeck, but introduce improvements such as liquid crystal rather than CRT displays and modernised systems. Power is from four 249kN (56,000lb) thrust Rolls-Royce Trent 556 turbofans.

The commercial launch for A340-500/-600 was at the 1997 Paris Airshow, the program's industrial launch was in December that year when Virgin Atlantic ordered eight A340-600s and optioned eight. The A340-600 was the first to fly, on April 23 2001. European certification was awarded in May 2002, US certification in July. Service entry with Virgin Atlantic followed July 2002's Farnborough Airshow.

The A340-500 first flew on February 2002 and service entry with Air Canada is planned for November 2003.

Thus far the new airliners have sold relatively slowly, a cause not helped by Swissair's collapse in October 2001 and subsequent cancellation of an order for nine A340-600s.

Photo: Virgin Atlantic's first A340-600. (Glenn Alderton)

Airbus A380

Country of origin: Europe (France, Germany, Spain and UK)

Type: High capacity, long range, twin deck, widebody airliner

Powerplants: A380-800 – Four 302kN (67,890lb) Rolls-Royce Trent 900 or Engine Alliance (GE & P&W) GP7200 turbofans. A380-800HGW – Four 311kN (69,915lb) Trent 900s or GP7200s.

Performance: A380-800 – Max cruising speed Mach 0.88. Long range cruising speed Mach 0.85. HGW range 15,100km (8150nm).

Weights: A380-800 – Operating empty 276,800kg (610,240lb), max takeoff 560,000kg (1,234,580lb). A380-800HGW – Max takeoff 586,000kg (1,291,900lb).

Dimensions: A380-800 – Wing span 79.80m (261ft 10in), length 73.00m (239ft 6in), height 24.10m (79ft 1in). Wing area 845.0m² (9095.5sq ft).

Capacity: A380-800 – Flightcrew of two. Airbus says seating for 555 passengers on two decks in three classes (10 abreast in economy on main deck, eight on upper deck), typical airline configurations likely to seat around 515. A380 has 49% more floor area than 747-400.

Production: 95 firm orders at late 2002.

History: The 555 seat, double deck Airbus A380 is the most ambitious civil aircraft program yet. When it enters service in 2006, the A380 will be the world's largest airliner.

Airbus first began studies on a very large 500 seat airliner in the early 1990s. Engineering studies of the then A3XX began in 1994. A 12 abreast single deck design was soon rejected for a twin deck configuration. Design aims included 15% lower direct operating costs per seat compared with the 747-400 and the ability to use existing airport infrastructure with little modifications to the airports.

Airbus formally launched the A380 on December 19 2000 after gaining 50 launch order commitments from five airlines (Emirates, Singapore, Air France, Qantas and Virgin Atlantic) and lessor ILFC. The out of sequence A380 designation was chosen as the '8' represents the twin decks. First flight is planned for early 2005, while service entry, with Singapore Airlines, is scheduled for March 2006.

The A380 will feature an advanced flightdeck with pull-out keyboards for the pilots, and a high degree of composite construction (including pioneering GLARE, an aluminium/glass fibre composite).

Several A380 models are planned. The basic aircraft is the A380-800 and high gross weight A380-800, with the longer range A380-800R planned. The 590 tonne MTOW 10,410km (5620nm) range A380-800F freighter will be able to carry a 150 tonne payload and is due to enter service in 2008 – launch customers are Emirates and FedEx. Future models will include the shortened, 480 seat A380-700, and the stretched, 656 seat A380-900.

Airbus froze the A380's general configuration design in early 2001. Metal cutting for the first A380 component occurred in January 2002. In 2002 more than 6000 people were working on A380 development.

A380 final assembly will take place in new facilities at Airbus' Toulouse, France, home, with interior fitment in Hamburg, Germany. Major A380 assemblies will be transported to Toulouse by ship, barge and road.

Photo: Lufthansa has ordered 15 A380s. (Airbus)

Airbus Corporate Jetliner

Country of origin: European consortium

Type: Long range large corporate jet

Powerplants: Two 120kN (27,000lb) International Aero Engines IAE V2527M-A5 turbofans (CFM International CFM56s optional).

Performance: Max cruising speed Mach 0.82. Max altitude 41,000ft. Range with 12 passengers up to 11,100km (6000nm), range with 40 passengers up to 8300km (4500nm).

Weights: Max takeoff 75,500kg (166,400lb).

Dimensions: Wing span 33.91m (111ft 3in), length 33.80m (110ft 11in), height 11.80m (38ft 8.5in). Wing area 122.4m² (1317.5sq ft).

Capacity: Flightcrew of two. Six standard layouts offered, seating from 10 to 39 passengers.

Production: First customer delivery December 1999, 14 delivered by mid 2002, by which time Airbus held orders and commitments for 30. Green airframe costs approx $US36m, outfitting $US4-10m.

History: The Airbus Corporate Jetliner, or ACJ, is a long range corporate jet development of the A319 airliner which competes directly with the Boeing Business Jet and dedicated long range corporate jets such as the Bombardier Global Express and Gulfstream V.

Airbus launched the ACJ at the 1997 Paris Airshow and the first ACJ rolled out in October 1998. The airframe was then due to be fitted with belly auxiliary fuel tanks and flight test instrumentation prior to making a first flight in May 1999. Certification (to FAA Part 121 and JAR OPS) was awarded in July 1999, with the first delivery, to the Al Kharafi Group, that December.

The ACJ was designed as a minimum change development of the A319. One of its key design features is that the A319CJ can be easily converted to an airliner, thus increasing the aircraft's potential resale value. The ACJ can be powered by either the IAE V2500 or CFM56, although in October 2000 Airbus signed an agreement with IAE to make the V2500 the 'reference' engine on the aircraft. As a consequence the V2500 powered ACJ is now offered to potential customers as a package.

The A319's containerised cargo hold means that the ACJ's auxiliary fuel tanks can be easily loaded and unloaded, giving operators flexibility to reconfigure the aircraft for varying payload/range requirements. Like the rest of the A320 single aisle family (plus the A330 and A340), the ACJ shares Airbus' common advanced six screen glass flightdeck with sidestick controllers (but with a new flight management system), plus fly-by-wire flight controls. It also features a standard integral airstair and has a higher cruising altitude than the A319 airliner.

Airbus supplies green ACJ airframes to the customer's choice of one of six outfitters – Air France Industries, Associated Air Center (Dallas), Jet Aviation (Basle), EADS Sogerma (Toulouse & Lake Charles, USA), Lufthansa Technik (Hamburg) and Ozark Aircraft Systems – for interior fitment. Interiors weigh 3.8 tonnes (8500lb) to 4.8 tonnes (10,700lb) and installation takes from four to eight months.

The first A319CJ order was announced in December 1997. Customers include Qatar Air, Aero Service Executive, the Italian and French air forces and DaimlerChrysler.

Photo: Qatar Air's ACJ. (Paul Merritt)

Air Tractor AT-301, AT-401 & AT-501

Air Tractor turbine models

Country of origin: United States of America

Type: Piston powered agricultural aircraft

Powerplant: AT-301 – One 447kW (600hp) Pratt & Whitney R-1340 radial piston engine driving a two blade prop. AT-401B – One remanufactured 447kW (600hp) P&W R-1340, two or three blade prop.

Performance: AT-301 – Max speed 266km/h (144kt), economical cruising speed 225km/h (122kt), working speed 193-225km/h (104-122kt). Range with max fuel and no reserves 869km (469nm). AT-401B – Max cruising speed 251km/h (135kt), cruising speed 230km/h (124kt), typical working speed 193-225km/h (104-122kt). Range with max fuel and no reserves 1015km (547nm).

Weights: AT-301 – Empty 1656kg (3650lb), loaded 3130kg (6900lb). AT-401B – Empty (spray equipped) 1950kg (4300lb), standard max takeoff 3565kg (7860lb), optional max takeoff 4082kg (9000lb).

Dimensions: AT-301 – Wing span 13.75m (45ft 2in), length 8.23m (27ft 0in), height 2.59m (8ft 6in). Wing area 25.1m² (270sq ft). AT-401B – Same except span 15.57m (51ft 1in). Wing area 28.4m² (306.0sq ft).

Capacity: Pilot only. Chemical spray hopper capacity of 1210 litres in AT-301, 1325 litres in AT-301A/B and 1515 litres in AT-401.

Production: More than 1700 Air Tractors of all models have been built, including more than 665 AT-301s, 270 AT-401s and 11 AT-501s.

History: The AT-301, AT-401 and AT-501 are the radial piston powered members of the series of the successful Air Tractor family.

The Air Tractor was designed by company founder Leland Snow who had earlier designed and built the Snow S-2 ag aircraft (which was later built by Rockwell and Ayres). Leland Snow today remains president of the Olney, Texas based company he established. Snow began work on the Air Tractor AT-301 in January 1971 (he formed Air Tractor in 1974). The prototype first flew in September 1973 and the type was awarded FAA certification in November of that year.

The AT-301 was similar in configuration to Snow's earlier S-2 series. It was powered by a remanufactured 447kW (600hp) Pratt & Whitney R-1340 (the R-1340 has been out of production since the mid '50s). Spray bars mounted below and behind the wing's leading edge dispensed the hopper's 1210 litre chemical capacity.

Air Tractor introduced the improved AT-301A, with a larger capacity 1325 litre capacity hopper, in 1981. The AT-301 and -301A were built side-by-side until 1987 when Air Tractor replaced the AT-301A with the slightly improved, shortlived AT-301B.

Meanwhile in 1986 Air Tractor developed the AT-301 based AT-401, with a 1.22m (4ft 0in) increased span wing, a 1514 litre capacity hopper and increased max takeoff weight. The AT-401 replaced the -301 in 1987 and remains in production as the AT-401B with remanufactured R-1340 and increased span wings with Hoerner wingtips. The AT-401A was a one-off with a PZL-3S radial flown in 1990. Orenda's V8 OE600A conversion for the AT-401 was certificated in late 2001.

The AT-500 prototype with a 16.15m (53ft 0in) wing span, three blade prop and higher landing gear debuted in 1985. It was the basis for the production 15.24m (50ft) span AT-501 (certificated mid 1987) and 11 were built to 1992 (they could be converted to turbine AT-502s).

Photo: An AT-401 in Air Tractor's standard yellow and blue colours.

Country of origin: United States of America

Type: Turboprop powered agricultural and firebombing aircraft

Powerplant: AT-502 – One 507kW (680shp) Pratt & Whitney Canada PT6A series turboprop, optionally a 560kW (750shp) PT6A, driving a three blade prop. AT-802 – One 966kW (1295shp) PT6-65AG or -67AG, or 1007kW (1350shp) PT6A-67AGR or -67AF driving a five blade prop.

Performance: AT-502 – Max speed 290kmh (155kt), typical operating speeds 195 to 235km/h (105 to 125kt). Initial rate of climb 1080ft/min. Range with max fuel 998km (538nm). AT-802 – Max speed 338km/h (182kt), max cruising speed 314km/h (170kt). Initial rate of climb 800ft/min. Range with max fuel 805km (434nm).

Weights: AT-502 – Empty 1870kg (4123lb), MTOW 4175kg (9200lb). AT-802 – Empty equipped 2903kg (6400lb), MTOW 7257kg (16,000lb).

Dimensions: AT-502 – Wing span 15.24m (50ft in), length 9.91m (32ft 6in), height 2.99m (9ft 10in). Wing area 27.9m² (300.0sq ft). AT-802 – Wing span 18.06m (59ft 3in) length 10.87m (35ft 8in), height 3.35m (11ft 0in). Wing area 37.3m² (401.0sq ft).

Capacity: Pilot only, two in tandem in AT-503A and AT-802.

Production: Turbo Air Tractor production includes 18 AT-302s, 86 -400s, 210 -402s, 520 -502s, 95 -602s, and 120 -802s and -802As.

History: The first turbine Air Tractor was the AT-301 based AT-302, which first flew in June 1977.

The AT-302 was powered by a 447kW (600shp) Avco Lycoming LTP 101-600, while the improved AT-301A, introduced in 1979, had a larger, 1514 litre hopper. Just 18 were built through to the mid 1980s.

The first Pratt & Whitney Canada PT6 powered model was the AT-400 Turbo Air Tractor, introduced in 1980. Powered by a 507kW (680shp) PT6A-15AG (or -27 or -28) it featured the AT-302A's 1514 litre hopper. The AT-400A is similar except the buyer supplies its used 410kW (550shp) PT6A-20. The AT-402 first flew in 1988 and features the increased span wings of the piston powered AT-401. The current AT-402A (introduced in 1997) has a 410kW (550shp) PT6A-11AG, joining the standard 507kW (680shp) PT6A powered AT-402B.

The first two seater Air Tractor was the AT-503. First flown in April 1986 it is based on the AT-400 and but features an 820kW (1100shp) PT6A-45R, five blade prop, 1892 litre hopper and tandem seats. It was initially developed for the US State Department for anti drugs work.

The single seat AT-502 is based on the AT-503 (first flight April 1987), and has a 15.24m (50ft) span wing (as on the piston AT-501) and a 507kW (680shp) PT6. The 502 remains in production alongside the AT-502A (first flight Feb 1992) with a far more powerful 820kW (1100shp) PT6A-45R driving a slow turning five blade prop, and the -502A based AT-502B with long span wings with Hoerner wingtips.

The 5.6 tonne MTOW 783kW (1050shp) or 966kW (1295shp) PT6 powered AT-602 (first flight December 1 1995) has a 818 litre hopper.

The heaviest and most powerful Air Tractors are the two seat (and dual controls) AT-802 and single seat AT-802A – the largest purpose designed single engine ag aircraft in production. First flight was in October 1990. The AT 802F is a twin seater optimised for firefighting. Total hopper capacity is 3066 litres.

Photo: An AT-502 gets airborne. (Andrew Peterson)

Antonov/PZL Mielec An-2 & SAMC Y-5

Countries of origin: Ukraine and Poland

Type: Biplane utility transport

Powerplants: An-2P – One 745kW (1000hp) PZL Kalisz ASz-61IR nine cylinder radial engine driving an AW-2 four blade variable pitch propeller. Y-5B – One 735kW (986hp) PZL Kalisz ASz-61IR-16 or Zhuzhou HS5 nine cylinder radial engine.

Performance: An-2P – Max speed 258km/h (139kt), economical cruising speed 185km/h (100kt). Range with a 500kg (1100lb) payload 900km (485nm). Y-5B – Max speed 220km/h (120kt), typical cruising speed 160km/h (85kt). Range 845km (455nm).

Weights: An-2P – Empty 3450kg (7605lb), max takeoff 5500kg (12,125lb). Y-5B – Max takeoff 5250kg (11,575lb).

Dimensions: Upper wing span 18.18m (59ft 8in), lower 14.14m (46ft 9in), length (tail down) 12.40m (40ft 8in), height (tail down) 4.01m (12ft 2in). Upper wing area 43.5m² (468.7sq ft), lower 28.0m² (301.2sq ft).

Capacity: Flightcrew of one or two pilots. Passenger accommodation for 12 at three abreast. Agricultural versions have large chemical hoppers with spray bars along the lower wing.

Production: More than 5000 An-2s were built in the Ukraine between 1948 and the mid 1960s, before production was transferred to PZL Mielec in Poland, where approx 12,000 were built through to the early 1990s, with a small number completed since then.

History: The An-2 biplane utility transport was originally designed to meet a USSR Ministry of Agriculture and Forestry requirement, and flew for the first time on August 31 1947.

Ukraine built An-2s entered production and service the following year, and were powered by 745kW (1000hp) ASh-62 radials. Soviet production continued through to the mid sixties by which time a number of variants had been developed, including the base model An-2P, An-2S and -2M crop sprayers, An-2VA water bomber, An-2M floatplane and the An-2ZA high altitude meteorological research aircraft.

Production responsibility was transferred to Poland's PZL Mielec in the 1960s, with the first example flying on October 23 1960. Aside from the An-2P, Polish versions include the An-2PK VIP transport, An-2PR for TV relay work, An-2S ambulance, An-2TD paratroop transport, An-2P cargo/passenger version, An-2 Geofiz geophysical survey version, 12 seat passenger An-2T and An-2TP with increased passenger headroom, and agricultural An-2R.

Chinese production as the Y-5 commenced with Nanchang in 1957, before being transferred to the Shijiazhuang Aircraft Manufacturing Company. The main Chinese version was the standard Y-5N which was built until 1986 after 221 had been built. The Y-5B specialist ag aircraft first flew in June 1989. Versions are the Y5B-100 with wingtip vanes, passenger Y-5B(K), agricultural or passenger Y-5B(D) and Y-5C parachutist version, ordered by the Chinese air force. Over 100 Y-5Bs have been built.

The An-3 Antonov built turboprop powered version first flew in the early 1980s powered by a 706kW (946shp) Omsk (Mars) TVD-10, but originally did not enter production. However a 1025kW (1375shp) TVD-20 powered An-3 received Russian certification in August 2000 and may enter production.

Photo: A Hungarian registered An-2. (Viktor László)

Antonov An-8, An-10 & An-12 & Xian Y-8

Countries of origin: Ukraine and China (Y-8)

Type: Turboprop freighter

Powerplants: An-12 – Four 2490kW (3495shp) Ivchenko AI-20K turboprops driving four blade constant speed AV-68 propellers. Y-8A – Four 3170kW (4250shp) Zhuzhou WJ6 turboprops.

Performance: An-12 – Max speed 777km/h (420kt), max cruising speed 670km/h (361kt). Range with max payload 3600km (1940nm), range with full fuel load 5700km (3075nm). Y-8A – Max speed 660km/h (357kt), economical cruising speed 530km/h (286kt). Range with max fuel load 5615km (3030nm), range with max payload 1275km (690nm).

Weights: An-12 – Empty 28,000kg (61,730lb), max takeoff 61,000kg (134,480lb). Y-8 – Empty equipped 35,490kg (77,237lb), max takeoff 61,000kg (134,480lb).

Dimensions: An-12 – Wing span 38.00m (124ft 8in), length 33.10m (108ft 7in), height 10.53m (34ft 7in). Wing area 121.7m² (1310sq ft). Y-8 – Same except for length 34.02m (111ft 8in), height 11.16m (36ft 8in). Wing area 121.9m² (1311.7sq ft).

Capacity: Flightcrew of two pilots, flight engineer, radio operator and navigator (the latter in the glazed nose). Can be configured to accommodate 14 passengers plus freight, with military versions carrying up to 90 troops. Max payload 20,000kg (44,090lb).

Production: An-12 production approximately 1200 aircraft. Xian has built over 60 Y-8s for military and civil use. In 2002 approximately 10 An-8s and 160 An-12s in commercial service.

History: The An-12 (NATO reporting name 'Cub') was developed to fulfil a Soviet air force requirement for a turboprop freighter.

The An-12 freighter and civil An-10 were developed in parallel and were based on the twin turboprop An-8. The An-8 first appeared in 1956 and was developed for Aeroflot. It is still in limited commercial service.

The prototype An-12 flew in 1958, powered by Kuznetsov NK-4 turboprops, and was essentially a militarised An-10 with a rear loading cargo ramp. Meanwhile approximately 500 An-10s were built, and they saw service between 1960 and 1972 exclusively with Aeroflot.

Production An-12s are powered by more economical AI-20 turboprops and were built through until 1973. In Soviet military service it was replaced by the Ilyushin Il-76 (described elsewhere). The An-12BP is the basic military transport version of the Cub. Other military versions have been used as Elint and ECM platforms.

The defensive rear gunner's turret is usually faired over on civil operated An-12s. Today large numbers remain in use with charter freight operators.

China's Xian began redesign work of the An-12 in 1969, resulting in a number of versions built by the Shaanxi Aircraft Company. Civil variants include the Y-8B and pressurised Y-8C, which was developed with cooperation from Lockheed (first flight was in 1990), export Y-8D with some western avionics, the Y-8F livestock carrier, Y-8F100 with improved engines, 2.2m (7ft 10in) stretched Y-8F200, and Y-8H aerial survey model.

Photo: A Chinese postal service Y-8. (Sam Chui)

Antonov An-22 Antheus

Country of origin: Ukraine

Type: Large capacity turboprop freighter

Powerplants: Four 11,185kW (15,000shp) Kuznetsov (now Kuibyshev) NK-12MA turboprops driving eight blade counter rotating propellers.

Performance: Max speed 740km/h (400kt), cruising speed 580-640km/h (313-345kt). Range with max fuel and 45 tonne (99,200lb) payload 10,950km (5905nm), range with max payload 5000km (2692nm).

Weights: Typical empty equipped 114,000kg (251,325lb), max takeoff 250,000kg (551,160lb).

Dimensions: Wing span 64.41m (211ft 4in), length 57.92m (190ft 0in), height 12.53m (41ft 1in). Wing area 345.0m² (3714sq ft).

Capacity: Flightcrew of up to six, comprising two pilots, navigator, flight engineer and a communications specialist. Up to 29 passengers can be accommodated on the upper deck behind the flight-deck. The unpressurised main cabin can house a range of oversize payloads such as main battle tanks and oil drilling equipment. Max payload is 80,000kg (176,350lb).

Production: Approximately 65 built, of which approximately 50 have been operated in Aeroflot colours. Just one example remained in commercial service in 2002, with the Antonov Design Bureau.

History: The massive An-22 is the largest turboprop powered aircraft yet built and was designed in response to a primarily Soviet military requirement for a strategic heavylift freighter.

The An-22 (NATO reporting name 'Cock') made its first flight on February 27 1965 – at that time it was comfortably the largest aircraft in the world. Production of the An-22 for the Soviet air force and Aeroflot continued through the 1960s until 1974. Early production was of the An-22, the definitive An-22A had less nose glazing. A 724 seat passenger variant did not make it off the drawing board.

Notable features of the An-22 include the NK-12 turboprops – which also power the Tupolev Tu-95/Tu-142 'Bear' family of bombers and maritime patrol aircraft and are the most powerful turboprop engines in service – comprehensive navigation and precision drop avionics, and massive undercarriage and tailplane.

The An-22 set 14 payload to height records in 1967, the pinnacle of which was the carriage of 100 tonnes (220,500lb) of metal blocks to an altitude of 25,748ft (7848m). It also established the record for a maximum payload lifted to a height of 2000m (6562ft), carrying a payload of 104,444kg (221,443lb). A number of class speed records were also set in 1972, including a speed of 608.5km/h (328kt) around a 1000km (540nm) circuit with a 50,000kg (110,250lb) payload. Further speed with payload records were established in 1974 and 1975.

As well as operations into the underdeveloped regions of Russia's northeast, Siberia and far east, Aeroflot An-22s were commonly used for military transport, their 'civilian' status allowing much freer access to landing and overflight rights.

Although just one An-22 was in use in 2002, the type's impressive payload capabilities means it remains a useful airlifter. The Antonov Design Bureau's single example is used for freight charters, alongside An-124s.

Photo: The An-22. (Peter Sweetten/Aviation Photography Worldwide)

Antonov An-24 & -26

Country of origin: Ukraine

Type: Regional airliners and freighters

Powerplants: An-24V – Two 1887kW (2530ehp) Ivchenko (Progress) AI-24A turboprops driving four blade constant speed propellers.

Performance: An-24V – Max cruising speed 500km/h (270kt), long range cruising speed 450km/h (243kt). Range with max payload 550km (296nm), range with max fuel 2400km (1295nm).

Weights: An-24V – Empty equipped 13,300kg (29,320lb), max takeoff 21,000kg (46,300lb).

Dimensions: An-24V – Wing span 29.20m (95ft 10in), length 23.53m (77ft 3in), height 8.32m (27ft 4in). Wing area 75.0m² (807sq ft).

Capacity: Flightcrew of two pilots and flight engineer, plus optional radio operator. Seating for up to 50 at four abreast. An-24T – Max payload 5700kg (12,566lb).

Production: Over 1200 An-24s built, most in the Ukraine. Approx 390 An-24s, 235 An-26s, 65 An-30s and 35 An-32s were in civil use in 2002.

History: The Antonov An-24 is the original aircraft in a prolific and highly successful family of twin turboprop civil and military transports that includes the military An-26 and Chinese built Y7.

The An-24 was designed to met a 1957 Aeroflot requirement for a 32-40 seat airliner with short field performance to replace the Il-14. Design features include wide span Fowler flaps and pressurised bonded/welded construction fuselage. The An-24 first flew in April 1960, by which time the design had grown to be a 44 seater courtesy of a rearranged cabin.

Aeroflot began training and route proving with the An-24 from September 1962, with service entry in September 1963 (between Moscow, Voronezh and Saratov). Aeroflot was the largest An-24 operator, with others going to Soviet client nation airlines such as Balkan, Cubana, Interflug and Tarom.

Versions of the An-24 include the 50 seat An-24V, An-24V Series II with more powerful engines, and the An-24T freighter. A small turbojet in the right engine nacelle to boost takeoff performance resulted in the An-24RT and An-24RV. The An-24P was designed to air drop firefighters near inaccessible forest fires. Ukrainian production ceased in 1978.

The An-24 was developed into the An-26 'Curl' military tactical transport with more powerful engines and redesigned tail, which itself evolved into the An-32 with enhancements for better hot and high performance. Over 200 An-26s are in civil service, with 1410 built.

The An-30 development was built in limited numbers and was designed largely for aerial survey and cartography work. This version is identifiable by its extensive nose glazing.

The An-32 first flew in 1976 and features much more powerful 3760kW (5042ehp) Progress engines for improved hot and high performance. The An-32's engines are mounted above the wing to give its larger diameter props adequate ground clearance.

China's Xian Aircraft Company has been building the An-24 since 1970 as the Y7, which is described separately.

Photo: A Podilla Avia An-26 freighter. (Dave Fraser)

Countries of origin: Ukraine and Poland

Type: Regional airliner and utility transports

Powerplants: An-28 – Two 715kW (960shp) PZL Rzeszów built RKBM/Rybinsk (Glushenkov) TVD-10B turboprops driving three blade propellers. M-28 – Two 820kW (1100shp) Pratt & Whitney Canada PT6A-65Bs driving five blade props. An-38-100 – Two 1118kW (1500shp) Honeywell TPE331-14GR-801E turboprops.

Performance: An-28 – Max cruising speed 350km/h (189kt), economical cruising speed 335km/h (181kt). Range with 20 passengers 510km (274nm), range with a full fuel load and 1000kg (455lb) payload 1365km (736nm). M-28 – Economical cruising speed 270km/h (146kt). Initial rate of climb 2657ft/min. Range with max fuel and 1000kg (2205lb) payload 1365km (735nm). An-38-100 – Max speed 405km/h (219kt), cruising speed 380km/h (205kt). Range with 27 passengers and reserves 600km (324nm).

Weights: An-28 – Empty equipped 3900kg (8598lb), max takeoff 6500kg (14,330lb). M-28 – Empty equipped 3917kg (8635lb), max takeoff 7000kg (15,432lb). An-38-100 – Empty 5300kg (11,684lb), max takeoff 8800kg (19,400lb).

Dimensions: An-28/M-28 – Span 22.06m (72ft 5in), length 13.10m (42ft 12in), height 4.90m (16ft 1in). Wing area 39.7m² (427.5sq ft). An-38 – Same except length 15.67m (51ft 5in), height 4.30m (14ft 1in).

Capacity: An-28/M-28 – Flightcrew of two. Typical passenger seating for 17 at three abreast and 72cm (28in) pitch. High density seating for 20. An-38 – Seating for 26 three abreast, optionally 27.

Production: Approx 200 An-28s built, with 80 in commercial service. Over 30 M-28s have been built. Five An-38s in service.

History: The An-28 was the winner of a competition against the Beriev Be-30 for a new light passenger and utility transport for Aeroflot's short haul routes. The An-38 is a stretched development

The An-28 is based on the earlier An-14. It combines the An-14's high wing layout, twin fins and rudders with a new and far larger fuselage and turboprop engines.

The An-28 made its first flight as the An-14M in September 1969 in the Ukraine, while a preproduction aircraft first flew in April 1975. Production of the An-28 was transferred to Poland's PZL Mielec in 1978, although it was not until July 22 1984 that the first Polish built production aircraft flew. The An-28's Soviet type certificate was awarded in April 1986.

PZL Mielec has been the sole source for production An-28s, and has developed the westernised M-28 Skytruck version powered by 820kW (1100shp) Pratt & Whitney Canada PT6A-65B turboprops with five blade Hartzell propellers, plus some western (Bendix-King) avionics. Originally designated the An-28PT, first flight was in July 1993 and it is in limited production. The M-28 received Polish certification equivalent to US FAR Part 23 in March 1996. The stretched M-28 Skytruck Plus is under development.

The An-38 is an Antonov developed stretched 26 seater which first flew on June 23 1994. Variants are the Honeywell TPE331 powered An-38-100 and An-38K convertible, and Omsk TVD-20 powered An-38-200. Russian certification was granted in April 1997.

Photo: The TPE331 powered An-38. (Greg Wood)

Countries of origin: Ukraine and Russia

Type: STOL capable freighter

Powerplants: Two 63.7kN (14,330lb) ZMKB Progress D-36 turbofans.

Performance: An-72 – Max speed 705km/h (380kt), cruising speed range 550 to 600km/h (295 to 325kt). Service ceiling 35,000ft. Range with max fuel and reserves 4800km (2590nm), with a 7500kg (16,535lb) payload 2000km (1080nm). An-74 – Speeds similar. Range with reserves and a 10,000kg (22,025lb) payload 1150km (620nm), or with a 1500kg (3310lb) payload 5300km (2860nm).

Weights: An-72 – Empty 19,050kg, max takeoff (from a 1800m/5900ft runway) 34,500kg (76,060lb). Max takeoff from a 600-800m (1970-2630ft) runway 27,500kg (60,625lb).

Dimensions: Wing span 31.89m (104ft 8in), length 28.07m (92ft 1in), height 8.65m (28ft 5in). Wing area 98.6m² (1062sq ft).

Capacity: Flightcrew of three (two pilots and a flight engineer) for the An-72. An-74 also has provision for a radio operator. Main cabin designed primarily for freight, in which role it can carry a payload of 10 tonnes (22,045lb) including four UAK-2.5 containers, or four 2.5 tonne (5510lb) PAV-2.5 pallets. An-72 can seat 68 on removable seats, while the An-74 when configured for combi passenger/freight tasks can carry eight support crew.

Production: Over 160 built, mostly for military customers. Approx 50 An-72s/An-74s in commercial use in 2002.

History: The An-72 was designed as a replacement for the An-26 tactical transport for the Soviet air force, but variants, particularly the An-74, are in use as commercial freighters.

The first of five flying An-72 prototypes first flew on August 31 1977, although the first of eight extensively revised preproduction An-72s with lengthened fuselage and longer span wings did not fly until December 1985. Included in this pre-series batch were two An-74s, designed to operate in polar regions and with greater fuel capacity and an increased max takeoff weight.

The most significant design feature of the An-72 and An-74 is the mouting of the engines forward and above the wing to use the Coanda effect to improve STOL performance. This utilises engine exhaust gases blown over the wing's upper surface to boost lift. Other features include multi slotted flaps, rear loading ramp and multi unit landing gear capable of operations from unprepared strips.

Versions of the An-72/74 family (NATO codename 'Coaler') include the An-72 base model with extended wings and fuselage compared to the prototypes, the An-72S VIP transport and An-72P maritime patrol aircraft.

An-74 variants include the base An-74, the increased MTOW and payload An-74-200 freighter and further improved An-74T-200A, the An-74TK-100 and -74TK-200 convertible passenger/freighter models (with seating for up to 52), and the An-74TK-200D Salon VIP transport. Production was transferred to Omsk in Russia in 1993.

The An-74TK-300 with new Progress D-426T1 turbofans mounted in pods under the wings made its official first flight in April 2001. A stretched variant, the An-74-400 or An-174, is under consideration.

Photo: The An-74TK-300 with D-426T1 turbofans at 2001's Paris Airshow. (Paul Merritt)

Antonov An-124

Country of origin: Ukraine

Type: Heavylift freighter

Powerplants: An-124 – Four 229.5kN (51,590lb) ZMKB Progress (Lotarev) D-18T turbofans.

Performance: An-124 – Max cruising speed 865km/h (468kt), typical cruising speeds 800 to 850km/h (430 to 460kt). Range with max payload 4500km (2430nm), ferry range with max fuel 16,500km (8900nm).

Weights: An-124 – Operating empty 175,000kg (385,800lb), max takeoff 405,000kg (892,875lb).

Dimensions: Wing span 73.30m (240ft 6in), length 69.10m (226ft 9in), height 20.78m (68ft 2in). Wing area 628.0m² (6760sq ft).

Capacity: Flightcrew of six – two pilots, two flight engineers, navigator and communications operator. Upper deck behind the flightdeck area features galley, rest room and two relief crew cabins. Upper deck behind the wing seats up to 88 passengers. Main deck cargo compartment can carry bulky and oversized cargos. An-124-100's payload 120 tonnes (military An-124s can lift 150t).

Production: About 60 An-124s have been built, of which 25 were in commercial use in 2000.

History: The massive An-124, the world's second largest aircraft behind the An-225 is commonly used for oversize freight charters.

The An-124 was developed primarily as a strategic military freighter (in which role it can carry missile units and main battle tanks). The prototype first flew on December 26 1982, a second prototype, named Ruslan (after a Russian folk hero), made the type's first western public appearance at the Paris Airshow in June 1985. Commercial operations began in January 1986, since which time the An-124 has set a wide range of payload records.

An-124 design features include nose and tail cargo doors, 24 wheel undercarriage allowing operations from semi prepared strips, the ability to 'kneel' to allow easier front loading, and a fly-by-wire control system.

The two major An-124 variants are the basic An-124 used by the military and similar Russian civil certificated An-124-100. Various upgrades have been proposed, including the three crew EFIS flightdeck equipped An-124-102 and the An-124FFF firebomber. Numerous re-engine studies have also been conducted, including using Rolls-Royce RB211-524Gs, General Electric CF6-80s (as the An-124-130) and even Aviadvigatel NK-93 propfans.

Antonov has developed a multistage life extension program for existing and new build An-124-100s, while after a break of five years deliveries of new build aircraft resumed in August 2000.

In mid 2002 Volga-Dnepr became the launch customer for the upgraded An-124-100M, ordering a new build -100M for delivery in the fourth quarter of 2003 and the conversion of its existing nine An-124s to the new standard. The -100M will feature a range of improvements including a four crew flightdeck with some western avionics, more efficient D-18T turbofans which will meet future Stage 4 noise limits, improved range and a 150 tonne payload

The stretched and six engined An-225 is described next.

Photo: An An-124-100 touches down. (Lee Archer)

Antonov An-225 Myria

Country of origin: Ukraine

Type: Six engine ultra heavy lift transport

Powerplants: Six 229.5kN (51,590lb) ZMKB Progress D-18T turbofans.

Performance: Cruising speed range 800 to 850km/h (430 to 460kt). Range with a 200,000kg (440,900lb) internal payload 4500km (2425nm). Range with a 100,000kg (220,450lb) internal payload 9600km (5180nm). Range with max fuel 15,400km (8310nm).

Weights: Max takeoff 600,000kg (1,322,750lb).

Dimensions: Wing span 88.40m (290ft), length 84.00m (275ft 7in), height 18.20m (59ft 9in). Wing area 905.0m² (9741sq ft).

Capacity: Flightcrew of six consisting of two pilots, a navigator, a communications specialist and two flight engineers. Accommodation for a relief crew plus a further 60 to 70 personnel provided in upper deck cabin behind the flightdeck. The maximum payload of 250 tonnes (551,150lb) can be carried internally in the 43m (141ft) long main cargo deck, or externally on two upper fuselage mounting beams.

Production: Thus far only one An-225 has been built, while work on a second has resumed.

History: The truly massive An-225 Myria (or Dream) is easily the world's largest aircraft, and the type holds a raft of international lifting records.

The An-124 based An-225 was designed to externally carry the Soviet Buran space shuttle orbiter. Design work on the An-225 commenced in mid 1985, culminating in the first flight on December 21 1988. On March 22 1989 the Myria set 106 records on a 3.5 hour flight on which it took off at a weight of 508,200kg (1,120,370lb), with a 156,300kg (344,576lb) payload, flying a 2000km (1080nm) closed circuit at an average speed of 813km/h (439kt), reaching an altitude of 40,485ft. The Myria subsequently made its first flight with the Buran orbiter mounted on its back in May that year.

The An-225 is a stretch of the earlier An-124 (itself the world's largest aircraft up until the appearance of the Myria), with a substantially lengthened fuselage, increased span wings, plus six (instead of four) D-18T turbofans. Other changes include the twin fins, deletion of the rear loading ramp, seven instead of five pairs of main undercarriage wheels on each side, and longitudinal mounting beams and faired attachment points to carry external loads, in particular the Buran orbiter. Like the An-124, the Myria uses fly-by-wire, and the two types share similar avionics suites.

The prototype was placed in storage at Gostomel in April 1994. In 1998 Antonov announced it planned to restore the aircraft to airworthiness and complete the second aircraft. The first aircraft made its first post restoration flight on May 7 2001. It has been redesignated An-225-100 and requires five flightcrew, features TCAS and its engines were treated to meet noise emission standards.

Antonov Airlines and Air Foyle offer the An-225 for commercial charter work.

Work on completing the second An-225 was continuing in 2002.

Photo: The refurbished An-225 participates in the 2001 Paris Airshow. (Paul Merritt)

Antonov An-140

Country of origin: Ukraine

Type: Turboprop regional airliner

Powerplants: An-140 – Two 1839kW (2466shp) Motor-Sich Al-30 Series 1 turboprops (licence built Klimov TV3-117s) driving six blade propellers, or two 1864kW (2500shp) Pratt & Whitney Canada PW127A turboprops.

Performance: An-140 with Al-30s – Max cruising speed 575km/h (310kt), economical cruising speed 520km/h (280kt). Range with 52 passengers 2100km (1133nm), range with a 6000kg (13,227lb) payload at 520km/h (280kt) 900km (486nm). An-140 with PW127s – Range with 52 passengers 2500km (1349nm).

Weights: An-140 – Max takeoff 19,150kg (42,218lb).

Dimensions: An-140 – Wing span 24.51m (80ft 5in), length 22.61m (74ft 2in), height 8.23m (26ft 11in).

Capacity: An-140 – Flightcrew of two. Typical passenger seating for 52 at four abreast and 75cm (30in) pitch or 48 at 81cm (32in) pitch. Forward starboard freight door allows 1900 to 3650kg (4188 to 8046lb) of palletised freight and 36 or 20 passengers to be carried in a combi configuration.

Production: Five on order with one in service in late 2002.

History: Antonov's An-140 is an all new 50 seat regional twin turboprop regional airliner developed to replace the ageing An-24.

Antonov announced development of the An-140 in 1993. The first An-140 prototype rolled out from the Kiev factory on June 6 1997 and flew for the first time on September 17 that year. The second flying prototype was completed in late 1998, while the first production standard An-140 flew on October 11 1999.

The An-140 is of conventional design and construction, with US and European certification planned in addition to Russian/CIS certification. The basic version is powered by Motor-Sich Al-20s which are licence built Klimov TV3-117VMA-SBM1s, while Pratt & Whitney Canada PW127As will be optional. The flightdeck features conventional instruments, the main cabin seats 52 in a four abreast configuration. The rear main passenger door features integral stairs, while a forward starboard side freight door allows cargo to be carried. The rear of the cabin also features a galley, coat stowage and a toilet.

Versions apart from the basic An-140 will include the An-140A for Aeroflot which will be powered by PW127As, the An-140T freighter which would have a large freight door on the rear port side, convertible An-140TK, the 3.80m (12ft 6in) stretched 68 seat An-140-100, and the An-142 with a rear loading freight. Military versions are also planned.

Series production of the An-140 is being undertaken at Kharkov by KhGAPP in the Ukraine and at Samara, Russia, by Aviacor. In 1996 Antonov signed an agreement with HESA of Iran for licence assembly of an An-140 model called the Iran 140 at a new plant at Esfahan. Initial Iran 140s will be assembled from supplied kits, with gradually increasing Iranian local content. The first flew in February 2001. Iran Asseman and Iran Air are expected to be customers.

Photo: An An-140 on approach to land at the 2002 Farnborough Airhsow. (Paul Merritt)

ATR 42

Countries of origin: France and Italy

Type: 42 seat turboprop regional airliner

Powerplants: ATR 42-300 – Two flat rated 1340kW (1800shp) Pratt & Whitney Canada PW120 turboprops driving four blade Hamilton Standard propellers. ATR 42-500 – Two PW127Es derated to 1610kW (2160shp) driving six blade Ratier-Fagiec/Hamilton Standard props.

Performance: ATR 42-300 – Max cruising speed 490km/h (265kt), econ cruising speed 450km/h (243kt). Range at max cruising speed 4480km (2420nm), or 5040km (2720nm) at econ cruising speed. ATR 42-500 – Cruising speed 563km/h (304kt). Max range 1850km (1000nm).

Weights: ATR 42-300 – Operating empty 10,285kg (22,674lb), max takeoff 16,700kg (36,817lb). ATR 42-500 – Operating empty 11,250kg (24,802lb), max takeoff 18,600kg (41,005lb).

Dimensions: Wing span 24.57m (80ft 8in), length 22.67m (74ft 5in), height 7.59m (24ft 11in). Wing area 54.5m^2 (586.6sq ft).

Capacity: Flightcrew of two. Maximum passenger accommodation for 50, 48 or 46 at 76cm (30in) pitch and four abreast. Typical seating arrangement for 42 at 81cm (32in) pitch.

Production: As at late 2002 total orders for all versions of the ATR 42 stood at 369 with 367 delivered.

History: Aerospatiale (now part of EADS) and Aeritalia (now Alenia) established Avions de Transport Regional or ATR in 1980 to develop a family of regional airliners. The program has proved very successful, the 600th ATR was delivered in early 2000, and is one of the west's most successful turboprop airliner programs.

The ATR 42 was the consortium's first aircraft and was launched in October 1981. The first of two ATR 42 prototypes first flew on August 16 1984 and Italian and French authorities granted certification in September 1985. The ATR 42 entered service on December 9 1985.

The ATR 42-300 was the standard production version of the ATR 42 family until 1996 and features greater payload range and a higher takeoff weight than the prototypes. The similar ATR 42-320 (also withdrawn in 1996) differed in having more powerful PW121 engines for better hot and high performance, while the ATR 42 Cargo is a quick change freight/passenger version of the 42-300.

The current production ATR 42-500 features a revised interior, more powerful PW127Es for a substantially increased cruising speed (565km/h/305kt) and driving six blade propellers, a 1850km (1000nm) maximum range, the EFIS flightdeck, elevators and rudders of the stretched ATR 72 (described separately), plus new brakes and landing gear and strengthened wing and fuselage for higher weights. The first ATR 42-500 delivery was in October 1995.

For a short time ATR was part of the Aero International (Regional) regional airliner consortium established in January 1996 to incorporate ATR, Avro and Jetstream. AI(R) was disbanded in mid 1998.

In mid 2000 ATR launched a freighter conversion program for both the 42 and 72, involving installing a forward freight door and modifying the cabin for freight. The ATR 42 Freighter can carry a 5.8 tonne payload. DHL Aviation Africa was the launch customer with the two converted ATR 42-300s redelivered in September and December 2000.

Photo: An ATR 42. (Toni Marimon)

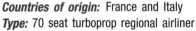

Countries of origin: France and Italy

Type: 70 seat turboprop regional airliner

Powerplants: ATR 72-200 – Two 1610kW (2160shp) Pratt & Whitney Canada PW124B turboprops driving four blade Hamilton Standard propellers. ATR 72-210 – Two 1850kW (2480shp) P&WC PW127s.

Performance: ATR 72-200 – Max cruising speed at 15,000ft 526km/h (284kt), economical cruising speed 460km/h (248kt). Range with reserves at max optional weight 1195km (645nm), range with 66 pax 2665km (1200nm).

Weights: Operating empty 12,500kg (27,558lb), max takeoff 21,500kg (47,400lb).

Dimensions: Wing span 27.05m (88ft 9in), length 21.17m (89ft 2in), height 7.65m (25ft 1in). Wing area 61.0m² (656.6sq ft).

Capacity: Flightcrew of two. Max seating for 74 passengers at four abreast and 76cm (30in) pitch. Typical seating for between 64 and 70 passengers, with seat pitch starting from 81cm (32in). With larger forward freight door fitted it can accommodate a payload of 7200kg (15,875lb) in 13 containers. ATR 52C – 7500kg (16,535lb) payload comprising pallets or five LD3 containers.

Production: As at late 2002 300 ATR 72s had been ordered, out of total ATR orders for 669, with 276 delivered.

History: The ATR 72 is a stretched development of the popular ATR 42 and was launched in January 1986.

The first of three ATR 72 development aircraft first flew on October 27 1988, followed by the awarding of French and then US certification in late 1989. Entry into service was on October 27 1989.

Significant differences between the ATR 72 and the smaller and older ATR 42 include a 4.50m (14ft 9in) fuselage stretch and reworked wings. The ATR 72's wings are new outboard of the engine nacelles and are 30% composite, comprising composite spars and skin panels and a carbon fibre wing box.

Aside from the baseline ATR 72-200, three developments have been offered, the ATR 72-210, ATR 72-500 and the ATR 52C. The ATR 72-210 has improved hot and high performance. It has more powerful PW127 engines for better takeoff performance.

The ATR 72-500 (for a time the ATR 72-210A) further improved hot and high model was certificated in early 1997. It features PW127Fs driving six blade composite Ratier-Fagiec/Hamilton Standard propellers.

The ATR 52C is an unlaunched freighter derivative with a redesigned tail to incorporate a rear loading ramp, intended for military and commercial operators. As with the ATR 42, a military maritime patrol version, known as the Petrel 72, has also been offered.

ATR has studied a number of developments which have not seen the light of day. The ATR 82, a 78 seat stretched development, would have been powered by two Allison AE 2100 turboprops (ATR studied turbofans for a time) and would have had a cruising speed as high as 610km/h (330kt). The ATR 82 was suspended in early 1996.

In 1998 the ATR 42/72 was also considered as the basis for the ATR AirJet regional jet family which would have featured the ATR's fuselage, a new wing and turbofan engines.

Photo: A KLM exel ATR 72. (ATR)

Country of origin: United Kingdom

Type: Two, three and four seat light aircraft

Powerplants: J/1 – One 75kW (100hp) Blackburn Cirrus. J/5B & J/5F – One 97kW (130hp) de Havilland Gipsy Major. J/5G – One 116kW (155hp) Blackburn Cirrus Major 3. All were inline four cylinder piston engines driving two blade fixed pitch propellers.

Performance: J/1 – Max speed 193km/h (104kt), cruising speed 160km/h (86kt). Initial rate of climb 568ft/min. Range with no reserves 515km (278nm). J/5G – Max speed 204km/h (110kt), cruising speed 177km/h (96kt). Initial rate of climb 710ft/min. Range with no reserves 780km (421nm). J/5F – Max speed 212km/h (114kt), cruising speed 180km/h (97kt). Initial rate of climb 705ft/min. Range with no reserves 435km (235nm).

Weights: J/1 – Empty 477kg (1052lb), max takeoff 840kg (1850lb). J/5B – Empty 605kg (1334lb), max takeoff 1090kg (2400lb). J/5G – Empty 620kg (1367lb), max takeoff 1110kg (2450lb). J/5F – Empty 600kg (1323lb), max takeoff 885kg (1950lb).

Dimensions: J/1 – Wing span 10.97m (36ft 0in), length 7.14m (23ft 5in), height 1.98m (6ft 6in). Wing area 17.2m² (185sq ft). J/5B – Same except for length 7.11m (23ft 4in), height 2.30m (7ft 6in). J/5G – Same except for length 7.06m (23ft 2in), height 2.30m (7ft 6in). J/5F – Same except for length 7.16m (23ft 6in), height 1.98m (6ft 6in). Wing area 15.2m² (164sq ft).

Capacity: Two pilots side by side, plus room for one or two passengers, depending on model type. Most J/5s seat four.

Production: Approximate production totals for the series are: J/1 – 420; J/1B – 87; J/1N – 43; J/2 – 44; J/4 – 26; J/5 – 58; J/5B – 92; J/5G – 92; J/5P – 24; J/5F – 56; J/5K, L, R & Q – 40 plus.

History: Auster traces its lineage back to the Taylorcraft Aeroplanes (England) company, which produced Taylorcrafts (described separately) under licence, and built over 1600 spotter (Air Observation Post) aircraft for Britain's Royal Air Force and Army, many of which were resold to private operators.

The first civil Auster (as Taylorcraft become known as in 1946) was the Mk 5 J/1 Autocrat, which was essentially similar to the military Taylorcraft Mk V, but had a Cirrus Minor 2 engine in place of the Mk 5's Lycoming, upholstered seats and other refinements.

The J/1 Autocrat served as the basis for a family of aircraft. The next to appear was the two seat side by side J/2 Arrow family, with a 56kW (75hp) Continental, which was further developed into the J/4 Archer with a Cirrus Minor engine (due to import restrictions on the US engine). The J/1N Alpha had less equipment and minor improvements. The J/1U Workmaster was an O-360 powered ag version.

Most Auster J/5 models were four seaters except for the initial J/5 which was an Autocrat with a more powerful engine, while the J/5B incorporated the enlarged four seat cabin. The J/5F Aiglet trainer was a fully aerobatic two seat trainer. The J/5D, introduced in 1959, was the last of the line and featured metal wing spars and ribs and Lycoming O-235 power (more than 160 were built, including 150 in Portugal by OGMA under licence). Auster was taken over by Beagle in 1960.

Photo: An O-235 powered Auster J/5D. (Peter Vercruijsse)

Aviat Husky A-1

Country of origin: United States of America

Type: Two seat utility light aircraft

Powerplant: A-1A – One 135kW (180hp) Textron Lycoming O-360-A1P flat four piston engine driving a two blade constant speed Hartzell propeller.

Performance: A-1/A-1A – Cruising speed at 75% power 225km/h (122kt), cruising speed at 55% power 212km/h (115kt). Stalling speed with flaps extended 67km/h (37kt). Initial rate of climb 1500ft/min. Service ceiling 20,000ft. Range with max fuel and reserves at 75% power cruising speed 1020km (550nm).

Weights: A-1A – Empty 540kg (1190lb), max takeoff (landplane) 857kg (1890lb), floatplane 984kg (2170lb).

Dimensions: A-1A – Wing span 10.82m (35ft 6in), length 6.88m (22ft 7in), height 2.01m (6ft 7in). Wing area 17.0m² (183.0sq ft).

Capacity: Seating for two in tandem.

Production: 450 A-1s built, approx 170 A-1As built.

History: The Aviat Husky utility is a very successful two seat light aircraft in the spirit of the popular Piper Super Cub. It also has the distinction of being the only all new light aircraft designed and placed into series production in the US in the mid to late 1980s.

The Husky was originally designed by Christen Industries, the company also responsible for the kit built Christen Eagle aerobatic biplane and previous owner of the Pitts Special aerobatic biplane series (described separately, Aviat now owns Pitts and Christen). Initial design work began in late 1985, with the aid of Computer Aided Design. The prototype Husky first flew in 1986 and US FAA certification was awarded on May 1 1987. Production deliveries followed shortly afterwards.

Husky design features include a braced high wing, seating for two in tandem and dual controls. The high wing arrangement was selected for good all round visibility, essential for the many observation and patrol roles the Husky is used for. The engine is a relatively powerful, for the Husky's weight, 135kW (180hp) Textron Lycoming O-360 flat four turning a constant speed two blade prop. The good power reserves and wing also give good field performance. Unlike most current light aircraft the Husky's structure features steel tube frames and Dacron covering over all but the rear of the fuselage, plus metal leading edges on the wings. Options include floats, skis and banner and glider hooks.

The basic Husky A-1 was replaced in production by the A-1A with increased span wing in 1998. The A-1B is similar to the A-1A but is designed for mission specific government agencies work and has an increased 907kg (2000lb) max takeoff weight.

With more than 600 built since production began, the Husky has quietly gone about becoming one of the largest selling light aircraft GA designs of recent times. Many are used for observation duties, fisheries patrol, pipeline inspection, border patrol, glider towing and a range of other utility missions. Notable users include the US Departments of the Interior and Agriculture and the Kenya Wildlife Service which bought seven for aerial patrols of elephant herds as part of the fight against illegal ivory poaching.

Photo: A Canadian registered Husky A-1. (Gary Gentle)

Aviat Pitts Special

Country of origin: United States of America

Type: Single and two seat competition aerobatic biplanes

Powerplants: S-1S – One 135kW (180hp) Lycoming IO-360 fuel injected flat four piston engine driving a two blade fixed pitch propeller. S-2C – One 195kW (260hp) Textron Lycoming AEIO-540 flat six driving a three blade constant speed Hartzell composite propeller.

Performance: S-1S – Max speed 283km/h (153kt), max cruising speed 227km/h (123kt). Initial rate of climb 2600ft/min. Service ceiling 22,300ft. Max range with no reserves 507km (275nm). S-2C – Max speed 313km/h (169kt), manoeuvring speed 248km/h (134kt). Initial rate of climb 2900ft/min. Service ceiling 21,000ft. Range at 55% power 555km (300nm).

Weights: S-1S – Empty 326kg (720lb), max takeoff 520kg (1150lb). S-2C – Empty 520kg (1150lb), max takeoff 771kg (1700lb).

Dimensions: S-1S – Wing span 5.28m (17ft 4in), length 4.71m (15ft 6in), height 1.91m (6ft 3in). Wing area 9.2m² (98.5sq ft). S-2C – Wing span upper 6.10m (20ft 0in), length 5.41m (17ft 9in), height 1.96m (6ft 8in). Wing area 11.8m² (127.5sq ft).

Capacity: S-1 series seats pilot only. S-2 series seats two, except for S-2S which seats pilot only.

Production: Current Aviat production is of the S-2C, over 50 built. Factory production includes 360 S-2Bs and 36 S-2S.

History: The designer of the original Pitts Special aerobatic biplane, Curtiss Pitts, could hardly have appreciated that his design would continue in production for many decades.

The original prototype of the S-1 Special first flew in September 1944. The aircraft was of steel tube construction with fabric covering over wooden spars, while the two wings were braced with wire. Power in early aircraft was supplied by 65 to 95kW (90 to 125hp) four cylinder Continentals or Lycomings. Later models were higher powered and of conventional metal construction.

Factory production of the basic single seat S-1 Special included the S-1S with a 135kW (180kW) Lycoming IO-360, driving a fixed pitch prop, and the S-1T. The S-1T was introduced to production in 1981, and features a 150kW (200hp) Lycoming (now Textron Lycoming) AEIO-360 driving a constant speed prop and symmetrical wings. Homebuilt versions of the S-1 include the S-1D and S-1E (for which plans or kits have also been offered), while the S-1S and S-1T are also available in kit form. The 225kW (300hp) S-1-11 Super Stinker remains availble to special order.

The two seat S-2 Special is of the same configuration as the single seat S-1 but is larger, and generally regarded as a more capable aerobatic aircraft due to its larger size and heavier weight, more power and aerodynamic changes. The S-2 has been offered in single seat 195kW (260hp) AEIO-540 powered S-2S form, as the two seat 150kW (200hp) IO-360 powered S-2A and the 195kW (260hp) AEIO-540 powered and fully aerobatic with two occupants S-2B.

The two seat S-2C is the only current factory production model and has aerodynamic changes including improved wing tip shape, flattened belly, refined engine cowl and redesigned windshield. It cruises 24km/h (13kt) faster than the S-2B.

Photo: An S-1S.

Aviation Traders ATL-98 Carvair

Country of origin: United Kingdom & USA

Type: Freighter

Powerplants: Four 1080kW (1450hp) Pratt & Whitney R-2000-7M2 Twin Wasp 14 cylinder twin row radial engines driving three blade Hamilton Standard Hydromatic variable pitch propellers.

Performance: Max speed 402km/h (217kt), max cruising speed 342km/h (185kt), economical cruising speed at 10,000ft 334km/h (180kt). Service ceiling at 33,110kg (73,000lb) 18,700ft. Range with max fuel and 4500kg (10,000lb) payload 5560km (3000nm). Range with 8035kg (17,700lb) payload 2745km (1480nm).

Weights: Empty equipped 18,762kg (41,365lb), max takeoff 33,475kg (73,800lb).

Dimensions: Wing span 35.82m (117ft 6in), length 31.27m (102ft 7in), height 9.09m (29ft 10in). Wing area 135.8m² (1462sq ft).

Capacity: Flightcrew of three. Maximum seating in a passenger configuration for 85 at five abreast at 86cm (34in) pitch. When used as a car ferry it was typically outfitted to carry five cars plus 22 passengers in the rear cabin.

Production: 21 Carvair conversions undertaken, the last completed in 1968. Two remained in commercial service in 2002: one in Georgia, USA and one with Phoebus Apollo, South Africa.

History: Aviation Traders developed the Carvair in response to Channel Air Bridge's requirement for an air ferry capable of transporting passengers and their cars between the United Kingdom and continental Europe.

The Carvair is a conversion of the Douglas DC-4 airliner (or C-54 Skymaster in military guise), which was readily available after World War 2, although its external appearance is quite different. The airframe from the wings rearward is that of a standard DC-4, except for a lengthened vertical tail for enhanced controllability. The major modifications performed on the forward fuselage centred on a new lengthened nose section with a hydraulically operated cargo door and an elevated flightdeck (somewhat similar in appearance to that which would appear on the Boeing 747 several years later) which allowed nose loading of cars.

The Carvair first flew on June 21 1961 and entered service in March 1962 with British United Air Ferries (into which Channel Air Bridge had been merged, it later became British Air Ferries and then British World Airways). Deliveries to other operators included three for Aer Lingus of Ireland and two for Aviaco of Spain, with other aircraft operated by French, Australian (Ansett) and Luxembourg carriers.

Aviation Traders also proposed a Carvair type conversion of the larger Douglas DC-6, DC-6B and DC-7, with the option of re-engining with Rolls-Royce Dart turboprops, although these plans never came to fruition.

In 2002 one Carvair is operated by Custom Air Service from Georgia in the USA (N89FA), while a second is in South Africa (9J-PAA) operated by Phoebus Apollo Executive Cargo. Both are ex Ansett machines.

Photo: Custom Air Service's Carvair pictured at Dallas in May 2002. (Josh Rawlin)

Ayres Turbo-Thrush

Country of origin: United States of America

Type: Agricultural aircraft

Powerplant: S2R-T34 – One 560kW (750shp) Pratt & Whitney Canada PT6A-34AG turboprop driving a three blade prop. 660 – Options of 917kW (1230shp) PT6A-65AG or 783kW (1050shp) PT6A-60 or 701kW (940shp) Honeywell TPE331-10 driving a five blade prop.

Performance: S2R-T34 – Max speed with spray equipment 256km/h (138kt), cruising speed at 50% power 240km/h (130kt), working speed range at 30 to 50% power 143 to 240km/h (82 to 130kt). Initial rate of climb 1740ft/min. Service ceiling 25,000ft. Ferry range at 40% power 1230km (665nm). 660 – Cruising speed 281km/h (152kt), working speeds 161-282km/h (87-152kt). Initial rate of climb 1250ft/min. Ferry range 966km (521nm).

Weights: S2R-T34 – Empty 1633kg (3600lb), max takeoff (ag category) 2720kg (6000lb). 660 – Empty 2381kg (5250lb), typical operating weights 5600kg (12,500lb).

Dimensions: S2R-T34 – Wing span 13.54m (44ft 5in), length 10.06m (33ft 0in), height 2.79m (9ft 2in). Wing area 30.3m² (326.6sq ft). 660 – Wing span 15.25m (50ft), length 10.22m (33ft 6in), height 2.80m (9ft 9in). Wing area 34.8m² (375sq ft).

Capacity: Pilot only, but optional second seat. Hopper capacities of 2498 litres (660US gal), 1930 ltr (510US gal) and 1515 ltr (400US gal).

Production: Approx 400 Turbo Thrushes built.

History: The Turbo Thrush family of turboprop agricultural aircraft was offered in three hopper capacity variants.

Ayres' first experience with the Thrush was when it contracted Serv-Aero Engineering to develop a turbine conversion of the Thrush Commander. The Thrush Commander/PT6 conversion first flew on September 9 1975 and Ayres marketed production conversions. Then in 1977 Ayres acquired from Rockwell the Thrush Commander-600 and -800 design rights and production facilities (in Albany, Georgia).

The initial production turbine S2R had a standard 560kW (750shp) PT6A-34 (with other PT6A models offered optionally) and a 1514 litre (400US gal) hopper. It remained in production through to 2001 with 373-507kW (500-680shp) PT6A or TPE331 turbines and has a 4222kg (9300lb) typical operating weight.

The 1930 litre (510US gal) capacity hopper first appeared on the piston R-1820 powered Bull Thrush. Today turbine 1930 litre (510US gal) hopper equipped Thrushes are offered with 507-917kW (680-1230shp) PT6As or 560-701kW (750-940shp) TPE331s. Typical operating weight is 4400kg (9700lb).

The last development was the 660 Turbo Thrush with its 2498 litre (660US gal) hopper. Again it was offered powered by either the PT6A or TPE331 turbines. The 660 Turbo Thrush was certificated in March 2000.

Two special missions developments are the S2R-T65 NEDS (Narcotics Eradication Delivery System) for the US State Department (who ordered 19 during the 1980s), and the TPE331 powered Vigilante surveillance and close air support version (ff 1989). The Sea Thrush firebomber was fitted with floats to scoop up water.

Ayres was shut down in August 2001.

Photo: A TPE331 powered Ayres Turbo Thrush.

BAC One-Eleven

Country of origin: United Kingdom

Type: Short haul airliner

Powerplants: Srs 200 – Two 45.9kN (10,330lb) Rolls-Royce Spey Mk 506 turbofans. Srs 400 – Two 50.7kN (11,400lb) Spey Mk 511s. Srs 500 – Two 55.6kN (12,500lb) Spey Mk 512-14DWs.

Performance: Max cruising speed 870km/h (470kt), econ cruising speed 742km/h (400kt). Series 200 – Range with typical payload 1410km (760nm). Srs 400 – Range with typical payload 2300km (1240nm). Srs 500 – Range with typical payload 2745km (1480nm).

Weights: Srs 200 – Empty 21,049kg (79,000lb), max takeoff 35,833kg (79,000lb). Srs 400 – Empty 22,493kg (49,857lb), max takeoff 40,153kg (88,500lb). Srs 500 – Operating empty 24,758kg (54,582lb), max takeoff 47,400kg (104,500lb).

Dimensions: Srs 200, 300, 400 – Wing span 26.97m (88ft 6in), length 28.50m (93ft 6in), height 7.47m (24ft 6in). Wing area 93.2m² (1003sq ft). Srs 500 – Wing span 28.50m (93ft 6in), length 32.61m (107ft 0in). Wing area 95.8m² (1031sq ft).

Capacity: Flightcrew of two. Srs 200, 300, 400 & 475 – Single class seating for up to 89 passengers. Srs 500 – typical seating for 97-109 passengers, max seating for 119.

Production: UK total 235, comprising 58 Srs 200s, nine Srs 300s, 70 Srs 400s, 86 Srs 500s and 12 production 475s. Nine 561s built in Romania. Approx 75 One-Elevens were in service in late 2002.

History: The One-Eleven can trace its origins back to the proposed Hunting H.107 jet airliner project of 1956.

Protracted development followed, but by 1961, when Hunting had been absorbed into the British Aircraft Corporation (BAC), a larger Rolls-Royce Spey turbofan powered design was finalised upon.

British United Airways placed a launch order for 10 of the new jets, then known as the BAC.111, in May 1961. The new aircraft first flew on August 20 1963, while the first production Series 200 first flew on December 19 1963. Certification was eventually awarded on April 6 1965, following a troubled flight test program during which one prototype crashed with the loss of its crew due to to deep stall from the rear engine and T-tail configuration. With the deep stall issue resolved, the BAC.111 entered service on April 6 1965.

Development of the basic Series 200 led to the higher weight Series 300, followed by the Series 400 designed for American requirements with a higher US equipment content.

The 4.11m (13ft 6in) stretched Series 500 could seat up to 119 and was the most popular One-Eleven model (with 86 built). It first flew (converted from a -400) on June 30 1967. The Series 475 was optimised for hot and high operations and combined the Series 500's more powerful engines with the earlier shorter length fuselage.

The last UK built One-Eleven (by this time a British Aerospace product) flew in 1982, when production was progressively being transferred to Romaero in Romania where nine were built.

In the mid 1990s Romaero worked on a Rolls-Royce Tay 650 powered development called the Airstar 2500. The Airstar was planned to fly in late 1996 but the program has been suspended.

Photo: A European Airlines 111-500. Note the hushkitted engines. (Rob Finlayson)

Beagle B.121 Pup

Country of origin: United Kingdom

Type: Two, three and four place light aircraft

Powerplant: 100 – One 75kW (100hp) Rolls-Royce Continental O-200-A flat four piston engine driving a two blade fixed pitch propeller. 150 – One 110kW (150hp) Lycoming O-320-A2B flat four. 160 – One 120kW (160hp) Lycoming IO-320.

Performance: 100 – Max speed 204km/h (110kt), max cruising speed 190km/h (103kt), economical cruising speed 153km/h (83kt). Initial rate of climb 575tft/min. Range with no reserves 916km (495nm). 150 – Max speed 222km/h (120kt), max cruising speed 211km/h (114kt), economical cruising speed 175km/h (95kt). Initial rate of climb 800ft/min. Range with no reserves 708km (382nm), range with optional additional fuel and no reserves 1019km (550nm).

Weights: 100 – Empty 482kg (1063lb), max takeoff 725kg (1600lb). 150 – Empty 522kg (1151lb), max takeoff 873kg (1925lb).

Dimensions: 100 – Wing span 9.45m (31ft 0in), length 6.99m (22ft 11in), height 2.29m (7ft 6in). Wing area 11.2m² (120sq ft). 150 – Same except length 7.06m (23ft 2in).

Capacity: 100 – Two side by side, plus two children behind. 150 – Three adults and one child.

Production: 173 Pups built, consisting of 66 Pup 100s, 98 Pup 150s, and 9 Pup 160s.

History: The Pup was one of two new designs to be produced by British Executive and General Aviation Ltd or Beagle, which was formed in October 1960 following the merger of Auster and Miles.

The Pup evolved from the Miles M.117 project, which was to have made extensive use of plastics. A range of conventional construction Pups was planned, from a 75kW (100hp) two seat trainer through to retractable undercarriage four seaters, a light twin and a fully aerobatic 155kW (210hp) military trainer, the Bull Pup. All would have featured metal construction.

The Pup made its first flight on April 8 1967 and deliveries of the initial Pup 100 began a year later in April 1968.

In the meantime Beagle had flown the first of the more powerful Pup 150s in October 1967. The 150 featured a 110kW (150hp) engine, as its designation reflects, and seating for an extra adult.

Another more powerful variant originally designed in response to an Iranian Civil Air Training Organisation requirement was the Pup 160. The Pup 160 featured a 120kW (160hp) IO-320 Lycoming, but only nine were built.

Continuing financial difficulties finally forced Beagle to close its doors in January 1970 after building 152 Pups, despite holding orders for an additional 276. As a consequence plans for the extended Pup based family came to nought. A further 21 near complete aircraft were subsequently assembled.

The Bulldog military basic trainer development first flew in May 1969. Scottish Aviation (which took over the design following Beagle's collapse) built 328 150kW (200hp) Lycoming IO-360 powered Bulldogs for a number of air forces, including Britain's Royal Air Force.

Scottish Aviation became part of British Aerospace in the late 1970s.

Photo: The Pup is one of the few light aircraft to feature control sticks and not control columns. This is a Pup 100. (Peter Vercruijsse)

Beagle B.206

Country of origin: United Kingdom

Type: Six/eight place cabin twin

Powerplants: B.206C – Two 230kW (310hp) Continental GIO-470-A geared, fuel injected flat six piston engines driving three blade constant speed propellers. B.206-S – Two 255kW (340hp) Continental GTSIO-520-C geared, turbocharged and fuel injected engines.

Performance: B.206C – Max speed 354km/h (191kt), max cruising speed 333km/h (180kt), economical cruising speed 298km/h (160kt). Initial rate of climb 1170ft/min. Range with no reserves 2905km (1570nm). B.206-S – Max speed 415km/h (224kt), max cruising speed 380km/h (205kt), economical cruising speed 301km/h (163kt). Initial rate of climb 1340ft/min. Range with no reserves 2462km (1330nm).

Weights: B.206C – Empty equipped 2381kg (5250lb), max takeoff 3401kg (7499lb). B.206-S – Empty equipped 2450kg (5400lb), max takeoff 3401kg (7499lb).

Dimensions: Wing span 13.96m (45ft 10in), length 10.26m (33ft 8in), height 3.43m (11ft 4in). Wing area 19.9m² (214sq ft).

Capacity: Standard seating for eight.

Production: Total production run of 79 aircraft included one 206X; one 206Y; two 206Z; 20 206R Bassets for the Royal Air Force; 11 B.206C; 43 206-S; and one Series 3.

History: The cabin class Beagle B.206's origins lie in a late 1950s Bristol project for a four seat twin.

Although the Bristol 220 was not built, when Bristol's managing director moved to the newly established Beagle in 1960 he took the design with him. Beagle then developed the 220 into the 206 and the prototype B.206X first flew on August 15 1961. The five/six seat, 195kW (260hp) Continental IO-470 powered prototype was considered too small and the design evolved into the B.206Y with 230kW (310hp) GIO-470 engines, greater wing span, a larger cabin with increased seating capacity, greater fuel capacity and increased weights.

This allowed the B.206 to meet a Royal Air Force requirement for a communications aircraft to transport V-bomber support crews. Twenty were ordered (not the originally planned buy of 80) in preference to the de Havilland Dove. In RAF service the B.206 was designated the CC.1 Basset, and deliveries began in May 1965.

Following the B.206Y were two evaluation B.206Z aircraft, then the initial civil production version, the Series 1 B.206C. Poor hot and high performance was in part responsible for slow sales and so Beagle developed the Series 2 B.206-S with more powerful turbocharged GTSIO-520 engines. The B.206-S also introduced a slightly revised cabin to seat eight with the entry door repositioned from above the wing to the rear port side fuselage. The B.206-S proved far more capable but was too late to compete in a marketplace already dominated by Cessna's 400 series and Piper's PA-31 Navajo.

A commuter airliner development was also built in prototype form, the 10 seat Series 3 with a further enlarged cabin. The Series 3 design died when Beagle entered liquidation in early 1970.

In the 1980s in the US, South Florida Aviation refurbished several 206s with 280kW (375hp) GTSIO-520-Ms, a new instrument panel and numerous other improvements

Photo: A Beagle 206-S. (Stewart Wilson)

Beechcraft Model 18

Country of origin: United States of America

Type: Light utility transport

Powerplants: Super H18 – Two 335kW (450hp) Pratt & Whitney R-985AN-14B Wasp Junior nine cylinder radial piston engines driving two blade constant speed propeller. Turboliner – Two 525kW (705ehp) AiResearch (Garrett) TPE331-1-101B turboprops driving three blade constant speed Hartzell propellers.

Performance: Super H18 – Max cruising speed 354km/h (191kt), economical cruising speed 298km/h (160kt). Initial rate of climb 1400ft/min. Service ceiling 21,400ft. Range with max fuel 2460km (1330nm). Turboliner – Max speed 450km/h (243kt), economical cruising speed 412km/h (222kt). Initial rate of climb 1520ft/min. Service ceiling 24,000ft. Range with max fuel and reserves 3340km (1800nm), range with max payload and reserves 555km (300nm).

Weights: Super H18 – Empty equipped 2650kg (5845lb), max takeoff 4490kg (9900lb). Turboliner – Empty (airliner) 2993kg (6600lb), max takeoff 5215kg (11,500lb).

Dimensions: Super H18 – Wing span 15.14m (49ft 8in), length 10.70m (35ft 3in), height 2.84m (9ft 4in). Wing area 33.5m² (360.7sq ft). Turboliner – Wing span 14.02m (46ft 0in), length 13.47m (44ft 3in), height 2.92m (9ft 7in). Wing area 34.8m² (374sq ft).

Capacity: Most Beech 18s seat two crew and seven to nine passengers in main cabin. Volpar Turboliner conversion seats up to 15.

Production: Over 9000 Beech 18s of all models built between 1937 and 1969, of which 2000 were built postwar. Wartime military production accounts for majority of Beech 18s built (approx 5000).

History: More than 9000 Beech 18s were built over an uninterrupted three decade long production run, making it Beech's most successful twin aircraft. While many of those were built against wartime military contracts, vast numbers went on to see civil service.

The prototype Beech 18 first flew on January 15 1937. The new aircraft followed conventional design wisdom at the time, including twin radial engines, metal construction and taildragger undercarriage, while less common were the twin tail fins. Early production aircraft were either powered by two 225kW (300hp) Jacobs L-6s or 260kW (350hp) Wright R-760Es. The Pratt & Whitney Wasp Junior became the definitive engine from the prewar C18S onwards.

The demands of World War 2 significantly boosted the already successful Beech 18's fortunes, with 5000 built as C-45s for the US Army Air Force for use as transports and multi engine pilot trainers.

Postwar, large numbers of C-45s entered civil service, while Beech resumed production of the C18S. Progressive development resulted in the D18S of 1946, the Continental powered D18C of 1947, the E18S of 1954, the G18S from 1959 and the H18 with optional tricycle undercarriage from 1962. Production ceased in 1969.

The Beech 18 has also been the subject of numerous conversions. Volpar offered tricycle undercarriage conversions, re-engining with TPE331 turboprops, and stretched fuselage and TPE331 powered conversions (described in the specs above). Hamilton meanwhile converted Beech 18s as Westwinds with Pratt & Whitney Canada PT6 turboprops and also offered stretched conversions.

Photo: A H18S. (Tony Arbon)

Beechcraft 35 Bonanza

Country of origin: United States of America

Type: Four & six seat high performance light aircraft

Powerplant: D35 – One 153kW (205hp) Continental E-185-11 flat six piston engine driving a two blade constant speed propeller. P35 – One 195kW (260hp) fuel injected Continental IO-470-N. V35TC – One 210kW (285hp) turbocharged and fuel injected Continental TSIO-520-D.

Performance: D35 – Max speed 306km/h (165kt), cruising speed 281km/h (152kt). Initial rate of climb 1100ft/min. Range with no reserves 1247km (673nm). P35 – Max speed 330km/h (178kt), cruising speed 306km/h (165kt). Initial rate of climb 1150ft/min. Range with optional fuel and no reserves 1955km (1056nm). V35TC – Max speed 386km/h (208kt), max cruising speed 360km/h (194kt), long range cruising speed 262km/h (141kt). Initial rate of climb 1225ft/min. Range with reserves & std fuel 917km (495nm), with opt fuel 1770km (955nm).

Weights: D35 – Empty 760kg (1675lb), max takeoff 1236kg (2725lb). P35 – Empty 841kg (1855lb), max takeoff 1418kg (3125lb). V35TC – Empty 907kg (2000lb), max takeoff 1542kg (3400lb).

Dimensions: D35 – Wing span 10.00m (32ft 10in), length 7.67m (25ft 2in). Wing area 16.5m² (177.6sq ft). P35 – Wing span 10.20m (33ft 6in), length 7.65m (25ft 1in). Wing area 16.8m² (181sq ft). V35TC – Wing span 10.20m (33ft 6in), length 8.04m (26ft 5in), height 2.31m (7ft 7in). Wing area 16.8m² (181sq ft).

Capacity: Models 35 through to J35 seat four people, K35 optional fifth passenger, later models from S35 onwards six people.

Production: Approximately 10,400 Model 35 Bonanzas of all variants were built between 1945 and 1982.

History: The distinctive Model 35 Bonanza is one of general aviation's most famous and prolific types, and enjoyed a production life spanning four decades.

The Bonanza first flew on December 22 1945. Featuring metal construction, retractable undercarriage and high performance, it heralded a new class of high performance GA aircraft. The design also featured the distinctive V-tail, incorporated for aerodynamic efficiency and reduced weight. Deliveries began in 1947.

Subsequent development led to a significant family of subtypes. Briefly these are the A35 of 1949 with a greater max takeoff weight; the B35 with a 146kW (196hp) E-185-8 engine; the 153kW (205hp) E-185-11 powered C, D and E models through to 1954; the F and G35 with third cabin window and 170kW (225hp) E-225-8 of the mid fifties; the 180kW (240hp) Continental O-470-G powered H35 of 1957; the fuel injected 187kW (250hp) powered J35; 1960's M35 with larger rear windows; and the N35 and P35 with a 195kW (260hp) IO-470-N and greater max takeoff weight.

Then followed the redeveloped S35 of 1964 with six seats and redesigned rear cabin, optional three blade prop, 215kW (285hp) IO-520-B engine and yet greater weights; the heavier V35; and turbocharged V35TC of 1966; V35A and V35A-TC of 1968 with increased rake windscreen; and the V35B and V35B-TC (just seven built) from 1970. The V35B remained in production until 1982 and underwent a number of detail changes in that time.

Photo: A V35 Bonanza. (Gary Gentle)

Beechcraft Queen Air

Country of origin: United States of America

Type: Utility, light executive transport and commuter airliner

Powerplants: 65 – Two 255kW (340hp) IGSO-480-A1E6 Lycoming fuel injected supercharged flat six piston engines driving three blade constant speed propellers. B80 – Two 285kW (380hp) Lycoming IGSO-540-A1D piston engines.

Performance: 65 – Max speed 385km/h (208kt), max cruising speed 344km/h (186kt), long range cruising speed 267km/h (144kt). Range with reserves and standard fuel 1682km (908nm), with optional fuel 2670km (1442nm). B80 – Max speed 400km/h (215kt), max cruising speed 362km/h (195kt), typical cruising speed 335km/h (181kt). Range with reserves 1950km (1053nm).

Weights: 65 – Empty 2324kg (5123lb), max takeoff 3719kg (8200lb). B80 – Empty 2394kg (5277lb), max takeoff 3992kg (8800lb).

Dimensions: Wing span 15.32m (50ft 3in), length 10.82m (35ft 6in), height 4.33m (14ft 3in). Wing area 27.3m² (294sq ft).

Capacity: One or two pilots and up to nine passengers in commuter configuration, or six passengers in executive transport role.

Production: 1001 Queen Airs of all models built (404 Model 65s & A65s, 42 Model 70s, 510 Model 80s and 45 Model 88s), including 71 A65s as the U-8F Seminole for the US Army.

History: The versatile Queen Air is Beech's largest and heaviest piston twin apart from the WW2 era radial powered Beech 18. It remained in production for two decades, and provided the basis for the very popular turboprop King Air (described under Raytheon).

The prototype Model 65 Queen Air first flew on August 28 1958, with deliveries of production aircraft beginning in late 1960. This first model combined the wings, undercarriage, Lycoming engines and tail surfaces of the Model E50 Twin Bonanza with a new and substantially larger fuselage. A Queen Air 65 established a new class altitude record of 34,882ft in 1960. Seventy-one were built for the US Army as the U-8F Seminole.

Many variants subsequently followed, including the 3630kg (8000lb) max takeoff weight Model 80 with more powerful 285kW (380hp) engines and swept fin and rudder, which flew in June 1961. The improved A80, the first to be offered as a commuter airliner, was introduced in 1964. The A80 had a redesigned nose and interior, increased wing span and a 227kg (500lb) greater takeoff weight.

The pressurised 88 first appeared in 1965. It combined the pressurised, circular window fuselage of the King Air 90 turboprop, the longer wingspan of the A80 and a 3992kg (8800lb) MTOW.

The B80 was the last major production model and appeared in 1966. It featured the longer span wing and the 88's max takeoff weight. In 11 seat commuter form it was marketed as the Queen Airliner.

The A65 (96 buit) was essentially a Model 65 with the swept fin and rudder of the Model 80, and entered production in 1967. The Model 70 featured the longer span wings, 3720kg (8200lb) max takeoff weight and 255kW (340hp) engines. It was built between 1969 and 1971.

Queen Air production ceased in 1977 with 1001 built.

Photo: The short lived model A65 Queen Air. (Lance Higgerson)

Beech Musketeer, Sierra & Sundowner

Country of origin: United States of America

Type: Four seat light aircraft

Powerplant: B19 – One 112kW (150hp) Lycoming O-320-E2D flat four piston engine driving a two blade fixed pitch propeller. C23 – One 135kW (180hp) Lycoming O-360-A4K. C23R – One 150kW (200hp) fuel injected Lycoming IO-360-A1B6 driving a variable pitch propeller.

Performance: B19 – Max speed 225km/h (169kt), long range cruising speed 182km/h (98kt). Initial rate of climb 700ft/min. Range with reserves 1420km (1064nm). C23 – Max speed 228km/h (123kt), long range cruising speed 182km/h (98kt). Initial rate of climb 700ft/min. Range with reserves 1168km (631nm). C23R – Max speed 262km/h (141kt), long range cruising speed 213km/h (115kt). Initial rate of climb 927ft/min. Range with reserves 1271km (686nm).

Weights: B19 – Empty 630kg (1390lb), max takeoff 1020kg (2250lb). C23 – Empty 681kg (1502lb), max takeoff 1111kg (2450lb). C24R – Empty 777kg (1713lb), max takeoff 1250kg (2750lb).

Dimensions: B19, C23 & C23R – Wing span 10.00m (32ft 9in), length 7.84m (25ft 9in), height 2.51m (8ft 3in). Wing area 13.6m² (146sq ft).

Capacity: Standard seating for four except two in Sport III.

Production: 4455 built, including 2390 Musketeers, I/II/III/Custom & Sundowners; 904 Sports; 793 Super R/Sierras; and 369 Supers.

History: Beechcraft's Musketeer family of four seaters competed with the more successful Cessna 172 and Piper Cherokee.

The bonded honeycomb construction wing, O-320 powered Musketeer first flew in October 1961 with deliveries beginning in late 1962 (for the 1963 model year). Some 553 were built in the first year, but none were built for the 1964 model year while Beech developed the improved A23 Musketeer II with a fuel injected 125kW (165hp) Continental IO-346 engine.

In the 1965 model year Beech offered a three model range (which it dubbed the Three Musketeers) – the A23A Musketeer Custom III with greater max takeoff weight, the reduced MTOW A23-19 Musketeer Sport III two seat trainer with a 110kW (150hp) Lycoming O-320, and the 150kW (200hp) IO-346 powered and increased MTOW A23-24 Musketeer Super III. For 1968 the Super III's Continental IO-346 was replaced by a 135kW (180hp) Lycoming O-360 to become the B23, while the Sport III became the Model 19A, both it and the Custom were certificated for aerobatics.

From the 1970 model year the three introduced a more rounded fuselage, more steeply raked windscreen and pointed propeller spinner. They were renamed the Musketeer B19 Sport, C23 Custom and A24 Super respectively, and were joined by the retractable undercarriage A24R Super R.

The Musketeer name was dropped in 1971, with the Custom renamed the Sundowner, the Super R the Sierra, and the Musketeer Sport becoming simply the Sport, while the Super was dropped.

The Sierra underwent significant changes for the 1974 model year becoming the B24R with a new cowling, quieter engine and more efficient prop. Further aerodynamic clean ups were introduced in 1977, the Sport was dropped in late 1978, while Sundowners and Sierras were built until 1983.

Photo: A C24R Sierra 200 (200 for 200hp). (Lance Higgerson)

Beechcraft 60 Duke

Country of origin: United States of America

Type: Four or six place light business twin

Powerplants: 60 – Two 285kW (380hp) Lycoming TIO-541-E1A4 turbocharged fuel injected flat six piston engines driving three blade constant speed Hartzell propellers. B60 – Two 285kW (380hp) Avco Lycoming TIO-541-E1C4s.

Performance: 60 – Max speed 460km/h (248kt), cruising speed 395km/h (214kt). Range with optional fuel and 45 minute reserves 1890km (1020nm). B60 – Max level speed 455km/h (246kt) at 23,000ft, max cruising speed 443km/h (239kt) at 25,000ft, cruising speed 431km/h (233kt) at 25,000ft. Initial rate of climb 1601ft/min. Service ceiling 30,000ft. Max range at 20,000ft with reserves 2078km (1122nm).

Weights: 60 – Empty equipped 1860kg (4100lb), max takeoff 3050kg (6725lb). B60 – Empty equipped 1987kg (4380lb), max takeoff 3073kg (6775lb).

Dimensions: Wing span 11.96m (39ft 3in), length 10.31m (33ft 10in), height 3.76m (12ft 4in). Wing area 19.8m² (212.9sq ft).

Capacity: Standard seating for four with optional fifth and sixth seats and toilet.

Production: Beechcraft built 584 Dukes between 1968 and 1982, including 113 60s, 121 A60s and 350 B60s.

History: Between the Beech Baron and Queen Air in size, performance and general capabilities, the Duke was a pioneer in the pressurised high performance light business twin class.

Beechcraft began design work on its new Model 60 in early 1965, with the first flight of the prototype on December 29 1966. US FAA certification was awarded on February 1 1968.

Duke design features include turbocharged Lycoming TIO-541 engines driving three blade propellers and a 0.32 bars (4.6psi) cabin pressure differential. A new fuselage with bonded honeycomb construction was mounted to Baron based wings and undercarriage. Optional fuel tanks in the wings were offered, increasing range.

Deliveries of the initial 60 model began in July 1968. Further development led to the improved A60 which appeared in 1970. It introduced an enhanced pressurisation system and longer life yet lighter turbochargers which increased the maximum altitude at which the engines could deliver maximum power, thus improving performance.

The definitive Duke model is the B60, with new interior arrangements and further improved turbochargers. It first appeared in 1974 and remained in production until 1982. The B60 accounted for about two-thirds of all Duke production, although the B60's production total of 350 is relatively small for a US GA type of its era.

From its appearance the Duke was regarded as something of a hot ship, attractive for its high performance in a relatively small package. However, this image did not translate into anything other than modest sales because of the Duke's relatively complex systems (turbochargers and pressurisation among them) and high operating costs.

Photo: A brightly painted Duke A60. (Keith Myers)

Beechcraft 76 Duchess

Country of origin: United States of America

Type: Four place light twin

Powerplants: Two 135kW (180hp) Lycoming 0-360-A1G6D flat four piston engines driving two blade constant speed propellers.

Performance: Max speed 317km/h (171kt), max cruising speed 307km/h (165kt), recommended cruising speed at 10,000ft 293km/h (158kt), long range cruising speed 280km/h (151kt). Initial rate of climb 1248ft/min. Max range with reserves 1445km (780nm).

Weights: Empty 1110kg (2446lb), max takeoff 1780kg (3900lb).

Dimensions: Wing span 11.58m (38ft 0in), length 8.85m (29ft 1in), height 2.89m (9ft 6in). Wing area 16.8m² (181.1sq ft).

Capacity: Seats for four.

Production: 437 Duchesses were built between 1978 and 1982.

History: Beechcraft's Model 76 Duchess was one of a new class of light four place twins developed in the mid 1970s.

The Duchess prototype, designated the PD289, made its first flight in September 1974, although a further 30 months of development work passed before the first production Model 76 first flew on May 24 1977. Certification was granted in early 1978, with first deliveries commencing that May.

The Duchess was positioned between the Bonanza and the Baron in the Beechcraft model range. Beech developed it for its Beech Aero Centers, and pitched it at the personal use light twin, light charter and multi engine training markets. Design aims included good low speed and single engine handling.

Aside from the prototype PD289, no variations of the Duchess 76 were built before production ended in 1982. All Duchesses therefore feature two Lycoming 0-360 engines (with counter rotating propellers), a T-tail (incorporated to reduce control forces and improve elevator response), entry doors on either side of the cabin, and electric trim and flap controls (the prototype PD289 featured manually operated flaps). The fuselage was based loosely on the single engine Sierra's, and like the Sierra and its Musketeer predecessors featured a bonded honeycomb construction wing. The Sierra and Duchess also share common structural components.

Beech offered three factory option packages on the Duchess – the Weekender, Holiday and Professional – and 11 factory installed avionics packages.

Beech developed the Duchess for low cost, high volume production, but the falling popularity of light twins, an economic recession and crippling product liability laws in the USA all contributed to a relatively short production run which wound up in 1982. Sales had peaked in 1979 when 213 were built.

Like its contemporaries the Grumman/Gulfstream American Cougar and Piper Seminole, the Duchess' success was hampered by poor timing. Ever increasing advances in engine efficiency, safety and reliability led to a rise in popularity for big high performance singles such as Beech's own Bonanza series, which lacked the maintenance overheads of two engines, but had comparable performance. However the Duchess did enjoy a degree of success as a twin engine trainer, to a greater extent than the Seminole and Cougar.

Photo: A Duchess on approach to land. (Glenn Alderton)

Beechcraft 77 Skipper

Country of origin: United States of America

Type: Two seat light aircraft

Powerplant: One 85kW (115hp) Lycoming 0-235-L2C flat four piston engine driving a two blade fixed pitch propeller.

Performance: Max speed 196km/h (106kt), max cruising speed 195km/h (105kt), long range cruising speed 158km/h (85kt). Initial rate of climb 720ft/min. Range with reserves 764km (413nm).

Weights: Empty 500kg (1103lb), max takeoff 760kg (1675lb).

Dimensions: Wing span 9.14m (30ft 0in), length 7.32m (24ft 0in), height 2.41m (7ft 11in). Wing area 12.1m² (129.8sq ft).

Capacity: Two seated side by side.

Production: Production of the Skipper ceased in 1981 after 312 had been built.

History: Beech developed the Skipper as a low expense two seat trainer in response to the growing costs (mainly fuel) of pilot training in the mid 1970s.

Starting life as the Beech PD (for Preliminary Design) 285, the new Skipper was intended to be a simple and cost effective new generation pilot training aircraft, combining low purchasing and operating costs with lightweight but sturdy construction. A PD285 prototype first flew on February 6 1975, but this differed from production aircraft in that it was powered by a 75kW (100hp) Continental 0-200 engine and featured a conventional low set tailplane.

Protracted development meant that the first of the definitive Model 77 Skippers did not fly until September 1978, by which time the 85kW (115hp) Lycoming 0-235 engine and T-tail had been settled upon. In the Beech product line-up the Skipper was to replace the two seat Model 19 Sport variant of the Musketeer family, production of which ended in 1978.

US FAA certification for the Skipper was awarded in April 1979, and the first production aircraft were delivered in May 1979 to Beechcraft's own Beech Aero Center pilot training centres.

Production lasted just three years until mid 1981 (at the time Beech said the halt in production was a "suspension" pending an improvement in market conditions). During that time little more than 300 Skippers had been built (at a rate of about 10 per month). Unsold Skipper stocks kept the type available for a further year.

The Skipper was in direct competition with Piper's very successful PA-40 Tomahawk and Cessna's 152. The Tomahawk was developed in a very similar time scale to the Skipper (entering service in early 1978) and both aircraft share a T-tail, low wing and canopy style cabin configuration (with 360° all round vision and a door on each side), and the Lycoming 0-235 powerplant. Of the three the Skipper was the least successful, being comfortably outsold by the Cessna and Piper products.

Other features of the Skipper design are a NASA developed GA(W)-1 high lift wing (the result of joint NASA and Beech research into high lift, supercritical aerofoils) bonded metal construction, tubular spars, and flap and aileron actuation by torque tubes rather than the more conventional cable and pulley system. New construction techniques were intended to reduce manufacturing costs.

Photo: 312 Beech Skippers were built. (Julien Moerenhout)

Beechcraft 99 Airliner

Country of origin: United States of America

Type: Commuter airliner

Powerplants: B99 – Two 505kW (680shp) Pratt & Whitney Canada PT6A-28 turboprops driving three blade constant speed Hartzell propellers. C99 – Two 535kW (715shp) PT6A-36s.

Performance: B99 – Max cruising speed 460km/h (247kt). Initial rate of climb 2090ft/min. Range at max cruising speed 1665km (900nm), range at cruising speed 1887km (1019nm). C99 – Max speed 496km/h (268kt) at 8000ft, cruising speed at 8000ft 461km/h (249kt). Range with max fuel and reserves 1686km (910nm).

Weights: B99 – Empty equipped 2620kg (5777lb), max takeoff 4944kg (10,900lb). C99 – Operating empty 3040kg (6700lb), max takeoff 5125kg (11,300lb).

Dimensions: B99 – Wing span 14.00m (45ft 11in), length 13.58m (44ft 7in), height 4.38m (14ft 4in). C99 – Same except for wing span 13.98m (45ft 11in). Wing area 26.0m² (279.7sq ft).

Capacity: Flightcrew of one or two. Typical passenger accommodation for 15 at two abreast. Baggage stowed in nose compartment and underbelly cargo pod. Some used as corporate aircraft.

Production: 239 Model 99s built, comprising 164 99s, A99s, A99-As and B99s between 1967 and 1975 and production of 75 C99s between 1980 and 1986.

History: The Beech 99 commuter airliner is an evolution of the successful Queen Air/King Air series, and shares the King Air's basic powerplant and layout, but with a stretched fuselage.

Beech began designing the 99 in the late 1960s, in part to find a replacement for its venerable Beech 18. In December 1965 Beech flew a stretched Queen Air development, which was subsequently re-engined with Pratt & Whitney Canada PT6A-20 turboprops to serve as the 99 prototype, first flying in this configuration in July 1966. Other features on the unpressurised 99 included an airstair incorporated in the main cabin door and an optional cargo door allowing it to carry a mix of passengers and freight, separated by a moveable bulkhead.

The first customer 99 Airliner was delivered in May 1968. At the time the 99 was Beech's largest aircraft yet and Beech was optimistically forecasting a production rate of 100 per year. Subsequent models were the flat rated 507kW (680shp) PT6A-27 powered A99, and the B99 with an increased gross weight. The 99 was available in two variants, the 99 Airliner and the 99 Executive, a corporate transport version with seating for between eight and 17 passengers.

Production of early models wound up in 1975. Then in 1979 Beech launched the improved Commuter C99 (plus the larger 1900, described separately) as part of a return to the commuter airliner market. A converted B99 fitted with P&WC PT6A-34 engines served as the C99 prototype, and flew in this form on June 20 1980.

Production aircraft featured PT6A-36 engines, and deliveries recommenced following certification, both in July 1981. Shortly afterwards it became known as the C99 Airliner.

C99 production ceased in 1986.

Photo: A German registered Beech 99 used for freight work. (Florian Kondziela)

Beechcraft Starship 2000

Country of origin: United States of America

Type: Corporate transport

Powerplants: Two 895kW (1200shp) Pratt & Whitney Canada PT6A-67A turboprops driving five blade constant speed propellers.

Performance: 2000 – Max cruising speed 622km/h (335kt), economical cruising speed 546km/h (295kt). Initial rate of climb 3225ft/min. Max range 2630km (1634nm). 2000A – Max cruising speed 621km/h (335kt), economical cruising speed 570kt (307kt). Initial rate of climb 2748ft/min. Range with reserves 2920km (1576nm).

Weights: 2000 – Empty equipped 4484kg (9887lb), max takeoff 6531kg (14,400lb). 2000A – Empty equipped 4574kg (10,085lb), max takeoff 6758kg (14,900lb).

Dimensions: Wing span 16.60m (54ft 5in), length 14.05m (46ft 1in), height 3.94m (12ft 11in). Wing area 26.1m² (280.9sq ft).

Capacity: Flightcrew of one or two pilots. Standard passenger layout for eight in 2000 or six in 2000A.

Production: Production ceased in early 1995 after three prototypes, 18 Starship 2000s and 32 Starship 2000As had been built. 49 in corporate use in 2002.

History: Despite its extensive use of modern technologies and innovative design the Starship was a commercial failure.

Conceived as a new generation light corporate transport in the King Air class, the Starship traces back to the 85% scale proof of concept demonstrator built by Scaled Composites, which first flew in August 1983. The prototype Starship 2000 proper made its first flight on February 26 1986, provisionally powered by PT6A-65 turboprops. A second prototype equipped with Collins avionics entered the flight test program in June 1986, while a third development aircraft took flight in January 1987. Initial US FAA certification was awarded on June 14 1988, while the first production example flew on April 25 1989.

The Starship incorporated many innovations. Foremost of these is its rear mounted laminar flow wing and variable geometry canards or foreplanes. The foreplanes sweep forward with flap extension for pitch trim compensation, designed to make it impossible for the Starship to stall on takeoff or landing.

The wing itself is constructed almost entirely of composites (something which attracted much criticism because of the associated difficulties of inspecting it thoroughly), and has tip mounted vertical tails. The rear mounted pusher engines mean low cabin noise levels, and their relatively close proximity to each other also improves single engine handling. The EFIS flightdeck has Collins avionics with colour and monochrome CRTs.

The improved Starship 2000A was certificated in April 1992. It introduced changes including seating for six instead of eight, a slightly higher max takeoff weight and increased range, partly overcoming performance shortfalls.

A lack of customer interest forced Beech to terminate Starship production in early 1995 after just 53 had been built (including three prototypes), a somewhat inglorious end to a technologically innovative and seemingly promising design.

Photo: The composite construction Starship 2000. (Howard Geary)

Bell 47

Country of origin: United States of America

Type: Two or three seat light utility helicopter

Powerplant: 47G – Various Lycoming flat six piston engines ranging in output from 150kW (200hp) to 210kW (280hp), including the 47G-3B-2A's 210kW (280hp) Lycoming TVO-435-F1A, driving two blade main and tail rotors. 47J Ranger – One 230kW (305hp) Lycoming VO-540-B1B flat six.

Performance: 47G-3B-2A – Max speed 169km/h (91kt), cruising speed 135km/h (73kt) at 5000ft. Initial rate of climb 880ft/min. Range 397km (214nm) at 6000ft. 47J Ranger – Max speed 169km/h (91kt), cruising speed 130km/h (70kt). Initial rate of climb 800ft/min. Range with max fuel and no reserves 413km (223nm).

Weights: 47G-3B-2A – Empty 858kg (1893lb), max takeoff 1340kg (2950lb). 47J Ranger – 785kg (1730lb), max takeoff 1340kg (2950lb).

Dimensions: 47G-3B-2A – Rotor diameter 11.32m (37ft 2in), fuselage length 9.63m (31ft 7in), height 2.83m (9ft 4in). Main rotor disc area 100.8m^2 (1085sq ft). 47J Ranger – Same except for fuselage length 9.90m (32ft 5in).

Capacity: 47G – Pilot and two passengers on a single bench seat. 47J Ranger – One pilot and three passengers.

Production: Bell built more than 4000 47s between the late 1940s and 1974. Agusta-Bell of Italy licence built over 1200; Kawasaki of Japan 239; and Westland of the UK 239.

History: The familiar and distinctive Bell 47 is an especially significant aircraft as it was one of the world's first practical helicopters.

The ubiquitous Bell 47 dates back to Bell's Model 30 of 1943, an experimental helicopter evaluated by the US Army (which ordered 10). The first subsequent prototype Bell Model 47 (with a car type cabin and two seats) first flew on December 8 1945. In May 1946, this early model Bell 47 became the first helicopter in the world to gain civil certification.

The first civil variants to see production were the similar Model 47B, and the 47B-3 with an open cockpit. The 47D followed and was the first model to feature the famous 'goldfish bowl' canopy and the distinctive uncovered tail boom. The Model 47E was similar but powered by a 150kW (200hp) Franklin engine.

The definitive Model 47G followed the 47E into production in 1953, and it was this variant, in a number of successively more powerful versions, that remained in production until 1974, testament to the utility and success of Bell's basic design. The 47G had optional metal rotor blades and was powered by a range of Lycoming engines outputting 150 to 210kW (200 to 280hp).

The Model 47H is based on the 47G, but with a fully enclosed fuselage and conventional cabin, and formed the basis for the 47J Ranger. The Ranger had a further enlarged cabin with seating for four, and entered production in 1956. The 47J-2 Ranger introduced powered controls and metal blades as standard, and was powered by a 195kW (260hp) VO-540.

Kawasaki in Japan licence built a development of the 47G, the KH-4 with more traditional style enclosed cabin.

Large numbers of Bell 47s have also seen military service.

Photo: A Bell 47G-5 fitted with floats. (Robert Wiseman)

Bell 206 JetRanger

Countries of origin: USA and Canada

Type: Light utility helicopter

Powerplant: 206B JetRanger II – One 300kW (400shp) Allison 250-C20 turboshaft driving a two blade main rotor and two blade tail rotor. 206B-3 JetRanger III – One 315kW (420shp) Rolls-Royce (Allison) 250-C20J.

Performance: 206B – Max cruising speed 219km/h (118kt). Initial rate of climb 1540ft/min. Range 702km (379nm). 206B-3 – Max speed 225km/h (122kt), max cruising speed 214km/h (115kt). Initial rate of climb 1280ft/min. Range with max fuel and no reserves 732km (385nm).

Weights: 206B – Empty 660kg (1455lb), max takeoff 1360kg (3000lb). 206B-3 – Empty 737kg (1635lb), max takeoff with external load 1521kg (3350lb), with internal load 1451kg (1500lb).

Dimensions: Main rotor diameter 10.16m (33ft 4in), fuselage length 9.50m (31ft 2in), height 2.91m (9ft 7in). Main rotor disc area 81.1m^2 (872.7sq ft).

Capacity: Total accommodation for five, including one pilot and one passenger in the front, and three behind them on the rear bench seat. Max internal payload (Model 206B) 635kg (1400lb), max external sling load 680kg (1500lb).

Production: Over 7725 military and civil versions of the JetRanger have been built by Bell in the USA and Canada, Agusta-Bell in Italy and other licensees. More than 4500 built for civilian customers.

History: The JetRanger is the world's most successful light single turbine helicopter and is used widely for utility and corporate work.

The JetRanger began as an unsuccessful Bell contender for a US Army competition for a light observation helicopter won by the Hughes 500. This first Model 206 made its first flight on December 8 1962, while the civil 206A, powered by a 235kW (317shp) Allison 250-C18A, flew on January 10 1966. Deliveries of the production JetRangers began late in that same year.

In the early 1970s Bell introduced the 206B JetRanger II with a 300kW (400shp) 250-C20 turboshaft, while conversion kits to upgrade earlier As to the new standard were made available.

The third major variant of the JetRanger is the 315kW (420shp) 250-C20B powered JetRanger III, with first deliveries commencing in late 1977. Once again Bell offered a conversion kit to update earlier JetRangers to the new standard. Other features introduced on the JetRanger III were a larger and improved tail rotor and minor modifications.

JetRanger production was transferred from Texas to Mirabel in Canada in 1986, where production of the JetRanger III continues, although only small numbers have been built in recent years.

The US Army did adopt the JetRanger as an observation helicopter as the OH-58 Kiowa due to rising costs and delivery difficulties with Hughes' OH-6, with deliveries from May 1968. The improved OH-58D flew in 1983 and featured a mast mounted sight and a four blade main rotor later adopted for the Bell 407 (described separately. Military 206Bs were also built in Australia for the Australian Army.

Photo: A TV work configured JetRanger. (Gary Gentle)

Bell 206L LongRanger

Countries of origin: USA and Canada

Type: Light utility helicopter

Powerplant: 206L LongRanger I – One 315kW (420shp) Allison 250-C20B turboshaft driving two blade main and tail rotors. 206L-1 LongRanger II – One 375kW (500shp) Allison 250-C28B. 206L-3 LongRanger III & 206L-4 LongRanger IV – One 485kW (650shp) Rolls-Royce 250-C30P.

Performance: 206L – Max speed 232km/h (125kt), cruising speed 229km/h (124kt). Hovering ceiling in ground effect 8200ft. Range 628km (339nm). 206L-1 – Same except for range 692km (374nm). 206L-3 – Max speed 241km/h (130kt), max cruising speed 203km/h (110kt). Range with no reserves 666km (360nm) at 5000ft. 206L-4 – Same except for range 661km (357nm) at 5000ft.

Weights: 206L – Empty 844kg (1861kg), max takeoff 1814kg (4000lb). 206L-1 – Empty 980kg (2160lb), max takeoff 1882kg (4150lb). 206L-3 – Empty 998kg (2200lb), max takeoff 1882kg (4150lb), or 1927kg (4250lb) with external sling load. 206L-4 – Empty 1031kg (2274lb), max takeoff 2018kg (4450lb), or 2064kg (4550lb) with external sling load.

Dimensions: Main rotor diameter 11.28m (37ft 0in), fuselage length 206L & 206L-1 10.13m (33ft 3in), 206L-3 10.44m (34ft 3in), 206L-4 9.81m (32ft 2in); height 3.14m (10ft 4in). Main rotor disc area 99.9m² (1075.2sq ft).

Capacity: Total seating for seven, including five passengers in main rear cabin, or four in an optional executive layout. Can accommodate two stretchers and two medical attendants for aerial ambulance.

Production: Over 1700 LongRangers have been delivered.

History: Bell developed the LongRanger to offer a light helicopter with greater capacity and utility than the JetRanger.

Bell announced its Model 206L, a stretched JetRanger, on September 25 1973, with a development aircraft first flying on September 11 1974. Production began in early 1975. The LongRanger seats a further two passengers compared to the JetRanger, and introduced a more powerful engine and 'Noda-Matic' transmission suspension system for less vibration and greater passenger comfort.

Subsequent versions have been the 206L-1 LongRanger II (introduced in 1978), the 206L-3 LongRanger III (introduced in 1982), and the current 206L-4 LongRanger IV, introduced in 1992. Each subsequent version features increasingly more powerful engines and other minor improvements.

LongRanger production, along with the JetRanger, was transferred to Mirabel in Canada in 1986 (although dynamic components continued to be built at Bell's Fort Worth, Texas plant, as is the case for all Canadian built Bells).

The LongRanger has found favour not only as a corporate transport, but with police and medical services worldwide, its extra cabin size providing a useful increase in utility.

During the mid 1990s Bell offered a twin engined LongRanger, the TwinRanger, while US company Tridair offers the twin engine Gemini ST conversion of the LongRanger (both are described separately). The LongRanger also forms the basis of the popular 407.

Photo: A 206L-1 LongRanger.

Bell TwinRanger & Tridair Gemini ST

Countries of origin: United States of America & Canada

Type: Twin engine light utility helicopters

Powerplant: Two 335kW (450shp) takeoff rated Allison 250-C20R turboshafts driving two blade main and tail rotors.

Performance: 206LT – Max cruising speed 217km/h (117kt), economical cruising speed 200km/h (108kt). Service ceiling 10,000ft. Hovering ceiling in ground effect 10,000ft, out of ground effect 6900ft. Range with max fuel and no reserves at long range cruising speed 463km (250nm). 206L-3ST – Max cruising speed 217km/h (117kt). Initial rate of climb 1550ft/min. Service ceiling 20,000ft. Hovering ceiling in ground effect 15,800ft. Range with max payload and max internal fuel 643km (347nm).

Weights: 206LT – Standard empty 1246kg (2748lb), max takeoff 2018kg (4450lb), or 2064kg (4550lb) with an external sling load. 206L-3ST – Empty 1175kg (2590lb), max takeoff 1928kg (4250lb).

Dimensions: Main rotor diameter 11.28m (37ft 0in), length overall 13.02m (42ft 9in), fuselage length 9.81m (32ft 3in), height 3.14m (10ft 4in). Main rotor disc area 99.9m² (1075.2sq ft).

Capacity: Typical seating for seven, plus pilot, in three rows (3+2+3). Executive configuration has club seating for four in main cabin.

Production: Gemini ST coversions commenced in early 1994. 13 206LTs built.

History: Bell's 206LT TwinRanger is a twin engined development of the 206L LongRanger, while Tridair helicopters in the USA offers its twin engine Gemini ST conversion for existing LongRangers.

The TwinRanger name predates the 206LT to the mid 1980s when Bell first looked at developing a twin engine version of the LongRanger. The Model 400 TwinRanger did fly (maiden flight was on April 4 1984) and it featured two Allison 250 turboshafts, the four blade main rotor developed for the military Bell 406/OH-58D Kiowa, shrouded tail rotor and a reprofiled fuselage. Bell suspended development of the 400 and the 440 (with a high degre of composites) in the late 1980s as it felt unable to achieve a protifable production rate of 120 units a year.

The 206LT TwinRanger is based on Tridair Helicopters' Gemini ST conversion program. Tridair announced it was working on a twin engine conversion of the LongRanger in 1989, and the prototype flew for the first time on January 16 1991. Full FAA certification was awarded in November and covers the conversion of LongRanger 206L-1s, L-3s and L-4s to Gemini ST configuration.

In mid 1994 the Gemini ST made history when it was certificated as the first Single/Twin aircraft, allowing it to operate either as a single or twin engine aircraft throughout all phases of flight. This unique certification allows it to operate with a single engine for maximum economy (for ferrying etc), with the extra redundancy and performance of a twin available when required.

Bell's 206LT TwinRanger was a new build production model equivalent to Tridair's Gemini ST and based on the LongRanger IV. The first example was delivered in January 1994. The last of 13 built was handed over in 1997. The TwinRanger has been replaced by the 427, described separately.

Photo: A TwinRanger. (Bell)

Bell 204, 205 & 214B

Country of origin: United States of America

Type: Medium twin utility helicopter

Powerplant: 204B – One 820kW (1100shp) Lycoming T5311A turboshaft driving two blade main and tail rotors. 205A-1 – One 932kW (1250shp) T5313B Lycoming turboshaft derated from 1050kW (1400shp).

Performance: 204B – Max speed 222km/h (120kt), max cruising speed 217km/h (117kt). Initial rate of climb 1600ft/min. Range with reserves 370km (200nm). 205A-1 – Max speed 204km/h (110kt), cruising speed 180km/h (97kt). Initial rate of climb 1680ft/min. Range 553km (300nm) at 8000ft.

Weights: 204B – Empty 2085kg (4600lb), max takeoff 4310kg (9500lb). 205A-1 – Empty 2414kg (5323lb), max takeoff 4765kg (10,500lb) with external load.

Dimensions: 204B – Main rotor diameter 14.63m (48ft 0in), fuselage length 12.69m (41ft 8in), height 4.45m (14ft 7in). Main rotor disc area 168.0m^2 (1808sq ft). 205A-1 – Same except for fuselage length 12.65m (41ft 6in).

Capacity: 204B – Total accommodation for 10, including one or two pilots, or 1360kg (3000lb) of freight. 205A-1 – Total accommodation for 15 including one or two pilots or 1815kg (4000lb) of cargo internally, or 2270kg (5000lb) externally in a sling. Air ambulance configuration for six stretchers and one or two medical attendants.

Production: Over 60 civil Model 204Bs had been delivered by 1967, while further examples were built by Agusta-Bell up until 1973. 12,000 Model 205s (including civil 205A-1s) were built by Bell and Agusta-Bell up to the early 1980s. Numerous ex military 204s and 205s converted for commercial use.

History: Bell's 204B and 205A-1 are the civil counterparts to the highly successful UH-1B and UH-1H Iroquois military helicopters.

Bell designed the 204 in response to a 1955 US Army requirement for a utility helicopter. The 204 was something of a quantum leap forward in helicopter design as it was one of the first to be powered by a turboshaft. The turboshaft engine radically improved the practicality of the helicopter due to its light weight and high power to weight ratio, lower fuel consumption, and lower maintenance and operating costs. The use of a turboshaft in the 204 allowed it to carry a useful payload over respectable ranges and at reasonable speeds, which resulted in the 204 and subsequent 205 becoming the most successful western helicopter series in terms of numbers built.

The UH-1B, equivalent to the 204B, was first delivered in March 1961. The subsequent Model 205A-1 is equivalent to the UH-1H, which, compared to the 204, is longer, larger, and has better performance and a more powerful engine.

In the civil world the 204 and 205 have been operated in a number of utility roles including as aerial cranes and for firebombing.

The 214B Biglifter is based on the 205 but is powered by a very powerful 2185kW (2930shp) Lycoming LTC4B turboshaft (with more than twice the output of the 205's T53). Its main use is as an aerial crane. Iran's Army took delivery of 287 during the 1970s while smaller numbers were built for civil customers through to 1981.

Photo: A 214B. (Lance Higgerson)

Bell 214ST

Country of origin: United States of America

Type: Medium twin utility helicopter

Powerplants: Two 1215kW (1625shp) General Electric CT7-2A turboshafts linked through a combining gearbox driving two blade main and tail rotors.

Performance: Max cruising speed 260km/h (140kt) at 4000ft, or 264km/h (143kt) at sea level. Max initial rate of climb 1780ft/min. Service ceiling with one engine out 4800ft. Hovering ceiling in ground effect 6400ft. Ferry range with auxiliary fuel 1020km (550nm), range with standard fuel and no reserves 805km (435nm).

Weights: Empty 4300kg (9481lb), max takeoff 7938kg (17,500lb).

Dimensions: Main rotor diameter 15.85m (52ft 0in), length overall rotors turning 18.95m (62ft 2in), fuselage length 15.03m (49ft 4in), height overall 4.84m (15ft 11in). Main rotor disc area 197.3m^2 (2124sq ft).

Capacity: Pilot and copilot and up to 16 or 17 passengers. Freight volume of 8.95m^3 (316cu ft). Can carry an external sling freight load of 3630kg (8000lb).

Production: The 214ST was in production from 1980 to 1990, during which time 100 were built.

History: Despite sharing a common model number with the 214 Huey Plus and Big Lifter (described separately), the Bell 214ST is a larger, much modified helicopter.

Bell's biggest helicopter yet (not counting the V-22 Osprey tiltrotor) was developed to meet an Iranian requirement for a larger transport helicopter with better performance in its hot and high environment than its 214 Isfahans. Bell based its proposal on the 214 but made substantial changes, resulting in what is essentially an all new helicopter with little commonality with the smaller 214 series.

The 214ST features two General Electric CT7 turboshafts (the commercial equivalent of the military T700), a stretched fuselage seating up to 17 in the main cabin, glassfibre main rotor blades, and lubrication free elastomeric bearings in the main rotor hub. The ST suffix originally stood for Stretched Twin, reflecting the changes over the 214, but this was later changed to stand for Super Transporter.

The 214ST was to have been built under licence in Iran as part of that country's plans to establish a large army air wing (other aircraft ordered in large numbers under this plan were the 214A Isfahan and AH-1J SeaCobra), but the Islamic revolution and fall of the Shah in 1979 put paid to these plans.

Undeterred, Bell continued development of the 214ST – which first flew in February 1977 – for civil and military customers. Three preproduction 214STs were built from 1978 and 100 production aircraft were built through to 1990.

Most 214ST sales were to military customers. Iraq was the 214ST's largest customer, taking delivery of 45 during 1987 and 1988, some most likely seeing service in the 1991 Gulf War.

Civil applications for the 214ST are numerous, including oil rig support, where its twin engine configuration and 17 passenger main cabin are useful assets.

Photo: The 214ST is Bell's largest helicopter, and differs considerably from the similarly designated 214A and 214B. (Robert Wiseman)

Bell 212 Twin Two-Twelve

Countries of origin: USA and Canada

Type: Medium twin utility helicopter

Powerplant: One 1340kW (1800shp) (derated to 960kW/1290shp) Pratt & Whitney Canada PT6T-3 or PT6T-3B Turbo Twin-Pac, comprising two coupled PT6 turboshafts sharing a common gearbox with a single output shaft, driving two blade main rotor and tail rotors.

Performance: Max speed 206km/h (111kt), long range cruising speed 193km/h (104kt). Initial rate of climb 1320ft/min. Range with standard fuel at long range cruising speed 450km (243nm).

Weights: Empty VFR configuration 2765kg (6097lb), IFR configuration 2847kg (6277lb); max takeoff (with or without an external load) 5080kg (11,200lb).

Dimensions: Main rotor diameter 14.69m (48ft 2in), length overall 17.46m (57ft 3in), fuselage length 12.92m (42ft 5in), height 4.53m (14ft 10in). Main rotor disc area 168.1m² (1809.6 sq ft).

Capacity: Total seating for 15, including one or two pilots. Max weight in an external sling load 2270kg (5000lb).

Production: Approximately 950 212s, including military aircraft, built through to 1998. Production totals augmented by Agusta-Bell licence production, although most were military versions. Bell production transferred to Canada in 1988.

History: The Model 212 is a twin engined development of Bell's earlier and highly successful Model 204 and 205 series.

Bell announced its decision to develop the Model 212 in early May 1968 in large part in response to a Canadian Armed Forces requirement for a twin engined development of the CUH-1H (Model 205) then entering military service in that country, and following successful negotiations with Pratt & Whitney Canada and the Canadian government. Development of the Model 212 was a joint venture between Bell, Pratt & Whitney Canada and the Canadian government, which provided financial support. The 212 (designated CUH-1N in Canadian and UH-1N in US military service) first flew in 1969 and was awarded commercial certification in October 1970. The first Canadian CUH-1Ns were handed over in May 1971.

The most significant feature of the Twin Two-Twelve is the PT6T Twin-Pac engine installation. This consists of two PT6 turboshafts mounted side by side and driving a single output shaft via a combining gearbox. The most obvious benefit of the new arrangement is better performance due to the unit's increased power output. However, the Twin-Pac engine system has a major advantage in that should one engine fail, sensors in the gearbox instruct the remaining operating engine to develop full power, thus providing a true engine out capability, even at max takeoff weight.

Aside from the twin engines, the 212 features only minor detail changes over the earlier Model 205 and UH-1H, including a slightly reprofiled nose. The 212 was also offered with a choice of IFR or VFR avionics suites. Production was transferred to Bell's Canadian factory in August 1988. The last was built in 1998.

Production of the 212 based 412 (described separately) continues.

Photo: The reprofiled nose and engine fairings help distinguish the 212 from the 205. (Peter Clark)

Bell 412

Countries of origin: USA and Canada

Type: Medium twin utility helicopter

Powerplants: 412 – One 1350kW (1800shp) (derated to 980kW/1308shp for takeoff) Pratt & Whitney Canada PT6T-3B Turbo Twin-Pac, consisting of two PT6 turboshafts linked through a combining gearbox, driving a four blade main rotor and two blade tail rotor. 412SP – One 1044kW (1400shp) takeoff rated PT6T-3B-1 Turbo Twin-Pac. 412EP – One 1342kW (1800shp) takeoff rated PT6T-3D Turbo Twin-Pac.

Performance: 412 – Max speed 240km/h (130kt) at sea level, cruising speed 235km/h (127kt). Max range 455km (245nm), or 835km (450nm) with auxiliary tanks. 412SP – Max speed 260km/h (140kt), max cruising speed 230km/h (124kt). Initial rate of climb 1350ft/min. Range with max payload and reserves 695km (374nm), max range with standard fuel 656km (354nm). 412EP – Max cruising speed 226km/h (122kt). Range at 5000ft 745km (402nm).

Weights: 412 – Empty equipped 2753kg (6070lb), max takeoff 5216kg (11,500lb). 412SP – Empty equipped (IFR) 3001kg (6616lb), max takeoff 5397kg (11,900lb). 412EP – Empty equipped (standard) 3079kg (6789lb), max takeoff 5397kg (11,900lb).

Dimensions: Main rotor diameter 14.02m (46ft 0in), length overall rotors turning 17.12m (56ft 2in), fuselage length 12.70m (41ft 9in), height 4.57m (15ft 0in). Main rotor disc area 154.4m² (1662sq ft).

Capacity: Total seating for 15, including one or two pilots. Maximum external sling load 2040kg (4500lb).

Production: Over 600 Bell 412s of all models, civil and military, have been built. Production of the 412 switched to Bell's Canadian plant in February 1989 after 213 had been built in the US.

History: The Bell 412 family is a four blade main rotor development of the 212 medium lift helicopter.

Bell announced development of the 412 on September 8 1978. Bell converted two 212s to 412 development aircraft, with the first of these flying in their new form in August 1979. The 412 was awarded VFR certification in January 1981, first delivery was the same month.

Subsequent development led to the 412SP, or Special Performance, with 55% increased fuel capacity, higher takeoff weight and more optional seating arrangements. The 412HP, or High Performance, superseded the 412SP in production in 1991. Features include improved transmission for better hovering performance.

The current standard production model is the 412EP, or Enhanced Performance. The 412EP features a PT6T-3D engine and a dual digital automatic flight control system fitted as standard, with optional EFIS displays. Fixed tricycle landing gear is optional.

Bell announced the proposed 412 Plus in 1999. It would have featured a 5647kg (12,450lb) max takeoff weight but was droppped in 2001.

Indonesia's Digantara (IPTN) has a licence to build the 412SP, which it calls the NBell-412. The licence covers up to 100 NBell-412s. AgustaWestland also holds a 412 licence and has built 250.

The 412 is in widespread use for a number of utility roles, including EMS and oil rig support. It is also in military service, including in Canada (which ordered 100 412EP based CH-146 Griffons).

Photo: An EMS configured 412. (Richard Koehne)

Bell 222 & 230

Bell 430

Countries of origin: Canada and USA

Type: Light twin corporate and utility helicopters

Powerplants: 222B – Two 505kW (680shp) Avco (Textron) Lycoming LTS 101-750C turboshafts driving two blade main and tail rotors. 230 – Two 520kW (700shp) takeoff rated Allison 250-C30G2 turboshafts.

Performance: 222B – Max cruising speed 240km/h (130kt). Initial rate of climb 1730ft/min. Hovering ceiling in ground effect 10,300ft. Range with no reserves 724km (390nm). 230 – Max cruising speed (with wheels) 261km/h (141kt), economical cruising speed (with wheels) 256km/h (138kt). Service ceiling 15,500ft. Hovering ceiling in ground effect 12,400ft. Range at economical cruising speed, with standard fuel, wheels and no reserves 558km (301nm), or 713km (385nm) with skids; range with wheels and auxiliary fuel, no reserves 702km (380nm).

Weights: 222B – Empty equipped 2076kg (4577lb), max takeoff 3472kg (8250lb). 230 – Empty with wheels 2312kg (5097lb), max takeoff 3810kg (8400lb).

Dimensions: 222B – Main rotor diameter 12.80m (42ft 0in), fuselage length 12.85m (42ft 2in), height 3.51m (11ft 6in). Main rotor disc area 128.7m² (1385.4sq ft). 230 – Main rotor diameter 12.80m (42ft 0in), length overall 15.23m (50ft 0in), fuselage length with wheels 12.87m (42ft 3in), with skids 12.81m (42ft 0in), height overall with skids 3.20m (12ft 2in). Main rotor disc area 128.7m² (1385.4sq ft).

Capacity: Standard seating for eight, including pilot, in four rows. Alternatively four in main cabin in club configuration.

Production: 184 Bell 222s built. 38 230s built 1992-95.

History: Bell announced the all new 222 twin, the first commercial light twin helicopter to be developed in the US, in April 1974.

The 222 first flew on August 13 1976. The new helicopter incorporated a number of advanced features including the Noda Matic vibration reduction system developed for the 214ST, stub wings housing the retractable undercarriage, and dual hydraulic and electrical systems.

The 222 was certificated in December 1979 and deliveries commenced in early 1980. Three initial versions were offered, the basic 222, the single/dual pilot IFR certificated corporate 222 Executive, and dual pilot IFR over-water certificated 222 Offshore.

Subsequent development led to the more powerful 222B with a larger diameter main rotor, introduced in 1982. Versions were the basic 222B, 222B Executive certificated for dual pilot IFR operations and with a corporate interior, and the 222B based 222UT Utility Twin, with skid landing gear.

The Bell 230 is a development of the 222 with two Allison 250 turboshafts instead of the 222's LTS 101s, plus other refinements. First flight of a 230, a converted 222, took place on August 12 1991, and Transport Canada certification was awarded in March 1992. The first delivery of a production 230 occurred that November and customers had a choice of skid or wheel undercarriage. Production ceased in 1995 after 38 had been built. The 230 has been replaced by the stretched, more powerful 430, described separately.

Photo: A Bell 222UT. (Martin Grimm)

Countries of origin: Canada and USA

Type: Light twin corporate utility helicopter

Powerplants: Two 584kW (783shp) takeoff rated, 521kW (699shp) max continuous rated Rolls-Royce 250-C40B turboshafts driving a four blade main rotor and two blade tail rotor.

Performance: Max cruising speed at sea level (with retractable gear or skids) 260km/h (140kt), economical cruising speed 256km/h (138kt) with retractable undercarriage, 237km/h (128kt) with skids. Service ceiling 18,340ft. Hovering ceiling in ground effect 11,350ft, out of ground effect 8750ft. Max range with reserves, standard fuel and retractable undercarriage 503km (272nm), with skids 644km (348nm).

Weights: Empty equipped 2406kg (5305lb) with retractable undercarriage, 2388kg (5265lb) with skids, max takeoff with internal load 4082kg (9000lb), max takeoff with sling load and optional MTOW with skids 4220kg (9300lb).

Dimensions: Main rotor disc diameter 12.80m (42ft 0in), length overall rotors turning 15.30m (50ft 3in), fuselage length incl tailskid 13.44m (44ft 1in), height to top of rotor head with wheels 3.72m (12ft 3in), with standard skids 4.03m (13ft 3in), optional skids 4.24m (13ft 11in). Main rotor disc area 128.7m² (1385.4sq ft).

Capacity: Typical seating configuration for 10 comprising pilot and passenger, with eight passengers in main cabin behind them in three rows of seats. Six and eight place executive layouts offered. In EMS role can carry one or two stretcher patients with four or three medical attendants respectively. Max hook capacity 1585kg (3500lb).

Production: Approximately 75 built.

History: Bell's 430 twin helicopter is a stretched and more powerful development of the 230.

Bell began preliminary design work on the 430 in 1991, even though the 230 itself had only flown for the first time in August that year. The 430 program was formally launched in February 1992. Two prototypes were modified from Bell 230s, and the first of these flew in its new configuration on October 25 1994. The second prototype featured the full 430 avionics suite, its first flight was on December 19 1994.

The first 430 production aircraft was completed in 1995, while Canadian certification was awarded on February 23 1996, allowing first deliveries from the middle of that year. Meanwhile 230 production had wound up in August 1995, making way for the 430.

Compared with the 230, the 430 features several significant improvements. Perhaps the most important of these is the new four blade, bearingless, hingeless, composite main rotor. Other changes include the 46cm (1ft 6in) stretched fuselage, allowing seating for an extra two passengers, 10% more powerful Rolls-Royce (Allison) 250 turboshafts (with FADEC) and an optional EFIS flightdeck. As well as the optional EFIS displays the 430 features as standard a Rogerson-Kratos Integrated Instrument Display System (IIDS), comprising two LCD displays to present engine information. The 430 is offered with either skids or retractable wheeled undercarriage.

Between August 17 and September 3 1996 Americans Ron Bower and John Williams broke the round the world helicopter record with a Bell 430, flying westwards from England.

Photo: Bell 430 with retractable undercarriage. (Andrew Povey)

Bell 407

Countries of origin: Canada and USA

Type: Light utility helicopter

Powerplants: One 605kW (814shp) takeoff rated, 520kW (700shp) max continuous rated Rolls-Royce 250-C47 turboshaft driving a four blade main rotor and two blade tail rotor.

Performance: Max cruising speed at sea level 237km/h (128kt), max cruising speed at 4000ft 243km/h (131kt), economical cruising speed at 4000ft 213km/h (115kt). Service ceiling 18,690ft. Hovering ceiling in ground effect 12,200ft, out of ground effect 10,400ft. Max range 577km (312nm). Endurance 3hr 42min.

Weights: Empty equipped 1178kg (2598lb), max takeoff with internal load 2268kg (5000lb), max takeoff with sling load 2495kg (5500lb).

Dimensions: Main rotor disc diameter 10.67m (35ft 0in), length overall rotors turning 12.70m (41ft 8in), fuselage length 9.77m (32ft 1in), height overall 3.56m (11ft 8in). Main rotor disc area 89.4m² (962.1sq ft).

Capacity: Typical seating configuration for seven comprising pilot and passengers, with five passengers in main cabin. Max hook capacity 1200kg (2645lb).

Production: Over 520 407s delivered by late 2002.

History: Bell's popular 407 is a development of its JetRanger and LongRanger light singles.

Development work on Bell's New Light Aircraft replacement for the LongRanger and JetRanger dates back to 1993. The end result was the 407, an evolutionary development of the LongRanger.

A modified 206L-3 LongRanger served as the concept demonstrator 407 and first flew in this form on April 21 1994, while the 407 was first publicly announced at the Las Vegas Heli-Expo in January 1995.

The 407 concept demonstrator mated the LongRanger's fuselage with the tail boom and dynamic system of the military OH-58D Kiowa (which has a four blade main rotor). Fake fairings were used to simulate the wider fuselage being developed for the production standard 407. The first preproduction 407 flew in June 1995, the first production 407 flew in November 1995. Customer deliveries commenced the following February.

Compared with the LongRanger, the 407 features the four blade main rotor developed for the OH-58, which uses composite construction, and the blades and hub have no life limits. Benefits of the four blade main rotor include improved performance and better ride comfort. The cabin is 18cm (8in) wider, increasing internal width and space, while the larger main cabin windows are 35% larger. Power is from a more powerful Rolls-Royce (Allison) 250-C47 turboshaft fitted with FADEC, allowing an increase in max takeoff weight and improving performance at hotter temperatures and/or higher altitudes. The tail boom is made from carbonfibre (in 1995 Bell studied fitting the 407 with a shrouded tail rotor). The instrument panel features Litton liquid crystal displays.

Bell looked at the 407T twin for a time, but opted instead to develop the all new twin PW206D powered 427.

Photo: The 407 became an overnight sales success, with around 520 delivered by late 2002. (Paul Sadler)

Bell 427

Countries of origin: Canada, USA and South Korea

Type: Light twin utility helicopter

Powerplants: Two 529kW (710shp) takeoff rated, 566kW (625shp) max continuous rated Pratt & Whitney Canada PW207D turboshafts driving a four blade main rotor and two blade tail rotor.

Performance: Max cruising speed at S/L 259km/h (140kt), econ cruising speed 246km/h (133kt). Hovering ceiling in ground effect 16,200ft, out of ground effect 13,900ft. Range with max fuel at econ cruising speed 730km (394nm). Max endurance 4hr.

Weights: Empty 1743kg (3842lb), max takeoff 2880kg (6350lb).

Dimensions: Main rotor diameter 11.28m (37ft 0in), length overall rotors turning 13.07m (42ft 11in), fuselage length 10.94m (35ft 11in). Height 3.49m (11ft 5in). Main rotor disc area 99.9m² (1075.2sq ft).

Capacity: Eight inc pilot in a 2+3+3 arrangement, or pilot and passenger side by side with seating for four in a club configuration. In medevac configuration two stretchers and two medical attendants.

Production: First deliveries January 2000.

History: Bell's latest helicopter, the 427 is a replacement for the 206LT TwinRanger and the cancelled 407T, which was to be a twin engine 407 (described separately).

When Bell first looked at a twin engine version of its new 407 light single, the company originally anticipated developing the 407T which would have been a relatively straightforward twin engine development (with two Allison 250-C22Bs). However, Bell concluded that the 407T would not offer sufficient payload/range performance, and so began studies of a new light twin.

The result was the all new 427, which Bell announced at the Heli Expo in Dallas in February 1996. Prior to this announcement Bell had signed a collaborative partnership agreement with South Korea's Samsung Aerospace Industries covering the 427. Samsung builds the 427's fuselage and tailboom, and may later assemble any 427s sold in South Korea and China at its Sachon plant. Bell builds the 427's flight dynamics systems at Fort Worth in Texas, with final assembly at Bell's Mirabel, Quebec plant.

The 427 was the first Bell designed entirely on computer (including using CATIA 3D modelling). Compared to the 407 the 427's cabin is 33cm (13in) longer, is largely of composite construction and lacks the roof beam which obstructs the cabin on the 206/206L/407.

Power is from two FADEC equipped Pratt & Whitney Canada PW206 turboshafts, driving the composite four blade main rotor and two blade tail rotor (based on those on the OH-58D Kiowa and Bell 407) through a new combining gearbox. The main rotor's soft-in-plane hub features a composite flexbeam yoke and elastomeric joints, eliminating the need for lubrication and any form of maintenance. The 427's glass cockpit features an integrated instrument display system (IIDS). A sliding main cabin door is optional.

First flight was on December 11 1997 and Canadian certification was awarded on November 19 1999. First customer deliveries followed US certification in January 2000. US FAA dual pilot IFR certification was awarded in May 2000.

Photo: A Bell 427 in Austria. (Elisabeth Klimesch)

Bell/Agusta AB139

Countries of origin: Italy & USA

Type: Medium lift helicopter

Powerplants: Two 1252kW (1679shp) takeoff rated Pratt & Whitney Canada PT6C-67C turboshafts driving a five blade main rotor and four blade tail rotor.

Performance: Max cruising speed 155kt (287km/h). Initial rate of climb 2000ft/min. Hovering ceiling out of ground effect 12,000ft. Max range with no reserves 750km (400nm). Endurance no reserves 3.9hr.

Weights: Max takeoff 6000kg (13,227lb). Useful load (external) 2700kg (6000lb).

Dimensions: Main rotor diameter 13.80m (45ft 3in), length overall rotors turning 16.65m (54ft 8in), height overall rotors turning 4.95m (16ft 3in). Main rotor disc area 149.6m² (1610.0sq ft).

Capacity: Flightcrew of one or two. Main cabin seating for up to 15 passengers on three rows of five seats (the first row rearward facing, the second and third rows forward facing). In EMS configuration can carry six stretcher patients and four medical attendants.

Production: First deliveries planned for early 2003. Launch orders from Bristow Helicopters placed in late 1999. The US Coast Guard will be an early operator.

History: The all new AB139 helicopter is the first product of the Bell/Agusta Aerospace Company (BAAC) joint venture to fly.

The new six tonne class AB139 is aimed at offshore oil rig support, corporate transport, and utility work, and will complement the Bell 212/412, as it is slightly larger with significantly improved performance. Military variants will also be offered. BAAC says the AB139 grew out of a comprehensive market survey which measured the requirements of operators in its size class.

The joint venture company publicly announced details of the AB139 on September 8 1998 at the Farnborough Airshow, while a mockup was displayed at the following year's Paris Airshow. The first pre-production AB139 first flew on February 3 2001, the second on June 4 and the third on October 22 that year. The first production machine first flew on June 24 2002, with certification and deliveries planned for early 2003.

Features of the new helicopter include a 291km/h (157kt) cruising speed, delivered courtesy of the twin PT6C engines and the five blade fully articulated main rotor and four bladed canted tail rotor, plus a Honeywell Primus Epic integrated glass cockpit, and a large, unobstructed main cabin with seating for 15.

Unlike the BA609 tiltrotor, AgustaWestland is the lead partner on the AB139, responsible for the new helicopter's design and development and production, while the manufacturing workshare is split 75:25 to the Italian manufacturer's benefit. Engine manufacturer Pratt & Whitney Canada and avionics provider Honeywell are risk sharing partners in the program, along with Kawasaki, for the transmission input module, Poland's PZL Swidnik, which is supplying airframe components, and landing gear and air-conditioning system supplier Liebherr of Germany. Final assembly will be undertaken at AgustaWestland's Vergiate plant, while Bell will establish a second line to build AB139s for North American customers.

Photo: The first production AB139. (Paul Merritt)

Bell/Agusta BA609

Country of origin: United States of America

Type: Six to nine seat corporate/utility tiltrotor

Powerplants: Two 1447kW (1940shp) Pratt & Whitney Canada PT6C-67A turboshafts driving three blade proprotors.

Performance: Provisional – Max cruising speed 510km/h (275kt), normal cruising speed 465km/h (260kt). Service ceiling 25,000ft. Max range, no reserves 1390km (750nm), range with aux fuel 1850km (1000nm).

Weights: Provisional – Max useful load 2500kg (5500lb), max takeoff 7258kg (16,800lb).

Dimensions: Proprotor diameter 7.9m (26ft), span between proprotor centres 10m (33ft), fuselage length 13.4m (44ft), width overall rotors turning 18.3m (60ft), height 4.6m (15ft).

Capacity: To be certificated for single pilot IFR operation. Main cabin seats six to nine passengers depending on configuration.

Production: Delivery timetable unclear at late 2002.

History: The Bell/Agusta BA609 is intended to become the first civil application of the revolutionary tiltrotor technology, taking advantage of Bell's experience with the military V-22 Osprey.

Bell pioneered the tiltrotor concept with the experimental XV-3 which first flew as early as 1957 and then with NASA developed the XV-15 experimental demonstrator which first flew in 1977. In conjunction with Boeing it is building the military V-22 Osprey for the US Marine Corps.

In November 1996 Bell and Boeing announced that they intended to use their expertise and experience with the V-22 to develop a nine seat civil tiltrotor. The Bell Boeing 609 was formally unveiled on November 18 1996, however in March 1998 Boeing announced its withdrawal from the program as a risk sharing partner to remain as a major subcontractor.

Then in September 1998 (at the Farnborough Airshow) Bell announced that Agusta would become a risk sharing development partner in the redesignated BA609. The two companies formed the Bell/Agusta Aerospace Company joint venture based in Fort Worth, Texas, which is also developing the AB139 twin (described separately). Bell has a majority holding in Bell/Agusta and has program lead on the BA609, while Agusta is leading development of the AB139. Production BA609s will be built at Bell's Amarillo, Texas Tiltrotor Assembly Center and at Agusta's facility near Milan in Italy.

The BA609 will incorporate advanced technologies such as a three LCD screen glass cockpit, fly-by-wire flight controls and a composite construction fuselage. Power will be from two PT6C-67A turboshafts. Unlike the V-22 it features a T-tail (with conventional elevators but no rudder). In May 2000 Bell/Agusta announced that Japan's Fuji Heavy Industries had been selected to build the BA609's composite fuselage.

First flight for the BA609 is now planned for early 2003 (somewhat delayed from the original announced schedule of first flight in mid 1999 and deliveries in 2001). Assembly of the first prototype was basically completed in 2001, but funding problems and issues with the larger, troubled V-22, have resulted in delays.

Photo: The BA609 undergoes ground running tests in December 2002.

Beriev Be-103 & KnAAPO SA-20P

Beriev Be-200

Country of origin: Russia

Type: Six seat amphibious light aircraft

Powerplants: Two 157kW (210hp) Teledyne Continental IO-360-ES4 flat six piston engine driving three blade propellers.

Performance: Max speed 265km/h (143kt), economical cruising speed 220km/h (119kt). Service ceiling 9840ft. Takeoff run on land 300m (985ft), takeoff run from water 550m (1805ft). Range with max payload 500km (270nm), range with max fuel 1850km (637nm).

Weights: Empty equipped 1540kg (3395lb), max takeoff 2270kg (5004lb).

Dimensions: Wing span 12.72m (41ft 9in), length 10.65m (34ft 11in), height 3.76m (12ft 4in). Wing area 25.1m² (270.2sq ft).

Capacity: Seating for six in pairs. Ambulance configuration accommodates pilot, stretcher patient and three seated passengers/medical attendants.

Production: Beriev estimates potential sales for up to 600, including over 200 for export. First customer was Russia's Border Guards.

History: The Beriev Be-103 is six seat piston twin powered amphibian, the KnAAPO SA-20P a single engine derivative.

The Beriev Aviation Company, based at Taganrog on Russia's Sea of Azoz, has specialised in amphibious aircraft design and development since 1948, and probably has more experience in this area than any other company today. Since the end of the Cold War Beriev has focused its efforts on civil aircraft which have export potential, including the Be-32, Be-200 and the uniquely configured Be-103.

Beriev began design work on the Be-103 in 1992. The first prototype was publicly displayed for the first time at the Gelendzhik Hydroaviation Show on the Black Sea in September 1996, before making its first flight on July 15 1997. Unfortunately this aircraft was short-lived, it crashed while practising for the Moscow Airshow on August 18 1997.

However by that stage a second prototype was well advanced and it first flew on November 17 1997. This aircraft made the Be-103's first flight from water on April 24 1998, but unfortunately it too crashed, on April 26 1999. Flight testing resumed when the first of three preproduction Be-103s first flew on February 19 1999. Russian AP-23 certification (equivalent to US FAR Part 23) was awarded in December 2001, while Beriev launched its US certification program in late 2002, which it hoped to achieve in the first quarter of 2003.

The Be-103's unique configuration features a low mounted, large area wing, with its two engines rear mounted on pylons on either side of the fuselage. The first prototype Be-103 was powered by VOKBM/Bakanov M-17F piston engines, while production aircraft will be powered by Teledyne Continental IO-360s. An enhanced development with a more powerful turbocharged Continental 230-260kW (310-350hp) TSIO-550 is under study.

KnAAPO (Komsomolsk-upon-Amur Aircraft Production Association) rolled outs its SA-20P variant powered by a single M-14 radial mounted above the fuselage in September 2002. Deliveries are planned for from 2004. The Rolls-Royce 250 turbine is under consideration as an alternate powerplant.

Photo: The short-lived first prototype Be-103. (Sebastian Zacharias)

Country of origin: Russia

Type: Firefighting and multirole amphibian

Powerplants: Two 73.6kN (16,550lb) ZMKB Progress D-436TP turbofans.

Performance: Max speed 720km/h (388kt), max cruising speed 700km/h (377kt), econ cruising speed 550km/h (297ky). Initial rate of climb 2755ft/min. Service ceiling 36,090ft. Range with 72 passengers 1850km (998nm), with 6500kg (14,330lb) freight payload 1850km (998nm). Range with max fuel 3850km (2078nm).

Weights: Max takeoff 42,000kg (92,594lb), max takeoff for firefighting 37,200kg (82,011lb).

Dimensions: Wing span 32.78m (107ft 7in), length 31.43m (103ft 2in), height 8.90m (29ft 3in). Wing area 117.4m² (1264.2sq ft).

Capacity: Flightcrew of two. In firefighting configuration can uplift 12 tonnes (26,460lb) of water. Alternative seating for 72 economy class, at four abreast. Ambulance configuration seats seven medical attendants and 30 stretcher patients. Can carry 7.5 tonnes (16,535lb) of freight in cargo configuration.

Production: Russia's ministry of emergency situations has ordered 7.

History: The Beriev Be-200 jet powered multirole amphibian is based on the larger military A-40 Albatross.

Beriev has extensive experience in building large amphibious aircraft, including the turboprop ASW Be-12 Tchaika and the Be-42 Albatross jet (NATO reporting name 'Mermaid').

The Be-200 is based on the Be-42 (which first flew in 1986) but is smaller overall and designed for civil roles, in particular firefighting. The all metal hull design is based on the Be-42's, and the Be-200 has a mildly swept wing with winglets, above fuselage mounted turbofan engines and a swept T-tail.

The airframe is strengthened to cope with the demands of water operations and firebombing and there is some use of advanced aluminium lithium alloys. The two crew flightdeck features an ARIA-2000 EFIS avionics suite (ARIA is a collaboration between the Russian avionics research institute and Honeywell). The ARIA-2000 suite includes specialist firefighting functions including an automatic glidescope and water source/drop zone memorisation.

Design work on the Be-200 began in 1989. It is being marketed by Betair, a collaboration between Beriev and Irkutsk in central Russia where the aircraft will be built.

After a number of delays the first flight took place on September 24 1998 from Irkutsk Aviation Production Organisation's airfield in Irkutsk, Siberia, however, the Be-200 has been hamstrung by funding shortfalls and delays. It was certificated for firefighting operations in August 2001. The second prototype first flew in August 2002, at which time EADS and Irkutsk Aircraft Production Association were in discussion over joint production and marketing.

The firebombing Be-200ChS version has been ordered by Russia's ministry of emergency situations for delivery from mid 2003. The Be-210 is a proposed 72 seat airliner version. The Rolls-Royce BR715 has been considered as an alternate powerplant.

Photo: The Be-200 was certificated for firefighting in August 2001. (Sebastian Zacharias)

Boeing Stearman

Boeing C-97 Stratofreighter

Country of origin: United States of America

Type: Two seat sport, utility and agricultural biplane

Powerplant: One 170kW (225hp) Lycoming R-680 seven cylinder radial piston engine driving a two blade fixed pitch propeller, or alternatively a 165kW (220hp) Continental W-670-6 or 170kW (225hp) Jacobs R-755-7 piston radial. Many later converted with a 335kW (450hp) Pratt & Whitney R-985-A6-1 radial piston engine.

Performance: Max cruising speed 200km/h (108kt), typical cruising speed range 148 to 170km/h (80 to 92kt). Initial rate of climb 1000ft/min. Service ceiling 11,200ft. Range with max fuel at 148km/h (80kt) cruising speed 605km (325nm).

Weights: Basic operating 940kg (2075lb), max takeoff 1275kg (2810lb), or max takeoff in ag configuration 2040kg (4500lb).

Dimensions: Wing span 9.80m (32ft 2in), length 7.62m (25ft 0in), height 2.79m (9ft 2in). Wing area 27.6m² (297.4sq ft).

Capacity: Typical seating for two in tandem, or single pilot only when used for agricultural work.

Production: Total production 8584. Postwar more than 2100 were converted for agricultural spraying work. Several hundred continue to fly with private owners.

History: The Boeing Stearman, the USA's primary basic trainer during WW2, is still widely used throughout the US and elsewhere as an historical recreational aeroplane.

This famous biplane began life as a design of the Wichita, Kansas based Stearman division of the United Aircraft conglomerate (at that time United Aircraft divisions also included Boeing and United Air Lines), which Boeing acquired as a wholly owned subsidiary in 1934. At the time of the takeover development on the X70 training biplane was well advanced, and Stearman continued work on the type under Boeing ownership. The prototype Stearman Model 75, as the X70 became, first flew in 1936. Later that year Stearman delivered the first production Model 35s, as the PT-13, to the US Army Air Corps. That service immediately found the Lycoming R-680 powered PT-13 to be an ideal basic trainer, the airframe was rugged and forgiving, and the slow turning radial engine reliable and reasonably economical.

America's entry into World War 2 brought with it massive requirements for pilot training and the US Army and Navy went on to buy thousands of PT-13s and Continental engined PT-17s and N2Ss. During the war almost all American pilots undertook basic training on the PT-13 or PT-17, and the type was exported to Canada (as the Kaydet), Britain and other nations. Apart from in Canada the Kaydet name was unofficially widely adopted for the type.

Postwar, the Stearman's rugged construction and good low speed handling saw large numbers converted for agricultural spraying work. Many conversions involved replacing the Stearman's fabric covering with metal (to avoid problems with chemical contamination), while many were fitted with more powerful 335kW (450hp) P&W R-985-A6-1 radials.

Today hundreds of Stearmans are still flown in private hands, although its crop spraying days are mostly over.

Photo: A Stearman in US Navy markings. (Lance Higgerson)

Country of origin: United States of America

Type: Freighter

Powerplants: KC-97G – Four 2610kW (3500hp) Pratt & Whitney R-4360-59B Wasp Major 28 cylinder radial piston engines driving four blade constant speed propellers.

Performance: KC-97G – Max speed 603km/h (325kt), cruising speed 482km/h (260kt). Service ceiling 35,000ft. Range with max fuel 6920km (3735nm).

Weights: KC-97G – Empty 37,450kg (82,500lb), max takeoff 79,450kg (175,000lb).

Dimensions: KC-97G – Wing span 43.05m (141ft 3in), length 35.81m (117ft 5in), height 11.67m (38ft 3in). Wing area 164.5m² (1769sq ft).

Capacity: Flightcrew of two pilots, flight engineer and, in military service, a navigator and radio operator. When configured for passengers can seat more than 100 (Stratocruisers in airline service typically seated 55). All surviving Stratofreighters used as freighters.

Production: Total military Model 367 production of 27 C-97s and 808 KC-97s, in addition to which 55 civil Model 377 Stratocruiser airliners were built. One Stratofreighter remained in commercial use in 2002.

History: Boeing's Stratofreighter formed the backbone of the US Air Force's Military Air Transport Service (MATS) during the early 1950s, and more than 800 were built for use as freighters and air-to-air refuellers.

The Model 367 Stratofreighter is based on the Boeing B-29 Superfortress, the most technologically advanced bomber to see service in World War 2, and an aircraft famous (or infamous) for dropping the atomic bombs on Japan in the closing stages of that conflict. The B-29 flew for the first time in September 1942, by which time Boeing had already studied a transport version, utilising the B-29's wing, engines, tail and lower fuselage, combined with a new upper fuselage section. The new double lobe fuselage shape was very distinctive, and also formed the basis for future Boeing jet airliner fuselage cross sections.

The US Army Air Force was impressed with Boeing's proposals and ordered three prototypes be built, the first of which flew on November 15 1944. Ten development YC-97s were subsequently ordered, the last of which represented production aircraft, featuring the more powerful R-4360 engines and taller tail developed for the B-50, an improved B-29. The first production C-97A was delivered in October 1949.

Development of the C-97 led to the C-97C, which was used for casualty evacuation, and the KC-97E, KC-97F and KC-97G aerial tankers. More than 590 KC-97Gs were built. The KC-97 was the US Air Force's primary tanker until replaced by the jet powered KC-135, the predecessor to the Boeing 707. Small numbers of 377 Stratocruiser airliners were also built, but the last of these have long been retired.

Many Stratofreighters survived their military service to be acquired by civilian operators for use as freighters and fire bombers. One still operates in Alaska with Hawkins and Power based at Fort Wainwright.

Photo: Hawkins and Power's C-97G. (Stephen Boreham)

Boeing 707

Boeing 720

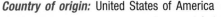

Country of origin: United States of America

Type: Medium to long range airliner and freighter

Powerplants: 707-120B – Four 75.6kN (17,000lb) Pratt & Whitney JT3D-1 turbofans. 707-320B – Four 80kN (18,000lb) JT3D-3s or four 84.4kN (19,000lb) JT3D-7s.

Performance: 707-120B – Max speed 1010km/h (545kt), max cruising speed 1000km/h (540kt), econ cruising speed 897km/h (484kt). Range with max fuel 8485km (4580nm). 707-320B – Max speed 1009km/h (545kt), max cruising speed 974km/h (525kt), long range cruising speed 885km/h (478kt). Range with max passengers 6920km (3735nm), range with 147 passengers 9265km (5000nm).

Weights: 707-120B – Operating empty 55,589kg (122,533lb), max takeoff 116,575kg (257,000lb). 707-320B – Empty 66,406kg (146,400lb), max takeoff 151,315kg (333,600lb).

Dimensions: 707-120B – Wing span 39.90m (130ft 10in), length 44.07m (144ft 6in), height 12.94m (42ft 5in). Wing area 226.3m² (2433sq ft). 707-320B – Wing span 44.42m (145ft 9in), length 46.61m (152ft 11in), height 12.93m (42ft 5in). Wing area 283m² (3050sq ft).

Capacity: Flightcrew of three or four. 707-120 – Max seating for 179, or 110 in two classes (44 first and 66 economy). 707-320B – Max seating for 219, or 189 single class at 81cm (32in) pitch, or 147 in two classes. Convertible or freighter versions – 13 A type containers.

Production: 878 707s built. In late 2002 approx 80 in commercial service, approx 10 in corporate use.

History: The 707's jet speed, long range, high seating capacity and operating economics revolutionised airliner travel when it was introduced into service in 1958. The 707 also laid the foundations for Boeing's subsequent dominance of the jet airliner market.

Recognising the jet engine's potential for commercial aviation, Boeing (at great financial risk) decided to develop a jet powered transport that could fulfil military tanker transport roles but also be easily adapted to become an airliner. The resulting prototype, the swept wing four jet designed Dash 80, first flew on July 16 1954. Impressed, the US Air Force ordered it into production as the KC-135 tanker/transport (more than 700 were built). The success of the KC-135 paved the way for the commercial 707, which was a similar but had a longer and widened fuselage.

The first production 707 (a 707-120 for Pan Am) flew on December 20 1957, and entered service later the following year. Developments of the 707-120 include the similar 707-220, the shorter -138 for Qantas, and the stretched 707-320, which flew in July 1959. The 707-320 and -120 were later fitted with JT3D turbofans (in place of the original JT3 turbojets) to become the 707-320B and the 707-120B respectively. The 707-320C was a convertible model, the 707-420 was powered by Rolls-Royce Conways, while the proposed CFM56 powered 707-700 upgrade was flight tested in the late 1970s but never entered production (although military 707 based E-3s and E-6s have CFM56s). Commercial 707 production ended in 1978, with military 707 airframes built through to 1990.

Today most 707s in service are freighter conversions or corporate transports. Many have been hushkitted

Photo: A 707-320C in Congo Airlines markings. (Rob Finlayson)

Country of origin: United States of America

Type: Medium range narrowbody airliner

Powerplants: 720B – Four 75.6kN (17,000lb) Pratt & Whitney JT3D-1 turbofans or four 80kN (18,000lb) JT3D-3s.

Performance: 720B – Max speed 1009km/h (545kt), max cruising speed 983km/h (530kt), economical cruising speed 896km/h (484kt). Range with maximum payload and no reserves 6687km (3610nm), range with max fuel 8428km (4550nm).

Weights: 720B – Operating empty 51,203kg (112,883lb), max takeoff 106,140kg (234,000lb).

Dimensions: Wing span 39.88m (130ft 10in), length 41.68m (136ft 9in), height 12.66m (41ft 7in). Wing area 234.2m² (2521sq ft).

Capacity: Flightcrew of three comprising two pilots and a flight engineer. Typical seating for 112 in two classes, max seating for 149.

Production: Between 1959 and 1969 Boeing built 65 720s and 89 720Bs (many 720s were converted to 720Bs). In 2002 two used as corporate transports.

History: The 720 is a smaller capacity, lighter, medium range variant of the 707, given its own model number to indicate significant engineering changes.

Introduced in 1959, the 720 (originally designated 707-020) retained the same basic structure as the 707-120, but was 2.54m (8ft 4in) shorter, which reduced seating to 112 in a typical two class arrangement. Other changes were made to the wing which introduced full span leading edge flaps, while a glove between the inner engines and the fuselage increased wing sweep and wing area and decreased the wing's thickness/chord ratio. The changes to the wing made it more aerodynamically efficient, permitting higher cruising speeds and lower minimum speeds (aiding field performance).

Like the early 707s the first 720s had JT3C turbojets, but needed less powerful models lacking water injection because of the 720's lighter weight. Compared with the 707-120 the 720 also had reduced fuel capacity and a lower max takeoff weight. But many components were interchangeable between the 720 and 707, while inside the cabin the 720 and 707 shared the same passenger interior and flightdeck.

The initial 720 (bound for launch customer United) first flew on November 23 1959. Certification was awarded on June 30 1960, and entry into service with United Airlines was on July 5 that year.

The availability of the far more fuel efficient Pratt & Whitney JT3D turbofan resulted in the 720B, which was powered by either JT3D-1s or -3s. First flight of the 720B was on October 6 1960, with certification awarded on March 3 1961. The 720B also featured a higher maximum zero fuel weight (significantly boosting payload/range) and an increased max takeoff weight due to the heavier turbofan engines.

Major 720 operators included American Airlines (a number of its 720s were converted to 720Bs with turbofan engines), United, Eastern, Northwest Orient and Western, while operators outside the US included Lufthansa and Avianca.

Today a handful are used as corporate transports, although none are understood to be in commercial service.

Photo: A corporate configured 720B. (Rob Finlayson)

Boeing 717

Country of origin: United States of America

Type: 100 seat regional airliner

Powerplants: 717-200BGW – Two 82.3kN (18,500lb) Rolls-Royce BR715 A1-30 turbofans. 717-200HGW – Same or optionally 89.9kN (20,000lb) or 93.4kN (21,000lb) BR715s.

Performance: 717-200BGW – Cruising speed 811km/h (438kt). Range with 106 passengers 2645km (1430nm). 717-200HGW – Cruising speed same. Range with 106 passengers 3815km (2060nm).

Weights: 717-200BGW – Operating empty 30,618kg (67,500lb), max takeoff 49,895kg (110,000lb). 717-200HGW – Operating empty 31,071kg (68,500lb), max takeoff 54,885kg (121,000lb).

Dimensions: Wing span 28.44m (93ft 3in), length 37.82m (124ft 0in), height 8.87m (29ft 1in). Wing area 93.0m² (1000.7sq ft).

Capacity: Flightcrew of two. Typical two class seating for 106 passengers at five abreast in main cabin. Single class seating for 117.

Production: At late 2002 162 717s had been ordered, of which 105 had been delivered.

History: The 100 seat 717 is the latest development of the DC-9/MD-80/MD-90 family and the only Douglas airliner which Boeing retained in its product line-up follow the 1997 merger with McDonnell Douglas. It is designed for high cycle, short range operations.

McDonnell Douglas first announced the MD-95 at the June 1991 Paris Airshow. At the time MDC anticipated a formal program launch by late 1991 and a first flight in July 1994. As it happened program launch was not until October 1995 when US airline ValuJet (now AirTran Airlines) ordered 50 and optioned 50.

In January 1998 Boeing (following the August 1997 Boeing/McDonnell Douglas merger) relaunched the MD-95 as the 717-200. First flight took place on September 2 1998, certification was awarded on September 1 1999 while the first delivery, to AirTran, was on September 23 that year.

Initially MDC studied powering the MD-95 with Pratt & Whitney JT8D-218s or Rolls-Royce Tays. In February 1994 however MDC announced it had chosen the new BMW Rolls-Royce (now just Rolls-Royce) BR715 over the JT8D-200 and an engine from the proposed 'Project Blue' teaming of General Electric, SNECMA, MTU and P&W.

Other 717-200 features include a fuselage 1.45m (4ft 9in) longer than the DC-9-30's, a wing based on the DC-9-34's, an advanced six LCD screen Honeywell EFIS flightdeck, and a cabin interior similar to that developed for the MD-90. It is offered in standard 717-200BGW (Basic Gross Weight) and extended range 717-200HGW (High Gross Weight) forms. In addition, 80 seat shortened 717-100 (formerly MD-95-20) and 130 seat stretched 717-300 (formerly MD-95-50) models have been studied, as has a business jet variant.

Companies participating in 717 production include Alenia (fuselage), Korean Air (nose), AIDC of Taiwan (empennage), ShinMaywa of Japan (engine pylons and horizontal stabilizers), Israel Aircraft Industries (undercarriage), and Fischer of Austria (interior).

Final assembly is at the old Douglas home of Long Beach. Boeing used the 717 to pioneer the moving production line which has since been successfully adapted for other Boeing models.

Photo: A 717 operated by QantasLink. (Rob Finlayson)

Boeing 727-100

Country of origin: United States of America

Type: Short to medium range narrowbody airliner

Powerplants: 727-100 – Three 62.3kN (14,000lb) Pratt & Whitney JT8D-7 turbofans.

Performance: Max speed 1017km/h (549kt), max cruising speed 977km/h (527kt), economical cruising speed 917km/h (495kt). Range with max payload 3260km (1760nm).

Weights: 727-100 – Empty equipped 36,560kg (80,602lb), max takeoff 72,570kg (160,000lb).

Dimensions: 727-100 – Wing span 32.92m (108ft 0in), length 40.59m (133ft 2in), height 10.36m (34ft 0in). Wing area 157.9m² (1700sq ft).

Capacity: Flightcrew of three (two pilots and flight engineer). Typical two class seating for 94, max seating for 131.

Production: Of the 582 727-100s built, approx 235 remained in commercial service in late 2002, with 40 more used as corporate jets.

History: The 727 short to medium range trijet is the world's second most successful jet airliner and an important part of the Boeing success story.

Boeing began initial design studies of a new short/medium range airliner in 1956, although for a time it appeared that it would not be built at all due to the company's financial position before sales of the 707 had taken off. Boeing persisted however and began serious development of the 727 in June 1959. The program was launched on the strength of orders for 80 from Eastern and United in 1960.

The 727 pioneered the rear trijet configuration, with power from three specially designed Pratt & Whitney JT8D turbofans (although Rolls-Royce Speys were originally considered). The trijet design was settled upon as it gave the redundancy of three engines, better climb performance than a twin and improved operating economics over a four engine jet. The 727 also introduced an advanced wing with outer leading edge Krueger flaps, inner leading edge slats and trailing edge triple slotted Fowler flaps. The 727 retained the 707's fuselage cross section, but with a redesigned smaller lower fuselage due to the need to carry less baggage on shorter range flights, and it has limited parts commonality with the 707 and 720. The 727 was also the first Boeing airliner to feature an APU (auxiliary power unit).

The prototype 727 first flew on February 9 1963, with certification granted in December that year. The first 727 entered service with Eastern Airlines on February 9 the following year.

Development of the initial 727-100 resulted in a small family of sub variants, including higher gross weight options for the basic passenger carrying 727, the 727-100C Convertible and 727-100QC Quick Change, both with a large freight door on the forward left hand side of the fuselage. Many were subsequently converted to pure freighters. The stretched 727-200 is described separately.

Production of the 727-100 ceased in 1973.

During the 1990s Dee Howard in the USA upgraded 45 727-100 freighters for express freight operator UPS with Rolls-Royce Tay turbofans, improving performance, reducing fuel consumption and allowing the aircraft to meet Stage 3 noise requirements.

Photo: A 727-100C of South Africa's Interair. (Rob Finlayson)

Boeing 727-200

Country of origin: United States of America

Type: Short to medium range narrowbody airliner

Powerplants: Three 64.5kN (14,500lb) Pratt & Whitney JT8D-9 turbofans, or 67.2kN (15,000lb) JT8D-11s, or 68.9kN (15,500lb) JT8D-15s or 71.1kN (16,000lb) JT8D-17s (Advanced only), or 77.3kN (17,400lb) JT8D-17Rs (Advanced only).

Performance: Advanced 727-200 – Max speed 1017km/h (549kt), max cruising speed 953km/h (515kt), economical cruising speed 865km/h (467kt). Range with max payload 3965km (2140nm), range with max fuel 4450km (2400nm).

Weights: Advanced 727-200 – Operating empty 45,360kg (100,000lb), max takeoff 95,030kg (209,500lb).

Dimensions: Wing span 32.92m (108ft 0in), length 46.69m (153ft 2in), height 10.36m (34ft 0in). Wing area 157.9m² (1700sq ft).

Capacity: 727-200 – Max seating for 189 at six abreast and 76cm (30in) pitch, typical two class seating for 14 premium class and 131 economy class passengers. 727-200F – Typical max payload comprises 11 2.23m x 3.17m (7ft 4in x 10ft 5in) pallets.

Production: 1831 727s built, including 1249 -200s. Approx 750 in commercial service, 16 as corporate transports at late 2002.

History: The 727-100 had been in service barely a year when Boeing began serious consideration of a stretched development.

Boeing announced it was developing the 727-200 in August 1965. The 727-200 was essentially a minimum change development of the -100, the only major change being the 6.10m (20ft) fuselage stretch, which increased maximum seating to 189 passengers. The 727-200's stretch consisted of two 3.05m (10ft) plugs, one forward and one rear of the wing. Otherwise the 727-100 and -200 shared common engines, fuel tank capacity and the same maximum takeoff weight.

The 727-200 first flew on July 27 1967, with certification granted in late November that year. The -200 was placed into service by launch customer Northeast Airlines (this airline was later acquired by Delta) the following month, by which time total 727 orders for both models exceeded 500.

The 727-200 proved very popular but was restricted by its relatively short range. Consequently, Boeing developed the increased range Advanced 727-200, which first flew in March 1972. Advanced model features included increased fuel capacity, and thus range, the option of more powerful engines, quieter engine nacelles and strengthened structure, and from 1976, a new interior. The Advanced remained the primary 727-200 production model until production ceased in 1984 (freighters and convertibles were also built). The last 727 built was a 727-200F for Federal Express.

The 727-200 remains popular with passengers and pilots but unmodified it does not meet Stage 3 noise requirements. A number of hushkit programs are on offer while Valsan converted 23 727s to its Stage 3 compliant Quiet 727 standard (before the company collapsed). This retrofit included installing JT8D-217s on the outer pylons and acoustic treatment of the centre engine. Large numbers have also been converted to freighters.

Photo: A 727-200 of South Africa's Kulula. (Rob Finlayson)

Boeing 737-100 & 737-200

Country of origin: United States of America

Type: Short range narrowbody airliner

Powerplants: 737-100 – Two 62.3kN (14,000lb) Pratt & Whitney JT8D-7 turbofans. 737-200 – Two 64.5kN (14,500lb) JT8D-9As, or two 68.9kN (15,500lb) JT8D-15s, or two 71.2kN (16,000lb) JT8D-17s, or two 77.4kN (17,400lb) JT8D-17Rs with automatic reverse thrust.

Performance: 737-100 – Max speed 943km/h (509kt), economical cruising speed 852km/h (460kt). Range with max fuel 2855km (1540nm). 737-200 – Max speed 943km/h (509kt), max cruising speed 927km/h (500kt), economical cruising speed 796km/h (430kt). Range with 115 passengers and reserves between 3520km (1900nm) and 4260km (2300nm) depending on weight options and engines.

Weights: 737-100 – Empty 25,878kg (57,000lb), max takeoff 49,940kg (110,000lb). 737-200 – Operating empty 27,448kg (60,600lb), MTOW 52,390kg (115,500lb) or opt 58,740kg (129,500lb).

Dimensions: 737-100 – Wing span 28.35m (93ft 0in), length 28.67m (94ft 0in), height 11.29m (37ft 0in). Wing area 91.1m² (980sq ft). 737-200 – Same except for length 30.53m (100ft 2in).

Capacity: Flightcrew of two. 737-100 – Typical single class seating for 100. 737-200 – Typical single class seating for 115, max seating for 130 at 74cm (29in) pitch. 737-200C & QC payload 15,545kg (34,270lb), consisting of pallets or containers.

Production: 1144 737-100s and 200s built, comprising 30 -100s and 1114 -200s, including 19 737-200 T-43A navigation trainers for the USAF and 104 737-200Cs. Approx 1 -100 and 720 -200s in commercial service in late 2002, plus 30 737-200 corporate transports.

History: The 737-100 and -200 are the first generation models of the world's most successful jet airliner family, Boeing's 737 twinjet.

Boeing conceived the 737 as a short range small capacity airliner to round out its jet airliner family beneath the 727, 720 and 707. Announced in February 1965, the 737 was originally envisioned as a 60 to 85 seater, although following consultation with launch customer Lufthansa, a 100 seat design was settled upon. Design features included two underwing mounted turbofans and 60% structural and systems commonality with the 727, including the same six abreast seating fuselage cross section (making it wider than the competing five abreast DC-9 and BAC 1-11).

The 737-100 first flew on April 9 1967 and entered service with Lufthansa in February 1968, while the last of 30 built was delivered to Malaysia-Singapore Airlines in October 1969.

By this time the larger capacity 1.93m (6ft 4in) stretched 737-200 was in service. The first 737-200 had flown for the first time on August 8 1967, with first delivery, to United, that December.

Developments of the -200 include the -200C convertible and quick change -200QC, while an unprepared airfield kit was also offered. The definitive Advanced 737-200 appeared in 1971, featuring minor aerodynamic refinements and other improvements.

Sales of the 737-200 far exceeded that of the shorter -100 and the 737-200 remained in production until 1988, by which time it had been superseded by the improved 737-300, after 1114 had been built. Many have been fitted with Stage 3 engine hushkits.

Photo: A RyanAir 737-200 advertising Jaguar cars. (Rob Finlayson)

Boeing 737-300

Country of origin: United States of America

Type: Short to medium range narrowbody airliner

Powerplants: Two 89.0kN (20,000lb) CFM International CFM56-3B-1 turbofans, or optionally two 97.9kN (22,000lb) CFM56-3B-2s.

Performance: Max cruising speed 908km/h (491kt), long range cruising speed 794km/h (429kt). Range with 128 passengers and standard fuel 3362km (1815nm), range with 128 pax and max fuel 4973km (2685nm). High gross weight version max range 6300km (3400nm) with 140 passengers.

Weights: Operating empty 32,881kg (72,490lb), standard max takeoff 56,740kg (124,500lb), high gross weight option 62,823kg (138,500lb).

Dimensions: Wing span 28.88m (94ft 9in), length 33.40m (109ft 7in), height 11.13m (36ft 6in). Wing area 105.4m² (1135sq ft).

Capacity: Flightcrew of two. Typical two class seating for 128 (eight premium class four abreast and 120 economy class six abreast), standard one class seating for 141 at six abreast and 81cm (31in) pitch, max seating for 149 at 76cm (30in) pitch.

Production: Grand total 737 orders stand at over 5160, of which 1113 were for the -300. Approximately 1080 737-300s were in airline service at late 2002, plus 5 used as corporate transports.

History: The 737-300 was the first and most popular of the three member second generation CFM56 powered 737 family, which also comprises the stretched 737-400 and shortened 737-500. Now dubbed the 737 Classic family, in all 3132 737s of the three models were built between 1984 and 1999, significantly contributing to make the 737 series the world's best selling airliner family.

Boeing announced it was developing the 737-300 in March 1981. This new variant started off as a simple stretch over the 737-200 but Boeing decided to adopt the CFM International CFM56 high bypass turbofan (jointly developed by General Electric and SNECMA) to reduce fuel consumption and comply with the then proposed International Civil Aviation Organisation Stage 3 noise limits.

Despite the all new engines and the 2.64m (104in) fuselage stretch, the 737-300 retains 80% airframe spares commonality and shares the same ground handling equipment with the 737-200. A number of aerodynamic improvements were incorporated to further improve efficiency including modified leading edge slats and a new dorsal fin extending from the tail. Another feature was the flattened, oval shaped engine nacelles for the larger fan diameter CFM56s, while the nosewheel leg was extended to increase ground clearance for the new engines.

Other internal changes included materials and systems improvements first developed for the 757 and 767 programs, including an early generation EFIS flightdeck with four colour CRT screens.

The 737-300 first flew on February 24 1984, with first deliveries in November that year. Through to 1999 1113 737-300s were built, and it forms the backbone of many airlines' short haul fleets across the globe. The final 737-300 was delivered to Air New Zealand on December 17 1999.

The 737-300's 1113 production run was just one unit short of the 737-200's 1114.

Photo: A 737-300 of KLM owned low fare carrier buzz. (Rob Finlayson)

Boeing 737-400

Country of origin: United States of America

Type: Short to medium range airliner

Powerplants: Two 97.9kN (22,000lb) CFM International CFM56-3B-2 turbofans, or optionally 104.5kN (23,500lb) CFM56-3C-1s.

Performance: Max cruising speed 912km/h (492kt), long range cruising speed 813km/h (439kt). Standard version range with max payload 4005km (2160nm), typical range with 146 passengers 3630km (1960km). High gross weight option range with 146 passengers 3850km (2080nm).

Weights: Standard version operating empty 34,564kg (76,200lb), max takeoff 62,820kg (138,500lb). High gross weight operating empty 34,827kg (76,780lb), max takeoff 68,040kg (150,000lb).

Dimensions: Wing span 28.88m (94ft 9in), length 36.45m (119ft 7in), height 11.13m (36ft 6in). Wing area 105.4m² (1135sq ft).

Capacity: Flightcrew of two. Typical two class seating for 146 (eight premium, 138 economy), typical all economy for 159 at 81cm (32in) pitch, or max seating for 168.

Production: Total 737-400 production of 486, with the last delivered in January 2000. Of those approx 470 were in airline service at late 2002, plus three were in use as corporate transports.

History: Boeing announced it was developing a new higher capacity version of the fast selling 737-300 in June 1986.

The new aeroplane, the 737-400, was developed as a 150 seat class 727 replacement. Although Boeing had initially built the 180 to 200 seat 757 to replace the successful 727, there still existed a considerable market for a near direct size replacement for the popular trijet. By developing the 737-400 as a minimum change stretch of the 737-300, Boeing was also able to offer considerable commonality, and thus cost, benefits to operators already with the 737-300, and to a lesser extent, the 737-200 in their fleets.

The major change to the 737-400 over the smaller -300 is a 3.05m (10ft 0in) fuselage stretch, consisting of a 1.83m (6ft 0in) stretch forward and a 1.22m (4ft 0in) plug rear of the wing. The stretch increases maximum passenger seating to 188. To cope with the increased weights, more powerful CFM56s are fitted. Other changes were minor, such as a tail bumper fitted to protect against over rotation at takeoff.

A higher gross weight longer range version was also offered. It introduced increased fuel capacity plus strengthened undercarriage and structures to cope with the greater weights, but was otherwise identical to the standard 737-400.

The 737-400 first flew on February 19 1988 and entered airline service in October that year with Piedmont. Of the 737-300/-400/-500 Classic family the -400 proved the second most popular, its larger capacity and transcontinental US range meaning it found a very useful market for Boeing as a 727 replacement.

The last 737-400 (and last 737 Classic) was delivered to CSA Czech Airlines on February 25 2000 (after rollout on December 9 1999). The -400 was replaced in the Boeing line-up by the Next Generation 737-800.

Photo: An Aeroflot 737-400. The 737-400 features two above wing emergency exits, rather than one on the -300. (Rob Finlayson)

Country of origin: United States of America

Type: Short to medium range airliner

Powerplants: Two 82.3kN (18,500lb) CFM International CFM56-3B-1 turbofans, or 89.0kN (20,000lb) CFM56-3C-1s.

Performance: Max cruising speed 912km/h (492kt), economical cruising speed 795km/h (430kt). Standard range with max passengers 2815km (1520nm), higher gross weight option range with max passengers 4444km (2400nm).

Weights: Operating empty (standard and high gross weight models) 31,983kg (70,510lb), standard max takeoff 52,390kg (115,500lb), high gross weight max takeoff 60,555kg (133,500lb).

Dimensions: Wing span 28.88m (94ft 9in), length 31.01m (101ft 9in), height 11.13m (36ft 6in). Wing area 105.4m² (1135sq ft).

Capacity: Flightcrew of two. Typical two class seating for 108 (eight first and 100 economy), or max single class seating for 132 at 76cm (30in) pitch.

Production: Total 737-500 production of 389, with the last delivered in 1999. Of those 378 were in airline service at late 2002, plus 3 serving as corporate transports.

History: The 737-500 was the shortest and smallest member of the second generation 737-300/-400/-500 Classic family, and the last to be developed.

When the new stretched 737-300 first appeared it was intended to supplement, rather than replace, the 737-200. However the evolution of the 737-300 into a family of models led to the development of a new model comparable in size to the 737-200, but offering better fuel economy and extensive commonality with the 737-300 and -400 models. This was the 737-500, known before its May 1987 formal launch as the 737-1000.

Like the preceding 737-300 and 737-400, the 737-500 is powered by CFM International CFM56s turbofans, in this case either 82.3kN (18,500lb) CFM56-3B-1s or 89.0kN (20,000lb) CFM56-3C-1s. All three second generation 737 models share extensive systems and structure commonality, and a common aircrew type rating. These benefits offer real cost savings to an airline with two or more variants of the family in its fleet.

The 737-500 is 31.01m (101ft 9in) in length, comparable to the 737-200's 30.53m (100ft 2in). Like the -300 and -400, a higher gross weight longer range version was offered, featuring auxiliary fuel tanks and uprated engines.

The 737-500's first flight occurred on June 30 1989, FAA certification was awarded on February 12 1990, with service entry later that same month. The last of 389 was delivered to All Nippon on July 21 1999.

The 737-500 appealed most to airlines with 737-400 and 737-300 fleets. Because the -500 is a shortened development of the -300, it still carries much of the structural weight needed for the higher weight models, which makes it less efficient than if it was designed specifically for its size category. However for 737-300/-400 operators, the extensive commonality benefits (including crewing) more than compensate for this.

Photo: An Air Ukraine 737-500. (Toni Marimon)

Country of origin: United States of America

Type: Short to medium range narrowbody airliners

Powerplants: 737-600 – Two 86.7kN (19,500lb) CFM56-7B18 turbofans, or 101kN (20,600lb) CFM56-7B22s on high gross weight version. 737-700 – Two 91.6kN (20,600lb) CFM56-7B20s or 101kN (22,700lb) CFM56-7B24s on HGW version.

Performance: Typical cruising speed Mach 0.785. Max certificated altitude 41,000ft. 737-600 – Range with 110 pax 2480km (1340nm) or 5648km (3050nm) for HGW version. 737-700 – Range with 126 pax 2852km (1540nm) or 6037km (3260nm) for HGW version.

Weights: 737-600 – Operating empty 37,104kg (81,800lb), max takeoff 56,245kg (124,000lb), HGW max takeoff 65,090kg (143,500lb). 737-700 – Operating empty 38,147kg (84,100lb), max takeoff 60,330kg (133,000lb), HGW max takeoff 70,080kg (154,500lb).

Dimensions: 737-600 – Wing span 34.31m (112ft 7in), length 31.24m (102ft 6in), height 12.57m (41ft 3in). Wing area 125.0m² (1344sq ft). -700 – Same except length 33.63m (110ft 4in), height 12.55m (41ft 2in).

Capacity: Two flightcrew. 737-600 – 110 two class passengers or 132 single class. 737-700 – 126 in two classes or 149 in a single class.

Production: 81 737-600s ordered and 47 delivered at late 2002; 816 737-700s ordered with 397 delivered at late 2002.

History: The 737-600 and -700 are the smaller members of Boeing's successful Next Generation 737-600/-700/-800/-900 family.

The improved Next Generation Boeing 737 family (originally covered by the 737-X designation) was launched in November 1993. The 737-700 was the first member of the new family to be developed, and is based on the 737-300, while the 737-600 is based on the 737-500.

The 737-700 rolled out on December 7 1996, was certificated in November 1997 and entered service (with Southwest) the following month. The 737-600 was launched on March 15 1995, first flew on January 22 1998, and entered service (with SAS) that September.

Among the many changes, the Next Generation 737s feature more efficient CFM56-7B turbofans. The CFM56-7 combines the core of the CFM56-5 with the CFM56-3's low pressure compressor and a 1.55m (61in) fan. The 737's new wing has greater chord, span and wing area, while the tail surfaces are also larger. The 2.4m (8ft) high winglets first developed for the Boeing Business Jet development are now offered as an option on the 737-700.

The Next Generation 737s cruise at Mach 0.78 to Mach 0.80, while the larger wing allows greater fuel tankage and transcontinental USA range. Other features include a 777 style EFIS flightdeck with six flat panel LCDs which can be programmed to present information as on the 777 or as on the 737-300/-400/-500 series, the latter allowing a common pilot type rating for the two 737 families.

The Boeing Business Jet or BBJ (described separately) is based on the fuselage of the 737-700 with the larger 737-800's wing. The BBJ's airframe also forms the basis for the convertible passenger/freighter variant of the -700, the 737-700QC, which has been ordered by the US Navy as the C-40A (to replace the DC-9 based C-9 Skytrain II). The C-40 first flew on April 17 2000.

Photo: An Air Algerie 737-600. (Rob Finlayson)

Boeing 737-800 & -900

Country of origin: United States of America

Type: Short to medium range narrowbody airliners

Powerplants: 737-800 – Two 107.6kN (24,200lb) CFM56-7B24s, or two 121.4kN (27,300lb) CFM56-7B27s on high gross weight versions. 737-900 – Two 117kN (26,300lb) CFM56-7B26s, or 121.4kN (27,300lb) or CFM56-7B27s in high gross weight versions.

Performance: Typical cruising speed Mach 0.785. Max certificated altitude 41,000ft. 737-800 – Standard range with 162 passengers 3685km (1990nm) or 5445km (2940nm) for high gross weight version. 737-900 – Standard range with 177 passengers 3815km (2060nm), high gross weight version 5083km (2458nm).

Weights: 737-800 – Operating empty 41,145kg (90,710lb), max takeoff 70,535kg (155,500lb), high gross weight max takeoff 79,015kg (174,200lb). 737-900 – Operating empty 42,493kg (93,680lb), max takeoff 74,840kg (164,000lb), HGW MTOW 79,015kg (174,200lb).

Dimensions: 737-800 – Wing span 34.31m (112ft 7in), length 39.47m (129ft 6in), height 12.55m (41ft 2in). Wing area 125.0m² (1344sq ft). 737-900 – Same except length 42.11m (138ft 2in).

Capacity: Flightcrew of two. 737-800 – Typical two class seating for 162 with 12 first class passengers at four abreast and 91cm (36in) pitch and 150 economy class at six abreast and 81cm (32in) pitch. Max single class seating for 189 at 76cm (30in) pitch. 737-900 – Typical two class seating for 177, with 12 first class at four abreast and 91cm (36in) pitch, max seating for 189 in a single class at 81cm (32in) pitch.

Production: 1015 737-800s ordered by late 2002 with 647 delivered. 48 737-900s were on order, with 26 delivered.

History: Boeing's Next Generation 737-800 and 737-900 are the largest members of the strong selling 737 family.

Like the -600 and -700, the -800 and -900 feature more efficient CFM56-7B turbofans, the new wing with greater chord, span and wing area, larger tail surfaces and the 777 style EFIS flightdeck with six flat panel LCDs which can present information as on the 777 or as on the 737-300/-400/-500 series, the latter allowing a common pilot type rating for the two 737 families. Winglets are popular options.

Until its launch on September 5 1994 the 737-800 was known as the 737-400X Stretch. Compared with the -400 the -800 is 3.02m (9ft 9in) longer, taking typical two class seating from 146 to 162, while range is significantly increased. The -800 has sold strongly since its launch, and at late 2002 was close to eclipsing the -200 as the biggest selling 737 model. First flight was on July 31 1997, first delivery (to Hapag Lloyd) was in April 1998.

The 737-900 is the largest and latest member of the 737 family, and was launched on September 10 1997 with an order for 10 from Alaska Airlines. A 1.57m (5ft 2in) plug forward of the wing and a 1.07m (3ft 6in) plug rear compared with the -800 increases seating to 177 in two classes (maximum seating is the same as the 737-800's due to emergency exit requirements). First flight was on August 3 2000, first delivery (to Alaska Airlines) was in April 2001.

Boeing is working on the increased MTOW 737-900X with new emergency exits which would allow seating for over 200 (twice that of the original 737-100) and increased range.

Photo: A winglet fitted Qantas 737-800. (Rob Finlayson)

Boeing Business Jets

Country of origin: United States of America

Type: Long range large capacity corporate jets

Powerplants: Two 117.4kN (26,400lb) CFM56-7 turbofans.

Performance: BBJ – Max cruising speed Mach 0.82, normal cruising speed Mach 0.80, long range cruising speed Mach 0.79. Initial cruise altitude 38,000ft, max certificated altitude 41,000ft. Range with eight passengers 11,480km (6200nm), with 25 passengers 11,075km (5980nm), with 50 passengers 10,205km (5510nm). BBJ 2 – Range with eight passengers 10,620km (5735nm), with 25 passengers 10,120km (5465nm), with 50 passengers 9140km (4935nm).

Weights: BBJ – Typical operating empty 42,895kg (94,570lb), max takeoff 77,560kg (171,000lb). BBJ 2 – Typical operating empty 45,730kg (100,815lb), max takeoff 79,015kg (174,200lb).

Dimensions: BBJ – Wing span incl winglets 35.79m (117ft 5in), length 33.63m (110ft 4in), height 12.05m (41ft 2in). Wing area 125.0m² (1345.5sq ft). BBJ 2 – Same except length 39.47m (129ft 6in).

Capacity: Flightcrew of two. BBJ – Interiors to customer preference. Typical configuration includes a crew rest area, forward lounge, private suite with double bed and private bathroom facilities including shower, 12 first class sleeper seats at four abreast and 152cm (60in) pitch, and rear galley and bathroom facilities. Alternatively rear cabin can seat 24 passengers at two abreast and feature a conference area or exercise gym, or up to 63 passengers at six abreast.

Production: By late 2002 BBJ orders stood at 65 with 57 delivered, with 8 BBJ 2s ordered and 7 delivered.

History: Boeing Business Jets offers two 737 based corporate jets, the 737-700 based BBJ and the 737-800 based BBJ 2.

Boeing Business Jets is a joint venture formed by Boeing and General Electric in July 1996 to develop and market a corporate version of the popular 737 airliner, initially focusing on the 737-700 based BBJ (or 737-700BBJ). The first BBJ rolled out from Boeing's Renton plant on August 11 1998 and flew for the first time on September 4 that year. On October 30 the US FAA awarded certification to the developed 737-700 airframe on which the BBJ is based. The first completed BBJ was delivered on September 4 1999.

The BBJ combines the Next Generation 737-700's airframe with the strengthened wing, fuselage centre section and landing gear of the larger and heavier 737-800, with three to 10 belly auxiliary fuel tanks. It features the Next Generation 737 flightdeck with six LCD screens, equipped with embedded dual GPS, TCAS, enhanced GPWS and Flight Dynamics head-up guidance system. Following their certification in September 2000, winglets became a standard option.

The BBJ 2 was launched in October 1999 and is based on the stretched 737-800 airframe, offering 25% greater cabin space (and 100% more baggage space) but has slightly reduced range. It is fitted with between three and seven auxiliary belly fuel tanks. The first BBJ 2 airframe was delivered for interior outfitting in March 2001.

Boeing supplies unfurnished or 'green' BBJ airframes to DeCrane of Georgetown, Delaware, for long range fuel tank installation. From DeCrane the BBJ is flown to a customer specified completion centre for interior fitout and exterior painting.

Photo: A Kazakhstan government BBJ. (Rob Finlayson)

Boeing 747-100 & -200

Country of origin: United States of America

Type: Long range high capacity widebody airliners

Powerplants: 747-200B – Four 243.5kN (54,750lb) Pratt & Whitney JT9D-7R4G2s, or four 233.5kN (52,500lb) General Electric CF6-50E2s, or 236.2kN (53,110lb) Rolls-Royce RB211-524D4s.

Performance: 747-200B – Max speed 981km/h (530kt) (with RR engines), economical cruising speed 907km/h (490kt). Range with 366 pax and reserves 12,778km (6900nm). 747-200F – Range with 90,270kg (200,000lb) payload 9075km (4900nm) with CF6-80C2s.

Weights: 747-200 – Operating empty with JT9Ds 169,960kg (374,400lb), with CF6-80C2s 172,730kg (380,800lb), with RB211s 174,000kg (383,600lb). Max takeoff 377,840kg (833,000lb). 747-200F – Operating empty with JT9Ds 155,220kg (342,200lb), max takeoff 377,840kg (833,000lb).

Dimensions: Wing span 59.64m (195ft 8in), length 70.66m (231ft 10in), height 19.33m (63ft 5in). Wing area 511m² (5500sq ft).

Capacity: Flightcrew of three (two pilots and flight engineer). Seating arrangements include 397 in three classes, 452 in two classes (32 first & 420 economy), all economy seating for 447 nine abreast or up to 500 ten abreast. 747-200F – Max payload of 112,400kg (247,800lb).

Production: 747-100/-200 in production to 1991. 167 -100s, 9 -100Bs, 29 -100SR, 224 -200Bs, 13 -200Cs, 69 -200Fs and 77 -200Ms built, plus 12 military aircraft. Approx 58 -100s and 300 -200s in service in late 2002.

History: The hugely significant 747 revolutionised airline transport. Far bigger than any airliner before it, the 747 slashed operating costs per seat and thus cut the cost of long haul international airline travel.

Boeing conceived the 747 in the mid 1960s when it missed out on a US Air Force contract for an ultra large strategic transport (which resulted in the Lockheed C-5 Galaxy), but had identified a market for a high capacity 'jumbo jet'. Boeing was able to draw upon design experience with the USAF transport and launched the new airliner on July 25 1966. First flight occurred on February 9 1969, certification was awarded on December 30 that year.

The basic 747-100 entered service with launch customer Pan American in January 1970. Progressive development of the 747 led to the 747-200B with higher weights, more powerful engines and longer range. The -200B first flew in October 1970, while nine higher weight 747-100Bs were built. Developments included the 747-200F freighter, the -100SR (short range) optimised for high cycle short sector operations and the -200C (Combi).

The 747, with its distinctive upper deck (initially used as a first class bar/lounge area before giving way to passenger seats) four double bogey main undercarriage units, and 360 plus seat passenger seating capacity was a huge leap in size over the 707s and DC-8s it would replace. It was the first aircraft to use high bypass ratio turbofans, and the first widebody, or twin aisle airliner, with nine or 10 abreast seating in economy class.

The 747 holds a place in the public eye unlike any other aircraft, and successfully opened up international air travel to millions.

Many 747-200s have been converted to freighters.

Photo: A Northwest Airlines 747-200. (Rob Finlayson)

Boeing 747SP

Country of origin: United States of America

Type: Long range high capacity widebody airliner

Powerplants: Four 218.4kN (48,750lb) Pratt & Whitney JT9D-7AW turbofans, or 222.8kN (50,100lb) Rolls-Royce RB211-524Bs or 229.5kN (51,600lb) RB211-524Cs, or 206.8kN (46,500lb) General Electric CF6-45A2s or CF6-50E2-Fs.

Performance: Max speed 1000km/h (540kt). Range with 331 passengers and baggage 10,840km (5855nm), range with 276 passengers 12,325km (6650nm), ferry range with max fuel and 13,610kg (30,000lb) payload 15,400km (8315nm).

Weights: Operating empty 147,420kg (325,000lb), max takeoff 317,515kg (700,000lb).

Dimensions: Wing span 59.64m (195ft 8in), length 56.31m (184ft 9in), height 19.94m (65ft 5in). Wing area 511m² (5500sq ft).

Capacity: Flightcrew of three comprising two pilots and one flight engineer. Max high density single class seating for 440, typical two class seating for 28 first class and 288 economy class passengers

Production: Just 43 747SPs were built, of which 14 were in commercial service in 2002. 13 were in use as corporate transports.

History: Boeing developed the 747SP ('Special Performance') in the mid 1970s as a longer range, shortened 747, trading passenger seating for extra range.

The 747SP first flew on July 4 1975, certification was awarded on February 4 1976 and first delivery (to Pan American) was in March 1976.

The 747SP's fuselage is shortened by 14.35m (47ft 1in) compared to other 747 models, while its vertical tail was increased in height to compensate for the shorter fuselage. Structurally the 747SP was lightened in some areas because of the significant reduction in gross weights. Overall though the 747SP retained 90% commonality of components with the 747-100 and -200. While shortening the 747's fuselage increased the fuel fraction and thus range, it also meant that seating capacity was reduced, typically to 316 in two classes.

The 747SP's range was well illustrated by the delivery flight of a South African Airways SP, which over March 23/24 1976 flew nonstop with 50 passengers from Paine Field in Washington State to Cape Town, South Africa, a distance of 16,560km (8940nm). This world nonstop record for a commercial aircraft stood until 1989 when a Qantas 747-400 flew 17,945km (9688nm) nonstop from London to Sydney.

Sales of the 747SP were modest despite the increased range, as the SP had poorer operating economics per seat compared to the 747-200. However the 747SP did pioneer a number of long range nonstop services that are now commonly flown by the 747-400.

Notable SP customers included South African Airways (who used the SP's extended range to bypass African nations that denied it landing rights while South Africa's apartheid policies were in place), Qantas and Pan Am, the latter pioneering nonstop trans Pacific Los Angeles/Sydney services.

In 2002 small numbers remained in airline service, with others used as corporate transports.

Photo: A JT9D powered Iran Air 747SP (Sam Chui)

Boeing 747-300

Country of origin: United States of America

Type: Long range high capacity widebody airliner

Powerplants: Four 243.5kN (54,750lb) Pratt & Whitney JT9D-7R4G2 turbofans, or 236.3kN (53,110lb) Rolls-Royce RB211-524D4s, or 233.5kN (52,500kN) General Electric CF6-50E2s, or 252.2kN (56,700lb) CF6-80C2B1s.

Performance: Max speed (with CF6-80s) 996km/h (538kt), max cruising speed 939km/h (507kt), economical cruising speed 907km/h (490kt), long range cruising speed 898km/h (485kt). Range with 400 passengers and reserves with JT9Ds 11,675km (6300nm), with CF6-50s 11,297km (6100nm), with CF6-80s 12,408km (6700nm), with RB211s 11,575km (6250nm).

Weights: Operating empty 174,134kg (383,900lb) with JT9Ds, 175,721kg (387,400lb) with CF6-50s, 176,901kg (390,000lb) with CF6-80s or 178,171kg (392,800lb) with RB211s. Max takeoff 351,535kg (775,000lb), or 356,070kg (785,000lb), or 362,875kg (800,000lb), or 371,945kg (820,000lb), or 377,840kg (833,000lb).

Dimensions: Wing span 59.64m (195ft 8in), length 70.66m (231ft 10in), height 19.33m (63ft 5in). Wing area 511m² (5500sq ft).

Capacity: 747-300 – Flightcrew of three, with two pilots and one flight engineer. Typical two class seating arrangement for 470 (50 business class including 28 on the upper deck and 370 economy class).

Production: 81 delivered 1983-90 with 75 in service in late 2002.

History: Boeing's 747-300 was the first 747 model with increased passenger capacity, introducing the distinctive stretched upper deck which can seat up to 69 economy class passengers.

The 747-300 was the end result of a number of Boeing studies which looked at increasing the 747's seating capacity. Concepts studied included fuselage plugs fore and aft of the wing increasing seating to around 600, or running the upper deck down the entire length of the fuselage. In the end Boeing launched the more modest 747SUD (Stretched Upper Deck) development on June 12 1980.

The 747SUD designation was soon changed to 747EUD (for Extended Upper Deck), and then 747-300. The new model first flew on October 5 1982 and was first delivered to Swissair on March 28 1983.

Compared to the -200, the -300's upper deck is stretched aft by 7.11m (23ft 4in), increasing economy class seating from 32 to a maximum of 69. The lengthened upper deck features two new emergency exit doors and allows an optional flightcrew rest area immediately aft of the flightdeck to be fitted. Access is via a conventional rather than spiral staircase as on the earlier models.

Otherwise the 747-300 is essentially little changed from the 747-200 and features the same takeoff weight and engine options. 747-300 variants include the 747-300M Combi and the short range 747-300SR built for Japan Air Lines for Japanese domestic services.

The extended upper deck was also offered as a retrofit to existing 747-100/-200s, although the only airline to take up this option was KLM. KLM later converted two to freighters, resulting in the first 747 freighters with the stretched upper deck. Boeing's own 747-300 freighter conversions, the 747-300 Special Freighter, was first delivered to Atlas Air in October 2000.

Photo: An Atlas 747-300 converted freighter. (Rob Finlayson)

Boeing 747-400 & 747-400ER

Country of origin: United States of America

Type: Long range high capacity widebody airliner

Powerplants: Four 252.4kN (56,750lb) Pratt & Whitney PW4056 turbofans or 266.9kN (60,000lb) PW4060s, or 275.8kN (62,000lb) PW4062s, 252.4kN (56,750lb) General Electric CF6-80C2B1Fs or 273.6kN (61,500lb) CF6-80C2B1F1s or -80C2B7Fs, or 258.0kN (58,000lb) Rolls-Royce RB211-524G or -524Hs, or 262.4 to 266.9kN (59 to 60,000lb) RB211-524G/H-Ts.

Performance: Max cruising speed 939km/h (507kt), long range cruising speed 907km/h (490kt). Design range with 420 three class pax at 396,895kg (875,000lb) MTOW 13,491km (7284nm) with PW4000s.

Weights: Standard operating empty with PW4056s 180,985kg (399,000lb), with CF6-80C2B1Fs 180,755kg (398,500lb), with RB211s 181,755kg (400,700lb); operating empty weights at optional MTOW with PW4056s 181,485kg (400,100lb), with CF6-80C2B1Fs 181,255kg (399,600lb), with RB211s 182,255kg (401,800lb). Max takeoff 362,875kg (800,000lb), or optionally 377,845kg (833,000lb), or 385,555kg (850,000lb), or 396,895kg (875,000lb).

Dimensions: Wing span 64.44m (211ft 5in), length 70.67m (231ft 10in), height 19.41m (63ft 8in). Wing area 541.2m² (5825sq ft).

Capacity: 747-400 – Flightcrew of two. Typical three class seating for 416 (23 first, 78 business and 315 economy). 747-400F – 113 tonnes – 30 pallets main deck, 32 LD1 containers in lower holds.

Production: Orders for the 747-400 as of late 2002 stood at 632 (incl 102 freighters) with 585 delivered. Total 747 sales stood at 1356.

History: Boeing launched the 747-400 in October 1985 and the first development aircraft first flew on April 29 1988. US certification (with PW4000s) was awarded in January 1989.

The 747-400 externally resembles the -300, but features a new, two crew flightdeck with six CRT displays, an increased span wing with winglets (the -400 was the first airliner to introduce winglets), new engines, recontoured wing/fuselage fairing, a new interior, lower basic but increased max takeoff weights, and greater range.

Variants include the basic passenger 747-400, the winglet-less 747-400 Domestic for Japanese short haul sectors (seating up to 568), the 747-400M Combi passenger/freight model, and the 747-400F Freighter (with original length upper deck).

On November 28 2000 Boeing launched the Longer-Range 747-400, or 747-400ER and 747-400ERF freighter, following a launch order for six from Qantas. The 747-400ER first flew on July 31 2002 and features the -400F's stronger wing, greater fuel capacity, a 412,770kg (910,000lb) max takeoff weight, a 14,205km (7670nm) range, LCD screens on the flightdeck, and a 777 based interior.

In February 2002 Boeing revealed the 747-400 Quiet Longer Range, or -400XQLR, which if launched would feature acoustically treated engine nacelles, raked wingtips and further increased range. Later that year Boeing announced it was working on the 14,800km (8000nm) range 747-800X, which would combine the XQLR's changes with a 2m (6.5ft) stretched fuselage, seating 20 to 40 extra passengers.

Boeing dropped the 747X and 747X Stretch in March 2001. The earlier 747-500X and -600X stretches were dropped in 1997.

Photo: The 747-400ER. (Boeing)

Boeing 757-200

Country of origin: United States of America

Type: Medium range narrowbody airliner

Powerplants: Two 178.8kN (40,200lb) Rolls-Royce RB211-535E4 turbofans, or 193.5kN (43,500lb) RB211-535E4-B2, or 162.8kN (36,600lb) Pratt & Whitney PW2037s, or 178.4kN (40,100lb) PW2040s, or 189.5kN (42,600lb) PW2043s.

Performance: Max cruising speed 914km/h (493kt), economical cruising speed 850km/h (460kt). Range with 201 passengers and PW2037s 4760km (2570nm), with PW2040s 7280km (3920nm), with RB211-535E4s 4400km (2375nm), with RB211-535E4-Bs 6845km (3695nm). 757-200PF – Speeds same. Range with 22,680kg payload and P&W engines 7195km (3885nm), with RR engines 6857km (3700nm).

Weights: Operating empty with PW2037s 58,325kg (128,580lb), with PW2040s 58,390kg (128,730lb), with RB211-535E4s 58,550kg (129,080lb), with RB211-535E4-Bs 58,620kg (129,230lb). Max takeoff with PW2037s or RB211-535E4s 99,790kg (220,000lb), with PW2040s or RB211-535E4-Bs 115,665kg (255,000lb) or 115,895kg (255,550lb).

Dimensions: Wing span 38.05m (124ft 10in), length 47.32m (155ft 3in), height 13.56m (44ft 6in). Wing area 185.3m² (1994sq ft).

Capacity: Flightcrew of two. 757-200 – Typical passenger arrangements vary from 178 two class (16 first & 162 economy), or 201 (12 first & 189 economy) or 208 (12 first and 196 economy) or 214 to 239 in all economy class. 757-200PF – Maximum of 15 standard 2.24 x 2.74m (88 x 108in) freight pallets on main deck.

Production: 987 757-200s had been ordered by late 2002, of which over 983 had been delivered. Total 757 sales stand at 1050.

History: Despite a slow sales start, the medium range single aisle 757 has become yet another sales success story for Boeing.

Boeing considered a number of proposals for a successor to the 727 trijet during the 1970s, with many of these designs featuring the nose and T-tail of the earlier jet. Boeing settled on a more conventional design featuring the same cross section as the 727 but with a considerably longer fuselage, an all new wing, nose and flightdeck, and fuel efficient high bypass turbofan engines.

Boeing launched the 757 in March 1979 following orders from British Airways and Eastern. Developed in tandem with the larger widebody 767, the two types share a number of systems and technologies, including a common early generation EFIS flightdeck.

First flight was on February 19 1982 and the 757 entered service in January the following year. Subsequent versions to appear are the 757-200PF Package Freighter, a pure freighter, and the 757-200M Combi (one built). The stretched 757-300 is described separately.

The 757-200SF (Special Freighter) is a freighter conversion of passenger 757-200s offered by Boeing Airplane Services. Pemco also offers freighter conversions.

Boeing has also studied the longer range 757-200ER which would feature the strengthened wing of the 757-300, up to four auxiliary fuel tanks and a 8520km (4600nm) range, and the 757 based BBJ 3.

The 1000th 757 was delivered to American Airlines on February 14 2002.

Photo: An Icelandair 757-200 converted freighter. (Rob Finlayson)

Boeing 757-300

Country of origin: United States of America

Type: Medium range narrowbody airliner

Powerplants: Two 193.5kN (43,500lb) Rolls-Royce RB211-535E4-B turbofans, or 178.8kN (40,200lb) RB211-535E4s, or 189.5kN (42,600lb) Pratt & Whitney PW2043s, or 178.4kN (40,100lb) PW2040s.

Performance: Cruising speed Mach 0.80. Range with PW2040s 4137km (2234nm), with PW2043s 6417km (3465nm), with RB211-535E4s 3805km (2055nm), or with RB211-535E4-Bs 6000km (3240nm).

Weights: Operating empty with RB211s 63,855kg (140,780lb), with PW2000s 63,655kg (140,330lb), max takeoff with PW2040s/535-E4s 108,860kg (240,000lb), with PW2043/535E4-Bs 123,605kg (272,500lb).

Dimensions: Wing span 38.05m (124ft 10in), length 54.43m (178ft 7in), height 13.56m (44ft 6in). Wing area 185.3m² (1994sq ft).

Capacity: Flightcrew of two. Typical two class arrangement seats 243 passengers (12 first and 231 economy class). Max seating for 279 in a high density configuration 71-74cm (28-29in) pitch.

Production: Total 757-300 orders stood at 63 at late 2002, of which 36 had been delivered.

History: The stretched, 240 seat Boeing 757-300 is the first significant variant of the basic 757-200 and was aimed in part at the European vacation charter operator market.

Although design work on the original 757 began in the late 1970s and its entry into service was in 1983, it wasn't until over a decade later in the mid 1990s that Boeing began to study a stretched development. This new 757 stretch was covered by the 757-300X designation until its launch at the Farnborough Airshow in England in September 1996.

The most obvious change over the 757-200 is the -300's 54.43m (178ft 7in) long fuselage, which is 7.11m (23ft 4in) longer than the standard aircraft (and only fractionally shorter than the 767-300). This fuselage stretch allows a 20% increase in seating to 225 to 279 passengers, depending on the interior configuration. Lower hold freight capacity is also increased by 40% over the 757-200 by virtue of the longer fuselage.

Another feature of the 757-300 is its new interior which is based on that developed for the Next Generation 737 models. Features include a new sculptured ceiling, larger overhead bins, indirect overhead lighting and vacuum toilets.

The 757-300 shares the -200's cockpit, wing, tail and powerplant options, although the -300 features strengthened structure and landing gear to cope with the increased weights, new wheels, tyres and brakes, and a tailskid.

The 757-300 first flew on August 3 1998, with certification awarded on January 27 1999. Entry into service with launch customer Condor (the charter arm of German carrier Lufthansa) was in March that year. Other customers include Icelandair, Northwest, American Trans Air, JMC Airlines and Continental.

The -300's 29 month development program from final configuration to planned first delivery was the fastest for any Boeing airliner (the 777-300 took 31 months for example).

Photo: A 757-300. (Rob Finlayson)

Boeing 767-200

Country of origin: United States of America

Type: Medium to long range widebody airliner

Powerplants: 767-200 – Two 213.5kN (48,000lb) Pratt & Whitney JT9D-7R4D turbofans, or 222.4kN (50,000lb) PW4050s, or 233.5kN (52,500lb) General Electric CF6-80C2B2s. 767-200ER – Two PW4050s (as above), or 231kN (52,000lb) PW4052s, or 252.4kN (56,750lb) PW4056s, or 257.7kN (57,900lb) CF6-80C2B4Fs.

Performance: 767-200 – Max cruising speed 914km/h (493kt), economical cruising speed 854km/h (461kt). Range of basic aircraft with JT9Ds 5855km (3160nm), medium range version with CF6s 7135km (3850nm). 767-200ER – Speeds same. Range with PW4056s 12,269km (6625nm), with CF6s 12,352km (6670nm).

Weights: 767-200 – Empty with JT9Ds 74,752kg (164,800lb), with CF6s 74,344kg (163,900lb). Operating empty with JT9Ds 80,920kg (178,400lb), with CF6s 80,510kg (177,500lb). Max takeoff 136,078kg (300,000lb), medium range max takeoff 142,881kg (315,000lb). 767-200ER – Empty with PW4056s 76,566kg (168,800lb), with CF6-80C2B4s 76,476kg (168,600lb), operating empty with PW4056s 84,415kg (186,100lb), with CF6-80C2B4Fs 84,370kg (186,000lb). Max takeoff with PW4056s or CF6-80C2B4Fs 175,540kg (387,000lb).

Dimensions: Wing span 47.57m (156ft 1in), length 48.51m (159ft 2in), height 15.85m (52ft 0in). Wing area 283.3m² (3050sq ft).

Capacity: Flightcrew of two. Typical two class seating for 18 premium and 198 economy class pax. Max seating for 290 at eight abreast and 76cm (30in) pitch. Underfloor cargo holds can accommodate up to 22 LD2 containers.

Production: Total 767 sales of 934 at late 2002. Total 767-200/200ER orders stood at 245, of which 240 had been delivered.

History: The narrowest widebody in service, Boeing's 767 started life in the late 1970s.

Boeing launched the 767 in July 1978 and developed it in tandem with the narrowbody 757 with which it shares a common two crew EFIS flightdeck (with six colour CRT displays) and many systems. The 767 also features a seven abreast (economy) fuselage and a new wing.

The 767 production program includes a high degree of international participation, with Japanese companies in particular having a large share of construction.

Initially Boeing intended to offer two versions, the longer 767-200 and short fuselage 767-100 (which was not launched as it was too close in capacity to the 757). The 767 first flew on September 26 1981, and entered service (with United) on September 26 1982 (certification with P&W engines was awarded on July 30 1982).

The longer range 767-200ER (Extended Range) version features higher weights and an additional wing centre section fuel tank. It first flew on March 6 1984, and service entry was two months later. The -200ER accounts for 117 of the total 245 767-200s ordered.

The last airliner 767-200/-200ER was delivered in 1994 until a November 1998 order from Continental. These had all been delivered by late 2002, but military orders for 767 tanker transports will keep the -200 in production.

Photo: An El Al 767-200ER. (Rob Finlayson)

Boeing 767-300

Country of origin: United States of America

Type: Medium to long range widebody airliner

Powerplants: Two 213.5kN (48,000lb) Pratt & Whitney JT9D-7R4 turbofans or 222.4kN (50,000lb) JT9D-7R4Es, or 222.4kN (50,000lb) PW4050s, or 233.5kN (52,000lb) PW4052s, or 213.5kN (48,000lb) General Electric CF6-80As or 213.5kN (48,000lb) CF6-80A2s, or 231.3kN (52,500lb) CF6-80C2B2s, or 257.5kN (57,900lb) CF6-80C2B4Fs, or 269.9kN (60,000lb) Rolls-Royce RB211-524Gs. 767-300ER – Same options or 252.4kN (56,750lb) PW4056s or 266.9kN (60,000lb) CF6-80C2B6s.

Performance: 767-300 – Max cruising speed 900km/h (486kt), econ cruising speed 850km/h (460kt). HGW version range with design payload and PW4050s 7835km (4230nm), with CF6-80C2B2s 7890km (4260nm). 767-300ER – Range with design payload with PW4060s 10,880km (5875nm), with CF6-80C2B4Fs 10,195km (5505nm).

Weights: 767-300 – Empty with PW4050s 79,560kg (175,400lb), with CF6-80C2B2s 79,379kg (175,000lb). Operating empty with PW4050s 87,135kg (192,100lb), with CF6-80C2B2s 86,955kg (191,700lb). Higher gross weight version max takeoff with PW4050s or CF6-80C2B2s 159,210kg (351,000lb). 767-300ER – Empty with PW4060s 81,374kg (179,400lb), with CF6-80C2B4s 80,603kg (177,700lb). Operating empty with PW4060s 90,535kg (199,600lb), with CF6-80C2B4s 90,175kg (198,800lb). Max takeoff with PW4060s 181,890kg (401,000lb), with CF6-80C2B4Fs 175,540kg (387,000lb).

Dimensions: Wing span 47.57m (156ft 1in), length 54.94m (180ft 3in), height 15.85m (52ft 0in). Wing area 283.3m² (3050sq ft).

Capacity: Flightcrew of two. Typical three class layout for 210, two class 269 (24 premium & 245 economy seven abreast) max seating for 350 at eight abreast. Underfloor capacity for 20 LD2s.

Production: 652 767-300s (comprising 104 -300s, 508 -300ERs & 40 -300Fs) ordered by late 2002, of which 607 had been delivered.

History: Boeing announced that it was developing a stretched development of the 767-200 in February 1983.

The resulting 767-300 features a 6.42m (21ft 1in) stretch consisting of fuselage plugs forward (3.07m/10ft 1in) and behind (3.35m/11ft) the wing centre section. The flightdeck and systems were carried directly over from the 767-200, the only other changes were minor, and related to the increased weights of the new version. Initially the max takeoff weight was the same as the later 767-200ER.

The 767-300 first flew on January 30 1986, and was awarded certification and entered service in September that year. The higher weight Extended Range ER version first flew on December 19 1986, while Rolls-Royce RB211-524G engines became available from 1989. A new 777 based interior was introduced in 2000.

In 1993 Boeing launched the 767-300F General Market Freighter. Changes include strengthened undercarriage and wing structure, a cargo handling system, no cabin windows and a main deck freight door. Capacity is 24 containers.

Boeing has studied the 14,170km (7650nm) range 767-300ERX with increased fuel, more powerful engines, and 767-400ER (described separately) flightdeck.

Photo: A Mas Air 767-300F freighter. (Rob Finlayson)

Boeing 767-400ER

Country of origin: United States of America

Type: Long range widebody airliner

Powerplants: Two 282.5kN (63,500lb) General Electric CF6-80C2B8Fs or 281.6kN (63,300lb) Pratt & Whitney PW4062 turbofans.

Performance: Typical cruising speed 854km/h (461kt). Design range at max takeoff weight with max passengers 10,418km (5625nm) with CF6-80C2B8Fs, 10,343km (5580nm) with PW4062s.

Weights: Operating empty with PW4062s 103,145kg (227,400lb), 103,100kg (227,300lb) with CF6-80C2B8Fs, max takeoff 204,120kg (450,000lb).

Dimensions: Wing span 51.92m (170ft 4in), length 61.36m (201ft 4in), height 16.86m (55ft 4in). Wing area 290.7m² (3129.0sq ft).

Capacity: Flightcrew of two. Typical three class arrangement for 245 passengers, comprising 20 first class at 152cm (60in) pitch, 50 business at 97cm (38in) and 175 economy at 81cm (32in). Typical two class seating for 305, single class seating for up to 375.

Production: As of late 2002 37 ordered, with all delivered.

History: Boeing's 767-400ER is a stretched, upgraded development of the popular 767-300ER.

Design work on the then 767-400ERX began in late 1996 when Boeing enlisted engineering support from the then independent McDonnell Douglas (Boeing and McDonnell Douglas merged in August 1997). The basic 767-400ER was formally launched in January 1997 when Delta Airlines ordered 21, while first flight was on October 9 1999. First delivery was to Delta on August 29 2000.

The most significant change with the 767-400ER is the 6.4m (21ft) fuselage stretch. The 767-400ER's wing is based on the 767-300's and features 2.34m (7ft 8in) long raked wingtips which improve aerodynamic efficiency. Winglets were originally considered but the wingtip extensions proved more efficient. The wing is also made from increased gauge aluminium with thicker spars. Other features include a new APU, new tailskid, increased weights, and all new, 46cm (18in) taller landing gear. The wheels, tyres and brakes are common with the larger 777.

Inside, the 767-400ER features a 777 style advanced flightdeck with six multifunction LCDs, which can present information in the same format as earlier 767s, allowing a common pilot type certificate, or as for the 777 and Next Generation 737s. The all new cabin interior is similar to that in the 777.

On September 13 2000 Boeing launched the Longer Range 767-400ER, which would have been delivered from mid 2004. The Longer Range 767-400ER would have featured new 320kN (72,000lb) Rolls-Royce Trent 600 or Engine Alliance GP7172 turbofans (which were proposed for the 747X), additional fuel carried in the horizontal tail and an increased max takeoff, allowing it to fly 11,390km (6150nm). Boeing effectively dropped the Longer Range 747-400ER program on March 29 2001, when it announced the proposed Sonic Cruiser and also cancelled the 747X and 747X Stretch versions.

At late 2002 all 767-400ER orders (21 from Delta and 16 from Continental, originally 26) had been fulfilled.

Photo: A Continental 767-400ER. (Rob Finlayson)

Boeing 777-200 & 777-200LR

Country of origin: United States of America

Type: Long and ultra long range widebody airliners

Powerplants: 777-200ER – General Electric options: 377kN (84,700lb) GE90-85Bs; 400kN (90,000lb) GE90-90Bs; 417kN (93,700lb) GE90-94Bs. Rolls-Royce options: 372kN (83,600lb) Trent 884s, 400kN (90,000lb) Trent 892s, or 415kN (93,400kN) Trent 895s. Pratt & Whitney options: 376kN (84,600lb) PW4084s; 401kN (90,200lb) PW4090s; 436kN (98,000lb) PW4098s.

Performance: Cruising speed 905km/h (490kt). -200ER – Range with GE90-85Bs 10,455km (5645nm); 14,065km (7595nm) with Trent 895s.

Weights: 777-200ER – Empty 142,430kg (314,000lb) with GE90-85Bs, 140,480kg (309,700lb) with Trent 895s, max takeoff 263,085kg (580,000lb) or 297,555kg (656,000lb).

Dimensions: 777-200 – Span 60.93m (199ft 11in), length 63.73m (209ft 1in), height 18.51m (60ft 9in). Wing area 427.8m² (4605sq ft).

Capacity: Flightcrew of two. Passenger seating for 305 in three classes or up to 440. Underfloor capacity for up to 32 LD3 containers.

Production: 497 777-200s ordered at late 2002 (inc 408 ERs & 3 LRs) with 375 delivered.

History: Boeing's advanced widebody 777 twin has been progressively developed into increasingly longer range developments.

The 777 was originally conceived as a stretched 767, but Boeing instead adopted an all new design with a unique fuselage cross section, fly-by-wire (a Boeing first), an advanced glass flightdeck with five liquid crystal displays, composites (10% by weight), and advanced and extremely powerful engines. The 777 was also offered with optional folding wings where the outer 6m/21ft of each would fold upwards.

The basic 777-200 as launched in October 1990 was offered in two versions, the basic 777-200 (initially A-Market) and the increased weight longer range 777-200IGW (Increased Gross Weight, initially B-Market). The IGW has since been redesignated 777-200ER.

The 777-200 first flew on June 12 1994, with FAA and JAA certification awarded on April 19 1995. The FAA awarded full 180 minutes ETOPS clearance for PW4074 -200s on May 30 that year. First customer delivery was to United Airlines in May 1995. The first 777-200IGW/ER was delivered to British Airways in February 1997.

The 777-100X was a proposed shortened ultra long range (16,000km/8635nm) model, dropped in favour of the 777-200X. The 777-200X evolved into the Longer-Range 777-200 which was formally launched along with the equivalent LR 777-300 on February 29 2000. However a luke warm market reception means Boeing has slowed development, with deliveries not likely until 2006.

The Longer-Range 777-200 would be one of the world's longest ranging airliners, capable of flying 16,405km (8860nm) – 18 hours flying time. It would achieve this with awesomely powerful 489kN (110,000lb) thrust GE90-110B1 turbofans, increased max takeoff weight and optional auxiliary fuel tanks. Other changes would include raked wingtips, new main landing gear, structural strengthening and optional crew and flight attendant rest stations above the cabin.

In late 2002 Boeing was studying the 13,900km (7500nm) range 777-250ERX, a slightly stretched -200 seating 300-320 passengers.

Photo: A Trent powered Emirates 777-200. (Rob Finlayson)

Boeing 777-300 & 777-300ER

Country of origin: United States of America

Type: Long and ultra long range high capacity widebody airliners

Powerplants: 777-300 – Either two 400kN (90,000lb) Pratt & Whitney PW4090 turbofans, or 436kN (98,000lb) PW4098s, or 409kN (92,000lb) Rolls-Royce Trent 892s. 777-300ER – Two 511kN (115,000lb) GE90-115Bs.

Performance: Typical cruising speed 893km/h (482kt). 777-300 – Range with 368 three class passengers 10,595km (5720nm). 777-300ER – Max range 13,427km (7250nm).

Weights: 777-300 – Operating empty with Trent 892s 155,675kg (343,200lb), max takeoff 299,370kg (660,000lb). 777-300ER – Max takeoff 341,105kg (752,000lb).

Dimensions: 777-300 – Wing span 60.93m (199ft 11in), or folded 47.32m (155ft 3in), length 73.86m (242ft 4in), height 18.51m (60ft 9in). Wing area 427.8m² (4605sq ft).

Capacity: Flightcrew of two. Typical passenger accommodation for 368 (30 first, 84 business and 254 economy) to 394 in three class arrangements, 400 to 479 in two class arrangements or up to 550 in an all economy high density configuration. Underfloor capacity for 20 standard LD3 containers or eight 2.55 x 3.17m (96 x 125in) pallets.

Production: 107 777-300s, including 46 ERs, ordered at late 2002, with 43 delivered.

History: Boeing's 777-300 is the world's largest twin engined aircraft, powered by the world's most powerful turbofan engines, and is the world's longest airliner and fastest widebody twin.

The stretched 777-300 was designed as a replacement for early generation 747s (747-100s and -200s). Compared to the older 747s the basic 777-300 has comparable passenger capacity and range, but burns one third less fuel and with 40% lower maintenance costs.

Compared with the 777-200 the -300 features a 10.13m (33ft 3in) stretch, comprising plugs fore and aft of the wings. The longer fuselage allows seating for up to 550 passengers in a single class high density configuration. The -300 also features a strengthened undercarriage, airframe and inboard wing. Other changes include a tailskid and ground manoeuvring cameras mounted on the horizontal tail and underneath the forward fuselage.

Boeing announced it was developing the 777-300 at the Paris Airshow in mid June 1995. The 777-300 first flew on October 16 1997 and made history on May 4 1998 when it was awarded type certification including an immediate 180min ETOPS approval. Service entry with Cathay Pacific was later in that month.

The Longer-Range 777-300 was being developed ahead of the 777-200LR – both were launched on February 29 2000. Both will feature a 341 tonne max takeoff weight, which, with auxiliary fuel, will give the 777-300ER a range of 13,427km (7250nm), comparable to the slightly larger 747-400. Common changes include 2m (6.5ft) raked wingtips, new main landing gear, structural strengthening and optional overheard crew and flight attendant rest stations above the cabin. The 777-300ER will be powered by the 511kN (115,000lb) GE90-115Bs – the world's most powerful jet engine.

First flight is due in early 2003.

Photo: The first 777-300ER leaves the paintshop in November 2002.

Boeing Vertol (Kawasaki) KV 107

Country of origin: United States of America

Type: Medium to heavylift utility helicopter

Powerplants: Two 930kW (1250shp) General Electric CT58-110-1 or Ishikawajima-Harima built CT58-IHI-110-1 turboshafts driving two three-blade rotors.

Performance: KV 107/II-2 – Max speed 270km/h (146kt), economical cruising speed 232km/h (125kt). Initial rate of climb 1440ft/min. Hovering ceiling out of ground effect 8800ft. Range with a three tonne (6600lb) payload and reserves 175km (95nm).

Weights: KV 107/II-2 – Empty equipped 4868kg (10,723lb), max takeoff 8618kg (19,000lb).

Dimensions: Diameter of each rotor 15.24m (50ft 0in), fuselage length 13.59m (44ft 7in), height 5.09m (16ft 9in). Rotor disc area (total) 364.6m² (3925sq ft).

Capacity: Flightcrew of two. Typical seating for 23 to 25 passengers in airliner configuration, or 12 passengers and freight in combi configuration. In an executive configuration seats six to 11 passengers in main cabin.

Production: Total BV/KV 107 production approximately 650, with almost all for military customers. Small numbers remain in commercial service.

History: Boeing Vertol's Model 107 is best known as the military CH-46 Sea Knight, but small numbers were built as airliners and utility transports for commercial customers.

The then independent Vertol company (previously Piasecki) designed the 107 in the late 1950s as a medium lift helicopter for US Army evaluation. Three prototype Lycoming turboshaft powered Vertol 107s were built (the Army ordered 10) designated YHC-1As, and first flight occurred on August 27 1958. By that time though the Army's interest had switched to what would become the Chinook and it did not order the 107. However in February 1961 Vertol (Boeing acquired Vertol in 1960) won a US Marine Corps competition with a developed General Electric T58-GE-8 powered version of the BV 107, and the type was ordered into production as the CH-46A Sea Knight.

The commercial 107 is based on the CH-46A powered by the CT-58-110 (equivalent to the military T58-GE-8). The first commercial 107 to fly was one of the three original development aircraft built for the US Army converted to the new standard, its first flight in the new configuration was on October 25 1960. Offered in two forms, the KV 107/II-1 utility transport and KV 107/II-2 airliner, only the latter was built. KV 107/II-2 customers included New York Airlines, who ordered three configured to seat 25, Columbia Helicopters in the US (Columbia still operates KV 107s) and Japan's Air Lift.

A more powerful 1045kW (1400shp) CT58-140-1 powered longer range KV 107/II-A-17 was offered and one was built for the Tokyo Police.

Japan's Kawasaki built all commercial 107s, and has held manufacturing rights to the 107 since 1965. Kawasaki has also built KV 107s for the Japanese military and Saudi Arabia.

Photo: A Japanese KV 107 in Australia where it was used in support of testing of a space re-entry vehicle. (Richard Koehne)

Boeing Commercial Chinook

Country of origin: United States of America

Type: Heavylift utility and airliner helicopter

Powerplants: Two 3040kW (4075shp) takeoff rated Lycoming AL 5512 turboshafts driving two three-blade rotors.

Performance: LR, MLR & ER – Max speed 278km/h (150kt), max cruising speed 270km/h (145kt), long range cruising speed 250km/h (135kt). Max initial rate of climb at MTOW 1180ft/min. Range – LR & MLR with max fuel 1150km (620nm), ER with max fuel 1918km (1035nm). UT – Max speed 260km/h (140kt), max cruising speed 260km/h (140kt), long range cruising speed 250km/h (135kt). Max initial rate of climb at MTOW 1500ft/min. Range with max internal load 425km (230nm).

Weights: LR – Empty 11,748kg (25,900lb), max takeoff 22,000kg (48,500lb), or 23,133kg (51,000lb) with an external load. ER – Empty 12,020kg (26,500lb), max takeoff same. MLR – Empty 11,113kg (24,500lb), max takeoff same. UT – Empty 9797kg (21,600lb), max takeoff 19,051kg (42,000lb), or 23,133kg (51,000lb) with an external sling load.

Dimensions: Rotor diameter (both) 18.29m (60ft 0in), length overall 30.18m (99ft 0in), fuselage length 15.87m (52ft 1in), height 5.68m (18ft 8in). Rotor disc area (total) 525.4m² (5655sq ft).

Capacity: Two pilots on flightdeck. Seating for 44 at four abreast in main cabin. Combi versions seat between eight and 32 with rear cabin loaded with freight, or between 22 and 32 with freight on one side of main cabin. Max internal load of LR and MLR models 9070kg (20,000lb), ER and UT models 8730kg (19,250lb). Max external sling load 12,700kg (28,000lb).

Production: Approximately a dozen Commercial Chinooks were built in the early to mid 1980s. Most remain in service.

History: The Boeing Helicopters Model 234 Commercial Chinook is a variant of the successful CH-47 Chinook military airlifter.

The Chinook was developed for the US Army and first flew in September 1961, and since then has been developed into a number of progressively improved variants and remains in production (over 1160 have been built). The Commercial Chinook was not launched until 1978, following a British Airways Helicopters order for three for North Sea oil rig support missions. The Commercial Chinook's first flight occurred on August 19 1980, certification was granted in June 1981, and service entry was the following month.

Largely identical in configuration to the CH-47, the Commercial Chinook retains the former's rear cargo ramp, but has a slightly reprofiled nose, commercial avionics and large passenger windows along both sides of the main cabin.

The initial orders were for the 234 LR Long Range, which compared with the CH-47 has roughly twice the fuel load, plus a 44 seat passenger interior based on that used in Boeing jetliners. A number of other versions were offered – the 234 ER Extended Range with additional tankage, the 234 UT Utility, and 234 MLR Multi purpose Long Range which can be used for either passenger or freight operations, or a combination of both.

Photo: A Taiwanese Fire Authority Commercial Chinook. (Charles Feng)

Bombardier Canadair CL-215 & CL-415

Country of origin: Canada

Type: Firebomber and utility amphibians

Powerplants: CL-215 – Two 1565kW (2100hp) Pratt & Whitney R-2800-CA3 18 cylinder radial piston engines driving three blade constant speed propellers. CL-415 – Two 1775kW (2380shp) Pratt & Whitney Canada PW123AF turboprops driving four blade constant speed Hamilton Standard props.

Performance: CL-215 – Max cruising speed 290km/h (157kt). Initial rate of climb 1000ft/min. Range at max cruising speed 1715km (925nm), at long range cruising speed 2095km (1130nm). CL-415 – Max cruising speed 376km/h (203kt), long range cruising speed 270km/h (145kt), patrol speed 240km/h (130kt). Initial rate of climb 1375ft/min. Ferry range with 500kg (1100lb) payload 2426km (1310nm).

Weights: CL-215 firebomber – Empty 12,220kg (26,941lb), max takeoff from water 17,100kg (37,700lb), from land 19,730kg (43,500lb). CL-415 firebomber – Operating empty 12,882kg (28,400lb), max takeoff from land 19,890kg (43,850lb), from water 17,168kg (37,850lb).

Dimensions: CL-215 – Wing span 28.60m (93ft 10in), length 19.82m (65ft 1in), height 8.98m (29ft 6in). Wing area 100.3m² (1080sq ft). CL-415 – Same except wing span over wingtips 28.63m (93ft 11in).

Capacity: Flightcrew of two, plus accommodation in special missions variants for a third flightdeck member, a mission specialist and two observers. Fire retardant capacity 6123kg (13,500lb). Passenger configuration for 30 at 79cm (31in) pitch, or in a combi configuration for 11, with firebombing tanks retained and freight in forward fuselage.

Production: Total CL-215 production of 125. Over 57 CL-415s have been ordered.

History: The piston CL-215 and turboprop CL-415 SuperScooper are purpose designed amphibious firebomber aircraft.

The CL-215 is powered by two Pratt & Whitney R-2800 radials, and is capable of scooping up 5455 litres (1200Imp gal/1440US gal) of water in 12 seconds from a water source such as a lake. The CL-215 first flew on October 23 1967, first delivery was to the French civil protection agency in June 1969. Production of batches of CL-215s continued through to 1990.

Originally the subsequent CL-215T was to be a straightforward turboprop powered development of the CL-215, and Canadair converted two aircraft in 1989 to act as development aircraft. The first of these flew on June 8 that year. Retrofit kits for CL-215s to the new standard were offered, but Canadair elected not to build new CL-215Ts, and instead developed the CL-415.

The primary improvement introduced on the CL-415 over the CL-215T is an EFIS avionics suite, while other improvements, some of which first appeared on the CL-215T, include winglets and finlets, higher weights and an increased capacity firebombing system. Like the CL-215 its principle mission is that of a firebomber, but various special mission (including SAR and maritime patrol) and transport configurations are available.

The CL-415 flew in December 1993 and was delivered from April 1994. The CL-415GR ordered by Greece has higher operating weights.

Photo: A CL-415. (Paul Sadler)

Bombardier CRJ100 & CRJ200

Country of origin: Canada

Type: Regional jet airliner

Powerplants: 100 – Two 41.0kN (9220lb) General Electric CF34-3A1 turbofans. 200 – Two 41.0kN (9220lb) CF34-3B1s.

Performance: 100 – High speed cruise 851km/h (459kt), typical cruising speed 786km/h (424kt). Range with max payload at long range cruising speed with reserves 1815km (980nm). 200LR – Speeds same. Range with max payload at long range cruising speed and reserves over 3713km (2005nm).

Weights: 100 – Empty 13,236kg (29,180lb), operating empty 13,653kg (30,100lb), max takeoff 21,523kg (47,450lb). 200LR – Empty 13,243kg (29,195lb), operating empty 13,740kg (30,292lb), max takeoff 24,040kg (53,000lb).

Dimensions: Wing span 21.21m (69ft 7in), length 26.77m (87ft 10in), height 6.22m (20ft 5in). Wing area 54.5m² (587.1sq ft).

Capacity: Flightcrew of two. Typical one class seating for 50 at four abreast and 79cm (31in) pitch. Max seating for 52. Corporate Jetliner corporate shuttle configurations seat from 18 to 30.

Production: 226 CRJ100s built, 445 CRJ200s delivered with 218 on order at late 2002, 14 CRJ440s delivered and 61 on order.

History: Bombardier's Canadair Regional Jet pioneered the 50 seat jet class, and has since become a runaway sales success.

The Canadair Regional Jet – or CRJ – was based on the Challenger corporate jet and was designed to offer the high speed advantages of much larger jets, with similar standards of service while at the same time offering operating economics, particularly over longer stage lengths, close to that of comparable size turboprops.

Canadair originally studied a 24 seat stretched regional airliner development of the CL-600 Challenger business jet up to 1981. Design studies for a stretched airliner based on the much improved CL-601 Challenger were first undertaken in 1987, leading Canadair to launch the Regional Jet program on March 31 1989. The first of three development aircraft first flew on May 10 1991. Transport Canada certification was awarded on July 31 1992, allowing the first customer delivery to Lufthansa that October.

Major changes over the Challenger apart from the stretched fuselage include a new wing optimised for airline operations, higher design weights, EFIS flightdeck with Collins Pro-Line 4 avionics suite, new undercarriage, additional fuel capacity and slightly more powerful CF34 engines.

The original CRJ100 series – the 100, 100ER and 100LR – was replaced by the 200 series (with more efficient engines) from 1996. The Series 200 is available in standard 200, long range 200ER with optional greater fuel capacity, and extended range Series 200LR forms, all with CF34-3B1s with improved fuel burn. The corporate shuttle Corporate Jetliner and the Challenger 800 (formerly Special Edition) business jet are also offered.

The CRJ440 is 44 seat variant built for Northwest, which has ordered 75. The first was delivered in January 2002.

The stretched CRJ700 and CRJ900 are described separately. Over 900 CRJs (including the CRJ700 and CRJ900) have been sold

Photo: A CRJ200 of South African Express. (Rob Finlayson)

Bombardier CRJ700 & CRJ900

Country of origin: Canada

Type: Regional jet airliners

Powerplants: CRJ700 – Two 56.4kN (12,670lb) or 61.3kN (13,790lb) with automatic power reserve General Electric CF34-8C1 turbofans. CRJ900 – Two 63.4kN (14,255lb) with APR CF34-8C5s.

Performance: CRJ700 – High speed cruise 860km/h (464kt), normal cruising speed 818km/h (442kt). Max certificated altitude 41,000ft. Range with 70 passengers and reserves 3124km (1687nm). ER variant range with 70 passengers and reserves 3674km (1984nm). CRJ900 – Speeds same. Range with 86 passengers 2774km (1498km), ER version range with 86 passengers 3208km (1732nm).

Weights: CRJ700 – Operating empty 19,269kg (42,480lb), standard max takeoff 32,999kg (72,750lb), ER max takeoff 34,020kg (75,000lb). CRJ900 – Operating empty 21,546kg (47,500lb). Max takeoff 36,514kg (80,500lb). CRJ900ER – Max takeoff 37,241kg (82,500lb).

Dimensions: CRJ700 – Wing span 23.01m (75ft 6in), length 32.41m (106ft 4in), height 7.29m (23ft 11in). CRJ900 – Same except length 36.19m (118ft 9in).

Capacity: CRJ700 – Flightcrew of two. Typical seating for 70 passengers at 79cm (31in) pitch and four abreast. Optionally can seat 72 or 78 passengers. CRJ900 – Standard seating for 86 or 90 passengers.

Production: 196 CRJ700s and 30 CRJ900s ordered at late 2002.

History: Bombardier's 70 seat CRJ700 and 90 seat CRJ900 are stretched developments of the fast selling 50 seat CRJ series.

Bombardier began development work on the CRJ700 in 1995, leading to a formal launch in January 1997 and first flight on May 27 1999. Service entry, with France's Brit Air, was in February 2001.

Compared with the 50 seat CRJ100/200, the CRJ700 is stretched by 4.72m (15ft 6in) with plugs forward and aft of the wing, while the cabin is 6.02m (19ft 9in) longer, aided by moving the rear pressure bulkhead 1.29m (4ft 3in) aft. The cabin windows are raised by 12cm (5in), the cabin floor is lowered slightly and the ceiling raised to provide 1.90m (6ft 3in) headroom. An underfloor baggage compartment beneath the forward fuselage and overwing emergency exits are added. Other changes include relocating the APU to the rear fuselage and redesigned overhead stowage bins.

Wing span is increased with a 1.83m (6ft 0in) wing root plug, while the leading edge is extended and high lift devices added. The main undercarriage units are lengthened and fitted with new wheels, tyres and brakes. The flightdeck features six liquid crystal displays presenting information from the Collins Pro Line 4 EFIS avionics suite.

Bombardier launched the further stretched, 90 seat class CRJ900 at the Farnborough Airshow in July 2000. A prototype converted from a CRJ700 development aircraft first flew on February 21 2001. Transport Canada certification was awarded in Setpember 2002, with deliveries due in early 2003.

Changes over the CRJ700 include the stretched fuselage (by 3.68m/12ft 1in), 5% more powerful engines, strengthened main landing gear, upgraded wheels and brakes, a strengthened wing, an additional underfloor baggage door and two additional overwing exits.

Photo: The CRJ900. (Bombardier)

Bombardier de Havilland Dash 8-100 & Q200

Country of origin: Canada

Type: Turboprop regional airliners

Powerplants: 100 – Two 1490kW (2000shp) Pratt & Whitney Canada PW120A turboprops driving four blade constant speed Hamilton Standard propellers. 100B – Two 1605kW (2150shp) PW121As. Q200 – Two 1605kW (2150shp) PW123C or PW123Ds.

Performance: 100A – Max cruising speed 490km/h (265kt), long range cruising speed 440km/h (237kt). Initial rate of climb 1560ft/min. Range with full passenger load, fuel and reserves 1520km (820nm), range with a 2720kg (6000lb) payload 2040km (1100nm). 100B – Same except max cruising speed of 500km/h (270kt). Q200 – Max cruising speed 546km/h (295kt). Initial rate of climb 1475ft/min. Range with 37 passengers 1795km (970nm).

Weights: 100A – Operating empty 10,250kg (22,600lb), max takeoff 15,650kg (34,500lb). 100B – Operating empty 10,273kg (22,648lb), max takeoff 16,465kg (36,300lb). Q200 – Operating empty 10,486kg (23,117lb), max takeoff 16,465kg (36,300lb).

Dimensions: Wing span 25.91m (85ft 0in), length 22.25m (73ft 0in), height 7.49m (24ft 7in). Wing area 54.4m^2 (585.0sq ft).

Capacity: Flightcrew of two. Typical passenger seating for 37 at four abreast and 79cm (31in) pitch, max seating for 40.

Production: At late 2002 299 Dash 8-100/Q100s and 94 Dash 8-200/Q200s ordered with 1 Q100 to be delivered.

History: Bombardier's de Havilland Dash 8 is the west's second most successful regional turboprop airliner family (after the Fokker F27).

De Havilland Canada began development of the Dash 8 in the late 1970s in response to what it saw as considerable market demand for a new generation 30 to 40 seat commuter airliner. The first of two preproduction aircraft first flew on June 20 1983, while Canadian certification was awarded on September 28 1984. The first customer delivery was to norOntair of Canada on October 23 1984.

Like the Dash 7 (described under de Havilland), the Dash 8 features a high mounted wing and T-tail, and has an advanced flight control system and large full length trailing edge flaps. The Dash 8 is powered by two Pratt & Whitney Canada PW120 series (originally designated PT7A) turboprops.

The initial Dash 8 Series 100 was followed by the Series 100A in 1990. The 100A introduced a revised interior with extra headroom and PW120A turboprops. The Series 100B was offered from 1992 with more powerful PW121s for better climb and airfield performance.

The improved performance Dash 8-200 was announced in 1992 and delivered from April 1995. It features more powerful PW123C engines which give a 56km/h (30kt) increase in cruising speed, as well as greater commonality with the stretched Dash 8-300. The 200B derivative has PW123Ds for better hot and high performance.

Since the second quarter of 1996 Dash 8s have been fitted with a computer controlled noise and vibration suppression system (or NVS). To reflect this the designation was changed to Dash 8Q (Q for 'quiet'). In 1998 that was changed again to Dash 8 Q100 and Dash 8 Q200 when a new interior was introduced as standard.

Dash 8 production was temporarily suspended in late 2002.

Photo: A QantasLink Dash 8-100. (Rob Finlayson)

Bombardier de Havilland Dash 8 Q300

Country of origin: Canada

Type: Turboprop regional airliner

Powerplants: 300A – Two 1775kW (2380shp) Pratt & Whitney Canada PW123 turboprops driving four blade propellers or optional 1865kW (2500shp) PW123Bs. Q300 HGW – Two 1865kW (2500shp) PW123Bs.

Performance: Q300 – Max cruising speed 532km/h (287kt). Initial rate of climb 1800ft/min. Service ceiling 25,000ft. Range with full passenger load and reserves 1538km (830nm), with 2720kg (6000lb) payload 1612km (870nm). Q300 HGW – Max cruising speed 528km/h (285kt). Range with 50 passengers 1625km (878nm), with 50 passengers and auxiliary fuel 2179km (1177nm).

Weights: 300 – Operating empty 11,657kg (25,700lb), standard max takeoff 18,642kg (41,100lb). Q300 HGW – Operating empty 11,743kg (25,888lb), max takeoff 19,505kg (43,000lb).

Dimensions: Wing span 27.43m (90ft 0in), length 25.68m (84ft 3in), height 7.49m (24ft 7in). Wing area 56.2m^2 (605sq ft).

Capacity: Flightcrew of two. Standard single class seating for 50 passengers at four abreast and 81cm (32in) pitch.

Production: Total orders for Dash 8-300s stood at over 209 by late 2002, of which 194 had been delivered.

History: With the success of the Dash 8-100 series, a stretched version with greater capacity was a logical development.

De Havilland Canada (now part of Bombardier) launched full scale development of a 50 seat stretched version of its Dash 8 during 1986, about two years after the standard fuselage length aircraft had entered service. The first series 300 aircraft was modified from the prototype Dash 8, and first flew in its new configuration on May 15 1987. Canadian certification was granted in February 1989, with the first delivery, to Time Air, following late that same month. US certification was awarded in June 1989.

The stretch comprises fuselage plugs forward and aft of the wing, increasing length by 3.43m (11ft 3in). The fuselage stretch increases typical seating capacity to 50 (at 81cm/32in pitch), or for up to 56 (at 74cm/29in pitch). In addition, the wings are greater in span. Other changes included a larger, repositioned galley, larger toilet, additional wardrobe, dual air conditioning packs, a new galley service door and optional APU.

The standard Dash 8-300 was followed in 1990 by the 300A which introduced optional higher gross weights, interior improvements (as on the Dash 8-100A), and standard PW123A engines (with PW123Bs optional). The 300B was introduced in 1992 and had 1865kW (2500shp) PW123Bs and the 300A's optional high gross weight as standard. The 300E had 1775kW (2380shp) PW123Es rated to 40 degrees, thus improving hot and high performance.

All Dash 8s built since the second quarter of 1996 have been fitted with a computer controlled noise and vibration suppression system (or NVS), consequently the Dash 8-300 was designated Dash 8Q-300. In 1998 the Dash 8 Q300 name was adopted when a new interior was introduced. The Q300 is offered in basic (PW123/PW123B powered) and optional high gross weight (PW123B powered) forms.

Photo: An Air Nippon Dash 8 Q300. (Rob Finlayson)

Bombardier de Havilland Dash 8 Q400

Country of origin: Canada

Type: 70 seat regional turboprop airliner

Powerplants: Two 3410kW (4573shp) takeoff rated Pratt & Whitney Canada PW150A turboprops driving six blade Dowty propellers.

Performance: Max cruising speed 648km/h (350kt). Max certificated ceiling 25,000ft, or optionally 27,000ft. Max range with 70 passengers and reserves 2520km (1360nm).

Weights: Operating empty 17,108kg (37,717lb), max takeoff 27,330kg (60,198lb), 27,995kg (61,720lb), or high gross weight 29,256kg (64,500lb).

Dimensions: Wing span 28.42m (93ft 3in), length 32.84m (107ft 9in), height 8.36m (27ft 5in). Wing area 63.1m² (679.0sq ft).

Capacity: Flightcrew of two. Can seat 70 passengers at 79cm (31in) pitch or 78 at 76cm (30in) pitch in a single class arrangement.

Production: Total Q400 firm sales at late 2002 stood at 74, of which 64 had been delivered.

History: Bombardier's 70 seat de Havilland Dash 8 Q400 (or Q400 for short) is the latest and longest member of the Dash 8 family, but with its new engines, avionics and systems, a modified wing and stretched fuselage is almost an all new aeroplane.

De Havilland was already working on a further stretch of the Dash 8 when Bombardier acquired the company from Boeing in 1992, although the program was not formally launched until June 1995. Rolled out on November 21 1997, the Q400 made its first flight on January 31 1998. Five Q400s were used in the 1900 flying hour flight test program, culminating in Canadian certification being awarded on June 14 1999 and US certification on February 8 2000. The first delivery, to launch customer SAS Commuter, was on January 20 2000, about 10 months later than originally planned.

The Q400 is pitched at the short haul regional airliner market for stage lengths of 550km (300nm) or less. Bombardier says the Q400's breakeven load factor for a 360km (195nm) stage length is just 29 passengers.

The Q400 features a new fuselage stretched 6.83m (22ft 5in) compared with the Q300 mated with a new horizontal tail. The fuselage's cross section and structure is based on the earlier Dash 8's but with two entry doors at the forward and aft ends of the fuselage on the left side, with emergency exit doors opposite them on the right side.

The Q400's inner wing section and wing fuselage wing join are new, while the outer wing has been strengthened. Power is from two FADEC equipped 3410kW (4573shp) Pratt & Whitney Canada PW150As driving six blade, slow turning Dowty propellers.

The Q400 is fitted with Bombardier's NVS active noise and vibration system which reduces cabin noise to levels comparable to the CRJ jet airliner. This is achieved through the use of computer controlled active tuned vibration absorbers (ATVAs) mounted on the airframe.

The flightdeck features five large Thales LCD colour displays which present information to the pilots in a similar format to earlier Dash 8s, allowing a common type rating.

Other new features include the main landing gear, wheels, tyres and brakes, a third hydraulic system and a bullet fairing at the tip of the fin.

Photo: A Team Lufthansa Q400. (Bombardier)

Bombardier Learjet 35, 36 & 31

Country of origin: United States of America

Type: Light corporate jets

Powerplants: Two 15.6kN (3500lb) Garrett TFE731-2-2B turbofans. 31A – Honeywell TFE731-2-3Bs.

Performance: 35A & 36A – Max speed 872km/h (470kt), max cruising speed 852km/h (460kt), economical cruising speed 774km/h (418kt). Service ceiling 41,000ft. Range with four passengers, max fuel and reserves 4070km (2195nm) for 35A, 4673km (2522nm) for 36A. 31A – Max cruising speed 891km/h (481kt), typical cruising speed at 45,000ft 832km/h (450kt). Max certificated altitude 51,000ft. Range with two crew, four passengers and IFR reserves 2344km (1266nm), or 2752km (1486nm) for 31A/ER.

Weights: 35A and 36A – Empty equipped 4590kg (10,120lb), max takeoff 8300kg (18,300lb). 31A – Empty 4651kg (10,253lb), operating empty 5035kg (11,100lb), max takeoff 7030kg (15,500lb), or optionally 7711kg (17,000lb). 31A/ER – Max takeoff 7711kg (17,000lb).

Dimensions: Wing span (over tip tanks) 12.04m (39ft 6in), length 14.83m (48ft 8in), height 3.73m (12ft 3in). Wing area 23.5m² (253.3sq ft). 31A – Same except for wing span 13.35m (43ft 10in). Wing area 24.6m² (264.4sq ft).

Capacity: Flightcrew of two. Seating for up to eight in main cabin in 35 and 31, or up to six in 36A. Some aircraft configured as package freighters.

Production: 676 Learjet 35s and 36s delivered. US Air Force and Air National Guard ordered 84 35As as C-21s. At late 2002 630 Learjet 35s, 15 36s, 35 31s and 200 31As were in service.

History: The Learjet 35 and 36 are stretched, turbofan powered developments of the initial Learjet models, the 23, 24 and 25.

The availability of the Garrett AiResearch TFE731 turbofan in the late 1960s led to a development of the Learjet 25 that was initially known as the 25B-GF (Garrett Fan). A testbed Lear 25 with a TFE731 on its left side flew in May 1971, while the definitive Learjet 35 prototype first flew on August 22 1973.

Aside from turbofans, the 35 and longer range 36 differ from the earlier Learjet 25 in having a 0.33m (1ft 1in) fuselage stretch. The Learjet 35 has seating for up to eight, but has less fuel than the longer range 36, which can only seat up to six, as both types share the same maximum takeoff weight. The 35 and 36 were certificated in July 1974.

Improvements to the two models led to the 35A and 36A from 1976, with higher standard max takeoff weights. Both models remained in production until 1994.

Development of the 35 and 36 range was taken one step further with the Learjet 31, which combines the 35/36's fuselage and powerplants with the more modern wing of the 55 (now also on the 60) and delta fins under the tail. A 31 development aircraft first flew in May 1987 and certification was awarded in August 1988.

The current production models are the improved 31A and 31A/ER, The extended range 31A/ER features a higher maximum takeoff weight and more fuel. A new interior with increased headroom was introduced in 1995. The 200th 31A was delivered in October 2000.

Bombardier acquired Learjet in 1990.

Photo: A German Learjet 31A. (Bombardier)

Bombardier Learjet 45 & 40

Country of origin: United States of America

Type: Small to mid size corporate jet

Powerplants: 45 – Two 15.7kN (3500lb) Honeywell TFE731-20 tur-bofans.

Performance: 45 – High speed cruise 867km/h (468kt), normal cruising speed 846km/h (457kt), long range cruising speed 778km/h (420kt). Max certificated altitude 51,000ft. Max range with four passengers and IFR reserves 3926km (2120nm).

Weights: 45 – Empty 5797kg (12,780lb), basic operating empty 6146kg (13,550lb), max takeoff 9298kg (20,500lb).

Dimensions: 45 – Wing span 14.58m (47ft 10in), length 17.81m (58ft 5in), height 4.37m (14ft 4in). Wing area 29.0m^2 (311.6sq ft).

Capacity: 45 – Flightcrew of two. Main cabin seating for eight or nine passengers (typically eight). 40 – Main cabin seating for seven.

Production: 45 – Approximately 200 delivered by late 2002. 40 – Deliveries due from 2004.

History: Bombardier's Learjet 45 is a popular small or 'super-light' sized corporate jet, and has been joined by the smaller Learjet 40.

Bombardier's Learjet division announced it was developing the Model 45 at the US NBAA's annual convention in Dallas in September 1992. First flight was on October 7 1995 (the 32nd anniversary of the first flight of the original Lear 23), and, after some delays, US FAA certification was granted on September 22 1997. The first customer aircraft was delivered in January 1998.

The 45 is effectively an all new aircraft, designed with the aid of 3D computer modelling. Design changes made early into the 45's design life included a larger fin and rudder, extended engine pylons, smaller delta fins, full span elevators, and single piece flaps.

Larger than the Learjet 31 and smaller than the 60, the 45 features a 1.50m (4.9ft) high and 1.55m (5.1ft) wide cabin which is designed to accommodate double club seating, a galley and a full width aft rest room. The wing spar is recessed beneath the cabin floor. Eight windows line each side of the cabin. The flightdeck features a four screen (two primary flight displays and two multifunction displays) Honeywell Primus 1000 integrated avionics suite, while an APU is standard.

Bombardier revealed the further improved 45XR at the Farnborough 2002 show. It will feature Honeywell TFE731-20BR engines and a 454kg (1000lb) increase in maximum takeoff weight, giving increased range. It will have a maximum range of 3885km (2098nm) with four passengers. Service entry is due in mid 2003.

Bombardier also announced the shortened Learjet 40 at the 2002 Farnborough Airshow. Compared to the 45 its shortened cabin seats one fewer passenger, with Bombardier claiming a maximum range of 3340km (1803nm) with four passengers. With full fuel and a maximum payload it will fly up to 3120km (1685nm) at Mach 0.73 (774 km/h/418kt).

The Learjet 40 prototype, a modified 45 shortened by 62cm (24.5in), flew on August 31 2002, while the first production Learjet 40 first flew on September 5. Certification and initial deliveries are planned for the first quarter of 2004.

Photo: The first production Learjet 40. (Bombardier)

Bombardier Learjet 55 & 60

Country of origin: United States of America

Type: Mid size corporate jets

Powerplants: 55 – Two 16.5kN (3700lb) Garrett TFE731-3A-2B tur-bofans. 60 – Two 20.5kN (4600lb) Pratt & Whitney Canada PW305As.

Performance: 55C – Max speed 884km/h (477kt), max cruising speed 843km/h (455kt), economical cruising speed 778km/h (420kt). Service ceiling 51,000ft. Range with two crew, four passengers and reserves 4442km (2397nm) for 55C/LR. 60 – High cruising speed 859km/h (464kt), normal cruising speed 839km/h (453kt), long range cruising speed 782km/h (422kt). Max certificated altitude 51,000ft. Range with two crew, four passengers and IFR reserves 4648km (2510nm).

Weights: 55C – Empty 5832kg (12,858lb), operating empty 6013kg (13,258lb), max takeoff 9525kg (21,000lb). 60 – Empty 6282kg (13,850lb), basic operating empty 6641kg (14,640lb), max takeoff 10,659kg (23,500lb).

Dimensions: 55 – Wing span 13.34m (43ft 9in), length 16.79m (55ft 1in), height 4.47m (14ft 8in). Wing area 24.6m^2 (264.5sq ft). 60 – Same except length 17.88m (58ft 8in),

Capacity: 55 – Flightcrew of two. Six different main cabin arrangements offered with seating ranging from four to eight. 60 – Flightcrew of two. Optional seating arrangements for six to nine passengers.

Production: Production of the Model 55 ceased in 1990 after 147 had been built. 140 55s in service at late 2002. Deliveries of Model 60 began in January 1993, with more than 245 in service by late 2002.

History: The Learjet 55 and its follow-on successor, the Learjet 60, are the largest members of the Learjet family, and date back to development work undertaken in the late 1970s.

In designing the 55, Learjet (or Gates Learjet as the company was then known) took the wing of the earlier Longhorn 28/29 series and married it to an all new, larger 10 seat fuselage. The original Model 55 Longhorn prototype first flew on November 15 1979. The first production aircraft meanwhile flew on August 11 1980, with the first delivered in late April 1981 (after FAA certification was granted in March that year).

Development of the 55 led to a number of sub variants, including the 55B which introduced a digital flightdeck, modified wings, improved interior, and most importantly, the previous optional higher takeoff weights becoming standard. The 55C introduced 'Delta Fins' which gave a number of performance and handling advantages, the 55C/ER is an extended range version with additional fuel in the tail cone (the additional tank can be retrofitted to earlier aircraft), while the 55C/LR introduced more fuel capacity.

The improved Learjet 60 first flew in its basic definitive form in June 1991 (the modified Learjet 55 prototype earlier served as a proof of concept aircraft for the 60 with Garrett engines). It differs from the 55 in having a 1.09m (43in) fuselage stretch and new Pratt & Whitney Canada PW305 turbofans. Certification of the 60 was awarded in January 1993, with first deliveries following shortly afterwards. A revised interior was introduced in 1998.

Photo: The 60 is the largest member of the Learjet family.

Bombardier Challenger 300

Countries of origin: Canada & USA

Type: Medium size corporate jet

Powerplant: Two 28.9kN (6500lb) with automatic power reserve Honeywell AS907 turbofans.

Performance: High speed cruising speed 870km/h (470kt) or Mach 0.82, normal cruising speed 850km/h (460kt) or Mach 0.80. Balanced field length 1510m (4950ft), landing distance 792m (2600ft). Max operating altitude 45,000ft, initial cruise altitude 41,000ft. Max range with eight passengers and NBAA IFR reserves at Mach 0.80 5740km (3100nm).

Weights: Basic operating empty 10,138kg (22,350lb), max takeoff 17,010kg (37,500lb).

Dimensions: Wing span 19.46m (63ft 10in), length 20.93m (68ft 8in), height 6.19m (20ft 4in). Wing area 48.5m² (522sq ft).

Capacity: Flightcrew of two. Typical cabin arrangement for eight, with a two seat lounge opposite two facing seats, with club seating for four behind them, or double club seating.

Production: First deliveries due in 2003.

History: Bombardier's all new Challenger 300 (formerly Continental Jet) is a transcontinental range eight seat corporate jet which will sit in the company's model line-up between the Learjet 60 and Challenger 604.

Bombardier revealed it was developing the then Continental Jet (design designation BD-100) at the NBAA's annual convention in Las Vegas in October 1998 and formally launched the aircraft at the Paris Airshow the following June. First metal for the prototype was cut in October 1999 with first flight on August 14 2001. Bombardier renamed the Continental Jet the Challenger 300 at the NBAA Convention in September 2002. Customer deliveries are due in 2003.

The Challenger 300 is powered by two Honeywell AS907 turbofans. The flightdeck features a Rockwell Collins Pro Line 21 avionics system displaying information on four large screen liquid crystal displays. The main cabin seats eight passengers in a standard double club arrangement and will feature a flat floor and stand-up headroom.

The Challenger 300 is largely built from conventional materials with limited use of composites for some non structural fairings. Flight controls are manual apart from fly-by-wire spoilers on the wings. The wings themselves feature a 27° sweepback and winglets.

Challenger 300 final assembly takes place at Bombardier's Learjet facilities in Wichita, Kansas. Fellow Bombardier subsidiaries Canadair and Shorts are also involved in the program – Canadair will build the cockpit, forward fuselage and primary flight controls, Shorts will build the centre fuselage.

Non Bombardier suppliers include Japan's Mitsubishi Heavy Industries which designed and is building the wing, and Taiwan's AIDC which builds the rear fuselage and tail. Boeing Australia builds the composite tailcone, Messier Dowty supplies the undercarriage, Huriel-Dubois the thrust reversers and GKN Westland the engine nacelles.

Photo: The fourth Challenger 300 made its first flight on April 9 2002. (Bombardier)

Bombardier Canadair 601 & 604 Challenger

Country of origin: Canada

Type: Long range corporate jets

Powerplants: 601 – Two 40.7kN (9140lb) General Electric CF34-3A turbofans. 604 – Two CF34-3Bs flat rated to 38.8kN (8729lb) without automatic power reserve, or 41.0kN (9220lb) with.

Performance: 601-1A – Max cruising speed 851km/h (460kt), typical cruising speed 819km/h (442kt), long range cruising speed 786km/h (424kt). Max operating altitude 45,000ft. Range with max fuel and reserves 6208km (3352nm). 601-3A – Normal cruising speed 851km/h (460kt). Ceiling 41,000ft. Range with max fuel, five pax and reserves 6236km (3365nm). 604 – Max cruising speed 882km/h (476kt), normal cruising speed 851km/h (459kt), long range cruising speed 787km/h (425kt). Certificated ceiling 41,000ft. Range with max fuel, five pax and reserves 7550km (4077nm) at long range cruising speed, 6980km (3769nm) at normal cruising speed.

Weights: 601-3A – Empty 9049kg (19,950lb), operating empty 11,605kg (25,585lb), max takeoff 19,550kg (43,100lb). 601-3A – Empty 9292kg (20,485lb), operating empty 11,566kg (25,500lb), max takeoff 19,550kg (43,100lb) or optionally 20,457kg (45,100lb). 604 – Empty 9806kg (21,620lb), operating empty 12,079kg (26,630lb), max takeoff 21,591kg (47,600lb), or optionally 21,863kg (48,200lb).

Dimensions: Wing span 19.61m (64ft 4in), length 20.85m (68ft 5in), height 6.30m (20ft 8in). Wing area 48.3m² (520.0sq ft).

Capacity: Flightcrew of two. Various seating options available depending on customer preference, maximum seating for 19.

Production: Challenger 601 production completed, with 66 601-1As, 134 601-3As and 59 601-3Rs delivered. Over 240 604s delivered. 500th Challenger (of all models) delivered in October 2000.

History: The Challenger 601 addressed the original CL-600 Challenger's weight problems and replaced the troubled ALF 502 turbofans, creating a highly successful full size corporate jet.

Troubles with the Avco Lycoming powered CL-600 Challenger (described under Canadair) led Canadair (now a division of Bombardier) to develop a vastly improved variant in the form of the General Electric CF34 powered Challenger 601. Another important change was the addition of winglets, which were also offered as a retrofit to earlier aircraft. The 601 first flew on April 10 1982 and for a time was offered alongside the CL-600. The CL-600 was dropped from the model line in 1983.

The improved 601-3A first flew in 1987, and introduced an EFIS glass flightdeck and upgraded engines. Available from 1989, the 601-3R was an extended range model with higher weights (the range increase modifications can also be retrofitted to 601-3As).

Further enhancements led to the Challenger 604. Improvements include an advanced Collins Pro-Line IV EFIS avionics system with colour displays, higher weights, CF34-3B turbofans and increased fuel tankage. Many other minor changes were incorporated based on Bombardier's experience with the Canadair Regional Jet. First flight with CF34-3A engines was in September 1994, first flight with the CF34-3B engines was on March 17 1995. Transport Canada certification was granted that September. First delivery was in January 1996.

Photo: An Australian registered Challenger 604. (Greg Wood)

Country of origin: Canada

Type: Ultra long range, high speed, high capacity corporate jet

Powerplants: Express – Two 65.6kN (14,750lb) Rolls-Royce BR710A2-20 turbofans.

Performance: Express – High speed cruise 935km/h (505kt) or Mach 0.88, normal cruising speed 904km/h (488kt) or Mach 0.85, long range cruising speed 850km/h (459kt) or Mach 0.80. Range with eight passengers, four crew and reserves at long range cruising speed 11,130km (6010nm), at normal cruising speed 9771km (5275nm). Range with max payload at normal cruising speed 8500km (4595nm), at long range cruise speed 9606km (5187km). 5000 – Max cruising speed Mach 0.89, normal cruising speed Mach 0.85. Range at Mach 0.85 8889km (4800nm).

Weights: Express – Operating empty 22,816kg (50,300lb), max takeoff 43,091kg (95,000lb) or 43,545kg (96,000lb). 5000 – Operating empty 22,838kg (50,330lb), max takeoff 39,780kg (87,700lb).

Dimensions: Express – Span over winglets 28.65m (94ft 0in), length 30.30m (99ft 5in), height 7.57m (24ft 10in). Wing area 94.95m² (1022sq ft). 5000 – Same except length 29.51m (96ft 10in).

Capacity: Express – Flightcrew of two plus one or two flight attendants. Typical arrangements seat from eight to 18 passengers. Can be fitted with a galley, crew rest station, work stations, a conference/lounge/dining area, a stateroom with a fold out bed, toilet, shower and wardrobe. High density 30 seat corporate shuttle configuration offered.

Production: At late 2002 110 Global Expresses were in service. Global 5000 first deliveries due late 2004.

History: The Global Express is a very long range corporate jet, the Global 5000 is a shortened development due to fly in 2003.

Bombardier's Canadair division announced development of the Global Express (engineering designation BD-700) in October 1991 at the annual NBAA conference in the USA. Officially launched on December 20 1993, it first flew on October 13 1996, with Canadian certification awarded on July 31 1998 followed by US certification that November. The first delivery to a customer of a completed aircraft was in July 1999.

The fly-by-wire Global Express shares the CRJ's fuselage cross section, but is otherwise an all new design. It features an advanced all new supercritical wing with a 35° sweep and winglets, plus a new T-tail. The engines are Rolls-Royce BR710s with FADEC. The advanced flightdeck features a six screen Honeywell Primus 2000 XP EFIS suite and is offered with optional head-up displays.

Five are being fitted with ground imaging radar for Britain's Royal Air Force under the ASTOR program.

Bombardier launched the shortened Global 5000 on February 5 2002, after publicly revealing the concept at the Dubai Airshow the previous October. Compared to the Global Express, the Global 5000 will feature a 1.22m shortened fuselage. It will be capable of transcontinental missions at Mach 0.89. First flight is due in the first quarter of 2003, with certification a year later and first deliveries in late 2004.

Photo: A Global Express demonstrator. (Charles Falk)

Country of origin: United States of America

Type: Light piston powered utility helicopters

Powerplant: B-2B – One 135kW (180hp) Textron Lycoming IVO-360-A1A fuel injected flat four piston engine driving a three blade main rotor and two blade tail rotor. 305 – One 225kW (305hp) Textron Lycoming IVO-540-B1A fuel injected flat six.

Performance: B-2B – Max level speed 161km/h (87kt), max cruising speed (at 75% power) 145km/h (78kt). Initial rate of climb 1900ft. Service ceiling 10,800ft. Hovering ceiling in ground effect 6700ft. Range with max fuel and reserves 400km (217nm). 305 – Max speed 193km/h (104kt), max cruising speed 177km/h (96kt). Initial rate of climb 975ft/min. Service ceiling 12,000ft. Hovering ceiling in ground effect 4080ft. Range with max fuel and reserves 354km (191nm).

Weights: B-2B – Empty 463kg (1020lb) or 481kg (1060lb) with floats, max takeoff 757kg (1670lb). 305 – Empty 815kg (1800lb), max takeoff 1315kg (2900lb).

Dimensions: B-2B – Main rotor diameter 7.24m (23ft 9in), length overall 8.53m (28ft 0in), fuselage length 6.62m (21ft 9in), height 2.06m (6ft 9in). Main rotor disc area 41.2m² (443.0sq ft). 305 – Main rotor diameter 8.74m (28ft 8in), length overall 10.03m (32ft 11in), fuselage length 7.44m (24ft 5in), height 2.44m (8ft 1in). Main rotor disc area 60.0m² (654.4sq ft).

Capacity: B-2 seats two side by side. 305 has seating for five with two forward individual seats and rear bench seat for three.

Production: Exact production unclear, but includes more than 400 B-2s. Production resumed in late 1996, with small numbers built since.

History: The Brantly B-2 light helicopter first flew in the early 1950s and returned to production in the early 1990s, while the larger five seat 305 dates to the early 1970s.

The original B-2 two seater was designed and built by N Brantly, and flew for the first time on February 21 1953. Certification was awarded in April 1959, with production deliveries following soon after. The initial production B-2 model featured a 135kW (180hp) VO-360-A1A flat four, the same basic powerplant fitted to the B-2 series through to the 1990s. The initial B-2 was followed by the improved B-2A with a redesigned cabin and the B-2B, which became the definitive production model.

Brantly also developed a larger five seat Model 305 based on the B-2, with a larger cabin and more powerful VO-540 engine. The 305 first flew in January 1964 and was certificated in July the following year.

Brantly production ceased in the early 1970s after more than 400 B-2s had been built. However production resumed in 1976 when the Hynes company acquired the design and production rights to what became the Brantly-Hynes B-2 and 305.

Brantly-Hynes continued low rate manufacture of both models through to the mid 1980s when it too ceased production. Then in 1989 James Kimura formed Brantly Helicopter Industries to build both models, and low rate production resumed for a time.

Brantly International Inc took over the B-2B's FAA production certificate in July 1996 and resumed low rate B-2B production at Vernon, Texas. A number of equipment improvements were incorporated.

Photo: A new production Brantly International B-2B. (Paul Sadler)

British Aerospace/Hawker Siddeley 748

Country of origin: United Kingdom

Type: Regional airliner and freighter

Powerplants: Srs 2A – Two 1700kW (2280ehp) Rolls-Royce Dart RDa.7 Mk 534-2 or Mk 535-2 turboprops driving four blade propellers. Super 748 – Two 1700kW (2280ehp) Dart Mk 552-2s.

Performance: Srs 2A – Cruising speed 452km/h (244kt). Range with max payload and reserves 1360km (735nm), range with max fuel and reserves 3130km (1690nm). Super 748 – Cruising speed 452km/h (244kt). Initial rate of climb 1420ft/min. Range with max payload and reserves 1715km (926nm), range with max fuel, 3360kg (7800lb) payload and reserves 2892km (1560nm).

Weights: Srs 2A – Operating empty 12,159kg (26,806lb), max takeoff 21,092kg (46,500lb). Super 748 – Empty 6676kg (14,720lb), max takeoff 12,430kg (27,400lb).

Dimensions: Srs 2A – Wing span 30.02m (98ft 6in), length 20.42m (67ft 0in), height 7.57m (24ft 10in). Wing area 75.4m² (810.8sq ft). Super 748 – Same except for wing span 31.23m (102ft 6in). Wing area 77.0m² (828.9sq ft).

Capacity: Flightcrew of two. Typical seating for between 48 and 51 passengers, at four abreast and 76cm (30in) pitch. Max seating for 58.

Production: Production ended in 1988 by which time 381 had been built, including 89 assembled in India, comprising 20 Srs 1, 85 Srs 2, 123 Srs 2A, 33 Srs 2B/Super 748 and 31 Andovers. Approx 100 in commercial use in 2002.

History: The HS.748 proved to be a quite successful turboprop airliner and today remains popular both as an airliner and freighter.

Avro designed the HS.748 in a bid to re-enter the civil market in anticipation of a decline in its military aircraft business (following Britain's famous 1957 Defence White Paper). Surfacing in 1958 as the Avro 748, the project became part of the Hawker Siddeley group when it formed in 1959 with the merger of several British aviation companies including Hawker and Avro. The new aircraft first flew on June 24 1960, with four prototype aircraft (two for static testing) built. The first production Series 1 flew on August 30 1961.

Series 1 production aircraft were powered by two 1400kW (1880ehp) Dart RDa.6 Mk 514 turboprops, and the first entered service in December 1961 with Skyways Airways.

The Series 2, in its 2, 2A and 2C (with large freight door) variants, was the most successful of the line, with the first flying on November 6 1961. The Series 2 introduced higher weights and more powerful engines. The Series 2B appeared in 1977, offering a range of aerodynamic and other improvements, including an increased wing span.

The most advanced 748 variant, the Super 748, first flew in July 1984. Based on the 2B, it also featured an updated flightdeck, improved efficiency and hushkitted Dart engines, and new galley and internal fittings. Production ended in 1988 with the last flying that December (with delivery the following month).

India's HAL licence built 89 748s between 1961 and 1984.

The Andover was a military variant with a rear loading freight door and 'kneeling' undercarriage. Small numbers of ex British and New Zealand air force Andovers are in commercial service.

Photo: A Horizon Airlines HS.748. (Denis Hill)

British Aerospace ATP

Country of origin: United Kingdom

Type: Turboprop powered regional airliner

Powerplants: ATP – Two 1978kW (2653shp) Pratt & Whitney Canada PW126A turboprops driving six blade propellers.

Performance: ATP – Max cruising speed 493km/h (266kt), econ cruising speed 437km/h (236kt). Range with max payload and reserves 630km (340nm), with 69 passengers and reserves 1480km (800nm).

Weights: ATP – Operating empty 14,193kg (31,290lb), max takeoff 22,930kg (50,550lb). J61 – Max takeoff 23,678kg (52,200lb).

Dimensions: Wing span 30.63m (100ft 6in), length 26.01m (85ft 4in), height 7.59m (24ft 11in). Wing area 78.3m² (842.84sq ft).

Capacity: Flightcrew of two. Typical one class seating for 64 to 68 in ATP or 70 in Jetstream 61 at four abreast and 79cm (31in) pitch. Combi versions can take passengers and freight.

Production: Total ATP and Jetstream 61 production of 65 (including 2 J61s) built between 1986 and 1993. Approx 35 are in service.

History: British Aerospace's ATP was a stretched development of the HS.748, but did not achieve the sales success of its smaller brethren and was effectively in production for barely five years.

British Aerospace announced it was developing an advanced derivative of the 748 in March 1984. The BAe ATP, or Advanced TurboProp, first flew on August 6 1986, while the first production aircraft flew in February 1988. Certification was granted in March 1988 and the ATP entered airline service that May.

Compared to the 748 the ATP features a stretched fuselage (with square rather than round windows) taking maximum seating up to 72 passengers, while Pratt & Whitney Canada PW126 turboprops drive slow turning six blade propellers. Much of the systems and equipment was new or significantly improved. The flightdeck has EFIS instrumentation, while the cabin interior was modernised. The nose was reprofiled and some sweep back was added to the vertical and horizontal tails.

The further improved Jetstream 61 (or J61) was marketed by the newly created Jetstream Aircraft division of British Aerospace in the mid 1990s. Apart from the name change it introduced a number of minor technical changes including an interior based on the Jetstream 41 (including the innovative armrests incorporated into the cabin walls for window seats), more powerful PW127D engines and increased operating weights giving higher speeds and longer range. The Jetstream 61 was certificated in June 1995, but marketing efforts ceased when AI(R) was formed because it was a direct competitor to the now disbanded consortium's far more successful ATR 72. Just two J61s were completed and they and 11 ATP airframes were scrapped.

The last three whitetail ATPs were not sold until late 1998, although production had effectively ceased in 1993.

BAE Systems and Sweden's West Air have jointly developed a freighter conversion of the ATP, the ATPF. It first flew on July 10 2002 and features a 2.64m (104in) wide x 1.73m (68in) large cargo door. Up to eight tonnes of payload – seven or eight LD3 containers or five LD4s – can be carried.

Photo: A British Airways CitiExpress ATP. (Lee Archer)

British Aerospace Jetstream 31 & 32

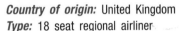

Country of origin: United Kingdom

Type: 18 seat regional airliner

Powerplants: J31 – Two 700kW (940shp) Garret TPE331-10 turboprops driving four blade props. Super 31 – Two 760kW (1020shp) TPE331-12UARs.

Performance: J31 – Max cruising speed 482km/h (260kt), long range cruising speed 426km/h (230kt). Initial rate of climb 2200ft/min. Range with 19 pax and reserves 1185km (640nm), 1760km (950nm) with 12 pax or 2130km (1150nm) with nine pax. Super 31 – Max cruising speed 490km/h (264kt), long range cruising speed 452km/h (244kt). Initial rate of climb 2240ft/min. Range with 19 pax and reserves 1192km (643nm).

Weights: J31 – Operating empty 4360kg (9613lb), max takeoff 6950kg (15,322lb). Super 31 – Operating empty 4578kg (10,992lb), max takeoff 7350kg (16,204lb).

Dimensions: Wing span 15.85m (52ft 0in), length 14.37m (47ft 2in), height 5.37m (17ft 6in). Wing area 25.1m² (270sq ft).

Capacity: Flightcrew of two. Main cabin seating for up to 19 at three abreast and 79cm (31in) pitch, or 12 passengers in a corporate shuttle configuration, or nine in an executive layout.

Production: Total J31 deliveries of 381, including 161 Super J31s. 189 in commercial service in late 2002.

History: The successful Jetstream 31 evolved from the Turbomeca Astazou powered Handley Page HP.137 Jetstream 1.

The HP.137 design was launched in 1965, and flew for the first time on August 18 1967. Initial Handley Page production aircraft were powered by 635kW (850hp) Astazou XIVs and named Jetstream 1 (36 built), but deliveries were delayed by excess weight and drag problems. To overcome these problems Handley Page developed the Jetstream 2 with more powerful 800kW (1073shp) Astazou XIVCs. However Handley Page folded in 1969, bringing to an end development of the more powerful Jetstream 2 and plans to market a civil version of the 3M in the USA.

Development of the Jetstream 2 resumed in 1970 as the Jetstream 200 under the control of the newly formed Jetstream Aircraft in collaboration with Scottish Aviation. Scottish Aviation later assumed overall responsibility for the Jetstream and built a number for Britain's military. Development continued after Scottish Aviation was merged into British Aerospace in 1977, and work on the Jetstream 31 (or J31) began in 1978. The first flight of the Garrett TPE331 powered Jetstream 31 (a converted HP.137) occurred on March 28 1980. UK certification was granted in June 1982.

Subsequent development led to the Super 31, certificated in October 1988. The Super 31 or J32 features uprated engines, higher weights and better performance. The last J31/J32 was built in 1993.

From 1997 British Aerospace (now BAE Systems) Asset Management has offered for sale or lease the upgraded J32EP (Enhanced Performance). Its minor aerodynamic and drag improvements enhance payload range and hot and high performance.

Canada's Aero Consutling Services has been developing a J31 cargo conversion kit, available from early 2003.

Photo: A Jetstream 32. Note underbelly pod. (Rob Finlayson)

British Aerospace Jetstream 41

Country of origin: United Kingdom

Type: 29 seat regional turboprop airliner

Powerplants: Two 1120kW (1500shp) AlliedSignal TPE331-14GR/HR turboprops driving five blade propellers on initial production aircraft, later two 1230kW (1650shp) TPE331-14s.

Performance: Max speed 547km/h (295kt), economical cruising speed 482km/h (260kt). Service ceiling 26,000ft. Range (initial production) with 29 passengers and reserves 1263km (681nm), definitive production standard 1433km (774nm).

Weights: Empty 6350kg (14,000lb), max takeoff initial production 10,433kg (23,100lb), definitive max takeoff 10,895kg (24,000lb).

Dimensions: Wing span 18.29m (60ft 0in), length 19.25m (63ft 2in), height 5.74m (18ft 10in). Wing area 32.6m² (350.8sq ft).

Capacity: Flightcrew of two. Main cabin seating for up to 29 at three abreast, seating for 27 with galley. Corporate shuttle configured J41s seat 16 at two abreast.

Production: Orders for the Jetstream 41 stood at 100 in May 1997 when BAe announced it was terminating production. 92 were in service in late 2002.

History: The 29 seat Jetstream 41 is a stretched and modernised development of the 19 seat Jetstream 31, and competed against the Embraer Brasilia, Dornier 328 and Saab 340.

The Jetstream 41 (or J41) is based on the J31, but features a 4.88m (16ft) fuselage stretch, consisting of a 2.51m (8ft 3in) plug forward of the wing and a 2.36m (7ft 9in) plug rear. The increased span wing (with reworked ailerons and flaps) is mounted lower on the fuselage so that it does not carry through the fuselage and interrupt the interior cabin aisle, unlike on the Jetstream 31. Other airframe modifications included a new reprofiled six piece windscreen and extended wing root fairing with greater baggage capacity. More powerful AlliedSignal TPE331 turboprops, mounted in new nacelles with increased ground clearance, drive advanced five blade McCauley propellers. The flightdeck has modern EFIS glass displays.

Development work on the J41 was announced in mid 1989, resulting in the type's first flight on September 25 1991. Three further aircraft were also used in the flight test program, with European JAA certification awarded on November 23 1992. The first delivery occurred two days later on November 25.

From mid 1994, all aircraft delivered benefited from various payload and range performance improvements, resulting from uprated engines and a higher maximum takeoff weight.

BAe established a separate Jetstream Aircraft division in mid 1993 to market the Jetstream 41. In January 1996 the J41 became part of the Aero International (Regional) stable, but in May 1997 BAe announced that it was terminating J41 production (the AI(R) consortium was disbanded in 1998). Just over 100 had been built when production was terminated.

Field Aircraft of the UK and Pilatus of Switzerland were risk sharing partners, while Gulfstream was tasked with building wingsets.

Photo: An Origin Pacific (New Zealand) Jetstream 41. (Rob Finlayson)

British Aerospace 146

Country of origin: United Kingdom

Type: Regional jet airliners

Powerplants: 146-100 – Four 30.0kN (6700lb) Textron Lycoming ALF 502R-3s or four 31.0kN (6970lb) ALF 502R-5 turbofans. 146-300 – Four 31.0kN (6900lb) Textron Lycoming ALF 502R-5s.

Performance: 146-100 – Cruising speed 767km/h (414kt), long range cruising speed 670km/h (361kt). Range with standard fuel 3000km (1620nm), range with max payload 1630km (880nm). 146-300 – Cruising speed 790km/h (426kt), long range cruising speed 700km/h (377kt). Range with standard fuel 2817km (1520nm), range with max payload 1927km (1040nm).

Weights: 146-100 – Operating empty 23,288kg (51,342lb), max takeoff 38,100kg (84,000lb). 146-300 – Operating empty 24,878kg (54,848lb), max takeoff 44,225kg (97,500lb).

Dimensions: 146-100 – Wing span 26.21m (86ft 0in), length 26.20m (86ft 0in), height 8.61m (28ft 3in). Wing area 77.3m² (832.0sq ft). 146-300 – Same except length 30.99m (101ft 8in), height 8.61m (28ft 3in).

Capacity: Flightcrew of two. 146-100 – Single class seating for 70 passengers at five abreast or 82 to 94 six abreast. 146-200 – Max seating 112 at six abreast, typical seating for 85 five abreast 146-200QT – Nine LD3 containers. 146-300 – Max seating 128 passengers at six abreast, typically 100 at five abreast.

Production: 37 146-100s, 113 146-200s and 71 146-300s built. 295 146s were in airline service in late 2002.

History: The BAe 146 family, which includes the Avro RJ (described separately) and the cancelled RJX, is likely to remain Britain's most successful jet transport program, with 395 built.

The then Hawker Siddeley announced in August 1973 it was designing the HS.146, a short range quiet airliner powered by four small turbofans, financed in part with British government aid. Serious development lasted just a few months before worsening recession made the project seem too risky. Work then continued on a limited scale until July 1978 when the project was officially relaunched by Hawker Siddeley successor British Aerospace.

The basic BAe 146-100 first flew on September 3 1981. Certification was granted in early 1983 with first deliveries following shortly afterwards in May 1983.

The 146-200 is essentially similar to its smaller stablemate, but has a 2.39m (7ft 8in) longer fuselage and heavier weights. The 146-200 first flew on August 1 1982, while the UK Civil Aviation Authority awarded the 146-200's type certificate on February 4 the following year.

The 146-300 is a further stretched derivative. An aerodynamic prototype based on the original prototype 146-100 flew for the first time on May 1 1987, with certification granted that September.

Both the 146-200 and -300 have been built in 'Quiet Trader' freighter and the 'Quick Change' convertible forms. BAE Systems may also develop a freighter conversion for passenger 146s

The last 146s were delivered in 1993, with series succeeded by the Avro RJ family (described next).

Photo: A buzz BAe 146-300. (Dave Fraser)

British Aerospace/BAE Systems Avro RJ

Country of origin: United Kingdom

Type: Regional jet airliners

Powerplants: RJ85 – Four 31.0kN (6970lb) Honeywell LF 507 turbofans. RJ100 – Four 31.1kN (7000lb) LF 507s.

Performance: RJ85 – Cruising speed 763km/h (412kt), long range cruising speed 720km/h (389kt). Range with standard fuel 2963km (1600nm), range with max payload 2129km (1150nm). RJ100 – Max operating speed Mach 0.73, cruising speed 763km/h (412kt), long range cruising speed 720km/h (389kt). Range with max fuel 2760km (1490nm), range with max payload 2129km (1150nm).

Weights: RJ85 – Operating empty 24,600kg (54,239lb), max takeoff 43,998kg (97,000lb). RJ100 – Operating empty 25,600kg (56,438lb), max takeoff initially 44,225kg (97,500lb), later 46,039kg (101,500lb).

Dimensions: RJ-85 – Wing span 26.21m (86ft), length 28.60m (93ft 10in), height 8.59m (28ft 2in). Wing area 77.3m² (832sq ft). RJ-100 – Wing span 26.21m (86ft 0in), length 30.99m (101ft 8in), height 8.61m (28ft 3in). Wing area 77.3m² (832sq ft).

Capacity: Flightcrew of two. RJ70 – Single class seating for 70 passengers at five abreast or 82 to 94 six abreast. RJ85 – Max seating 112 at six abreast, typical seating for 85 five abreast RJ100 – Max seating 128 at six abreast, typically 100 at five abreast.

Production: 170 RJs built.

History: The Avro RJ series are upgraded developments of the BAe 146 family, and like the 146 was built in three fuselage length variants – the RJ70, RJ85 and RJ100.

BAe first offered the improved RJ70 and RJ80, both of which are based on the 146-100, in 1990. They would have seated 70 and 80 passengers respectively, but instead these designs matured into the Avro series.

The 146-200 based Avro RJ85 was the first member of the new family to fly, on March 23 1992. The biggest member of the family, the 146-300 based RJ100, first flew on May 13 1992. The 146-100 based RJ70 was delivered from late 1993 but just 12 were sold.

RJ improvements over the 146 include more reliable and efficient FADEC equipped AlliedSignal (now Honeywell) LF 507 engines, new 'Spaceliner' cabin interior and a digital flightdeck. Weight and drag savings were introduced in 1996.

The RJ100 was also marketed as the RJ115 with extra emergency exits to seat 116 to 128 in a high density six abreast configuration. None were built. The Avro Business Jet was also offered.

The RJ series was originally marketed and manufactured by Avro Aerospace, a separate BAe company, so named as RJ production was undertaken at the former Avro factory near Manchester (most 146s were built at Hatfield). Avro was also part of the short-lived AI(R) consortium with ATR and Jetstream.

The last RJ was delivered in 2002.

The improved RJX with new Honeywell AS977 turbofans was cancelled on November 27 2001 in the wake of BAE Systems' post September 11 concerns of poor sales prospects after the prototype RJX-85's first flight that April. Just 14 had been ordered prior to program cancellation.

Photo: An Air Botnia RJ85. (BAE Systems)

BN Group (Britten-Norman) Islander

Countries of origin: United Kingdom & Romania

Type: Commuter airliner and light utility transport

Powerplants: BN-2A – Two 195kW (260hp) Lycoming O-540-E4C flat sixes. BN2B-20 – Two 225kW (300hp) Textron Lycoming IO-540K1B5s.

Performance: BN-2A – Max speed 273km/h (147kt), max cruising speed 257km/h (140kt), econ cruising speed 246km/h (133kt). Initial rate of climb 970ft/min. Service ceiling 13,200ft. Range at econ cruise 1400km (755nm). BN2B-20 – Max speed 280km/h (150kt), max cruising speed 264km/h (142kt), econ cruising speed 245km/h (132kt). Initial rate of climb 1130ft/min. Service ceiling 17,200ft. Range at econ cruise and std fuel 1136km (613nm), with opt fuel 1965km (1060nm).

Weights: BN-2A – Empty equipped 1627kg (3588lb), max takeoff 2993kg (6600lb). BN2B-20 – Empty equipped 1925kg (4244lb), max takeoff 2993kg (6600lb).

Dimensions: Wing span 14.94m (49ft 0in), length 10.86m (35ft 8in), height 4.18m (13ft 9in). Wing area 30.2m² (325.0sq ft).

Capacity: Flightcrew of two pilots or pilot and passenger on flight-deck, with seating for eight in main cabin. No centre aisle.

Production: Almost 1300 delivered. Approx 70 BN2Ts built.

History: The BN-2 (now BN2) Islander was Britten-Norman's second original design, work on which began during 1963.

The Islander was developed by John Britten and Desmond Norman as a Dragon Rapide replacement, with the emphasis on designing a rugged aircraft with good field performance, low operating costs and ease of maintenance. The prototype was powered by two 155kW (210hp) IO-360s and flew on June 13 1965.

The first production Islanders were powered by 195kW (260hp) IO-540s. Simply designated BN-2, the first flew in 1967. Twenty-three were built before production switched to the BN-2A, which introduced fairings to the main undercarriage legs, wing leading edge and flap droop, and an increased max takeoff weight. From 1970 the base A model was the BN-2A-6, the BN-2A-7 had extended wingtips, while the BN-2A-2 and BN-2A-3 were powered by the 225kW (300hp) IO-540, the latter with the extended wingtips.

In 1972 BN released the 195kW (260hp) powered BN-2A-26 and extended wingtips BN-2A-27, and the 225kW (300hp) BN-2A-20 and extended wingtips BN-2A-21. All four models had higher weights.

Further improvements came with the BN2B range with higher weights, improved interior and instrument panel and shorter diameter props. The -26, -27, -20 and -21 variants were available as before. The -27 and -21 were later dropped while the -20BN2B-20 and BN2B-26 remain in production. Approx 160 have been built.

The turboprop (Allison/Rolls-Royce 250) powered BN2T Turbine Islander has been built since 1981. Most of the 70 or so built have been for military customers. The Turbine 4000 is a further development.

Britten Norman was bought by Omani interests in May 2000 and renamed BN Group. BN Group aircraft are built by Romaero in Romania before being ferried to the UK for completion. Romero has built over 500 Islanders for Britten Norman since 1969.

BN Group signed a new contract with Romero in July 2002 for 24 further Islander airframes to be supplied over a two year period.

Photo: A BN-2A-26 Islander. (Gerard Williamson)

Britten-Norman Trislander

Country of origin: United Kingdom

Type: Commuter airliner

Powerplants: Three 195kW (260hp) Lycoming O-540-E4C5 flat six piston engines driving two blade constant speed Hartzell propellers. An optional 1.56kN (350lb) auxiliary rocket for takeoff was offered.

Performance: Max speed 290km/h (156kt), cruising speed at 75% power 267km/h (144kt), cruising speed at 50% power 241km/h (130kt). Initial rate of climb 980ft/min. Service ceiling 13,150ft. Max range 1610km (868nm).

Weights: Empty equipped 2650kg (5843lb), max takeoff 4536kg (10,000lb).

Dimensions: Wing span 16.15m (53ft 0in), length 15.01m (49ft 3in), height 4.32m (14ft 2in). Wing area 31.3m² (337.0sq ft).

Capacity: Usually one pilot and passenger on flightdeck. Seating for 16 passengers two abreast at 79cm (31in) pitch in main cabin.

Production: UK production total 74.

History: Britten Norman adopted a unique three engined configuration for the Trislander when it developed this stretched version of the Islander.

Britten-Norman research revealed a market for a stretched development of the Islander, and the company concluded that such an aircraft would need a 50% increase in internal capacity. The company's novel approach to the need for more power for the enlarged Islander was to add a third engine, rather than two engines of increased power output. A nose mounted engine was considered, but due to the Islander's nose configuration, Britten-Norman settled on mounting the engine on the vertical tail, resulting in the BN-2A Mk III Trislander.

The tail mounted engine involved significant modification to the tail and strengthening of the rear fuselage. Other changes over the Islander include a 2.29m (7ft 6in) fuselage stretch forward of the wing, new main landing gear and larger diameter wheels and tyres.

The first Trislander was converted from the second Islander prototype, and it first flew in its new form on September 11 1970. Early production Trislanders were also conversions of Islanders, while subsequent Trislanders were built on the same production line as the Islander. The first production Trislander flew on March 6 1971, certification was granted on May 14, and the first delivery to a customer occurred on June 29 that year.

Britten-Norman Trislander production originally ceased in 1982 after 73 were ordered (by which stage the company had been acquired by Pilatus). Plans to produce the Trislander in the USA as the Tri-Commutair by the International Aviation Corporation, and in Australia never came to fruition. However one of 12 kits built for the Tri-Commutair project was assembled in Guernsey in the UK and flew in March 1996.

In May 1999 Britten-Norman announced it had an order for three new Trislanders for China Northern Airlines. These were to feature new avionics (including GPS and weather radar) and a modern interior. The order fell through but BN Group was looking for new customers to relaunch Trislander production.

Photo: The uniquely configured Trislander. (BN Group)

Canadair CL-44

Country of origin: Canada

Type: Medium range airliner and freighter

Powerplants: CL-44D-4 – Four 4270kW (5730shp) Rolls-Royce Tyne 515/50 turboprops driving four blade propellers.

Performance: CL-44D-4 – Max cruising speed 647km/h (349kt), cruising speed 621km/h (335kt). Service ceiling 30,000ft. Range with max payload 4625km (2500nm), range with max fuel 8990km (4855nm).

Weights: CL-44D-4 – Operating empty 40,345kg (88,952lb), max takeoff 95,250kg (210,000lb).

Dimensions: CL-44D-4 – Wing span 43.37m (142ft 4in), length 41.73m (136ft 11in), height 11.18m (36ft 8in). Wing area 192.7m² (2075sq ft).

Capacity: Flightcrew of two pilots and one flight engineer. CL-44D-4 – Max single class seating for 178 passengers (or 214 in the CL-44J). Max payload 29,959kg (66,048kg).

Production: A total of 27 civil CL-44s built (incl one CL-400 conversion), and 12 military CC-106 Yukons, many of which later entered civil service. One Guppy conversion was in service in 2002.

History: The Bristol Britannia based Canadair CL-44 resulted from a mid 1950s Royal Canadian Air Force requirement for a maritime patrol aircraft.

What resulted was the CP-107 Argus. The Argus differed from the Britannia in a number of significant respects – it was powered by Wright Turbo Compound radial engines (selected in place of turboprops to give better endurance at low level), and had a redesigned unpressurised fuselage incorporating a weapons bay. With Canadair already producing the Argus, it was a relatively simple matter to offer a Britannia based design to meet an RCAF requirement for a freighter.

The freighter became the CC-106 Yukon (or to Canadair the CL-44D). Twelve were built, featuring Rolls-Royce Tyne turboprops, lengthened fuselage and wings and a conventional side loading large freight door. The first Yukon flew on November 15 1959.

Canadair then began to offer the Yukon to commercial customers and developed the CL-44D-4, which featured the hinged tail which considerably simplified loading. The first CL-44D-4 flew on November 16 1960, and at that time the model was the largest commercial freighter on offer in the world.

Most CL-44s in civil service have been used as freighters, but Icelandic airline Loftleidir operated three CL-44D-4s plus a single CL-44J as airliners. The J, or the CL-400, differed from the D-4s in that it featured a 4.62m (15ft 2in) fuselage stretch. Only one was built, two Loftleidir CL-44D-4s were also converted to CL-44Js.

One CL-44 was converted by Conroy Aircraft in the US as a large volume freighter with a new enlarged fuselage (similar to the Boeing 377 Super Guppy conversions), and it flew after conversion for the first time on November 26 1969. This aircraft is the last CL-44 of any type in use in 2002.

Several ex military Yukons found their way into civil service after retirement in 1973.

Photo: Teeside, England based Johnson International Airlines operates this Conroy converted CL-44. (Don Boyd)

Canadair CL-600 Challenger

Country of origin: Canada

Type: Medium to long range corporate jet

Powerplants: Two 33.6kN (7500lb) Avco Lycoming ALF 502L turbofans.

Performance: Max speed 904km/h (488kt), max cruising speed 890km/h (480kt), long range cruising speed 800km/h (432kt). Max operating altitude 45,000ft. Range with reserves (later build aircraft) 6300km (3402nm), or 5925km (3200nm) (earlier build aircraft).

Weights: Early build aircraft – Operating empty 10,353kg (22,825lb), max takeoff 18,325kg (40,400lb). Later build aircraft – Empty 8369kg (18,450lb), operating empty 10,285kg (22,675lb), max takeoff 18,201kg (40,125lb).

Dimensions: Wing span 18.85m (61ft 10in), length 20.85m (68ft 5in), height 6.30m (20ft 8in). Wing area 41.8m² (450sq ft).

Capacity: Flightcrew of two. Various customer seating options including 14, 15, 17 or 18 passenger configurations.

Production: 83 Challenger CL-600s built between 1978 and 1983. 81 were in service in late 2002.

History: The Canadair Challenger had a troubled early history but formed the basis for what became a very successful business jet.

In 1976 Canadair purchased the exclusive production, development and marketing rights to an all new business jet developed by Learjet designer Bill Lear. Known as the LearStar 600, this design was first conceived in 1974. Notable for its large size cabin, the LearStar promised long range and good operating economics and was also one of the first aircraft to be designed with a supercritical wing. Lear initially planned that the LearStar would be a trijet, but the design had evolved to become a twin by the time Canadair purchased the rights to it.

Canadair launched development of the LearStar design as the CL-600 Challenger on October 29 1976 with 53 firm orders. Canadair made a small number of changes to the design including repositioning the horizontal tailplane to the top of the fin.

Three development Challengers were built, the first flying on November 8 1978, the others flying in March and July the following year. However the first aircraft crashed in a deep stall accident and while certification was granted in August 1980, temporary restrictions limited maximum takeoff weight to 14,970kg (33,000lb) and maximum speed to 587km/h (317kt), with flight into known icing conditions and the use of thrust reversers prohibited.

A major weight and drag reduction program pared back the Challenger's weight, improving range. The General Electric CF34 powered Challenger CL-601 (described under Bombardier) further addressed performance shortfalls and overcame problems with the CL-600's ALF 502 turbofan.

One version that failed to see the light of day was the CL-610 Challenger E, which would have featured a fuselage stretch allowing seating for 24 passengers, but Canadair suspended development in 1981.

CL-600 production ceased in 1983, in favour of the much improved CL-601. The 600 can be distinguished from the 601 (and current 604 – described under Bombardier) by its different nacelles and its lack of winglets, although some have had winglets retrofitted.

Photo: A CL-600 Challenger gets airborne.

Country of origin: France

Type: Single and two seat aerobatic light aircraft

Powerplant: 10 B – One 135kW (180hp) Textron Lycoming AEIO-360-B2F fuel injected flat four piston engine driving a two blade fixed pitch prop. 21 – One 150kW (200hp) AEIO-360-A1B driving a two blade variable pitch prop. 232 – One 224kW (300hp) AEIO-540-L1B5 flat six driving a three or four blade c/s prop.

Performance: 10 B – Max speed 270km/h (146kt), max cruising speed at 75% power 250km/h (135kt). Initial rate of climb 1575ft/min. Service ceiling 16,400ft. Range with max fuel 1000km (540nm). 21 – Max cruising speed at 75% power 265km/h (143kt). Initial rate of climb 2755ft/min. Endurance with max fuel two hours. 232 – Max speed 339km/h (183kt). Initial rate of climb 3000ft/min. Service ceiling 15,000ft. Range with max fuel 1200km (647nm).

Weights: 10 B – Empty equipped 550kg (1213lb), max takeoff in aerobatic category 760kg (1675lb), or 830kg (1829lb) in utility category. 21 – Empty 500kg (1103lb), max takeoff 620kg (1367lb). 232 – Empty 590kg (1300lb), max takeoff 816kg (1800lb).

Dimensions: 10 B – Wing span 8.06m (26ft 5in), length 7.16m (23ft 6in), height 2.55m (8ft 5in). Wing area 10.9m² (116.8sq ft). 21 – Wing span 8.08m (26ft 6in), length 6.46m (21ft 3in), height 1.52m (5ft 0in). Wing area 9.2m² (99.0sq ft). 231 – Wing span 8.08m (26ft 6in), length 6.75m (22ft 2in), height 1.90m (6ft 3in). Wing area 9.9m² (106.1sq ft).

Capacity: Two side by side in CAP 10, all others pilot only.

Production: More than 290 CAP 10s and 10Bs, 40 CAP 21s, approximately 30 231s and 231 EXs and 35 232s built.

History: The successful CAP series of aerobatic aircraft dates back to the Piel C.P.30 Emeraude of the early 1960s.

Claude Piel designed the two seat Emeraude in France in the early 1960s for kit builders, but more than 200 were built in four different factories across Europe. The Emeraude first flew in 1962 and was built in basic 50kW (65hp) Continental A65 power C.P.30 form and 65kW (90hp) Continental C90 C.P.301 Super Emeraude form.

One of the companies to build the Emeraude was CAARP, a company owned by Auguste Mudry. CAARP used the basic Emeraude design as the basis for the CAP 10, which was a similar aircraft other than its 135kW (180hp) Lycoming IO-360 engine and stressing for aerobatic flight. The prototype CAP 10 first flew in August 1968. CAARP built 30 CAP 10s for the French air force before Mudry started production for civil orders in 1972 at his other aviation company, Avions Mudry.

The CAP 10 remains in production. From 1999 the 10 B form with an enlarged tail (certified 1970) was replaced by the 10 C with carbon fibre spar. The CAP 20 meanwhile was a single seat development with a 150kW (200hp) AEIO-360 engine.

The updated CAP 21 replaced the CAP 20 in 1981. The CAP 21 combined the fuselage of the CAP 20 with an all new wing and new undercarriage, and forms the basis for the similar CAP 231, CAP 231 EX (with a carbon fibre wing) and the current production CAP 232.

Akrotech Europe (owned by Aeronautique Service) took over the CAP series in early 1997 following Mudry's bankruptcy. Akrotech renamed itself CAP Aviation in January 1999.

Photo: An Australian registered CAP 232. (Michael Johnson)

Country of origin: United States of America

Type: Two seat light aircraft

Powerplants: 150 & 150M – One 75kW (100hp) Continental O-200-A flat four piston engine driving a two blade fixed pitch prop. A152 Aerobat – One 81kW (108hp) Lycoming O-235-N2C.

Performance: 150 – Max speed 200km/h (108kt), optimum cruising speed 196km/h (106kt). Initial rate of climb 640ft/min. Service ceiling 15,300ft. Range 563km (304nm). 150M – Max speed 201km/h (109kt), max cruising speed 196km/h (106kt), economical cruising speed 159km/h (86kt). Initial rate of climb 670ft/min. Service ceiling 12,250ft. Max range with no reserves 909km (490nm), or 1424km (769nm) with optional fuel. A152 – Max speed 200km/h (108kt), cruising speed 195km/h (105kt). Initial rate of climb 715ft/min. Range 575km (310nm).

Weights: 150 – Empty 447kg (985lb), max takeoff 681kg (1500lb). 150M – Empty 458kg (1010lb), max takeoff 726kg (1600lb). A152 – Empty 513kg (1131lb), max takeoff 760kg (1675lb).

Dimensions: 150 – Wing span 10.17m (33ft 4in), length 6.56m (21ft 6in), height 2.11m (6ft 11in). Wing area 14.8m² (159.5sq ft). 150M – Wing span 10.21m (33ft 6in), length 6.58m (21ft 7in), height 2.39m (7ft 10in). Wing area 14.6m² (157sq ft). A152 – Wing span 10.17m (33ft 4in), length 7.25m (24ft 1in), height 2.59m (8ft 6in). Wing area 14.9m² (160sq ft).

Capacity: Seating for two side by side.

Production: Total 150 and 152 production of 31,289 over 27 years, comprising 6860 US built 152s, 589 French built 152s, 22,082 US built 150s and 1758 French built 150s.

History: The introduction of the Cessna 150 marked Cessna's return to the two seat trainer market after a six year absence and resulted in the most prolific and successful two seat trainer line in history.

Development of the original 150 began in the mid 1950s, resulting in a first flight in September 1957. This all new aircraft followed the Cessna trends of a strut braced high wing, all metal construction and tricycle undercarriage. Production began in September 1958.

A continuous process of model improvement followed, although throughout the 150 model life the Continental O-200-A powerplant remained unchanged. One of the most significant model changes was the 150D of 1964 which introduced the wraparound rear window. The 150F (1966) introduced the swept back fin and rudder, the 150K (1970) conical wingtips.

Most versions were built in Standard, Commuter and Trainer forms with differing equipment levels, while licence production in France was undertaken by Reims (the FRA150 had a 97kW/130hp Rolls-Royce Continental O-240). Aerobat versions were stressed for limited aerobatic work (+6g, -3g).

The 152 was a response to availability problems with 80/87 octane fuel, and mated the 150 with a Lycoming O-235 running on 100 Octane (initially a 82kW/110hp O-235-L, later a 81kW/108hp O-235-N). The 152 replaced the 150 from 1977 and remained in production until late 1985. It too was progressively updated, offered in A152 Aerobat form and was built in France (as the F152 and FA152).

Photo: A Reims Cessna FRA150L Aerobat. (Paul Sadler)

Cessna 170

Country of origin: United States of America

Type: Four seat light aircraft

Powerplant: 170 – One 108kW (145hp) Continental C145-2 flat six piston engine driving a two blade fixed pitch McCauley propeller. 170B – One 108kW (145hp) Continental O-300-A.

Performance: 170 – Max speed 225km/h (122kt), max cruising speed 195km/h (106kt). Initial rate of climb 690ft/min. Service ceiling 15,000ft. Range 952km (514nm). 170B – Max speed 230km/h (124kt), max cruising speed 195km/h (106kt). Initial rate of climb 690ft/min. Service ceiling 15,500ft. Range 950km (513nm).

Weights: 170 – Empty 554kg (1220lb), max takeoff 998kg (2200lb). 170B – Empty 547kg (1205lb), max takeoff 998kg (2200lb).

Dimensions: Wing span 10.97m (36ft 0in), length 7.61m (24ft 11.5in), height 2.01m (6ft 7in). Wing area 16.2m² (174sq ft).

Capacity: Typical seating for four.

Production: 5173 Cessna 170s were built between 1948 and 1957, including 730 170s and 1537 170As.

History: A larger four seat development of the earlier Cessna Model 140, the four seat 170 was in production for almost a decade, and was the predecessor to the successful and long running 172 series.

Cessna developed the 170 as a low cost four seater to round out its product line. The prototype Cessna 170 (NX41691) first flew in September 1947, while the first production 170 flew on February 27 1948. Notable features included the six cylinder 110kW (145hp) Continental C145 engine (later redesignated O-300A), extensive metal instead of fabric covering and the characteristic Cessna braced high wing.

The first production Cessna 170s were delivered from March 1948, but this model was soon replaced by the improved 170A. The primary improvement with the 170A was metal instead of fabric covered wings with larger flaps, but it also featured a single strut under each wing (instead of two) and an increased tail area (identical to that used on the larger Cessna 195).

The third and final major variant appeared in 1953. The Cessna 170B featured the most significant revisions to the line, including the large semi Fowler wing flaps (first developed for the military L-19 Bird Dog and dubbed 'Para-lift' by Cessna marketing) that were to become characteristic of later single engine Cessna models, revised tail wheel steering, larger rear windows and revised and lengthened engine cowling.

The 170 remained in production until 1957, by which stage its popularity had waned and sales of the new 172 had taken off. The early 172 was a direct development of the 170, but introduced tricycle undercarriage and squared off vertical tail surfaces. The 170's most popular year was 1952 when 1186 were built.

The 170 laid the foundation for Cessna's two most successful single engine light aircraft lines, the 172 and 182, plus the 180 and 185. As well as the 172 tricycle undercarriage development, the 170 also formed the basis for the 180, which started as a more powerful, higher performance version of the 170, while the subsequent 182 was originally a tricycle undercarriage 180.

Photo: A Cessna 170B. (Peter Vercruijsse)

Cessna 180 & 185

Country of origin: United States of America

Type: Four to six seat utility light aircraft

Powerplant: 180 – One 168kW (225hp) Continental O-470-A flat six piston engine driving a two blade constant speed McCauley prop. 180G – One 172kW (230hp) O-470-R. A185F – One 225kW (300hp) fuel injected IO-520-D driving a three blade constant speed prop.

Performance: 180 – Max speed 267km/h (144kt), cruising speed 260km/h (140kt). Initial rate of climb 1150ft/min. Service ceiling 20,000ft. Range 1247km (673nm). 180G – Max speed 273km/h (147kt), max cruising speed 260km/h (141kt), long range cruising speed 195km/h (105kt). Initial rate of climb 1090ft/min. Service ceiling 19,600ft. Range with no reserves 1490km (804nm). A185F – Max speed 283km/h (153kt), max cruising speed 272km/h (147kt), long range cruising speed 207km/h (111kt). Initial rate of climb 1075ft/min. Service ceiling 17,900ft. Range with reserves 1575km (850nm).

Weights: 180 – Empty 690kg (1520lb), max takeoff 1158kg (2550lb). 180G – Empty 692kg (1525lb), max takeoff 1270kg (2800lb). A185F – Empty 783kg (1727lb), max takeoff 1520kg (3350lb).

Dimensions: 180 – Wing span 10.98m (36ft 0in), length 7.98m (26ft 2in), height 2.29m (7ft 6in). Wing area 16.2m² (174sq ft). 180G – Wing span 11.02m (36ft 2in), length 7.77m (25ft 6in), height 2.29m (7ft 6in). Wing area 16.2m² (174sq ft). A185F – Wing span 10.92m (35ft 10in), length 7.81m (25ft 8in). Wing area 16.2m².

Capacity: 180 has standard seating for four, 180 Skywagon and 185 have seating for six. 180H has optional 1360kg (3000lb) cargo pod. Often used with rear seats removed for cargo work. 185 Ag Carryall is fitted with a 571 litre (126Imp gal/151US gal) chemical hopper.

Production: Total 180 production of 6210. Total 185 production 4339 aircraft including 265 U-17A and 215 U-17B military variants and 109 Ag Carryalls.

History: The 180 started life as a more powerful development of the 170 four seater 'tourer', but evolved into a family of useful utility aircraft that was in production for over three decades.

The first 180s were essentially Model 170s with a more powerful 170kW (225hp) O-470-A engine. The first of the type flew in 1952 and deliveries began in February the following year. The 180's career as a high performance single was short lived due to the arrival of the tricycle undercarriage equipped 180 based 182 in 1956, but by then the type had established itself a useful niche as a utility aircraft.

Progressive updating of the line led to a range of updated models including the 170kW (230hp) 180A, and 1964's 180G with a third cabin window which from 1966 was offered as a six seater, by then having the same fuselage as the more powerful 185 Skywagon. The Skywagon name was applied to the 180 in 1969. The 180 remained in production until 1981.

The first 185 Skywagon flew in July 1960. It differed from the 180 in having a more powerful engine (195kW/260hp) and larger cabin, allowing six seats. Updated models include the 225kW (300hp) A185E from 1967 and the versatile Ag Carryall (introduced in late 1971) with removable chemical spraying equipment. From 1980 the previously optional three bladed prop became standard equipment.

Photo: A float equipped 185. (Peter Vercruijsse)

Cessna 172 Skyhawk (O-300 models)

Country of origin: United States of America

Type: Four seat light aircraft

Powerplants: 172 – One 108kW (145hp) Continental O-300-A flat six piston engine driving a two blade fixed pitch McCauley propeller. 175A – One 130kW (175hp) Continental GO-300-C geared flat six. 172F – One 108kW (145hp) Continental O-300-C.

Performance: 172 – Max speed 217km/h (117kt), cruising speed 200km/h (108kt). Initial rate of climb 660ft/min. Service ceiling 15,100ft. Range with no reserves 1000km (539nm). 175A – Max speed 236km/h (128kt), max cruising speed 225km/h (121kt), long range cruising speed 170km/h (91kt). Initial rate of climb 850ft/min. Service ceiling 15,900ft. Range with no reserves 957km (517nm). 172F – Max speed 222km/h (120kt), max cruising speed 211km/h (114kt), long range cruising speed 164km/h (88kt). Initial rate of climb 645ft/min. Service ceiling 13,100ft. Max range with no reserves 1158km (625nm).

Weights: 172 – Empty 572kg (1260lb), max takeoff 998kg (2200lb). 175A – Empty 607kg (1339lb), max takeoff 1066kg (2350lb). 172F – Empty 599kg (1320lb), max takeoff 1043kg (2300lb).

Dimensions: 172 – Wing span 10.92m (35ft 10in), length 8.20m (26ft 11in), height 2.59m (8ft 6in). Wing area 16.2m² (175sq ft). 175A – Wing span 10.97m (36ft 0in), length 8.08m (26ft 6in), height 2.72m (8ft 11in). 172F – Wing span 11.02m (36ft 2in), length 8.07m (26ft 6in), height 2.72m (8ft 11in).

Capacity: Typical seating for four in all models.

Production: Approx 15,800 civil Continental powered 172s built. Approx 2190 175 Skylarks built.

History: The Cessna 172 is without doubt the most successful mass produced light aircraft in history. From 1955 through to 1967 the Skyhawk was powered by the six cylinder Continental O-300, before this engine was replaced by the four cylinder Lycoming O-320.

The Cessna 172 started life as a tricycle undercarriage development of the 170, with a basic level of standard equipment. First flight was in November 1955. The 172 became an overnight sales success and over 1400 were built in 1956, its first full year of production.

The basic 172 remained in production until replaced by the 172A of early 1960. The 172A introduced a swept back tail and rudder, while the 172B of late 1960 introduced a shorter undercarriage, equipment changes and for the first time the Skyhawk name.

The 172D of 1963 introduced the cut down rear fuselage with wraparound rear window. The 172F introduced electric flaps and was built in France by Reims Cessna as the F172 through to 1971. It also formed the basis for the US Air Force's T-41A Mescalero primary trainer (over 850 T-41s were built in four models). The 172G of 1966 introduced a more pointed spinner, while the 172H (built until late 1967) was Cessna's last Continental powered 172.

The 175 Skylark was powered by a 130kW (175hp) geared GO-300, while the GO-300 powered P172D Powermatic of 1963 had a constant speed prop. The 1966 R172E had a Continental IO-360 and a constant speed prop. It was built in France as the FR172.

The O-320 powered 172 models are described separately.

Photo: A Cessna 172E Skyhawk. (Bill Lines)

Cessna 172 Skyhawk (O-320 models)

Country of origin: United States of America

Type: Four seat light aircraft

Powerplants: 172M – One 112kW (150hp) Lycoming O-320-E2D flat four piston engine driving a two blade fixed pitch propeller. R172 Hawk XP – One 145kW (195hp) Continental IO-360-KB fuel injected flat six driving a two blade constant speed propeller.

Performance: 172M – Max speed 232km/h (125kt), max cruising speed 222km/h (122kt), long range cruising speed 188km/h (102kt). Initial rate of climb 645ft/min. Service ceiling 13,000ft. Max range with no reserves and standard fuel 1125km (608nm), with optional fuel 1408km (760nm). R172 – Max speed 246km/h (133kt), max cruising speed 241km/h (130kt), long range cruising speed 177km/h (95kt). Initial rate of climb 870ft/min. Service ceiling 17,000ft. Max range with 45min reserves and standard fuel 1065km (575nm), with optional fuel 1510km (815nm).

Weights: 172M – Empty 624kg (1375lb), max takeoff 1043kg (2300lb). R172 – Empty 710kg (1565lb), max takeoff 1157kg (2550lb).

Dimensions: 172M – Wing span 10.92m (35ft 10in), length 8.21m (26ft 11in), height 2.68 (8ft 10in). Wing area 16.3m² (175sq ft). R172 – Span 10.92m (35ft 10in), length 8.28m (27ft 2in), height 2.68m (8ft 10in).

Capacity: Typical seating for four in all models.

Production: Approx 22,000 basic Lycoming powered 172s were built 1968-1985.

History: In the late 1960s Cessna re-engined its already highly successful 172 four seater with the four cylinder Lycoming O-320. These O-320 powered models were the most successful to bear the Skyhawk name.

Cessna re-engined the 172 with the Lycoming O-320-E, which compared with the O-300 had two less cylinders (and thus lower overhaul costs), a 200 hour greater TBO, improved fuel efficiency and more power. Even so, Cessna thought 172 production would be shortlived as the similarly powered but more modern 177 Cardinal was released at the same time. However the Lycoming powered 172 was a great success and far outsold and outlived its 'replacement'.

The first O-320 Skyhawk was the 172I introduced in 1968. The 1969 172K introduced a redesigned fin, reshaped rear windows and optional increased fuel capacity, while 1970's 172K sported conical camber wingtips and a wider track undercarriage. The 172L in production in the 1971/72 model years was the first to feature the enlarged dorsal fin fillet.

The 172M of 1973/76 gained a drooped wing leading edge for improved low speed handling. The 172M was also the first to introduce the optional 'II' package of higher standard equipment. Also in 1976 Cessna stopped marketing the aircraft as the 172.

The 172N was powered by a 120kW (160hp) O-320-H designed to run on 100 octane fuel, but the engine proved troublesome and was replaced by the similarly rated O-320-D in the 172P of 1981. The P was the last basic 172 model, remaining in production until 1985.

Higher performance 172s include the R172 Hawk XP, powered by a 145kW (195hp) Continental IO-360 and the 135kW (180hp) Lycoming O-360 powered, retractable undercarriage 172RG Cutlass.

Photo: A 172RG Cutlass. (Paul Sadler)

Cessna 172R Skyhawk & 172S Skyhawk SP

Cessna 177 Cardinal

Country of origin: United States of America

Type: Four seat light aircraft

Powerplants: 172R – One 120kW (160hp) Textron Lycoming IO-360-L2A fuel injected flat four piston engine driving a two blade fixed pitch McCauley propeller. 172S – One 135kW (180hp) IO-360-L2A.

Performance: 172R – Max cruising speed at sea level 228km/h (123kt), cruising speed at 75% power at 8000ft 226km/h (122kt). Initial rate of climb from sea level 720ft/min. Service ceiling 13,500ft. Range 1272km (687nm). 172S – Max cruising speed at sea level 233km/h (126kt), cruising speed at 75% power at 8500ft 229km/h (124kt). Initial rate of climb 730ft/min. Range 880km (475nm).

Weights: 172R – Empty 726kg (1600lb), max takeoff 1111kg (2450lb). 172S – Operating empty 730kg (1610lb), max takeoff 1160kg (2555lb)

Dimensions: Wing span 11.00m (36ft 1in), length 8.20m (26ft 11in), height 2.72m (8ft 11in). Wing area 16.3m² (175.5sq ft).

Capacity: Typical seating for four.

Production: Approx 1800 172Rs/172Ss delivered.

History: The hot selling Cessna 172R Skyhawk was one of three models Cessna returned to production in the mid 1990s after a decade long break from piston engine light aircraft manufacture.

Recession and crippling product liability laws in the USA forced Cessna to stop production of light aircraft in 1985. Following the passing in August 1994 of the General Aviation Revitalisation Act (in the USA) Cessna announced it would resume light aircraft production.

The new 172R Skyhawk features a fuel injected Textron Lycoming IO-360-L2A engine which Cessna says is significantly quieter than the O-320 it replaced as it produces its max power at only 2400rpm. Other changes include a new interior with contoured front seats which adjust vertically and recline, an all new multi level ventilation system, standard four point intercom, interior soundproofing, and energy absorbing 26g seats with inertia reel harnesses.

The 172R features epoxy corrosion proofing, stainless steel control cables, a dual vacuum pump system, tinted windows, long range fuel tanks, backlit instruments with non glare glass and an annunciator panel. 172R options include two avionics packages (one with GPS, the other with IFR GPS and a single axis autopilot) and wheel fairings.

An engineering prototype 172R (a converted 1978 172N) powered by an IO-360 first flew in April 1995, while the first new build pilot production 172R first flew on April 16 1996. This aircraft was built at Wichita, while production 172Rs are built at an all new factory in Independence, Kansas.

The higher performance 172S Skyhawk SP delivered from July 1998 features an IO-360-L2A (as on the 172R) but rated at 135kW (180hp) by increasing rpm. It also features a 45kg (100lb) increase in useful payload, a new prop and standard leather interior.

In 2000 Cessna released the limited Millennium Edition Skyhawk SP, featuring a new interior, optional IFR GPS, new paint and other detail improvements. Further improvements for all Cessna piston aircraft were announced in October 2000, including an optional 13cm (5in) multifunction liquid crystal display, and a revised interior.

Photo: A 172R. (Paul Sadler)

Country of origin: United States of America

Type: Four seat light aircraft

Powerplant: 177 – One 112kW (150hp) Lycoming O-320-E2D flat four piston engine driving a two blade fixed pitch McCauley propeller. 177B – One 135kW (180hp) Lycoming O-360-A1F6D driving a two blade constant speed McCauley prop. 177RG – One 150kW (200hp) Lycoming IO-360-A1B6 fuel injected flat four.

Performance: 177 – Max speed 227km/h (123kt), cruising speed 210km/h (113kt). Initial rate of climb 670ft/min. Service ceiling 12,700ft. Range 1215km (655nm). 177B – Max speed 250km/h (136kt), cruising speed 230km/h (124kt). Initial rate of climb 840ft/min. Service ceiling 14,600ft. Range 1120km (604nm). 177RG – Max speed 290km/h (156kt), long range cruising speed 223km/h (120kt). Initial rate of climb 925ft/min. Service ceiling 17,100ft. Max range with reserves 1657km (895nm).

Weights: 177 – Empty 608kg (1340lb), max takeoff 1067kg (2350lb). 177B – Empty 680kg (1495lb), max takeoff 1135kg (2500lb). 177RG – Empty 800kg (1671lb), max takeoff 1270kg (2800lb).

Dimensions: 177 – Wing span 10.85m (35ft 8in), length 8.22m (27ft 0in), height 2.77m (9ft 1in). Wing area 16.2m² (174sq ft). 177B – Wing span 10.82m (35ft 6in), length 8.44m (27ft 8in), height 2.62m (8ft 7in). Wing area 16.2m² (174sq ft). 177RG – Same except for length 8.31m (27ft 3in).

Capacity: Typical seating for four.

Production: 4240 177s built between 1968 and 1978, including 1490 RGs (including 176 RGs by Reims in France).

History: The Cessna 177 Cardinal was developed in the mid 1960s as an all new replacement for the 172 family.

Announced in late 1967, this new aircraft featured a wide cabin, a rear set flush riveted high wing for good visibility in turns, a single piece all moving tailplane, a high level of standard equipment and the 110kW (150hp) O-320-E recently installed on the 172 driving a fixed pitch prop. Offered in two versions, the standard 177 and up-spec Cardinal, it entered the marketplace priced around 10% more than the then current 172 model.

While not a failure, the 177 failed to attract anywhere near the sales volume of the 172 (in its first full year – 1968 – 601 were built, about half the number of 172s built that year). A perceived lack of power was addressed with the 135kW (180hp) O-360-A powered 177A introduced in late 1968. The increase in engine power and hence performance lifted the 177B into a more upmarket four seater market niche between the 172 and 182.

The 1970 model 177B introduced a revised aerofoil, conical camber wingtips, cowl flaps and a constant speed propeller. An up market version known as the Cardinal Classic appeared in 1978 with full IFR instrumentation and luxury interior fittings.

The 177RG was announced in December 1970, and, as its designation suggests, featured hydraulically actuated retractable undercarriage, plus a 150kW (200hp) fuel injected IO-360-A engine and a constant speed prop.

Both the 177B and 177RG remained in production until 1978.

Photo: An American registered 177RG Cardinal. (Gary Gentle)

Cessna 182 Skylane

Country of origin: United States of America

Type: Four seat light aircraft

Powerplants: 182 – One 170kW (230hp) Continental O-470-R flat six piston engine driving a two blade constant speed propeller. TR182 – One 175kW (235hp) Lycoming O-540-L3C5D turbocharged flat six. 182R – One 170kW (230hp) Continental O-470-U.

Performance: 182 – Max speed 257km/h (140kt), cruising speed 253km/h (136kt). Initial rate of climb 1200ft/min. Service ceiling 20,000ft. Range 1078km (582nm). TR182 – Max speed 346km/h (187kt), economical cruising speed 232km/h (125kt). Initial rate of climb 1040ft/min. Service ceiling 20,000ft. Range 1870km (1010nm). 182R – Max speed 275km/h (149kt), cruising speed 246km/h (133kt). Initial rate of climb 865ft/min. Service ceiling 14,900ft. Range with max fuel and reserves 1898km (1025nm).

Weights: 182 – Empty 735kg (1621lb), max takeoff 1160kg (2550lb). TR182 – Empty 837kg (1845lb), max takeoff 1406kg (3100lb). 182R – Empty 786kg (1733lb), max takeoff 1406kg (3100lb).

Dimensions: 182 – Wing span 10.98m (36ft 0in), length 25.17m (25ft 2in), height 2.80m (9ft 2in). Wing area 16.2m² (174sq ft). TR182 & 182R – Wing span 10.92m (35ft 10in), length 8.53m (28ft 0in), height 2.82m (9ft 3in). Wing area 16.2m² (174sq ft).

Capacity: Typical seating for four.

Production: 21,864 182s (including 169 R182s by Reims) built.

History: The popular, relatively high performance Cessna 182 began life as a tricycle development of the 180.

The first Model 182 appeared in 1956 while the Skylane name was first introduced with the 1958 182A development to denote an optional higher level of equipment. Major changes were introduced with 1960's 182C, including a third window on each side of the cabin, a swept vertical tail and a 45kg (100lb) increase in gross weight. The 182D of 1961 had shorter undercarriage and a redesigned engine cowl.

The 182E of 1962 introduced the cut down rear fuselage with wrap around rear window, improved O-470-R engine, more fuel and optional autopilot. The 182F had more fuel and could seat six with an optional rear cabin seat for two children. The 182G to 182L models introduced detail changes (some 182Js, as A182s, were built in Argentina). The 182M (1970) has an increased takeoff weight, the 182N (1972) introduced the 'Camber Lift' wing with bonded leading edge and tubular spring steel main undercarriage legs. The 182P (1977) introduced the O-470-U which ran on 100 octane fuel. The 182Q and 182R had a bonded wing with integral fuel tanks.

The retractable undercarriage Skylane RG arrived in 1977, giving a significant speed increase. A further performance boost came with the introduction of the turbocharged 175kW (235hp) Lycoming O-540-L engine on the T182RG, which became available from 1979. The AiResearch turbocharger meant that max power could be delivered right up to the 182's service ceiling of 20,000ft. A turbocharged fixed gear model was also offered, but only small numbers were built.

Cessna 182 production initially ceased in 1985, the new build 182S, 182T and T182T are described separately.

Photo: A 182H Skylane. (Glenn Alderton)

Cessna 182S/T Skylane & T182T Turbo Skylane

Country of origin: United States of America

Type: Four seat light aircraft

Powerplants: 182S/T – One 172kW (230hp) Textron Lycoming IO-540-AB1A5 flat six piston engine driving a three blade constant speed propeller. T182T – One 175kW (235hp) TIO-540-AK1A turbocharged flat six.

Performance: 182T – Max speed at sea level 276km/h (149kt), cruising speed at 80% power 267km/h (144kt). Initial rate of climb 924ft/min. Service ceiling 18,100ft. Range with reserves at 75% power at 6000ft 1565km (845nm), at 55% power at 10,000ft 1793km (968nm). T182T – Max speed at S/L 326km/h (176kt), cruising speed at 88% power at 12,000ft 293km/h (158kt). Initial rate of climb 1040ft/min. Max range 1798km (971nm).

Weights: 182T – Standard empty 875kg (1928lb), max takeoff 1406kg (3100lb). T182T – Standard empty 929kg (2048lb).

Dimensions: 182T – Wing span 10.97m (36ft 0in), length 8.84m (29ft 0in), height 2.84m (9ft 4in). Wing area 16.3m2 (175.5sq ft).

Capacity: Typical seating for four.

Production: 182S deliveries began April 1997. T182T and 182T deliveries began May 2001. Over 1000 built by late 2002.

History: The 182S, 182T and T182T Skylane are new production models of Cessna's popular 182.

The popularity of Cessna's 182 is well illustrated by its 20,000+ production run through to 1985 (second only to the 172). So it's not surprising that the 182 was one of three models Cessna decided to return to production following the signing of the General Aviation Revitalisation Bill in the USA in 1994.

The new production 182S was based on the 182R but features a new powerplant, a Textron Lycoming IO-540 driving a three blade propeller, in place of the earlier Continental IO-470 (Textron owns both Cessna and Lycoming). Numerous detail changes and improvements were also incorporated, including a metal instrument panel, Honeywell avionics, and interior improvements.

Cessna built three preproduction 182S Skylanes at its Wichita, Kansas facility, the first of which first flew on July 16 1996. US FAA certification was awarded on October 3 1996 and the first production 182S was delivered from Cessna's new Independence, Kansas plant (built specifically for new production of Cessna singles) in April 1997.

In April 2000 Cessna introduced the limited edition Millennium Edition Skylane, featuring a new interior with leather seats, optional IFR GPS, new paint and other detail improvements.

In October 2000 Cessna announced the improved 182T and the reintroduction of a turbocharged Skylane with the T182T. Both feature aerodynamic improvements including redesigned wingtips, while the T182T, like the original turbocharged Skylane, features a TIO-540, improving rate of climb, takeoff and high altitude performance.

T182T Turbo Skylane and 182T deliveries began in May 2001. They incorporate improvements for all Cessna piston singles announced in October 2000, including an optional 13cm (5in) multifunction liquid crystal display, and a revised interior.

Photo: A 182S Skylane. (Lance Higgerson)

Cessna 205, 206 & 207

Country of origin: United States of America

Type: Six seat utility light aircraft

Powerplant: 205 – One 195kW (260hp) Continental IO-470-S fuel injected flat six piston engine, driving a two blade constant speed McCauley prop. TU206F – One 210kW (285hp) Continental TSIO-520-C turbocharged and fuel injected flat six driving a two or three bladed c/s prop. 207A – One 225kW (300hp) Continental IO-520-F fuel injected flat six driving a three blade c/s McCauley prop.

Performance: 205 – Max speed 278km/h (150kt), max cruising speed 262km/h (140kt), long range cruising speed 183km/h (99kt). Initial rate of climb 965ft/min. Service ceiling 16,100ft. Range with no reserves 2050km (1110nm). TU206F – Max speed 321km/h (174kt), max cruising speed 296km/h (160kt), long range cruising speed 274km/h (148kt). Initial rate of climb 1030ft/min. Service ceiling 26,300ft. Range at long range cruising speed 1327km (717nm). 207A – Max speed 278km/h (150kt), max cruising speed 266km/h (144kt), long range cruising speed 220km/h (118kt). Initial rate of climb 810ft/min. Service ceiling 13,300ft. Range with standard fuel and reserves 871km (470nm), with optional fuel and reserves 1280km (690nm).

Weights: 205 – Empty 795kg (1750lb), max takeoff 1497kg (3300lb). TU206F – Empty 880kg (1940lb), max takeoff 1634kg (3600lb). 207A – Empty 951kg (2095lb), max takeoff 1730kg (3812lb).

Dimensions: 205 – Wing span 11.15m (36ft 7in), length 8.46m (27ft 9in), height 2.75m (9ft 0in). Wing area 16.30m² (175.5sq ft). TU206F – Wing span 10.92m (35ft 10in), length 8.54m (28ft 0in), height 2.95m (9ft 8in). Wing area 16.18m² (174sq ft). 207A – Same as 206 except for length 9.80m (32ft 2in).

Capacity: 205 & 206 seat six, 207 seats seven or eight.

Production: 574 205s, 7556 206s, and 790 207s were built.

History: In concept the 205/206/207 line began life as a six seat utility flying station wagon.

The initial 205 was a fixed undercarriage derivative of the 210B Centurion, optimised for utility roles. Introduced to the Cessna lineup in 1962, the 205 was powered by the same IO-470 engine as the 210B and featured an additional small cargo door on the left side of the fuselage to allow access to the rear seats for removal and the baggage compartment.

The 205 was replaced in 1963 by the more powerful IO-520 powered 206, which featured larger double cargo doors on the right fuselage side and was known as the Super Skywagon. Continuous product improvement followed, including adding a turbocharged and fuel injected model, while the prefix 'Super' was dropped in 1969, and the Stationair name was adopted in 1971. Production ceased in 1985, however in 1994 Cessna announced it planned to return the 206 into production.

The 207 Skywagon featured a 1.07m (3ft 6in) fuselage stretch (allowing seating for seven) and became available from 1969. Known as the Stationair 7 from 1978, it was replaced by the 207A Stationair 8 from 1979 which had seating for an eighth occupant. Production ended in 1984.

Photo: A 207 Stationair. (Theo Van Loon)

Cessna 206H & T206H

Country of origin: United States of America

Type: Six seat utility light aircraft

Powerplant: 206H – One 224kW (300hp) Textron Lycoming IO-540-AC1A driving a three blade c/s prop. T206H – One 231kW (310hp) turbocharged TIO-540-AJ1A.

Performance: 206H – Max speed 278km/h (150kt), cruising speed at 75% power at 6500ft 143kt (265km/h). Initial rate of climb 920ft/min. Service ceiling 16,000ft. Range at 75% power 1120km (605nm), at 55% power 1352km (730nm). T206H – Max speed 330km/h (178kt), cruise speed at 75% at 20,000ft 306km/h (165kt). Initial rate of climb 1050ft/min. Service ceiling 27,000ft. Range at 75% power at 20,000ft 1052km (568nm), max range 1281km (692nm).

Weights: 206H – Empty 974kg (2146lb), max takeoff 1632kg (3614lb). T206H – Empty 1031kg (2274lb), max takeoff 1632kg (3614lb).

Dimensions: 206H & T206H – Wing span 10.97m (36ft 0in), length 8.62m (28ft 3in), height 2.83m (9ft 4in). Wing area 16.3m² (175.5sq ft).

Capacity: 206 seats six.

Production: Deliveries began December 1998. Approx 400 206Hs & T206Hs delivered by late 2002.

History: The popular 206 utility was the third piston single Cessna returned to production at the company's new Independence plant in Kansas in the 1990s.

Two versions are offered, the normally aspirated 206H and turbocharged T206H. The T206H first flew on August 6 1996, powered by a TIO-580, while the normally aspirated 206H, powered by an IO-580, followed on November 6. Cessna decided to switch to the TIO-540 and IO-540 because of reliability concerns which delayed production. The 206H was certificated on September 9 1998, the T206H on October 1. Deliveries began that December, with 10 206Hs for the Uruguayan air force.

Apart from the new engines, the 206H and T206H introduced a range of other improvements over earlier 206s, including new Honeywell avionics, epoxy corrosion proofing, cabin interior improvements and numerous detail changes.

Optional equipment on the 206H and T206H includes stabiliser abrasion boots, a cargo pod, propeller anti-ice system and oversized tyres and wheel fairings. A floatplane conversion kit is also offered.

As with the 172 and 182, Cessna offered Millennium Edition models of the 206 and T206. These featured a redesigned interior with leather seats, Honeywell KLN 94 IFR GPS, new exterior paint scheme and polished spinner.

From the 2001 model year the 206H and T206H introduced aerodynamic improvements including redesigned wingtips, improved landing gear fairings, plus interior enhancements with sculptured composite side panels with integrated armrests and cupholders, and a 12 volt electrical port for laptop computers or portable GPS units. An optional a 12.7cm (5in) Honeywell colour multifunction liquid crystal display was also introduced.

Photo: A float equipped 206H. (Cessna)

Cessna 210 Centurion

Country of origin: United States of America

Type: High performance four to six seat light aircraft

Powerplant: 210L – One 225kW (300hp) Continental IO-520-L fuel injected flat six piston engine driving a three blade constant speed McCauley prop. T210M – One 230kW (310hp) fuel injected and turbocharged TSIO-520R, driving a constant speed three blade prop. P210R – One 240kW (325hp) turbocharged and fuel injected TSIO-520-CE.

Performance: 210L – Max speed 324km/h (175kt), max cruising speed 317km/h (171kt), long range cruising speed 249km/h (134kt). Initial rate of climb 950ft/min. Service ceiling 17,300ft. Max range with reserves 1972km (1065nm). T210M – Max speed 380km/h (205kt), max cruising speed 367km/h (198kt), long range cruising speed 260km/h (140kt). Initial rate of climb 1030ft/min. Service ceiling 28,500ft. Range at long range cruising speed 1455km (785nm). P210R – Max speed 417km/h (225kt) at 20,000ft, max cruising speed 394km/h (213kt) at 23,000ft. Initial rate of climb 1150ft/min. Service ceiling 25,000ft. Range with reserves and optional fuel 2205km (1190nm).

Weights: 210L – Empty 1015kg (2238lb), max takeoff 1725kg (3800lb). T210M – Empty 1022kg (2250lb), max takeoff 1725kg (3800lb). P210R – Empty 1120kg (2470lb), MTOW 1860kg (4100lb).

Dimensions: 210 – Wing span 11.21m (36ft 9in), length 8.59m (28ft 2in). Wing area 16.3m² (175.5sq ft). T210M – Wing span 11.21m (36ft 9in), length 8.59m (28ft 2in), height 2.87m (9ft 5in). Wing area same. P210R – Wing span 11.84m (38ft 10in), length 8.59m (28ft 2in), height 2.95m (9ft 8in). Wing area 17.2m² (185.5sq ft).

Capacity: Typical seating for four with optional seating for extra two children in some models, or seating for six adults in later versions.

Production: 9240 built including 843 P210s.

History: During its production life the Cessna 210 was at the top of the Cessna single piston engine model lineup, positioned between the 182 and the 310 twin.

The 210 first flew in January 1957 and it was the first single engine Cessna aircraft to feature retractable undercarriage and swept back vertical tail surfaces. The 210 entered production in late 1959, and from that time the line was constantly updated.

Notable early upgrades include the 210B which introduced the wraparound rear windows, the 210D with a more powerful (213kW/285hp) engine and introduced the Centurion name, and the turbocharged T210F. The 210G dispensed with the traditional strutted wing in favour of a cantilever wing, increased fuel capacity, restyled rear windows and enlarged tail surfaces. The 210K had a 224kW (300hp) IO-520-L. Continual development of the 210 and T210 range continued through until production ceased in 1985.

A significant development of the T210 was the high performance, pressurised P210 which first appeared in 1978. The pressurisation system (based on that in the 337 Skymaster) meant that the cabin's internal altitude was equivalent to 8000ft when flying at 17,350ft. P210s can be identified by their four small cabin windows.

Photo: The P210 was the first pressurised single to reach quantity production. (Keith Myers)

Cessna 188 Ag Wagon series

Country of origin: United States of America

Type: Agricultural aircraft

Powerplant: Ag Truck – One 225kW (300hp) Continental IO-520-D fuel injected flat six piston engine driving a two blade fixed pitch or three blade constant speed McCauley propeller. Ag Husky – One 230kW (310hp) Continental TSIO-520-T turbocharged and fuel injected flat six driving a three blade constant speed McCauley prop.

Performance: Ag Truck – Max speed 196km/h (106kt), max cruising speed 187km/h (101kt). Initial rate of climb 465ft/min. Service ceiling 7800ft/min. Range with max fuel and reserves at 75% power 465km (252nm). Ag Husky – Max speed 209km/h (113kt), max cruising speed (75% power) 196km/h (106kt). Initial rate of climb 510ft/min. Certificated service ceiling 14,000ft. Range with max fuel and reserves at max cruising speed 402km (217nm).

Weights: Ag Truck – Empty 1015kg (2235lb), max takeoff 1495kg (3300lb), max takeoff restricted ag category 1905kg (4200lb). Ag Husky – Empty 1045kg (2305lb), max takeoff restricted ag category 1995kg (4400lb).

Dimensions: Ag Truck – Wing span 12.70m (41ft 8in), length 7.90m (25ft 11in), height 2.49m (8ft 2in). Wing area 19.1m² (205sq ft). Ag Husky – Same except for length 8.08m (26ft 6in).

Capacity: Pilot only in all models. Standard hopper capacity of 757 litres (166Imp gal/200US gal) for Ag Wagon & Ag Pickup; Ag Truck & Ag Husky have a 1059 litre (233Imp gal/280US gal) capacity.

Production: Approximate total of 3975 including 53 Ag Pickups, 1589 Ag Wagons, 1949 Ag Trucks and 385 Ag Huskies.

History: The successful Ag Wagon 188 series was Cessna's only purpose designed agricultural aircraft.

Cessna's Model 188 resulted from research and consultation with agricultural aircraft operators conducted in the early 1960s. The design Cessna settled upon was of the conventional agricultural aircraft arrangement with a braced low wing (unique among Cessna singles) with seating for the pilot only. Like other ag aircraft the chemical hopper is made of fibreglass and the rear fuselage is of semi monocoque construction and sealed to reduce the potential for damage from chemical contamination.

The prototype Cessna 188 Ag Wagon first flew on February 19 1965, while type approval was awarded the following February. The 188 was initially offered in two forms, the 170kW (230hp) Continental O-470-R powered 188 (which was named the Ag Pickup from 1972) and the 250kW (300hp) Continental IO-520-D powered 188A Ag Wagon.

The 1972 model year also saw the introduction of the most successful 188 model, the Ag Truck. The Ag Truck has the same powerplant as the Ag Wagon, but a larger hopper and a higher max takeoff weight. The ultimate 188 model is the Ag Husky, which was introduced in 1979. It features a turbocharged TSIO-520-T and a further increased max takeoff weight.

Production of the Ag Pickup was suspended in 1976, the Ag Wagon in 1981, and the Ag Truck and Ag Husky in 1985, when all Cessna light aircraft manufacturing was suspended.

Photo: An A188 Ag Wagon. (Les Bushell)

Cessna 310 & 320

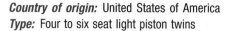

Country of origin: United States of America

Type: Four to six seat light piston twins

Powerplants: 310B – Two 180kW (240hp) Continental O-470-M flat six piston engines driving two blade constant speed McCauley propellers. T310P – Two 213kW (285hp) turbocharged and fuel injected TSIO-520-Bs. 310R – Two 213kW (285hp) Continental IO-520-MBs.

Performance: 310B – Max speed 383km/h (207kt), cruising speed 291km/h (157kt). Initial rate of climb 1800ft/min. Service ceiling 19,800ft. Range no reserves 1617km (873nm). T310P – Max speed 442km/h (237kt), max cruising speed 418km/h (226kt) at 20,000ft, long range cruising speed 288km/h (156kt) at 10,000ft. Initial rate of climb 1862ft/min. Service ceiling 28,600ft. Range at max cruise (no reserves and std fuel) 1226km (662nm) at 10,000ft, 3146km (1699nm) at 20,000ft. 310R – Max speed 383km/h (207kt), max cruising speed 360km/h (195kt), long range cruising speed 267km/h (144kt). Initial rate of climb 1662ft/min. Service ceiling 19,750ft. Max range with reserves 1170km (632nm), with reserves and optional fuel 2840km (1535nm).

Weights: 310B – Empty equipped 1436kg (3166lb), max takeoff 2190kg (4830lb). T310P – Empty 1493kg (3292lb), max takeoff 2268kg (5400lb). 310R – Empty equipped 1480kg (3260lb), max takeoff 2495kg (5500lb).

Dimensions: 310B – Wing span 10.88m (35ft 9in), length 8.23m (27ft 0in), height 3.20m (10ft 6in). Wing area 16.3m² (175sq ft). T310P – Wing span 11.25m (36ft 11in), length 8.92m (29ft 3in), height 3.02m (9ft 11in). Wing area 16.6m² (179sq ft). 310R – Wing span 11.25m (36ft 11in), length 9.74m (32ft 0in), height 3.25m (10ft 8in). Wing area 16.6m² (179sq ft).

Capacity: Typical seating for four or five, with an optional sixth seat.

Production: 6013 310s and 320s built, including 575 320s and 196 for the US Army (160 U-3As) and Air Force (36 U-3Bs).

History: The sleek Cessna 310 was the first twin engine design from Cessna to enter production after WW2.

The 310 first flew on January 3 1953. The modern lines of the new twin were backed up by innovative features such as engine exhaust thrust augmentor tubes and the storage of all fuel in tip tanks. Deliveries commenced in late 1954.

The first significant upgrade to the 310 line came with the 310C of 1959, which introduced more powerful 195kW (260hp) IO-470-D engines. The 310D of 1960 featured swept back vertical tail surfaces. An extra cabin window was added with the 310F. A development of the 310F was the turbocharged 320 Skyknight, with TSIO-470-B engines and a fourth cabin side window. The Skyknight was in production between 1961 and 1969 (the 320E was named the Executive Skyknight), when it was replaced by the similar Turbo 310.

The 310G introduced the 'stabila-tip' tip tanks, while the 310K replaced the rear two windows on each side with a single unit. Subsequent significant developments include the 310Q and turbocharged T310Q with redesigned rear cabin with a skylight window, and the final 310R and T310R with lengthened noses. Production ended in 1980.

Photo: A Cessna 310R. (Paul Sadler)

Cessna 336 & 337 Skymaster

Country of origin: United States of America

Type: Six seat light piston twins

Powerplants: 337D – Two 157kW (210hp) Continental IO-360-C fuel injected flat six piston engines driving two blade c/s props. T337G – Two 170kW (225hp) turbocharged and fuel injected TSIO-360-Cs.

Performance: 337D – Max speed 320km/h (173kt), max cruising speed at 75% power 306km/h (167kt), econ cruising speed 232km/h (125kt). Initial rate of climb 1200ft/min. Service ceiling 19,500ft. Range at max cruise with no reserves and std fuel 1223km (660nm), with opt fuel 1706km (921nm). T337G – Max speed 402km/h (217kt), max cruising speed 380km/h (205kt), long range cruising speed 273km/h (147kt). Initial rate of climb 1250ft/min. Operational ceiling 20,000ft. Range with no reserves 2422km (1308nm) at 16,000ft.

Weights: 337D – Empty 1204kg (2655lb), max takeoff 1995kg (4400lb). T337G – Empty 1444kg (3184lb), MTOW 2132kg (4700lb).

Dimensions: 337D – Wing span 11.58m (38ft 0in), length 9.07m (29ft 9in), height 2.84m (9ft 4in). Wing area 18.7m² (201sq ft). T337G – Wing span 11.63m (38ft 2in), length 9.07m (29ft 9in), height 2.84m (9ft 4in). Wing area 18.7m² (201sq ft).

Capacity: Typical seating for six. Optional underbelly cargo pod.

Production: 336 total production of 195 between 1962 and 1964. 337 production comprised 1859 337s, 332 pressurised 337s and 513 military versions. Reims built 67 standard and 27 pressurised 337s.

History: Cessna's 336 and 337 Skymaster twins were designed to overcome conventional twins' problems of engine out asymmetric flight handling characteristics through their distinctive push-pull engines and twin boom configuration.

Cessna called the layout concept 'Center Line Thrust', as the nose mounted tractor and rear fuselage mounted pusher engines eliminated asymmetric handling problems normally experienced when one of a twin's engines fails. The concept was recognised by the US FAA which created a new centre thrust rating for pilots to be rated on the type.

The fixed undercarriage Model 336 first flew on February 18 1961, but significant improvements to the design were made before production aircraft were delivered. Changes included more powerful engines, a larger fuselage with seating for six, and revised wing, tail and rear engine cowling. The 336 was delivered from mid 1963 and production lasted until late 1964 when it was replaced by the 337 Super Skymaster ('Super' was later dropped) which was released in February 1965.

The improved 337 Super Skymaster ('Super' was dropped in 1972) introduced retractable undercarriage, more powerful 160kW (210hp) engines, a dorsal air intake for the rear engine, variable cowl flaps, repositioned forward engine and cowl for improved visibility, and higher weights.

The turbocharged T337 was first released in the 1967 model year, dropped in 1972 and relaunched in 1978, while the ultimate 337 was the T337G Pressurised Skymaster, introduced from August 1972.

Development of the 337 continued in France by Reims after Cessna production ended in 1980, resulting in the FTB337 STOL and the military FTMA Milirole. Cessna also built more than 500 337s as O-2s for the US Air Force, used largely in the Forward Air Control role.

Photo: A 337G Super Skymaster. (Gordon Reid)

Cessna 411, 401 & 402

Country of origin: United States of America

Type: Freighter, 10 seat commuter, or six to eight seat business twins

Powerplants: 411A – Two 255kW (340hp) Continental GTSIO-520-C turbocharged, geared and fuel injected flat six piston engines driving three blade constant speed propellers. 402C – Two 240kW (325hp) turbocharged and fuel injected TSIO-520-VBs.

Performance: 411A – Max speed 431km/h (233kt), max cruising speed 396km/h (214kt), long range cruising speed 283km/h (153kt). Initial rate of climb 1900ft/min. Service ceiling 26,000ft. Range with std fuel (no res) 2003km (1081nm), with opt fuel 2310km (1247nm). 402C – Max speed 428km/h (230kt), max cruising speed 394km/h (213kt), long range cruising speed 304km/h (164kt). Initial rate of climb 1450ft/min. Ceiling 26,900ft. Range at econ cruising speed 2360km (1273nm).

Weights: 411A – Empty 1973kg (4350lb), max takeoff 2948kg (6500lb). 402C – Empty (Businessliner) 1845kg (4069lb), max takeoff 3107kg (6850lb).

Dimensions: 411 – Wing span 12.15m (39ft 10in), length 10.20m (33ft 6in), height 3.52m (11ft 7in). Wing area 18.6m² (200sq ft). 402C – Wing span 13.45m (44ft 2in), length 11.09m (36ft 5in), height 3.49m (11ft 6in). Wing area 21.0m² (225.8sq ft).

Capacity: 411 & 401 – Standard seating for six with a centre aisle between the four main cabin seats. 402 – Six to eight seats in corporate configured Businessliner, 10 seats or freight in Utililiner.

Production: 301 Cessna 411s, 404 Cessna 401s and 1535 402s built.

History: Cessna's 411 eight seat cabin class twin competed with the previously dominant market leader, the Beech Queen Air.

The 411 was more modern than the Queen Air, lighter, smaller and faster. The prototype first flew in July 1962 and differed from the following production aircraft in having two blade props and direct drive engines. Production aircraft featured geared GTSIO-520-C engines driving three blade props.

Deliveries began in October 1964. Optional features for corporate configured aircraft included folding tables, a toilet and refreshment centre. The 411 was followed up by the 411A from 1967 with lighter and more efficient props and optional extra fuel capacity.

Production of the 411 ceased in 1968, replaced by the 401 and 402, which had first been introduced in late 1966. These developments of the 411 were lighter, less powerful and had direct drive engines, and thus were less costly to operate. While the 401 and 402 were essentially the same aircraft, the 401 was optimised for corporate transport and was fitted with fewer seats than the 402, which was configured for commuter and freighter work. A number of versions of both models were developed with minor refinements, including the 402A, which had a lengthened nose, square windows and an optional 10th seat.

The 402B replaced the 401 and 402A from mid 1972, and was offered in Businessliner corporate and Utililiner convertible passenger/freighter configurations and introduced rectangular cabin windows. The 402C appeared in late 1978 and featured the longer span wings from the 414A and 421C (without tip tanks) and more powerful engines. It remained in production until 1985.

Photo: A Cessna 402C. (Gerard Williamson)

Cessna 421 & 414

Country of origin: United States of America

Type: Pressurised six to eight seat cabin twins

Powerplants: 421C – Two 280kW (374hp) Continental GTSIO-520-L geared, turbocharged and fuel injected flat six piston engines driving three blade constant speed McCauley propellers. 414A – Two 230kW (310hp) TSIO-520-NBs.

Performance: 421C – Max speed 478km/h (258kt), max cruising speed 447km/h (241kt) at 25,000ft, long range cruising speed 356km/h (192kt) at 25,000ft. Initial rate of climb 1940ft/min. Service ceiling 30,200ft. Max range at 25,000ft with reserves and standard fuel 2016km (1089nm) or 2748km (1484nm) with optional fuel. 414A – Max speed 436km/h (235kt), cruising speed 420km/h (227kt), economical cruising speed 340km/h (183kt). Initial rate of climb 1520ft/min. Service ceiling 30,800ft. Range with reserves at economical cruising speed 2460km (1327nm), at max cruising speed 2036km (1100nm).

Weights: 421C – Empty equipped 2298kg (5067lb), MTOW 3379kg (7450lb). 414A – Empty 1976kg (4356lb), MTOW 3062kg (6750lb).

Dimensions: 421C – Wing span 12.53m (41ft 2in), length 11.09m (36ft 5in), height 3.49m (11ft 6in). Wing area 20.0m² (215sq ft). 414A – Wing span 13.45m (44ft 2in), length 11.09m (36ft 5in), height 3.49m (11ft 6in). Wing area 21.0m² (225.8sq ft).

Capacity: Standard seating for six, optional seating for eight in 421 and 414A, seven in 414.

Production: 1901 Model 421s and 1055 Model 414s built, production of both ceased in 1985.

History: The lineage of the 421 and 414 traces back to the 411, the 421 beginning life as a pressurised development of the 411.

The prototype 421 first flew in October 1965 (three years after the 411). In comparison to the 411 on which it was based, the 421 introduced a cabin pressurisation system (with a differential of 0.3 bar/4.2psi), more powerful geared and turbocharged GTSIO-520-D engines (the turbochargers also drove the pressurisation system) and a higher max takeoff weight. Deliveries of production 421s began in May 1967, Cessna claiming the 421 as the cheapest pressurised twin available.

Minor improvements were introduced with the 421A in 1969. The 421B Golden Eagle of 1970 featured a number of significant changes including lengthened nose (by 71cm/2ft 4in) and wing span, and GTSIO-520-H engines which retained their power rating to a higher altitude than before. The 421C Golden Eagle was available from late 1975, introducing a bonded wet wing with no tip tanks, higher vertical tail, more efficient props and new trailing link undercarriage.

The 414 was developed as a less powerful, lighter, simpler and lower cost 421. First flown in 1968, it entered production in 1969. It features the fuselage of the 401 and 402 (both lighter developments of the 411) with the 421's pressurised fuselage, plus direct drive, rather than geared engines. The 414A Chancellor appeared in 1978, introducing the bonded wet wing without tip tanks and the Golden Eagle's longer nose. It remained in production until 1985.

Photo: A 421B Golden Eagle. (Lance Higgerson)

Cessna 404 Titan

Country of origin: United States of America

Type: Ten seat corporate and utility piston twin

Powerplants: Two 280kW (375hp) Continental GTSIO-520-M geared, turbocharged and fuel injected flat six piston engines driving three blade constant speed McCauley propellers.

Performance: Max speed 430km/h (238kt), max cruising speed 402km/h (217kt) at 20,000ft, 369km/h (199kt) at 10,000ft, economical cruising speed 302km/h (163kt) at 20,000ft, 259km/h (140kt) at 10,000ft. Initial rate of climb 1940ft/min. Service ceiling 26,000ft. Range with 936kg (2064lb) useable fuel and reserves at 75% power at 20,000ft 2717km (1466nm), at 10,000ft 2501km (1350nm), at economical cruising speed at 20,000ft 3410km (1840nm), at 10,000ft 3404km (1837nm).

Weights: Empty 2192kg (4834lb) for Ambassador, 2205kg (4861lb) for Courier, 2133kg (4702lb) for Freighter, max takeoff (all variants) 3810kg (8400lb).

Dimensions: Wing span 14.12m (46ft 4in) or 14.23m (46ft 8in) in late production aircraft, length 12.04m (39ft 6in), height 4.04m (13ft 3in). Wing area 22.5m² (242sq ft).

Capacity: Pilot and copilot on flightdeck, seating for eight or nine in main cabin.

Production: 378 Titans built between 1976 and 1982.

History: In July 1975 Cessna announced it was developing a new piston twin suitable for airline, freight and corporate work. It would be capable of taking off with a 1560kg (3500lb) payload from a 770m (2530ft) strip, and be similar in concept to the successful 402, but larger overall.

The resulting Model 404 Titan was Cessna's largest piston twin. It shares the same basic fuselage as the turbine powered 441 Conquest which was developed concurrently, but differs in having geared 280kW (375hp) piston engines and it is unpressurised. Other features include a bonded wet wing (then appearing on a number of 400 series Cessna twins) and the trailing link main undercarriage design shared with the Conquest.

The prototype Titan first flew on February 26 1975, production deliveries began in October the following year. Throughout the Titan's model life (Cessna dropped references to the 404 model number in its marketing in the late 1970s) it was offered in three major versions, each differing in internal equipment fit.

The base aircraft was the Titan Ambassador, configured for passenger operations, the Titan Courier was convertible from passenger to freight configurations, and the Titan Freighter was a pure cargo aircraft. The Titan Freighter featured a strengthened floor, cargo doors and walls and a ceiling made from impact resistant polycarbonate material. All were offered with II and III avionics equipment levels (as with other Cessna twins). The fully IFR III pack avionics suite included a weather radar.

The Titan underwent minor modifications from 1980 when the wing span was increased and the wingtips redesigned, but production continued only until 1982, by which time 378 had been built.

Photo: Titans are popular charter and special missions workhorses worldwide. (Richard Hall)

Cessna Corsair, Conquest I & II & Caravan II

Countries of origin: USA and France (Caravan II)

Type: Turboprop powered executive transports

Powerplants: 441 – Two 474kW (636shp) Garrett TPE331-8-410S/402S turboprops driving either Hartzell or McCauley props. F406 – Two 373kW (500shp) Pratt & Whitney Canada PT6A-112 turboprops driving three blade McCauley propellers.

Performance: 441 – Max speed 547km/h (295kt), max cruising speed 543km/h (293kt). Initial rate of climb 2435ft/min. Service ceiling 37,000ft. Max range with reserves at long range cruising speed 3048km (1646nm), range with max payload and reserves 2724km (1471nm). F406 – Max cruising speed 455km/h (246kt). Initial rate of climb 1850ft/min. Service ceiling 30,000ft. Range with max fuel at max cruising speed 2135km (1153nm).

Weights: 441 – Empty 2588kg (5706lb), max takeoff 4468kg (9850lb). F406 – Std empty 2283kg (5033lb), MTOW 4468kg (9850lb).

Dimensions: 441 – Wing span 15.04m (49ft 4in), length 11.89m (39ft 0in), height 4.01m (13ft 1in). Wing area 23.6m² (253.6sq ft). F406 – Wing span 15.08m (49ft 6in), length 11.89m (39ft 0in), height 4.01m (12ft 7in). Wing area 23.5m² (252.8sq ft).

Capacity: 425 – Typical accommodation one or two pilots and four passengers in corporate configured main cabin, optional passenger seating for six. 441 – One or two pilots and up to nine passengers.

Production: Over 230 Corsair/Conquest Is delivered by the end of 1987 by which time production had been suspended. 370 Model 441s were built. Approx 100 F406-5s built thus far.

History: The Corsair and Conquest I, and the 441 Conquest II are the turboprop powered equivalents of the 421 Golden Eagle and 404 Titan respectively. The Reims Caravan II is an unpressurised development.

The Model 441 Conquest was the first to be developed, it was designed concurrently with the piston engined 404 Titan in the mid 1970s. Development was announced in November 1974, and the first flight occurred in August 1976. First customer deliveries were from September 1977. The 441 shares a common fuselage with the Titan, but has a longer span (bonded and wet) wing, a pressurised fuselage, and most significantly, Garrett TPE331 turboprop engines. A PT6A powered 441, the 435, flew during 1986, but did not enter production.

The 425 Corsair meanwhile was introduced to the Cessna model lineup from 1980. Based on the Model 421 Golden Eagle, it differs from its donor aircraft in having turboprop engines (in this case PT6As). Design work on the Corsair began in 1977, first flight was on September 12 1978 and first deliveries took place in November 1980. From 1983 Cessna renamed the Corsair the Conquest I, while the Conquest became the Conquest II. Production of both ceased in 1986.

The French built Reims Aviation F406 Caravan II meanwhile is essentially an unpressurised Conquest II but powered by 373kW (500shp) PT6A-112s. The F406 first flew on September 22 1983 with deliveries from late 1984. The Caravan II is the only Cessna 400 series twin currently in production, Reims offers it in a variety of configurations including 12 passenger airliner, freighter and Vigilant maritime patrol and special missions versions.

Photo: A 441 Conquest II. (Rob Finlayson)

Cessna 340 & 335

Country of origin: United States of America

Type: Six seat business twins

Powerplants: 340A – Two 230kW (310hp) Continental TSIO-520-NB turbocharged and fuel injected flat six piston engines driving three blade constant speed McCauley propellers. 335 – Two 225kW (300hp) TSIO-520-EBs.

Performance: 340A – Max speed 452km/h (244kt), max cruising speed 425km/h (230kt), economical cruising speed 315km/h (170kt) at 25,000ft. Initial rate of climb 1650ft/min. Service ceiling 29,800ft. Range with reserves at economical cruising speed 2603km (1405nm), at max cruising speed 774km (418nm). 335 – Max speed 425km/h (230kt), max cruising speed 390km/h (211kt), economical cruising speed 313km/h (169kt). Initial rate of climb 1400ft/min. Service ceiling 26,800ft. Range at max cruising speed 2016km (1088nm), range at economical cruising speed 2542km (1372nm).

Weights: 340A – Empty 1780kg (3921lb), max takeoff 2719kg (5990lb). 335 – Empty equipped 1800kg (3963lb), max takeoff 2719kg (5990lb).

Dimensions: Wing span 11.62m (28ft 1in), length 10.46m (34ft 4in), height 3.84m (12ft 7in). Wing area 17.1m² (184sq ft).

Capacity: Typical seating for six, including one pilot.

Production: 1287 340s and 64 335s were built. The 340 was in production between 1971 and 1984, the 335 between 1979 and 1981.

History: The Cessna 340 at its release joined the Beechcraft Duke as the only other six seat pressurised piston twin from a major manufacturer, positioned in Cessna's product line between the 310 and the eight seat 414 and 421.

Development of the 340 began in 1969, but the loss of the prototype early in 1970 set back the development program so that production deliveries did not begin until early 1971. The resulting aircraft borrowed heavily from other Cessna twins of the time including the wings from the 414 and the 310's undercarriage and a similar tail unit. Design features of the new aircraft included a pressurisation system with a differential of 0.29bars (4.2psi) that kept the cabin's internal altitude at 8000ft while the aircraft was at 20,000ft, an all new fail safe fuselage and an integral airstair door.

Initial production 340s were powered by two 210kW (285hp) turbocharged Continental TSIO-520-K engines. The 340A, first introduced in 1976, featured two 230kW (310hp) TSIO-520-NBs, while other improvements included reduced diameter props and a slight increase in weights. The 340A was offered in optional 340A II and 340A III forms with various levels of IFR avionics fitted.

The Cessna 335 is an unpressurised, lighter weight and thus lower cost development of the 340, available from 1979. Aside from being unpressurised it differed from the 340 in having 225kW (300hp) TSIO-520-EB engines, but externally the two were identical. Cessna marketing claimed the 335 was the lowest priced cabin class business twin on the market, but just 64 335s were built before production was terminated in 1980.

Production of the 340 continued until 1984. The peak production year was 1979 when 200 340s were built.

Photo: A Cessna 340. (Lance Higgerson)

Cessna T303 Crusader

Country of origin: United States of America

Type: Six seat corporate and utility transport

Powerplants: Two 185kW (250hp) Continental TSIO-520-AE turbocharged and fuel injected flat six piston engines driving three blade constant speed counter rotating McCauley propellers.

Performance: Max speed 400km/h (216kt) at 18,000ft, max cruising speed 363km/h (196kt), economical cruising speed 333km/h (180kt). Initial rate of climb 1480ft/min. Service ceiling 25,000ft. Range with max fuel and reserves at 71% power at 20,000ft 1658km (895nm), at econ cruising speed and 10,000ft 1890km (1020nm).

Weights: Empty 1526kg (3364lb), max takeoff 2336kg (5150lb).

Dimensions: Wing span 11.90m (39ft 0.5in), length 9.27m (30ft 5in), height 4.06m (13ft 4in). Wing area 17.6m² (189.2sq ft).

Capacity: Normal seating for pilot and five passengers with central aisle between seats. Can be configured with a club seating arrangement for four in the main cabin, or for aerial ambulance or freighter work.

Production: In production between 1981 and 1985, 297 Crusaders were sold.

History: Cessna's Model 303 started life as a four seat twin, intended for the light transport and training role.

A prototype four seat Cessna 303 first flew on February 14 1978. Powered by two 120kW (160hp) Lycoming O-320 engines and featuring extensive use of bonded structures and a supercritical wing section, it would have competed against the Beech Duchess, Grumman GA-7 (Cougar) and Piper Seminole. However, a reappraisal of market demand for the aircraft led to Cessna rethinking the 303 design, and the outcome was a larger six seater aircraft aimed at charter and corporate users which could replace the Cessna 310 in the company's product line-up (Cessna 310 production wound up in 1980).

The new model, designated the T303 for its turbocharged (and fuel injected) Continental TSIO-520 engines, first flew on October 17 1979. Certification was granted in August 1981, and first production deliveries commenced in October 1981. For a time the T303 was named the Clipper, but this was changed to Crusader as Pan Am held the rights to the Clipper name.

The T303 was Cessna's first entirely new piston twin in over a decade, and incorporated a number of advanced features. These included bonded structures around the integral fuel tank and counter rotating propellers, while standard equipment included integral airstairs and a full IFR avionics suite (Cessna claimed the latter as a first for its class).

Only minor changes were introduced during production, including the addition of anti ice equipment as an option in 1982, and in 1983 the rear cabin bulkhead was moved aft slightly which increased baggage space and allowed the addition of a cargo door.

Production of the Crusader wound up in 1985 as part of the general decline in light aircraft sales during that period, terminating prematurely what looked to be a promising program. The cancellation also put paid to rumours that Cessna planned to develop more powerful, pressurised, and turboprop powered versions of the aircraft.

Photo: A Chilean registered Crusader. (Alvaro Romero)

Cessna Citation Mustang

Country of origin: United States of America

Type: Light corporate jet

Powerplants: Two 6kN (1350lb) thrust class FADEC equipped turbofans (Cessna to select between Pratt & Whitney Canada PW615 and Williams International FJ33.)

Performance: Provisional – Cruising speed at 603km/h (340kt) at 35,000 ft. Takeoff distance at MTOW 951m (3120ft). Max certificated ceiling 41,000ft. Range VFR with 45 minute reserves 2408km (1300nm).

Weights: Takeoff weight 3530-3720kg (7800-8200lb). Payload with maximum fuel (single pilot) 272kg (600lb).

Dimensions: Provisional – Wing span 12.97m (42ft 3in), length 11.86m (38ft 11in), height 4.18m (13ft 9in).

Capacity: Standard seating for six including one pilot. Club four seating in main cabin, with standard aft bench seat with centre storage console and fold down arm rest. Provisional cabin dimensions height 1.37m (4ft 6in), width 1.42m (4ft 8in), length (forward pressure bulkhead to aft pressure bulkhead) 4.36m (14ft 3in). Baggage capacity volume 1.27m³ (45.0 cu ft).

Production: At late 2002 Cessna held over 300 Mustang orders. Planned production rate 150 to 200 a year. 2002 introductory price $US2.3m.

History: Cessna's latest business jet will be its smallest, the six seat Citation Mustang which is pitched at the owner pilot market

Cessna launched the Mustang at the National Business Aviation Association's annual convention in Orlando, Florida in September 2002. The new jet proved an instant success – by the end of the show Cessna had signed orders for nearly 200 Mustangs backed by $US10,000 deposits.

The Mustang is due to fly in May 2005, with US FAA certification expected in June 2006. Once in full swing production will average 150 to 200 units a year, although at late 2002 Cessna had not decided whether to assemble the Mustang at its Wichita or Independence plants.

The all metal Mustang will be powered by two FADEC equipped 6kN (1350lb) class turbofans, with Cessna due to decide between the Pratt & Whitney Canada PW615 and the Williams International FJ33 by early 2003. The fuselage and T-tail layout bears a strong family resemblance with the CJ1, but the Mustang is slightly smaller, with an all new high aspect ratio straight wing.

The Mustang's flightdeck will be dominated by three large colour displays – two primary flight displays and a centre multifunction display, integrating traffic, weather and terrain data to reduce pilot workload. At late 2002 Cessna had yet to select the avionics supplier.

Cessna will keep Mustang production costs down by keeping optional equipment to a minimum.

The Mustang competes against turbine singles such as the slightly larger and slower EADS Socata TBM700 and Beech King Air C90. It is significantly larger and more expensive than the Eclipse 500.

Photo: The Citation Mustang is due to fly in 2005. (Cessna)

Cessna CitationJet & CJ1

Country of origin: United States of America

Type: Light corporate jets

Powerplants: CitationJet & CJ1 – Two 8.45kN (1900lb) Williams Rolls-Royce FJ44-1A turbofans.

Performance: CitationJet – Max cruising speed at 3990kg (8800lb) AUW 704km/h (380kt). Initial rate of climb 3311ft/min. Certificated ceiling 41,000ft. Range with max fuel and reserves 2750km (1485nm). CJ1 – Max cruising speed at 3990kg (8800lb) AUW 706km/h (381kt). Certificated ceiling 41,000ft. Range with pilot, three passengers and IFR reserves 2315km (1250nm).

Weights: CitationJet – Empty 2794kg (6160lb), max takeoff 4717kg (10,400lb). CJ1 – Empty equipped 3016kg (6650lb), max takeoff 4808kg (10,600lb).

Dimensions: CitationJet & CJ1 – Wing span 14.26m (46ft 10in), length 12.98m (42ft 7in), height 4.18m (13ft 8in). Wing area 22.3m² (240.0sq ft).

Capacity: CitationJet & CJ1 – Two flightdeck positions, one for pilot, other for a copilot or passenger. Main cabin seats five in standard layout – one sideways facing seat at front of cabin and club four arrangement behind.

Production: 359 production CitationJets built to early 2000 when replaced by CJ1. 500th CitationJet/CJ1 delivered June 2002. Over 150 CJ1s delivered by late 2002.

History: The Cessna CitationJet and CJ1 are highly successful light business jets.

Cessna launched the new Model 525 CitationJet at the annual US National Business Aviation Association convention in 1989 to fill the void left by the out of production Citation I. First flight occurred on April 29 1991, a second preproduction aircraft flew November 20 1991, FAA certification was awarded on October 16 1992 and the first delivery was on March 30 1993.

The CitationJet is effectively an all new aircraft. The basic Citation forward fuselage is coupled with a new T-tail and a new supercritical laminar flow wing (with thicker skins to decrease dimpling and buckling), sitting on a trailing link main undercarriage. Power is from two Williams Rolls FJ44 turbofans (with paddle thrust reversers) – developed in partnership by cruise missile engine manufacturer Williams International and Rolls-Royce. The CitationJet's fuselage is 27cm (11in) shorter than the Citation/Citation I's, while cabin height is increased courtesy of a lowered centre aisle. It features EFIS avionics and is certificated for single pilot operation.

At the 1998 NBAA convention Cessna revealed the improved CJ1 and stretched CJ2 (described separately). The CJ1 has replaced the CitationJet and introduced a Collins Pro Line 21 EFIS avionics suite (with two 203 x 253mm colour displays – a third is optional) and a moderate increase in maximum takeoff, ramp and landing weights.

The first CJ1 flew in late 1999, FAA certification was awarded in February 2000, and the first production CJ1 delivered on March 31 2000 (to the Commercial Envelope Company).

Photo: Over 500 CitationJets and CJ1s have been delivered since 1993. (Robert Wiseman)

Cessna CJ2 & CJ3

Country of origin: United States of America

Type: Light corporate jets

Powerplants: CJ2 – Two 10.7kN (2400lb) Williams Rolls-Royce FJ44-2C turbofans. CJ3 – Two 12.4kN (2780lb) FJ44-3s.

Performance: CJ2 – Max cruising speed at 33,000ft 759km/h (410kt), econ cruising speed 615km/h (332kt). Initial rate of climb 3870ft/min. Service ceiling 45,000ft. Range with max fuel and reserves 2863km (1546nm). CJ3 – Max cruising speed 772km/h (417kt). Time to 45,000ft just over 35min. Range with four passengers 3080km (1665nm)

Weights: CJ2 – Empty equipped 3402kg (7500lb), max takeoff 5613kg (12,375lb). CJ3 – Basic empty 3701kg (8160lb), max ramp weight 6290kg (13,870lb).

Dimensions: CJ2 – Wing span 15.09m (49ft 6in), length 14.29m (46ft 11in), height 4.24m (13ft 11in). Wing area 24.5m² (264.0sq ft). CJ3 – Wing span 16.13m (52ft 11in), length 15.61m (51ft 2in), height 4.62m (15ft 2in).

Capacity: One or two pilots. CJ2 – Main cabin seats six in standard club arrangement. CJ3 – Main cabin seating for six.

Production: First CJ2 delivery November 2000, with 200th delivered in September 2002. In September 2002 NetJets committed to buy 50 CJ3s.

History: The CJ2 and CJ3 are stretched developments of the highly popular Cessna CitationJet/CJ1.

Compared to the donor CJ1, the CJ2 is stretched, faster and more powerful. A CitationJet was converted to act as the CJ2 prototype and first flew as such on April 27 1999. The first production aircraft rolled out in mid February 2000, with certification awarded on June 21 2000 with first customer deliveries from that November. Less than two years later the 200th had been delivered.

The CJ2 features an 89cm (35in) cabin and 43cm (17in) tailcone stretch allowing standard seating for six in the main cabin. Like the CJ1 it features Rockwell Collins Pro Line 21 EFIS avionics, plus uprated FJ44-2C engines, increased span wings, larger area tail, six cabin windows per side and greater range.

In September 2002 at the annual NBAA convention, Cessna announced it was developing the further stretched CJ3, which it says is faster, larger and more powerful than earlier CJs. It will feature a 61cm (2ft) longer cabin giving more passenger room, longer span wings, and more powerful FJ44-3 turbofans with dual channel FADEC. The CJ3's advanced avionics system will include Rockwell Collins' Pro-Line 21 suite linked to a file server allowing cursor control of the three flat panel displays, displaying information such as electronic charts, approach plates and graphical weather.

The prototype CJ3 is due to fly in the second quarter of 2003. Certification is planned for the second quarter of 2004, with deliveries in the third quarter.

At $US5.45m the CJ3 will be priced above the stablemate older Citation Bravo, which will remain in production for the time being as it features two extra seats and slightly more payload and range (but is also much heavier).

Photo: A computer generated image of the CJ3. (Cessna)

Cessna Citation & Citation I

Country of origin: United States of America

Type: Light corporate jets

Powerplants: Citation – Two 9.79kN (2200lb) Pratt & Whitney JT15D-1 turbofans. Citation I – Two 9.79kN (2200lb) JT15D-1A1Bs.

Performance: Citation – Max speed 647km/h (350kt), max cruising speed 644km/h (348kt). Initial rate of climb 3350ft/min. Service ceiling 38,400ft. Range with eight people on board and reserves at high speed cruise 2250km (1215nm). Citation I – Cruising speed 662km/h (357kt). Initial rate of climb 2720ft/min. Range with max fuel, 710kg (1560lb) payload and reserves 2460km (1328nm).

Weights: Citation – Empty 2455kg (5408lb), max takeoff 4920kg (10,850lb). Citation I – Empty equipped 3008kg (6631lb), max takeoff 5380kg (11,850lb).

Dimensions: Citation – Wing span 13.32m (43ft 9in), length 13.26m (43ft 6in), height 4.36m (14ft 3in). Wing area 24.2m² (260sq ft). Citation I – Same except for wing span 14.35m (47ft 1in). Wing area 25.9m² (278.5sq ft).

Capacity: Two pilots for Citation and Citation I, single pilot for Citation I/SP. Optional main cabin layouts for five, six or seven passengers.

Production: Over 690 Citations, Citation Is and I/SPs were built between 1971 and 1985. Approx 640 in service in late 2002

History: The highly popular Citation and Citation I pioneered the entry level light business jet market, and their success formed the basis for the world's largest family of corporate jets.

Cessna became the first of the big three American manufacturers (Piper, Beech and Cessna) to develop a jet powered transport. In October 1968 Cessna announced its plans to build a new eight place jet powered business aircraft that would be capable of operating into airfields already served by light and medium prop twins. The new jet was dubbed the Fanjet 500 and the prototype first flew on September 15 1969. Soon after Cessna renamed the Fanjet Citation.

A relatively long development program followed, during which time a number of key changes were made to the design including a longer forward fuselage, repositioned engine nacelles, greater tail area and added horizontal tail dihedral. In this definitive form the Citation was granted FAA certification on September 9 1971.

Improvements including higher gross weights and thrust reversers were added to the line in early 1976, followed shortly after by the introduction of the enhanced Citation I later that same year. Citation I improvements included higher weights, JT15D-1A engines and an increased span wing.

A further model to appear was the Citation I/SP, which is certificated for single pilot operation. The I/SP was delivered in early 1977.

Production of the Citation I ceased in 1985, its place in the Citation line left vacant until the arrival of the CitationJet (described separately) some years later.

Direct developments of the Citation were the Citation II (now Citation Bravo) and Citation V (now Citation Encore).

Photo: This shot shows to good effect the Citation/Citation I's low ground clearance and tailplane dihedral. This is a Citation I. (Gary Gentle)

Cessna Citation II & Bravo

Country of origin: United States of America

Type: Light corporate jets

Powerplants: S/II – Two 11.1kN (2500lb) Pratt & Whitney Canada JT15D-4Bs turbofans. Bravo – Two 12.8kN (2887lb) Pratt & Whitney Canada PW530As.

Performance: S/II – Cruising speed 746km/h (403kt). Initial rate of climb 3040ft/min. Range with two crew, four passengers and reserves 3223km (1739nm). Range with max fuel 3700km (1998nm). Bravo – Max cruising speed 745km/h (402kt). Max initial rate of climb 3195ft/min. Max certificated altitude 45,000ft. Range with four passengers and reserves 3704m (2000nm).

Weights: S/II – Empty equipped 3655kg (8060lb), max takeoff 6850kg (15,100lb). Bravo – Empty 3992kg (8750lb), max takeoff 6713kg (14,800lb).

Dimensions: S/II – Wing span 15.91m (52ft 3in), length 14.39m (47ft 3in), height 4.57m (15ft 0in). Wing area 31.8m² (342.6sq ft). Bravo – Wing span 15.90m (52ft 2in), length 14.39m (47ft 3in), height 4.57m (15ft 0in). Wing area 30.0m² (322.9sq ft).

Capacity: S/II – Flightcrew of two. Main cabin can be optionally configured to seat 10, but standard interior layout for six. Can be configured as an air ambulance with one or two stretchers and up to four medical attendants. Bravo – Standard seating for seven with max seating for 10 in main cabin.

Production: 733 Citation IIs built through to late 1994. Bravo deliveries began Feb 1997, approx 240 delivered by late 2002.

History: The early success of the original Citation led Cessna to develop a larger capacity model in the mid 1970s.

Cessna announced the stretched Citation II in September 1976. The fuselage was extended by 1.14m (3ft 9in) to increase maximum seating capacity to 10, while more powerful Pratt & Whitney Canada JT15D-4 engines and greater fuel tankage meant higher cruise speeds and longer range. Increased baggage capacity and increased span wings were also added.

The new Model 550 Citation II first flew on January 31 1977 and FAA certification for two pilot operation was awarded in March 1978. The II/SP is certificated for single pilot operation.

Major improvements were made to the design with the arrival of the Model S550 Citation S/II. Announced in October 1983, this improved version first flew on February 14 1984. Certification, including an exemption for single pilot operation, was granted that July. Improvements were mainly aerodynamic, including a new wing designed using supercritical technology plus JT15D-4B turbofans. The S/II initially replaced the II from 1984, but the II returned to the line-up from late 1985, and both variants remained in production until the introduction of the Bravo.

The Bravo features new P&WC PW530A turbofans, a modern Honeywell Primus EFIS avionics suite, a revised interior based on that introduced in the Citation Ultra and other improvements such as trailing link main undercarriage. The Bravo first flew on April 25 1995 and was granted certification in August 1996. First delivery was in February 1997.

Photo: A Citation II. (Theo van Loon)

Cessna Citation V, Ultra & Encore

Country of origin: United States of America

Type: Small to mid size corporate jets

Powerplants: V – Two 12.9kN (2900lb) Pratt & Whitney Canada JT15D-5A turbofans. Ultra – Two 13.6kN (3045lb) JT15D-5Ds. Ultra Encore – Two 14.9kN (3360lb) P&WC PW535As.

Performance: V – Cruising speed 790km/h (427kt). Initial rate of climb 3650ft/min. Range with six passengers, two crew and reserves 3558km (1920nm). Ultra – Max cruising speed 796km/h (430kt). Initial rate of climb 4100ft/min. Certificated ceiling 45,000ft. Range with five passengers 3630km (1960nm). Encore – Max cruising speed at mid cruise weight 798km/h (431kt). Certificated ceiling 45,000ft. Max range with IFR reserves 3150km (1700nm).

Weights: V – Empty equipped 4004kg (8828lb), max takeoff 7212kg (15,900lb). Ultra – Empty 4196kg (9250lb), operating empty 4377kg (9650lb), max takeoff 7393kg (16,300lb). Encore – Empty approx 4526kg (9977lb), max takeoff 7544kg (16,630lb).

Dimensions: V & Ultra – Wing span 15.91m (52ft 3in), length 14.90m (48ft 11in), height 4.57m (15ft 0in). Wing area 31.8m² (342.6sq ft). Encore – Same except height 4.63m (15ft 1in).

Capacity: V – Typical seating for eight passengers. Ultra/Encore – Standard seating arrangement for seven.

Production: 262 Citation Vs built through to mid 1994. Approx 340 Ultras built. Over 70 Encores delivered by late 2002.

History: The Citation V, Citation Ultra and Encore are stretched and improved developments of the Citation II.

Cessna publicly announced it was developing a stretched development of the Citation II at the annual NBAA convention in New Orleans in 1987. Earlier in August that year the first engineering prototype Model 560 Citation V had successfully flown. A preproduction prototype flew in early 1986, while US certification was granted on December 9 1988. Deliveries began the following April.

The Citation V was based on the Citation II/SP, but differences over the smaller jet include more powerful Pratt & Whitney Canada JT15D-5A turbofans and a slight fuselage stretch, allowing seating in a standard configuration for eight passengers. The Citation V proved quite popular, with 262 built through to mid 1994 before production switched to the modernised Ultra.

Cessna announced development of the upgraded Citation V Ultra in September 1993. FAA certification was granted in June 1994, allowing for deliveries of production aircraft to commence soon after. Compared with the Citation V, the Ultra features more powerful 13.6kN (3045lb) Pratt & Whitney Canada JT15D-5D engines and Honeywell Primus 1000 EFIS avionics with three CRT displays (two primary flight displays and one multifunction display).

The Citation Encore is a new development announced at the 1998 NBAA convention. Compared with the Ultra the Encore introduces new Pratt & Whitney Canada PW535 engines, plus trailing link main undercarriage, more fuel and payload, updated interior and improved systems. The Ultra's Primus 1000 EFIS avionics suite is retained.

The Encore first flew on July 9 1998, certification was awarded on May 26 2000 with service entry on September 29 2000.

Photo: The Encore is the latest development of the Citation V. (Cessna)

Cessna Citation III, VI & VII

Country of origin: United States of America

Type: Medium size corporate jets

Powerplants: III & VI – Two 16.2kN (3650lb) Garrett TFE731-3B-100S turbofans. VII – Two 18.2kN (4080lb) AlliedSignal TFE731-4R-2Ss.

Performance: III & VI – Max cruising speed 874km/h (472kt). Initial rate of climb 805ft/min. Range with two crew and four passengers and reserves 4348km (2346nm). VII – Max cruising speed 881km/h (476kt). Initial rate of climb 4442ft/min. Range with six passengers and reserves 4110km (2220nm).

Weights: III & VI – Empty 5357kg (11,811lb), operating empty 5534kg (12,200lb), max takeoff 9980kg (22,000lb). VII – Empty 5316kg (11,720lb), max takeoff 10,183kg (22,450lb).

Dimensions: Wing span 16.31m (53ft 6in), length 16.90m (55ft 6in), height 5.12m (16ft 10in). Wing area 29.0m² (312.0sq ft).

Capacity: Flightcrew of two. Typical main passenger cabin seating for six, or optionally up to nine.

Production: Total of 202 Citation IIIs delivered when production ceased in 1992. A total of 39 Citation VIs had been built when production ceased in 1995, while 119 VIIs were built to September 2000.

History: The Cessna Model 650 Citation III was designed as a high performance, mid size long range corporate jet to supplement the much smaller Citation I and II.

Development of this all new, larger Citation began in 1978. As it evolved, the III had little in common with the previous Citation models other than the name. The new design featured a swept supercritical wing optimised for high speed long range flight, new Garrett TFE731 turbofans, a T-tail, and a new fuselage.

The new jet made its first flight on May 30 1979 with a second prototype flying on May 2 1980. Certification was granted on April 30 1982, first customer deliveries occurring the following year. The Citation III set two time to height records for its class in 1983 and a class speed record by flying from Gander to Le Bourget in 5hr 13min.

Production improvements to the Citation III were first proposed in the cancelled Citation IV. This model was announced in 1989 and was to feature more range and better short field performance.

Instead Cessna developed the Citation VI and VII. The Citation VI was offered as a low cost development of the III with a different avionics package and a standard interior layout. First flight of the Citation VI took place in 1991 but only 39 were built when production wound up in May 1995.

The Citation VII meanwhile features a number of improvements including more powerful engines for improved hot and high performance. The first Citation VII prototype flew in February 1991 and the type was certificated in January 1992. The 119th and last Citation VII (and Cessna Model 650) was rolled out from Cessna's Wichita's facilities on September 15 2000. This last aircraft was delivered to United Foods, which also took delivery of the first Citation III. The VII will be replaced in Cessna's model line-up by the Citation Sovereign.

Photo: A Cyprus registered Citation III. (Francis Nickelson)

Cessna Citation Excel

Country of origin: United States of America

Type: Small to mid size corporate jet

Powerplants: Two 16.9kN (3804lb) Pratt & Whitney Canada PW545A turbofans.

Performance: Max cruising speed at 35,000ft 795km/h (429kt). Initial rate of climb 3790ft/min. Max certificated altitude 51,000ft. Range with four passengers and two crew 3852km (2080nm).

Weights: Empty equipped 5579kg (12,300lb), max takeoff 9071kg (20,000lb).

Dimensions: Wing span 16.98m (55ft 10in), length 15.79m (51ft 10in), height 5.24m (17ft 3in). Wing area 34.5m² (369.7sq ft).

Capacity: Flightcrew of two. Choice of four interior configurations with seating for up to 10 passengers in main cabin. Typical arrangement seats seven passengers. Cabin also features a forward refreshment centre and aft lavatory.

Production: First delivery July 1998, 100th delivered in August 2000. Approx 275 in service by late 2002.

History: The popular Citation Excel combines the cabin width and standup headroom cabin dimensions of the Citation X in a new small/medium size package.

The new Excel followed from customer consultation and advances in engine and airframe technology. The basis of the Excel is a shortened Citation X fuselage (the same fuselage cross section as was used in the Citation III, VI and VII), combined with a modified unswept supercritical wing based on the Citation V Ultra's, the Citation V's cruciform tail configuration and new Pratt & Whitney Canada PW545A turbofans.

Other design features include trailing link main undercarriage units and a standard Honeywell Primus 1000 three 20 x 18cm (8 x 7in) screen EFIS avionics package (two primary flight displays, one for each pilot, and a multifunction display).

Cessna claims the Citation Excel's cabin is the largest of any light business jet. It features standup headroom and a dropped aisle that runs the length of the main cabin. Seated head and elbow room is greater than that in the Citation II and V, while the cabin length is similar to the Citation III, VI and VII. Standard seating is for seven, an option is double club seating for eight. A baggage compartment is in the rear fuselage.

The Excel was one of the first applications for the new generation PW500 series engines. The Excel's 16.9kN (3804lb) PW545As (derated from 19.9kN/4450lb, with a TBO of 5000 hours) are fitted with Nordam thrust reversers as standard and the engines allow it to cruise at 801km/h (432kt).

Cessna announced it was developing the Excel at the NBAA convention in October 1994. Prototype construction began in February 1995 and it flew for the first time on February 29 1996. The first production Excel rolled out in November 1997 and the type was certificated in April 1998, with deliveries beginning mid that year at which stage over 200 were on order.

Cessna delivered the 100th Excel in August 2000, by which time the company was building one every three days.

Photo: The Cessna Excel. (Martin Flanagan)

Cessna Citation Sovereign

Country of origin: United States of America

Type: Mid size corporate jet

Powerplants: Two 25.3kN (5690lb) Pratt & Whitney Canada PW306C turbofans.

Performance: Max cruising speed 822km/h (444kt), econ cruising speed 796km/h (430kt). Certificated ceiling 47,000ft. Time to 43,000ft 26min. Takeoff distance at max takeoff weight 1220m (4000ft). Range with eight passengers 4630km (2500nm).

Weights: Approx empty 7711kg (17,400kg), max takeoff 13,608kg (30,000lb).

Dimensions: Wing span 19.24m (63ft 1in), length 19.35m (63ft 6in), height 6.07m (19ft 11in). Wing area 47.9m² (516.0sq ft).

Capacity: Flightcrew of two. Typical seating for eight passengers in a double club arrangement, max seating for 11.

Production: First customer deliveries scheduled for early 2004.

History: Cessna is developing the new Citation Sovereign mid size corporate jet to meet what it sees as a large replacement market for ageing business aircraft such as the Falcon 10, Westwind and Sabreliner.

Cessna revealed the Citation Excel based Model 680 Citation Sovereign at the October 1998 NBAA exhibition in Las Vegas. At that time certification was planned for the second quarter of 2002 with deliveries in the third quarter of that year, but delays will now see deliveries in early 2004. The prototype Sovereign made its first flight on February 27 2002, and FAA certification is planned for late 2003.

The Sovereign is based on the Excel's fuselage and shares some common systems but features an all new wing and numerous other differences. Cessna looked at an all new fuselage cross section for the Sovereign but opted instead to stretch the Excel fuselage (by 1.5m/4.9ft) to keep down costs and reduce development time. Even so Cessna claims the Sovereign's eight seat cabin will have 40% more volume than the Bombardier Learjet 60 and 18% more than the Raytheon Hawker 800XP.

The Sovereign is powered by two FADEC equipped 25.3kN (5690lb) Pratt & Whitney Canada PW306C turbofans. The PW306 was selected in part as it also powers the 328JET regional airliner which should give maintenance and reliability benefits because of the airline industry's more rigorous operating demands.

The mildly swept wing is an all new, supercritical design, based on Cessna's experience with the Citation III and X. The horizontal stabiliser is also slightly swept. The Sovereign will enjoy good field performance, being able to operate from 1220m (4000ft) runways at max takeoff weight. Another feature is trailing link main undercarriage.

The Sovereign is equipped with a Honeywell Epic CDS avionics suite, with four 20 x 25cm (8 x 10in) colour flat panel liquid crystal displays, a digital dual channel autopilot and flight director, dual long range navigation systems and dual attitude/heading reference systems. Other standard equipment includes TCAS and an EGPWS (enhanced ground proximity warning system).

Photo: The Citation Sovereign prototype on its February 27 2002 first flight. (Cessna)

Cessna Citation X

Country or origin: United States of America

Type: Long range, high speed, mid size corporate jet

Powerplants: Two 28.7kN (6442lb) Rolls-Royce AE 3007C turbofans, from 2001 30.1kN (6764lb) AE 3007C-1s.

Performance: Max cruising speed at mid cruise weight Mach 0.91 (934km/h/504kt) at 37,000ft. Initial rate of climb 4000ft/min. Max certificated altitude 51,000ft. Range with reserves 6020km (3250nm).

Weights: Typical empty equipped 9705kg (21,400lb), max takeoff 16,195kg (35,700lb). MTOW from 2001 16,389kg (36,100lb).

Dimensions: Wing span 19.48m (63ft 11in), length 22.00m (72ft 2in), height 5.77m (18ft 11in). Wing area 49.0m² (527.0sq ft).

Capacity: Flightcrew of two. Main cabin seating for up to 12 passengers seated on individual seats and couches in a high density configuration. Other interiors to customer preference, including eight passenger seats in a double club arrangement.

Production: First production Citation X delivered in June 1996. Approx 200 Citation Xs had entered service by late 2002.

History: The Citation X (as in the Roman numeral, not the letter, and Cessna's Model 750) is Cessna's largest, fastest and longest range Citation yet, and is the fastest corporate jet in service.

The design objective behind the Citation X was transcontinental USA and trans Atlantic range in a mid size package that cruises faster than any other business jet available. This high speed cruise capability means the X can save up to one hour's flight time on transcontinental US flights, flying from Los Angeles to New York with normal wind conditions in 4 hours 10 minutes. Cessna also says the Citation X consumes less fuel than current jets on such a transcontinental flight.

The X's FADEC equipped Rolls-Royce (formerly Allison) AE 3007A turbofans are very powerful for an aircraft of the X's size, while the highly swept (37°) wings are also long in span. Other design features include the fuselage cross section of the Citation III/VI/VII but with more efficient use of internal space that allows greater head and shoulder room, an area ruled, waisted rear fuselage, trailing link main undercarriage units and a Honeywell Primus 2000 EFIS avionics suite with five colour CRT displays.

Cessna announced that it was developing the Citation X in October 1990 at that year's NBAA conference. The prototype flew for the first time on December 21 1993, certification was granted on June 3 1996, with the first customer delivery (to golfer Arnold Palmer) that month.

A Citation X was the 2500th Citation to be delivered, handed over on September 10 1997. The USA's National Aeronautics Association awarded its prestigious Collier Trophy to the Citation X design team in February 1997.

From January 2001 Xs feature slightly more powerful engines, giving better field performance, and a 182kg (400lb) increase in maximum takeoff weight. Previously optional equipment, such as TCAS (Traffic Collision Avoidance System) and EGPWS (Enhanced Ground Proximity Warning System), also became standard.

Photo: A Citation X owned by adventurer Steve Fossett. (Greg Wood)

Cessna Caravan & Grand Caravan

Country or origin: United States of America

Type: Single turboprop utility transport

Powerplant: 208A – One 450kW (600shp) Pratt & Whitney Canada PT6A-114 turboprop driving a three blade variable pitch Hartzell propeller. 208-675, 208B Super Cargomaster & Grand Caravan – One 505kW (675shp) PT6A-114A.

Performance: 208A – Max cruising speed 340km/h (184kt). Initial rate of climb 1215ft/min. Range max fuel and reserves 2066km (1115nm). 208B Super Cargomaster – Max cruising speed 317km/h (171kt). Initial rate of climb 770ft/min. Range with max fuel and reserves 2000km (1080nm). Grand Caravan – Max cruising speed 337km/h (182kt). Initial rate of climb 975ft/min. Range with max fuel and reserves 1667km (900nm).

Weights: 208A – Empty 1725kg (3800lb), max takeoff 3310kg (7300lb). 208B Super Cargomaster – Empty 2073kg (4570lb), max takeoff 3970kg (8750lb). Grand Caravan – Empty equipped 2250kg (4965lb), max takeoff 3970kg (8750lb).

Dimensions: 208A – Wing span 15.88m (52ft 1in), length 11.46m (37ft 7in), height 4.32m (14ft 2in). Wing area 26.0m² (279.4sq ft). 208B – Same except for length 12.67m (41ft 7in).

Capacity: 208A – Pilot and typically nine passengers, or up to 14 with an FAA FAR Part 23 waiver. Cargo capacity 1360kg (3000lb). Super Cargomaster – Cargo capacity for 1587kg (3500lb). Grand Caravan – One pilot and up to 14 passengers.

Production: Over 1300 delivered by late 2002 (1000th Grand Caravan delivered Dec 12 2002).

History: Tthe useful Caravan is a very popular utility workhorse.

Design work for the Caravan dates back to the early eighties. First flight of a prototype occurred on December 9 1982 and certification was granted in October 1984. When production began the following year it became the first all new single engine turboprop powered aircraft to enter production.

The Caravan has had a close association with US package freight specialist Federal Express (FedEx), on whose request Cessna especially developed two pure freight versions. The first of these was the 208A based Cargomaster (40 delivered), the second was the stretched 208B Super Cargomaster (260 delivered). The first Super Cargomaster flew on March 3 1986 and features a 1.22m (4ft) stretch and greater payload capacity, including an under fuselage cargo pannier. FedEx's aircraft lack cabin windows.

The Super Cargomaster formed the basis for 208B Grand Caravan, which first flew in 1990 and is powered by a 505kW (675shp) PT6A-114 (which also powers Super Cargomasters built from 1991). It can seat up to 14 passengers.

Announced at the 1997 NBAA convention, the 208-675 or Caravan 675 has replaced the basic 208A. It combines the standard length airframe with the more powerful PT6A-114 of the 208B.

Underbelly cargo pods and floats are offered as options on the Caravan family, and the type is easily converted from freight to passenger configurations. A military/special mission version of the 208A, dubbed the U-27, has also been offered.

Photo: A Grand Caravan over New Zealand. (Peter Clark)

Chichester-Miles Leopard

Country of origin: United Kingdom

Type: High performance jet powered four seat light aircraft

Powerplants: Prototype – Two 1.33kN (300lb) Noel Penny NPT 301 turbofans. 2nd aircraft – Two 3.11kN (700lb) Williams International FJX turbofans. Production aircraft – Two Williams International FJX-2s.

Performance: Prototype aircraft – Max cruising speed 655km/h (354kt). Initial rate of climb 2350ft/min. Range with no reserves 1300km (700nm). Production aircraft (estimated) – Max speed 869km/h (469kt), max and econ cruising speed at 45,000ft 804km/h (434kt). Initial rate of climb 6430ft/min. Service ceiling 55,000ft. Range with max payload 2780km (1500nm), range with max fuel 3545km (1915nm).

Weights: Prototype – Basic empty 795kg (1750lb), max takeoff 1155kg (2550lb). Production aircraft (estimated) – Empty equipped 998kg (2200lb), max takeoff 1815kg (4000lb).

Dimensions: Prototype – Wing span 7.16m (23ft 6in), length 7.54m (24ft 9in), height 2.06m (6ft 9in). Wing area 5.9m² (62.9sq ft). Production aircraft – Wing span 7.62m (25ft 0in), length 7.85m (25ft 9in). Wing area 5.97m² (64.3sq ft).

Capacity: Standard seating for four.

Production: Prototype and preproduction aircraft only built at the time of writing, with design of production aircraft continuing.

History: The Leopard is arguably the most advanced high performance light aircraft yet designed and flown.

The sleek Leopard dates back to the early 1980s when Ian Chichester-Miles, a former Chief Research Engineer at BAe Hatfield, established Chichester-Miles Consultants. CMC completed construction of a Leopard mockup in early 1982 and then contracted Designability Ltd to perform detail design work and build a prototype.

CMC originally hoped that the prototype Leopard would fly in early 1987, however various delays meant that it did not fly until December 12 1988. Since then development has progressed slowly.

The program suffered a setback when engine supplier Noel Penny ceased trading, and all flying stopped while a preproduction aircraft powered by Williams International FJX turbofans was designed and built. This aircraft was displayed at the 1996 Farnborough Airshow and flew for the first time on April 9 1997.

Production Leopards will incorporate a number of advanced design features including all composite construction; supercritical, laminar flow, swept wings; liquid deicing and decontamination system along the wings and tailplane; and EFIS avionics (the prototype features simpler avionics and pressurisation systems and liquid deicing on the tailplane only). The preproduction Leopard incorporates most of these features bar the FJX-2 engines. The Leopard also does not feature spoilers or ailerons, instead roll, pitch and yaw control is provided by the all moving fin and differentially actuated tailplanes.

The first production standard Leopard was due to fly in 2004-05, pending availability of its FJX-2 engines. Proposed production versions include the six seat 3705km (2000nm) range Leopard Jet 6 with oval side windows and side entry door and military trainer Leopard T-Jet.

Photo: The second development Leopard. (Paul Merritt)

Cirrus Design SR20

Country of origin: United States of America

Type: Four seat high performance light aircraft

Powerplant: One 150kW (200hp) Teledyne Continental IO-360-ES fuel injected flat six piston engine driving a two or three blade Hartzell propeller.

Performance: Cruising speed at 75% power 295km/h (160kt). Initial rate of climb 920ft/min. Service ceiling 17,500ft. Range with reserves 1480km (800nm).

Weights: Empty 885kg (1950lb), max takeoff 1315kg (2900lb).

Dimensions: Wing span 10.85m (35ft 7in), length 8.00m (26ft 3in), height 2.82m (9ft 3in). Wing area 12.6m² (135.0sq ft).

Capacity: Typical seating for four.

Production: At late 2002 approx 260 SR20s delivered.

History: Cirrus Design's SR20 is an all new, modern high performance four seat light aircraft.

Cirrus Design Corporation began life manufacturing kit aircraft. The company's piston or turbine powered kit built VK30 four seater in fact forms the basis of the SR20, even though the VK30 features a pusher engine. The VK30 first flew in February 1988 but kit production ceased in 1993 to allow Cirrus to relocate its manufacturing facilities to Duluth, Minnesota, and to concentrate on a developing family of fully certificated and factory built GA aircraft.

Details of the SR20 were publicly announced at the Oshkosh EAA Convention in July 1994. The SR20 features composite construction, a 26cm (10in) Avidyne Flight Max colour multifunction liquid crystal display (It displays a contoured "map" with colour coded terrain, geographical features, aviation information with Stormscope), side mounted control yokes, a 150kW (200hp) Teledyne Continental IO-360 flat six piston engine with a single lever operating both mixture and throttle, and a luxury car-like interior.

The SR20 is also fitted standard with a ballistic recovery system (BRS) parachute (a first for a certificated production aircraft), while various energy absorbing features have been designed into the airframe to reduce deceleration loads and increase its ability to absorb energy in the event of an impact.

Apart from its high levels of technology, Cirrus claims that the SR20 offers significant improvements over current four seaters in the areas of performance, price, interior cabin space and internal noise levels.

The SR20 prototype first flew on March 31 1995. FAA FAR Part 23 certification was awarded on October 23 1998 (delayed because Cirrus decided to redesign the wing to lower the stall speed and improve lateral control). First delivery was on July 20 1999.

In mid 2001 Cirrus introduced into production the improved SR20A with 45kg (100lb) increased max takeoff weight, repositioned landing light and optional enhanced HSI.

In April 2002 Cirrus announced the SR20 Version 2.0 for 2003. It will feature slight performance improvements and redundant electrical systems allowing for the elimination of vacuum systems. Optional Version 2.1 and 2.2 avionics packages mirror those offered on the higher performance SR22 (described separately).

Photo: A US registered SR20. (Gerard Frawley)

Cirrus Design SR22 & SR21tdi

Country of origin: United States of America

Type: Four seat high performance light aircraft

Powerplant: SR22 – One 230kW (310hp) Teledyne Continental IO-550-N flat six piston engine driving a three blade constant speed Hartzell propeller. SR21tdi – One 172kW (230hp) SMA SR 305 turbocharged jet fuel burning diesel piston engine.

Performance: SR22 – Cruising speed at 75% power 333km/h (180kt). Initial rate of climb 1400ft/min. Range at 75% power 1377km (744nm), range at economical cruising speed over 1850km (1000nm).

Weights: SR22 – Empty 1021kg (2250lb), max takeoff 1542kg (3400lb).

Dimensions: SR22 – Wing span 11.73m (38ft 6in), length 7.92m (26ft 0in), height 2.80m (9ft 2in). Wing area 13.5m² (144.9sq ft).

Capacity: Typical seating for four.

Production: At late 2002 over 375 SR22s delivered.

History: The SR22 is a higher performance development of Cirrus Design's very successful SR20. The SR22 also forms the basis of the turbo diesel jet fuel burning SR 305 powered SR21tdi, which is particularly aimed at European customers.

The SR22 is based closely on the SR20 but features a much more powerful 230kW (310hp) Teledyne Continental IO-550-N, giving a quick 333km/h (180kt) cruising speed at 75% power.

Other than the more powerful engine, the SR22 features minor airframe changes including extended wingtips and fuselage mounted vortex generators. Like the SR20, it features the Cirrus Airframe Parachute System. It also features all electric instrumentation (now incorporated on the SR20), meaning no vacuum system.

The SR22 was publicly unveiled in October 2000, with type certification on November 30 that year. First customer delivery was on February 6 2001.

In July 2002 Cirrus announced the SR22 will be offered with an optional glass cockpit (for delivery from the third quarter of 2003), featuring an Avidyne FlightMax Entegra primary flight display (in addition to the standard Avidyne Flightmax multifunction display). The 26cm (10.4in) diagonally across Entegra display presents standard flight instrumentation including attitude direction indicator, horizontal situation indicator, altitude, airspeed, vertical speed and moving map. The artificial horizon display stretches across the width of the screen. The Entegra also incorporates a fully integrated air data/attitude and heading reference system to provide information such as true airspeed and winds.

Cirrus announced the turbocharged diesel SMA SR 305 powered SR21tdi development at the AERO Airshow in Friedrichshafen, Germany on April 26 2001. The diesel cycle 172kW (230hp) SR 305 burns Jet-A or jet fuel, and is particularly pitched at Europe where avgas is expensive and not as widely available. First deliveries were planned for mid 2003.

Cirrus says the SR21tdi will feature "SR22-like" performance at higher altitudes while burning "significantly" less fuel. It will cruise at over 315km/h (170kt) at 12,000ft.

Photo: An SR22 in flight. (Cirrus)

Commander 114B & 115

Country of origin: United States of America

Type: Four seat high performance light aircraft

Powerplant: 115 – One 195kW (260hp) Textron Lycoming IO-540-T4B5 fuel injected flat six piston engine driving a three blade constant speed McCauley propeller. 114TC – One 200kW (270hp) turbocharged and fuel injected TIO-540-AG1A.

Performance: 115 – Max speed 304km/h (164kt), cruising speed at 75% power 296km/h (160kt), economical cruising speed at 65% power 287km/h (155kt). Initial rate of climb 1070ft/min. Range at 75% power 1585km (855nm), range at 65% power 1742km (940nm), at 55% power 1862km (1005nm). 114TC – Max speed 364km/h (197kt), cruising speed at 75% power 328km/h (177kt). Initial rate of climb 1050ft/min. Service ceiling 25,000ft. Range at 75% power 1240km (670nm), at 65% power 1445km (780nm).

Weights: 115 – Empty 954kg (2102lb), max ramp 1480kg (3260lb). 114TC – Empty 1018kg (2245lb), max takeoff 1500kg (3305lb)

Dimensions: Wing span 9.98m (32ft 9in), length 7.59m (24ft 11in), height 2.57m (8ft 5in). Wing area 14.1m² (152sq ft).

Capacity: Typical seating for four.

Production: Approx 160 Commander 114B/TC/ATs built. Deliveries of 115s began in mid 2000.

History: The Commander 114B and 115 are modernised developments of the Rockwell Commander 114.

The Rockwell Commander 114 was itself a more powerful development of the Commander 112 of 1970, one of only two new GA designs from Rockwell. Unfortunately for Rockwell, the 150kW (200hp) powered 112 was widely regarded as underpowered. To address concerns with the 112, Rockwell developed the 114 which incorporated a number of improvements plus, most importantly, a 195kW (260hp) six cylinder engine.

The 112 and 114 remained in production with Rockwell until 1979. In 1981 Rockwell's General Aviation Division was sold to Gulfstream Aerospace. Gulfstream held the manufacturing rights for the Commander family but never built the 112 or 114, instead selling the rights to the newly formed Commander Aircraft Company in 1988.

Under Commander Aircraft Company's stewardship, the basic 114 design was improved and updated considerably. The main changes to the Commander 114B over the original 114 included a restyled engine cowling to reduce drag and other aerodynamic improvements, a quieter and more efficient three blade McCauley Black Mac propeller, and a new luxury leather and wool interior.

The revised Commander 114B was issued a new Type Certificate on May 4 1992 and production aircraft were delivered from later that year.

Commander also offered the 114AT optimised for pilot training and the turbocharged 200kW (270hp) TIO-540 powered 114TC, which entered service in 1995.

On March 29 2000 Commander announced the introduction of the improved Commander 115 series, which is available in 115, 115TC and 115AT forms. Engine, airframe and systems improvements and an upgraded avionics package are incorporated while range is significantly increased.

Photo: The turbocharged Commander 114TC. (Commander)

Curtiss C-46 Commando

Country of origin: United States of America

Type: Freighter

Powerplants: C-46 – Two 1495kW (2000hp) Pratt & Whitney R-2800-34 Double Wasp 18 cylinder radial piston engines driving three blade constant speed propellers. C-46R – Two 1565kW (2100hp) Pratt & Whitney R-2800 C or CA series radial pistons.

Performance: C-46 – Typical cruising speed 300km/h (162kt). Range with 2585kg (5700lb) payload 1880km (1017nm). C-46R – Max speed 435km/h (235kt), max cruising speed 378km/h (204kt). Service ceiling 22,000ft. Range with max fuel 2897km (1564nm).

Weights: C-46 – Operating empty 14,970kg (33,000lb), max payload 5265kg (11,630lb), max takeoff 21,772kg (48,000lb). C-46R – Empty 13,290kg (29,300lb), max takeoff 22,680kg (50,000lb).

Dimensions: Wing span 32.92m (108ft 0in), length 23.27m (76ft 4in), height 6.60m (21ft 8in). Wing area 126.2m² (1358sq ft).

Capacity: Flightcrew of two pilots and optional flight engineer. Typical accommodation for freight, but in an airliner configuration can seat 36, or in military configuration 50 troops.

Production: 3182 Commandos built for US armed forces (as the C-46 for the USAAF and R5C for the USN). Many hundreds subsequently converted for civil service. Approx 15 in service as of late 2002.

History: The Curtiss Commando came into widespread civilian service as both an airliner and a freighter after a large number were built as transports for the US military during World War 2, although the original Curtiss design was intended as an airliner.

The Curtiss CW-20 was originally intended as a competitor to the highly successful Douglas DC-3, which was the preeminent airliner of the time and was designed to operate on routes of up to 1000km (540nm), which at the time accounted for 90% of the US domestic airline system. The CW-20 featured two 1270kW (1700hp) Wright R-2600 Twin Cyclone radial engines, twin vertical tails and a pressurised double lobe, or 'double bubble' fuselage. Accommodation would have been for 36 passengers plus four crew.

The CW-20 first flew on March 26 1940. In July that year an impressed US Army Air Force ordered 20 unpressurised CW-20s, which it named the C-46 Commando. The first production aircraft was completed in May 1942, by which time the powerplant choice had been switched to the P&W R-2800, and the first deliveries to the USAAF occurred that July.

Initially the C-46 was troubled with reliability problems in military service, but these were soon overcome and the Commando proved to be a useful transport with its relatively cavernous freight hold.

A proposed postwar commercial version was the CW-20E, but it failed to attract customer interest and thus all Commandos to enter civilian service were ex military aircraft. Many were purchased by American operators for freight work while several hundred operated in Latin America. One postwar conversion was the Riddles Airlines C-46R which had more powerful engines and better performance. Thirty or so were converted.

In 2002 C-46s were operational in Alaska and Canada, with others possibly flying in Bolivia.

Photo: A C-46 freighter in Alaska. (Rob Finlayson)

Convair CV-240, 340 & 440

Country of origin: United States of America

Type: Short haul commercial transports

Powerplants: CV-240 – Two 1490kW (2000hp) Pratt & Whitney R-2800-CA18 Double Wasp piston radial engines driving three blade constant speed propellers. CV-340 – Two 1790kW (2400hp) R-2800-CB16 Double Wasps. CV-440 – Two 1865kW (2500hp) R-2800-CB16 or -CB17 Double Wasps.

Performance: CV-240 – Cruising speed 435km/h (235kt). Range with max fuel 2900km (1565nm). CV-340 – Cruising speed 457km/h (247kt). Typical range with max payload 935km (505nm). CV-440 – Max cruising speed 483km/h (261kt), economical cruising speed 465km/h (250kt). Service ceiling 24,900ft. Range with max payload 756km (408nm), range with max fuel 3106km (1677nm).

Weights: CV-240 – Empty 12,520kg (27,600lb), max takeoff 18,956kg (41,790lb). CV-340 – Empty 13,375kg (29,486lb), max takeoff 21,320kg (47,000lb). CV-440 – Empty 15,110kg (33,314lb), max takeoff 22,544kg (49,700lb).

Dimensions: CV-240 – Wing span 27.97m (91ft 9in), length 22.76m (74ft 8in), height 8.20m (26ft 11in). Wing area 75.9m² (817sq ft). CV-340 – Wing span 32.12m (105ft 4in), length 24.13m (79ft 2in), height 8.58m (28ft 2in). Wing area 85.5m² (920sq ft). CV-440 – Same as CV-340 except for length 24.84m (81ft 6in).

Capacity: CV-240 – Flightcrew of two or three. Passenger seating for up to 40, or a 4240kg (9350lb) payload. CV-340 – Flightcrew of two or three. Passenger seating for up to 52, or a 6075kg (13,391lb) payload. CV-440 – Flightcrew of two or three. Passenger seating for up to 52, or a 5820kg (12,836lb) payload.

Production: 176 CV-240s, 133 civil and 99 military (C-131 Samaritan) CV-340s and 153 CV-440s were built.

History: The Convair CV-240, 340 and 440 series was one of the closest designs to come near to being a Douglas DC-3 replacement as despite a glut of cheap DC-3s in the postwar years this family of airliners achieved considerable sales success.

Design of the original CV-110 was initiated in response to an American Airlines request for a DC-3 replacement. American found the CV-110 (which first flew on July 8 1946) to be too small and asked that the CV-110 be scaled up in size, and this resulted in the CV-240 ConvairLiner. The CV-240 was arguably the most advanced short haul airliner of its day, and first flew on March 16 1947 and entered service on June 1 1948.

The success of the CV-240 led to the 1.37m (4ft 6in) stretched CV-340, which first flew on October 5 1951, and the CV-440 (often called the Metropolitan) which incorporated some aerodynamic improvements and first flew on October 6 1955.

The CV-240, CV-340 and CV-440 sold in large numbers, mainly to airlines in North America, and formed the backbone of many airlines' short to medium haul fleets. Today the small numbers that remain in service are mainly used as freighters.

Many of the surviving aircraft have been converted with turboprops, and these conversions are discussed in the following entry.

Photo: A Portuguese registered Convair 440 operated by the UK's Atlantic Airways, part of Coventry based Air Atlantique. (Dave Fraser)

Convair CV-540, 580, 600, 640 & CV5800

Country of origin: United States of America

Type: Short haul turboprop converted commercial transports

Powerplants: CV-580 – Two 2800kW (3750shp) Allison 501-D13H turboprops driving four blade propellers. CV-640 – Two 2255kW (3025hp) Rolls-Royce R.Da.10/1 Darts. CV5800 – Two 3430kW (4600shp) Allison 501-D22Gs.

Performance: CV-580 – Max cruising speed 550km/h (297kt) at 20,000ft. Range with 2270kg (5000lb) payload 3650km (1970nm), range with max fuel 4773km (2577nm). CV-640 – Cruising speed 483km/h (260kt). Range with max payload 1979km (1069nm), range with max fuel 3138km (1695nm).

Weights: CV-580 – Operating empty 13,732kg (30,275lb), max takeoff 26,371kg (58,140lb). CV-640 – Operating empty 13,733kg (30,275lb), max takeoff 25,855kg (57,000lb). CV5800 – Operating empty 15,043kg (33,166lb), max takeoff 28,576kg (63,000lb).

Dimensions: CV-580 – Wing span 32.12m (105ft 4in), length 24.84m (81ft 6in), height 8.89m (29ft 2in). Wing area 85.5m² (920sq ft). CV5800 – Same except for length 29.18m (95ft 9in).

Capacity: Flightcrew of two or three. Passenger seating for up to 56 at four abreast and 76cm (30in) pitch. CV5800 – Seating for 76.

Production: 170 CV-340s and CV-440s converted to CV-580s, 38 CV-240s converted to CV-600s, 27 CV-340s and CV-440s converted to CV-640s. 85 CV-580s, 13 CV-600s and CV-640s were in commercial service in late 2002. Two CV5800 conversions in service.

History: The original piston Convairs have been the subject of a number of turboprop modification programs.

As early as 1950 the potential of turboprop powered CV-240s was recognised, leading to first flight of the Allison 501 powered CV-240 Turboliner that December, while an Allison 501D powered YC-131C conversion of the CV-340 for the US Air Force first flew on June 19 1954. One other early conversion occurred in 1954 when D Napier and Sons in Britain converted CV-340s with that company's 2280kW (3060hp) Eland N.El.1 turboprops as the CV-540. Six -540s were converted for Allegheny Airlines in the USA, although these aircraft were later converted back to piston power. Canadair meanwhile built 10 new aircraft with Eland engines for the Royal Canadian Air Force from 1960.

The most popular Convair conversions were those done by PacAero in California for Allison, and this involved converting CV-340s and CV-440s to CV-580s with Allison 501D turboprops, plus modified tail control surfaces and a larger tail area. The first such conversion flew on January 19 1960, although it was not until June 1964 that a converted aircraft entered service (with Frontier Airlines).

Convair's own conversion program involved Rolls-Royce Darts, and the first of these flew on May 2 1965. Thus converted CV-240s became CV-600s, while CV-340s and CV-440s became CV-640s.

Kelowna Flightcraft in Canada has offered the most ambitious Convair conversion program, the CV5800, which stretches a CV-580 by 4.34m (14ft 3in) and reverts to the CV-440's original tail unit. Production conversions also have the options of a new freight door and new avionics. Two are in service with Contract Air Cargo in the US.

Photo: A Convair CV-580 at Valdez, Alaska. (Christian Hanuise)

Country of origin: France

Type: Light corporate jet

Powerplants: 10 & 100 – Two 14.4kN (3230lb) Garrett TFE731-2 turbofans.

Performance: 10 – Max cruising speed 912km/h (492kt). Range with four passengers and reserves 3560km (1920nm). 100 – Max cruising speed same. Range with four passengers and reserves 3480km (1880nm).

Weights: 10 – Empty equipped 4880kg (10,760lb), max takeoff 8500kg (18,740lb). 100 – Empty equipped 5055kg (11,145lb), max takeoff 8755kg (19,300lb).

Dimensions: Wing span 13.08m (42ft 11in), length 13.86m (45ft 6in), height 4.61m (15ft 2in). Wing area 24.1m² (259sq ft).

Capacity: Flightcrew of two on flightdeck. Main cabin is typically configured to seat four in an executive club seating arrangement. Main cabin can seat up to seven in Falcon 10 or eight in Falcon 100 in a high density layout. Can be configured for air ambulance, aerial photography and navaid calibration missions.

Production: In addition to three prototypes, 226 Falcon 10s and Falcon 100s (including seven military MERs & 31 Falcon 100s), were built between 1973 and 1990, of which 170 10s and 34 100s were in corporate use in late 2002.

History: The smallest of Dassault's corporate jet family, the Falcon 10 and Falcon 100 series (Mystère 10 and Mystère 100 in France) sold in good numbers during a production run that lasted almost two decades.

In concept a scaled down Falcon/Mystère 20, the Falcon 10/100 was an all new design except for similar high lift wing devices. It was conceived in the late 1960s, the second member of the Dassault Falcon family to be developed. Dassault originally intended the Falcon 10 be powered by two General Electric CJ610 turbojets, and a CJ610 powered prototype first flew on December 1 1970.

Flight testing was delayed until May 1971 while changes were made to the wing design, including increasing the wing sweepback angle. The second prototype was the first to be powered by Garrett TFE731 turbofans, and it completed its first flight on October 15 1971. Flight testing was completed with the aid of a third prototype, and French and US certification was awarded in September 1973. Deliveries of production aircraft began that November.

Almost all Falcon 10 production was for civil customers, but the French navy ordered seven, designated the Mystère 10 MER, as multi purpose pilot trainers. Missions include simulation of targets for Super Etendard pilots and instrument training.

The improved Falcon 100 replaced the Falcon 10 in production in the mid 1980s. Certificated in December 1986, changes included an optional early EFIS glass cockpit, a higher maximum takeoff weight, a fourth cabin window on the right side and a larger unpressurised rear baggage compartment.

Production of the Falcon 100 ceased in 1990 with the last delivered that September.

Photo: A French registered Falcon 10 approaches Geneva. (Charles Falk)

Country of origin: France

Type: Mid size corporate jet

Powerplants: 20 – Two 20.0kN (4500lb) General Electric CF700-2D-2 turbofans. 200 – Two 23.1kN (5200lb) Garrett ATF 3-6A-4Cs.

Performance: 20 – Max cruising speed 863km/h (466kt), economical cruising speed 750km/h (405kt). Service ceiling 42,000ft. Range with max fuel and reserves 3300km (1780nm). 200 – Max cruising speed 870km/h (470kt), economical cruising speed 780km/h (420kt). Service ceiling 45,000ft. Range with max fuel, eight passengers and reserves 4650km (2510nm).

Weights: 20 – Empty equipped 7530kg (16,600lb), max takeoff 13,000kg (28,660lb). 200 – Empty equipped 8250kg (18,290lb), max takeoff 14,515kg (32,000lb).

Dimensions: Wing span 16.32m (53ft 7in), length 17.15m (56ft 3in), height 5.32m (17ft 6in). Wing area 41.0m² (441.33sq ft).

Capacity: Flightcrew of two. Typical seating for between eight and 10 passengers, up to 14 in a high density configuration.

Production: 38 200s and 476 20s (including HU-2Js) delivered. In 2002 427 Falcon 20s and 32 Falcon 200s remained in use.

History: The Mystère or Falcon 20 and 200 family remains Dassault's most successful business jet program thus far, with more than 500 built and most still in service.

Dassault, the famous French fighter manufacturer, launched development of what would become the Mystère 20 in December 1961. State owned Sud Aviation became a program partner in June 1962, with responsibility for building the fuselage and tail.

The first prototype, powered by 14.7kN (3300lb) Pratt & Whitney JT12A-8 turbojets, first flew on May 4 1963. Production Mystère 20s (or Falcon 20s outside France) were powered with General Electric CF700s. The first GE powered 20 flew on New Year's Day 1965. Production continued until 1983.

A notable variant was the Falcon 20DC package freighter developed for Federal Express (which it used to inaugurate services with in April 1973). Thirty-three new and used Falcons were converted with a large forward port side freight door and strengthened floor

The Falcon 200, announced at the 1979 Paris Airshow, is powered by Garrett ATF 3-6A-4C. A converted Falcon 20 served as the prototype, and first flew with the new engines on April 30 1980. French DGAC certification was awarded in June 1981.

Apart from the Garrett engines, the Falcon 200 (initially the 20H) introduced greater fuel capacity and much longer range, redesigned wing root fairings and some systems and equipment changes. The 200 remained in production until 1988.

The Guardian is a maritime surveillance variant of the Falcon 200 sold to the French navy (as the Gardian) and the US Coast Guard (HU-25).

AlliedSignal (now Honeywell) has offered a Falcon 20 re-engine program with its TFE731 turbofan. From 1991 over 90 Falcon 20s were re-engined with 21.1kN (4750lb) TFE731-5ARs or -5BRs.

In 1973 Dassault flew the prototype Falcon 30, a 30 seat regional airliner stretched development of the 20, but it did not enter production.

Photo: A Ukraine registered Falcon 20. (Rob Finlayson)

Dassault Falcon 50

Country of origin: France

Type: Long range mid size corporate jet

Powerplants: 50 – Three 16.5kN (3700lb) AlliedSignal TFE731-3 turbofans. 50EX – Three 16.5kN (3700lb) Honeywell TFE731-40s.

Performance: 50 – Max cruising speed 880km/h (475kt), long range cruising speed 797km/h (430kt). Max operating altitude 45,000ft. Range with eight passengers and reserves 5715km (3084nm). 50EX – Range with eight passengers at Mach 0.80 5602km (3025nm), at Mach 0.75 6083km (3285nm).

Weights: 50 – Empty equipped 9150kg (20,170lb), standard max takeoff 17,600kg (38,800lb), or optionally 18,500kg (40,780lb). 50EX – Empty equipped 9603kg (21,270lb), standard max takeoff 18,007kg (39,700lb), optional max takeoff 18,497kg (40,780lb).

Dimensions: Wing span 18.86m (61ft 11in), length 18.52m (61ft 11in), height 6.98m (22ft 11in). Wing area 46.8m² (504.1sq ft).

Capacity: Flightcrew of two pilots. A number of cabin seating arrangements offered. Seating for eight or nine with aft toilet, or for up to 12 with forward toilet. Max accommodation for 19. Can accommodate three stretchers and two medical attendants in a medevac role.

Production: 245 Falcon 50s and 70 50EXs in service in late 2002.

History: The trijet Falcon 50 is a long range corporate jet that grew out of the earlier twinjet Mystère/Falcon 20 and 200.

The Dassault Falcon 50 was developed for long range trans Atlantic and transcontinental flights, using the Falcon 20 as the design basis. However, to meet the 6440km (3475nm) range requirement significant changes mean that the Falcon 50 is for all intents and purposes an all new aircraft.

Key features include three 16.6kN (3700lb) Garrett TFE731 turbofans mounted on a new area ruled tail, plus a new supercritical wing of greater area than that on the 20 and 200. Falcon 20 components carried over include the nose and fuselage cross section.

The prototype Falcon 50 first flew on November 7 1976, although it wasn't until March 7 1979 that FAA certification was granted. In the meantime the design had been changed to incorporate the supercritical wing, although the original wing's basic planform was retained. A second prototype first flew on February 18 1978, a first preproduction aircraft following on June 13 1978. First customer deliveries began in July 1979.

In April 1995 Dassault announced the long range Falcon 50EX with more fuel efficient TFE731-40 turbofans, 740km (400nm) greater range (at Mach 0.80) than the base Falcon 50 and a new EFIS flightdeck based on the Falcon 2000's with Collins Pro Line 4 avionics. The 50EX also features as standard equipment items offered as options only on the standard Falcon 50.

The Falcon 50EX's maiden flight was on April 10 1996, with French and US certification in November and December 1996 respectively. First delivery (to Volkswagen) was in the following January. (Earlier 50s can be upgraded with the TFE731-40 engines.)

The Surmar is a maritime patrol version of the 50 ordered by the French navy (fitted with a FLIR and search radar).

Photo: A Falcon 50EX. (Dassault)

Dassault Falcon 900

Country of origin: France

Type: Large intercontinental range corporate jet

Powerplants: 900B – Three 21.1kN (4750lb) AlliedSignal TFE731-5BRs. 900EX – Three 22.3kN (5000lb) Honeywell TFE731-60s.

Performance: 900B – Max cruising speed 927km/h (500kt), economical cruising speed Mach 0.75. Max certificated altitude 51,000ft. Range with eight passengers and reserves at Mach 0.80 7150km (3860nm). 900EX – Range with eight passengers at Mach 0.80 8020km (4330nm), at long range cruising speed 8335km (4500nm).

Weights: 900B – Empty equipped 10,255kg (22,611kg), max takeoff 20,640kg (45,500lb). 900EX – Empty equipped 10,830kg (23,875lb), max takeoff 21,909kg (48,300lb).

Dimensions: Wing span 19.33m (63ft 5in), length 20.21m (66ft 4in), height 7.55m (24ft 9in). Wing area 49.0m² (527.43sq ft).

Capacity: Flightcrew of two. Main passenger cabin seating for eight and 15 passengers, or up to 18 in a high density configuration.

Production: Over 295 Falcon 900s (inc 7 900Cs & 70 900EXs) in service in 2002.

History: The Falcon 900 intercontinental range trijet is a substantially revised development of the Falcon 50.

Dassault announced it was developing a new intercontinental range large size business jet based on the Falcon 50 on May 27 1983 at the Paris Airshow. The prototype, *Spirit of Lafayette*, flew for the first time on September 21 1984. A second prototype flew on August 30 1985. French certification was awarded on March 14 1986, FAA certification followed on March 21, and first customer deliveries occurred in December that year.

While of similar overall configuration to the Falcon 50, the Falcon 900 introduced an all new wider and longer fuselage which can seat three passengers abreast. The main commonality with the Falcon 50 is the wing, which despite being designed for a considerably lighter aircraft, was adapted almost directly unchanged. In designing the Falcon 900 Dassault made use of computer aided modelling, while the aircraft's structure incorporates a degree of composite materials.

From 1991 the standard production model was the Falcon 900B, which differs from the earlier 900 in having more powerful engines and increased range. Earlier production 900s could be retrofitted to 900B standard.

The Falcon 900EX is a longer range development launched in October 1994. It features TFE731-60s, a Honeywell Primus 4000 EFIS avionics suite, optional Flight Dynamics head-up displays, increased fuel capacity and greater range. Its first flight was on June 1 1995 and first delivery was in May 1996.

The latest Falcon 900 model is the 900C, revealed in 1998. The C is a development of the B but incorporates the advanced Honeywell Primus avionics of the 900EX. The 900C replaced the 900B in the Falcon product line with first deliveries in early 2000.

From 2003 the 900EX will introduce Dassault's EASy avionics operating system with four colour displays, cursor control devices and multifunction keyboards.

Photo: A Saudi gorvernment Falcon 900B. (Charles Falk)

Dassault Falcon 2000

Country of origin: France

Type: Transcontinental range mid to large size corporate jet

Powerplants: 2000 – Two 26.3kN (5918lb) CFE (General Electric & Honeywell) CFE738-1-1B turbofans. 2000EX – Two 31.1kN (7000lb) Pratt & Whitney Canada PW308Cs.

Performance: 2000 – Max cruising speed Mach 0.84 or 891km/h (481kt), normal cruising speed Mach 0.80 or 850km/h (459kt), long range cruising speed Mach 0.80 or 850km/h (459kt). Max certificated altitude 47,000ft. Range at 0.80 Mach with six passengers 5633km (3040nm). 2000EX – Normal cruising speed Mach 0.80 or 850km/h/ 459kt. Range at 0.80 Mach with six passengers 7041km (3800nm).

Weights: 2000 – Empty equipped 9405kg (20,735lb), standard max takeoff 16,238kg (35,800lb), optional max takeoff 16,556kg (36,500lb). 2000EX – Max takeoff 18,478kg (40,700lb).

Dimensions: Wing span 19.33m (63ft 5in), length 20.22m (66ft 4in), height 7.06m (23ft 2in). Wing area 49.0m² (527.6sq ft).

Capacity: Flightcrew of two. Main cabin seating typically for eight passengers, or up to 12 in a high density layout.

Production: Over 180 in service in late 2002.

History: The Falcon 2000 is a twin engine, slightly smaller development of the Falcon 900 trijet.

The Falcon 2000 shares the 900's wing and forward fuselage, but there are a number of design changes. From the start the Falcon 2000 was designed with a range of 5560km (3000nm) in mind, which is less than the intercontinental 900's range. This removed the need for the redundancy of three engines for long range overwater flights, allowing the two new CFE738 engines to be fitted, with considerable maintenance and operating economics benefits over a trijet configuration. The CFE738 engine was developed specifically for the Falcon 2000 by CFE, a partnership of General Electric and AlliedSignal (now Honeywell). Meanwhile, the 2000's fuselage is 1.98m (6ft 6in) shorter than the 900. Another noticeable design change between the 900 and 2000 is the area ruled rear fuselage.

The wing, compared to the 900's, features a modified leading edge and the inboard slats have been removed, while the cockpit features a Collins four screen EFIS avionics system with optional Flight Dynamics head-up displays.

Dassault announced it was developing the Falcon 2000, then known as the Falcon X, in June 1989. First flight occurred on March 4 1993 and certification was awarded in November 1994. The first customer delivery occurred in March 1995.

In October 2000 at that year's NBAA convention Dassault launched the extended range Falcon 2000EX. The 2000EX will be powered by Pratt & Whitney Canada PW308C engines with a 1732kg (3815lb) increase in fuel capacity, giving it a 7040km (3800nm) range, 25% better than the standard 2000, allowing westbound nonstop flights from Europe to the east coast of the USA.

First flight was on October 25 2001 with customer deliveries in early-mid 2003. The standard 2000 will remain in production alongside the 2000EX. The 2000EX will be offered with Dassault's EASy avionics operating system from early-mid 2004.

Photo: The Falcon 2000. (Dassault)

Dassault Falcon 7X

Country of origin: France

Type: Transcontinental range large corporate jet

Powerplants: Three 27kN (6100lb) Pratt & Whitney Canada PW307A turbofans.

Performance: Max operating speed Mach 0.9, typical cruising speed Mach 0.85. Range with eight passengers at Mach 0.80 with NBAA IFR reserves 10,560km (5700nm).

Weights: Basic operating empty 15,027kg (33,100lb), max takeoff 28,920kg (63,700lb).

Dimensions: Wing span 25.13m (82ft 6in), length 23.19m (76ft 1in), height 7.77m (25ft 6in).

Capacity: Flightcrew of two. Main cabin seating typically for 12, with crew rest area, three lounges, galley, lavatories and baggage compartment. Cabin height 1.88m (6ft 2in), cabin length 11.92m (39ft 1in). Baggage volume 4.4m³ (157cu ft). Cabin altitude 6000ft.

Production: Deliveries following certification in 2006. Estimated market over 400.

History: The Falcon 7X is Dassault's latest and will be its largest and fastest member of the Falcon business jet family.

Dassault launched the Falcon 7X, then called Falcon Next, at the Paris Airshow in June 2001. The new jet is due to fly in early 2005 with certification in 2006.

The 7X shares the same fuselage cross section as the Falcon 900 but its cabin will be 20% larger, while the nose is redesigned with fewer but larger cockpit transparencies. Power is from three Pratt & Whitney Canada PW307 turbofans, mounted, like the Falcon 50 and 900, on and in the rear fuselage. The PW307 is a close relative to the Falcon 2000EX's PW308.

The key to the 7X's performance will be its all new supercritical wing designed for transonic speed cruise. Compared to the Falcon 900's wing, the 7X's unit will feature increased sweep, 40% more area, a higher aspect ratio and a 35% lift-to-drag ratio. It will feature two section leading edge flaps.

Falcon 7X will feature Dassault's new EASy advanced flightdeck with four large 36cm (14.1in) colour screens, which aims to reduce pilot workload and improve situational awareness. Based on Honeywell's Primus Epic platform, EASy features include flightpath based symbology, intuitive displays and map merging. The 7X will also feature sidestick controllers and fly-by-wire flight controls with flight envelope protection (as on Airbus airliners).

The 7X's 10,560km (5700nm) range allows it to operate such nonstop city pairs as Paris-Tokyo, New York-Riyadh and San Francisco-Moscow. The 7X is cheaper, slightly smaller and will not quite have the range of the Bombardier Global Express and Gulfstream V/5000.

Falcon 7X suppliers will include Honeywell (avionics, APU), Messier Dowty (landing gear), EADS Socata (part of the upper fuselage, body fairing), Latecoere (part of the fuselage), EADS CASA (horizontal stabiliser), Sonaca (wing leading edge), Fokker (trailing edge movable surfaces) and Hurel Hispano and Aermacchi (nacelles and thrust reversers).

Photo: The Falcon 7X is being designed with the aid of computational fluid dynamics. (Dassault)

De Havilland Canada DHC-1 Chipmunk

Country of origin: Canada

Type: Two seat light aircraft

Powerplant: One 108kW (145hp) de Havilland Gipsy Major 8 four cylinder inverted inline piston engine driving a two blade fixed pitch wooden propeller.

Performance: Max speed at sea level 223km/h (120kt), cruising speed 200km/h (108kt). Initial rate of climb 900ft/min. Service ceiling 17,200ft. Max range 450km (243nm). Endurance 2.3 hours.

Weights: Empty 526kg (1158lb), max takeoff 914kg (2014lb).

Dimensions: Wing span 10.46m (34ft 4in), length 7.75m (25ft 5in), height 2.13m (7ft 0in). Wing area 15.9m² (172sq ft).

Capacity: Seating for two in tandem. Small numbers were modified for crop spraying and fitted with a chemical hopper in place of the front cockpit.

Production: 1291 Chipmunks built, including 217 in Canada, 60 under licence in Portugal and 1014 in Britain. Most built originally for military customers, but hundreds now fly with private owners.

History: De Havilland Canada's Chipmunk – affectionately known as the Chippie – was designed to replace the Royal Air Force's ageing Tiger Moth two seat basic trainer biplane (described separately).

With a full design workload (courtesy of the revolutionary Comet jet airliner project among others), de Havilland handed design responsibility for the new trainer to its Canadian subsidiary, de Havilland Canada. DHC's first aircraft was the design responsibility of W J Jakimuk who had emigrated to Canada from Poland in 1940 and was previously responsible for designing the PZL 24 and PZL 50 Jastrab fighters and the DH.95 Flamingo airliner.

His new aircraft was designated the DHC-1 Chipmunk and first flew on May 22 1946. Features of the design included a de Havilland Gipsy Major engine and all metal construction (but with fabric covered control surfaces). First deliveries were in 1947.

Canadian built DHC-1B-1s and DHC-1B-2s (60 built for the RCAF) were known as the T.30 in British service, and many featured clear view blown canopies. However the bulk of Chipmunk production was undertaken by de Havilland in Britain. British production models included the initial T.10 and T.20 for the RAF, and civilian T.21.

Civilianised versions of RAF aircraft became available in large numbers from the late 1950s, with civilianised T.10s becoming Mk.22s, while Mk.22As were modified ex RAF T.10s with greater fuel capacity.

Farm Aviation Services in the UK heavily modified five Chipmunks with a hopper tank in place of the forward cockpit for spraying duties, these aircraft were designated Mk.23s. Three similar conversions were performed in Australia by Sasin/Aerostructures as the SA29 Spraymaster.

Today the Chipmunk remains a very popular sport and private aircraft, while a small number are still used for pilot training and tailwheel endorsements. Some have also been extensively modified with the installation of Lycoming or Continental engines, blown canopies and wheel spats.

Photo: A Chipmunk in a natural metal finish. (Keith Anderson)

De Havilland Canada DHC-2 Beaver

Country of origin: Canada

Type: STOL utility transport

Powerplant: Mk I – One 335kW (450hp) Pratt & Whitney R-985 Wasp Junior nine cylinder radial piston engine driving a two blade variable pitch prop. Mk III – One 578eshp Pratt & Whitney Canada PT6A-6 or PT6A-20 turboprop driving a three blade constant speed propeller.

Performance: Mk I – Max speed 225km/h (121kt), max cruising speed 217km/h (117kt), normal cruising speed 201km/h (109kt). Initial rate of climb 1020ft/min. Service ceiling 18,000ft. Max range with reserves 1252km (676nm). Mk III – Max speed 274km/h (148kt), max cruising speed 253km/h (137kt), long range cruising speed 225km/h (122kt). Initial rate of climb 1185ft/min. Service ceiling 20,000ft. Max range with reserves 1090km (588nm).

Weights: Mk I – Empty 1293kg (2850lb), max takeoff 2313kg (5100lb). Mk I seaplane – Operating empty 1506kg (3316lb), max takeoff 2309kg (5090lb). Mk III – Empty 1175kg (2590lb), max takeoff 2436kg (5370lb).

Dimensions: Mk I – Wing span 14.63m (48ft 0in), length 9.25m (30ft 4in), height 2.75m (9ft 0in). Wing area 23.1m² (250sq ft). Mk I – seaplane – Same except for length 9.98m (32ft 9in), height 3.18m (10ft 5in). Mk III – Same as Mk I except for length 10.74m (35ft 3in).

Capacity: Standard seating for eight including the pilot, seating for 11 in Turbo Beaver. The 'Ag-Beaver' is fitted with a 0.99m³ (35cu ft) chemical hopper.

Production: 1692 Beavers built between 1948 and 1968, including approximately 60 Turbo Beavers. 974 were delivered to the US military and many others delivered to foreign military air arms. Several hundred remain in service with civilian operators.

History: The Beaver was de Havilland Canada's first purpose designed utility aircraft and its most successful program sales wise (both military or civil), with almost 1700 built over two decades.

Beaver development work began in 1946 with considerable input from the Ontario Department of Lands and Forests. A prototype flew on August 16 1947, with seating for five or six. The production Beaver was slightly larger to seat an extra two passengers, with civil certification awarded in March 1948.

The only major development of the Beaver (aside from a single prototype powered by a 410kW/550hp Alvis Leonides 502/4 radial engine) was the Turbo Beaver. First flown in December 1963 it featured a Pratt & Whitney (then United Aircraft Canada) PT6A-6 turboprop, which offered lower empty and higher takeoff weights, and even better STOL performance. The Turbo Beaver's cabin was also longer due to a forward fuselage extension, allowing maximum accommodation for 11, including the pilot. Externally, the Turbo Beaver had a much longer and reprofiled nose, and a larger swept vertical tail.

About 60 new build Turbo Beavers were built (the first was delivered to the Ontario Department of Lands in December 1964) while DHC also offered conversion kits enabling piston powered Beavers to be upgraded to Turbo standard. Many after-market conversions have also been performed. Others have been fitted with Garrett TPE331s.

Photo: A Beaver floatplane. (Paul Sadler)

De Havilland Canada DHC-3 Otter

Country of origin: Canada

Type: STOL utility transport

Powerplant: One 447kW (600hp) Pratt & Whitney R-1340-S1H1-G or R-1340-S3H1-G nine cylinder radial piston engine driving a three blade Hamilton Standard constant speed propeller.

Performance: Max speed 257km/h (140kt), economical cruising speed at sea level 195km/h (105kt). Initial rate of climb 850ft/min. Service ceiling 18,800ft. Max range with reserves 1520km (820nm), range with a 950kg (2100lb) payload and reserves 1410km (760nm).

Weights: Landplane – Basic operating 2010kg (4431lb), max take-off 3629kg (8000lb). Floatplane – Basic operating 2219kg (4892lb), max takeoff 3614kg (7967lb).

Dimensions: Wing span 17.69m (58ft 0in), length 12.80m (41ft 10in), height 3.83m (12ft 7in), floatplane height 4.57m (15ft 0in). Wing area 34.8m² (375sq ft).

Capacity: Flightcrew of one or two. Normal main cabin seating for nine passengers, max seating for 10. As an aerial ambulance can carry six stretchers and four passengers or three stretchers and seven passengers.

Production: A total of 460 Otters built including for military air arms in 11 nations.

History: The Otter was conceived to be capable of performing the same roles as the earlier and highly successful Beaver, but was bigger, and was the second in de Havilland Canada's successful line of rugged and useful STOL utility transports.

Although the same overall configuration of the Beaver, the Otter is much larger overall. The Otter began life as the King Beaver, but compared to the Beaver is longer, has greater span wings and is much heavier. Seating in the main cabin is for 10 or 11, whereas the Beaver seats six. Power is supplied by a nine cylinder, 450kW (600hp) Pratt & Whitney R-1340 Wasp radial. Like the Beaver the Otter can be fitted with skis and floats. The amphibious floatplane Otter features a unique four unit retractable undercarriage, with the wheels retracting into the floats.

De Havilland Canada began design work on the DHC-3 Otter in January 1951, the company's design efforts resulting in the type's first flight on December 12 1951. Canadian certification was awarded in November 1952.

De Havilland Canada demonstrated the Otter to the US Army, and subsequently that service went on to become the largest DHC-3 operator (designated U-1). Other military users included Australia, Canada, India and Norway.

Small numbers of Otters were converted to turbine power by Cox Air Services of Alberta, Canada. Changes included a Pratt & Whitney Canada PT6A turboprop, a lower empty weight of 1692kg (3703lb) and a higher maximum speed of 267km/h (144kt). It was called the Cox Turbo Single Otter. A number of other after-market PT6 conversions have also been offered.

The Otter found a significant niche as a bush aircraft and today it remains highly sought after.

Photo: A turbine floatplane conversion of the Otter gets airborne. (Paul Sadler)

De Havilland Canada DHC-4 Caribou

Country of origin: Canada

Type: STOL utility transport

Powerplants: DHC-4A – Two 1080kW (1450shp) Pratt & Whitney R-2000-7M2 14 cylinder twin row radial piston engines driving three blade propellers.

Performance: DHC-4A – Max speed 347km/h (187kt), normal cruising speed 293km/h (158kt). Initial rate of climb 1355ft/min. Service ceiling 24,800ft. Range with max payload 390km (210nm), range with max fuel 2105km (1135nm).

Weights: DHC-4A – Basic operating 8293kg (18,260lb), standard max takeoff 12,930kg (28,500lb), military overload max takeoff 14,195kg (31,300lb).

Dimensions: Wing span 29.15m (95ft 8in), length 22.13m (72ft 7in), height 9.68m (31ft 9in). Wing area 84.7m² (912sq ft).

Capacity: Flightcrew of two. Can carry almost four tonnes (8000lb) of cargo in freighter configuration, or seat approximately 30 passengers.

Production: Caribou production ended in 1983 after 307 had been built, most for military customers. A small number survive in commercial service in 2002.

History: De Havilland's Caribou rugged STOL utility was primarily a military tactical transport that in commercial service found itself a small niche.

De Havilland Canada designed the DHC-4 in response to a US Army requirement for a tactical airlifter to supply the battlefront with troops and supplies and evacuate casualties on the return journey. With assistance from Canada's Department of Defence Production DHC built a prototype demonstrator that first flew on July 30 1958.

Impressed with the DHC-4's STOL capabilities and potential, the US Army ordered five for evaluation as YAC-1s and went on to become the largest Caribou operator, taking delivery of 159. The AC-1 designation was later changed to CV-2, and then C-7 when the US Army's CV-2s were transferred to the US Air Force in 1966. US and Australian Caribou saw extensive service during the Vietnam conflict. In addition some US Caribou were captured by North Vietnamese forces and remained in service with that country through to the late 1970s. Other notable military operators included Canada, Malaysia, India and Spain.

The majority of Caribou production was for military operators, but the type's ruggedness and excellent STOL capabilities also appealed to a select group of commercial users. US certification was awarded on December 23 1960. Ansett-MAL, which operated a single example in the New Guinea highlands, and AMOCO Ecuador were early customers, as was Air America (a CIA front in South East Asia during the Vietnam War era for covert operations). Other Caribou entered commercial service after being retired from their military users.

Today only a handful are in civil use as the Caribou's thirsty twin row radial engines make commercial operations uneconomic where its STOL performance is not important. A turboprop development of the Caribou, the DHC-5 Buffalo, was quite successful as a military airlifter but was not sold to commercial operators.

Photo: The civil Caribou fleet is dwindling. (Paul Howard)

De Havilland Canada DHC-6 Twin Otter

Country of origin: Canada

Type: STOL turboprop regional airliner and utility transport

Powerplants: 100 – Two 431kW (578shp) Pratt & Whitney Canada (formerly United Aircraft of Canada) PT6A-20 turboprops driving three blade propellers. 300 – Two 460kW (620shp) P&WC PT6A-27s.

Performance: 100 – Max cruising speed 297km/h (160kt). Range with max fuel 1427km (771nm), range with 975kg (2150lb) payload 1344km (727nm). 300 – Max cruising speed 338km/h (182kt). Initial rate of climb 1600ft/min. Range with 1135kg (2500lb) payload 1297km (700nm), range with a 860kg (1900lb) payload and wing tanks 1705km (920nm).

Weights: 100 – Basic operating empty 2653kg (5850lb), max take-off 4763kg (10,500lb). 300 – Operating empty 3363kg (7415lb), max takeoff 5670kg (12,500lb).

Dimensions: 100 – Wing span 19.81m (65ft 0in), length 15.09m (49ft 6in), height 5.94m (19ft 6in). Wing area 39.0m² (420sq ft). 300 – Same except for length 15.77m (51ft 9in), or 15.09m (49ft 6in) for floatplane variants.

Capacity: Flightcrew of two. Standard regional airliner interior seats 20 at three abreast and 76cm (30in) pitch.

Production: 115 Series 100s, 115 Series 200s and 614 Series 300s built. 600 in service in 2002.

History: The Twin Otter remains popular for its rugged construction and useful STOL performance, and after the Bombardier CRJ is Canada's most successful commercial aircraft program.

Development of the Twin Otter began in January 1964 when de Havilland Canada started design work on a new STOL twin turbo-prop commuter airliner (seating between 13 and 18) and utility transport based on the piston single DHC-3 Otter. The new aircraft was designated the DHC-6 and prototype construction began in No-vember that year, resulting in the type's first flight on May 20 1965. After receiving certification in mid 1966, the first Twin Otter entered service with long time de Havilland Canada supporter the Ontario Department of Lands.

Design features included a stretched Otter fuselage, a longer span Otter based wing with double slotted trailing edge flaps and ailerons that can act in unison to boost STOL performance, and twin PT6A turboprops. The first production aircraft were Series 100s. Com-pared with the later Series 200s and 300s, the 100s are distinguish-able by their shorter, blunter noses.

The main addition to the Series 200, which was introduced in April 1968, was the extended nose, which, together with a reconfigured storage compartment in the rear cabin, greatly in-creased baggage stowage area.

The definitive Series 300 was introduced from the 231st produc-tion aircraft in 1969. It too featured the lengthened nose, but also introduced more powerful engines, thus allowing a 450kg (1000lb) increase in takeoff weight and a 20 seat interior. Production ceased in late 1988. In addition, six 300S enhanced STOL performance DHC-6-300s were built in the mid 1970s.

Examples of all models have been fitted with skis and floats.

Photo: A pair of float fitted Canadian Twin Otters. (Paul Sadler)

De Havilland Canada Dash 7

Country of origin: Canada

Type: STOL turboprop regional airliner

Powerplants: Four 835kW (1220shp) Pratt & Whitney Canada PT6A-50 turboprops driving four blade propellers.

Performance: Max cruising speed 428km/h (230kt), long range cruising speed 400km/h (215kt). Service ceiling 21,000ft. STOL takeoff distance at 18,600kg (41,000lb) TO weight 670m (2260ft). Range with 50 passengers and reserves 1270km (690nm), range with standard fuel and three tonne payload 2168km (1170nm). 150 – Range with 50 passengers at max cruising speed 2110km (1140nm), with max fuel 4670km (2525nm).

Weights: 100 – Operating empty 12,560kg (27,690lb), max takeoff 19,958kg (44,000lb). 150 – Operating empty 12,465kg (27,480lb), max takeoff 21,320kg (47,000lb).

Dimensions: Wing span 28.35m (93ft 0in), length 24.58m (80ft 8in), height 7.98m (26ft 2in). Wing area 79.9m² (860.0sq ft).

Capacity: Flightcrew of two. Max seating for 54 at four abreast and 74cm (29in) pitch, 50 passengers at 81cm (32in) pitch. In freighter configuration can carry five standard pallets.

Production: 111 Dash 7s were built between 1977 and 1988. 64 were in commercial service as of late 2002.

History: The four engine de Havilland Canada Dash 7 remains unri-valled because of its impressive STOL performance and low noise.

The Dash 7 (or DHC-7) was designed as a STOL (short takeoff and landing) 50 seat regional airliner capable of operating from strips as short as 915m (3000ft) in length. (At the time it was envisaged that many cities would develop inner city 'STOL ports'.) Design features include an advanced wing and four Pratt & Whitney Canada PT6A turboprops. Double slotted trailing edge flaps run the entire span of the high mounted wing, substantially increasing the lifting surface available for takeoff. Extra lift is also generated by the airflow over the wing from the relatively slow turning propellers. The wings also feature two pairs of spoilers each – the inboard pair also operate as lift dumpers, the outboard pair can act differentially in conjunction with the ailerons to boost roll control.

Financial backing from the Canadian Government allowed the launch of the DHC-7 program in the early 1970s, resulting in the first flight of the first of two development aircraft on March 27 1975. The first production Dash 7 flew on March 3 1977, the type was certifi-cated on May 2 1977 and it entered service with Rocky Mountain Airways on February 3 1978.

The standard passenger carrying Dash 7 is the Series 100, while the type was also offered in pure freighter form as the Series 101. The only major development of the Dash 7 was the Series 150, which featured a higher max takeoff weight and greater fuel capac-ity, boosting range. The Series 151 was the equivalent freighter. However just one Series 150 was built, for Canada's Department of the Environment for ice reconnaissance.

Dash 7 production ended in 1988 with the last delivered to Aus-tria's Tyrolean Airways in December 1988, following Boeing's takeo-ver of de Havilland Canada.

Photo: A Dash 7 of Canadian operator Trans Capital. (Gary Gentle)

De Havilland DH.82 Tiger Moth

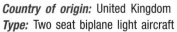

Country of origin: United Kingdom

Type: Two seat biplane light aircraft

Powerplant: DH.82A – One 97kW (130hp) de Havilland Gipsy Major 1 inline and inverted four cylinder piston engine driving a fixed pitch two blade wooden propeller.

Performance: DH.82A – Max speed 175km/h (95kt), max cruising speed 160km/h (87kt), economical cruising speed 145km/h (78kt). Initial rate of climb 673ft/min. Service ceiling 13,600ft. Range with max fuel 459km (248nm).

Weights: DH.82A – Empty 506kg (1115lb), max takeoff 828kg (1825lb).

Dimensions: Wing span 8.94m (29ft 4in), length 7.29m (23ft 11in), height 2.70m (8ft 10in). Wing area 22.2m² (239sq ft).

Capacity: Seating for two in tandem open cockpits. Flown solo from rear cockpit due to weight and balance considerations.

Production: 8492 Tiger Moths built, including 5161 in the UK (including 1153 prewar), 1747 in Canada, 1085 in Australia, 345 in New Zealand, 91 in Portugal, 37 in Norway and 23 in Sweden.

History: The much loved Tiger Moth was produced in large numbers for WW2 service as a basic pilot trainer, and today is a highly sought after recreational aircraft.

The DH.82 Tiger Moth is a development of de Havilland's successful Moth line of biplanes. Based on the DH.60T Moth Trainer, the Tiger Moth first flew on October 26 1931. Like the earlier Moth and Gipsy Moth the new aircraft was a two place biplane and featured a Gipsy Major engine and wooden and metal construction. Difficulty bailing out in an emergency was a problem with the earlier aircraft, and this was addressed through repositioning the struts forward of the front cockpit. To counter centre of gravity problems that would have resulted, the wings were given a modest sweepback angle.

The DH.82 attracted the interest of Britain's Royal Air Force, and the first of what would ultimately be several thousand Tiger Moths entered service with the RAF in 1932. Initial production DH.82s were powered by 90kW (120hp) engines, while the DH.82A introduced in 1937 featured a 97kW (130hp) engine, and was the most produced version. Most prewar production was for military orders, although some civil machines were built.

As Britain's standard basic pilot training aircraft, production of the Tiger Moth increased greatly during WW2, and 4000 were built in the UK. During the war large numbers were also built in Canada (as the DH.82C with a Gipsy Major IC or 120kW/160hp Pirate D.4 engine), Australia and New Zealand.

Postwar, surplus military Tiger Moths proved extremely popular with private owners. Many examples were converted for agricultural work, particularly in Australia and New Zealand, while small numbers of the four seat Jackaroo conversion were built from 1957.

Today the Tiger Moth remains very popular for recreational flying while some earn their keep operating joyflights. In some countries Tiger Moth populations are in fact growing as retired machines are restored and returned to the air.

Photo: The Tiger Moth is popular for its relaxed pace, open cockpit flying. (Michael Johnson)

De Havilland DH.104 Dove

Country or origin: United Kingdom

Type: Eight seat commuter airliner and executive transport

Powerplants: Dove 1 – Two 245kW (330hp) de Havilland Gipsy Queen 70-3 supercharged inverted six cylinder inline engines driving three blade constant speed propellers. Dove 8 – Two 300kW (400hp) Gipsy Queen 70 Mk.3s.

Performance: Dove 1 – Max speed 338km/h (182kt), max cruising speed 322km/h (174kt), long range cruising speed 266km/h (144kt). Initial rate of climb 750ft/min. Service ceiling 20,000ft. Max range 1610km (890nm). Dove 8 – Max speed 370km/h (200kt), max cruising speed 338km/h (183kt), long range cruising speed 300km/h (163kt). Initial rate of climb 1135ft/min. Service ceiling 21,700ft. Max range 1416km (765nm).

Weights: Dove 1 – Empty 2563kg (5650lb), max takeoff 3856kg (8500lb). Dove 8 – Empty 2869kg (6325lb), MTOW 4060kg (8950lb).

Dimensions: Wing span 17.37m (57ft 0in), length 11.96m (39ft 3in), height 4.06m (13ft 4in). Wing area 31.1m² (335sq ft).

Capacity: Two pilots. Main cabin seating for eight passengers, max cabin seating for 11 in a modified cabin arrangement.

Production: 544 built, including 200 for military operators. 17 Riley 400 conversions performed. Small numbers remain in service.

History: The Dove was Britain's first successful postwar civil aircraft, and one of the few successful Brabazon Committee projects.

The Brabazon Committee was established during WW2 to define requirements for British postwar civil aircraft. While the government established committee was responsible for a number of failures such as the Bristol Brabazon, it also resulted in the highly successful Vickers Viscount and the de Havilland Dove.

The DH.104 Dove was developed in response to a requirement for a small feederliner for UK and Commonwealth domestic services. The resulting aircraft featured new versions of the Gipsy Queen engine, a raised flightdeck and separate passenger cabin and all metal construction. The Dove first flew on September 25 1945.

Steady sales as a regional airliner and corporate transport (particularly in the US) were boosted by big military orders (RAF versions were known as the Devon, Royal Navy aircraft the Sea Devon).

The Dove remained in production until the mid 1960s (by which time it was a Hawker Siddeley product), and a number of variants were built. These were the initial Series 1, the executive interior Series 2, the military Series 4, the Series 5 with greater range and more powerful engines, the Series 6 (and 6A for the US) executive version of the Series 5, Series 6BA with more powerful engines, Series 7 (Series 7A for the US) with more powerful engines and raised Heron style flightdeck, and Series 8 (8A or Custom 800 in the US) with five seat interior.

In the USA Riley Aeronautics offered Dove conversions with two 300kW (400hp) Lycoming IO-720 engines fitted with turbochargers. The conversion is known as the Riley 400 (later Riley Turbo Exec 400), and customers could fit a swept back tail, a new instrument panel and a steel spar capped wing. The first Riley 400 flew in 1963. Max cruising speed was 474km/h (255kt).

Photo: A Riley 400 converted Dove. (David Daw)

Diamond DA 40 Diamond Star

Country of origin: Austria

Type: Four seat light aircraft

Powerplants: DA 40-180 – One 134kW (180hp) Textron Lycoming IO-360-M1A flat four piston engine driving a three blade MTV-12-B/180-7 constant speed propeller. DA 40-TDI – One 100kW (135hp) Thielert Centurion 1.7 jet fuel burning turbo diesel flat four.

Performance: DA 40-180 – Max level speed 287km/h (155kt), cruising speed at 75% power 272km/h (147kt), economical cruising speed 222km/h (120kt). Initial rate of climb 1070ft/min. Max certified altitude 16,400ft. Range with standard fuel and reserves 1100km (594nm), with optional fuel and reserves 1480km (799nm). DA 40-TDI – Max speed 285km/h (154kt), cruising speed at 80% power at 12,000ft 278km/h (150kt), cruising speed at 60% at 12,000ft 250km/h (135kt). Initial rate of climb 730ft/min. Range with standard fuel and reserves 1400km (750nm), with optional fuel and reserves 2030km (1100nm).

Weights: DA 40-180 – Empty 700kg (1543lb), max takeoff 1150kg (2535lb). DA 40-TDI – Empty 750kg (1653lb), max takeoff same.

Dimensions: Wing span 11.94m (39ft 5in), length 8.01m (26ft 3in), height 2.00m (6ft 7in). Wing area 13.5m² (145.3sq ft).

Capacity: Standard seating for four.

Production: Over 280 DA 40-180s on order. DA 40-TDI deliveries from early 2003.

History: The DA 40 Diamond Star is a composite construction four place light single now offered in avgas and jet fuel burning forms.

Diamond Aircraft was formed in 1981 as Hoffman Flugzeugbau, and following bankruptcy reformed as Hoffman Aircraft in 1984 and was renamed Diamond Aircraft in 1996. The DA 40 is its first FAR/JAR Pt 23 certificated aircraft, its earlier products include the H-36 Dimona, HK 36 Super Dimona and the Rotax 912 and Continental IO-240 powered DA 20 Katana two seater (built in Canada).

Diamond formally launched the DA 40 on April 23 1997 at the Aero 97 airshow in Germany. The Rotax 914 powered proof of concept DA 40-V1 first flew on November 5 1997, the second prototype DA 40-V2 with a IO-240 followed shortly after. The third prototype, with a Textron Lycoming IO-360, the production powerplant, flew in 1998. Five further prototypes followed, with JAA JAR 23 certification awarded on October 25 2000. FAA and JAA IFR certification was awarded in April 2001.

The DA 40-180 is based loosely on the DA 20 but features a larger fuselage with seating for four and a slightly longer span wing. The airframe is made from glassfibre reinforced plastics with carbonfibre reinforcement in some areas. Power is from a Lycoming IO-360 with Lasar electronic fuel injection. Standard fuel capacity is 155 litres, optional fuel capacity is 200 litres.

The turbo diesel Thielert Centurion 1.7 powered DA 40-TDI flew on November 28 2001. Despite 'only' producing 100kW (135hp) the Centurion 1.7 gives the DA 40-TDI cruise performance comparable to the DA 40-180 and even better range, while burning just 17 litres of fuel (either jet fuel or diesel) an hour. Deliveries are expected from early 2003.

Photo: A DA 40-180 Diamond Star in flight.

Diamond DA 42 TwinStar

Country of origin: Austria

Type: Four seat light twin

Powerplants: Two 100kW (135hp) Thielert Centurion 1.7 avtur burning turbo diesel four cylinder piston engines driving three blade MTV-6A-129 hydraulic constant speed propellers.

Performance: Cruising speed at 95% power at 12,000ft 376km/h (203kt), economical cruising speed 334km/h (180kt). Initial rate of climb 1700ft/min. Max operating altitude 20,000ft. Range at 60% power with standard fuel 1912km (1061nm), with optional fuel tanks 2677km (1485nm).

Weights: Empty 1030kg (2270lb), max takeoff 1650kg (3673lb). Payload 620kg (1366lb).

Dimensions: Wing span 13.42m (44ft), length 8.5m (27.8ft), height 2.6m (8.5ft). Wing area 16.5m² (177.2sq ft).

Capacity: Standard seating for four.

Production: Deliveries expected from early 2004. Base price $US360,000

History: The Diamond DA 42 TwinStar is an all new four place carbonfibre construction light twin powered by jet fuel burning turbo diesel engines.

Austria's Diamond Aircraft unveiled the DA 42 at the May 2002 Berlin Airshow. The new aircraft flew on December 9 2002, leading to European JAA certification in late 2003 and US FAA certification and first deliveries in mid 2004.

The TwinStar's design objectives include high speed cruise at very low throttle settings and good low speed handling. It is loosely modelled on Diamond's DA 40 Diamond Star four place single (see opposite), and features an all composite airframe with a high aspect ratio wing with winglets.

The heart of the TwinStar is its two Thielert Centurion 1.7 (formerly TAE 125) turbo diesel four cyclinder engines, which are designed to run on either diesel or Jet-A1/jet fuel. Germany based Thielert's Centurion turbo diesel engine was certificated in early 2002 and is based on a Mercedes-Benz automotive design. Diamond expects the DA 42's two engines will burn just 45 litres an hour while cruising at a very fast 333km/h (180kt). Standard fuel capacity is 200 litres, while optional long range tanks take maximum fuel capacity to 280 litres.

The engines drive slow turning three blade constant speed propellers, which combined with the engines' low noise emissions and the DA 42's fast climb rate will result in a low ground noise signature. The engines also feature electronic fuel management, automatic prop controls and auto feather.

The Twin Star will feature dual controls and an optional EFIS glass cockpit with three vertical format colour LCDs. The basic aircraft will be equipped with conventional IFR avionics, and has a project price of $US360,000.

Diamond Aircraft says the DA 42 will be suitable for flight training as well as private and business use.

Downstream Diamond may also offer the TwinStar with conventional powerplants, but at late 2002 no decision had been made.

Photo: The prototype DA 42 Twin Star.

Dornier Do 27

Country of origin: Germany

Type: Four to six seat STOL utility light aircraft

Powerplant: Do 27H-2 – One 255kW (340hp) Lycoming GSO-480-B1B6 flat six piston engine driving a three blade Hartzell propeller. Do 27Q-5 – One 200kW (270hp) GSO-480-B1A6 driving a two blade prop.

Performance: Do 27H-2 – Max speed 245km/h (132kt), high speed cruise 212km/h (115kt), economical cruising speed 180km/h (97kt). Initial rate of climb 965ft/min. Service ceiling 22,000ft. Range with max fuel and no reserves 1360km (735nm). Do 27Q-5 – Max speed 232km/h (125kt), 75% power cruising speed 211km/h (114kt), 60% power cruising speed 190km/h (103kt), economical cruising speed 175km/h (95kt). Initial rate of climb 650ft/min. Service ceiling 10,800ft. Range with max fuel and no reserves 1102km (595nm).

Weights: Do 27H-2 – Empty equipped 1170kg (2580lb), max takeoff 1848kg (4070lb). Do 27Q-5 – Empty equipped 1130kg (2490lb), max takeoff 1848kg (4070lb).

Dimensions: Do 27H-2 & Q-5 – Wing span 12.00m (39ft 5in), length 9.60m (31ft 6in), height 2.80m (9ft 2in). Wing area 19.4m² (208.8sq ft).

Capacity: Pilot and passenger side by side with between four and six passengers behind them on two facing bench seats. Can carry freight with rear seats removed.

Production: Total Do 27 production of over 620.

History: The Dornier Do 27 was the first military aircraft to be manufactured in quantity in what was West Germany after World War 2, and was also built in small numbers for civil customers.

The Do 27 traces back to the Do 25, which Professor Claude Dornier (Dornier was responsible for the Do 17 medium bomber in WW2) designed in Spain to meet a Spanish military requirement for a light general purpose utility aircraft. Two prototype Do 25s were built, the first powered by a 110kW (150hp) ENMA Tigre G-IVB engine and first flew on June 25 1954. CASA then built 50 production aircraft as Do 27As for the Spanish air force (designated C.127).

Subsequently the German military ordered the Do 27 in large numbers. In all 428 were delivered to Germany's armed forces from the mid 1950s to 1960. Small numbers were built for other military customers, and others for commercial use.

Features of the Do 27 design include a flat six Lycoming engine, a wide and relatively roomy cabin, all metal construction apart from fabric covered double slotted flaps and ailerons on the wings (the ailerons are split, the inner portions can also act as flaps), wide track undercarriage and excellent STOL performance. The STOL performance in particular suited the Do 27 for use in developing countries, and several have seen service in Africa.

Do 27 models include the initial Do 27A and dual control Do 27B for Germany; the Do 27H series that was based on the A-4 but with a more powerful engine and three blade prop; and the Do 27Q series, equivalent to the Do 27A.

The Do 27 T-1 was built in prototype form only, it featured a Turbomeca Astazou turboprop. Do 27 production ceased in 1966. In addition over 60 twin engine Do 28s were built in the early 1960s (powered by two 216kW/290hp Lycoming IO-540s).

Photo: A Do 27. (Sebastian Zacharias)

Dornier Do 28 & 128

Country of origin: Germany

Type: STOL utility transports

Powerplants: Do 28D-2 – Two 285kW (380hp) Lycoming IGSO-540-A1E flat six piston engines driving three blade constant speed Hartzell propellers. 128-6 – Two 300kW (400shp) Pratt & Whitney Canada PT6A-110 turboprops driving three blade Hartzell propellers.

Performance: Do 28D-2 – Max speed 325km/h (175kt), max cruising speed 306km/h (165kt), economical cruising speed 241km/h (130kt). Initial rate of climb 1160ft/min. Service ceiling 25,200ft. Range with max payload 1050km (566nm). 128-6 – Max speed 340km/h (183kt), max cruising speed 330km/h (178kt), econ cruising speed 256km/h (138kt). Initial rate of climb 1260ft/min. Service ceiling 32,600ft. Range with max fuel at econ cruising speed 1825nm (985nm), with a 805kg (1774lb) payload 1460km (788nm).

Weights: Do 28D-2 – Empty 2328kg (5132lb), max takeoff 3842kg (8470lb). 128-6 – Empty 2540kg (5600lb), max takeoff 4350kg (9590lb).

Dimensions: Do 28D-2 – Wing span 15.55m (51ft 0in), length 11.41m (37ft 5in), height 3.90m (12ft 10in). Wing area 29.0m² (312sq ft). 128-6 – Same except for wing span 15.85m (52ft 0in).

Capacity: One or two pilots on flightdeck and seating in main cabin for 10 or 12 seats two abreast with a centre aisle.

Production: Total Do 28 and 128-2 production was over 200 units including military orders, total 128-6 production approximately 25.

History: The Dornier Do 28 Skyservant was the second aircraft to bear the Do 28 designation, but is similar only in overall configuration to the first Do 28.

Dornier's original Do 28 first flew in 1959 and was a twin engined development of the high wing single engine Do 27 utility (powered by two 216kW/290hp Lycoming IO-540s). The Do 28 Skyservant first flew on February 23 1966, and while it retained the earlier Do 28's high wing and unique fuselage side mounted engine configuration, was a completely new aircraft. Other design features of this unusual looking aircraft were the fixed tailwheel undercarriage, with the faired mainwheels mounted beneath the engines. FAA certification was granted on April 19 1968.

The Do 28 was developed into a number of progressively improved variants, from the original D, through the D-1 and D-2, to the 128-2, introduced in 1980. Each variant introduced a number of detail changes. Most Do 28 production was for military customers, notably Germany, although a small number were delivered to commercial operators.

An initial turboprop version of the Do 28, designated the Do 28D-5X, first flew in April 1978, fitted with two Avco Lycoming LTP 101-600-1As derated to 300kW (400shp).

However production turboprop Dornier 128-6s feature Pratt & Whitney Canada PT6As, with the first such configured aircraft flying in March 1980. Only about two dozen were built between then and 1986, when production ceased, and again most aircraft were for military customers.

Photo: A Chilean registered Do 28. (Alvaro Romero)

Dornier 228

Country of origin: Germany

Type: 15-19 seat regional airliner and STOL utility transport

Powerplants: 100 – Two 535kW (715shp) Garrett TPE331-5 turbo-props driving four blade constant speed Hartzell propellers. 212 – Two 560kW (776shp) Garrett/AlliedSignal TPE331-5-252Ds.

Performance: 100 – Max cruising speed 432km/h (233kt). Initial rate of climb 2050ft/min. Service ceiling 29,600ft. Range at max cruising speed 1730km (934nm), or 1970km (1064nm) at long range cruising speed. 212 – Max cruising speed 434km/h (234kt), cruising speed 408km/h (220kt). Initial rate of climb 1870ft. Service ceiling 28,000ft. Range with max pax and reserves at max cruising speed 1037km (560nm), range with a 775kg (1710lb) payload and reserves at long range cruising speed 2445km (1320nm).

Weights: 100 – Operating empty 3235kg (7132lb), max takeoff 5700kg (12,570lb). 212 – Empty 3258kg (7183lb), operating empty 3739kg (8243lb), max takeoff 6400kg (14,110lb).

Dimensions: 100 – Wing span 16.97m (55ft 7in), length 15.03m (49ft 3in), height 4.86m (15ft 9in). Wing area 32.0m^2 (345sq ft). 212 – Same except for length 16.56m (54ft 4in).

Capacity: Flightcrew of two. 100 – Typical passenger seating for 15. 212 – Typical passenger seating for 19 at two abreast and 76cm (30in) pitch. 228-212 based 228 Cargo has a max payload of 2340kg (5159lb). 212 based ambulance accommodates six stretchers and up to nine attendants or passengers.

Production: 238 Dornier 228s of all models built, with 112 in commercial service in late 2002. Indian licence production of more than 80 228s (mostly for the Indian military).

History: In terms of civil sales the 228 turboprop was been Dornier's most successful postwar design.

The Dornier 228 incorporates the fuselage cross section of the earlier Do 28 and 128 combined with an all new supercritical wing and TPE331 turboprops. Two fuselage length versions, the 100 and 200, were developed concurrently, the 100 offering better range, the 200 more payload. The 100 was the first to fly, on March 28 1981, the first 200 followed on May 9 that year. The first 228 entered service in August 1982.

Composites were used in a number of areas of the 228 including upper wing skins, nose and tail. At one stage Dornier also planned to offer the Pratt & Whitney Canada PT6A as an optional powerplant, but this never eventuated.

Dornier 228 developments include the 228-101 with reinforced structure and landing gear for higher weights, the corresponding 228-201 version of the -200, the 228-202 built under licence production in India with HAL to meet that country's Light Transport Aircraft requirement, and the 228-212.

The -212 was the last Dornier production aircraft, its improvements include higher operating weights, structural strengthening and a lower empty weight, improvements to enhance STOL performance and modern avionics. The last of 238 Dornier built 228s was completed in 1999. HAL licence production continues.

Photo: A Dornier 228-200 of Air Wales. Note open pilot's door. (David Fraser)

Douglas DC-3

Country of origin: United States of America

Type: Short range airliner and utility transport

Powerplants: Two 895kW (1200hp) Pratt & Whitney R-1830-S1C3G Twin Wasp 14 cylinder twin row radial piston engines driving three blade variable pitch propellers, or two 895kW (1200hp) Wright SGR-1820 Cyclone nine cylinder radials.

Performance: Max speed 346km/h (187kt), economical cruising speed 266km/h (143kt). Initial rate of climb 1130ft/min. Range with max fuel 2420km (1307nm), range with max payload 563km (305nm).

Weights: Typical operating empty 8030kg (17,720lb), max takeoff 12,700kg (28,000lb).

Dimensions: Wing span 28.96m (95ft 0in), length 19.66m (64ft 6in), height 5.15m (16ft 11in). Wing area 91.7m^2 (987sq ft).

Capacity: Flightcrew of two. Seating for between 28 and 32 passengers at four abreast or 21 three abreast.

Production: 10,655 built in the USA, including 430 for commercial operators prior to US entry to WW2. 2500 or so built in Russia under licence. Approximately 400 remained in service in 2002.

History: Over six decades after its first flight several hundred DC-3s remain in commercial service worldwide. Durability, longevity and profitability are but three of this historically significant aircraft's virtues.

The DC-3 is a direct descendant of the one-off Douglas Commercial 1 (DC-1) and subsequent DC-2 (198 built) which made their first flights in 1933 and 1934 respectively. In 1934 American Airlines requested that Douglas develop a larger more capable version of the DC-2 for transcontinental US sleeper flights. The resulting DC-3 (or DST – Douglas Sleeper Transport as it then was) first flew on December 17 1935.

The DC-3 was an almost instant sales success, and it became the mainstay of the US domestic airline network in the years prior to World War 2. Aside from passenger comfort and appeal, the DC-3 offered profitability, with the result that over 400 had been sold to airlines prior to late 1941.

The entry of the United States into WW2 in December 1941 had a profound effect on the fortunes of the already successful DC-3. The US Army Air Force's requirements for transport aircraft were admirably met by the in-production DC-3, with the result that as the C-47 Skytrain it became the standard USAAF transport during the war. More than 10,000 were built for service with US and allied air arms.

After the war most C-47s became surplus and were sold off at bargain prices. The result was that demilitarised C-47s became the standard postwar aircraft of almost all the world's airlines and the backbone of the world airline industry well into the 1950s. Its availability and reliability meant it proved extremely popular. Even by the early 1960s 1500 or so remained in airline service.

A postwar update of the DC-3, the Super DC-3, involving a stretched airframe and more powerful engines, was commercially unsuccessful in the face of cheap second hand DC-3s and the more advanced Convair 340 and Martin 2-0-2/-4-0-4. The Super DC-3 first flew in June 1949 and some were built for the US Navy as the R4D-8 and for a US domestic airline, and a few remain in service.

Photo: A Swiss registered DC-3. (Charles Falk)

Douglas DC-4

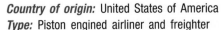

Country of origin: United States of America

Type: Piston engined airliner and freighter

Powerplants: Four 1080kW (1450shp) Pratt & Whitney Twin Wasp 14 cylinder twin row radial piston engines driving three blade constant speed propellers.

Performance: Max speed 451km/h (244kt), cruising speed 365km/h (197kt). Service ceiling 22,300ft. Range with a 5200kg (11,440lb) payload 4023km (2172nm).

Weights: Empty 19,660kg (43,300lb), MTOW 33,112kg (73,000lb).

Dimensions: Wing span 35.81m (117ft 6in), length 28.60m (93ft 10in), height 8.38m (27ft 6in). Wing area 135.6m² (1460sq ft).

Capacity: Flightcrew of three, standard passenger seating for 44, max seating for 86. Most surviving aircraft configured as freighters.

Production: Total DC-4 production comprised one DC-4E, 78 commercial DC-4s, 1162 military C-54 Skymasters and 42 Canadair developed Merlin powered derivatives. Almost 80 remain in commercial service, most as freighters.

History: The original DC-4 dates back to a 1936 United Air Lines requirement for a four engined long range airliner.

United looked to Douglas to fulfil the requirement, resulting in the highly ambitious DC-4E (E for experimental). This four engined behemoth was flight tested in 1939. It was over twice the size of the DC-3 (its wingspan was 42.17m/138ft 3in, and length 29.76m/97ft 7in), had triple tail surfaces, tricycle undercarriage, was pressurised and potentially could fly nonstop from Chicago to San Francisco.

However all the ground breaking new technology on the DC-4E meant that it was costly, complex and had higher than anticipated operating costs, so instead Douglas developed an all new the design, the smaller and simpler definitive DC-4.

The new DC-4 was developed under the darkening clouds of WW2, and upon the USA's entry into the war all DC-4s then on the production line (US airlines had ordered 61 off the drawing board) were requisitioned for the US military. Consequently the first DC-4 flew for the first time on February 14 1942 in military markings as the C-54 Skymaster. The DC-4 was found to admirably suit the USAAF's requirement for a long range cargo transport, and 1162 were built through the war years (some were built for the US Navy as the R5D).

As was the case with the DC-3, the end of war meant that many C-54s were made surplus and over 500 were leased or sold to the world's airlines in 1945/46. In addition Douglas built a further 78 DC-4s (designated DC-4-1009) to new orders, the first of which was delivered to Western Air Lines in January 1946. Over the years the survivors have been passed down to charter and freight airlines, and today about 80 survive in service as freighters.

Notable developments of the DC-4 include Aviation Trader's much modified Carvair freighter while Canadair built a number with Rolls-Royce Merlin engines and pressurised fuselages. The DC-4 also formed the basis for the larger DC-6 and DC-7 which are described separately (the DC-4 was the first airliner to introduce a circular section, constant diameter fuselage which made stretching the basic aircraft relatively simple).

Photo: A DC-4 firebomber in California. (Tony Zeljeznjak)

Douglas DC-6

Country of origin: United States of America

Type: Piston engined airliner and freighter

Powerplants: DC-6 – Four 1340kW (1800hp) Pratt & Whitney R-2800-CA15 Double Wasp 18 cylinder twin row radial piston engines (with a maximum output of 1790kW/2400hp with water injection) driving three blade constant speed Hamilton Standard propellers. DC-6B – Four 1685kW (2500hp) R-2800-CB17s.

Performance: DC-6 – Cruising speed 501km/h (270kt). Initial rate of climb 1070ft/min. Max range 7376km (3983nm). DC-6B – Cruising speed 507km/h (274kt). Service ceiling 25,000ft. Range with max payload 4835km (2610nm), range with max fuel 7595km (4100nm).

Weights: DC-6 – Empty 23,840kg (52,567lb), max takeoff 44,129kg (97,200lb). DC-6B – Empty 25,110kg (55,357lb), max takeoff 48,534kg (107,000lb).

Dimensions: DC-6 – Wing span 35.81m (117ft 6in), length 30.66m (100ft 7in), height 8.66m (28ft 5in). Wing area 135.9m² (1463sq ft). DC-6B – Same except length 32.18m (105ft 7in).

Capacity: DC-6 – Flightcrew of three or four. Passenger seating typically for 48 to 56, but most aircraft now operated as freighters equipped to carry freight. DC-6B – Typical passenger seating for 54, with max seating for 102, but now usually configured for freight.

Production: Total DC-6 production of 665, comprising 174 DC-6s, 73 DC-6As, 288 DC-6Bs, 105 C-118s and 25 R6Ds. Approximately 100 remain in service.

History: The DC-6 was developed in response to a military airlift requirement and went on to become Douglas' most successful four engined piston airliner.

During the latter stages of WW2 Douglas began work on a developed DC-4 for postwar commercial use. However the improved DC-4 (which would feature a 2.11m/6ft 11in fuselage stretch and P&W R-2800 Double Wasp engines) soon attracted the attention of the US Army Air Force, which devised a requirement which the new transport was developed against. A prototype was built, designated XC-112, but it did not fly until February 15 1946, by which time the war was over and the military requirement no longer stood.

However US airlines had already shown strong interest in the new transport, with launch orders for the DC-6 placed in September 1944. The first production DC-6 first flew in June 1946 and service entry, with United Air Lines, occurred on April 27 1947. However early service use was not smooth with the fleet grounded for four months from November that year after two internal fuselage fires.

The availability of the more powerful R-2800 engines with water/methanol injection prompted Douglas to develop the further stretched DC-6A Liftmaster freighter (first flight September 29 1949) and the equivalent passenger DC-6B (first flight February 2 1951). The DC-6C, the last DC-6 model to be developed, was a convertible passenger/freight version of the DC-6A.

Meanwhile renewed military interest in the DC-6 was sparked by the Korean War, with the result that large numbers of USAF C-118s and USN R6D-1s were built. Many of these were later sold to civilian operators.

Photo: A DC-6 freighter departs Anchorage, Alaska. (Paul Merritt)

Douglas DC-7

Country of origin: United States of America

Type: Piston engine airliner and freighter

Powerplants: DC-7F & DC-7C – Four 2535kW (3400hp) Wright R-3350-EA1 or -EA4 Turbo Compound 18 cylinder radial piston engines driving four blade constant speed propellers.

Performance: DC-7F – Typical cruising speed 555km/h (300kt). Range with max fuel and no reserves 7130km (3850nm). DC-7C – Typical cruising speed 555km/h (330kt). Range with max payload 5810km (3135nm), range with max fuel and no reserves 9077km (4900nm).

Weights: DC-7F – Basic operating 30,030kg (66,200lb), max takeoff 57,153kg (126,000lb). DC-7C – Basic operating 36,287kg (80,000lb), max takeoff 64,865kg (143,000lb).

Dimensions: DC-7F – Wing span 35.81m (117ft 6in), length 33.24m (108ft 11in), height 8.71m (28ft 7in). Wing area 136.0m² (1463sq ft). DC-7C – Wing span 38.86m (127ft 6in), length 34.21m (112ft 3in), height 9.70m (31ft 10in). Wing area 152.0m² (1637sq ft).

Capacity: Flightcrew of three. DC-7/DC-7B could seat up to 99 in a high density configuration, the DC-7C up to 105. Capacity of DC-7F conversion of the DC-7B is 15,700kg (34,600lb).

Production: DC-7 production was 338, comprising 105 DC-7s, 112 DC-7Bs and 121 DC-7Cs. Approximately 40 remain in service.

History: Douglas' largest and last piston engined airliner, the DC-7 was one of the first airliners capable of nonstop trans Atlantic crossings between New York and London.

Originally the DC-7 designation applied to a commercial development of the C-74 Globemaster I that Pan Am had ordered. Instead the DC-7 arose from an American Airlines requirement for a stretched longer range DC-6 to compete with TWA's Lockheed Super Constellations on nonstop transcontinental US services. The resulting aircraft had the same wing as the DC-6, with a stretched DC-6 fuselage (by 1.02m/3ft 4in), more powerful Wright Turbo Compound engines (with exhaust driven turbochargers) and extra fuel allowing nonstop transcontinental US flights in both directions.

The prototype DC-7 first flew on May 18 1953, and the type entered service with American between New York and Los Angeles that November. Production of the initial DC-7 was solely for US domestic operators. The extended range DC-7B had extra fuel capacity in extended nacelle tanks and higher weights, allowing Pan American to inaugurate nonstop New York/London services from June 1955.

While the DC-7B could fly New York/London nonstop, wind conditions usually forced reverse services to make a refuelling stop at Gander. Consequently Douglas developed the DC-7C 'Seven Seas'. The DC-7C featured extra fuel capacity, a further 1.02m (3ft 4in) fuselage stretch, extended span wings (by 3.05m/10ft) with new centre section, more powerful engines, taller vertical tail surfaces, and a higher max takeoff weight. As a result it could cross the North Atlantic nonstop in either direction. It entered service in April 1956, although sales were restricted by the coming availability of jets.

Today a small number DC-7s survive, mainly as freighters. Douglas offered DC-7F conversions from 1959 (the DC-7F described above is based on the DC-7B). Others are used for firebombing.

Photo: Turks Air's DC-7B freighter. (Jonathan Derden)

Douglas DC-8 Series 10 to 50

Country of origin: United States of America

Type: Medium to long range airliner and freighter

Powerplants: Series 50 – Four 80.1kN (18,000lb) Pratt & Whitney JT3D-3 turbofans.

Performance: Series 50 – Max cruising speed 933km/h (504kt). Range with max payload 9205km (4970nm), max range 11,260km (6078nm).

Weights: Series 50 – Operating empty 60,020kg (132,325lb), max takeoff 147,415kg (325,000lb).

Dimensions: Wing span 43.41m (142ft 5in), length 45.87m (150ft 6in), height 12.91m (42ft 4in). Wing area 257.6m² (2773sq ft) on early aircraft, 266.5m² (2868sq ft) on later aircraft.

Capacity: Flightcrew of three. Mixed class seating for 132, typical all economy seating for 144, or up to 179 in high density single class layout. A number of aircraft are converted for VIP/executive use. Freighter versions can carry approximately 15 tonnes (34,000lb) of cargo consisting of pallets or containers.

Production: 295 Series 10, 20, 30, 40 and 50 DC-8s built between the late 1950s and 1968. Approximately 25 DC-8-50s remained in commercial service in 2002.

History: The popular DC-8 was Douglas' first jet powered airliner, and the USA's second successful jet transport behind the Boeing 707.

Despite its strong hold on the world airliner market in the early 1950s, and the appearance of the jet powered de Havilland Comet in 1949, Douglas moved cautiously into the field of jet powered transports, a decision which was to cost it dearly in lost potential sales over the following decades.

Douglas announced it was developing the jet powered DC-8 airliner in June 1955, a year after the first flight of the Boeing Model 367-80 prototype, the 707 predecessor. The first DC-8 flew on May 30 1958, five months before the 707 entered service with Pan Am. A concerted flight test program involving nine aircraft led to certification being awarded on August 31 1959. Entry into commercial service with launch customers United and Delta was on September 18 that year.

Unfortunately for Douglas, the earlier availability of the 707 meant that initial sales of the DC-8 were relatively slow. However the emergence of Douglas' design had already forced Boeing to widen the fuselage width of the 707, and unlike the Boeing the DC-8 was offered in domestic and intercontinental versions from the start.

Versions of the initial short fuselage DC-8 were: the Series 10, the initial domestic version with 60.1kN (13,500lb) P&W JT3C-6 turbojets – 28 were built for Delta and United; the similar Series 20 but with more powerful 74.7kN (16,800lb) JT4A-9 turbojets; the intercontinental Series 30 and Series 40, powered by JT4A-11s or Rolls-Royce Conways respectively; and the Series 50, perhaps the definitive short fuselage model and a direct competitor to the 707-320B/C, with 80.1kN (18,000lb) JT3D-3 turbofans. Convertible 50CF and pure freight 50AF Jet Trader versions were also offered, while others were subsequently converted to freighters.

The short fuselage DC-8s were replaced in production by the substantially larger stretched DC-8 Super Sixty series.

Photo: A DC-8-50F freighter. (Keith Gaskell)

Douglas DC-8 Super 60 & 70 Series

Country of Origin: United States of America

Type: Long range medium capacity airliner and freighter

Powerplants: DC-8-61 & 62 – Four 80.1kN (18,000lb) Pratt & Whitney JT3D-3B turbofans. DC-8-63 – Four 84.5kN (19,000lb) JT3D-7s. DC-8-70 series – Four 97.9kN (22,000lb) CFM Intl CFM56-2C5s.

Performance: DC-8-60 – Max cruising speed 965km/h (521kt). Range with max payload DC-8-61 6035km (3256nm); DC-8-62 9620km (5210nm); DC-8-63 7240nm (3907nm). DC-8-70 – Max cruising speed 887km/h (479kt), economical cruising speed 850km/h (459kt). Range with max payload (Super 73) 8950km (4830nm).

Weights: DC-8-61 – Operating empty 67,538kg (148,897lb), max takeoff 147,415kg (325,000lb). DC-8-62 – Operating empty 64,366kg (141,903lb), max takeoff 151,950kg (335,000lb). DC-8-63 – Operating empty 69,739kg (153,749lb), max takeoff 158,760kg (350,000lb). DC-8-73 – Operating empty 75,500kg (166,500lb), max takeoff 162,025kg (355,000lb).

Dimensions: DC-8-61 & 71 – Wing span 43.41m (142ft 5in), length 57.12m (187ft 5in), height 12.92m (42ft 5in). Wing area 267.9m² (2884sq ft). DC-8-62 & 72 – Span 45.23m (148ft 5in), length 47.98m (157ft 5in), height 12.92m (42ft 5in). Wing area 271.9m² (2927sq ft). DC-8-63 & 73 – Wing span 45.23m (148ft 5in), length 57.12m (187ft 5in), height 12.92m (45ft 5in). Wing area 271.9m² (2927sq ft).

Capacity: Flightcrew of three. Max seating capacity 259 or standard seating for between 180 and 220 in Series 61, 63, 71 & 73. Super 62 & 72 standard seating for 189. Super 60 and 70 freighters payload between 40,405kg (89,000lb) and 49,585kg (109,217lb).

Production: 262 Super 60 series built with 110 70 series conversions. Approx 82 Super 60s and 96 Super 70s in service in late 2002.

History: The successful DC-8 Super 60 airliners are stretched developments of the DC-8 Series 50. The Super 70s are Super 60s re-engined with CFM56 high bypass turbofans.

Douglas announced the DC-8 Super Sixty series in April 1965. The first, a DC-8-61, first flew on March 14 1966, followed by the first flights of the DC-8-62 on August 29 1966 and the DC-8-63 on April 10 1967. The DC-8-61 differed from the earlier DC-8-50 in having two fuselage plugs which increased length by 11.18m (36ft 8in), increasing max seating capacity to 259 (the largest of any single aisle airliner prior to the 757-300) and underfloor freight capacity by 80%. Intended for domestic operations, its max takeoff weight was identical to the DC-8-50.

The Super 62 was intended for long range operations and featured only a modest 2.04m (6ft 8in) stretch compared to the Series 50, greater wing span, revised engine nacelles and pylons and significantly increased fuel capacity. The Super 63 meanwhile combined the DC-8-61's fuselage with the DC-8-62's wings. It was the final DC-8 variant in production, the last was delivered in May 1972.

McDonnell Douglas initiated a re-engining program of Super 60 series aircraft with CFM International CFM56 engines in the early 1980s, known as the Super 70 Series. The first converted airframe flew in August 1981. The Super 70 aircraft are considerably quieter than their predecessors, with better fuel economy and range.

Photo: A DC-8-71F. (Sam Chui)

EADS CASA C-212 Aviocar

Country of origin: Spain

Type: STOL turboprop regional airliner and utility transport

Powerplants: C-212C – Two 580kW (775shp) Garrett AiResearch TPE331-5-251C turboprop engines driving four blade propellers. Series 300 – Two 670kW (900shp) Honeywell TPE331-10R-513Cs.

Performance: C-212C – Max speed 370km/h (199kt), max cruising speed 359km/h (194kt), economical cruising speed 315km/h (170kt). Range with max fuel and 1045kg (2303lb) payload 1760km (950nm), range with max payload 480km (258nm). Series 300 – Max operating speed 370km/h (200kt), max cruising speed 354km/h (191kt), economical cruising speed 300km/h (162kt). Range with 25 passengers and reserves at max cruising speed 440km (237nm), with 1700kg (3770lb) payload 1435km (775nm).

Weights: C-212C – Empty 3700kg (8157lb), max takeoff 6300kg (13,890lb). Series 300 – Empty 3780kg (8333lb), operating empty 4560kg (10,053lb), max takeoff 7700kg (16,975lb).

Dimensions: C-212C & Series 200 – Wing span 19.00m (62ft 4in), length 15.20m (49ft 11in), height 6.30m (20ft 8in). Wing area 40.0m² (430.6sq ft). Series 300 – Wing span 20.28m (66ft 7in), length 16.15m (53ft 0in), height 6.60m (21ft 8in). Wing area 41.0m² (441.3sq ft).

Capacity: Flightcrew of two. Max passenger seating for 26 at three abreast, or 24 with lavatory. Freighter version can accommodate three LD3 containers or two LD2s or two LD727/DC-8s. Max payload 2700kg (5950lb).

Production: Over 460 Aviocars of all models built. IPTN in Indonesia has built over 90 NC-212s under licence.

History: The C-212 was initially conceived as a light STOL transport for the Spanish air force, but also found a handy market niche and is highly regarded for its utility in underdeveloped regions.

The C-212 was designed to replace the Spanish air force's mixed transport fleet of Douglas C-47 Dakotas and Junkers Ju 52s still in service in the 1960s, but a civil variant was always intended. Design work began in the late 1960s, the first prototype made its first flight on March 26 1971. Preproduction examples followed, before the type entered air force service in 1974. The first commercial version was delivered in July 1975.

The basic civil version was designated the C-212C, the military version the C-212-5. Production of these models ceased in 1978, CASA switching to the Series 200 with more powerful engines and higher operating weights. The first Series 200, a converted C-212C prototype, flew for the first time in its new configuration on April 30 1978. A third development of the Aviocar is the Series 300 which first flew in 1984 and was certificated in late 1987. Improvements to this model are newer engines and winglets.

The latest development is the C-212-400, which first flew on April 4 1997. It features TPE331-12JR engines which maintain their power output to a higher altitude for improved hot and high performance and an EFIS flightdeck. Utility and airliner configurations are offered. The Patrullero maritime patrol variant is offered in a number of mission specific configurations.

Photo: A C-212-400 Patrullero of Spain's Ministry of Agriculture, Fisheries and Food. (EADS)

EADS CASA/IAe CN-235

Countries of Origin: Spain and Indonesia

Type: Utility transport and 45 seat regional airliner

Powerplants: Two 1395kW (1870shp) General Electric CT7-9C turboprops driving four blade constant propellers.

Performance: CN-235-100 – Max speed 509km/h (275kt), max cruising speed 454km/h (245kt). Initial rate of climb at sea level 1780ft/min. Range with max payload and reserves at 18,000ft 796km (430nm).

Weights: CN-235-100 – Operating empty 9800kg (21,605lb), max takeoff 15,100kg (33,290lb).

Dimensions: Wing span 25.81m (84ft 8in), length 21.40m (70ft 3in), height 8.18m (26ft 10in). Wing area 59.1m² (636.17sq ft).

Capacity: Flightcrew of two. Passenger accommodation in airliner version for 45 four abreast. Quick change convertibles can carry mixtures of passengers and LD2 or LD3 containers. Cargo version can carry four LD3s or five LD2s or palletised freight.

Production: Out of total orders for 251 CN-235s, 24 have been to civil customers. Over 26 are currently in airline service.

History: The CN-235 regional airliner and military transport was designed and developed under the Airtech banner as a 50:50 joint venture between CASA of Spain (now part of EADS) and Indonesian Aerospace (formerly IPTN).

One prototype was built in both countries and these rolled out simultaneously on September 10 1983. The Spanish prototype flew first, on November 11 1983, with the Indonesian built aircraft following on December 30 that year. Certification by Spanish and Indonesian authorities and first deliveries (from the Indonesian line) occurred in December 1986. Commercial service entry was in March 1988.

Final assembly lines for the CN-235 are in Spain and Indonesia, but all other manufacture is not duplicated. EADS (CASA) builds the centre and forward fuselage, wing centre section and inboard flaps, and engine nacelles, while Indonesian Aerospace (IAe) builds outer wings and flaps, ailerons, the rear fuselage and the tail unit.

The initial production CN-235-10 was soon replaced by the CASA built CN-235-100 and IPTN's CN-235-110, incorporating CT7-9C engines in place of CT7-7As, and new composite engine nacelles. The CASA CN-235-200 and similar IAe CN-235-220 have increased operating weights, better field performance and greater range, with structural improvements and improved leading edge flaps and rudder. The CN-235-220 was certificated in March 1992. CASA and IAe now develop their own CN-235 variants independently.

Other variants on the CN-235 theme are the CN-235 QC quick change variant capable of carrying passengers or freight or both; IAe's CN-235 MPA maritime patrol aircraft and CASA's CN-235MP Persuader (which while primarily aimed at military customers, have customs and boarder patrol applications); and the widely ordered CN-235 M multirole military freighter. IAe has marketed military CN-235s as the Phoenix. CASA has developed the stretched C-295 primarily for military use.

The CN-235 has succeeded in achieving only a small number of commercial orders, mostly from Indonesian and Spanish operators. In contrast it has won a significant number of military orders.

Photo: A Merpati CN-235 airliner. (John Sise)

EADS Socata Tampico, Tobago & Trinidad

Country of origin: France

Type: Four/five seat light aircraft

Powerplant: TB 9 Tampico Club – One 120kW (160hp) Textron Lycoming O-320-D2A flat four piston engine driving a two blade fixed pitch Sensenich propeller. TB 21 Trinidad GT – One 185kW (250hp) Textron Lycoming TIO-540-AB1AD turbocharged fuel injected flat six piston engine driving a two blade (three optional) c/s Hartzell prop.

Performance: TB 9 – Max speed 226km/h (122kt), max cruising speed 198km/h (107kt), economical cruising speed 194km/h (105kt). Initial rate of climb 750ft/min. Max certificated altitude 11,000ft. Max range 1030km (555nm). TB 21 GT – Cruising speed at 75% power 352km/h (190kt), econ cruising speed 313km/h (169kt), economical cruising speed 291km/h (157kt). Initial rate of climb 1130ft/min. Service ceiling 25,000ft. Max range 1916km (1035nm).

Weights: TB 9 – Empty 647kg (1426lb), MTOW 1060kg (2335lb). TB 21 GT – Operating empty 867kg (1911lb), MTOW 1400kg (3086lb).

Dimensions: TB 9 – Wing span 9.76m (32ft 0in), length 7.70m (25ft 3in), height 3.02m (9ft 11in). Wing area 11.9m² (128.1sq ft). TB 21 – Span 9.97m (32ft 9in), length 7.75m (25ft 5in), height 2.85m (9ft 4in).

Capacity: Typical seating for four or five, with pilot and passenger on front bucket seats and two or three passengers on rear bench seat.

Production: Over 1900 TBs built incl over 470 Tampicos, over 725 Tobagos & 680 Trinidads/Trinidad TCs. GT series delivered from 2000.

History: Socata's popular 'Caribbean' TB series spans from the basic fixed gear Tampico Club to the turbocharged Trinidad TC.

Design work on the TB singles began in the mid 1970s. The first prototype, a TB 10 but powered by a 120kW (160hp) Lycoming O-320, flew for the first time on February 23 1977. Production began in 1979.

Three distinct versions of the TB series have been built. The TB 9 Tampico is marketed as a trainer and is powered by a four cylinder 120kW (160hp) Lycoming O-320. Until the late 1980s it was available with a fixed pitch propeller as the Tampico FP, or with a constant speed prop as the Tampico CS. Both the Tampico FP and CS had a more up market interior than the later TB 9 Tampico Club, which has a two blade fixed pitch Sensenich prop. The Tampico Sprint was launched in 1997 and introduced faired, trailing link undercarriage and a new prop, increasing cruising speed by 18km/h (10kt).

The TB 10 Tobago and TB 200 Tobago XL feature faired undercarriage, higher weights, a higher level of interior equipment, more powerful engines and constant speed props. The Tobago is powered by a 135kW (180hp) O-360, the TB 200 Tobago XL a 150kW (200hp) fuel injected IO-360.

The TB 20 Trinidad and TB 21 Trinidad TC feature retractable gear, the Trinidad powered by a 185kW (250hp) IO-540, the TC a similarly rated turbocharged TIO-540. The TB 20C has a port side freight door.

In early 2000 Socata switched production to the improved GT (Generation Two) series of all four models. The GTs feature the slightly enlarged cabin and aerodynamic improvements – including upturned wingtip and curved dorsal fillet – developed for the MR series.

Photo: A TB 21 Trinidad GT. (EADS Socata)

EADS Socata MS 200 FG & RG

Country of origin: France

Type: Four/five seat light aircraft

Powerplant: One 172kW (230hp) Morane Renault SR 305 turbocharged and intercooled direct injection flat four piston engine (compression ratio 19:1) running on jet fuel driving a three blade constant speed Hartzell propeller.

Performance: MS 200 FG – Cruising speed at 10,000ft 248km/h (134kt). Initial rate of climb over 750ft/min. Service ceiling 17,000ft. Max range 1845km (996nm). MS 200 RG – Cruising speed at 15,000ft 350km/h (189kt). Initial rate of climb over 1100ft/min. Service ceiling 23,000ft. Max range 2655km (1433nm).

Weights: Weights not published at late 2002.

Dimensions: Wing span 9.97m (32ft 9in), length 7.75m (25ft 5in), height 2.85m (9ft 4in).

Capacity: Typical seating for four or five.

Production: Deliveries due to begin in 2003.

History: Socata's MS 200 light single development of the TB series is one of the first applications for new technology Morane Renault direct injection diesel piston engines which run on jet fuel/avtur.

Morane Renault is the marketing name for the Societe de Motorisations Aeronautiques (SMA), jointly established in 1997 by Socata parent Aerospatiale and Renault Sport, the motorsport arm of the French car manufacturer, to develop new technology piston engines.

Morane Renault initially planned three new diesel direct injection turbocharged engines, the direct drive 135kW (180hp) MR 180, and the geared 185kW (250hp) MR 250 and 225kW (300hp) MR 300. Instead Morane Renault concentrated on the 172kW (230hp) SR 305 and the 221kW (296hp) SR460. The major benefit of these engines is that they will run on jet fuel, which is cheaper and more readily available than Avgas. The engines are computer controlled, allowing the use of a single power lever on aircraft they power.

The MR engines will cost about the same as conventional piston engines, but operating costs are predicted to be as much as 30 to 40% lower due to a 3000 hour TBO (time between overhaul), lower maintenance costs, better fuel efficiency and the affordability of jet fuel. Noise emissions are also lower.

A Morane Renault engine got airborne for the first time aboard a modified Socata Trinidad on March 3 1998. This was an MR 250 derated to 150kW (200hp) due to a gearbox limitation. The production SR 305 received French DGAC certification in April 2001.

Socata's new Morane singles will be among the first applications for the new technology engines. The MS 200 FG (previously MS 180) will feature fixed undercarriage and a 172kW (230hp) SR 305 driving a three blade propeller. The MS 200 RG is similar save its retractable undercarriage. First deliveries are planned for 2003.

Socata is also developng the MS 300 Epsilon II, a MR 300 powered development of its Epsilon two seat trainer.

Like the GT series of the TB family, the MS 200 will feature an enlarged cabin, with single piece carbonfibre/honeycomb roof and revised window pillars, and aerodynamic improvements, including upturned wingtip and curved dorsal fillet.

Photo: The Trinidad testbed with the MR 250 engine.

EADS Socata TBM 700

Country of origin: France

Type: Single engine corporate turboprop

Powerplant: One 522kW (700shp) flat rated Pratt & Whitney Canada PT6A-64 turboprop driving a four blade c/s Hartzell propeller.

Performance: TBM 700 – Max cruising speed 555km/h (300kt), economical cruising speed 450km/h (243kt). Initial rate of climb 2380ft/min. Max certificated altitude 30,000ft. Range with max payload and reserves at max cruising speed 1666km (900nm), at economical cruising speed 2000km (1079nm). Range with max fuel at max cruising speed 2500km (1350nm), at economical cruising speed 2870km (1550nm). TBM 700C2 – Speeds same. Max range (NBAA IFR reserves) at economical cruising speed with max payload 1184nm (2193km), range with max fuel 1678nm (3107km).

Weights: TBM 700 – Empty equipped 1860kg (4101lb), max takeoff 2984kg (6578lb). TBM 700C2 – Basic empty 2110kg (4651lb), max takeoff 3354kg (7394lb).

Dimensions: Wing span 12.68m (41ft 7in), length 10.64m (34ft 11in), height 4.35m (14ft 3in). Wing area 18.0m² (193.8sq ft).

Capacity: Pilot and one passenger (or copilot) on flightdeck. Main cabin seating for up to five, or typical accommodation for four in a club arrangement. The TBM 700 is also offered as a freighter.

Production: More than 185 built by late 2002. Total of 25 ordered for the French air force and army.

History: Socata's TBM 700 is a high performance single engine turboprop powered light business and corporate transport.

The TBM 700 was developed by Socata (then Aerospatiale's General Aviation division, now part of EADS) in France and Mooney in the USA, hence the TBM designation. The two formed TBM SA to build and market the TBM 700, with development responsibility for the project split 70/30 between Socata and Mooney respectively.

The first of three TBM 700 prototypes first flew on July 14 1988. French certification was granted in January 1990. Mooney withdrew from the program shortly after the delivery of the first production aircraft in December 1990.

The pressurised TBM 700 is of conventional design and construction, with a small amount of composite materials used in some areas. Flight controls, flaps and most of the empennage and fin are made from Nomex honeycomb and metal sheets. Leading edges and undercarriage doors meanwhile are made from a carbon and fibreglass composite. Entry to the cabin is through a split upward/downward opening door in the rear port fuselage.

Apart from the base aircraft the TBM 700 has been offered as the TBM 700B with large cabin door and the TBM 700C freighter with a freight door and separate port side cockpit door. A French customer placed the TBM 700C into service in November 1999. Development of the stretched TBM 700S ceased in 1995.

The latest variant is the TBM 700C2, with increased takeoff weight and hence improved payload range. Other features include a some airframe strengthening, a new interior and increased baggage compartment space. It was announced at Oshkosh in July 2002, with deliveries due by the end of that year.

Photo: A TBM 700 in flight. (Paul Merritt)

Eclipse 500

Country of origin: United States of America

Type: Six seat light twin corporate jet

Powerplant: Prototype – Two 3.4kN (770lb) Williams International EJ22 turbofans.

Performance: Prototype – Max cruising speed 658km/h (355kt). Stalling speed 115km/h (62kt). Rate of climb 2680ft/min. Time to 35,000ft 20min. Max altitude 41,000ft. Range at high speed cruise with pilot and three passengers and NBAA IFR reserves 2409km (1300nm). Max range 2965km (1600nm), max range with optional wingtip tanks 3382km (1825nm).

Weights: Prototype – Empty 1225kg (2700lb), max takeoff 2132kg (4700lb)

Dimensions: Wing span 11m (36.0ft), length 10.1m (33.1ft), height 3.3m (11.0ft).

Capacity: Standard seating for six, including pilot. Club seating for four behind pilot and second pilot/passenger. Optional toilet.

Production: 1350 firm orders and 715 options held at late 2002. Anticipated deliveries of 140 in 2004, 500 in 2004 and 900 in 2006. 2002 price tag $US855,000.

History: The six seat Eclipse 500 is an ambitious attempt at pioneering a new class of light corporate jet.

Albuquerque, New Mexico based Eclipse Aviation was formed in May 1998 and raised $US60m in initial funding in June 1999, when it began work on the 500. The project was officially announced in March 2000, with the preliminary design review completed that September. The prototype Eclipse 500 was rolled out on July 13 2002, and made its first flight on August 26 that year.

The key to the Eclipse 500 was to be its two Williams International EJ22 turbofans, and these engines are fitted to the prototype. Eclipse had an exclusivity arrangement with Williams covering supply of the tiny FADEC equipped 3.4kN (770lb) turbofans, but withdrew from this agreement in late November 2002. Instead 2002 Eclipse said it was working to find a new engine supplier.

This hiccup will effect Eclipse's timetable of certification in late 2003 and first deliveries in January 2004. A new schedule was due be announced when a new engine supplier was selected.

The 500 is made from aluminium, with major assemblies such as the cabin, aft fuselage, wings and engine mounts joined using friction stir welding (a rapidly rotating pin between two pieces of aluminium creates friction which softens but not melts the metal, resulting in a seamless join). The low mounted wing features high lift Fowler style flaps and a pneumatic de-icing system. Wingtip fuel tanks will become optional. The aircraft sits on trailing link main landing gear, which, along with the split tail cone speed brakes, are electromechanically actuated. Flight controls are mechanical.

The Eclipse will be certificated for single pilot operation. The standard integrated architecture glass cockpit features two primary flight displays and one large multifunction display. It features sidestick controllers, autothrottle, dual three axis autopilot, weather radar, ADS-B, terrain avoidance warning and RVSM.

Photo: The prototype Eclipse 500 makes its first flight on August 26 2002. (Eclipse Aviation)

Embraer EMB-110 Bandeirante

Country of origin: Brazil

Type: 15-18 seat turboprop regional airliner

Powerplants: Two 560kW (750shp) Pratt & Whitney Canada PT6A-34 turboprops driving three blade constant speed Hartzell propellers.

Performance: EMB-110P – Max speed 460km/h (248kt), max cruising speed 417km/h (225kt), economical cruising speed 326km/h (176kt). Initial rate of climb 1788ft/min. Service ceiling 22,500ft. Range at long range cruising speed with reserves 2000km (1080nm). EMB-110P2A/41 – Max cruising speed 413km/h (222kt), economical cruising speed 341km/h (184kt). Range with max fuel 1964km (1060nm).

Weights: EMB-110P – Empty equipped 3515kg (7751lb), max takeoff 5700kg (12,566lb). EMB-110P2A/41 – Operating empty 3590kg (7915lb), max takeoff 5900kg (13,010lb).

Dimensions: Wing span 15.33m (50ft 3in), length 15.10m (50ft 4in), height 4.92m (16ft 2in). Wing area 29.1m² (313sq ft).

Capacity: Flightcrew of two. Typical passenger seating for 18 at three abreast, max seating for 21 at 74cm (29in) pitch.

Production: 500 Bandeirantes built, the last of which were delivered to the Brazilian military in 1990. Over 180 remain in airline service.

History: The Embraer EMB-110 Bandeirante (often dubbed 'Bandit'), was Embraer's first successful commercial aircraft program.

The EMB-110 was developed at the Brazilian Institute of Research and Development against a Brazilian Ministry of Aeronautics specification for a general purpose light transport suitable for military and civilian duties. The new design was developed with the assistance of well known French designer Max Holste, and the first of three YC-95 prototypes first flew on October 26 1968.

Embraer (or Empresa Brasilera de Aeronáutica SA) was established the following year, and development and production of the C-95 became one of the company's first responsibilities. The first production standard EMB-110 Bandeirante (Portuguese for Pioneer) flew on August 9 1972, and the first entered airline service in April 1973.

Initial Bandeirante models were the 12 seat transport EMB-110, the aerial photography EMB-110B and maritime patrol EMB-111 for the Brazilian air force; the initial airline version, the 15 seat EMB-110C; and the seven seat EMB-110E executive transport.

The 18 seat enlarged EMB-110P gave rise to the main production models, the convertible EMB-110P1 with larger rear door and the passenger EMB-110P2 with airstair, which both appeared in 1977. The P1/41 and P2/41 introduced a higher maximum takeoff weight.

From 1983 Embraer built the EMB-110P1A, P1A/41, P2A and P2A/41, which featured dihedral on the tailplane among other minor improvements. The EMB-110P1A/41 and P2A/41 versions of the P1A were certificated to US FAA SFAR-41 standards.

Bandeirante production ceased in May 1990, the final aircraft being delivered to the Brazilian air force although a further two were completed in 1992 for the Colombian air force. Today the Bandeirante's virtues of reliability and good operating economics means that it remains popular with its operators.

Photo: Over 180 Bandeirantes are in service. (Lance Higgerson)

Embraer EMB-120 Brasilia

Country of origin: Brazil

Type: 30 seat turboprop regional airliner

Powerplants: Two 1340kW (1800shp) Pratt & Whitney Canada PW118 or PW118A turboprops driving four blade Hamilton Standard propellers.

Performance: EMB-120 – Max cruising speed 555km/h (300kt) with PW118s, or 574km/h (310kt) with PW118As, long range cruising speed 482km/h (260kt). Initial rate of climb 2120ft/min. Service ceiling 30,000ft with PW118s, or 32,000ft with PW118As. Range with max passengers and reserves 1020km (550nm) with PW118s, or 926km (500nm) with PW118As. EMB-120ER – Max cruising speed 555km/h (300kt) with PW118s, or 580km/h (313kt) with PW118As, long range cruising speed 500km/h (270kt). Initial rate of climb 2500ft/min. Service ceiling 29,000ft with PW118s, or 32,000ft with PW118As. Range with max pax and reserves 1556km (840nm) with PW118s, or 1500km (810nm) with PW118As.

Weights: EMB-120 – Empty equipped 7100kg (15,655lb), max takeoff 11,500kg (25,353lb). EMB-120ER – Empty equipped 7140kg (15,741lb), max takeoff 11,990kg (26,433lb).

Dimensions: EMB-120 – Wing span 19.78m (64ft 11in), length 20.00m (65ft 8in), height 6.35m (20ft 10in). Wing area 39.4m² (424.42sq ft). EMB-120ER – Same except for length 20.07m (65ft 10in).

Capacity: Flightcrew of two. Standard main cabin seating for 30 at three abreast and 79cm (31in) pitch. Optional passenger seating for 24 or 26 with greater baggage/cargo space.

Production: 352 Brasilias built, with the last delivered in September 1999. Over 290 in service in 2002.

History: The 30 seat Brasilia has proved to be a popular regional turboprop airliner, enjoying strong sales in the face of fierce competition from the slightly larger Saab 340 and Dash 8.

Embraer first began design work on a new regional turboprop airliner in the late 1970s when the company studied stretching its EMB-121 Xingu corporate turboprop to a 25 seat regional airliner. While this was the first aircraft to bear the EMB-120 designation (it was named the Araguaia), the production EMB-120 is an all new aircraft.

Design studies of the definitive EMB-120 began in September 1979, the PW115 powered prototype first flew on July 27 1983. Entry into service was in October 1985 with Atlantic Southcoast Airlines.

Versions of the EMB-120 include: the initial production EMB-120; the Reduced Takeoff weight EMB-120RT; the Extended Range EMB-120ER; the EMB-120 Cargo freighter; mixed passenger/freight EMB-120 Combi; and EMB-120 Convertible. Hot and high versions of these models (offered from 1986) have PW118A engines, which retain their power ratings to a higher altitude.

From 1994 the standard Brasilia production model was the EMB-120ER Advanced (first delivered to Skywest Airlines in May 1993). The ER Advanced incorporates a range of external and interior improvements and an increased maximum takeoff weight. Production ceased in 1999.

The fuselage of the EMB-120 is also used by the very successful ERJ regional jet family.

Photo: A Brasilia in flight. (Embraer)

Embraer EMB-121 Xingu

Country of origin: Brazil

Type: Twin turboprop corporate transport

Powerplants: Xingu I – Two 505kW (680shp) Pratt & Whitney Canada PT6A-28 turboprops driving three blade constant speed Hartzell propellers. Xingu II – Two 559kW (750shp) PT6A-135s driving four blade props.

Performance: Xingu I – Max cruising speed 450km/h (243kt), econ cruising speed 365km/h (197kt). Initial rate of climb 1400ft/min. Service ceiling 26,000ft. Range with max fuel 2352km (1270nm). Xingu II – Max cruising speed 474km/h (256kt), economical cruising speed 380km/h (205kt). Initial rate of climb 1800ft/min. Service ceiling 28,000ft. Range with max fuel 2278km (1230nm), with max payload 1630km (880nm).

Weights: Xingu I – Empty equipped 3620kg (7984lb), max takeoff 5670kg (12,500lb). Xingu II – Empty equipped 3710kg (8179lb), max takeoff 5670kg (12,500lb).

Dimensions: Wing span 14.45m (47ft 5in), length 12.25m (40ft 2in), height 4.74m (15ft 7in). Wing area 27.5m² (296.0sq ft).

Capacity: Flightcrew of one or two, plus typical main cabin seating for five or six passengers, max seating in main cabin for nine. The cabin features a standard toilet and galley.

Production: Total Xingu I & II production 105 aircraft, including military orders, comprising 89 Xingu Is and 16 Xingu IIs. Over 60 currently in use as corporate transports, largely in Europe and South America, including French military aircraft.

History: The Xingu corporate transport combined the Bandeirante's wing with an all new fuselage, but was only built in small numbers.

The Xingu first flew on October 10 1976, with a production aircraft following on May 20 1977. The first customer delivery occurred later that same year (to the Copersucar-Fittipaldi Formula One racing team). Design features included a wing based on that on the EMB-110P2 but with reduced span and modified tips, and Pratt & Whitney Canada PT6A turboprops.

The major customer for the Xingu I was the French military, with a total order for 41 (for aircrew training and liaison duties for the air force and navy), which accounted for almost half of all EMB-121 production.

Several derivatives of the Xingu design were proposed, including the original EMB-120, the Araguaia, a commuter airliner which would have seated 25, and the EMB-123 Tapajós. The Tapajós would have had more powerful 835kW (1120shp) PT6A-45 engines (which also would have powered the Araguaia), increased wing span and a lengthened fuselage.

A more modest development did enter production, the EMB-121B Xingu II. This introduced more powerful PT6A-135 engines, four blade props, increased fuel tankage and small strakes added to each side of the tail cone. Similar in size, powerplant and performance to the Raytheon Beech King Air B200, the Xingu II made its first flight on September 4 1981. Embraer introduced an improved interior for the Xingu II in 1984.

Production ceased in August 1987 after 105 Xingus had been built.

Photo: A Xingu I. (Embraer)

Embraer ERJ 135, ERJ 140 & Legacy

Embraer ERJ 145

Country of origin: Brazil

Type: 37 and 44 seat regional jet airliners & corporate jet (Legacy)

Powerplants: ERJ 135LR – Two 33.0kN (7426lb) Rolls-Royce AE 3007A1/3 turbofans. ERJ 140LR – Same.

Performance: ERJ 135LR – Max cruising speed 834km/h (450kt). Service ceiling 37,000ft. Range with 37 passengers 3138km (1700nm). ERJ 140LR – Same except range with 44 passengers 3019km (1630nm).

Weights: ERJ 135LR – Operating empty 11,420kg (25,176lb), max takeoff 20,000kg (44,092lb). ERJ 140LR – Operating empty 11,740kg (25,882lb), max takeoff 21,100kg (46,517lb).

Dimensions: ERJ 135 & Legacy – Wing span 20.04m (65ft 9in), length 26.34m (86ft 5in), height 6.75m (22ft 2in). Wing area 51.2m² (550.9sq ft). ERJ 140 – Same except length 28.45m (93ft 5in).

Capacity: Flightcrew of two. ERJ 135 – Flightcrew of two. Standard seating for 37 passengers at three abreast. ERJ 140 – Standard seating for 44 passengers at three abreast.

Production: By late 2002 firm ERJ 135 orders stood at 122 with 89 delivered. 174 ERJ 140s on order, with 52 delivered. 66 firm Legacy orders at late 2002.

History: The ERJ 135 and more recent ERJ 140 are shortened developments of the 50 seat ERJ 145, while the Legacy is a corporate jet development of the ERJ 135.

Embraer launched the ERJ 135 on September 16 1997 with the prototype flying just nine and a half months later on July 4 1998. A second prototype first flew in October 1998, US FAA certification was awarded on July 16 1999 and first delivery was to Continental Express on July 23 1999.

The ERJ 135 is a fairly straightforward development of the 145. Both 135 prototypes were converted from ERJ 145 prototypes, requiring little modification other than the removal of two fuselage plugs totalling 3.50m (11ft 6in) in length. The only other notable change is the derated Rolls-Royce (Allison) AE 3007 turbofans. Like the ERJ 145 therefore, the 135 also features a Honeywell Primus 1000 avionics suite with five large multifunction displays in the cockpit and three abreast passenger seating.

Also in common with the ERJ 145, the 135 is offered in standard ERJ 145ER and extended range ERJ 145LR forms. The LR features an additional fuel tank and slightly uprated engines.

In September 1999 Embraer launched the third member of its regional jet family, the 44 seat ERJ 140. The ERJ 140 is also a minimum change development, and differs from the 135 and 145 only in its fuselage length and seating capacity. First flight was on June 27 2000 and deliveries began in late July 2001.

The 140 is largely aimed at US airlines who have to contend with pilot labour agreement restrictions on the numbers of 50 seater jets they can operate. American Eagle was the launch customer.

Meanwhile at Farnborough 2000 Embraer launched development of the ERJ 135 based Legacy corporate jet. First flight (of a converted ERJ 125) was on March 31 2001. The Legacy features additional fuel giving a range with 10 passengers of 5930km (3200nm).

Photo: A British Midland ERJ 135. (Embraer)

Country of origin: Brazil

Type: 50 seat regional jet airliner

Powerplants: ERJ 145ER – Two 31.3kN (7040lb) Rolls-Royce AE 3007A turbofans. ERJ 145LR – Two 33.0kN (7426lb) AE 3007A1s.

Performance: High speed cruising speed 833km/h (450kt). Service ceiling 37,000ft. ERJ 145ER – Range with 50 passengers at long range cruising speed 2445km (1320nm). ERJ 145LR – Range with 50 passengers 2870km (1550nm).

Weights: ERJ 145ER – Operating empty 11,667kg (25,722lb), max takeoff 20,600kg (45,415lb). ERJ 145LR – Operating empty 12,007kg (26,470lb), max takeoff 22,000kg (48,500lb).

Dimensions: Wing span 20.04m (65ft 9in), length 29.87m (98ft 0in), height 6.75m (22ft 2in). Wing area 51.2m² (550.9sq ft).

Capacity: Flightcrew of two. Standard passenger accommodation for 50 at three abreast. Can seat 48 or 49 with wardrobe fitted.

Production: First deliveries late December 1996. At late 2002 orders stood at 581, of which 446 had been delivered.

History: The 50 seat ERJ 145 regional jet has become a runaway sales success, following a chequered early development history.

Embraer began working on 50 seat regional jet concepts in the late 1980s. The original EMB-145 (now renamed ERJ 145) was launched in mid 1989 and would have been a stretched and jet engined EMB-120 Brasilia (with the two turbofans mounted forward of the wing as on most low wing turboprops). But by 1990 Embraer was studying a modified design as wind tunnel testing revealed that the original configuration would not meet performance objectives. Changes included a mildly swept wing with winglets and conventional below wing mounted engines.

By late 1991 Embraer had frozen the definitive ERJ 145 design with rear fuselage mounted engines, T-tail and no winglets. Other features include Rolls-Royce AE 3007A turbofans and Honeywell's Primus 1000 EFIS avionics with five colour screens in the flightdeck. The Brasilia's three abreast fuselage cross section was retained.

The ERJ 145 first flew on August 11 1995, with first deliveries from December 1996 to Continental Express. Continental's initial order for 25 was a major fillup for the program and opened the floodgates for a number of major sales.

Embraer has developed three ERJ 145 models, the initial ERJ 145ER, the higher max takeoff weight longer range ERJ 145LR introduced in 1998 and most recently the ERJ 145XR (Extra Long Range). The 145XR was launched first flew on June 29 2001 and entered service in October 2002. It features uprated yet more fuel efficient 36kN (8110lb) engines, winglets, 24,100kg (53,131lb) max takeoff weight, a max cruising speed of 0.8 Mach (852km/h/460kt) and increased fuel capacity for a 3705km (2000nm) range.

Other ERJ 145 developments are two radar platforms for the Brazilian air force (the AEW EMB-145 SA and remote sensing EMB-145RS), and the ERJ 135, 140 and Legacy, described separately.

Under an agreement signed in December 2002, the ERJ 145 family will be built under licence in China by the Harbin Embraer Aircraft Industry Company. First deliveries are planned from late 2003.

Photo: An ERJ 145XR. (Embraer)

Embraer 170, 175, 190 & 195

Country of origin: Brazil

Type: 70, 78, 98 and 108 seat regional airliners

Powerplants: Embraer 170 – Two 62.3kN (14,000lb) General Electric CF34-8E turbofans. 190 – Two 82.3kN (18,500lb) CF34-10Es.

Performance: 170 – Max cruising speed Mach 0.80 or 870km/h (470kt). Standard range with max passengers at long range cruising speed 3334km (1800nm), LR range at same conditions 3889km (2100nm). 190 – Speed same. Standard range with max passengers at long range cruising speed 3334km (1800nm), LR range at same conditions 4260km (2300nm). ERJ 195 – Speed same. Standard range with max passengers at long range cruising speed 2593km (1400nm), LR range at same conditions 3334km (1800nm).

Weights: 170 – Basic operating 20,150kg (44,422lb), standard max takeoff 35,450kg (78,153lb), LR max takeoff 36,850kg (81,239lb). 190 – Basic operating 26,200kg (57,760lb), standard max takeoff 45,990kg (101,389lb), LR max takeoff 48,500kg (106,922lb). 195 – Basic operating 27,100kg (59,744lb), standard max takeoff 46,990kg (103,593lb), LR max takeoff 48,990kg (108,003lb).

Dimensions: 170 – Wing span over winglets 26.00m (85ft 4in), length 29.90m (98ft 1in), height 9.67m (31ft 9in). 190 – Wing span over winglets 28.72m (94ft 3in), length 36.24m (118ft 11in), height 10.28m (33ft 9in). 195 – Same as 190 except length 38.65m (126ft 10in).

Capacity: Flightcrew of two. 170 – Standard seating for 70 at four abreast. 175 – Standard seating for 78. 190 – Standard seating for 98. 195 – Std seating for 108.

Production: At late 2002 82 170s & 30 195s were on firm order.

History: The Embraer 170 and 190 series are all new entrants into the top end of the regional jet airliner market, with seating capacities spanning from 70 to 108.

Embraer announced the ERJ 170 and ERJ 190 – now Embraer 170 and Embraer 190 – in February 1999, and formally launched the program on June 14 that year at the Paris Airshow.

The first member of the family is the 70 seat Embraer 170, which rolled out on October 29 2001 (when the ERJ prefix was dropped) and first flew on February 19 2002. Six aircraft were being used in the flight test program, which, after some small delays, will allow first deliveries – to Swiss – in the second quarter of 2003.

The 6.25m (8ft 5in) stretched Embraer 190 will seat 98 passengers, the further stretched Embraer 195 – 2.41m (7ft 11in) longer than the 190 – will seat 108. The Embraer 195 will fly first, in late 2003, the 190 following a year later. Embraer is also building the Embraer 175, stretched by 1.77m (5ft 10in) over the Embraer 170, with deliveries to India's Jet Airways from the third quarter of 2002.

All three variants are offered in standard and LR (long range) variants. A corporate jet version of the 170 is also proposed.

Features of the family include new FADEC equipped GE CF34 engines (the most powerful CF34 variants), a new four abreast 'double bubble' fuselage cross section, a moderately swept wing with winglets (added to the design in mid 2000), fly-by-wire flight controls, and Honeywell Primus Epic EFIS avionics.

Photo: An Embraer 170 in flight. (Embraer)

Embraer (Neiva) Ipanema

Country of origin: Brazil

Type: Agricultural aircraft

Powerplants: EMB-200 – One 194kW (260hp) Lycoming O-540-H2B5D flat six piston engine driving a two blade fixed pitch McCauley propeller. EMB-202 – One 225kW (300hp) Textron Lycoming IO-540-K1J5D driving a two blade (optional three blade) constant speed propeller. Teledyne Continental IO-550-D optional.

Performance: EMB-200 – Max cruising speed at 67% power 211km/h (114kt). Initial rate of climb 705ft/min. Range with max fuel and no reserves 941km (507nm). EMB-202 (normal category) – Max speed 230km/h (124kt), max cruising speed at 75% power 213km/h (115kt). Initial rate of climb 930ft/min. Range at 6000ft with no reserves 938km (506nm).

Weights: EMB-200 – Max takeoff normal category 1550kg (3417lb), max takeoff restricted category 1800kg (3968lb). EMB-202 – Empty 1020kg (2249lb), max takeoff weights same.

Dimensions: EMB-200 – Wing span 11.20m (36ft 9in), length (tail up) 7.43m (24ft 5in), height 2.20m (7ft 3in). Wing area 18.0m² (193.8sq ft). EMB-202 – Same except wing span 11.69m (38ft 4in). Wing area 19.9m² (214.6sq ft).

Capacity: Pilot only. EMB-200 hopper capacity 680 litres. EMB-202 hopper capacity 750kg (1653lb) or 950 litres.

Production: Over 800 of all models sold, including 49 EMB-200s, 24 EMB-200As, 200 EMB-201s, 3 EMB-201Rs, and 402 EMB-201As. Production transferred to Embraer subsidiary Neiva in 1980.

History: The Embraer/Neiva Ipanema agricultural aircraft has been a great success, with other 850 sold.

Brazil's Department of Aviation began designing the Ipanema in May 1969 in response to a Brazilian Ministry of Agriculture requirement for an agricultural spraying aircraft. Responsibility for the design was transferred to Embraer on January 2 1970 and the first prototype EMB-200 first flew on July 30 that year. Brazilian certification was awarded on December 14 1971.

Features of the EMB-200 included a low mounted wing, a 194kW (260hp) O-540 flat six engine and a 680 litre hopper, whose contents are dispensed from spray booms mounted behind the wing trailing edges or a dusting system below the centre fuselage. The EMB-200A was similar except for its variable pitch propeller.

The EMB-201 was built between 1974 and 1977 and introduced the more powerful fuel injected 225kW (300hp) IO-540 engine. The EMB-201A first flew on March 10 1977 and incorporated a new wing profile with new winglets, revised cockpit layout and aerodynamic changes. The EMB-201R was optimised for glider towing, just three were built for the Brazilian air force academy's gliding club.

The current production EMB-202 was introduced in 1992. It has a longer span wing, increased capacity hopper, and optional three blade prop and optional 225kW (300hp) Teledyne Continental IO-550-D. Large winglets are a recent addition.

In October 2002 Neiva unveiled an alcohol powered version of the EMB-202 it is working on with Brazil's Centro Technologivo Aerospacial, Lycoming and Hartzell.

Photo: The alcohol powered Ipanema prototype. (Embraer)

Enstrom F28, 280 & 480

Country of origin: United States of America

Type: Three and five seat light helicopters

Powerplant: F28A – One 155kW (205hp) Lycoming HIO-360-C1B flat four piston engine driving a three blade main rotor and two blade tail rotor. 280FX – One 170kW (225hp) Textron Lycoming HIO-360-F1AD with Rotomaster turbocharger. 480 – One 215kW (285shp) takeoff rated Rolls-Royce 250-C20W turboshaft.

Performance: F28A – Max cruising speed 161km/h (87kt). Initial rate of climb 950ft/min. Service ceiling 12,000ft. Hovering ceiling in ground effect 5600ft. Range with max fuel 380km (205nm). 280FX – Max speed 189km/h (102kt), economical cruising speed 172km/h (93kt). Initial rate of climb 1450ft/min. Certificated ceiling 12,000ft. Hovering ceiling out of ground effect 8700ft. Range with max fuel and no reserves 483km (260nm). 480 – Cruising speed 211km/h (114kt) at 1293kg (2850lb). Initial rate of climb 1500ft/min. Service ceiling 13,000ft. Hovering ceiling out of ground effect 12,200ft. Max range 806km (435nm).

Weights: F28A – Empty 657kg (1450lb), max takeoff 975kg (2150lb). 280FX – Empty equipped 719kg (1585lb), max takeoff 1179kg (2600lb). 480 – Empty 760kg (1675lb), max takeoff 1292kg (2850lb).

Dimensions: F28A – Main rotor diameter 9.75m (32ft 0in), length overall 8.94m (29ft 4in), fuselage length 8.56m (28ft 1in), height to top of rotor hub 2.79m (9ft 2in). Main rotor disc area 74.7m² (804sq ft). 280FX – Same except for length overall 8.92m (29ft 3in). 480 – Main rotor diameter 9.75m (32ft 0in), fuselage length 9.09m (29ft 10in), height to main rotor hub 2.92m (9ft 7in).

Capacity: Three seats in the F28 and 280, five seats in 480. Can also be fitted with agricultural spraying gear.

Production: Production of all versions exceeds 1000. Approximately 45 480s built.

History: This long running line of three, four and five place light helicopters dates back to the late 1950s and remains in production.

The Enstrom Helicopter Corporation was first formed in 1959, and the three place F28 was its first product. The first F28 prototype first flew on November 12 1960, with the production prototype flying in May 1962. Since that time numerous developments of the basic design have been built. These include the F28A which appeared in 1968; the Model 280 Shark from 1973, an improved version with a reprofiled airframe which supplemented the F28A in production; and the turbocharged F28C and 280C, which were certificated in 1975.

The prototype for the Allison (now Rolls-Royce) 250 turboshaft powered 480 five seater and TH-28 three seat trainer first flew in 1989 after a proof of concept 280FX powered by an Allison 250-C20W began test flying the previous year. The 480 was certificated in June 1993, the TH-28, which Enstrom unsuccessfully entered into a recent US Army competition for a new pilot training helicopter, was certificated in 1992 and is aimed at training and light patrol work.

Current Enstrom production models are the F28F Falcon which first appeared in 1981; the FLIR pod equipped F28F-P Sentinel which is optimised for police work; the three seat 280FX Shark which was certificated in early 1988; and the turbine powered 480 and TH-28.

Photo: An Enstrom 280FX Shark. (Dave Prossor)

Eurocopter AS 350 Ecureuil

Country of origin: France

Type: Light utility helicopter

Powerplant: AS 350B – One 546kW (732shp) Turbomeca Arriel 1D1 turboshaft (transmission takeoff rating 440kW/590shp) driving a three blade main rotor and two blade tail rotor. AS 350D – One 460kW (615shp) Textron (Avco) Lycoming LTS 101-600A2. AS 350B3 – One 632kW (848shp) Arriel 2B (transmission takeoff rating 500kW/671shp).

Performance: AS 350B2 – Max cruising speed 246km/h (133kt). Max rate of climb 1752ft/min. Hovering ceiling out of ground effect 8360ft. Range with max fuel 670km (362nm). AS 350D – Max cruising speed 230km/h (124kt). Max inclined rate of climb 1575ft/min. Range with max fuel and no reserves 760km (410nm). AS 350B3 – Max cruising speed 248km/h (134kt). Initial rate of climb 1791ft/min. Hovering ceiling out of ground effect 12,240ft. Range with max fuel 666km (360nm).

Weights: AS 350B2 – Empty 1171kg (2582lb), max takeoff 2250kg (4960lb). AS 350D – Empty 1070kg (2359lb), max takeoff 1950kg (4300lb), or 2100kg (4630lb) with a sling load. AS 350B3 – Empty 1175kg (2590lb), max takeoff 2250kg (4960lb).

Dimensions: Main rotor diameter 10.69m (35ft 1in), length with rotors turning 12.94m (42ft 6in), fuselage length 10.93m (35ft 11in), height overall 3.14m (10ft 4in). Main rotor disc area 89.8m² (966.1sq ft).

Capacity: Standard seating for six, including two forward seats and a four place rear bench seat.

Production: Approx 3000 AS 350s of all types (including military Fennecs) ordered by late 2002. In addition Helibras in Brazil has built over 300 Esquilos under licence.

History: Europe's most successful civil helicopter, the Ecureuil (or Squirrel) is in extensive civil and military use worldwide undertaking a variety of wide ranging missions.

Aerospatiale's development of the AS 350 Squirrel in the early 1970s culminated in the first flights of the Avco Lycoming LTS 101 powered prototype on June 27 1974 and the Turbomeca Arriel powered prototype on February 14 1975. These aircraft were followed by eight pre-production examples, the first of which flew in late 1977.

Deliveries began in April 1978. Initial models offered were the Arriel powered AS 350B, which was marketed outside North America, and the LTS 101 powered AS 350C AStar sold in the USA. The AS 350C was soon replaced by the D, with a more powerful engine.

Subsequent developments include the hot and high AS 350B1 with a 510kW (684shp) Arriel 1D; the AS 350BA which was certificated in 1991 and was in production through to 1998 and is fitted with the larger main rotors of the AS 350B2 (AS 350Bs can be retrofitted to BA standard); and the AS 350B2 (marketed in North America as the SuperStar) with a more powerful Arriel 1D1 turboshaft, and the main and tail rotors developed for the twin engine AS 355F Ecureuil 2 (described separately) and certificated in April 1989.

The AS 350B3 first flew on March 4 1997 and is a hot and high optimised model. Its most important change is a more powerful Arriel 2D engine. Deliveries began in January 1998.

Military Ecureuils are marketed as the AS 550 Fennec.

Photo: An AS 350B2. (Paul Sadler)

Eurocopter AS 355 Ecureuil 2

Country of origin: France

Type: Twin engined light utility helicopter

Powerplants: AS 355F – Two 315kW (420shp) Allison 250-C20F turboshafts driving a three blade main rotor and two blade tail rotor. AS 355N – Two 302kW (406shp) max continuous rated Turbomeca TM 319 1A Arrius turboshafts.

Performance: AS 355F – Max cruising speed 224km/h (121kt). Initial rate of climb 1280ft/min. Hovering ceiling in ground effect 5900ft. Service ceiling 11,150ft. Range with max fuel and no reserves 703km (380nm). AS 355N – Max cruising speed 222km/h (120kt), economical cruising speed 217km/h (117kt). Initial rate of climb 1260ft/min. Hovering ceiling out of ground effect 2460ft. Range with max fuel 722km (390nm).

Weights: AS 355F – Empty 1305kg (2877lb), max takeoff 2540kg (5600lb) or 2600kg (5732lb) with external sling load. AS 355N – Empty 1436kg (3166lb), max takeoff 2600kg (5732lb).

Dimensions: Main rotor diameter 10.69m (35ft 1in), length overall rotors turning 12.94m (42ft 6in), fuselage length 10.91m (35ft 10in), height 3.14m (10ft 4in). Main rotor disc area 89.8m² (966.1sq ft).

Capacity: Standard seating for six, including two forward seats and a four place rear bench seat. Can be configured for police, ambulance, EMS and media missions.

Production: Orders for military AS 555s and civil AS 355s total over 880. Helibras of Brazil has built over 25 AS 355s under licence.

History: The twin engined AS 355 Ecureuil 2 offers greater performance, carrying capability and the increased redundancy of twin engines compared to the single engined AS 350.

Development of the first twin engine Ecureuil began early in the model's development life, with the first flying on September 28 1979. This prototype was powered by two Allison 250-C20F turboshafts, supplying power to the main and tail rotors through a combining gearbox. Put into production as the AS 355E, it was essentially a twin engined version of the AS 350 with detail changes made to the fuselage structure, fuel system, transmission and main rotor blades to support the twin engine configuration. In common with the AS 350, the AS 355 features the maintenance free Starflex main rotor hub, while the main rotor blades are of composite construction.

The AS 355F replaced the AS 355E from early 1982, and introduced new wider chord main rotor blades and a higher max takeoff weight. The AS 355F was followed by the F1 in January 1984 and F2 in December 1985, which introduced progressively higher maximum takeoff weights.

The current production model is the AS 355N Ecureuil 2 which introduced twin Turbomeca TM 319 Arrius turboshafts. It was certificated in 1989 and first deliveries took place from early 1992. It is marketed in North America as the TwinStar.

As with the single engined AS 550, the twin engine military AS 555 is marketed as the Fennec (the AS 555SN is fitted with a chin mounted search radar for ASW).

Photo: An AS 355F media helicopter. Note gyro stabilised turret mounted camera under the nose. (Paul Sadler)

Eurocopter EC 130B

Country of origin: France

Type: Light utility helicopter

Powerplants: One 632kW (847shp) takeoff rated, 543kW (728shp) max cont rated Turbomeca Arriel 2B1 turboshaft driving a three blade main rotor and Fenestron shrouded tail rotor.

Performance: Max operating speed 235km/h (127kt). Initial rate of climb 2290ft/min. Service ceiling 23,000ft. Hovering ceiling in ground effect 19,280ft, out of ground effect 17,460ft.

Weights: Empty 1360kg (3000lb), max takeoff internal load 2400kg (5291lb).

Dimensions: Main rotor diameter 10.69m (35ft 1in), length overall rotors turning 12.64m (41ft 6in), fuselage length 10.68m (35ft 1in), height to top of fin 3.61m (11ft 10in). Main rotor disc area 89.8m² (966.1sq ft).

Capacity: Standard seating for seven with three seats in front row and four seats behind. Medium density seating for eight with four seats in front row and four seats behind. In EMS configuration: pilot, one or two stretcher patients and one or two medical attendants, or two pilots, one stretcher patient and two medical attendants.

Production: First delivery February 2001, approx 50 delivered by late 2002.

History: The EC 130B is a development of the AS 350 Ecureuil but has a new enlarged cabin seating up to eight and Eurocopter's trademark Fenestron shrouded tail rotor.

Eurocopter developed the EC 130B in secrecy, not announcing the program until it handed over the first customer aircraft at the February 2001 HeliExpo. The first EC 130B prototype first flew in June 1999, and JAA and FAA certification was awarded in December 2000. The first production model is the EC 130B4.

The EC 130B is based on the AS 350B3, with the same Arriel 2B engine (with the addition of FADEC), Starflex main rotor and driveshaft. From the Eurocopter parts bin comes EC 120 windscreen side panels, doors and skid landing gear, a Fenestron shrouded tail rotor based on that on the EC 135, and a dual hydraulic system from the AS 355N twin.

The EC 130B's enlarged cabin has 23% more volume than the AS 350 and seats six or seven (one or two more than in the Ecureuil) on energy absorbing seats. The baggage locker is also 10% larger, and air conditioning is optional.

Standard VFR instrumentation includes a double LCD colour screen VEMD (Vehicle and Engine Multifunction Display) and GPS with colour map. FADEC allows the matching of rotor speed to flight conditions to reduce noise.

The large cabin and low noise emissions of the Fenestron shrouded tail rotor make the EC 130B well suited to sight seeing in sensitive areas.

Early EC 130B4 operators include Blue Hawaiian, Rocky Mountain Helicopters and Mont Blanc Helicopters. Series production got under way in September 2001 after four preproduction aircraft had been delivered.

Photo: The EC 130B4 prototype. The EC 130's AS 350 origins are well disguised by the Fenestron and widened cabin. (Eurocopter)

Eurocopter AS 332 & EC 225 Super Puma

Country of origin: France

Type: Medium lift utility helicopter

Powerplants: AS 332L – Two 1325kW (1755shp) Turbomeca Makila turboshafts driving a four blade main rotor and five blade tail rotor. AS 332L2 – Two 1375kW (1845shp) takeoff rated Turbomeca Makila 1A2 turboshafts.

Performance: AS 332L – Max cruising speed 277km/h (150kt). Max inclined rate of climb 1810ft/min. Hovering ceiling in ground effect 9840ft. Range 850km (635nm). AS 332L2 – High speed cruise 277km/h (150kt), economical cruising speed 252km/h (136kt). Rate of climb at 130km/h (70kt) 1447ft/min. Hovering ceiling out of ground effect 9380ft. Range with max fuel, economical cruising speed and no reserves 1490km (805nm), with standard fuel and same conditions 850km (460nm). Endurance 4hr 54min.

Weights: AS 332L – Empty 4370kg (9635lb), MTOW 9000kg (19,840lb). AS 332L2 – Empty 4686kg (10,331lb), MTOW 9300kg (20,502lb).

Dimensions: AS 332L – Main rotor diameter 15.08m (49ft 6in), length overall rotors turning 18.70m (61ft 4in), fuselage length 15.52m (50ft 11in), height overall 4.92m (16ft 1in). AS 332L2 – Main rotor diameter 16.20m (53ft 2in), length overall rotors turning 19.50m (63ft 11in), height overall 4.97m (16ft 4in). Main rotor disc area 206.1m^2 (2218.7sq ft).

Capacity: Flightcrew of one (VFR ops), or two (IFR ops) pilots. AS 332 seating for 17, AS 332L and AS 332L2 max seating for 24.

Production: Military and civil orders for all variants of the Super Puma total more than 550.

History: The Super Puma medium lift twin helicopter is a larger development of the Puma (described under Aerospatiale), and is particularly popular for offshore oil rig support work.

The original SA 330 Puma, on which the Super Puma is based, first flew in April 1965. The first Super Puma flew in September 1978 and was essentially a more powerful version of the Puma, featuring 1270kW (1700shp) Turbomeca Makila turboshafts, new avionics, composite rotor blades and an enlarged fuselage. For a time Aerospatiale planned to fit the Super Puma with a Fenestron shrouded tail rotor, but testing revealed no significant performance benefits. Commercial versions were designated AS 332Cs.

The AS 332L (or SA 332L before 1980) Super Puma introduced a stretched fuselage (by 76.5cm/2.5ft), first flew on October 10 1980 and was certificated in 1983. The updated AS 332L1 with Makila 1A1 engines appeared in 1986. Bristow Helicopters ordered 31 customised AS 332Ls named Tiger for its North Sea offshore oil rig work.

The AS 332L has been replaced by the AS 332L2. The L2 Super Puma Mk 2 (known as the Cougar in military guise) features a further fuselage stretch permitting an additional row of seats, EFIS flight instrumentation, spheriflex rotor heads and longer main rotor blades with parabolic tips. It was certificated in 1992.

The EC 225 Mk 2+ first flew on November 30 2000. It features Makila 1A4 engines (with FADEC), new main gearbox, a five blade main rotor, and a new glass cockpit with four LCDs. First delivery to launch customer CHC is due in mid 2003.

Photo: An AS 332L2. (Eurocopter)

Eurocopter AS 365N Dauphin 2 & EC 155

Country of origin: France

Type: Twin engine mid sized utility helicopter

Powerplants: AS 365N2 – Two 550kW (739shp) Turbomeca Arriel 1C2 turboshafts driving a four blade main rotor and Fenestron shrouded tail rotor. EC 155B – Two 635kW (851shp) takeoff rated Arriel 2C1s driving a five blade main rotor and Fenestron shrouded tail rotor.

Performance: AS 365N2 – Max cruising speed 285km/h (154kt), economical cruising speed 260km/h (140kt). Initial rate of climb 1380ft/min. Hovering ceiling in ground effect 8365ft, out of ground effect 5905ft. Range with standard fuel 900km (485nm). EC 155B – Max cruising speed 269km/h (145kt), economical cruising speed 265km/h (143kt). Hovering ceiling out of ground effect 2840ft. Max range with standard fuel 830km (448nm).

Weights: AS 365N2 – Empty 2240kg (4940lb), max takeoff 4250kg (9370lb). EC 155B – Empty 2528kg (5187lb), MTOW 4800kg (10,582lb).

Dimensions: AS 365N2 – Main rotor diameter 11.94m (39ft 2in), length overall rotor turning 13.68m (44ft 11in), height 3.98m (13ft 1in). Main rotor disc area 111.9m^2 (1205sq ft). EC 155 – Main rotor diameter 12.60m (41ft 4in), length overall rotor turning 14.30m (46ft 11in), fuselage length 12.73m (41ft 9in), height 4.35m (14ft 3in). Main rotor disc area 124.7m^2 (1342.1sq ft).

Capacity: One pilot (VFR) or two pilots (IFR), and max seating for 13 passengers (with one pilot). Standard passenger seating for eight or nine. EC 155 – Standard seating for 14 including one or two pilots.

Production: Approx 700 AS 365/366/565s ordered. Approx 50 EC 155s ordered. Licence production in China as the Harbin Z-9.

History: The AS 365N Dauphin 2 is one of Eurocopter's most successful designs and has found widespread use in corporate, police, media, EMS and search and rescue roles worldwide.

The AS 365N is a much improved development of the original SA 365C Dauphin 2 (described under Aerospatiale). The AS 356N introduced more powerful Arriel 1C turboshafts, enlarged tail surfaces, revised transmission, main rotor, rotor mast fairing and engine cowling, and retractable tricycle undercarriage. The AS 365N first flew on March 31 1979. Deliveries began in early 1982.

The US Coast Guard took delivery of 99 AS 365N based HH-65 Dolphins. These aircraft are powered by Textron (Avco) Lycoming LTS 101s and are optimised for the USCG's search and rescue role.

Deliveries of the improved AS 365N2 commenced in 1990. It features upgraded Arriel 1C2 engines, improved gearbox, increased max takeoff weight, redesigned cabin doors, revised interior and optional EFIS instrumentation. The AS 365N3 is a hot and high development with FADEC equipped Arriel 2Cs. Deliveries began in December 1998.

Military AS 365Ns are offered as AS 565 Panthers.

The improved EC 155B (initially AS 365N4) development was announced at the 1997 Paris Airshow. It features twin Arriel 2Cs equipped with FADEC, a five blade Spheriflex main rotor and a 40% larger main cabin, achieved with bulged doors. First flight was on June 17 1997, with French and German certification awarded in December 1998. First delivery was in March 1999.

Photo: An AS 365N3. (Paul Sadler)

Eurocopter BO 105

Country of origin: Germany

Type: Five seat light utility helicopter

Powerplants: BO 105 CBS & BO 105 CBS-5 – Two 313kW (420shp) Rolls-Royce 250-C20B turboshafts driving a four blade main rotor and two blade tail rotor.

Performance: BO 105 CBS-4 – Max cruising speed 240km/h (129kt), long range cruising speed 204km/h (110kt). Initial rate of climb 1457ft/min. Hovering ceiling out of ground effect 1500ft. Range with standard fuel and max payload 555km (300nm), ferry range with auxiliary fuel tanks 1020km (550nm). BO 105 CBS-5 – Max cruising speed 245km/h (132kt). Initial rate of climb 1870ft/min. Hovering ceiling out of ground effect 7960ft. Range 596km (321nm).

Weights: BO 105 CBS-4 – Empty 1300kg (2868lb), max takeoff 2500kg (5511lb).

Dimensions: Main rotor diameter 9.84m (32ft 4in), length incl rotors 11.86m (38ft 11in), fus length 8.81m (28ft 11in), height to top of main rotor mast 3.02m (9ft 11in). Main rotor disc area 76.1m^2 (818.6sq ft).

Capacity: Total seating for five, including two pilots or one pilot and passenger in front bucket seats, and three passengers on rear bench seat. Behind rear seats and below the engine is a freight/baggage compartment, accessible by two rear fuselage clamshell doors.

Production: Almost 1400 BO 105s of all models, including military versions, delivered thus far, including licence production in Canada, Indonesia, the Philippines and Spain.

History: In widespread military and civilian service, the BO 105 was MBB's (now part of Eurocopter) most successful helicopter design.

Construction of the first of three prototypes began in 1964, the first of which made the type's first flight on February 16 1967. This aircraft was powered by 236kW (317shp) Allison 250-C18 turboshafts and featured a conventional main rotor hub, but the subsequent prototypes incorporated a new rigid hub with feathering hinges, plus composite blades and MAN-Turbo 6022 engines. The BO 105 reverted back to Allison 250 power with the second of two pre-production aircraft flying in this form in January 1971.

Initial production was of the BO 105C which was available from 1970. The Allison 250-C20 powerplant became standard from 1973. The BO 105 CB was introduced in 1975, and became the standard production model. It introduced uprated engines and a strengthened transmission. The BO 105 is now built in BO 105 CBS form with a slight 25cm (10in) fuselage stretch and extra window, allowing an additional passenger to be carried.

The BO 105 D has IFR instrumentation and was developed for the British offshore oil rig support market. The BO 105 L has more powerful engines and higher takeoff weight. The BO 105 LSA-3 is a hot and high version with Rolls-Royce (Allison) 250-C28C engines and built exclusively in Canada by Eurocopter Canada. The BO 105 LSA-3 Super Lifter has been developed for aerial crane work and has a 2850kg (6283lb) max takeoff weight.

The BO 105 CBS-5 (formerly EC Super Five) is an upgraded BO 105 CBS with new main rotor blades. It was certificated in late 1993 and has been the main production model since then.

Photo: A BO 105 CBS-5. (Eurocopter)

Eurocopter EC 120 B Colibri

Countries of origin: France, Germany, China and Singapore

Type: Five place light utility helicopter

Powerplants: One 376kW (504shp) takeoff rated, 335kW (449shp) max continuous Turbomeca TM 319 Arrius 2F turboshaft driving a three blade main rotor and eight blade Fenestron shrouded tail rotor.

Performance: Max cruising speed 226km/h (122kt). Initial rate of climb 1300ft/min. Service ceiling 17,024ft. Range with no reserves 731km (3954nm). Endurance at 120km/h (65kt) 4hr 10min.

Weights: Empty 960kg (2116lb), max takeoff 1715kg (3781lb), max takeoff with a sling load 1800kg (3968lb).

Dimensions: Main rotor diameter 10.00m (32ft 9in), length overall rotor turning 11.52m (37ft 10in), fuselage length 9.60m (31ft 6in), height 3.40m (11ft 2in). Main rotor disc area 78.6m^2 (845.4sq ft).

Capacity: Typical seating for five, with pilot and passenger side by side with three passengers on rear bench seat. Could be configured for special missions roles. Max sling load 700kg (1543lb).

Production: First Colibri delivery (to Japan) in January 1998. 300th delivered November 8 2002.

History: Eurocopter's solution to develop a new light helicopter lay in forming a partnership with CATIC (Harbin) of China and Singapore Technologies Aerospace of Singapore.

Eurocopter (then Aerospatiale), CATIC and STA launched definition development of a new light helicopter, then designated P120L, in February 1990. The teaming arrangements for the helicopter saw Aerospatiale/Eurocopter take a 61% program share and leadership, CATIC with 24% and STAe with 15%. A development go-ahead contract for the new aircraft was signed in October 1992 (by which time Aerospatiale's helicopter activities had been merged into Eurocopter) and the EC 120 designation was announced in January 1993 (the Colibri [or Hummingbird] name came later). Design definition was completed in mid 1993.

Within the Eurocopter/CATIC/STAe partnership, Eurocopter is responsible for the design and manufacture of the rotor system and transmission, final assembly (at Marignane in France), flight testing and certification. CATIC builds the EC 120's fuselage, landing gear and fuel system, while STAe's areas of responsibility covers the tailboom, fin and doors.

Notable Colibri design features include a three blade main rotor with a Spheriflex hub integrated with the driveshaft and transmission, composite main and tail rotor blades and skid landing gear, a metal construction fuselage and a new eight blade Fenestron shrouded tail rotor. The Turbomeca TM 319 Arrius 1F turboshaft was selected to power at least the first 300 Colibris. The Colibri's cabin features standard seating for five including the pilot.

The first of two EC 120 prototypes first flew on June 9 1995 from Eurocopter France's Marignane facility. French DGAC certification was awarded in June 1997, while the first production Colibri first flew in December that year. First delivery was in January 1998, the 100th was delivered in May 2000, the 300th in November 2002.

A second assembly line is due to be established in Australia to assemble Colibris for the Asia Pacific region.

Photo: An Austrian registered EC 120 B Colibri. (Eurocopter)

Eurocopter/Kawasaki BK 117 & EC 145

Countries of origin: Germany and Japan

Type: Twin engine utility helicopter

Powerplants: BK 117 B-2 – Two 410kW (550shp) takeoff max cont rated Honeywell LTS 101-750B-1 turboshafts driving a four blade main rotor and two blade tail rotor. EC 145 – Two 550kW (738shp) takeoff rated, 516kW (692shp) max cont rated Turbomeca Arriel 1E2s.

Performance: BK 117 B-2 – Max cruising speed 248km/h (134kt). Initial rate of climb 1900ft/min. Hovering ceiling out of ground effect 7500ft. Range with standard fuel 540km (290nm), with internal long range fuel tank 706km (381nm). EC 145 – Max level speed 268km/h (145kt). Service ceiling 15,000ft. Range with max fuel 700km (378nm). Endurance 3hr 25min.

Weights: BK 117 B-2 – Empty 1745kg (3846lb), max takeoff 3350kg (7385lb). EC 145 – Max takeoff 3550kg (7826lb), max takeoff with external sling load 3650kg (8046lb).

Dimensions: BK 117 – Main rotor diameter 11.00m (36ft 1in), length overall 13.00m (42ft 8in), fuselage length 9.91m (32ft 6in), height rotors turning 3.85m (12ft 8in). Main rotor disc area 95.0m² (1023sq ft). EC 145 – Same except fuselage length 10.27m (33ft 8in).

Capacity: One pilot and max seating for 10 passengers. Executive configuration seats six, standard MBB/Eurocopter configuration seats seven, standard Kawasaki version seats nine.

Production: Approx 420 BK 117s built, with 290 from Eurocopter/ MBB and 130 from Kawasaki. Indonesia's IPTN licence built three BK 117s as NBK-117s. First EC 145 delivered April 2002.

History: The BK 117 was developed under a joint collaborative effort between MBB of Germany (now part of Eurocopter) and Kawasaki of Japan, resulting in production lines in both countries.

The BK 117 program replaced the independently developed BO 107 and Kawasaki KH-7 design studies. The BK 117 retains the former's overall configuration, with Eurocopter responsible for the helicopter's rotor system (a scaled up version of the BO 105's four blade rigid main rotor), tail unit, hydraulic system and power controls. Kawasaki has responsibility for the fuselage, transmission and undercarriage.

The BK 117 first flew on June 13 1979, the first production aircraft (built in Japan) flew December 1981, certification was awarded in December 1982, and first deliveries took place early in 1983. Initial production was of the BK 117 A-1, while the BK 117 A-3 with higher max takeoff weight and enlarged tail rotor with twisted blades was certificated in March 1985. The BK 117 A-4 introduced from 1987 features an increased transmission limit at takeoff power, improved tail rotor head and, on German built aircraft, increased fuel.

The BK 117 B-1 (certificated in 1987) has more powerful engines, the BK 117 B-2 has an increased max takeoff weight. The BK 117 C-1 is a German development with Turbomeca Arriel engines.

The upgraded C-1 based EC 145 (formerly BK 117 C-2) first flew in mid 1999. Improvements include a reprofiled EC 135 style nose, redesigned tail rotor and new avionics. It is stretched by 40cm and features a 3550kg (7819lb) max takeoff weight.

The first delivery was on April 24 2002.

Photo: A French Securite Civile EC 145. (Eurocopter)

Eurocopter EC 135

Countries of origin: Germany and France

Type: Seven seat light twin turbine utility helicopter

Powerplants: Either two 435kW (583shp) takeoff rated Turbomeca Arrius 2B1 or two 463kW (621shp) takeoff rated Pratt & Whitney Canada PW206B turboshafts driving a four blade main rotor and 10 blade shrouded Fenestron tail rotor.

Performance: Max cruising speed 256km/h (138kt). Max initial rate of climb 1500ft/min. Hovering ceiling out of ground effect 10,200ft. Range with standard fuel at sea level 620km (335nm) with Arrius 2Bs or 620km (340nm) with PW206Bs, ferry range with long range tanks 878km (474nm). Endurance with standard fuel 3hr 24min with Arrius 2B1s, 3hr 33min with PW206s.

Weights: Empty 1490kg (3284lb), max takeoff 2835kg (6250lb) or 2900kg (6393lb) with an external sling load.

Dimensions: Main rotor diameter 10.20m (33ft 6in), length overall rotor turning 12.16m (39ft 11in), fuselage length 10.20m (33ft 7in), height 3.62m (11ft 11in). Main rotor disc area 81.7m² (879.5sq ft).

Capacity: Designed for single pilot operation. Alternative cabin layouts are for five (two forward & three rear) or seven (two + three + two) in passenger roles. Alternative EMS layouts for one stretcher, three medical attendants and the pilot, or two stretchers, two attendants and pilot. Stretchers loaded through rear clamshell doors.

Production: 250th EC 135 delivered late October 2002.

History: The EC 135 light twin was developed from the BO 108 technology demonstrator.

The original MBB BO 108 was intended as an advanced technology helicopter demonstrator, and incorporated a range of high technology features including a hingeless main rotor (Sikorsky and Boeing adopted this design for their military RAH-66 Comanche), all composite bearingless tail rotor, shallow transmission (allowing greater cabin height) with special vibration absorbers, composite structures, improved aerodynamics, modern avionics and EFIS instrumentation. The first BO 108 was powered by Allison 250-C20R-3 turboshafts and flew on October 15 1988.

The success of the BO 108 test program led to MBB's announcement in January 1991 that it would develop a production version of the 108 with Arrius or PW206 engines as a replacement for the BO 105, with certification planned for 1994 and first deliveries in 1995. However the formation of Eurocopter (in January 1992) gave the program access to Aerospatiale's Fenestron shrouded tail rotor technology which was then incorporated into the design.

The combination of the BO 108 and the Fenestron led to the definitive EC 135, which first flew on February 15 1994. German certification was granted on June 14 1996, while US approval was given on July 31 that year, the same day as the first customer delivery.

The initial PW206 powered model is designated EC 135P1, the EC 135T1 has the Arrius 2B1. The EC 135P2 features the improved PW207, but designated PW206B2 (with better single engine performance) and was delivered from late 2001. The EC 135T2 features the improved Arrius 2B2 was introduced in September 2002.

The military EC 635 is also on offer.

Photo: A US registered EC 135. (Eurocopter)

Extra 230, 300 & 200

Country of origin: Germany

Type: Unlimited competition aerobatic aircraft

Powerplant: 230 – One 150kW (200hp) Textron Lycoming AEIO-360 flat four piston engine driving a two blade c/s Mühlbauer propeller. 300 – One 225kW (300hp) Textron Lycoming AEIO-540-L1B5 flat six driving a three (or optionally four) blade Mühlbauer c/s prop.

Performance: 230 – Max speed 352km/h (190kt). Initial rate of climb 2950ft/min. Endurance with max fuel 2hr 30min. 300 – Max speed 343km/h (185kt), max manoeuvring speed 293km/h (158kt). Initial rate of climb 3300ft/min. Range with reserves 974km (526nm).

Weights: 230 – Empty 440kg (970lb), max takeoff 560kg (1235lb). 300 – Empty 630kg (1389lb), max aerobatic takeoff 870kg (1918lb), max takeoff 950kg (2094lb).

Dimensions: 230 – Wing span 7.40m (24ft 3in), length 5.82m (19ft 2in), height 1.73m (5ft 8in). 300 – Wing span 8.00m (26ft 3in), length 7.12m (23ft 4in), height 2.62m (8ft 7in). Wing area 10.7m^2 (115.17sq ft). 300S – Same except for wing span 7.50m (24ft 7in), length 6.65m (21ft 9in). Wing area 10.4m^2 (112sq ft).

Capacity: 300 and 200 seat two, 230 and 300S seat pilot only.

Production: Extra 230 production ceased in 1990. Approximately 230 Extra 300s delivered since 1988, approx 30 200s since 1996.

History: Extra's aerobatic light aircraft were designed from the outset for unlimited aerobatic competition flying.

The original Extra 230 was designed by company founder Walter Extra to meet the requirements of competition aerobatic pilots with the Swiss Aero Club. First flight occurred during 1983. Unusually for an aircraft of its type the Extra 230 features a wooden wing with dacron covering, while as on other aerobatic competition aircraft the 230's wing has 0° incidence for sustained inverted flight. Production ceased in 1990 as Extra couldn't source the correct type of wood.

Design work on the larger, two seat Extra 300 began in early 1987, culminating in the first flight of a prototype on May 6 1988 and certification in May 1990. Production began in October 1988.

Small numbers of Extra 260s were also built in the early 1990s. These aircraft were essentially downsized Extra 300s with seating for a pilot only and powered by a 195kW (260hp) IO-540 flat six. The Extra 260 was not certificated, the six that were built were able to fly under special permits.

The single seat Extra 300S first flew on March 4 1992 and was certificated that same month. The 300S differs from the 300 in having a single seat, shorter span wings and more powerful ailerons, while retaining the same powerplant and basic fuselage. The 300L has a low mounted wing. The strengthened 330L has a 245kW (330hp) AEIO-580 and larger control surfaces, and first flew in January 1998. The 330LX two seater first flew in early 1999.

Both the 300 and 300S are stressed for +10/-10g flight with a single pilot, have additional transparencies in the lower sides of the fuselage below the wings for pilot visibility, and a single piece canopy.

Extra's latest product is the 150kW (200hp) AEIO-360 powered Extra 200 two seater. It first flew in April 1996. Of similar construction to the 300, it replaced the earlier 230.

Photo: An Extra 300L. (Brian Maginnity)

Extra 400

Country of origin: Germany

Type: High performance six seat light aircraft

Powerplant: One 261kW (350hp) Teledyne Continental TSIO-550-C Voyager liquid cooled, turbocharged and intercooled flat six piston engine driving a four blade constant speed MTV-14-D/195-30a propeller (three blade prop optional).

Performance: Max speed 480km/h (259kt), max cruising speed 435km/h (235kt). Initial rate of climb 1400ft/min. Max operating altitude 25,000ft. Range at 55% power 2148km (1160nm).

Weights: Basic operating empty 1389kg (3062lb), max takeoff 2000kg (4409lb).

Dimensions: Wing span 11.50m (37ft 9in), length 9.57m (31ft 5in), height 3.09m (10ft 2in). Wing area 14.3m^2 (153.5sq ft)

Capacity: Standard seating for six – pilot and passenger side by side with club four seating behind.

Production: Approx 20 Extra 400s have been built, including two prototypes.

History: The Extra 400 is a very high performance pressurised six seat light aircraft which so far has sold in only small numbers

Dinslaken, Germany based Extra announced development of the 400 in February 1993, and designed the aircraft in cooperation with Holland's Delft University. The prototype first flew on April 4 1996, and German certification was awarded on April 23 1997. A second prototype, with downward turned winglets and ventral strakes, flew in April 1998, but unfortunately this aircraft crashed on delivery to its customer later that year.

The high wing, T-tail, retractable undercarriage Extra 400 is made largely from composites, including carbonfibre and glass fibre. The aircraft's fuselage is made in two halves which are joined down the centreline. The wings too are built in two top and bottom parts and feature large Fowler flaps, giving a stalling speed in landing configuration of just 110km/h (59kt).

Power is from a watercooled, turbocharged and intercooled Teledyne Continental TSIO-550 Voyager flat six piston unit driving a four blade propeller. (An advantage of watercooling is the lack of shock cooling, allowing an emergency descent rate of 3500ft/min.)

The Extra 400 features a comprehensive IFR avionics suite with two glass displays, with a dual Garmin GPS and Meggitt autopilot package optional. A Honeywell RDR 2000 colour weather radar is optional, housed in a streamlined pod mounted under the port wingtip. The wing and tail are fitted with de-icing boots, allowing flight into known icing conditions. The cabin pressure differential is 0.38 bar (5.5lb/sq in). Entry to the roomy cabin is via a single door on the port side which splits in the middle – the top half raising upwards, the bottom half lowering down and containing integral stairs.

Despite its high performance the Extra 400 has neutral handling characteristics and good visibility ahead and to the sides for the pilot.

A turboprop powered variant has been considered but so far not been built.

Photo: The Extra 400 first prototype, which was retired in 1997.

Explorer Aircraft 500R, 500T & 750R

Countries of origin: Australia & USA

Type: Light utility aircraft

Powerplants: 500R – One 447kW (600hp) Orenda OE600A water cooled V8 piston engine driving a three blade propeller. 500T – One 447kW (600shp) Pratt & Whitney Canada PT6A-135B driving a four blade propeller. 750T – One 560kW (750shp) PT6A-60A driving a four blade propeller.

Performance: 500R – Cruising speed 324km/h (175kt). Initial rate of climb 1000ft/min. Service ceiling 25,000ft. Max range 1760km (950nm). 500T – Max cruising speed 371km/h (200kt), cruising speed 333km/h (180kt). Other figures as per 500R. 750T – Cruising speed 352km/h (190kt). Initial rate of climb 1200ft/min. Service ceiling 25,000ft. Max range 1668km (900nm).

Weights: 500R & 500T – Empty 1725kg (3800lb), max takeoff 2812kg (6200lb). 750R – Empty 2267kg (5000lb), max takeoff 4082kg (9000lb).

Dimensions: 500R & 500T – Wing span 14.43m (47ft 4in), length 9.68m (31ft 9in), height 4.72m (15ft 6in). Wing area 18.4m² (197.6sq ft). 750T – Wing span 17.7m (58ft), length 12.3m (40ft 6in), height 4.72m (15ft 6in).

Capacity: Explorer 500R and 500T seat 10 (including pilot), Explorer 750T will seat 16 (including pilot). 500R & 500T payload 1090kg (2400lb), 750T payload 1816kg (4000lb).

Production: 500T deliveries planned from 2005.

History: The all new Explorer family of light utility aircraft was originally developed in Australia by Aeronautical Engineers Australia (AEA) but will be placed into production in the USA by Explorer Aircraft Inc.

AEA and Explorer Aircraft founder Peter Swannell first began looking at a new utility aircraft in the late 1980s, and initially considered developing a stretched and more powerful Cessna 206 conversion. But by 1993 Swannell had started design work on an all new aircraft, which evolved to become the Explorer 350R, an eight seater powered by a Teledyne Continental TSIO-550 flat six.

The proof of concept Explorer 350R first flew on January 23 1998. Apart from its 260kW (350hp) TSIO-550 engine, design features included a metal frame fuselage with a carbonfibre shell, conventional all metal wings and tail surfaces and retractable undercarriage.

The Explorer's basic configuration is optimised for its intended utility roles, with a high mounted, braced wing, rectangular and constant section, fuselage flat floor cabin, and large cabin windows.

Initially the Explorer 350R was intended to be the first production member of a family of utility aircraft. Instead Explorer Aircraft is focussing on the 10 seat PT6 turboprop powered 500T. The Orenda V8 piston powered 500R (which will share the same airframe with the 350R), and the stretched, 16 seat PT6 powered 750T, may follow.

Explorer Aircraft formed in Denver, Colorado in the US in mid 1999 to develop and build the Explorer range, and then relocated to Jasper, Texas in mid 2001. The proof of concept 350R was re-engined with a PT6A and flew as the 500R in June 2000. Certification of the 500T is scheduled for 2005. Decisions on whether or not to build the 350R, 500R and 750T have not been made.

Photo: The Explorer 500T. (Gordon Reid)

Fairchild (Swearingen) Merlin

Country of origin: United States of America

Type: Turboprop corporate transport

Powerplants: IIB – Two 495kW (665shp) AiResearch (Garrett) TPE331-1-151G turboprops driving three blade constant speed propellers. IIIC – Two 670kW (900shp) Garrett TPE331-10U-503G turboprops driving four blade constant speed Dowty propellers.

Performance: IIB – Max cruising speed 475km/h (257kt). Initial rate of climb 2570ft/min. Service ceiling 29,000ft. Range with max fuel 2872km (1550nm). IIIC – Max cruising speed 556km/h (300kt). Initial rate of climb 2650ft/min. Range with max standard fuel at max cruising speed with six people on board 3590km (1938nm).

Weights: IIB – Empty 2926kg (6452lb), max takeoff 4540kg (10,000lb). IIIC – Empty equipped 3695kg (8150lb), max takeoff 5670kg (12,500lb).

Dimensions: IIB – Wing span 13.98m (45ft 11in), length 12.22m (40ft 1in), height 4.37m (14ft 4in). Wing area 26.0m² (279.74sq ft). IIIC – Wing span 14.10m (46ft 3in), length 12.85m (42ft 2in), height 5.13m (16ft 10in). Wing area 25.8m² (277.5sq ft).

Capacity: IIB – Flightcrew of one or two, with typical main cabin seating for six in executive layout or up to eight. III – Seating in main cabin for up to 11, or eight in a corporate configuration. Merlin IV seats up to 12 passengers in main cabin in a corporate configuration.

Production: Includes 33 Merlin IIAs, 87 Merlin IIBs, 92 Merlin III and IIIAs and 10 Merlin 300s. 65 IIs, 160 IIIs and 82 IVs in service in 2002.

History: The Merlin series of turboprop executive transports was Swearingen's first manufacturing program.

Prior to building the original Merlin II, Swearingen specialised in converting existing aircraft into corporate transports. The Merlin II (or SA26-T) for example is based on the Beech Queen Air and Twin Bonanza. The Merlin combined the wing of the Queen Air with the Twin Bonanza's undercarriage and an all new Swearingen designed pressurised fuselage and tail. The first Merlins were powered by two 300kW (400hp) Lycoming TIGO-540s, while the Merlin IIA was powered by Pratt & Whitney Canada PT6A-20 turboprops. The prototype IIA first flew on April 13 1965 and 33 were built before production switched to the AiResearch TPE331 powered Merlin IIB.

The improved and slightly larger Merlin III combined the Merlin II's fuselage but stretched slightly and with a new tail; and the wings and landing gear of the Metro II airliner (described separately) and more powerful engines. The Merlin III (or SA226-T) was certificated on July 27 1970. The improved IIIA introduced additional windows and avionics and systems changes, it was followed by the IIIB and then in 1981 (by which time Fairchild had acquired Swearingen) the IIIC, incorporating the wing from the Metro III.

The Merlin III was followed by the Merlin 300 which introduced aerodynamic improvements including winglets. Only 10 were built.

The Merlin IV designation applies to corporate configured versions of the Metro series of commuter airliners. The Merlin IVA designation covers the corporate versions of the original Metro II (which used a stretched Merlin II's fuselage coupled with a new wing, undercarriage and tail), the IVB is the executive equivalent of the Metro III, and the Merlin 23 is equivalent to the Metro 23.

Photo: A Swearingen Merlin IIIB. (Rob Finlayson)

Fairchild Metro II, III & 23

Country of origin: United States of America

Type: 19 seat regional airliner

Powerplants: Metro II – Two 700kW (940shp) Garrett AiResearch TPE331-3UW-303G turboprops driving three blade constant speed propellers. 23 – Two 745kW (1000shp) AlliedSignal TPE331-11U-612Gs, or 820kW (1100shp) TPE331-12UARs.

Performance: II – Max cruising speed 473km/h (255kt), long range cruising speed 450km/h (242kt). Service ceiling 27,000ft. Range with 19 passengers and reserves at max cruising speed 346km (187nm), with 15 pax and reserves at max cruising speed 1100km (595nm). 23 – Max cruising speed 542km/h (293kt). Service ceiling 25,000ft. Range with 19 passengers and reserves 2065km (1314nm), with 2268kg (5000lb) payload and reserves 988km (533nm).

Weights: II – Empty 3380kg (7450lb), max takeoff 5670kg (12,500lb). 23 – Operating empty 4309kg (9500lb), max takeoff 7484kg (16,500lb).

Dimensions: II – Wing span 14.10m (46ft 3in), length 18.09m (59ft 4in), height 5.08m (16ft 8in). Wing area 25.8m² (277.5sq ft). 23 – Same except for wing span 17.37m (57ft 0in). Wing area 28.7m² (309.0sq ft).

Capacity: Flightcrew of two. Passenger seating for 19 at two abreast and 76cm (30in) pitch. Merlin IV and 23 also seat 12 to 14 passengers in a corporate configuration. The Expediter I and 23 are freighters.

Production: 1028 Metros built, 395 in commercial service in 2002.

History: After a slow start to sales in the early 1970s, the Metro 19 seat commuter became one of the most popular of its class.

The Metro traces back to the Swearingen Merlin I executive transport. From the Merlin I Swearingen developed the turboprop powered II and III formed the basis of the new Metro commuter airliner. The Metro was Swearingen's first complete inhouse design and development work began in the late 1960s, resulting in the SA-226TC Metro's first flight on August 26 1969. The design was similar in appearance and layout to the earlier Merlins, and featured a pressurised fuselage, TPE331 turboprop engines and double slotted trailing edge flaps. Certification was awarded in June 1970 and the first example entered commercial service in 1973.

The Metro II superseded the I from 1975, with improvements to reduce cabin noise levels. The equivalent executive aircraft is the Merlin IV. In 1981 Fairchild introduced the Metro III (by which time Fairchild had taken over Swearingen), which was certificated to SFAR-41B allowing greater takeoff weights, while more efficient engines (including the option of Pratt & Whitney Canada PT6As on the IIIA) and greater wing span made the III more economical to operate. The Expediter freighter is based on the III.

The final production Metro model was the 23. Certificated to FAR Part 23 (Amendment 34) standards (hence the Metro 23 designation) it features a higher takeoff weight, more powerful engines and systems improvements first introduced on the military C-26. The Metro 23 EF has a bulged lower fuselage for greater baggage capacity, while the Merlin 23 and Expediter 23 models were also offered. In 1996 Fairchild studied a Metro with a significantly higher fuselage allowing stand-up headroom (in the style of the Beech 1900D).

Metro production wound up in 1999.

Photo: A Metro 23. (Martin Flanagan)

Fairchild Dornier 328

Country of origin: Germany

Type: 30 seat regional turboprop airliner

Powerplants: Two 1625kW (2180shp) takeoff rated Pratt & Whitney Canada PW119B turboprops driving six blade Hartzell propellers.

Performance: 328-110 – Max cruising speed 620km/h (335kt). Design cruising altitude 25,000ft or optionally 31,000ft. Range with 30 passengers and reserves at max cruising speed and 25,000ft cruising altitude 1665km (900nm), at 31,000ft 1850km (1000nm).

Weights: 328-110 – Operating empty 8920kg (19,665lb), max takeoff 13,990kg (30,842lb).

Dimensions: Wing span 20.98m (68ft 10in), length 21.22m (69ft 8in), height 7.24m (23ft 9in). Wing area 40.0m² (430.6sq ft).

Capacity: Flightcrew of two. Typical passenger seating for 30 to 33 at three abreast, max seating for 39 at four abreast.

Production: Total 328 production of 112, incl 105 production aircraft. 95 in service in late 2002.

History: The 30 seat Dornier 328 is a modern regional turboprop airliner with high cruising speeds and advanced systems.

Development of the 328 traces back to Dornier's mid 1980s market research that indicated there existed a substantial market for regional airliners in the 30 seat class through to 2005. Firm 328 development work began in December 1988, culminating in the first development aircraft's first flight on December 6 1991.

The 328 was awarded certification in October 1993. First customer deliveries also occurred in October 1993.

The 328 design incorporated an all new fuselage section for three abreast seating (offering more width per passenger than the 727/737) combined with the same basic supercritical wing of the earlier Dornier 228. Clean aerodynamics give the 328 excellent high speed cruise and climb performance. Composite materials are used in a number of areas (particularly the tail) to reduce weight and the blades on the Hartzell props are composite. The flightdeck features a five screen Honeywell Primus 2000 EFIS avionics system, while with heads-up displays the 328 can be qualified for Cat IIIa landings.

Industrial partners on the 328 included Daewoo Heavy Industries (fuselage), Aermacchi (nose), Westland (nacelles) and Israel Aircraft Industries (wing), accounting for 40% of the aircraft's construction.

Variants of the 328 are the initial production standard 328-100, the standard 328-110 with heavier weights and greater range, the 328-120 with improved short field performance and the 328-130 with progressive rudder authority reduction with increasing airspeed.

Fairchild Aerospace acquired 80% of Dornier in mid 1996 to form Fairchild Dornier.

At various times Dornier and Fairchild Dornier studied 50 seat stretches of the 328, but all were abandoned. Dornier also studied building a 328 demonstrator powered by hydrogen. The liquid hydrogen fuel would have been stored in two external tanks under the wings and outboard of the engines.

The last 328 was delivered to Air Alps Aviation in Austria in October 1999. The 328JET rejional jet development is described separately in the next entry.

Photo: A 328-100 of Austria's Welcome Air. (Toni Marimon)

Fairchild Dornier 328JET & Envoy 3

Country of origin: Germany

Type: 32 seat regional jet airliner

Powerplant: Two 26.9kN (6050lb) Pratt & Whitney Canada PW306B turbofans.

Performance: 328JET – Max cruising speed 750km/h (405kt). Service ceiling 35,000ft. Range with payload and reserves 1370km (740nm), high gross weight version range with max payload and reserves 1666km (900nm). Envoy 3 – Range with optional long range fuel tank 3705km (2000nm).

Weights: 328JET – Standard operating empty 9344kg (20,600lb), standard max takeoff 15,200kg (33,510lb), high gross weight operating empty 4394kg (20,710lb), HGW max takeoff 15,660kg (34,524lb).

Dimensions: Wing span 20.98m (68ft 10in), length 21.28m (69ft 10in), height 7.24m (23ft 9in). Wing area 40.0m^2 (430.6sq ft).

Capacity: Flightcrew of two. Standard seating for 32 to 34 passengers three abreast at 79cm (31in). Envoy 3 seats 12 to 14 in a typical corporate configuration, or up to 19.

Production: At the time of Fairchild Dornier entering bankruptcy protection in 2002 142 328JETs were on order. Production wound up in mid 2002 with 82 built.

History: The Fairchild Dornier 328JET was a pioneer of the 30 seat regional jet class.

Fairchild Aerospace took over Dasa's 80% stake in Dornier in mid 1996. Soon after Fairchild Dornier (for a time called Fairchild Aerospace) launched the 328JET, a jet engined development of the 328 turboprop, in February 1997.

The 328JET features FADEC equipped Pratt & Whitney Canada PW306 turbofans mounted in underwing pods. Otherwise the 328JET was designed to be a minimum change development of the 328 turboprop. Just two fuselage frames (which the wing and landing gear attach to) required strengthening. A 10cm (4in) extension to the trailing edge flaps cuts aerodynamic drag. Other changes include strengthened landing gear and brakes, slight changes to the software of the Honeywell Primus 2000 EFIS avionics suite, and an APU is standard.

The first 328JET prototype was converted from the second 328 turboprop, and was rolled out on December 6 1997. It first flew from Munich in Germany on January 20 1998. Certification and first deliveries were in July 1999.

Fairchild Dornier considered two stretched developments of the 328JET, the 50 seat 528JET and the 42 to 44 seat PW306B powered 428JET. The 428JET was formally launched in May 1998 and would have been assembled in Israel by IAI, but Fairchild Dornier suspended the program in August 2000 due to not being able to make a viable business case. The Envoy 3 was a corporate jet/corporate shuttle development.

On July 1 2002 Fairchild Dornier was declared insolvent and entered administration, with a buyer to be sought for its programs to stave off liquidation. If buyers are not found by April 2003 the company will be shut down and its assets sold.

Photo: A Skyways Airlines/Midwest Express 328JET on approach to land. (Don Boyd)

Fairchild Dornier 728 & 928

Country of origin: Germany

Type: Regional jet airliners

Powerplants: 728 – Two 60.4kN (13,572lb) General Electric CF34-8D3 turbofans. 928 – Two 82.3kN (18,500lb) CF34-10D5s, 928-200 85.2kN (19,150lb) CF34-10D6s.

Performance: 728 – Max cruising speed at 35,000ft Mach 0.805 or 859km/h (464kt). Max altitude 41,000ft. 728-100 range with 70 passengers 2648km (1430nm), 728-200 range with 70 passengers 3481km (1880nm). 928 – Max cruising speed at 33,000ft Mach 0.8 or 864km/h (467kt). 928-100 range with 95 passengers 4986km (1520nm), 928-200 range with 95 passengers 4075km (2200nm).

Weights: 728 – Operating empty 20,880kg (46,032lb), max takeoff 35,200kg (77,602lb), ER max takeoff 37,900kg (83,555lb). 928 – Operating empty 24,440kg (53,881lb), max takeoff 47,870kg (105,535lb), ER max takeoff 49,700kg (109,570lb).

Dimensions: 728 – Wing span 27.13m (89ft 0in), length 27.04m (88ft 9in), height 9.04m (29ft 8in). Wing area 75.0m^2 (807.3sq ft). 928 – Wing span 28.81m (94ft 6in), length 30.96m (101ft 7in), height 9.97m (32ft 9in). Wing area 84.4m^2 (908.5sq ft)

Capacity: Flightcrew of two. Typical seating for 70 to 85 passengers at five abreast in 728, 100 in 928.

Production: 125 728s and 928s on firm order before Fairchild Dornier entered insolvency protection in April 2002.

History: The 728 family was the product of Fairchild Dornier's ambitious bid to develop a range of 70-100 regional jet airliners, however the company entered insolvency protection in April 2002 and the future of the project now looks in doubt.

Fairchild Dornier launched its new family of regional jets on May 19 1998, with provisional launch orders from Crossair and Lufthansa for 120 new aircraft. The lead aircraft in the program was the 70 to 85 seat 728JET, later just 728, which rolled out on March 21 2002 (about two years after the original schedule due to revisions to the design). It had not flown when in April 2002 Fairchild Dornier entered insolvency protection under an administrator and work on the project was suspended. At late 2002 a Russian company was showing interest in buying Fairchild Dornier and restarting the 728 program, but if a sale is not completed by April 2003, the company will be liquidated.

Design features of the 728 family include General Electric's FADEC equipped CF34-8D (selected ahead of the SNECMA/Pratt & Whitney Canada SPW 14), Honeywell Primus Epic integrated EFIS avionics suite with flat panel LCDs, fly-by-wire flight control system, and a common crew type rating. EADS CASA was responsible for building the wings and empennage.

The stretched 928 (928JET) was due to fly in late 2003 for an entry into service in early 2005. It would feature a two plug fuselage stretch, more powerful engines and increased span wing, and seat 100 passengers. The 55 to 63 seat 528JET with shortened fuselage and derated engines was also offered.

Fairchild Dornier was also developing a corporate version of the 728, the Envoy 7, for delivery from mid 2004.

Photo: The 728 rollect out in March 2002. (Fairchild)

Fokker F27 & Fairchild F-27 & FH-227

Country of origin: Netherlands and USA

Type: 44-52 seat turboprop regional airliners

Powerplants: Mk 200/500/600 – Two 1730kW (2320ehp) Rolls-Royce Dart Mk 536-7R turboprops driving four blade Dowty Rotol propellers. FH-227E – Two 1715kW (2300shp) Dart 532-7Ls.

Performance: Mk 500 – Normal cruising speed 480km/h (260kt). Service ceiling 29,500ft. Range with 52 passengers and reserves 1741km (1935nm). FH-227 – Max cruising speed 473km/h (255kt), economical cruising speed 435km/h (236kt). Range with max payload 1055km (570nm), range with max fuel 2660km (1440nm).

Weights: Mk 500 – Empty 12,243kg (26,992lb), operating empty 12,684kg (27,964lb), max takeoff 20,410kg (44,996lb). FH-227 – Operating empty 10,398kg (22,923lb), max takeoff 20,639kg (45,500lb).

Dimensions: Mk 500 – Wing span 29.00m (95ft 2in), length 23.06m (82ft 3in), height 8.71m (28ft 7in). Wing area 70.0m² (753.5sq ft). FH-227 – Same except length 25.50m (83ft 8in), height 8.41m (27ft 7in).

Capacity: Flightcrew of two. Seating for 44 at four abreast and 76cm (30in) pitch in original fuselage length versions (Mks 100, 200, 300, 400, 600 & F-27). Standard seating for 52 and max seating for 60 at 72cm (28.5in) pitch in Mk 500. FH-227 seats 52 at 79cm (31in) pitch, or a maximum of 56.

Production: 581 F27s, 128 F-27s and 78 FH-227s built. Fokker production comprised 85 Mk 100s, 138 Mk 200s, 13 Mk 300s, 218 Mk 400 & 600s, 112 Mk 500s and six F27MPA Maritimes. 209 Fokker built F27s and 18 Fairchild F-27s and 19 FH-227s in service in late 2002. 19 F27s/F-27s/FH-227s used as corporate transports.

History: More Fokker F27 Friendships, including the Fairchild built F-27 and FH-227, were built than any other western turboprop airliner.

The Fokker F27 started life as the P275 design study in 1950, a 32 seater powered by two Rolls-Royce Dart turboprops. With the aid of Dutch government funding the P275 evolved into the F27, which first flew on November 24 1955. This original prototype was powered by Dart 507s and would have seated 32, by the time the second prototype flew in January 1957 the fuselage length had grown to allow seating for 36.

By this stage Fokker had signed an agreement that would see Fairchild build Friendships in the USA. The first aircraft to enter service was in fact a Fairchild built F-27 (note hyphen), in September 1958.

Fairchild F-27s differed from the initial Fokker F27 Mk 100s in having basic seating for 40, a lengthened nose capable of housing a weather radar, American avionics and additional fuel capacity.

Developments included the Mk 200/F-27A with more powerful engines, combi Mk 300/F-27B and primarily military Mk 400 versions, the Mk 500 with a 1.50m (4ft 11in) fuselage stretch taking seating to 52 (first flight November 15 1967), and Mk 600 quick change freight/passenger aircraft.

Fairchild independently developed the stretched FH-227, which first flew on January 27 1966, almost two years earlier than the Mk 500. The FH-227 featured a 1.83m (6ft 0in) stretch over standard length F27/F-27s, taking standard seating to 52.

Photo: A BAC Express F27-500. (Rob Finlayson)

Fokker 50

Country of origin: Netherlands

Type: Turboprop regional airliner

Powerplant: Series 100 – Two 1864kW (2500shp) Pratt & Whitney Canada PW125B turboprops driving six blade Dowty propellers. Series 300 – Two 2050kW (2750shp) PW127Bs.

Performance: Series 100 – Max cruising speed 532km/h (287kt), economical cruising speed 454km/h (245kt). Max operating altitude 25,000ft. Range with 50 passengers and reserves 2055km (1110nm), or 2822km (1524nm) for optional high gross weight version. Series 300 – Typical cruising speed 526km/h (284kt). Range with 50 passengers and reserves at high speed cruise 2033km (1097nm), or 3017km (1628nm) for high gross weight option at long range cruise.

Weights: Series 100 & 300 – Operating empty 12,520kg (27,602lb), max takeoff 19,950kg (43,980lb), or optionally 20,820kg (45,900lb).

Dimensions: Wing span 29.00m (95ft 2in), length 25.25m (82ft 10in), height 8.32m (27ft 4in). Wing area 70.0m² (753.5sq ft).

Capacity: Flightcrew of two. Standard seating for 50 at four abreast and 81cm (32in) pitch. Max high density seating for 58. Available with convertible passenger/freight configurations.

Production: 205 Fokker 50s built. Last delivered in May 1997. At late 2002 169 in commercial service and four used as corporate transports.

History: The Fokker 50 was the successor to Fokker's highly successful and long running F27 Friendship.

Fokker announced it was developing the 50 seat Fokker 50, together with the 100 seat jet powered Fokker 100, in November 1983. The Fokker 50 is based on the fuselage of the F27-500 Friendship, but is a thoroughly revised design. Foremost of the improvements was the new generation Pratt & Whitney Canada PW125 turboprops driving advanced six blade props, giving a 12% higher cruising speed and greater fuel economy, and improved range. Other improvements include new avionics and an EFIS glass cockpit, limited use of composites, small 'Foklet' winglets, and more, but smaller, square main cabin windows.

Two prototypes were built based on F27 airframes (despite the fact that over 80% of Fokker 50 parts were new or modified), the first flying on December 28 1985. The first production aircraft flew on February 13 1987, certification was granted in May 1987, and first customer delivery, to Lufthansa Cityline, was in August that year.

The basic Fokker 50 production model was the Series 100. The Series 120 has three, instead of four doors. The hot and high optimised Series 300 has more powerful PW127B turboprops, and was announced in 1990. It has higher cruising speeds and better field performance, particularly at altitude.

The only significant development of the Fokker 50 to see the light of day was the Fokker 60 Utility, a stretched utility transport version ordered by the Royal Netherlands Air Force. Fokker built four for the Netherlands air force and looked at offering a passenger variant. The Fokker 60 was stretched by 1.62m (5ft 4in).

Fokker collapsed due to financial problems on March 15 1996 and the last Fokker 50 was delivered to Ethiopian Airlines in May 1997.

Photo: A Fokker 50 of Thai operator Air Andaman. (Rob Finlayson)

Fokker F28 Fellowship

Country of origin: Netherlands

Type: Regional jet airliner

Powerplants: Mk 3000 & 4000 – Two 44.0kN (9900lb) Rolls-Royce RB183-2 Spey Mk 555-15P turbofans.

Performance: 3000 – Max cruising speed 843km/h (455kt), economical cruising speed 678km/h (366kt). Range at high speed cruise with 65 passengers 2743km (1480nm), at long range cruise with 65 passengers 3170km (1710nm). 4000 – Speeds same. Range at high speed cruise with 85 passengers 1900km (1025nm), at long range cruising speed with 85 passengers 2085km (1125nm).

Weights: 3000 – Operating empty 16,965kg (37,400lb), max takeoff 33,110kg (73,000lb). 4000 – Operating empty 17,645kg (38,900lb), max takeoff 33,110kg (73,000lb).

Dimensions: 3000 – Wing span 25.07m (82ft 3in), length 27.40m (89ft 11in), height 8.47m (27ft 10in). Wing area 79.0m² (850sq ft). 4000 – Same except for length 29.61m (97ft 2in).

Capacity: Flightcrew of two. Max seating for 85 at five abreast and 74cm (29in) pitch in Mk 4000, or 65 in Mk 3000. Mk 3000 offered with a 15 seat executive interior.

Production: Total F28 sales of 241, including some to military customers. As at late 2002 approx 149 remained in commercial service.

History: The F28 Fellowship jet was developed to complement Fokker's highly successful F27 Friendship turboprop.

Fokker began development of the F28 in 1960 after perceiving a market for a higher performance (ie jet engined) and greater capacity airliner in comparison with the F27. First details of the F28 were made public in April 1962, at which stage it was to have been a 50 seater powered by two Bristol Siddeley BS.75 turbofans. By the time the F28 was launched in November 1965 it had grown to a 65 seater with simplified Rolls-Royce Spey turbofans (called the Spey Junior).

The first of three F28 prototypes first flew on May 9 1967, with certification award and first customer delivery (to LTU) both occurring on February 24 1969.

The F28 was developed into a range of models. Initial production was of the Mk 1000, which could typically seat between 55 and 65, and was powered by 43.8kN (9850lb) Spey Mk 555-15 turbofans. The Mk 2000 was essentially similar but featured a 2.21m (7ft 3in) fuselage stretch, increasing maximum seating to 79.

The Mks 5000 and 6000 were based on the 1000 and 2000 respectively, but introduced a longer span wing (by 1.49m/4ft 11in) and wing leading edge slats. Neither version attracted much sales interest – no 5000s and just two 6000s were built. A proposed variant that was not built was the Mk 6600, which would have been stretched by a further 2.21m (7ft 3in), allowing for seating for 100 in a high density layout. It was aimed at Japanese airlines.

The final production models were the 3000 and 4000, again based on the 1000 and 2000 respectively. Both introduced a number of improvements, while the addition of two extra above wing emergency exits on the 4000 increased maximum seating to 85. Freight door equipped convertible versions of each model were offered, and are identified by a C suffix. The last F28 was delivered in July 1987.

Photo: An Air Niugini F28-4000. (Tim Dath)

Fokker 100

Country of origin: Netherlands

Type: 100 seat regional jet

Powerplants: Two 61.6kN (13,850lb) Rolls-Royce Tay Mk 620-15 or 67.2kN (15,100lb) Mk 650-15 turbofans.

Performance: Max cruising speed 845km/h (456kt), long range cruising speed 737km/h (453kt). Range with 107 passengers and Tay 620s 2505km (1323nm), or high gross weight version with Tay 650s 3167km (1710nm).

Weights: Tay 620 – Operating empty 24,375kg (53,738lb), max takeoff 43,090kg (95,000lb). With Tay 650s – Operating empty 24,541kg (54,103lb), max takeoff 45,810kg (101,000lb).

Dimensions: Wing span 28.08m (92ft 2in), length 35.53m (116ft 7in), height 8.50m (27ft 11in). Wing area 93.5m² (1006.4sq ft).

Capacity: Flightcrew of two. Max single class high density seating for 122. Standard single class seating for 107 at five abreast and 81cm (32in) pitch. Two class seating for 12 first class passengers at four abreast and 91cm (36in) pitch, and 85 economy class passengers; or 55 business class at five abreast and 86cm (34in) pitch, and 50 economy class pax. Fokker 100QC Quick Change max payload of 11,500kg (25,353lb), comprising five LD9/LD7 containers and one half size container, or up to 11 LD3 containers.

Production: 283 Fokker 100s had been built when production ceased in early 1997. 263 in service in late 2002.

History: The Fokker 100 is a 100 seat jet airliner based on the F28 Fellowship, but stretched and modernised.

Fokker announced it was developing the Fokker 100 simultaneously with the Fokker 50 turboprop in November 1983. First flight occurred on November 30 1986, certification was awarded in November 1987 and the first customer delivery, to Swissair, occurred in February 1988.

The Fokker 100 is based on the basic F28 airframe, with the most important and obvious change being the stretched fuselage, increasing maximum seating to 122, compared with 85 in the F28-4000 (on which the 100 is based). Other changes include more economical Rolls-Royce Tay turbofans (which, unlike the F28's Speys, conform to Stage 3 noise limits), revised wing design with greater span and aerodynamic efficiency (Fokker claimed it to be 30% more efficient than the F28's), a modern EFIS glass flightdeck, redesigned cabin interior plus other systems and numerous equipment changes.

The Fokker 100 was offered in a number of versions including higher gross weight options of the standard airliner, the Fokker 100QC Quick Change airliner or freighter with a large forward freight door, and the Fokker Executive Jet 100 corporate shuttle or VIP transport, fitted with luxury interiors to customer requirements. It also formed the basis for the shorter Fokker 70, while the 130 seat class Fokker 130 was studied for a time.

Fokker collapsed in 1996 due to on-going financial problems and wound up production early the following year. Rekkof (Fokker spelt backwards) Restart unsuccessfully attempted to re-open the Fokker 70 and 100 lines.

Photo: A Portugalia Fokker 100 gets airborne. (Toni Marimon)

Fokker 70

Country of origin: Netherlands

Type: 70 seat regional jet airliner

Powerplants: Two 61.6kN (13,850lb) Rolls-Royce Tay Mk 620 turbofans.

Performance: High speed cruise Mach 0.77. Range with 79 passengers and baggage at standard weights 2010km (1085nm), or 3410km (1840nm) for high gross weight option with extra fuel.

Weights: Operating empty 22,673kg (49,985lb), max takeoff standard aircraft 36,470kg (80,997lb), or optionally 38,100kg (83,996lb), or 39,915kg (87,997lb).

Dimensions: Wing span 28.08m (92ft 2in), length 30.91m (101ft 5in), height 8.50m (27ft 11in). Wing area 93.5m² (1006.4sq ft).

Capacity: Flightcrew of two. Standard single class passenger accommodation for 79 at five abreast at 81cm (32in) pitch. Fokker Executive Jet 70 interiors were fitted to customer requirements.

Production: 48 Fokker 70s built. Last delivered in April 1997. 43 in service in late 2002.

History: The Fokker 70 is a shortened development of the popular 100 seat class Fokker 100.

Fokker began development of the new derivative airliner in November 1992 despite the absence of firm orders, hopeful of snaring a large share of the forecast 2000 plus aircraft in the 70 to 125 seat class required through to 2010, and the replacement F28 market. The Fokker 70's 30.91m (101ft 4in) length is close to that of the F28-4000's 29.61m (97ft 2in).

The first Fokker 70 was in fact the second Fokker 100 prototype which was modified by removing two fuselage plugs – one forward and one rear of the wing. Modification of this aircraft began in October 1992 (before the November 1992 program go-ahead), resulting in the Fokker 70's first flight on April 4 1993. The first production Fokker 70 first flew in July 1994 and certification was awarded on October 14 1994. The first Fokker 70 delivery (an Executive Jet 70) was to Ford in the USA later that month.

A design aim of the Fokker 70 was to retain as much commonality with the larger Fokker 100 as possible. As a result they share essentially identical wings, airframes (except for length, and the removal of two emergency overwing exits on the Fokker 70) and systems, plus similar EFIS flightdecks. The Fokker 70 was offered with two flightdecks, one optimised for the 70's regional airline operations, the other essentially identical to the Fokker 100's to give operators of both types commonality. The Fokker 70 and 100 also share identical Tay Mk 620 powerplants, although the Tay Mk 650 that was offered for the 100 was not available on the 70. The 70 and 100 were built on a common production line.

As with the Fokker 100, a corporate shuttle, the Fokker Executive Jet 70, was offered (and attracted a small number of orders). The Fokker 70A was optimised for US carriers, while the Fokker 70ER (announced in late 1994) had extra fuel capacity and extended range.

With Fokker's collapse in 1996, the Fokker 70/100 production line closed in early 1997. Second hand examples are highly sought after.

Photo: A Malev Fokker 70. (Rob Finlayson)

Found FBA-2 Bush Hawk

Country of origin: Canada

Type: Five seat light utility aircraft

Powerplants: Hawk XP – One 225kW (300hp) Textron Lycoming IO-540-L1C5 flat six piston engine driving a three blade Hartzell prop.

Performance: Hawk XP landplane – Cruising speed at 75% power 278km/h (150kt). Initial rate of climb 1120ft/min. Service ceiling 18,000ft. Max range 1630km (880nm). Max endurance 8.5hr. Hawk XP floatplane – Cruising speed at 75% power 240km/h (130kt). Initial rate of climb 1050ft/min. Service ceiling 15,000ft. Max range 1315km (710nm). Endurance 8.5hr.

Weights: Hawk XP landplane – Empty 863kg (1900lb), max takeoff 1590kg (3500lb). XP floatplane – Empty 1022kg (2250lb), max takeoff 1680kg (3700lb).

Dimensions: Wing span 10.97m (36ft 0in), length (landplane) 8.08m (26ft 6in), length (floats) 8.74m (28ft 8in), height (landplane) 2.51m (8ft 3in), height (floats) 4.17m (13ft 8in). Wing area 16.7m² (180.0sq ft).

Capacity: Standard seating for five.

Production: 27 initial FBA-2Cs built in 1964-65. First FBA-2C1 delivered May 2001, approx 40 built. Production at late 2002 running at one aircraft a month, with the company holding a two year order backlog. Production to double to two a month in 2004.

History: The Found FBA-2C Bush Hawk taildragger is a new production utility aircraft with an old pedigree, dating to the original FBA-2 of the 1960s, which in turn was based on 1949's FBA-1.

Found Brothers Aviation was formed in 1946 to design and build the FBA-1 bush aircraft. Just one was built, flying in 1949, before design work on the FBA-2 began the following year. Work progressed slowly due to a lack of funds, with the prototype FBA-2 (with tricycle undercarriage) flying in 1959. Certification was awarded in 1964, when production of the FBA-2C began. Found built 27 before it decided to concentrate on the larger Centennial Model 100, but the company wound up operations in 1967.

Found Aircraft Canada was formed in May 1996 to return the all metal FBA-2 to production. The company has a 930m² (10,000sq ft) production facility at Parry Sound Municipal Airport, 200km north of Toronto. The prototype FBA-2C1 was converted from an existing aircraft, fitted with an IO-540-D, flying in its new form in November 1996. Two preproduction aircraft flew in October 1998 and March 1999 respectively. The first new production FBA-2C1 first flew on March 2 2000, the first delivery was in May 2001.

Transport Canada's type certificate for the original FBA-2C was reinstated in 1997. The FBA-2C1 was certificated in Canada in March 1999 and in the US in March 2000.

Compared to the original FBA-2C, the 2C1 Bush Hawk has been re-engineered to meet current certification standards, with primary structures now fail safe. Other changes include new landing gear, flush cargo door sills, a 378 litre wet wing and a 195 or 225kW (260 or 300hp) Textron Lycoming IO-540. Floats and tundra tyres are optional.

The Hawk XP (with 225kW/300hp IO-540) entered service in mid 2001 and has Fowler flaps, improving field performance, and removable rear seats. A tricycle gear variant will be introduced in 2004.

Photo: The first production new build FBA-2C1. (Rodney Kozar)

Fuji FA-200 Aero Subaru

Country of origin: Japan

Type: Four seat light aircraft

Powerplant: FA-200-160 – One 120kW (160hp) Lycoming O-320-D2A flat four piston engine driving a two blade fixed pitch McCauley propeller. FA-200-180 – One 135kW (180hp) fuel injected IO-360-B1B driving a two blade constant speed McCauley prop.

Performance: FA-200-160 – Max speed 222km/h (120kt), max cruising speed 196km/h (106kt), long range cruising speed 164km/h (89kt). Initial rate of climb 680ft/min. Service ceiling 11,400ft. Max range with no reserves 1520km (820nm). FA-200-180 – Max speed 233km/h (126kt), max cruising speed 204km/h (110kt), long range cruising speed 167km/h (90kt). Initial rate of climb 760ft/min. Service ceiling 13,700ft. Range with no reserves 1400km (755nm).

Weights: FA-200-160 – Empty 620kg (1366lb), max takeoff 1059kg (2335lb). FA-200-180 – Empty 650kg (1433lb), max takeoff 1150kg (2535lb).

Dimensions: FA-200-160 – Wing span 9.42m (30ft 11in), length 7.96m (26ft 1in), height 2.02m (6ft 8in). Wing area 14.0m² (150.7sq ft). FA-200-180 – Same except for length 7.98m (26ft 2in).

Capacity: Typical seating for four.

Production: 299 Aero Subarus built between 1965 and 1986. Series production lasted until 1977, when the Aero Subaru became available by firm order only through to 1986.

History: The Fuji FA-200 Aero Subaru was the first wholly Japanese designed light aircraft to enter series production, with the majority built for export.

The FA-200 was a product of the Fuji Heavy Industries industrial conglomerate (which was formed through the merger of six different concerns, including WW2 fighter manufacturer Nakajima, and also builds Subaru cars). Design work began in 1964 and a prototype, the FA-200-II, first flew on August 12 1965.

The basic FA-200 was expected to form the basis of a family of light aircraft including the two seat side-by-side trainer FA-200-I powered by a 85kW (115hp) Lycoming O-235 and the single seat F-204 agricultural version. However only the four seat tourer, as represented by the prototype, entered production. This aircraft was of conventional low wing and fixed undercarriage design, and was certificated for aerobatics at reduced weights.

Three versions of the FA-200 entered production, the first being the 120kW (160hp) powered FA-200-160, which was also certificated with reduced weights in the utility category with three seats, and the in aerobatic category with two seats. The FA-200-180 was essentially similar but powered by a 135kW (180hp) fuel injected IO-360. Deliveries of both versions began in March 1968.

The FA-200-180AO joined the lineup from mid 1973. This was a reduced specification version of the FA-200-180 with a fixed pitch propeller and caburetted Lycoming O-360 engine.

The Aero Subaru remained in production until 1977 when 274 had been built. It then remained available to special order through to 1986, by which time a further 25 had been built.

Photo: An Australian registered Lycoming O-320 powered FA-200-160. (Gerard Frawley)

GAF N22 & N24 Nomad

Country of origin: Australia

Type: STOL utility transport

Powerplants: Two 313kW (420shp) Allison 250-B17C turboprops driving three blade Hartzell propellers.

Performance: N22B – Typical cruising speed 311km/h (168kt). Service ceiling 21,000ft. Range with standard fuel, reserves and operating at 90% power 1352km (730nm). Search mission endurance at 259km/h (140kt) at 5000ft up to 8 hours.

Weights: N22B – Basic empty 2150kg (4741lb), max takeoff 3855kg (8500lb). N24A – Operating empty 2377kg (5241lb), max takeoff 4268kg (9400lb).

Dimensions: N22B – Wing span 16.52m (54ft 2in), length 12.56m (41ft 2in), height 5.52m (18ft 1.5in). Wing area 30.1m² (324.0sq ft). N24A – Same except length 14.36m (47ft 1in).

Capacity: Accommodation for one or two pilots (certificated for single pilot operation). Seating in main cabin at two abreast for 12 (N22) or 16 (N24). Searchmaster B patrol aircraft is fitted with a Bendix RDR 1400 search radar and has a normal crew of four. The more sophisticated Searchmaster L has a Litton LASR (AN/APS-504) search radar with 360 degree coverage in an undernose radar.

Production: Production ceased in late 1984 when 172 Nomads for civil and military customers had been built, including two prototypes. Approx 17 remain in service with commercial operators.

History: The Nomad STOL utility transport was developed by Australia's Government Aircraft Factory from the late 1960s to help provide the facility with work after construction of licence built Mirage jet fighters was completed.

The Nomad N2 prototype first flew on July 23 1971, followed by the second prototype on December 5 that year. First deliveries of the production N22 (to the Philippines military) began in 1975.

Features of the new utility design included retractable undercarriage, two Allison 250 turboprops, a braced, high mounted wing with full span double slotted flaps, and a square sided fuselage.

The initial N22 was followed by the N22B with an increased maximum takeoff weight, which was certificated in 1975. The N22 also formed the basis for the Searchmaster coastal patrol aircraft which apart from military users also saw service with Australian and US customs services. The Floatmaster was a N22B fitted with Wipaire floats with retractable undercarriage.

The N22 was stretched by 1.14m (3ft 9in) resulting in the N24. Aimed more at regional airlines (and marketed as the Commuterliner) than utility operators, the main cabin could seat 16. Versions of the N24 offered included the Cargomaster freighter and the Medicmaster aerial ambulance.

Nomad production ceased in 1984, as much due to mismanagement by the Australian government departments entrusted with its development as any faults with the aircraft. However the aircraft is largely unloved in its home country.

It is interesting to note that GAF was renamed ASTA (Aerospace Technologies of Australia), which was acquired by Rockwell in 1996 and hence was subsequently inherited by Boeing late that year.

Photo: An N22 Nomad. (Lenn Bayliss)

Gippsland Aeronautics GA-200 Fatman

Country of origin: Australia

Type: Two seat agricultural aircraft

Powerplant: GA-200 – One 195kW (260hp) Textron Lycoming O-540-H2A5 flat six piston engine driving a two blade fixed pitch McCauley propeller, or alternatively a 185kW (250hp) O-540-A1D5.

Performance: GA-200 – Long range cruising speed 185km/h (100kt). Initial rate of climb 970ft/min.

Weights: GA-200 – Operating empty 770kg (1698lb), certificated max takeoff 1315kg (2899lb), max takeoff in ag operation 1700kg (3748lb).

Dimensions: Wing span 11.93m (39ft 2in), length in flying attitude 7.48m (24ft 7in), height on ground over cockpit 2.33m (7ft 8in). Wing area 19.6m² (211.0sq ft).

Capacity: Seating for two side-by-side. Hopper capacity 800 litres (211US gal/176Imp gal).

Production: Approx 60 built by late 2002.

History: The Gippsland Aeronautics GA-200 Fatman is an Australian developed ag aircraft.

The GA-200 is Gippsland Aeronautics' first inhouse design, and results from more than two decades of experience in modifying other aircraft. In particular Gippsland Aeronautics has extensive experience in modifying the Piper Pawnee, but despite the visual similarity the GA-200 is an all new design.

Features of the GA-200 include a braced low mounted wing, a Textron Lycoming O-540 flat six engine and 800 litre (211US gal/176Imp gal) integral chemical hopper forward of the cockpit. It is of conventional construction with a low mounted braced wing. The single slotted flaps can be extended for tighter turns during spraying.

Australian CAA certification in normal and agricultural categories to US airworthiness standards was awarded on March 1 1991. US FAA certification to FAR Pt 23 was awarded in October 1997.

The GA-200 is offered in standard agricultural aircraft and Ag-trainer form. The Ag-trainer is an ag pilot trainer fitted with a smaller chemical hopper and dual controls.

The GA-8 has won a number of export orders, including several to China. Others have been built for customers in New Zealand and the USA. Aircraft sold in the US have their airframe sections shipped from Australia with components such as the engine and avionics fitted locally.

Gippsland Aeronautics studied a development of the GA-200 powered by an Australian developed magnesium block V8 engine that would have run on unleaded mogas (the GA-200 already has Australian approval to operate using premium grade unleaded mogas for its O-540). However the company instead focussed its efforts on the more powerful GA-200C powered by an uprated 225kW (300hp) O-540 and an increased max takeoff weight. A hopper upgrade to 1060 litres (280USgal/233Imp gal). The prototype GA-200C first flew in early 1998 and it is now the standard production model.

Production continues at a low rate, with the GA-8 Airvan the focus of Gippsland Aeronauctics' efforts.

Photo: A GA-200 on Lord Howe Island, off Australia's east coast. (Peter Phillipps)

Gippsland Aeronautics GA-8 Airvan

Country of origin: Australia

Type: Eight seat utility light aircraft

Powerplants: One 225kW (300hp) IO-540-K1A5 Textron Lycomng fuel injected flat six driving a two blade constant speed Hartzell prop.

Performance: Never exceed speed 342km/h (185kt) IAS, long range cruising speed 222km/h (120kt). Takeoff distance 550m (1800ft). Initial rate of climb 788ft/min. Max range 1355km (730nm).

Weights: Empty 997kg (2200lb), max takeoff 1815kg (4000lb).

Dimensions: Wing span 12.37m (40ft 7in), length 8.79m (28ft 10in), height 2.82m (9ft 3in). Wing area 19.3m² (208.0sq ft).

Capacity: Single pilot and passenger side-by-side with up to six passengers in the main cabin behind them. Main cabin can also configured to carry freight or two stretchers and a medical attendant.

Production: First Airvan delivered December 2000. Approx 30 built.

History: The GA-8 Airvan has been designed as a utility transport to replace the popular Cessna 206/207 series and other workhorses such as the de Havilland Canada Beaver.

Design work on the Airvan began in early 1994 and prototype construction commenced soon after. This prototype first flew on March 3 1995 and publicly appeared at the Australian International Airshow and Aerospace Expo at Avalon near Melbourne later that month after having completed just eight flying hours.

At that time Gippsland Aeronautics anticipated that the Airvan could be certificated within 12 months. Unfortunately the prototype crashed during spinning trials in February 1996, pushing back the planned certification and entry into service dates.

The prototype Airvan was powered by a 185kW (250hp) Textron Lycoming O-540 driving a two blade propeller. A second prototype flew in August 1996, powered by a 225kW (300hp) IO-540. This was to be replaced with a 225kW (300hp) IO-580, while production Airvans feature an IO-540-K as detailed above. Useable fuel capacity is 332 litres.

Other Airvan design features include its strut braced, high mounted two spar wing which is based on the unit on the GA-200 ag aircraft, the square sided large volume fuselage with a large sliding freight door on the port side and flat floor, and fixed landing gear designed for rough field operations.

The first production Airvan (the fifth Airvan built) flew in November 2000, while full Australian certification was awarded on December 18 2000. The first delivery, to Fraser Island Air, followed soon after, on December 22.

Gippsland has developed a cargo pod for the Airvan with a capacity of 0.5m³ (18cu ft). It will carry in excess of 180kg (400lb) and items up to 2.4m (8ft) in length.

Gippsland is also studying a range of Airvan developments, including the 335kW (450shp) Rolls-Royce 250-B17F turboprop powered GA-10 Tasker, and a higher performance piston model with an IO-580. Others include a turbocharged version and a model powered by a jet fuel burning diesel engine. A floatplane option is also under development.

Photo: An Airvan undergoing evaluation by the US Civil Air Patrol in Colorado. (Gippsland Aeronautics)

Grob G 115

Country of origin: Germany

Type: Two seat basic and aerobatic trainer

Powerplant: G 115A – One 85kW (115hp) Textron Lycoming O-235-H2C flat four piston engine driving a two blade fixed pitch or optional c/s Hoffmann prop. G 115D – One 135kW (180hp) Textron Lycoming fuel injected AEIO-360 driving a two blade c/s prop.

Performance: G 115A – Max speed 220km/h (119kt), cruising speed 205km/h (110kt). Initial rate of climb 690ft/min. Range with max fuel 1000km (540nm). G 115D – Max speed 270km/h (146kt), cruising speed 250km/h (135kt). Initial rate of climb 1500ft/min. Range with no reserves 963km (520nm).

Weights: G 115A – Basic empty 590kg (1300lb), max takeoff 850kg (1874lb). G 115D – Basic empty 660kg (1455lb), MTOW 920kg (2028lb).

Dimensions: G 115A – Wing span 10.00m (32ft 10in), length 7.36m (24ft 2in), height 2.75m (9ft 0in). Wing area 12.2m^2 (131.4sq ft). G 115D – Wing span 10.00m (32ft 10in), length 7.44m (24ft 5in), height 2.75m (9ft 0in). Wing area 12.2m^2 (131.4sq ft).

Capacity: Standard seating for two.

Production: 110 G 115s and G 115As built by late 1992. Production switched to the G 115C and G 115D in late 1993. Over 200 have been built of all models.

History: Grob is well known for its sailplanes and powered gliders, and its G 115 is the first aircraft made from glass fibre reinforced plastics to be certificated by the US FAA.

Development of the G 115, sometimes referred to as the T-Bird, dates back to the early 1980s and Grob's two earlier two seat trainers. The initial G 110 first flew in 1982 and was built in small numbers, while the G 112 flew in 1984 in prototype form only. The two types formed the basis of the G 115, the prototype (powered by an O-235 engine) of which made its first flight in November 1985. The first prototype was representative of the production G 115 model, a second prototype differed in having a constant speed propeller, a taller fin and rudder and relocated tailplane, and represented the G 115A. The G 115 and G 115A remained in production until 1990. The line re-opened with improved models in late 1992.

Grob G 115 models include: the 115B, essentially a 115A with a more powerful 120kW (160hp) O-320 engine (which can be retrofitted to earlier A models); the G 115C with the same O-320, plus fuel in the wings and other minor improvements; the similar G 115C1 Acro; 135kW (180hp) O-360 powered G 115C2; the fully aerobatic 135kW (180hp) AEIO-360G powered 115D which can also be used as a glider tug; and 120kW (160hp) AEIO-320 powered G 115D2. The G 115 Bavarian was built for a US flying club. It features fuel in the wing, a revised instrument panel and more glass.

The current model is the G 115E with its fuselage built entirely from carbonfibre. It has been ordered by Britain's RAF for its University Air Squadrons and Air Cadets, and by the Egyptian air force.

Another aircraft to bear the G 115 designation is the G 115TA Acro, but this is similar to other G 115s in name and basic configuration only. Powered by a 195kW (260hp) AEIO-540, it was aimed primarily at military customers. Twelve were built.

Photo: A Grob G 115D.

Grumman American AA-1

Country of origin: United States of America

Type: Two seat light aircraft

Powerplant: AA-1A – One 81kW (108hp) Lycoming O-235-C2C flat four piston engine driving a two blade fixed pitch propeller. AA-1C – One 85kW (115hp) O-235-L2C.

Performance: AA-1A – Max speed 222km/h (120kt), max cruising speed 203km/h (110kt), long range cruising speed 180km/h (97kt). Initial rate of climb 765ft/min. Service ceiling 13,750ft. Range with no reserves 805km (435nm). AA-1C – Max speed 233km/h (126kt), max cruising speed 217km/h (117kt), long range cruising speed 178km/h (96kt). Initial rate of climb 700ft/min. Max range with reserves 648km (350nm).

Weights: AA-1A – Empty 442kg (975lb), max takeoff 680kg (1500lb). AA-1C – Empty 485kg (1066lb), max takeoff 726kg (1600lb).

Dimensions: Wing span 7.47m (24ft 6in), length 5.87m (19ft 3in), height 2.32m (7ft 7in). Wing area 9.4m^2 (101sq ft).

Capacity: Typical seating for two.

Production: Over 1100 built by American Aviation of all models. Grumman production of over 600.

History: What became Grumman's first light aircraft came from the drawing board of noted kit aircraft designer Jim Bede.

The AA-1 began life as the Bede BD-1, a compact design using just 385 parts and bonded honeycomb construction. The original BD-1 was powered by a 65kW (90hp) Continental C90-14, and first flew on July 11 1963. Unlike other Bede designs however the BD-1 was not intended for kit builders, instead Bede renamed his company the American Aviation Corporation, and placed the BD-1 in series production at the company's Cleveland plant.

Production aircraft differed from the prototype in having a revised wing layout and vertical tail, a wider track undercarriage and a more powerful Lycoming O-235. First production aircraft were designated the AA-1 Yankee and the first were delivered in 1968, the last in 1971.

The Yankee was replaced in production by the AA-1A Trainer, with a modified wing and equipped for pilot training. It first flew on March 25 1970 and was certificated in January 1971. A superior spec deluxe version of the AA-1A, the Tr-2, had an upmarket interior trim, wheel fairings and more comprehensive standard avionics fit. It was introduced in October 1971.

Following Grumman Corporation's acquisition of American Aviation, all AA-1s and Tr-2s were produced under the Grumman American Aviation Corporation banner. The first new development from the new company was the AA-1B, a revised Trainer with greater takeoff weights.

Grumman introduced the further improved AA-1C, T-Cat and Lynx in 1978 with greater takeoff weights, a more powerful O-235 engine and revised tail surfaces. The AA-1C was the standard production model, the T-Cat and Lynx offering progressively higher levels of standard equipment.

Gulfstream acquired Grumman American in 1978, and discontinued AA-1 production shortly afterwards.

Photo: A Tr-2. (Gary Gentle)

Grumman American AA-5

Country of origin: United States of America

Type: Four seat light aircraft

Powerplants: AA-5 – One 110kW (150hp) Lycoming O-320-E2G flat four piston engine driving a two blade fixed pitch propeller. AG-5B – One 135kW (180hp) Textron Lycoming O-360-A4K.

Performance: AA-5 – Max speed 240km/h (130kt), max cruising speed 225km/h (122kt), typical cruising speed 207km/h (112kt). Initial rate of climb 660ft/min. Service ceiling 12,650ft. Range with reserves 805km (435nm). AG-5B – Max cruising speed 265km/h (143kt). Service ceiling 13,800ft. Range with max fuel at 75% power 1020km (550nm).

Weights: AA-5 – Empty 545kg (1200lb), max takeoff 998kg (2200lb). AG-5B – Empty 595kg (1310lb), max takeoff 1088kg (2400lb).

Dimensions: Wing span 9.60m (31ft 6in), length 6.71m (22ft 0in), height 2.40m (8ft 0in). Wing area 13.0m² (140sq ft).

Capacity: Standard seating for four.

Production: Production totals include over 1000 Tigers, plus over 100 American General Aircraft AG-5Bs.

History: The AA-5 four seater is a larger development of the two seat AA-1 – the two share 60% structural commonality.

The first AA-5 prototype (built by American Aviation) flew on August 21 1970. Differences from the AA-1 included the stretched fuselage allowing seating for four, greater span wing, higher max takeoff weight and more powerful 110kW (150hp) Lycoming O-320 engine. Production deliveries began in December 1971, at which time two basic models were offered, the standard AA-5 and the upmarket Traveler. The Traveler featured a comprehensive instrument fit with dual controls. The Traveler was instantly popular, especially with its higher cruising speeds compared to other 110kW (150hp) powered light singles such as the 172.

Significant improvements were introduced when Grumman American (following Grumman's 1972 acquisition of American Aviation) released the AA-5B. Performance was boosted considerably with a more powerful 135kW (180hp) Lycoming O-360 (giving performance more like that of 150kW/200hp powered retractable gear singles), while the maximum takeoff weight was increased. Other revisions included increased span horizontal tail surfaces, larger rear cabin windows, greater fuel capacity, revised wheel fairings and deletion of the ventral fin fitted to earlier Traveler models. An up spec model with a greater standard equipment list was also sold as the Tiger. The AA-5B was offered alongside the AA-5.

The basic AA-5 was modernised in 1976 with the aerodynamic improvements introduced on the AA-5B, optional extra fuel and other improvements to boost speed slightly. Base aircraft of this model were the AA-5A, the corresponding higher level standard equipment model was the Cheetah.

Production of the AA-5A and AA-5B continued through the late 1970s until 1978 when Gulfstream purchased Grumman American. The production rights to the series were then put up for sale. Over a decade later the American General Aircraft Corporation restarted production of a revised AA-5B in 1990 as the AG-5B. However American General ceased trading in mid 1994 due to poor sales.

Photo: An AA-5B registered in Belgium. (Peter Vercruijsse)

Grumman/Schweizer Ag-Cat

Country of origin: United States of America

Type: Agricultural aircraft

Powerplants: G-164A Super Ag-Cat – One 335kW (450hp) Pratt & Whitney R-985 series nine cylinder radial piston engine driving a two blade constant speed propeller. G-164B Ag-Cat Super-B Turbine – Choice of 373kW (500shp) Pratt & Whitney Canada PT6A-11AG, or 510kW (680shp) PT6A-15AG, or 560kW (750shp) PT6A-34AG turboprops, driving a three blade constant speed prop.

Performance: G-164A – Max speed 237km/h (128kt), typical working speed range 130 to 160km/h (70 to 86kt). Initial rate of climb 1080ft/min. Super-B Turbine with PT6A-15AG – Working speed 210km/h (113kt). Range with max fuel 318km (172nm).

Weights: G-164A – Empty equipped for spraying 1220kg (2690lb), max certificated takeoff 2040kg (4500lb). Super-B Turbine – Empty equipped for spraying 1429kg (3150lb), max takeoff 3184kg (7020lb).

Dimensions: G-164A – Wing span 10.95m (35ft 11in), length 7.11m (23ft 4in), height 3.27m (10ft 9in). Wing area 20.5m² (328sq ft). Super Turbine B – Wing span upper 12.92m (42ft 5in), lower 12.36m (40ft 7in); length 8.41m (27ft 8in), height 3.68m (12ft 1in). Wing area 36.5m² (392.7sq ft).

Capacity: Usually pilot only. Hopper capacity 1514 litres (400US gal/333Imp gal). Some converted with a second cockpit (seating two) for joyflights.

Production: Schweizer built 2628 under contract for Grumman between 1959 and 1979, including more than 400 G-164s, 1330 G-164As and 833 G-164Bs. Some built under licence in Ethiopia.

History: The Ag-Cat biplane is a purpose designed agricultural aircraft, built between 1959 and the late 1990s.

The Grumman designed G-164 Ag-Cat biplane first flew on May 27 1957. Some 400 initial G-164 Ag-Cats were delivered from 1959, fitted with a variety of radial engines including various Continentals, the 180kW (240hp) Gulf Coast W-670-240, the 185kW (245hp) Jacobs L-4 or 205 to 225kW (275 to 300hp) Jacobs R-755 engines.

The G-164A followed. In its basic A/450 form it was powered by a 335kW (450hp) Pratt & Whitney R-985, and featured a greater maximum takeoff weight and additional fuel. The A/600 has a 450kW (600hp) R-1340 engine. The B/450 is based on the A/450 but with increased span wings, while the B/525 is powered by a 390kW (525hp) Continental/Page R-975.

The longer fuselage 450kW (600hp) R-1340 powered C/600 meanwhile forms the basis for the Pratt & Whitney Canada PT6A powered Turbo Ag-Cat D.

Recent models included the 450kW (600hp) R-1340 powered Super-B/600 and the PT6A powered Ag-Cat Super-B Turbine (various PT6A models were offered ranging from 375 to 560kW/680 to 750shp).

Schweizer built all production Ag-Cats until 1992, firstly under contract for Grumman between 1959 and 1979, and again from 1981 when it bought the design and production rights. In 1995 Schweizer sold the Ag-Cat's manufacturing rights to the Ag-Cat Corp of Malden, Missouri, who built small numbers of Ag-Cat Super-B turbines until entering bankruptcy.

Photo: A G-164 Ag-Cat on floats. (Eric Allen)

Grumman G-21 Goose

Country of origin: United States of America

Type: Eight seat utility amphibian

Powerplants: G-21A – Two 335kW (450hp) Pratt & Whitney R-985-AN-6 Wasp nine cylinder piston radial engines driving two blade c/s. Turbo-Goose – Two 505kW (680shp) Pratt & Whitney Canada PT6A-27 turboprops driving three blade props.

Performance: G-21A – Max speed 323km/h (175kt), cruising speed 307km/h (166kt). Initial rate of climb 1300ft/min. Service ceiling 22,000ft. Range with max fuel 1285km (695nm). Turbo-Goose – Max speed 390km/h (210kt). Service ceiling 20,000ft. Range with standard fuel 2575km (1390nm).

Weights: G-21A – Empty 2460kg (5425lb), max takeoff 3630kg (8000lb). Turbo-Goose – Empty equipped 3040kg (6700lb), max takeoff weight 5670kg (12,500lb).

Dimensions: G-21A – Wing span 14.95m (49ft 0in), length 11.70m (38ft 4in), height 3.66m (12ft 0in). Wing area 34.8m² (375sq ft). Turbo-Goose – Wing span 15.49m (50ft 10in), length 12.06m (39ft 7in). Wing area 35.1m² (377.6sq ft).

Capacity: Flightcrew of two. Main cabin passenger seating for six or seven in piston engined Goose, Turbo-Goose seats up to 12.

Production: Total Goose production exceeded 300 aircraft, most of which were originally delivered to military customers. Production ceased in 1945. Small numbers of radial and turbine powered Gooses remain in service worldwide.

History: The Goose began life before WW2 as Grumman's first design intended for civilian use, but most of the type's production ultimately was against military orders placed during the war.

The Goose's first flight occurred in June 1937. Grumman's already extensive experience in building carrier based fighters for the US Navy was reflected in the Goose's rugged construction, features of which included a braced tailplane and deep two step hull. Retractable undercarriage was another feature. Initial civil production machines were designated the G-21A.

The arrival of WW2 saw the Goose (a name originally bestowed on the aircraft by Britain's Royal Air Force) enter military service with a number of allied air arms, the largest operator being the US Navy. Military orders from the US, Britain and Canada accounted for much of the Goose's 300 unit production run.

Postwar, surplus Gooses found their way into service with commercial operators worldwide, their amphibious capability and rugged construction ensuring their popularity in the coming decades.

Some Goose aircraft have been converted to turboprop power, McKinnon Enterprises (initially based in the US, and then Canada) first fitted G-21s with four 255kW (340hp) Lycoming GSO-480 six cylinder geared and turbocharged piston engines as the G-21C and G-21D, and then with two Pratt & Whitney Canada PT6As.

Turbo Goose Turbine models were the G-21C and G-21D with PT6A-20s, and then the 507kW (680shp) PT6A-27 powered G-21G Turbo-Goose with a range of improvements (options included enlarged windows and increased fuel capacity) and the more straightforward Turboprop Goose conversion.

Photo: A US registered G-21A Goose. (Gordon Reid)

Grumman G-44 Widgeon

Country of origin: United States of America

Type: Light utility amphibian

Powerplants: G-44A – Two 150kW (200hp) Ranger 6-440C-5 six cylinder, inverted, inline piston engines driving two blade propellers. Super Widgeon – Two 200kW (270hp) Lycoming GO-480-B1D flat sixes driving three blade constant speed Hartzell propellers.

Performance: G-44A – Max speed 257km/h (139kt), typical cruising speed 209km/h (113kt). Initial rate of climb 1000ft/min. Super Widgeon – Max speed 306km/h (165kt), typical cruising speed 282km/h (152kt). Initial rate of climb 1750ft/min. Service ceiling 18,000ft. Range with max fuel and reserves 1600km (865nm).

Weights: G-44A – Empty 1470kg (3240lb), max takeoff 2052kg (4525lb). Super Widgeon – Empty 1724kg (3800lb), max takeoff 2500kg (5500lb).

Dimensions: Wing span 12.19m (40ft 0in), length 9.47m (31ft 1in), height 3.48m (11ft 5in). Wing area 22.8m² (245sq ft).

Capacity: Maximum accommodation for six, including pilot.

Production: More than 266 Widgeons built, including 176 for military use during World War 2, and postwar 50 Grumman built G-44As and 40 SCAN-30 French built G-44As. McKinnon converted more than 50 G-44s to Lycoming powered Super Widgeon configuration.

History: The smallest of Grumman's amphibians developed, the Widgeon was conceived as a light personal and executive transport, following the success of the larger Goose.

The prototype Widgeon first flew in July 1940, but America's entry into WW2 soon after stalled plans for civilian production. The first production Widgeon was the military J4F-1, a three seat anti submarine patrol and utility version for the US Navy. The US Navy and US Army Air Force ordered large numbers of Widgeons throughout the war years, others saw service with the US Coast Guard and 15 were supplied to Britain's Royal Navy, that service originally calling the aircraft Gosling. In all, 176 Widgeons were built for military service during the conflict.

After the war, Grumman refined the Widgeon for commercial use by altering the hull profile for improved handling on water and increasing seating capacity for up to six. Grumman built 50 of these as the G-44A, while a further 40 were built in France as the SCAN-30. Most SCAN-30s were delivered to customers in the USA.

US firm McKinnon Enterprises offered conversions during the 1960s for both the Grumman Goose and Widgeon. McKinnon's Super Widgeon conversion involved fitting G-44As with Lycoming GO-480 flat six cylinder engines driving three blade Hartzell propellers, significantly boosting top speed and climb performance, with more range through improved fuel economy and extra fuel capacity. Other changes incorporated on the Super Widgeon were IFR avionics, enlarged cabin windows, more soundproofing, an emergency escape hatch, and optional retractable wingtip floats. Modifications to the hull and structure meanwhile allowed an increase in the Super Widgeon's maximum takeoff weight.

Small numbers of Widgeons and Super Widgeons still fly, most in private hands.

Photo: A McKinnon Super Widgeon. (Gordon Reid)

Grumman G-73 Mallard

Country of origin: United States of America

Type: Utility amphibious transport

Powerplants: G-73 – Two 450kW (600hp) Pratt & Whitney R-1340-S3H1 Wasp nine cylinder piston radial engines driving three blade constant speed propellers. G-73T – Two 530kW (715shp) Pratt & Whitney Canada PT6A-27 or PT6A-34 turboprops.

Performance: G-73 – Max speed 346km/h (187kt), cruising speed 290km/h (157kt). Initial rate of climb 1290ft/min. Service ceiling 23,000ft. Range with max fuel 2220km (1655nm). G-73T – Max cruising speed 354km/h (191kt), economical cruising speed 346km/h (187kt). Initial rate of climb 1350ft/min. Service ceiling 24,500ft. Range with max fuel and no reserves 2595km (1400nm), with max payload and no reserves 1388km (750nm).

Weights: G-73 – Empty 4240kg (9350lb), max takeoff 5783kg (12,750lb). G-73T – Empty equipped 3970kg (8750lb), max takeoff 6350kg (14,000lb).

Dimensions: G-73/G-73T – Wing span 20.32m (66ft 8in), length 14.73m (48ft 4in), height on undercarriage 5.72m (18ft 9in). Wing area 41.3m² (444sq ft).

Capacity: Crew of two. Main cabin seating for up to 10 passengers. Many aircraft used as executive transports with customised interiors.

Production: 59 Mallards built between 1946 and 1951. Small numbers later converted to turboprop power.

History: Grumman developed the G-73 Mallard amphibian for commercial use.

The Mallard was developed in the immediate postwar years. It is similar in configuration to Grumman's earlier amphibious designs the Goose and the Widgeon, and features twin radial engines on a high mounted wing with underwing floats, retractable undercarriage and an unswept tail. Unlike the earlier aircraft the Mallard features tricycle undercarriage, a stressed skin two step hull and fuel can be carried in the wingtip tanks.

The Mallard prototype first flew on April 30 1946, and the type entered service shortly afterwards in September that year with a Canadian operator. The Mallard was designed for regional airline operations with two pilots and 10 passengers, but most of the 59 delivered were for corporate use. Today only a small number remain in use, but their unique amphibious capability means they remain popular, particularly with tourist operators.

Like the earlier and smaller Goose, the Mallard has been fitted with Pratt & Whitney Canada PT6A turboprops. Frakes Aviation in the USA re-engined a small number of Mallards as G-73Ts in the early 1970s, their PT6A-27s substantially boosting performance and operating economy. The first Frakes conversion first flew in 1969 and an FAA supplemental type certificate was awarded in October 1970.

In early 1994 an ambitious plan emerged which would see the Mallard re-enter production in the Czech Republic. Aero and Levov of the Czech Republic and Duncan Aviation of the USA hoped to raise the necessary capital to restart the line in the late 1990s. These plans later lapsed.

Photo: Few, if any, aircraft can match the Mallard's amphibian qualities and load carrying capability. (Greg Wood)

Grumman G-111 Albatross

Country of origin: United States of America

Type: Amphibious airliner and light utility transport

Powerplants: Two 1100kW (1475hp) Wright R-1820-982C9HE3 nine cylinder radial piston engines driving three blade constant speed propellers.

Performance: Max speed 380km/h (205kt), max cruising speed 362km/h (195kt), long range cruising speed 200km/h (108kt). Initial rate of climb (with METO power) 1250ft/min. Range with 28 passengers and reserves 750km (405nm) from water or 505km (273nm) from land, max ferry range with no reserves 2740km (1480nm).

Weights: Operating empty 10,660kg (23,500lb), max takeoff from land 13,970kg (30,800lb), max takeoff from water 14,130kg (31,150lb).

Dimensions: Wing span 29.46m (96ft 8in), length 18.67m (61ft 3in), height 7.87m (25ft 10in). Wing area 96.2m² (1035sq ft).

Capacity: Flightcrew of two. G-111 conversion seats 28 passengers in main cabin at 81cm (32in) pitch.

Production: Production for military customers of 418, built between 1947 and 1961. Grumman purchased 57 ex military Albatrosses for conversion to civil G-111 configuration in the early 1980s, but only 12 were converted. Other ex USN Albatrosses fly in private hands.

History: The Albatross is easily the largest of Grumman's series of utility amphibians, and was the only one originally developed specifically for military service.

The Albatross resulted from a late 1940s US Navy requirement for a general purpose amphibious transport. The first Albatross prototype flew on October 24 1947, with more than 400 production HU-16s subsequently delivered to the US Navy, US Coast Guard and 12 other nations. Military Albatross missions included general reconnaissance, maritime patrol, anti submarine warfare (in which role it could be armed with torpedoes and depth charges) and search and rescue.

In the late 1970s, Grumman and major US flying boat operator Resorts International began work on a program to convert the Albatross for civil airline service. The conversion incorporated numerous changes to the basic Albatross, including a 28 seat passenger interior, a galley and provision for a flight attendant, upgraded avionics and other improved systems. The airframes were also stripped down, inspected, components were replaced or repaired, and the whole airframe was zero timed. Military equipment was removed and the engines were stripped down and rebuilt.

The first such G-111 Albatross conversion flew for the first time on February 13 1979 and US FAA certification was awarded in April 1980.

Grumman purchased 57 Albatrosses for conversion and foresaw a potential market for up to 200 modified amphibians, however this prediction proved somewhat optimistic. In all only 12 aircraft were converted, all for Resorts International.

A further developed version powered by Garrett TPE331 turboprops and a firebomber were also studied but not developed. Later in 1986 Frakes International proposed re-engining Albatrosses with Pratt & Whitney Canada PT6A or PW120 turboprops, but these plans also fell through.

Photo: A G-111 Albatross at Fort Lauderdale, Florida. (Toni Marimon)

Grumman G-159 Gulfstream I

Country of origin: United States of America

Type: Corporate transport and regional airliner

Powerplants: Two 1485kW (1990hp) Rolls-Royce Dart Mk 529-8X or -8E turboprops driving four blade Rotol propellers.

Performance: I – High speed cruise 560km/h (302kt), economical cruising speed 463km/h (250kt). Range with a 1245kg (2740lb) payload, max fuel and reserves 4087km (2206nm). I-C – Max cruising speed 555km/h (300kt). Range with max payload 805km (435nm).

Weights: I – Empty equipped 9942kg (21,900lb), max takeoff 15,935kg (35,100lb). I-C – Empty 10,747kg (23,639lb), max takeoff 16,300kg (36,000lb).

Dimensions: I – Wing span 23.92m (78ft 6in), length 19.43m (63ft 9in), height 6.94m (22ft 9in). Wing area 56.7m² (610.3sq ft). I-C – Same except for length 22.97m (75ft 4in), height 7.01m (23ft 0in).

Capacity: I – Flightcrew of two. Typical corporate layouts seat between 10 and 14 passengers. Commuter airliner seating for 19 or high density seating for up to 24. I-C – Flightcrew of two. Seating for between 32 and 38 at three abreast.

Production: 200 Gulfstream Is built when production ceased in February 1969 in favour of the jet powered Gulfstream II. Approximately 100 remained in corporate use in 2002 while a further 36 were in airline service. Five Gulfstream G-1C conversions performed. In 2002 two were in use as corporate transports.

History: Grumman developed the Gulfstream I turbine powered executive transport to replace the many hundreds of war surplus piston twins performing such missions in the mid 1950s.

Design work began in 1956, with first flight of the Gulfstream I prototype occurring on August 14 1958. FAA Type certification was awarded on May 21 1959 and deliveries of production aircraft followed from that June. Notably, the Gulfstream I was the first US twin engined corporate transport to be certificated to cruise at 30,000ft.

As the first in the Gulfstream line, the GI established the basic fuselage cross section that carries through today. Other features were the Rolls-Royce Dart turboprops (beginning a long standing association with RR that remains to this day) giving the I good high speed cruise performance, and an auxiliary power unit allowing independent operations from remote strips, providing power for the air conditioning and electrical systems prior to engine start.

While primarily designed as a corporate transport, a large number of the standard fuselage Gulfstream Is were also used as commuter airliners, seating up to 24 passengers. Military Gulfstream Is were built for the US Navy (navigator training TC-4s) and US Coast Guard (VIP VC-4s). Production of the standard fuselage I ceased in 1969.

In 1979, by which time Grumman's design rights had been purchased by the newly established Gulfstream American Corporation, Gulfstream began offering stretched airliner conversions of the base GI. These aircraft were stretched by 3.25m (10ft 8in), allowing seating for up to 38 passengers at three abreast. Called the G-159C Gulfstream I-C, the first conversion flew on October 25 1979, and production conversions (five were undertaken) were delivered from November 1980.

Photo: A US registered Gulfstream I. (Wally McLeod)

Grumman Gulfstream II & Gulfstream III

Country of origin: United States of America

Type: Long range large corporate jet

Powerplants: Gulfstream II & III – Two 50.7kN (11,400lb) Rolls-Royce Spey turbofans.

Performance: GII – Max cruising speed 935km/h (505kt), economical cruising speed 795km/h (430kt). Initial rate of climb 4350ft/min. Range with max fuel and reserves 6880km (3715nm). GIII – Max cruising speed 928km/h (500kt), economical cruising speed 818km/h (442kt). Initial rate of climb 3800ft/min. Max operating ceiling 45,000ft. Range with eight passengers 7600km (4100nm).

Weights: GII – Operating empty 16,740kg (36,900lb), max takeoff 29,710kg (65,500lb). GIII – Empty 14,515kg (32,000lb), operating empty 17,235kg (38,000lb), max takeoff 31,615kg (69,700lb).

Dimensions: GII – Wing span 20.98m (68ft 10in), length 24.36m (79ft 11in), height 7.47m (24ft 6in). Wing area 75.2m² (809.6sq ft). GIII – Wing span 23.72m (77ft 10in), length 25.32m (83ft 1in), height 7.43m (24ft 5in). Wing area 86.8m² (933sq ft).

Capacity: Flightcrew of two. Main cabin seating for up to 19 in GII or 21 in GIII in a high density configuration, eight to 12 in a typical corporate configuration.

Production: Total Gulfstream II and III production amounted to 464 aircraft, comprising 258 GIIs and 206 GIIIs. 243 GIIs and 197 GIIIs were in corporate service in 2002.

History: Collectively the most successful members of the Gulfstream corporate aircraft family, the Gulfstream II and Gulfstream III are Spey powered large business jets.

The Rolls-Royce Dart turboprop powered Grumman Gulfstream I proved to be quite successful as a large long range corporate transport, while the availability of an appropriately sized turbofan in the form of the Rolls-Royce Spey meant that a jet powered successor was a logical development. Grumman launched this aircraft, named the Gulfstream II (or GII), in May 1965.

While based on the original Gulfstream I – the GII shares the same forward fuselage and cross section – there are more differences than similarities. The most obvious difference is the two rear mounted Spey turbofans, others include a new swept wing and T-tail. A similar size fuselage to the GI seats 10 in a typical executive configuration.

No prototype GII was built, instead the first to fly was a production standard aircraft, which recorded its maiden flight on October 2 1966. Certification and first production deliveries occurred on October 19 and December 6 1967 (to National Distillers & Chemical Corporation) respectively.

The improved Gulfstream III followed Gulfstream American's purchase of Grumman's GA lines in 1978. The Gulfstream III first flew on December 2 1979. Changes compared with the GII include a revised wing of greater span and area with drag reducing winglets, more fuel tankage and thus range, a reprofiled nose and a 97cm (3ft 2in) fuselage stretch. Gulfstream IIBs are GIIs retrofitted with the GIII's wing.

Production deliveries of GIIIs began in late 1980 and continued until 1986 when production ceased in favour of the Gulfstream IV.

Photo: A Canadian registered GIII. (Robert Wiseman)

Gulfstream IV, G300 & G400

Country of origin: United States of America

Type: Long range large corporate jet

Powerplants: Two 61.6kN (13,850lb) Rolls-Royce Tay Mk 611-8 turbofans.

Performance: IV – Normal cruising speed 850km/h (460kt). Initial rate of climb 4000ft/min. Range with max payload 6732km (3633nm), range with eight passengers 7815km (4220nm). IV-SP – Max cruising speed 936km/h (505kt), normal cruising speed 850km/h (460kt). Initial rate of climb 4122ft/min. Max certificated altitude 45,000ft. Range with max payload 6182km (3338nm), range with eight passengers 7815km (4220nm).

Weights: IV – Empty 16,102kg (35,500lb), max takeoff 33,203kg (73,200lb). IV-SP – Empty same, max takeoff 33,838kg (74,600lb).

Dimensions: Wing span 23.72m (77ft 10in), length 26.92m (88ft 4in), height 7.45m (24ft 5in). Wing area 88.3m^2 (950.4sq ft).

Capacity: Flightcrew of two. Main cabin seating for between 14 and 19, plus flight attendant.

Production: Approximately 470 Gulfstream IVs and IV-SPs delivered by late 2002. Military C-20s built for the US.

History: The Gulfstream IV is a significantly improved, larger, longer ranging and advanced development of the earlier II and III.

The most significant improvement with the GIV over the earlier Gulfstream models are the Rolls-Royce Tay turbofans, which bring significant fuel burn and noise emission improvements despite their higher thrust output than the II and III's Speys. Other changes include a stretched fuselage and substantially revised wing, greater fuel capacity and range, increased span tailplane and an EFIS avionics suite with six colour CRT displays.

Design work on the IV began in early 1983, with the first of four production prototypes making the type's first flight on September 19 1985. FAA certification was awarded on April 22 1987. The improved Gulfstream IV-SP (SP = Special Performance), with higher payload and landing weights and improved payload range performance, replaced the IV from September 1992.

A third development is the special mission SRA-4. Designed primarily for military roles (such as maritime patrol and electronic surveillance, depending on equipment fit) it is also offered as a freighter for priority cargo transport (operated by the US Navy and Marines as C-20G operations support aircraft capable of accommodating 26 passengers or three freight pallets).

Both the Gulfstream IV and IV-SP have set a number of records. A Gulfstream IV flew west around the world over 36,800km (19,890nm) in June 1987 in a time of 45hr 25min, setting 22 class world records, another flew east around the world in February 1988, setting 11 class world records.

In September 2002 Gulfstream launched two new developments, the G300 and G400. The 6665km (3600nm) range G300 is aimed at Gulfstream III operators, and will enter service in 2003.

The 7600km (4100nm) range G400 – effectively the IV-SP rebadged – will also enter service in 2003. A head-up display will be standard equipment.

Photo: A Swiss registered Gulfstream IV. (Rob Finlayson)

Gulfstream V, G500 & G550

Country of origin: United States of America

Type: Ultra long range large corporate jet

Powerplants: GV – Two 65.6kN (14,750lb) Rolls-Royce BR710-48 turbofans. G550 – Two 68.4kN (15,383lb) BR710s.

Performance: GV – Max cruising speed 924km/h (499kt), long range cruising speed 850km/h (459kt). Initial rate of climb 4188ft/min. Initial cruise altitude 41,000ft, max certificated altitude 51,000ft. Max range with four crew and eight passengers and reserves at design cruising speed 12,045km (6500nm), flight time for which would be approximately 14hr 28min. G550 – Max range at Mach 0.80 12,500km (6750km)

Weights: GV – Basic operating with four crew 21,228kg (46,800lb), max takeoff 40,370kg (89,000lb). G550 – Max takeoff 41,277kg (91,000lb).

Dimensions: GV – Span over winglets 28.50m (93ft 4in), length 29.39m (96ft 5in), height 7.87m (25ft 10in). Wing area 105.6m^2 (1137.0sq ft).

Capacity: Flightcrew of two. GV – Typical passenger load of eight but seats 15 to 19. Typically equipped with a crew rest room, a business work station, a dining/conference area with seating for four, a three seat couch that converts into a bed, five other reclining seats, two galleys and a restroom fitted with a toilet and shower.

Production: 100th GV delivered late 2000.

History: The Gulfstream V is the largest of the Gulfstream line of corporate transports, designed to fly intercontinental distances.

Gulfstream Aerospace first announced it was studying a stretch of the Gulfstream IV at the annual NBAA convention in October 1989, while the program was officially launched at the 1992 Farnborough Airshow. First flight was on November 28 1995. Provisional FAA certification was awarded in December 1996, full certification was granted in April 1997. First customer delivery was on July 1 1997.

The Gulfstream V is based on the Gulfstream IV, but features a number of substantial changes to suit its different design objectives. The fuselage is stretched, but perhaps the two most important changes are the new wing and new Rolls-Royce BR710 turbofans (the GV was the first application for this engine). The all new wing is built by Northrop Grumman, and is optimised for high speed flight (it was developed using Computer Aided Design and NASA developed computational fluid dynamics). The flightdeck is built around a six screen Honeywell EFIS avionics suite and features head-up displays.

The improved Gulfstream V-SP first flew on July 18 2002, with deliveries from late 2003. Improvements include a 227kg (500lb) increase in max takeoff weight, aerodynamic improvements for better range at higher cruising speeds – 9265km (5000nm) at Mach 0.87 or 12,507km (6750nm) at Mach 0.80 – slightly reduced takeoff length, reconfigured main cabin, a seventh fuselage window on the forward right-hand side, and Gulfstream's new PlaneView flightdeck including improved head-up displays, CNS/ATM compatibility, and forward looking infrared camera.

In September 2002 Gulfstream relaunched the basic Gulfstream V, with some improvements as the G500, for delivery in 2004, while the V-SP has been renamed the G550.

Photo: A Gulfstream V in flight (Gulfstream)

Gulfstream G100, G150 & IAI Astra

Gulfstream G200

Country of origin: Israel

Type: Small to mid size corporate jet

Powerplants: 1125 – Two 16.2kN (3650lb) Garrett TFE731-3B-100G turbofans. G100 – Two 18.9kN (4250lb) Honeywell TFE731-40R-200Gs.

Performance: 1125 – Max cruising speed 862km/h (465kt). Initial rate of climb 3560ft/min. Service ceiling 41,500ft. Range with long range tanks and four passengers at Mach 0.72 cruising speed 5760km (3110nm). G100 – Normal cruising speed 850km/h (459kt), long range cruising speed 796km/h (430kt). Certificated altitude 45,000ft. Range with four passengers 5000km (2700nm).

Weights: 1125 – Basic operating empty 5747kg (12,670lb), max takeoff 10,660kg (23,500lb). G100 – Basic operating empty incl 2 crew 6638kg (14,635lb), max takeoff 11,181kg (24,650lb).

Dimensions: Wing span 16.05m (52ft 8in), length 16.94m (55ft 7in), height 5.53m (18ft 2in). Wing area 29.4m² (316.6sq ft). SPX – Same except wing span over winglets 16.64m (54ft 7in).

Capacity: 1125 & G100 – Flightcrew of two. Typical seating for six passengers, with max seating for nine.

Production: Approx 140 Astras delivered by late 2002.

History: The IAI 1125 Astra is a comprehensively upgraded development of the successful 1124 Westwind, with a number of key changes to improve performance and increase cabin volume. It is now part of the expanded Gulfstream stable, designated G100.

Israel Aircraft Industries began work on an improved development of its model 1124, initially known as the 1125 Westwind, in the early 1980s, with the first flight on March 19 1984. The first production Astra flew in March 1985, and the first customer delivery took place in mid 1986 after certification had been granted in August the previous year.

The Astra is based on the basic Westwind II fuselage and tail, mated with an all new high speed swept wing (initially lacking winglets), repositioned low on the fuselage (as opposed to mid mounted on the Westwind), where it does not intrude on internal cabin space. Headroom is increased by 20cm (8in). Other changes include a lengthened nose for greater avionics space and more extensive use of composites (mainly for control surfaces).

The original 1125 Astra was replaced in production by the Astra SP. The SP was announced in 1989 and features a revised interior, upgraded avionics, EFIS cockpit and some minor aerodynamic refinements. Thirty-seven were built before it was replaced by the SPX.

The SPX, G100 from September 2002, first flew in August 1994 and features more powerful FADEC equipped 18.9kN (4250lb) Honeywell TFE731-40Rs, winglets and Collins Pro Line 4 avionics.

IAI builds the G100 in Israel and the 'green' airframes are flown to Lincoln, Nebraska in the US for interior outfitting. Gulfstream acquired Galaxy Aerospace, which held the SPX and Astra type certificates and was responsible for marketing, in May 2001.

In September 2002 Gulfstream announced the improved G150, based on the G150 but with an enlarged fuselage and seating for six to eight. It will be powered by TFE731s, cruise at Mach 0.75 and have a range of 5000km (2700nm). Deliveries are due in 2005.

Photo: The Astra SPX. (IAI)

Country of origin: Israel

Type: Super mid size corporate transport

Powerplants: Two 26.9kN (6040lb) Pratt & Whitney Canada PW306A turbofans.

Performance: Typical cruising speed 871km/h (470kt), long range cruising speed 797km/h (430kt). Max operating altitude 45,000ft. Max range with four passengers and reserves 6708km (3620nm).

Weights: Basic operating 8709kg (19,200lb), max takeoff 15,808kg (34,850lb).

Dimensions: Wing span 17.70m (58ft 1in), length 18.97m (62ft 3in), height 6.53m (21ft 5in). Wing area 34.3m² (369.0sq ft).

Capacity: Flightcrew of two. Seating for eight or more in executive style arrangements, or up to 18 in a three abreast corporate shuttle configuration.

Production: First deliveries January 2000. Approx 70 delivered by late 2002.

History: The Gulfstream G200 mid size corporate jet is built by IAI and was originally marketed and supported by Galaxy Aerospace Inc, which was acquired by Gulfstream in May 2001.

Design work on the G200 (initially called the Galaxy) began in the early 1990s and formal program launch was announced in September 1993. In 1995 a co-production arrangement was terminated that would have seen Yakovlev in Russia responsible for the design and manufacture of the Galaxy's fuselage, while IAI would be the main contractor responsible for final assembly, integration and marketing. Subsequently SOGERMA of France was selected to manufacture production Galaxy fuselages and tails.

The Galaxy was first expected to fly in 1996 but this was delayed until December 25 1997. A second prototype flew in May 1998 while the first production aircraft first flew in October that year. US FAA and Israeli certification was issued in December 1998. The first customer aircraft was delivered to TTI Industries in January 2000. (A Galaxy delivered to Lion Industries in Zurich in July 1999 was leased back by Galaxy Aerospace for use as a demonstrator.)

The G200's swept high speed wing is based on that on the Astra/G100, but otherwise the G200 is a new design. It features a new 'widebody' fuselage, significantly wider and longer than the G100's, with standup room. The rear fuselage is area ruled to reduce drag, while the wing features winglets. The G200 also features an EFIS Collins Pro Line 4 cockpit and nonstop trans Atlantic range.

IAI selected the Pratt & Whitney Canada PW306A turbofans for the Galaxy in January 1993 after studying competing designs from Allison (the AE 3007) and AlliedSignal/General Electric (the CFE738). The PW306A is a growth development (with increased fan diameter, improved hot end material and a forced mixer in the exhaust) of the PW305 series that powers the Hawker 1000 and Learjet 60.

IAI assembles and test flies G200s in Israel at its Tel Aviv facilities, while interior completion takes place at Gulfstream's Dallas Love Field facility. (Before Gulfstream's acquisition of the project, Galaxy Aerospace undertook completions and deliveries from a new facility at Alliance Airport, Fort Worth, Texas.)

Photo: A Swiss registered Galaxy/G200. (Charles Falk)

Countries of origin: United States of America

Type: Four place light twin

Powerplants: GA-7 – Two 119kW (160hp) Lycoming O-320-D1D flat four piston engines driving two blade constant speed propellers. TB 360 – Two 135kW (180hp) Textron Lycoming O-360-A1G6.

Performance: GA-7 – Max speed 311km/h (168kt), max cruising speed 296km/h (160kt), typical cruising speed 260km/h (140kt). Initial rate of climb 1150ft/min. Service ceiling 17,400ft. Max range with no reserves 2170km (1170nm). TB 360 – Max speed 322km/h (174kt), cruising speed at 75% power 306km/h (165kt), at 45% power 222km/h (120kt). Initial rate of climb 1400ft/min. Service ceiling 20,000ft. Range with max fuel at 75% power 1480km (800nm), at 45% power 2110km (1140nm).

Weights: GA-7 – Empty 1174kg (2588lb), MTOW 1725kg (3800lb).

Dimensions: GA-7 – Wing span 11.23m (36ft 10in), length 9.09m (29ft 10in), height 3.16m (10ft 4in). Wing area 17.1m² (184.0sq ft).

Capacity: Standard seating for four.

Production: GA-7s were built in 1978 and 1979.

History: The GA-7 Cougar light twin saw limited production with Gulfstream in the late 1970s.

The GA-7 prototype first flew on December 20 1974, but three years passed before production began. By this time Grumman's light aircraft lines had been acquired by Gulfstream, which delivered production GA-7s from February 1978.

The GA-7 design featured two 120kW (160hp) Lycoming O-320s and bonded honeycomb construction as used on the Grumman AA-1 and AA-5. The initial GA-7 design featured a sliding cockpit canopy and two cabin windows per side. Changes for production aircraft included the adoption of a conventional cabin roof enclosing an enlarged cabin with an entry door on the right hand side. The prototype's single spar wing design was changed to a twin spar design allowing an integral wet wing fuel tank, and on production GA-7s the main undercarriage units retracted outwards, rather than inwards.

Gulfstream built two basic variants, the standard GA-7 and the GA-7 Cougar with a more comprehensive avionics fit and improved interior fittings. However sales of both aircraft were slow, in part because of the GA-7's relatively low combined power output of 240kW (320hp). Production ceased in 1979 with Gulfstream's departure from light aircraft manufacture.

In 1995 Socata purchased the rights to the GA-7 with the intention of placing it back into production as the TB 320 Tangara. In June 1996 Socata announced its plans to redevelop the aircraft as the TB 360 Tangara with 135kW (180hp) O-360s.

Three modified GA-7s were flown as Tangara prototypes, the first had a 120kW (160hp) and a 135kW (180hp) engine and flew in mid 1996, the third, which first flew in February 1997, was in full TB 360 configuration. French certification was awarded in December 1997 but in 1999 Socata announced it was suspending development due to strong demand for its other products, and that instead it was looking for a partner to place the TB 360 into production. No progress has since been reported.

Photo: A Grumman Cougar. (Bill Lines)

Country of origin: China

Type: Commuter airliners and utility transports

Powerplants: Y-11B – Two 260kW (350hp) Teledyne Continental TSIO-550-B flat six piston engines driving three blade variable pitch props. Y-12 (II) – Two 460kW (620shp) Pratt & Whitney Canada PT6A-27 turboprops driving three blade constant speed Hartzell props.

Performance: Y-11B – Max speed 265km/h (143kt), max cruising speed 235km/h (127kt), economical cruising speed 200km/h (108kt). Initial rate of climb 1100ft/min. Service ceiling 19,685ft. Range with max payload 300km (163nm), with max fuel 1080km (590nm). Y-12 (II) – Max cruising speed 292km/h (157kt), economical cruising speed 250km/h (135kt). Initial rate of climb 1595ft/min. Service ceiling 22,960ft. Range at economical cruising speed with max fuel and reserves 1340km (725nm).

Weights: Y-11B – Empty equipped 2505kg (5250lb), max takeoff 3500kg (7715lb). Y-12 (II) – Max takeoff 5300kg (11,685lb).

Dimensions: Y-11B – Wing span 17.08m (56ft 1in), length 12.12m (39ft 9in), height 5.19m (17ft 0in). Wing area 34.2m² (367.7sq ft). Y-12 (II) – Wing span 17.25m (56ft 7in), length 14.86m (48ft 9in), height 5.68m (18ft 8in). Wing area 34.3m² (368.88sq ft).

Capacity: Flightcrew of two. Main cabin seats six to eight passengers in Y-11. Y-12 can seat up to 17 at three abreast and 75cm (30in) pitch.

Production: Approx 40 Y-11s, two prototype and one production Y-11Bs and over 120 Y-12s built. 35 Twin Pandas on order.

History: Harbin's piston powered Y-11 and turboprop Y-12 are Chinese developed regional airliners and utility transports.

Design of the type 11 transport aircraft, or Yun-shu 11 (Y-11), began during the mid 1970s to develop a replacement for the Antonov An-2 utility biplane in Chinese service (licence built in China as the Y-2). A prototype was built and flown at Shenyang in 1975, while production began at what is now the Harbin Aircraft Manufacturing Company in 1980. Features include two radial engines, capability for rough field operations and STOL performance. Y-11s have seen service as commuter airliners and have also been configured and used for ag spraying.

The Y-11B is an improved development powered by Teledyne Continental engines to overcome single engine altitude performance shortfalls. The first Y-11B's maiden flight was on December 25 1990.

The Y-12 is a turboprop powered development and has been built in greater numbers than the Y-11. Work on a turboprop powered Y-11 began in the early 1980s, and a Pratt & Whitney Canada PT6A powered and enlarged cabin Y-12 prototype (previously the Y-11T) first flew on August 16 1984. Current production is of the Y-12 (II), while the further improved Y-12 (IV) was granted US certification in March 1995.

Canadian Aerospace Group (CAG) has plans to offer a developed Y-12 as the Twin Panda, which it aims at the Twin Otter replacement market. The Twin Panda is based on the Y-12 (IV) but features more powerful PT6A-34 engines, strengthened landing gear, and upgraded avionics and interior. Production Twin Pandas would be built in China and outfitted in Canada prior to delivery.

Photo: A Harbin Y-11B. (Sebastian Zacharias)

Hawker Siddeley HS.125

Country of origin: United Kingdom

Type: Mid size corporate jet

Powerplants: Srs 400 – Two 14.9kN (3360lb) Rolls-Royce Viper 522 turbojets. Srs 600 – Two 16.7kN (3750lb) Rolls-Royce Viper 601 turbojets.

Performance: Srs 400 – Long range cruising speed 724km/h (390kt). Initial rate of climb 4800ft/min. Range with 454kg (1000lb) payload and reserves 2835km (990nm). Srs 600 – Long range cruising speed 810km/h (427kt). Initial rate of climb 4900ft/min. Range with max fuel and reserves 3020km (1630nm).

Weights: Srs 400 – Typical operating empty 5557kg (12,260lb), max takeoff 10,569kg (23,300lb). Srs 600 – Max takeoff 11,340kg (25,000lb).

Dimensions: Srs 400 – Wing span 14.32m (47ft 0in), length 14.42m (47ft 5in), height 5.26m (17ft 3in). Wing area 32.8m² (353sq ft). Srs 600 – Same except length 15.37m (50ft 6in).

Capacity: Flightcrew of two. Various optional interior configurations offered depending on customer preference. Max main cabin seating for 12 in Srs 400 or 14 in Srs 600.

Production: Total sales of HS.125s up to and including the Series 600 reached 358, including the Srs 2 Dominie for Britain's RAF. More than 240 remained in use in 2002.

History: The Hawker Siddeley HS.125 was one of the most popular first generation business jets and in developed form remains in production with Raytheon (refer separate entry).

The HS.125 started life as a de Havilland project before that company became part of the Hawker Siddeley group. As the DH.125 this mid size corporate jet first flew on August 13 1962. For a time the DH.125 was named the Jet Dragon, while just eight initial Series 1 production aircraft were built before deliveries switched to the more powerful Series 1A (the A suffix denoting North America) and Series 1B (the B denoting sales for world markets). A total of 77 was built. The Series 2 meanwhile was a military navigation trainer derivative built for Britain's Royal Air Force as the Dominie.

The improved Series 3A and 3B (29 built) had a higher gross weight, while the 3A-R and 3B-R (36 built) were heavier still with extra fuel for greater range.

When de Havilland merged into Hawker Siddeley, the Series 4, which featured numerous minor refinements, was marketed as the Series 400A and 400B and 116 were built.

The final Viper turbojet powered 125 built was the Series 600A and 600B. The Series 600 features a stretched fuselage taking standard main cabin seating from six to eight, or up to 14 in a high density configuration. Other changes included more powerful Rolls-Royce Viper 601-22 turbojets, lengthened vertical tail and ventral fin, and a fuel tank in the extended dorsal fin.

The 600 first flew on January 21 1971 and it became the standard production model until the Garrett TFE731 turbofan powered 700 series was introduced (described separately) in 1976. Some Series 600s were re-engined with TFE731s as HS.125-600Fs.

Photo: A HS.125 Series 600B. The HS.125 was one of the British aviation industry's most successful postwar designs.

Helio Courier

Country of origin: United States of America

Type: Four/six seat STOL utility light aircraft

Powerplants: H-250 – One 185kW (250hp) Lycoming O-540-A1A5 flat six piston engine driving a three blade constant speed propeller. H-295 – One 229kW (295hp) geared GO-480-G1D6.

Performance: H-250 – Max speed 257km/h (140kt), max cruising speed 245km/h (132kt), long range cruising speed 214km/h (116kt). Initial rate of climb 830ft/min. Service ceiling 15,200ft. Range with standard fuel and no reserves 1035km (560nm), with optional fuel 2073km (1120nm). H-295 – Max speed 270km/h (145kt), max cruising speed 265km/h (143kt), long range cruising speed 240km/h (130kt). Initial rate of climb 1150ft/min. Service ceiling 20,500ft. Range with standard fuel and no reserves 1060km (575nm), with optional fuel 2220km (1200nm).

Weights: H-250 – Empty 890kg (1960lb), max takeoff 1542kg (3400lb). H-295 – Empty 943kg (2080lb), max takeoff 1542kg (3400lb).

Dimensions: H-250 & H-295 – Wing span 11.89m (39ft 0in), length 9.45m (31ft 0in), height 2.69m (8ft 10in). Wing area 21.5m² (231sq ft).

Capacity: Early models up to the H-250 could seat four, the H-395 five or six, the H-250 and subsequent models six.

Production: More than 500 Couriers of all models built, including 130 U-10s for the US Air Force.

History: The Helio Courier has proven to be a versatile utility aircraft, highly regarded for its superb STOL abilities.

The Courier traces back to a much modified experimental development of the two seat Piper Vagabond known as the Koppen-Bolinger Helioplane. This Helioplane featured numerous aerodynamic modifications to enhance low speed handling and STOL performance, and many of its features were subsequently incorporated into the all new and much larger Courier.

The Courier was initially known as the Helioplane Four and first appeared in 1952. In its original form it was powered by a 197kW (264hp) Lycoming GO-435 and seated four. First flight occurred during 1953 and deliveries of the initial production model, the H-391B, got underway in 1954. Subsequent development led to a number of derivatives, beginning with the H-392 Strato Courier of 1957. Intended for high altitude photographic work, the H-392 was powered by a 255kW (340hp) supercharged GSO-435.

The H-395, featuring a 220kW (295hp) GO-485 and seating for five or six, was the first major production version and it appeared in 1957. The H-395A was similar but its engine could operate on 80 octane fuel, making it suitable for operations in remote areas. Next came the H-250 (with a 185kW/250hp O-540) and H-295 Super Courier (220kW/295hp GO-480) from 1965, and the tricycle undercarriage HT-295 from 1974. The H-250 remained in production until 1972, the H-295 until 1976.

A development of the H-295 with an eight cylinder 300kW (400hp) Lycoming IO-720, the Courier 800, plus the 260kW (350hp) TIO-540 powered Courier 700, were put into production by the newly established Helio Aircraft Company from 1983, but production was limited and ceased in the late 1980s.

Photo: The Lycoming O-540 powered H-250 Courier. (Theo van Loon)

Hiller UH-12

Country of origin: United States of America

Type: Light utility helicopter

Powerplant: UH-12E4T – One 315kW (420shp) Allison 250-C20B turboshaft driving two blade main and tail rotors. UH-12E3 – One 255kW (340hp) Textron Lycoming VO-540-C2A flat six piston engine.

Performance: UH-12E4T – Max speed 154km/h (83kt). Range with auxiliary tanks 565km (305nm). UH-12E3 – Max speed 154km/h (83kt), cruising speed 145km/h (78kt). Initial rate of climb 1290ft/min. Service ceiling 15,000ft. Hovering ceiling out of ground effect 6800ft. Range with reserves 278km (150nm), or 585km (316nm) with optional fuel.

Weights: UH-12E4T – Empty 750kg (1650lb), max takeoff 1406kg (3100lb). UH-12E3 – Empty 798kg (1759lb), MTOW 1406kg (3100lb).

Dimensions: UH-12E4T – Main rotor diameter 10.80m (35ft 5in), length overall 12.41m (40ft 9in), fuselage length 9.08m (29ft 10in), height 3.08m (10ft 2in). Main rotor disc area 92.0m^2 (990.0sq ft). UH-12E3 – Same except fuselage length 8.69m (28ft 6in).

Capacity: Seating for three on a bench seat, or for four (two forward and two behind) in UH-12E4 and -12E4T.

Production: Over 2300 of all versions built, including military H-23s.

History: The UH-12 series of light helicopters has had one of the longest and most sporadic production runs in history.

The UH-12 first flew in 1948. The initial variant was the Model 12 which was powered by a 133kW (178hp) Franklin 6V4-178-B33 engine. The Model 12A followed from 1952, it introduced a semi enclosed cockpit, while the distinctive goldfish bowl cockpit first appeared on the 12C, which also introduced all metal rotor blades (the 12C, plus the 12A and 12B were powered by a 150kW/200hp or 155kW/210hp engine). The definitive UH-12E was first delivered from May 1959.

Developments of the UH-12E include the four seat UH-12E4 with a stretched fuselage and the Allison 250 turboshaft powered UH-12ET and UH-12E4T. Kits were offered allowing the conversion of -12Es into -12E4s, while piston powered aircraft could be retrofitted with the Allison turboshaft. Large numbers of military Hillers were also built for the US military as H-23 Ravens.

The production history of the UH-12 is chequered, with design and initial production undertaken by the original Hiller company. Hiller, and then Fairchild Hiller, built over 2000 up until the late 1960s. The newly formed Hiller Aviation acquired design and production rights in 1973 and restarted UH-12E production. Hiller Aviation was then acquired by Rogerson Aircraft in 1984, the first UH-12Es manufactured under the new company banner coming off the line in mid 1984. Rogerson subsequently changed its name to Rogerson Hiller, and relaunched UH-12E production in 1991.

The final chapter of the UH-12 story so far opened in mid 1994 when the original designer and owner Stanley Hiller, in conjunction with Thai investors, acquired the program from Rogerson. The new Hiller Aircraft Corporation planned to build small numbers of UH-12E3s (the first, a conversion of an existing UH-12E, flew on June 2 1995) for its Thai partners, and also flew the Allison 250 turboprop powered UH-12E3T, but did not resume production.

Photo: The UH-12E has proven successful worldwide.

Hindustan Advanced Light Helicopter

Country of origin: India

Type: Medium utility helicopter

Powerplants: Prototypes – Two 746kW (1000shp) takeoff rated Turbomeca TM 333-2B turboshafts driving a four blade main rotor and a four blade tail rotor. Production civil aircraft – Two 970kW (1300shp) LHTEC CTS 800s.

Performance: Max speed 290km/h (156kt), max cruising speed 245km/h (132kt). Initial rate of climb 2360ft/min. Service ceiling 19,680ft. Hovering ceiling in ground effect over 9840ft. Range with max fuel 800km (430nm), range with a 700kg (1543lb) payload 400km (215nm). Endurance 4hr.

Weights: Army version – Empty equipped 2500kg (5511lb), max takeoff 4000kg (8818lb). Naval version – Empty 2500kg (5511lb), max takeoff 5000kg (11,023lb).

Dimensions: Main rotor diameter 13.20m (43ft 4in), length overall rotors turning 15.87m (52ft 1in), fuselage length tail rotor turning 13.43m (44ft 1in), height overall tail rotor turning with skids 4.98m (16ft 4in), with wheels 4.91m (16ft 2in). Main rotor disc area 136.9m^2 (1473.0sq ft).

Capacity: Flightcrew of two. Main cabin seating for 10 to 14, depending on configuration. Max external sling load army variant 1000kg (2205lb), naval variant 1500kg (3307lb).

Production: The Indian government plans to buy 307 for that country's military. HAL foresees civil and military domestic sales of 650.

History: The Advanced Light Helicopter is the first indigenous helicopter design of the growing Indian aircraft industry, and will be built in different versions for the Indian Army, Navy, Coast Guard and Air Force, as well as for civil customers.

In the early 1980s India approached Germany's MBB (now Eurocopter Deutschland) to help it design and build a mid size multirole helicopter for both military and civil use. Subsequently a cooperation agreement was signed in July 1984, covering design support, development and production. Design work began in November that year, while the first flight of the first of four prototypes was on August 20 1992.

ALH design features include a hingeless four blade main rotor with swept back tips and composite construction main and tail rotor blades. The first three prototypes are powered by TM 333s, which will also power production aircraft (the CTS 800 was planned as an option, until the US blocked supply due to India's refusal to sign a nuclear test ban treaty).

The Advanced Light Helicopter will be built in two military versions, one for the Indian air force and army, and one for the navy. Army and air force versions will feature skids, and will be used for ground attack, troop transport and SAR. Naval versions will be fitted with retractable tricycle undercarriage and a folding tail boom. The civil version will feature tricycle landing gear and will be certificated to western standards.

The Indian government plans to buy around 300 ALHs for its military, to replace a variety of helicopters including Chetaks and Cheetahs. The first firm order, for 100, was placed in late 1996. First deliveries were due in 2002.

Photo: The first prototype ALH, Z 3182. (Hindustan)

IAI Arava

Country of origin: Israel

Type: STOL utility transport

Powerplants: 201 – Two 560kW (750shp) Pratt & Whitney Canada PT6A-34 turboprops driving three blade constant speed Hartzell propellers.

Performance: 201 – Max speed 326km/h (176kt), max cruising speed 320km/h (172kt), economical cruising speed 310km/h (168kt). Initial rate of climb 1290ft/min. Service ceiling 25,000ft. Range with max payload and reserves 260km (140nm), max range with a 1585kg (3500lb) payload and reserves 1000km (540nm).

Weights: 201 – Operating empty 4000kg (8816lb), max takeoff 6804kg (15,000lb).

Dimensions: 201 – Wing span 20.96m (68ft 9in), length 13.03m (42ft 9in), height 5.21m (17ft 1in). Wing area 43.7m² (470.2sq ft).

Capacity: Flightcrew of two. Seating for 19 passengers four abreast in an airline configuration in 101B, 20 in 102 and 24 in 201. 201 can carry 2350kg (5184lb) of freight. 102 can carry up to 12 passengers in an executive configuration, other configurations offered include aerial ambulance, mapping and mineral exploration.

Production: Total Arava production of more than 90 mainly for military customers. In 2002 nine in service as corporate transports, others in commercial service.

History: The Arava STOL utility transport was IAI's first design to enter production that was intended for both military and civil customers, but was built in only small numbers.

IAI began design work on the Arava in 1966. Design objectives included STOL performance, the ability to operate from rough strips, and the carriage of 25 troops or bulky payloads. To achieve this the Arava design was of a fairly unusual configuration, featuring a barrel-like short but wide fuselage, the rear of which is hinged and swings open for easy loading and unloading, plus long span wings, twin tails mounted on booms that run from the engine nacelles, and two Pratt & Whitney Canada PT6A turboprops.

The Arava first flew on November 27 1969, while a second prototype flew for the first time on May 8 1971. US FAA certification for the initial Arava 101 was granted in April 1972.

The Arava 101 was not put into production, but formed the basis for the 101B, 102 and 201 production models. The 101B was marketed in the USA as the Cargo Commuterliner and differed from the 101 in having an improved 19 seat interior in passenger configuration and more powerful PT6A-36s. The 102 had a 20 seat passenger interior, or alternatively a 12 passenger executive interior or all freight configuration.

The 201 is primarily a military version. More than 70 were built, mainly for air arms of developing nations. The final Arava development was the 202, which is easily recognised by its large Whitcomb winglets, boundary layer fences inboard of each wingtip and slightly stretched fuselage. The winglets and boundary layer fences were offered as a kit for retrofitting to existing Aravas.

Arava production ceased in the late 1980s.

Photo: A Tierra del Fuego Island government operated Arava at Ushuaia, Argentina. (Juan Pablo Marini)

IAI Westwind

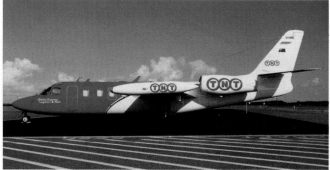

Country of origin: Israel

Type: Small to mid size corporate jet

Powerplants: 1123 – Two 13.8kN (3100lb) General Electric CJ610-9 turbojets. 1124A – Two 16.5kN (3700lb) Garrett TFE731-1-100G turbofans.

Performance: 1123 – Max cruising speed 870km/h (470kt), economical cruising speed 755km/h (408kt). Initial rate of climb 4040ft/min. Service ceiling 45,000ft. Max range 3410km (1840nm), range with max payload 2575km (1390nm). 1124A – Max speed 868km/h (469kt), economical cruising speed 723km/h (390kt). Range with max payload and reserves 4430km (2390nm), range with four passengers and max fuel 5385km (2905nm).

Weights: 1123 – Operating empty 5330kg (11,750lb), max takeoff 9390kg (20,700lb). 1124A – Operating empty 6010kg (13,250lb), max takeoff 10,660kg (23,500lb).

Dimensions: 1123 & 1124A – Wing span 13.65m (44ft 5in), length 15.93m (52ft 3in), height 4.81m (15ft 10in). Wing area 28.6m² (308.3sq ft).

Capacity: Flightcrew of two. Standard seating for seven in typical corporate layout, max seating for 10. Many configured as freighters.

Production: 150 1121s built. More than 250 Westwinds built, incl 36 with turbojets. 51 1121s, 25 1123s and 242 1124s in service in 2002.

History: The IAI Westwind has become one of the success stories of the small but effective Israeli aviation industry.

The Westwind started life as the Aero Commander 1121 Jet Commander, a General Electric CJ610 turbojet powered small executive jet based on Aero Commander's successful piston and turboprop twin line (described under Rockwell). The first 1121 flew on January 27 1963, with deliveries of slightly stretched production aircraft from January 1965. However North American shortly afterwards acquired Aero Commander, and as it was already building the Sabreliner (described under Rockwell), the Jet Commander had to be sold because of competition laws, so design and production rights for the Jet Commander were sold to Israel Aircraft Industries (IAI) in 1967.

IAI continued production of the Jet Commander as the improved 1121A and 1121B Commodore Jet – total US/Israeli 1121 production was 150, production was transferred to Israel between 1967 and mid 1969. IAI then developed the 1123 Westwind (originally Commodore Jet Eleven 23) with a stretched fuselage allowing seating for 10 passengers. The Westwind first flew on September 28 1970. Thirty-six turbojet powered 1123s were built before production transferred to the Garrett TFE731 turbofan powered 1124 (known as the Westwind I from 1981), the first of which were delivered in mid 1976. The 1124N Sea Scan was announced in 1976 and is a radar equipped maritime patrol and surveillance derivative.

Development of the basic 1124 led to the 1124A Westwind 2 with improved hot and high performance, better fuel economy and longer range. Delivered from May 1980, changes over the 1124 included a modified wing section, winglets, flat cabin floor and other interior improvements. Production ceased in 1987 in favour of the 1125 Astra (now the Gulfstream 100).

Photo: A 1124 Westwind used for package freight. (Richard Hall)

Ibis Aerospace Ae270

Countries of origin: Czech Republic & Taiwan

Type: Turboprop utility & corporate transport

Powerplants: Ae270 HP – One 634kW (850shp) PT6A-66A driving a four blade propeller.

Performance: Ae270 HP – Max cruising speed at 25,000ft 500km/h (270kt). Initial rate of climb 1900ft/min. Certificated ceiling 30,000ft. Range with reserves 2985km (1610nm).

Weights: Ae270 HP – Empty 2300kg (5070lb), max takeoff 3800kg (8380lb).

Dimensions: Wing span 13.82m (45ft 4in), length 12.23m (40ft 1in), height 4.78m (15ft 8in). Wing area 21.0m^2 (226.0sq ft).

Capacity: Flightcrew of one or two pilots. Main cabin seating for up to eight in a passenger configuration, or six or seven forward facing seats or four seats in a club arrangement in corporate configurations. Can be configured for freight or in an aeromedical configuration with two stretchers.

Production: 69 on order at late 2002. Deliveries planned for early 2004.

History: The single engine Ibis Ae270 turboprop is aimed at corporate, commuter airliner and utility operators, and is being developed by Czech and Taiwanese interests.

The Ae270 was originally designed by Czech Republic based Aero, a company better known for its L-29 and L-39 military jet trainers (in fact Aero has built more jet trainers than any other company in the world). Aero announced it was working on the L-270 (as the Ae270 was then designated) in 1990, with design configuration finalised the following year. Aero had planned to build two L-270 models, the basic Motorlet M 601 E powered, unpressurised, fixed landing gear Ae270 U, and the pressurised, retractable undercarriage, P&WC PT6A-42 powered Ae270 MP equipped with Bendix-King avionics. In 1993 Aero adopted the Ibis name for the aircraft and refined the two models with the Ae270 MP evolving to become the Ae270P with AlliedSignal avionics, with the Ae270 U becoming the Ae270 W.

After some delays, in 1997 Aero and Taiwan's AIDC formed Ibis Aerospace as a 50:50 joint venture company to develop and produce the Ae270. Under the new joint venture company arrangement final assembly will take place in the Czech republic, while the wings and landing gear will be built in Taiwan.

The Ae270 P prototype was rolled out on December 10 1999 with first flight on July 25 2000. A second prototype flew on January 11 2002.

At the NBAA's annual convention in New Orleans in October 2000 Ibis announced development of the improved performance Ae270 HP. The Ae270 HP, which will be the production standard, has a more powerful PT6A-66A engine and will cruise at higher speeds. EFIS avionics will be standard. The third prototype was built to this configuration, and flew in late 2002. Certification is planned for late 2003.

Ibis plans a production rate of two aircraft per month from the first quarter of 2004.

Photo: The third prototype Ae270 on its first flight. The Ae270 is sized between the TBM700 and PC-12. (Ibis Aerospace)

Ilyushin Il-18

Country of origin: Russia

Type: Medium range turboprop airliner

Powerplants: Il-18D – Four 3170kW (4250shp) Ivchenko Al-20M turboprops driving four blade propellers.

Performance: Max cruising speed 675km/h (365kt), economical cruising speed 625km/h (337kt). Range with max payload and reserves 3700km (1995nm), with max fuel and reserves 6500km (3510nm).

Weights: Empty equipped (with 90 seats) 35,000kg (77,160lb), max takeoff 64,000kg (141,095lb).

Dimensions: Wing span 37.40m (122ft 9in), length 35.90m (117ft 9in), height 10.17m (33ft 4in). Wing area 140m^2 (1507sq ft).

Capacity: Flightcrew of five comprising two pilots, flight engineer, navigator and radio operator. Initial Il-18s seated 75, the Il-18B 84, Il-18C 90 to 100, Il-18D and Il-18E 110 or max 122 at six abreast.

Production: Estimated production of over 600 aircraft for civilian operators, all initially delivered to airlines in the former Soviet Union, Eastern Europe, China, Cuba and various client states in Africa and Asia. Approximately 45 remained in service in 2002.

History: The Ilyushin Il-18 enjoyed one of the longest production runs of any turboprop airliner in the world and played a significant role in developing air services in Russia's remote regions in the 1960s and 1970s.

The Il-18 was developed in response to a mid 1950s Aeroflot requirement for an economical 75 to 100 seat medium range airliner. The prototype Il-18 (named *Moskva*) was powered by four 2985kW (4000shp) Kuznetsov SN-4 turboprops and flew for the first time on July 4 1957. The first Il-18 entered Aeroflot service on April 20 1959. The first international service – Moscow-London – was flown in October 1959.

Initial production Il-18s could seat 75 passengers and the first 20 were powered by the Kuznetsov engines before the 2985kW (4000shp) Ivchenko Al-20 became the standard powerplant on the Il-18B. From there on only minor changes characterised the Il-18's development life.

The Il-18B was the first major production model and featured a reconfigured interior to seat 84 passengers. The Il-18V entered service in 1961. It became the standard Aeroflot version and could seat up to 111 passengers, depending on configuration.

The Il-18D and domestic Il-18E were developed from the Il-18I prototype and introduced more powerful 3170kW (4250ehp) Al-20Ms, and could seat up to 122 passengers due to the rear cabin pressue bulkhead being moved further aft. The Il-18D is similar to the E but has extra fuel capacity with an additional centre section tank. During winter Aeroflot's Il-18Es would be reconfigured with fewer seats with the addition of a rear coat closet. On the Il-18D and E the APU is in the belly of the fuselage, rather than in the tail.

Il-18 production ceased in 1968.

The Il-18 has the NATO reporting name of 'Coot'. Like the Lockheed Electra, the Il-18 also formed the basis of a maritime patrol and anti submarine warfare aircraft, the Il-38 'May'.

Most Il-18s are now flown by secondary and charter operators.

Photo: A Russian registered Il-18 at Sharjah. (Rob Finlayson)

Ilyushin Il-62

Country of origin: Russia

Type: Medium to long range medium capacity airliner

Powerplants: Il-62 – Four 103.0kN (23,150lb) Kuznetsov NK-8-4 turbofans. Il-62M – Four 107.9kN (24,250lb) Soloviev D-30KU turbofans.

Performance: Il-62 – Cruising speed 820 to 900km/h (440kt to 485kt). Range with max payload and reserves 6700km (3610nm), range with 10 tonne (22,045lb) payload 9200km (4965nm). Il-62M – Speeds same. Range with max payload 7800km (4210nm), range with 10 tonne (22,045lb) payload 10,000km (5400nm).

Weights: Il-62 – Empty 66,400kg (146,390lb), operating empty 69,400kg (153,000lb), max takeoff 162,200kg (375,150lb). Il-62M – Operating empty 71,500kg (157,360lb), max takeoff 165,500kg (363,760lb).

Dimensions: Wing span 43.20m (141ft 9in), length 53.12m (174ft 4in), height 12.35m (40ft 6in). Wing area 279.6m² (3009sq ft).

Capacity: Flightcrew of five comprising two pilots, flight engineer, navigator and radio operator. Max seating for 174 in Il-62M, 186 in Il-62 and 195 in Il-62MK at six abreast in two cabins. Alternative configurations include 114 at five abreast, or 85 first class passengers.

Production: Over 250 of all models built, of which over 75 were exported. Production ceased in 1994. Approx 83 in service in 2002.

History: The four engined Il-62 was the Soviet Union's first long range jet airliner.

The prototype Ii-62 was first unveiled in September 1962, and like the contemporary British Vickers VC10 (which had first flown four months earlier) its design featured a T-tail and four rear mounted engines. Due to the unavailability of the chosen Kuznetsov NK-8 turbofans this aircraft made the type's first flight, in January 1963, powered by four 75.0kN (16,750lb) Lyulka AL-7 turbojets. Other design features included a wing sweep of 35°, three section ailerons, double slotted trailing edge flaps, two upper surface spoilers and fixed drooping leading edge extension on the outer two-thirds of the wings to combat limited control at low speed, a characteristic of T-tail aircraft. The four engines are rear mounted either side of the fuselage in pairs with only the outer two engines fitted with thrust reversers.

Prolonged development due to deep stall problems (something encountered by other T-tail aircraft) and problems with the NK-8 turbofan meant the Il-62 did not enter passenger revenue service until March 1967, while its first intercontinental service was in September 1967 between Moscow and Montreal.

The improved Il-62M appeared at the 1971 Paris Airshow and introduced more economical Soloviev D-30KU turbofans, increased fuel capacity, greatly improving payload-range performance, as well as an improved flightdeck and modified mechanised cargo holds capable of housing containers. The Il-62M entered service in 1974.

The Il-62MK was announced in 1978. It features an increased max takeoff weight of 167,000kg (368,170lb) which allows a maximum of 195 passengers to be carried.

Low rate production of the Il-62 ceased in 1994 when the final two aircraft were completed.

Photo: An Aviaenergo Il-62M. (Toni Marimon)

Ilyushin Il-76

Country of origin: Russia

Type: Freighter

Powerplants: Il-76T – Four 117.7kN (26,455lb) Aviadvigatel (Soloviev) D-30KP turbofans. Il-76MF – Four 156.9kN (35,275lb) Aviadvigatel PS-90AN turbofans.

Performance: Il-76T – Max speed 850km/h (460kt), cruising speed 750 to 800km/h (405 to 430kt). Max range with reserves 6700km (3615nm), range with 40 tonne (88,185lb) payload 5000km (2700nm). Il-76TD – Speeds same. Range with max payload 3650km (1970nm), with 20 tonne (44,090lb) payload 7300km (3940nm). Il-76MF – Cruising speed range 750 to 780km/h (405 to 420kt). Range with 40 tonne (88,185lb) payload 5200km (2805nm).

Weights: Il-76T – Max takeoff 170,000kg (374,785lb). Il-76TD – Max takeoff 190,000kg (418,875lb). Il-76MF – Operating empty 101,000kg (222,665lb), max payload 52,000kg (114,640lb), max takeoff 200,000kg (440,925lb).

Dimensions: Il-76T – Wing span 50.50m (165ft 8in), length 46.59m (152ft 10in), height 14.76m (48ft 5in). Wing area 300.0m² (3229.2sq ft). Il-76MF – Same except length 53.20m (174ft 6in).

Capacity: Flightcrew of five including two pilots, flight engineer, navigator and radio operator, plus two freight handlers. Il-76MP firefighting conversion can carry 44 tonnes (97,000lb) of fire retardant in two tanks.

Production: Over 800 Il-76s of all models built, most for the Russian military. Approx 295 were in commercial service in 2002.

History: The Ilyushin Il-76 (NATO reporting name 'Candid') was developed to replace the Antonov An-12, mainly for military use.

Development under the design leadership of G V Novozhilov in the late 1960s resulted in the type's first flight on March 25 1971. Series production commenced in 1975 and the first examples entered Aeroflot service that year.

The Il-76 features a high mounted wing, four engines, T-tail, rear loading ramp and freight doors. It also designed for short field operations from austere strips and to this end features wide span triple slotted trailing edge flaps, upper surface spoilers and near full span leading edge slats, and it rides on 20 low pressure tyres, the front nose unit featuring four wheels, the main wheel bogies having two rows of four tyres each. Freight handling is largely mechanised, requiring only two freight handlers which can be carried as part of the standard crew complement of seven.

Civil versions developed from the basic Il-76 include the Il-76T with additional fuel; the Il-76TD with increased takeoff and payload weights and D-30KP-2s which retain their power output to higher altitudes; and the Il-76MP firefighter. Military Il-76MDs (equivalent to the TD) are also in commercial service.

The stretched Aviadvigatel PS-90AN powered Il-76MF, which first flew on August 1 1995, would be built in Tashkent. Stage 3 compliant, it was originally intended for the Russian air force, but in 2002 the project was moribund due to a lack of funding. Civil aircraft would be designated Il-96TF.

Ilyushin has also planned to build a CFM56-5 powered version of the Il-76MF, which would be designated Il-76MF-100.

Photo: An Il-76TD. (Lars Wahlstrom)

Ilyushin Il-86

Country of origin: Russia

Type: Medium range widebody airliner

Powerplants: Four 127.5kN (28,660lb) KKBM (Kuznetsov) NK-86 turbofans.

Performance: Max cruising speed 950km/h (513kt), typical cruising speed between 900km/h (485kt) and 950km/h (513kt). Design range with 40 tonne (88,185lb) payload 3600km (1945nm), with max fuel 4600km (2485nm).

Weights: Max takeoff 208,000kg (458,560lb).

Dimensions: Wing span 48.06m (157ft 8in), length 59.94m (195ft 4in), height 15.81m (51ft 10in). Wing area 320m² (3444sq ft).

Capacity: Flightcrew of three comprising two pilots and flight engineer, with provision for a navigator. Max seating for 350 at nine abreast. Mixed two class seating for 234 comprising 28 six abreast in forward cabin and 206 eight abreast in other two cabins. Lower deck freight holds can accommodate up to 16 standard LD3 containers if some lower deck carry-on baggage racks are omitted.

Production: 103 built (including four military command posts). Approximately 83 were in service in late 2002, all with Russian and CIS operators and one Chinese airline.

History: Russia's first widebody airliner, the Ilyushin Il-86 has endured a chequered career. It has suffered from poor fuel economy, and failed to meet its modest design range, and was built in relatively small numbers.

Antonov, Tupolev and Ilyushin were asked to respond to Aeroflot's requirement for a widebody airliner, with Ilyushin's design proving successful. Il-86 development was announced at the 1971 Paris Airshow. Development was protracted and the first examples did not enter service until almost a decade later in late 1980.

The Il-86 initially was similar in configuration to the narrowbody Il-62, with four rear mounted turbofans and a T-tail. However the same problems that affect most T-tail designs – such as poor low speed handling, plus the heavy structural weight needed to support the four engines – caused a rethink, resulting in the adoption of a conventional tail and under wing mounted engine configuration.

Although a conventional design, one unusual feature of the Il-86 is that – where airport aerobridges are not provided – passengers can board the aircraft via airstairs leading to a lower deck baggage stowage area, before climbing a fixed internal staircase to the main passenger cabin.

The Il-86 prototype was unveiled in 1976. The first of two prototypes first flew on December 22 1976, while the first production aircraft flew on October 24 1977. Airline service began in December 1980 (Aeroflot had previously hoped to have it in service in time for the 1980 Moscow Olympic Games). Just over 100 had been built when production ended in 1994, the only change to the design to that time being a slight increase in max takeoff weight.

Plans to equip the Il-86 with CFM International CFM56 turbofans to dramatically improve fuel economy and range and reduce noise levels to within ICAO Stage 3 limits have been discussed at various times, but the cost of such an upgrade has always proved prohibitive.

Photo: An AJT Air International Il-86. (Steve Allsopp).

Ilyushin Il-96-300 & Il-96-400T

Country of origin: Russia

Type: Medium to long range widebody airliner

Powerplants: Four 156.9kN (35,275lb) Aviadvigatel (Soloviev) PS-90A turbofans.

Performance: Cruising speed 850 to 900km/h (460 to 485kt). Range with max payload and reserves 7500km (4050nm), with 30 tonne (66,140lb) payload 9000km (4860nm), with 15 tonne (33,070lb) payload 11,000km (5940nm).

Weights: Operating empty 117,000kg (257,940lb), max takeoff 216,000kg (476,200lb).

Dimensions: Wing span over winglets 60.11m (197ft 3in), length 55.35m (181ft 7in), height 17.55m (57ft 7in). Wing area 391.6m² (4215.0sq ft).

Capacity: Flightcrew of three, comprising two pilots and flight engineer. Basic single class seating for 300 at nine abreast in two cabins. Aeroflot aircraft being refurbished with new interiors seating 12 first, 21 business class and 180 economy class passengers. Forward lower freight hold accommodates six LD3 containers or pallets, rear hold accommodates 10 LD3s or pallets.

Production: 11 Il-96-300s in commercial service at late 2002, with 21 on order.

History: The Il-96-300 is a long range widebody airliner based on the older, larger Il-86.

Development of Russia's second widebody airliner began in the mid 1980s, resulting in the Il-96's first flight on September 28 1988. In all, three flying prototypes were built, plus two airframes to use for static and ground testing. Commonality in some areas with the Il-86 allowed a 1200 flight hour certification program, resulting in Russian certification being awarded on December 29 1992. The Il-96-300 entered service with Aeroflot Russian International Airlines the following year. Initial reliability was poor.

The Il-96-300 features a triplex fly-by-wire flight control system, a six screen EFIS flightdeck (however a flight engineer is retained, unlike modern western designs), some composite construction (including the flaps and main deck floors), and increased span wing and winglets. The PS-90A turbofans comply with ICAO Stage 3 noise limits (the Il-86's engines do not) and the Il-86's unique lower deck airstair design was deleted.

The Il-96-300 also formed the basis for the cancelled stretched and westernised Il-96M and Il-96T which feature a fuselage stretch, Pratt & Whitney PW2337 turbofans, and Rockwell Collins avionics including a modern two crew six screen EFIS flightdeck.

The Il-96MO prototype, a converted Il-96-300, first flew on April 6 1993, while a production Il-96T freighter was rolled out on April 26 1997. Russian certification for the Il-96T was awarded on March 31 1998, followed by US FAA certification on June 2 1999.

Ilyushin cancelled the Il-96M program in mid 2001 after it failed to organise funding for production. Instead it has converted the Il-96T to Il-96-400T standard with Russian avionics and PS-90A engines. Uncompleted Il-96M airframes could be refurbished as Il-96-400Ts.

Photo: An Il-96-300. (Toni Marimon)

Ilyushin Il-103

Country of origin: Russia

Type: Four/five seat light aircraft

Powerplants: One 157kW (210hp) Teledyne Continental IO-360-ES2B fuel injected flat six piston engine driving a two blade variable pitch Hartzell propeller.

Performance: Max speed 220km/h (119kt), cruising speed 180km/h (97kt). Initial rate of climb 623ft/min. Max range with pilot, 270kg (595lb) payload and reserves 800km (432nm).

Weights: Empty 900kg (1984lb), max takeoff (utility) 1285kg (2832lb).

Dimensions: Wing span 10.56m (34ft 8in), length 8.00m (26ft 3in), height 3.13m (10ft 4in). Wing area 14.7m² (158.4sq ft).

Capacity: Seating for four or five, with rear bench seat for either two or three.

Production: Approximately 30 have been built, production appears to have ceased in 2000, but may be resumed.

History: The Il-103 light aircraft was developed to meet both eastern and western certification standards.

The Il-103 was originally conceived in response to a Russian requirement for 500 military and civil basic trainers. Program go-ahead for this new tourer and trainer was given in 1990. First flight was originally planned for the second half of 1993, although this was delayed until May 17 1994.

The Il-103 is fairly conventional in design and construction. It is powered by a 157kW (210hp) Teledyne Continental IO-360 driving a two blade variable pitch propeller, but has a surprisingly slow cruising speed compared with similarly powered western light aircraft. It features fixed tricycle undercarriage with a castoring nosewheel and anti lock brakes on main wheels, control sticks with columns optional, and a 200 litre fuel capacity.

Il-103 construction is largely of aluminium, but the firewall frame and wingroot attachments are made from titanium, and the wingtips are from bonded glass fibre reinforced plastic.

Ilyushin has received both Russian and US FAA FAR Part 23 certification. Russian AP-23 certification (equivalent to FAR Part 23) was awarded in February 1996, with first deliveries to local customers taking place later that year, while US certification was awarded in December 1998.

The Il-103 was developed in three basic models. The basic Il-103-01 is for the Russian market. The Il-103-10 was the export version with upgraded avionics, while the Il-103-11 was for export but with partially upgraded avionics compared to the Russian baseline fit. A fourth model, the Il-103SKh crop sprayer, flew in 2000.

Ilyushin also looked at certificating the Il-103 with a 1460kg (3218lb) max takeoff weight and a development with a 194kW (260hp) class Teledyne Continental or Textron Lycoming engine.

The Il-103's first export sale was an order for five for the Peruvian air force. Others were ordered by Russian aero clubs and flying schools. However production appears to have ceased in 2000, and the status of the Il-103 remains unclear.

Photo: The first prototype Il-103 with big brother Il-96M in the background. (Rob Finlayson)

Ilyushin Il-114

Countries of origin: Russia & Uzbekistan

Type: Turboprop regional airliner

Powerplants: Il-114 – Two 1840kW (2466shp) Klimov TV7-117S turboprops driving six blade SV-34 propellers

Performance: Il-114 – Max speed 500km/h (270kt), cruising speed 470km/h (254kt). Range with 64 passengers and reserves 1000km (540nm), with a 1500kg (3300lb) payload 4800km (2590nm).

Weights: Il-114 – Operating empty 15,000kg (33,070lb), max takeoff 23,500kg (50,045lb).

Dimensions: Il-114 – Wing span 30.00m (98ft 5in), length 26.88m (88ft 2in), height 9.32m (30ft 7in). Wing area 81.9m² (881.6sq ft).

Capacity: Flightcrew of two. Seating for 64 at four abreast and 75cm (30in) pitch. Il-114T freighter can carry a 6500kg (14,315lb) payload 1000km (540nm).

Production: Total 15 built or substantially completed by early 1998. No reports of new production since. Two Il-114Ts in service with Uzbekistan Airways, one in service with Vyborg Airlines.

History: The Ilyushin Il-114 was designed to replace ageing fleets of turboprop airliners, including the Antonov An-24, in service on regional routes within the USSR.

Ilyushin finalised the Il-114's basic design and configuration in 1986, although the first prototype did not fly until March 29 1990. In total, three prototypes were built plus two static test airframes, with the original intention being to achieve certification and service entry in 1993. However the test program was delayed, caused at least in part by the crash of one of the prototypes on takeoff during a test flight in mid 1993. Russian certification was finally awarded on April 26 1997.

The Il-114 is of conventional configuration, but 10% of its structure by weight is of composites and advanced metal alloys, including titanium. It features low noise six blade composite propellers, and it can operate from unpaved airfields.

The Il-114 is the basic airliner and forms the basis for a number of developments. The Il-114T is a freighter developed for Uzbekistan Airlines. It is fitted with a 3.31 x 1.78m (10ft 10in x 5ft 10in) freight door in the rear port fuselage and a removable roller floor. The Il-114T entered service with Uzbekistan Airlines in 1998. The Il-114-N200S would feature a rear loading freight ramp.

The Il-114-100 (formerly Il-114PC) is powered by Pratt & Whitney Canada PW127 turboprops, increasing fuel economy and range. Ilyushin and P&WC signed a joint venture covering Il-114-100 development in June 1997 and the first example first flew on January 26 1999. Russian certification was awarded on December 27 that year.

The Il-114M would feature more powerful TV7M-117 engines and increased max takeoff weight allowing a payload of 7000kg (15,430lb) to be carried. The Il-114MA would feature the increased MTOW and P&WC engines, giving a cruising speed up to 650km/h (351kt).

The Il-114P would be a military maritime patrol variant while the Il-114FK is designed for elint, reconnaissance and cartographic work and would feature a glazed nose and raised flightdeck.

The Il-114 is assembled in Tashkent in Uzbekistan, but none appear to have been built since 1998.

Photo: The PW127 powered Il-114-100. (Paul Merritt)

Kaman K-Max

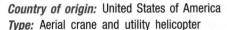

Country of origin: United States of America

Type: Aerial crane and utility helicopter

Powerplant: One 1119kW (1500shp) Honeywell T53-17A-1 turboshaft flat rated to 1007kW (1350shp) for takeoff driving two intermeshing two blade main rotors.

Performance: Never exceed speed 185km/h (100kt) or 130km/h (75kt) with an external load. Initial rate of climb 2500ft/min. Hovering ceiling out of ground effect 29,120ft. Range with max fuel 494km (267nm), range with max fuel and external load 396km (214nm).

Weights: Operating empty 2334kg (5145lb), max takeoff without jettisonable load 2948kg (6500lb), with jettisonable external load 5443kg (12,000lb).

Dimensions: Rotor diameter (each) 14.73m (48ft 4in), length overall rotors turning 15.85m (52ft 0in), fuselage length 12.73m (41ft 9in), height to centre of hubs 4.14m (13ft 7in). Total rotor disc area 340.9m^2 (3669.0sq ft).

Capacity: Accommodates pilot only but certificated with fuselage side mounted external seats (one either side). Designed to lift external loads such as Bambi firefighting buckets. The K-Max's maximum hook lifting capability is 2720kg (6000lb).

Production: The first K-Max delivered in Jan 1994. Over 31 built.

History: Kaman's first civil helicopter since the Ka-225 was certificated in 1949, the K-Max is a specialised helicopter designed specifically for aerial crane work.

The unusual looking K-2100 K-Max is easily identified by its characteristic intermeshing main rotors. The two main rotors have the dual advantages of allowing a low rotor disc area loading and that all the engine's power produces lift, and none is 'wasted' driving an anti torque tail rotor. The two main rotors are also fitted with trailing edge servo flaps that control the blades' angle of attack, negating the need for hydraulic power.

Power is supplied by a Honeywell (formerly AlliedSignal and Lycoming) T53-17A-1 turboshaft (equivalent to the military T53-L-703), the T53 also powers the Bell UH-1 Iroquois series (and the equivalent commercial Bell 204 and 205, described separately). The extremely high power to weight ratio of the K-Max means it can lift loads of up to 2720kg (6000lb).

The prototype K-Max first flew on December 23 1991. Certification was delayed somewhat by an early decision to improve the rotor system to increase performance margins, changes including lengthening the main rotors' diameters and increasing the rating of the transmission. US FAA certification was awarded in September 1994.

Recognising that the K-Max's high power to weight ratio may place inexperienced operators in difficult situations, Kaman took a very cautious approach to marketing the aircraft and leased out the first six production aircraft while flight experience was gained.

As an aerial crane the K-Max is suited to firefighting operations carrying various size Bambi buckets, logging, construction, surveying and aerial spraying. It was also demonstrated to the US Navy in the vertrep (vertical replenishment) role (due to USN requirements Kaman certificated the K-Max for IFR operations, awarded in 1999).

Photo: The K-Max features intermeshing twin rotors. (Bob Bell)

Kamov Ka-26 & Ka-226

Country of origin: Russia

Type: Light twin utility helicopters

Powerplants: Ka-26 – Two 240kW (325hp) Vedeneyev M-14V-26 radial piston engines driving two counter rotating main rotors.

Performance: Ka-26 – Max level speed 170km/h (90kt), max cruising speed 150km/h (80kt), economical cruising speed 90 to 110km/h (60 to 70kt), typical agwork operating speeds 30 to 115km/h (15 to 62kt). Service ceiling 9840ft. Range with seven passengers and reserves 400km (215nm), max range with auxiliary fuel tanks 1200km (647nm). Endurance at economical cruising speed 3hr 40min.

Weights: Ka-26 – Basic aircraft operating empty 1950kg (4300lb), max takeoff 3250kg (7165lb).

Dimensions: Ka-26 – Main rotor diameter (each) 13.00m (42ft 8in), fuselage length 7.75m (25ft 5in), height 4.05m (13ft 4in). Disc area of each main rotor 132.7m^2 (1430sq ft).

Capacity: Ka-26 – Seating for eight including one pilot and passenger separated from modular main cabin which seats six. For agwork can be fitted with a 900kg (1985lb) capacity hopper and spraybars in place of cabin. In air ambulance configuration can accommodate two stretchers and three seated casualties or medical attendants. For freight work it can carry a sling load or be operated with an open platform in place of the cabin module.

Production: Ka-26 – Approx 850 built for civil and military operators.

History: The unusually configured Kamov Ka-26 remains in widespread civil service in many former Soviet states.

The Ka-26 (which has the NATO reporting name 'Hoodlum') first flew in prototype form in 1965, but it did not enter service until 1970. More than 850 were built, mostly for civil applications.

The Ka-26 features two counter rotating main propellers, a Kamov design characteristic that negates the need for an anti torque tail rotor. Other features include the two podded radial piston engines mounted either side of the fuselage, and the removable and exchangeable rear fuselage model.

The interchangeable cabin means that the Ka-26 can perform a wide variety of missions, including passenger and freight transport, air ambulance, aerial survey, and search and rescue, among others, with a special mission specific rear fuselage pod fitted as needed. The fuselage pod can also be removed and the aircraft instead equipped with a chemical hopper and booms for crop spraying, or it can work as an aerial crane and can also carry sling loads of freight.

Ka-26 production evidently ceased in the late 1970s, although the design was developed into the turbine powered and modernised Ka-126 which first flew in 1986. Development of the Ka-126 continued into the mid 1990s but production was never undertaken.

Kamov is currently working on the improved Ka-226A Sergei. Enhancements include a new rotor system with hingeless hubs and glass fibre blades, and changes to the airframe including a reprofiled nose. Power is from two 335kW (450shp) Rolls-Royce 250-C20R/2 turboshafts. First flight was on September 4 1997. Kamov plans to achieve US certification for the Ka-226.

Photo: The Ka-226. (Sabastian Zacharias)

Kamov Ka-32

Country of origin: Russia

Type: Medium utility helicopter

Powerplants: Ka-32T – Two 1635kW (2190shp) Klimov TV3-117V turboshafts driving two counter rotating three blade main rotors.

Performance: Ka-32T – Max speed 250km/h (135kt), max cruising speed 230km/h (125kt). Service ceiling 16,400ft. Hovering ceiling out of ground effect 11,480ft. Range with max fuel 800km (430nm). Endurance with max fuel 4hr 30min.

Weights: Ka-32T – Empty 6500kg (14,330lb), normal loaded 11,000kg (24,250lb), max flight weight with sling 12,600kg (27,775lb).

Dimensions: Ka-32T – Main rotor diameter (each) 15.90m (52ft 2in), fuselage length 11.30m (37ft 1in), height 5.40m (17ft 9in). Rotor disc area (each) 198.5m² (2138sq ft).

Capacity: Pilot and navigator on flightdeck. Main cabin seats 16 passengers, or can be configured for freight carriage or as an air ambulance. Max internal payload is 4000kg (8820lb), max sling load weight is 5000kg (11,025lb).

Production: Approx 170 Ka-32s delivered, with approx 130 in service. A number have been leased by western companies and others operate throughout the globe on charter from their Russian owners.

History: The Kamov Ka-32 (NATO reporting name 'Helix-C') is a utility helicopter based on the military Ka-27.

Kamov began design work on the Ka-27 in 1969, its principle design objective being to provide a shipborne anti submarine warfare helicopter to replace the Ka-25 ('Hormone'). The Ka-27 prototype first flew in December 1974 and served as a prototype for the planned military and civil (Ka-32) variants. The Ka-27 was first noted in Soviet navy service in 1981, the same year that the first civil Ka-32 was publicly exhibited at Minsk. The Ka-27 and -32 feature the same overall configuration of the Ka-25, including the Kamov trademark of counter rotating propellers (negating the need for a tail rotor), plus twin vertical tails.

A number of versions of the basic Ka-32 have appeared thus far. The Ka-32T is the standard utility version, and is in use for a range of missions including passenger transport, air ambulance or flying crane. Although it features only basic avionics, it has been produced in greater numbers than the other Ka-32 derivatives. The Ka-32S meanwhile is fitted with a comprehensive IFR avionics suite for operations in poor weather conditions. Equipped for maritime operations, it is used from icebreakers, for maritime search and rescue, and offshore oil rig support, among other tasks.

The Ka-32K is optimised for use as a flying crane and features a retractable gondola beneath the fuselage for a second pilot who can manoeuvre the aircraft for accurate positioning. The Ka-32A is similar to the Ka-32T but is certificated (awarded in June 1993) to the Russian equivalent of US FAR Pt 29/Pt 33 airworthiness standards, and is offered with advanced avionics. In May 1998 the Ka-32A11BC was certificated by Transport Canada to FAR Pt 29, the first time a Russian helicopter had been awarded western certification.

Kamov is now working on the improved Ka-32M with 1839kW (2466shp) TV3-117VMA-SB3 turboshafts.

Photo: The Canadian certificated Ka-32A11BC.

Kazan Ansat

Country of origin: Russia

Type: Twin utility helicopter

Powerplant: Prototype – Two 477kW (640shp) takeoff rated, 418kW (560shp) max continuous rated Pratt & Whitney Canada PW206C turboshafts driving a four blade main rotor and two blade tail rotor. Production aircraft will have PW206Ks.

Performance: Max speed 285km/h (153kt), max cruising speed 250km/h (135kt). Initial rate of climb S/L 3150ft/min. Service ceiling 14,760ft. Hovering ceiling in ground effect 9180ft, out of ground effect 8540ft. Range with max normal fuel 540km (290nm), ferry range with auxiliary tanks 1300km (700nm). Endurance 3hr 30min.

Weights: Empty equipped 1900kg (4189lb), normal max takeoff 3000kg (6613lb), max takeoff 3300kg (7275lb).

Dimensions: Main rotor diameter 11.50m (37ft 9in), length overall rotors turning 13.76m (45ft 2in), fuselage length 11.06m (36ft 5in), height 3.40m (11ft 2in). Main rotor disc area 103.9m² (1118.0sq ft).

Capacity: Seating for up to 11 including pilot and passenger beside pilot. In EMS configuration can accommodate two stretcher patients and three medical attendants. Corporate configuration seats five in main cabin. Max external payload 1300kg (2865lb).

Production: Two prototypes flying by late 2002. Various Russian organisations have announced intentions to buy Ansats, including the border guards and Gazprom.

History: The Ansat is the first inhouse design of Russian helicopter manufacturer Kazan, an organisation that has built over 4000 Mi-8s and Mi-17s.

Tartarstan's Kazan Helicopters established its design bureau in 1993, beginning work on a new multirole light twin helicopter after surveying the needs of Russian helicopter operators. Early design goals include a 3.3 tonne max takeoff weight and compliance with US FAR Part 29 certification.

Kazan displayed a fuselage mockup of the Ansat (which in Tartar means 'easy' or 'plain') at the 1995 Paris Airshow. A revised engineering mockup, used for engine ground running tests, was shown at the 1997 Paris show. The first prototype was displayed at the 1998 Farnborough Airshow and made its first flight on August 17 1999. The second, revised prototype (with a redesigned nose with) was completed in late 2001.

Ansat design features included its twin Pratt & Whitney Canada PW206C turboshafts with FADEC (production aircraft will feature PW206Ks licence built in Russia), an Avionika quadruplex fly-by-wire flight control system linked to a roll, direction, pitch and collective pitch control system, four blade glass fibre construction main rotor and hingeless hub, Russian avionics including a colour multifunction display (with western avionics to be optional), skid undercarriage, and a baggage bay behind the cabin. A weather radar can be mounted in the nose, and the engine inlets fitted with sand filters. Another option is an emergency floatation system.

Kazan expected to finalise certification testing of the Ansat before the end of 2003.

Photo: The second prototype Ansat features a reprofiled nose compared to the first aircraft. (Kazan)

Lake LA-4, Buccaneer & Renegade

Country of origin: United States of America

Type: Four/six seat amphibious light aircraft

Powerplant: LA-4 – One 135kW (180hp) Lycoming O-360-A1A flat four piston engine driving a two blade fixed pitch propeller. LA-4-200 – One 150kW (200hp) fuel injected IO-360-A1B. Turbo 270 – One 185kW (250hp) turbocharged TIO-540-AA1AD flat six.

Performance: LA-4 – Max speed 217km/h (117kt), max cruising speed 210km/h (114kt), typical cruising speed 200km/h (109kt). Initial rate of climb 800ft/min. Service ceiling 14,000ft. Max range 1010km (545nm). LA-4-200 – Max speed 248km/h (134kt), max cruising speed 240km/h (130kt), long range cruising speed 213km/h (115kt). Initial rate of climb 1200ft/min. Ceiling 14,700ft. Max range 1327km (717nm). Turbo 270 – Max cruising speed 287km/h (155kt). Service ceiling 23,800ft. Max range no reserves at 55% power 2075km (1120nm).

Weights: LA-4 – Empty 715kg (1575lb), max takeoff 1090kg (2400lb). LA-4-200 – Empty 705kg (1555lb), MTOW 1220kg (2690lb). Turbo 270 – Empty equipped 875kg (1930lb), max takeoff 1383kg (3050lb).

Dimensions: LA-4 & LA-4-200 – Wing span 11.58m (38ft 0in), length 7.59m (24ft 11in), height 2.84m (9ft 4in). Wing area 15.8m² (170.0sq ft). Turbo 270 – Wing span 11.68m (38ft 4in), length 8.64m (28ft 4in), height 3.05m (10ft 0in). Wing area 15.2m² (164.0sq ft).

Capacity: Four in LA-4 and Buccaneer; six in Renegade and Turbo Renegade.

Production: Over 1000 built, including over 300 Renegades.

History: This LA-4 series is the world's most successful family of amphibious light aircraft (exceeding Republic's Seabee).

The LA-4 series dates back to the Colonial C-1 Skimmer, a three place light amphibian which first flew in July 1948. The C-1 eventually entered production powered by a 110kW (150hp) Lycoming O-320 in 1955, and small numbers of it and the four seat 135kW (180hp) O-360 powered C-2 Skimmer IV were built before Lake Aircraft purchased the manufacturing and design rights in October 1959.

Lake's prototype LA-4P was a development of the Skimmer IV, and first flew in November 1959. Put into production in August 1960, the production LA-4 differed from the Skimmer IV in having greater wing span, strengthened structure and higher weights. The LA-4 remained in production until 1972 (small numbers of seaplane only LA-4Ts were built), by which stage the improved LA-4-200 Buccaneer had been in production for two years. The LA-4-200 had a more powerful engine, extra fuel and higher weights.

The LA-250 Renegade was certificated in 1983. It introduced a number of changes over the Buccaneer including the more powerful six cylinder IO-540 engine and a lengthened fuselage with seating for six. It was joined by the turbocharged (TIO-540-AA1AD powered) Turbo 270 Renegade. The Special Edition Seafury and Special Edition Turbo Seafury were based on the Renegade and Turbo Renegade respectively, and featured enhancements for salt water operations. Production ceased in the mid 1990s.

In 2002 Lake Aircraft was purchased by Wadi Rahim, who planned to restart production of the Renegade and Turbo Renegade, under the Sun Lake Aircraft banner.

Photo: An LA-4-200 Buccaneer. (Paul Sadler)

Lancair Columbia 300, 350 & 400

Country of origin: United States of America

Type: High performance four seat light aircraft

Powerplant: 300 – One 225kW (300hp) Teledyne Continental IO-550-N2B flat six piston engine driving a three blade constant speed Hartzell prop.

Performance: 300 – Normal cruising speed at 75% power 353km/h (191kt). Initial rate of climb 1340ft/min. Service ceiling 18,000ft. Range 2038km (1100nm).

Weights: 300 – Empty 998kg (2200lb), max takeoff 1542kg (3400lb).

Dimensions: 300 – Wing span 11.00m (36ft 1in), length 7.67m (25ft 2in), height 2.74m (9ft 0in). Wing area 13.1m² (141.2sq ft).

Capacity: Standard seating for four.

Production: 300 – More than 300 on order by late 2000. 56 delivered when production suspended in July 2002. Production resumed late that year. 350 & 400 – First deliveries planned for early 2003.

History: Lancair's Columbia 300, 350 and 400 are high performance, composite construction factory built aircraft from a company famous for its high performance kit aircraft.

The Columbia 300 is Lancair's first production aircraft, but the Redmond, Oregon based Lancair was established in 1984 by Lance Neibauer, and has built more than 1500 high performance aircraft kits.

Lancair announced it was developing the Columbia, then designated the LC-40, in 1996. An aerodynamic prototype began test flying in July 1996 while the first certification prototype first flew in early 1997. The type's first public appearance was at the 1997 Oshkosh Airshow as the Columbia 300. Certification was awarded on October 1 1998. Deliveries of production aircraft (built at a new factory at Redmond's Bend Municipal Airport) began in February 2000. Financial problems forced Lancair to cease production temporarily in mid 2002 until a new financial backer invested in the company.

The Columbia 300 features composite construction allowing a smooth, low drag external finish. Power is from a six cylinder 225kW (300hp) Continental IO-550. The 300 features a 402 litre (106US gal/ 82Imp gal) fuel capacity, IFR avionics and fixed undercarriage.

In July 2002 Lancair revealed the improved Lancair 350, an all electric version of the 300, with a dual bus, dual battery electrical system eliminating the need for vacuum pumps.

Lancair announced turbocharged Columbia 400 in early 2000. The 400 is based on the 300 but features a twin turbocharged, twin intercooled 231kW (310hp) Teledyne Continental TSIO-550-G, giving a cruising speed of 426km/h (230kt) at 18,000ft. Like the 350, it is all electric with no vacuum system. First flight was in June 2000.

The 350 and 400 are offered with an optional glass cockpit. The Avidyne Flightmax Entegra integrated flightdeck features a primary flight display (PFD) and an EX5000 multifunction display. The PFD displays standard flight instrumentation including attitude direction, horizontal situation indicator, altitude, airspeed and vertical speed. The MFD can display a moving map with terrain, and in the future will be able to display datalinked traffic and weather information.

A FADEC engine management system, allowing single lever control for power, mixture and the prop, will be introduced later.

Photo: The Columbia 300 in flight. (Lancair)

Learjet 23, 24, 25, 28 & 29

Country of origin: United States of America

Type: Light corporate jets

Powerplants: 23 – Two 12.7kN (2850lb) General Electric CJ610-4 turbojets. 25D & 29 – Two 13.1kN (2950lb) CJ610-8As.

Performance: 23 – Max speed 860km/h (465kt), max cruising speed 850km/h (460kt), economical cruising speed 817km/h (440kt). Range with max fuel and reserves 2660km (1436nm). 25D – Cruising speed 860km/h (465kt). Range with four passengers and reserves 2663km (1438nm). 29 – Max speed 883km/h (477kt), max cruising speed 836km/h (452kt), economical cruising speed 756km/h (408kt). Service ceiling 51,000ft. Range with four passengers, max fuel and reserves 2550km (1376nm).

Weights: 23 – Empty 2974kg (6550lb), max takeoff 5675kg (12,500lb). 25D – Empty equipped 3465kg (7640lb), MTOW 6805kg (15,000lb). 29 – Empty 3730kg (8224lb), MTOW 6805kg (15,000lb).

Dimensions: 23 – Wing span 10.84m (35ft 8in), length 13.18m (43ft 3in), height 3.73m (12ft 3in). Wing area 21.5m² (231.8sq ft). 25D – Same except for length 14.50m (47ft 7in). 29 – Same as 25 except for wing span 13.35m (43ft 10in). Wing area 24.6m² (264.5sq ft).

Capacity: 23 & 24 – Two on flightdeck. Max seating in main cabin for six, typical seating for four. 25 & 28 – Flightcrew of two. Main cabin seating for up to eight passengers. 29 – Flightcrew of two and seating for six passengers.

Production: 745 turbojet power Learjets built, comprising 363 23/24s; 373 25s; five 28s and four 29s. In late 2002 34 23s, 211 24s, 314 25s, five 28s and four 29s were in service worldwide.

History: One of the world's largest, fastest, best selling and well known series of business jets, the Learjet family began with the original six to eight seat Learjet 23 which first flew on October 7 1963.

The 23 was designed and conceived by William (Bill) Lear in Switzerland as the SAAC-23, later named the Learjet 23. The diminutive 23 pioneered a new market for the light business jets, and proved very successful. The first production 23 was delivered in October 1964, but was replaced by the improved Model 24 in 1966 after 104 had been built. The 24, which introduced uprated engines and a number of detail changes, first flew in February 1966 and was delivered from the middle of that year. Developments of the 24 included the 24D, E and F, introducing improvements such as increased weights, thrusts, and range.

The Learjet 25 introduced a 1.27m (4ft 2in) fuselage stretch allowing seating for up to eight passengers and was first flown on August 12 1966. A number of improved developments of the 25 were built, including the B, D, F and G.

The unsuccessful Learjet 28 and 29 Longhorns were based on the 25 but introduced a new, increased span wing fitted with winglets. This improved fuel efficiency and overall performance, particularly payload range and fuel economy. The Longhorn 28 seats up to eight passengers, the Longhorn 29 sacrifices two seats for extra range. They are otherwise similar. Production of the family ceased in 1982.

Learjets are known for their tight accommodation. Max internal cabin width is just 1.50m (4ft 11in), max height 1.32m (4ft 4in).

Photo: The diminutive Learjet 23. (Gary Gentle)

Let L-200 Morava

Country of origin: Czech Republic

Type: Four/five seat light twin

Powerplants: L-200A – Two 155kW (210hp) Walter Minor M337 fuel injected inverted inline piston engines driving two blade variable pitch propellers. L-200D – Same except three blade constant speed props.

Performance: L-200A – Max speed 305km/h (165kt), max cruising speed 293km/h (158kt), long range cruising speed 256km/h (138kt). Initial rate of climb 1150ft/min. Service ceiling 20,340ft. Range with max fuel 1770km (955nm). L-200D – Max speed 290km/h (157kt), max cruising speed 282km/h (152kt), long range cruising speed 256km/h (138kt). Initial rate of climb 1260ft/min. Service ceiling 18,700ft. Range with max fuel 1710km (923kt).

Weights: L-200A – Empty 1275kg (2810lb), max takeoff 1950kg (4300lb). L-200D – Empty 1330kg (2932lb), max takeoff 1950kg (4300lb).

Dimensions: Wing span 12.31m (40ft 5in), length 8.61m (28ft 3in), height 2.25m (7ft 4in). Wing area 17.3m² (186sq ft).

Capacity: Typical seating for four or five, with pilot and passenger in individual seats and two or three passengers on rear bench seat.

Production: Total L-200 production over 1000, including approximately 160 L-200As.

History: The Let L-200 Morava retractable four seat light twin was one of the few light aircraft to be exported from behind the Iron Curtain during the Cold War era, although in small numbers.

Ladislav Smrek of the Czechoslovakian State Aircraft Factory designed the L-200 in the mid 1950s to replace the early postwar vintage Aero 45 and 145 light twins. His resulting design is similar in many ways to its contemporary western twins, with a four or five place cabin, a low wing, wingtip tanks, metal construction and retractable undercarriage. However the Morava is distinguishable by its twin tails, standard thermal wing de-icing equipment and inverted inline engines.

The prototype XL-200 Morava first flew on April 8 1957. The XL-200 prototype and a series of preproduction L-200s were powered by 120kW (160hp) Walter Minor 6-III inline sixes. Initial production was of the L-200A, which differed from the L-200 in being powered by two 155kW (210hp) fuel injected M337s, and had greater weights, a reprofiled cabin and hydraulically (rather than electrically) operated undercarriage and flaps.

Let built 160 L-200s before production switched to the improved L-200D. Features include a strengthened undercarriage, improved hydraulic and electrical systems and constant speed three blade propellers. The L-200D remained in production until 1969, and a number were licence built in Slovenia (then part of Yugoslavia). A turboprop powered development was studied but not built.

Most L-200 production was for customers within the Soviet Bloc – Aeroflot for example operated several hundred in a range of roles including air taxi, air ambulance and communications duties. However small numbers were exported to western Europe, the USA and elsewhere.

Photo: An Australian registered L-200A. (Bill Lines)

Let L 410 & L 420

Country of origin: Czech Republic

Type: 19 seat turboprop regional airliners

Powerplants: L 410 UVP-E – Two 560kW (750shp) Motorlet M 601 E turboprops driving five blade Avia propellers. L 420 – Two 580kW (775shp) M 601 Fs.

Performance: L 410 UVP-E – Max cruising speed 388km/h (210kt), economical cruising speed 365km/h (197kt). Initial rate of climb 1378ft/min. Service ceiling 24,300ft. Range with max fuel (including wingtip tanks), 920kg (2030lb) payload and reserves 1318km (707nm). 420 – Max cruising speed 390km/h (210kt). Initial rate of climb 1400ft/min. Range with max payload 560km (302nm), range with a 1015kg (2237lb) payload and max fuel including tip tanks 1358km (733nm), range with max fuel excluding tip tanks 940km (507nm).

Weights: L 410 UVP-E – Empty 3920kg (8720lb) to 4020kg (8863lb), operating empty 4120kg (9083lb) to 4180kg (9215lb), max takeoff 6600kg (14,550lb). L 420 – Basic empty 4065kg (8962lb), operating empty 4225kg (9314lb), max takeoff 6600kg (14,550lb).

Dimensions: Wing span over tip tanks 19.98m (65ft 7in), span excluding tip tanks 19.48m (63ft 11in), length 14.43m (47ft 4in), height 5.83m (19ft 2in). Wing area 34.9m² (375.2sq ft).

Capacity: Flightcrew of two. Typical commuter passenger seating for 17 or 19 at three abreast. Executive version seats 15 plus flight attendant. Cargo version equipped to handle special containers. Air ambulance version configured for six stretcher patients and six sitting passengers, either injured or medical attendants.

Production: Almost 1100 L 410s of all variants built, including 31 L 410As, 110 L 410Ms and 560 L 410 UVP-Es, with over 310 in service. One L 420 built.

History: The L 410 is very successful commuter which was first built in response to Soviet requirements, but sold widely around the globe.

Design studies of the original 15 seat L 410 began in 1966. The resulting design was named the Turbolet, and was developed to be capable of operations from unprepared strips. The powerplant chosen was the all new Walter or Motorlet M 601, but this engine was not sufficiently developed enough to power the prototypes, and Pratt & Whitney Canada PT6A-27s were fitted in their place. First flight occurred on April 16 1969, and series production began in 1970. Initial production L 410s were also powered by the PT6A, and it was not until 1973 that production aircraft L 410Ms featured the M 601.

The basic L 410 was superseded from 1979 by the L 410 UVP with a 47cm (1ft 7in) fuselage stretch, M 601B engines and detail refinements. The UVP was in turn replaced by the definitive UVP-E with improved M 601Es and five blade props, and the toilet and baggage compartments were repositioned allowing more efficient seating arrangements for up to 19 passengers.

The L 420 is an improved variant with more powerful M 601F engines, higher weights and improved performance designed to meet western certification requirements. It first flew on November 10 1993 and was awarded US FAA certification in March 1998.

Ayres took control of Let in September 1998 but Let ceased aircraft production in mid 2000 due to financial problems.

Photo: A Philippines L 410 UVP-E. (Greg Wood)

Liberty XL-2

Countries of origin: UK and USA

Type: Two seat light aircraft

Powerplants: One 93kW (125hp) Teledyne Continental IOF-240 flat four piston engine driving a two blade fixed pitch Dowty carbonfibre propeller.

Performance: Max cruising speed 245km/h (132kt), cruising speed at 55% power 222km/h (120kt), stalling speed flaps deployed 83km/h (45kt). Takeoff and landing run 229m (750ft). Range at 55% power with reserves 926km (500nm).

Weights: Empty (VFR equipped) 476kg (1050lb), max takeoff 750kg (1653lb).

Dimensions: Wing span 8.53m (28ft 0in), length 6.28m (20ft 6in), height 2.26m (7ft 4in). Wing area 10.4m² (112.0sq ft).

Capacity: Standard seating for two, side by side.

Production: Over 60 on firm order at late 2002. Basic price $US116,500.

History: The Liberty XL-2 is a new two seat touring aeroplane aimed at owner pilots.

The XL-2 is based on the British Europa kitplane, with modifications to make it suitable for series production. Certification planned to US FAA FAR Part 23 standard. Design work on the XL-2 began in 1997, although the project was not publicly revealed until May 2000. In October that year at the AOPA USA convention, Montrose, California based Scaled Technology Works was announced as Liberty's production partner on the XL-2, responsible for building and flight testing the aircraft.

The prototype XL-2 made its official first flight on April 2 2001. FAA certification was originally planned for mid 2002 but was delayed due to Liberty's decision to fit the XL-2 with a larger 105 litre fuel tank and the FADEC equipped version of the Teledyne Continental IOF-240 piston engine. XL-2 certification was expected in April 2003, which would make it the first piston single certificated with FADEC.

The Powerlink FADEC IOF-240 allows a single lever power control and features computer controlled electronic fuel injection. Fuel burn at 55% power is 21.8 litres an hour. The specifically designed two blade Dowty prop is made from carbonfibre.

A Vision Microsystems VM1000FX digital engine information system is standard. Various avionics packages will be offered, including two levels of IFR fit.

The XL-2's airframe is a mixture of steel, aluminium and carbonfibre. A welded tubular steel chassis takes the loads from the engine, landing gear and wing. The wing and fuselage skins are made from carbonfibre, while the flying controls feature bonded aluminium skins. A revised nose cowling, improving aerodynamics and cooling efficiency, was incorporated into the design in mid 2002.

The XL-2 promises to be a roomy and capable two seat tourer. The cabin is 121cm (48in) wide. The XL-2's 274kg (603lb) useful payload is designed to allow two occupants, full fuel and baggage for touring. A 45kg (100lb) capacity baggage bay is located behind the seats. Leather seats are optional.

Photo: The XL-2 in flight. (Liberty Aerospace)

Lockheed Martin L-100 Hercules

Country of origin: United States of America

Type: Medium range freighter

Powerplants: L-100-30 – Four 3362kW (4508shp) Allison 501-D22A turboprops driving four blade constant speed propellers.

Performance: L-100-30 – Max cruising speed 571km/h (308kt). Range with max payload 2472km (1334nm), range with no payload 8950km (4830nm).

Weights: L-100-30 – Operating empty 35,260kg (77,736lb), max takeoff 70,310kg (155,000lb).

Dimensions: L-100-30 – Wing span 40.41m (132ft 7in), length 34.37m (112ft 9in), height 11.66m (38ft 3in). Wing area 162.1m² (1745.0sq ft).

Capacity: L-100-30 – Flightcrew of three or four. Max payload of 23,158kg (51,054lb) comprising pallets or containers.

Production: Approximately 35 civil standard L-100s are in commercial service. Some ex US Air Force C-130s are in commercial use, including as firebombers.

History: Lockheed's L-100 freighters are the civil equivalents of the venerable military C-130 Hercules, and have proven to be of great utility, particularly in developing countries.

Lockheed initiated design of the Hercules in response to a 1951 US Air Force requirement for a turboprop powered freighter. This resulted in the C-130 Hercules, which first flew in prototype form on August 23 1954. Design features included the high mounted wing, four Allison 501/T56 turboprops and the rear loading freight ramp. The USAF ordered the C-130 into series production in September 1952, and since that time more than 2200 have been built.

The C-130's appeal to freight operators led Lockheed to develop a civil version. The first commercial versions were based on the C-130E model, and a demilitarised demonstrator first flew in April 1964. This initial civil development, the Model 382, was awarded civil certification in February 1965. This model was soon followed up by the 382B, or the L-100, which introduced an improved freight handling system.

Sales of these initial versions were slow, leading Lockheed to develop the 2.54m (8ft 4in) stretched L-100-20 (Model 382E), which offered better freight capacity and operating economics. The L-100-20 was certificated in October 1968, but was soon followed by the even longer L-100-30. The -30 was 2.03m (6ft 8in) longer than the -20, first flew in August 1970, and was delivered from December that year. Most civil Hercules sales have been of the L-100-30 variant. The last L-100 was built in 1992, while the last military Allison 501/T56 powered C-130 was delivered in 1996.

The L-100J would be a commercial derivative of the new generation C-130J Hercules II. Improvements would include new Rolls-Royce AE 2100 advanced turboprop engines driving six blade props, two crew glass flightdeck and significantly lower maintenance and operating costs. The C-130J first flew on April 5 1996, while US FAA civil certification was awarded in September 1998. The L-100J would be based on the stretched fuselage C-130J-30 but in 2000 the program was frozen as Lockheed Martin focussed on the military variants.

Photo: An L-100-30 operated by Safair of South Africa. (Craig Murray)

Lockheed L-188 Electra

Country of origin: United States of America

Type: Turboprop airliner and freighter

Powerplants: L-188C – Four 2800kW (3750shp) Allison 501-D13 turboprops driving four blade constant speed propellers.

Performance: L-188C – Max cruising speed 652km/h (352kt), econ cruising speed 602km/h (325kt). Service ceiling 27,000ft. Range with max payload 3450km (1910nm), with max fuel 4023km (2180nm).

Weights: L-188C – Operating empty 27,895kg (61,500lb), max takeoff 52,664kg (116,000lb).

Dimensions: Wing span 30.18m (99ft 0in), length 31.81m (104ft 6in), height 10.01m (32ft 10in). Wing area 120.8m² (1300sq ft).

Capacity: Flightcrew of three. Single class seating for up to 104 passengers. Most aircraft now configured as freighters, max payload weight is approximately 12 tonnes (26,000lb).

Production: 170 Electras built, including 55 L-188Cs. Approx 40 in commercial service in late 2002, two used as corporate transports.

History: Lockheed's Electra provided a number of airlines with their introduction to turbine powered aircraft. Today it remains popular with freight operators.

The Lockheed L-188 Electra was developed to meet a 1954 American Airlines requirement for a domestic short to medium range 75 to 100 seat airliner. In June 1955 American ordered 35 of Lockheed's design, the L-188. Many other airlines shared American's interest in the L-188, and by the time the first prototype flew on December 6 1957, the order book stood at 144. Service entry was with Eastern Airlines (due to a pilots' strike at American) on January 12 1959.

However, any optimism Lockheed felt about a strong sales future would have been short lived, as a number of crashes in 1959 and 1960 (two of which where the aircraft broke up in flight) contributed to a number of order cancellations.

As an interim measure following the crashes, speed restrictions were imposed. Investigations uncovered a design defect with the engine mountings where the wing would shake and eventually brake up. Lockheed undertook a significant modification program where the nacelles, nacelle mountings and wing structure were strengthened, and the speed restrictions were eventually lifted in 1961. After that the Electra proved reliable and popular in service, but the damage had been done and production wound up in 1961 after 170 had been built.

The L-188A was the basic production aircraft, and accounted for most Electra sales. The L-188C entered service with KLM in 1959 and had greater fuel capacity and higher weights, and thus improved payload range performance.

Most Electras currently in service are configured as freighters. From 1967 Lockheed converted 41 Electras to freighters or convertible freighter/passenger aircraft, fitting a strengthened floor and a large cargo door forward of the wing on the left side. Other companies have also converted Electras to freighters. However, a small number remain in passenger service.

The Electra also formed the basis for the P-3 Orion maritime patrol aircraft – more than 600 were built.

Photo: An Atlantic Airlines Electra freighter. (Rob Finlayson)

Lockheed L-1011 TriStar

Country of origin: United States of America

Type: Medium to long range widebody airliner

Powerplants: L-1011-1 – Three 187kN (42,000lb) Rolls-Royce RB211-22B turbofans. L-1011-200 – Three 213.5kN (48,000lb) RB211-524s or 222.4kN (50,000lb) -524B or B4s.

Performance: L-1011-1 – Max cruising speed 973km/h (526kt), economical cruising speed 890km/h (463kt). Max range 5760km (3110nm). L-1011-200 – Speeds same. Range with max pax payload 6820km (3680nm), range with max fuel 9111km (4918nm).

Weights: L-1011-1 – Operating empty 109,045kg (240,400lb), max takeoff 195,045kg (430,000lb). L-1011-200 – Operating empty 112,670kg (248,000lb), max takeoff 211,375kg (466,000lb).

Dimensions: Wing span 47.34m (155ft 4in), length 54.17m (177ft 8in), height 16.87m (55ft 4in). Wing area 320.0m² (3456.0sq ft).

Capacity: Flightcrew of three. Max seating for 400 at 10 abreast and 76cm (30in) pitch. Typical two class seating for 256 at six abreast and nine abreast. Underfloor holds can accommodate 16 LD3s.

Production: Total TriStar production of 250, of which 200 were standard fuselage length -1, -100, -200 and -250 models. Approx 107 TriStars in commercial service in 2002, of which 70 were standard fuselage models, including 11 freighters.

History: The Lockheed TriStar was the second widebody airliner to be launched, and although it was dogged with early financial and development problems, particularly with the engine, it went on to gain an excellent reputation in service for its reliability, economy of operation and low noise emissions.

The L-1011 TriStar was the last Lockheed airliner to be developed and was launched in March 1968 in response to an American Airlines requirement (that also resulted in the DC-10) for a large capacity medium range airliner. Lockheed initially studied a twin engined layout, but it was decided that three engines would be necessary to ensure the new aircraft could take off at max weights from existing runways.

Work on the L-1011 prototype began early in 1969, resulting in a November 16 1970 first flight. The engine choice of Rolls-Royce's advanced three shaft design RB211 however dogged the TriStar's early career. Rolls-Royce went bankrupt in February 1970 largely due to higher than estimated RB211 development costs, severely harming both Lockheed and the TriStar sales program. The problems were fixed after the British government nationalised Rolls-Royce, guaranteeing the supply of production engines. Despite its initial problems the RB211 proved to be reliable and efficient.

The domestic L-1011-1 (which was built in greater numbers than any other TriStar variant) entered service with Eastern and TWA in April 1972. Subsequent models were the -100 with more fuel and higher weights, the -200 with higher thrust engines, and the long range -500, described separately. The -250 was a conversion of the -1 with RB211-524B4 engines (as on the -500) for US carrier Delta. Other L-1011-1 conversions were the L-1011-50 with increased max weight and the L-1011-150 with improved range. A small number have been converted to freighters.

Photo: ATA operates 12 standard length L-1011s. (Trent Jones)

Lockheed L-1011-500 TriStar

Country of origin: United States of America

Type: Long range widebody airliner

Powerplants: Three 222.4kN (50,000lb) Rolls-Royce RB211-524B or -525B4 turbofans.

Performance: Max cruising speed 960km/h (518kt), economical cruising speed 894km/h (483kt). Range with max pax payload 9905km (5345nm), range with max fuel 11,260km (6100nm).

Weights: Operating empty 111,310kg (245,500lb), max takeoff 231,330kg (510,000lb).

Dimensions: Wing span 50.09m (164ft 4in), length 50.05m (164ft 3in), height 16.87m (55ft 4in). Wing area 329.0m² (3540.0sq ft).

Capacity: Flightcrew of three. Max seating for 330 in a single class 10 abreast layout at 76cm (30in) pitch. Typical two class seating for 24 premium class at six abreast and 222 economy at nine abreast. Underfloor cargo holds can accommodate 19 standard LD3 containers.

Production: 50 L-1011-500s built, 33 were in commercial service in late 2002. Three used as corporate transports.

History: Lockheed developed the shortened fuselage L-1011-500 as a long range, smaller capacity TriStar based on the L-1011-200.

Launched in August 1976, the key changes incorporated in the -500 over the standard L-1011s are the 4.11m (13ft 6in) shorter fuselage, greater takeoff weights and more powerful RB211-524 engines. The shortened fuselage reduces seating capacity to a maximum of 330, 70 less than the standard length TriStars, while the below deck galleys that had been a feature of the L-1011 family were replaced with conventional main deck units.

Other improvements include enhanced wing-to-fuselage and fuselage-to-rear engine intake fairings, automatic braking and automatic thrust control. Most have three, rather than four, doors/emergency exits on each side of the fuselage. The design changes combine to give the -500 a maximum range of 11,260km (6100nm), approximately 2000km (1300nm) further than the long range -200.

The L-1011-500 first flew on October 16 1978 and entered service with British Airways in May 1979.

Soon after the -500 also introduced the active aileron improvements first pioneered on the Advanced TriStar, which was the original prototype TriStar fitted with a number of advanced features intended for introduction to the TriStar production line. The Advanced TriStar incorporated increased span wings to reduce drag, with active, automatic operation of the ailerons used to cope with the increased weight and aerodynamic loads instead of strengthening the wing structure.

The first -500 with active ailerons and extended wingtips flew in November 1979 and deliveries of -500s with the new wing tip extension began the following year, while in 1981 it became a standard feature. Lockheed began retrofitting the active aileron wingtip extension to all previously built L-1011-500s from 1981. Production ceased in 1983 after 50 had been built, although the last 500 was not delivered until 1985.

Nine ex Pan Am and British Airways -500s are operated by Britain's Royal Air Force as long range tanker-transports.

Photo: An BWIA West Indies Airways L-1011-500. (Lee Archer)

Lockheed JetStar

Country of origin: United States of America

Type: Large size corporate jet

Powerplants: JetStar – Four 14.7kN (3300lb) Pratt & Whitney JT12A-8 turbojets. JetStar II – Four 16.5kN (3700lb) Garrett TFE731-3 turbofans.

Performance: JetStar – Max speed 911km/h (492kt), economical cruising speed 816km/h (440kt). Range with max fuel and reserves 3595km (1940nm). JetStar II – Max cruising speed 880km/h (475kt), econ cruising speed 817km/h (440kt). Initial rate of climb 4200ft. Service ceiling 36,000ft. Range with max fuel and reserves 5132km (2770nm), range with max payload and reserves 4818km (2600nm).

Weights: JetStar – Operating empty 10,012kg (22,074lb), max takeoff 19,051kg (42,000lb). JetStar II – Operating empty 10,967kg (24,178lb), max takeoff 19,844kg (43,750lb).

Dimensions: Wing span 16.60m (54ft 5in), length 18.42m (60ft 5in), height 6.23m (20ft 5in). Wing area 50.4m² (542.5sq ft).

Capacity: Flightcrew of two. Seating for eight to 10 passengers.

Production: 164 turbojet powered JetStars built by mid 1973. Lockheed built 40 new build turbofan powered JetStar IIs from 1976. Garrett AiResearch converted 53 JetStars to JetStar 731 configuration. Approx 20 JT12 powered JetStars, 38 JetStar IIs and 42 JetStar 731s in service at late 2002.

History: The four engined JetStar was initially designed as a private venture but was also selected to fulfil a US Air Force requirement for a multi engined crew trainer and light transport.

The first JetStar prototype first flew on September 4 1957. Two prototypes were built powered by two Bristol Siddeley Orpheus turbojets, one of these was re-engined with four Pratt & Whitney JT12s in 1959 when an agreement to licence assemble the Orpheus in the United States could not be negotiated. The JT12 was selected for production aircraft, and the first of these flew in mid 1960.

Civil certification for the JetStar was awarded in August 1961, making the JetStar the first civil certificated business jet. Meanwhile the JetStar entered service with the USAF in late 1961 as the VC-140 VIP transport and in 1962 as the C-140 navaid calibration aircraft – the service had dropped its plans to use the aircraft as an aircrew trainer.

The JT12 turbojet powered JetStar was built through until mid 1973. The initial Dash 6 JetStar (or JetStar 6) with 10.7kN (2400lb) JT12A-6s and then 11.4kN (2570lb) JT12A-6As was replaced by the more powerful 14.7kN (3300lb) JT12A-8 powered Dash 8 JetStar (or JetStar 8) from 1967.

The improved JetStar II features four Garrett (previously AiResearch) TFE731 turbofans with their significantly improved fuel consumption, giving the aircraft better operating economics and range, plus lower noise levels. The first JetStar II flew on August 18 1976, with certification following in December that year. The II remained in production until 1979.

AiResearch meanwhile had already flown its own TFE731 powered conversion of the JetStar in July 1974. The first production AiResearch 731 JetStar conversion flew in March 1976.

Photo: A Lockheed JetStar 731. (Peter Tonna)

Luscombe Model 8 Silvaire

Country of origin: United States of America

Type: Two seat light aircraft

Powerplant: 8A – One 50kW (65hp) Continental A-65 flat four piston engine driving a two blade fixed pitch propeller. 8F Special – One 65kW (90hp) Continental C-90 flat four.

Performance: 8A – Max speed 185km/h (100kt), cruising speed at 75% power 165km/h (90kt). Initial rate of climb 900ft/min. Range 595km (320nm). 8F – Max speed 206km/h (111kt), max cruising speed 193km/h (104kt). Initial rate of climb 900ft/min. Range 804km (435nm).

Weights: 8A – Empty 302kg (665lb), max takeoff 545kg (1200lb). 8F Special – Empty 395kg (870lb), max takeoff 635kg (1400lb).

Dimensions: 8A & 8F Special – Wing span 10.68m (35ft 0in), length 6.10m (20ft 0in), height 1.78m (5ft 10in). Wing area 13.0m² (140.0sq ft).

Capacity: Seating for two side by side.

Production: Over 7500 Model 8s built between 1938 and 1960.

History: The Luscombe 8 Silvaire was a highly successful two seat high wing light aircraft which remains popular as a classic aircraft.

Prior to introducing the Silvaire into production in 1937, Luscombe had built a small number of two seat high wing light aircraft, the most popular of which was the Phantom, which was powered by a 108kW (145hp) Warner Super Scarab radial engine. The initial Model 8A Silvaire was similar to the Phantom in configuration but differed in that it was powered by a 50kW (65hp) Continental A-65 engine. A more up-market model was built from 1939, with more standard equipment and improved cabin trim. The 8B was similar to the 8A other than it was powered by a 50kW (60hp) Lycoming.

In 1941 Luscombe released the 8C which featured a 55kW (75hp) Continental engine, and the 8D, which differed in having wingtip fuel tanks. Over 1200 Model 8s were built through to early 1942 when production ceased due to the United States' entry into WW2.

After the war in late 1945 Luscombe resumed Silvaire production to meet the booming demand experienced by all US light aircraft manufacturers as returned military pilots wanted to continue flying in civilian life. From 1946 all Luscombes featured a new metal wing with a single strut. The first Silvaire to feature the new wing was the 8E, which was powered by a 65kW (85hp) Continental C-85-12 engine.

The final Silvaire production model was the 8F, which featured a 65kW (90hp) Continental C-90. The 8A Sky Pal meanwhile was a lower powered variant of the 8F with a Continental C-65.

Financial difficulties forced Luscombe to cease trading in 1949. US company Temco took over production and built a small number before it too ceased production in 1950. Finally, some Silvaires were built in Colorado between 1955 and 1960.

In 1998 Renaissance Aircraft revealed plans to reintroduce the 8F to production. Georgia based Renaissance's 8F features a 110kW (150hp) Textron Lycoming O-320 driving a metal propeller, dramatically improving performance, giving an estimated top speed of 243km/h (131kt) and a max rate of climb of 1500ft/min. A Luscombe built 8F was refurbished to serve as the prototype in 1999, manufacture of the first new build 8F was underway in 2002. Options include wheel spats, leather interior and IFR avionics.

Photo: A Silvaire at Hillsboro Airport, Oregon. (Keith Myers)

Maule M-4 to M-7

Country of origin: United States of America

Type: Four-five seat STOL light aircraft

Powerplant: M-4C – One 108kW (145hp) Continental O-300-A flat six piston engine driving a two blade fixed pitch propeller. MX-7-235 – One 175kW (235hp) Textron Lycoming O-540-J1A5D flat six or fuel injected IO-540-W1A5D driving a two or three blade prop.

Performance: M-4C – Max speed 245km/h (132kt), max cruising speed 233km/h (125kt). Initial rate of climb 700ft/min. Service ceiling 12,000ft. Max range no reserves 1130km (610nm). MX-7-235 (with IO-540) – Max speed 273km/h (147kt), max cruising speed 257km/h (140kt). Initial rate of climb 2000ft/min. Service ceiling 20,000ft. Range 790km (425nm), range with aux fuel 1496km (807nm).

Weights: M-4C – Empty 500kg (1100lb), max takeoff 953kg (2100lb). MX-7-235 – Empty 669kg (1475lb), max takeoff 1247kg (2750lb).

Dimensions: M-4C – Wing span 9.04m (29ft 8in), length 6.71m (22ft 0in), height 1.89m (6ft 3in). Wing area 14.2m² (152.5sq ft). MX-7-235 – Wing span 9.40m (30ft 10in), length 7.16m (23ft 6in), height 1.93m (6ft 4in). Wing area 15.4m² (165.6sq ft).

Capacity: Standard seating for four, M-7-235 has seats for five.

Production: More than 2000 of all variants produced.

History: The origins of this rugged series of STOL light aircraft lie in the Bee Dee M-4 (named after its designer Belford D Maule).

Although the M-4, which first flew on September 8 1960, was planned to be a kitbuilt aircraft, it was placed into series production.

The first of the line was the M-4 series, which was in production between 1962 and 1973. The initial M-4, or later M-4C Jetasen, was quite basic, featuring a 108kW (145hp) O-300 and fixed pitch prop. Other M-4 variants were the 155kW (210hp) Continental IO-360 powered M-4-210C Rocket and the 118kW (220hp) Franklin 6A-350 powered M-4-220C Strata-Rocket.

The M-5 series went into production in 1973 and featured a large swept back vertical tail surface, four cabin doors, optional extra fuel and the cambered wingtips first introduced on later series M-4s. Variants included the Franklin powered M-5-220C and Lycoming O-540 powered M-5-225C Lunar Rockets; the Continental powered M-5-210C and M-5-180C (with a four cylinder O-360); and the turbocharged Lycoming TIO-360 powered M-5-210TC.

The M-6 was only built in small numbers but introduced changes such as greater wing span and fuel tankage.

Maule Aircraft Production ceased in 1975, while Maule Air Inc was formed in 1984 to build the M-5 and improved M-7.

The M-7, which introduced a stretched cabin and increased fuel capacity, forms the basis of a prolific family of subvariants. Current production M-7s are built with five powerplant options: the 120kW (160hp) O-320 powered MX-7-160 and tricycle undercarriage MXT-7-160 family; the 134kW (180hp) M/MX/MXT-7-180; 175kW (235hp) M-7-235 and MT-7-235 series; the 194kW (260hp) O-540/ IO-540 powered M-7-260 and MT-7-260 range; and 313W (420shp) Rolls-Royce 250-B17C turboprop powered M and MT-7-420. Numerous subvariants are offered.

In late 2002 Maule was installing an SR 305 diesel in a M-7.

Photo: An M-5-235C Lunar Rocket. (Les Bushell)

McDonnell Douglas DC-9-10, -20 & -30

Country of origin: United States of America

Type: Short range airliners

Powerplants: -10 – Two 54.5kN (12,250lb) Pratt & Whitney JT8D-5 turbofans. -30 – Two 64.5kN (14,500lb) JT8D-9s, or two 66.7kN (15,000lb) JT8D-11s, or two 71.2kN (16,000lb) JT8D-17s.

Performance: -10 – Max cruising speed 903km/h (488kt), economical cruising speed 885km/h (478kt). Range with max payload 1055km (570nm). -30 – Max cruising speed 907km/h (490kt), long range cruise 798km/h (430kt). Range at high speed cruise with 64 passengers and reserves 2150km (1160nm), range at long range cruise with 80 passengers and reserves 3095km (1670nm).

Weights: -10 – Operating empty 22,635kg (49,900lb), max takeoff 41,140kg (90,700lb). -30 – Empty 25,940kg (57,190lb), max takeoff 54,885kg (121,000lb).

Dimensions: -10 – Wing span 27.25m (89ft 5in), length 31.82m (104ft 5in), height 8.38m (27ft 6in). Wing area 86.8m² (934sq ft). -30 – Same except for length 36.37m (119ft 4in), wing span 28.47m (93ft 5in). Wing area 93.0m² (1000.7sq ft).

Capacity: Flightcrew of two. -10 – Seating for 80 in a single class at five abreast and 86cm (34in) pitch. Max seating for 90. -30 – Max seating for 115 five abreast and 81cm (32in) pitch, standard single class seating for 105. DC-9-30CF can carry over eight cargo pallets.

Production: 976 DC-9s of all models built including 137 -10s, 10 -20s and 662 -30s (including military C-9s). 97 DC-9-10s, 4 DC-9-20s and 381 DC-9-30s in airline service at late 2002. 1 DC-9-10, 8 DC-9-15s and 3 DC-9-30s used as corporate jets at late 2002.

History: No other airliner in history has undergone more development than the prolific DC-9/MD-80/MD-90/717 series, which started life with the 70 seat DC-9-10 of the early sixties.

Douglas developed the DC-9 as a short range airliner complementing the much larger DC-8. Development was launched on April 8 1963, with a launch order from Delta following soon after. The DC-9 was an all new design, featuring rear fuselage mounted engines, a T-tail, moderately swept wings and seats for up to 90 passengers in a five abreast fuselage.

Construction of the prototype began in July 1963 with first flight on February 25 1965. Certification and service entry was on November 23 and December 8 1965, respectively.

From the outset the DC-9 had been designed with stretched larger capacity developments in mind. The first stretch resulted in the biggest selling DC-9, the 4.54m (14ft 11in) longer, 105 seat DC-9-30, which entered service with Eastern on February 1 1967. Subsequent stretched versions are described separately.

Small numbers of developed versions of the DC-9-10 were also built. The DC-9-20 featured the DC-9-10's fuselage with the -30's more powerful engines and longer span wings, giving better hot and high performance. The DC-9-15 was basically a -10 but with more fuel and higher weights. Factory built convertibles and pure freighters were also offered, while a number of DC-9-30s have been converted to freighters, and/or are having Stage 3 hushkits fitted, further extending their useful service lives.

Photo: An Aerocaribe DC-9-30. (Sam Chui)

McDonnell Douglas DC-9-40 & -50

Country of origin: United States of America

Type: Short to medium range airliners

Powerplants: -40 – Two 64.5kN (14,500lb) Pratt & Whitney JT8D-9 turbofans, or two 69.0kN (15,500lb) JT9D-15s, or two 71.2kN (16,000lb) JT8D-17s. -50 – Two 69.0kN (15,500lb) JT8D-15s, or two 71.2kN (16,000lb) JT8D-17s.

Performance: -40 – Max cruising speed 898km/h (485kt), long range cruising speed 820km/h (443kt). Range at high speed cruise with 70 passengers and reserves 1725km (930nm), range with 87 passengers and reserves at long range cruising speed 2880km (1555nm). -50 – Speeds same except for max speed 926km/h (500kt). Range at long range cruising speed with 97 passengers and reserves 3325km (1795nm).

Weights: -40 – Empty 26,612kg (58,670lb), MTOW 54,885kg (121,000lb). -50 – Empty 28,068kg (61,880lb), MTOW 54,885kg (121,000lb).

Dimensions: -40 – Wing span 28.47m (93ft 5in), length 38.28m (125ft 7in), height 8.53m (28ft 0in). Wing area 93.0 m² (1000.7sq ft). -50 – Same except for length 40.72m (133ft 7in).

Capacity: Flightcrew of two. -40 – Seating for up to 125 passengers at five abreast. -50 – Seating up to 139 passengers at five abreast and 79cm (31in) pitch.

Production: Total DC-9 production of 976, including 71 Series 40s and 96 Series 50s. Approximately 53 -40s and 46 -50s remained in service in late 2002.

History: The DC-9-40 and DC-9-50 are stretched developments of the DC-9-30 and predecessors to the later further lengthened MD-80 and MD-90 series.

The DC-9-40 was developed in response to a Scandinavian Airline System (SAS) requirement for a larger capacity development of the DC-9. Compared with the DC-9-30, the DC-9-40 is 1.91m (6ft 4in) longer, raising seating capacity in a single class configuration to 125. Apart from the fuselage stretch and more powerful engine options, the -40 was much the same as the -30. First flight occurred on November 28 1967, and the -40 entered service with SAS on March 12 the following year.

The DC-9-50 is the largest member of the DC-9/MD-80/MD-90/717 family to bear the DC-9 designation. Launched in mid 1973 and delivered from August 1975, the DC-9-50 is a further 2.44m (8ft 0in) longer than the DC-9-40, or 4.34m (14ft 3in) longer than the DC-9-30, and has maximum seating for 139 passengers. The DC-9-50 introduced a new look cabin interior designed to make more efficient use of the space available and give the impression of greater space, plus other improved features such as an improved anti skid braking system and quieter engines compared with the DC-9-40.

The DC-9-40 and -50 sold only in fairly modest numbers before the arrival of the further stretched MD-80 series. The largest DC-9-40 customer was SAS, while Northwest continues to operate a large fleet of DC-9-40s and -50s (it is currently the largest DC-9 operator in the world).

Photo: A Northwest DC-9-40 on pushback from a bleak Toronto. (Gary Gentle)

McDonnell Douglas MD-80

Country of origin: United States of America

Type: Short to medium range airliner

Powerplants: MD-81 – Two 82.3kN (18,500lb) Pratt & Whitney JT8D-209 turbofans. MD-88 – Two 93.4kN (21,000lb) JT8D-219s.

Performance: MD-81 – Max speed 925km/h (500kt), long range cruising speed 813km/h (440kt). Range with 155 passengers and reserves 2897km (1564nm). MD-88 – Speeds same. Range with 155 passengers and reserves 4850km (2620nm).

Weights: MD-81 – Operating empty 35,329kg (77,888lb), max takeoff 63,505kg (140,000lb), or 67,810kg (149,500lb) with JT8D-217As. MD-88 – Operating empty 35,369kg (77,976lb), max takeoff 67,810kg (149,500lb).

Dimensions: Wing span 32.87m (107ft 10in), length 45.06m (147ft 10in), height 9.02m (29ft 7in). Wing area 112.3m² (1209sq ft).

Capacity: Two flightcrew. Max seating for 172. Typical two class seating for 142 (14 premium and 128 economy class).

Production: MD-80 series (incl MD-87) orders totalled 1191 aircraft, of which over 1035 (exc MD-87) were in service in 2002.

History: The popular MD-80 series was a stretched and improved development of the McDonnell Douglas DC-9.

In 1975 McDonnell Douglas tested a standard DC-9 was fitted with improved, more efficient, higher bypass ratio JT8D-200 series turbofans. MDC originally proposed fitting the new engines (which meet Stage 3 noise limits) to a development designated the DC-9-55, which would have featured two JT8D-209s and a 3.86m (12ft 8in) stretched fuselage over the -50.

Instead MDC developed the DC-9 Super 80 (or DC-9-80), combining the new engines with a further stretched fuselage, increased span wing and other improvements. Launched in October 1977, the Super 80 first flew on October 18 1979. Certification for the initial Super 80 model, the 81, was granted on August 16 1980. The first customer delivery was to Swissair in September 1980.

McDonnell Douglas renamed the DC-9-80 the MD-80 in 1983. The generic MD-80 designation applies to the series with separate designations for different model types. The specific MD-80 models are the initial MD-81, the MD-82 with more powerful JT8D-217s, the extended range MD-83 with extra fuel and more efficient JT8D-219s, and the MD-88 (first flight August 1987) with the JT8D-219s, weights and fuel capacity of the MD-82 with an EFIS flightdeck and redesigned cabin interior, plus other improvements. The shorter fuselage but longer range MD-87 is described separately.

Early sales of the Super 80 were slow until American Airlines placed an initial order for 67 MD-82s (with options on 100) in early 1984. It became a highly successful program – the 1000th MD-80 was delivered in March 1992. (American remains the largest MD-80 operator with 266 MD-82s and 95 MD-83s.)

Boeing and McDonnell Douglas merged in 1997. That December Boeing announced its decision to cease MD-80 and MD-90 production once current orders were fulfilled. The 1191st and last MD-80, an MD-83 named *Spirit of Long Beach,* was delivered to TWA on December 21 1999.

Photo: A Swiss MD-83. (Swiss)

Country of origin: United States of America

Type: Short to medium range airliner

Powerplants: Two 89.0kN (20,000lb) Pratt & Whitney JT8D-217C turbofans. Other JT8D-200 series engines were available optionally.

Performance: Max speed 925km/h (500kt), long range cruising speed 811km/h (438kt). Range with 130 passengers and reserves 4393km (2372nm), or optionally 5248km (2833nm). Range with max fuel 5522km (2980nm), or optionally 6764km (3650nm).

Weights: Operating empty with standard fuel 33,237kg (73,274lb), operating empty with optional fuel 33,965kg (74,880lb), max takeoff 63,505kg (140,000lb), optionally 67,810kg (149,500lb).

Dimensions: Wing span 32.86m (107ft 10in), length 39.75m (130ft 5in), height 9.30m (30ft 6in). Wing area 112.3m² (1209.0sq ft).

Capacity; Flightcrew of two. Max seating for 139 passengers at five abreast at 81cm (32in) pitch. Two class seating for 117.

Production: Of total MD-80 sales of over 1100, 75 were for MD-87s. 69 were in commercial service in 2002, two were in use as corporate transports.

History: The MD-87 is a shortened version of the successful MD-80 series, with typical seating for 117.

A reversal of the trend from the DC-9 to the MD-80 series, the MD-87 combines the advanced features introduced on the MD-80 (most notably the more fuel efficient, quieter Pratt & Whitney JT8D-200 engines) with a 5.3m (17ft 5in) shorter fuselage which is similar in length to the DC-9-30.

The MD-87 features a 39.75m (130ft 5in) fuselage length; plus an EFIS flightdeck (the MD-87 was the first aircraft of the MD-80 series to introduce EFIS, with two dual flight management systems and glass displays) and an optional Sundstrand Head-Up Display; Pratt & Whitney JT8D-217C turbofans (which are approximately 2% more efficient than the -217A); the cruise performance package improvements introduced on late production MD-80s, including the extended low drag tail cone, fillet fairing between the engine pylons and the fuselage and low drag flap hinge fairings; and increased height fin to compensate for the shorter fuselage.

The MD-87 was optionally available with extra front and rear cargo compartment auxiliary fuel tanks to extend range, and other engines in the JT8D-200 series. In other respects the MD-87 is similar to the rest of the MD-80 series.

McDonnell Douglas launched development of the MD-87 on January 3 1985, following the placement of launch orders from Finnair and Austrian in December 1984. First flight took place on December 4 1986 and US FAA certification was granted on October 21 1987.

MD-87 sales were relatively small and mainly to traditional Douglas customers. Notable operators include Iberia (with 24), SAS (18), Aeromexico (10) and Japan Air System/Japan Airlines (eight). Smaller operators include Spanair, Spirit Airlines and Austrian.

By the time Boeing and McDonnell Douglas merged in August 1997 all MD-87 orders had been fulfilled and Boeing ceased marketing the type.

Photo: Iberia is the largest MD-87 operator. (Toni Marimon)

Country of origin: United States of America

Type: Short to medium range narrowbody airliner

Powerplants: MD-90-30 – Two 111.2kN (25,000lb) International Aero Engines V2525-D5 turbofans.

Performance: MD-90-30 – Typical cruising speed 809km/h (437kt). Range with 153 passengers 3862km (2085nm), or 4023km (2172nm) for standard -30ER, or 4425km (2389nm) for long range -30ER.

Weights: MD-90-30 – Operating empty 39,915kg (88,000lb) max takeoff 70,760kg (156,000lb).

Dimensions: Wing span 32.87m (107ft 10in), length 46.51m (152ft 7in), height 9.33m (30ft 7in). Wing area 112.3m² (1209.0sq ft).

Capacity: Flightcrew of two. Two class seating for 12 premium class and 141 economy class passengers in MD-90-30, or max single class seating for 172.

Production: Total MDC/Boeing MD-90 production of 114, completed in 2000. 105 were in service in 2002. Three MD-90-30Ts built in China under the Trunkliner program.

History: The MD-90, a stretched, IAE V2500 powered development of the MD-80, is the largest member of the Douglas/McDonnell Douglas/Boeing DC-9/MD-80/MD-90/717 family.

McDonnell Douglas launched the MD-90 program in November 1988, first flight occurred on February 22 1993, and certification was awarded on November 16 1994. Launch customer Delta took delivery of the first of 31 MD-90s it ordered on February 25 1995 (Delta is now replacing them with 737-800s).

The MD-90's most significant change over the MD-80 is its two V2500 turbofans. Interestingly, at 111kN (25,000lb) thrust, the MD-90's V2500s are the largest, heaviest and most powerful engines to be rear mounted on any airliner.

Other changes over the MD-80 include the 1.45m (4ft 9in) fuselage stretch forward of the wing, allowing seating for an extra 10 passengers (in a two class arrangement). The stretch is forward of the wing to compensate for the extra weight of the engines. The MD-90 also features an EFIS glass flightdeck based on that in the MD-88, and other improvements such as a revised passenger interior.

The basic MD-90 model is the MD-90-30, while the extended range MD-90-30ER has an increased max takeoff weight and optional auxiliary fuel tank (just two were built, for Egypt's AMC Aviation). The MD-90-50 was offered but not ordered. It was a further extended range version with a higher maximum takeoff weight and extra fuel. The MD-90-50 based MD-90-55 high capacity variant would have been capable of seating 187 passengers in a single class with two extra doors in the forward fuselage to meet emergency evacuation requirements.

Under a 1992 agreement SAIC in China was to build 20 MD-90-30T Trunkliners (with double bogey main landing gear) under licence. However China abandoned the Trunkliner program in mid 1998 and just three MD-90-30Ts were completed.

Following the 1997 merger of Boeing and McDonnell Douglas, Boeing decided to cancel MD-90 production once outstanding orders were fulfilled. The last of 114 US built MD-90s was completed in 2000.

Photo: A MD-90 in Japan Air System colours. (Glenn Alderton)

McDonnell Douglas DC-10 & Boeing MD-10

Country of origin: United States of America

Type: Medium to long range widebody airliner

Powerplants: DC-10-10 – Three 178kN (40,000lb) General Electric CF6-6D turbofans, or 182.4kN (41,000lb) CF6-6D1s. DC-10-30 – Three 218kN (49,000lb) CF6-50As, 226.9kN (51,000lb) CF6-50Cs, or 233.5kN (52,500lb) CF6-50C1s or C2s, or 240.2kN (54,000lb) CF6-50C2Bs. DC-10-40 – Three 219.6kN (49,400lb) Pratt & Whitney JT9D-20s, or 235.8kN (53,000lb) JT9D-59As.

Performance: DC-10-30 – Max speed 982km/h (530kt), max cruising speed 908km/h (490kt). Range with max fuel and no payload 12,055km (6505nm), range with max payload 7415km (4000nm). DC-10-40 – Range with max fuel and no payload 11,685km (6305nm), range with max payload (& JT9D-59As) 7505km (4050nm).

Weights: DC-10-30 – Empty 121,198kg (267,197lb), max takeoff 263,085kg (580,000lb). DC-10-40 – Empty 122,951kg (271,062lb), max takeoff 259,450kg (572,000lb).

Dimensions: Wing span 50.40m (165ft 5in), length 55.50m (182ft 1in), height 17.70m (58ft 1in). Wing area 367.7m² (3958.0sq ft).

Capacity: Flightcrew of three. Max seating for 380 passengers at nine abreast and 81cm (32in) pitch. Mixed class seating arrangements vary between 250 and 270. DC-10-30F – 23 pallets on main deck.

Production: 386 civil DC-10s built with 262 in airline service in late 2002. FedEx has 18 MD-10s in service.

History: The DC-10 was designed in response to the same American Airlines requirement as the Lockheed TriStar, and, despite a sometimes troubled past, was the more successful of the two.

Originally conceived as a twinjet, the DC-10 gained a third engine at the base of its vertical tail to meet an American Airlines requirement that the aircraft be capable of operating from existing runways. The DC-10 subsequently was launched in February 1968 with orders from American and United. First flight took place on August 29 1970.

The first transcontinental range DC-10-10s entered service with American in August 1971. By then work was already underway on the intercontinental range DC-10-30 which introduced more powerful engines, additional fuel tanks and a third main undercarriage unit.

Most DC-10s built were -30s (including convertible -30CFs and pure freight -30Fs), while the -40 is a Pratt & Whitney JT9D powered variant ordered by Northwest and JAL. The United States Air Force ordered 60 CF6 powered DC-10s as KC-10 Extender tanker transports.

A number of major and catastrophic accidents marred the DC-10's service record in the mid to late 1970s, but the various causes of these accidents were overcome and the DC-10 went on to operate successfully and reliably. Production ceased in 1989.

The Boeing MD-10 conversion initiated for FedEx sees DC-10s fitted with a two crew Honeywell VIA 2000 EFIS flightdeck with six LCD screens. The instrument panel layout is identical to that in the MD-11, and pilots can be qualified to fly the two interchangeably. First flight was on April 4 1999. The first was delivered on May 9 2000 (the same day the conversion was certificated). Some 89 MD-10 conversions for FedEx are planned, with 18 delivered at late 2002.

Photo: An Aero Lyon DC-10-30. (Rob Finlayson)

McDonnell Douglas (Boeing) MD-11

Country of origin: United States of America

Type: Long range widebody airliner

Powerplants: Three 266.9kN (60,000lb) Pratt & Whitney PW4460s, 276kN (62,000lb) PW4462s, or 273.6kN (61,500lb) General Electric CF6-80C2D1F turbofans.

Performance: MD-11 – Max cruising speed 945km/h (510kt), economical cruising speed 876km/h (473kt). Range with 298 passengers and reserves 12,633km (6821nm). MD-11F – Range 7242km (3910nm). MD-11 Combi – Range with 183 passengers, six freight pallets and reserves 12,392km (6691nm). MD-11ER – Range with 298 passengers 13,408km (7240nm).

Weights: MD-11 – Operating empty 130,165kg (286,965lb) with CF6s, standard max takeoff 273,314kg (602,555lb), optional 285,990kg (630,500lb). MD-11F – Operating empty 113,920kg (251,150lb), max takeoff same. MD-11 Combi – Operating empty 131,035kg (288,885lb) passenger, max takeoff same. MD-11CF – Operating empty passenger configuration 131,525kg (289,965lb), freighter configuration 115,380kg (254,372lb), max takeoff same. MD-11ER – Max takeoff 285,989kg (630,500lb).

Dimensions: Wing span 51.66m (169ft 6in), length 61.21m (200ft 10in) with PW4460s, 61.62m (202ft 2in) with CF6s, height 17.60m (57ft 9in). Wing area 338.9m² (3648.0sq ft).

Capacity: Flightcrew of two. MD-11 – Max single class seating for 410, can seat 298 in three classes, 323 in two.

Production: 200 MD-11 ordered (comprising 136 MD-11, 5 MD-11C and 59 MD-11F). 183 were in service in late 2002.

History: The McDonnell Douglas MD-11 is a slightly stretched and re-engined evolution of the DC-10 trijet.

Launched on December 30 1986, the MD-11 was the result of a two year study to find a replacement for the DC-10. First flight was on January 10 1990, certification was granted in November that year, and service entry with Finnair was in that December.

Compared to the DC-10, the MD-11 introduced a 5.71m (18ft 9in) fuselage stretch, winglets, modified tail with less sweepback, an advanced two crew six screen EFIS flightdeck, restyled main cabin interior and new engine options. Variants offered were the longer range MD-11ER available from early 1996, MD-11F freighter, and MD-11C Combi and MD-11CF convertible passenger/freighter models. Many airliner MD-11s have since been converted to freighters

A multi stage performance improvement program (PIP) cut weight and reduced drag as the MD-11 initially failed to meet performance targets.

McDonnell Douglas studied various MD-11 developments with fuselage stretches and even underfloor panorama deck seating. In 1996 MDC revealed the the MD-XX with a new wing. Two versions were proposed, one with the standard MD-11 fuselage and a 15,565km (8400nm) range, the other a stretched 375 seater.

In November 1997 following the Boeing/McDonnell Douglas merger Boeing announced that the MD-11 would be kept in production, primarily as a freighter. However in June 1998 Boeing reversed that decision. The last MD-11 built, a MD-11F for Lufthansa Cargo, was delivered on February 23 2001.

Photo: An Alitalia MD-11. (Sam Chui)

MD Helicopters/Hughes 500

Country of origin: United States of America

Type: Light utility helicopters

Powerplant: 500C – One 207kW (278shp) Allison 250-C20 turboshaft driving a four blade main rotor and two blade tail rotor. MD 530F – One 280kW (375shp) max cont rated Rolls-Royce 250-C30 driving a five blade main rotor and two or optionally four blade tail rotor.

Performance: 500C – Max cruising speed 232km/h (125kt), long range cruising speed 217km/h (117kt). Initial rate of climb 1700ft/min. Hovering ceiling in ground effect 13,000ft. Range 605km (325nm). MD 530F – Max cruising speed 249km/h (135kt), economical cruising speed 228km/h (123kt). Initial rate of climb 2070ft/min. Service ceiling 18,700ft. Range standard fuel no reserves 429km (232nm).

Weights: 500C – Empty 493kg (1088lb), max takeoff 1157kg (2550lb). MD 530F – Empty 722kg (1591lb), max takeoff 1406kg (3100lb), max overload takeoff 1610kg (3550lb), max takeoff with sling load 1700kg (3750lb).

Dimensions: 500C – Main rotor diameter 8.03m (26ft 4in), fuselage length 7.01m (23ft 0in), height 2.48m (8ft 2in). MD 530F – Main rotor diameter 8.33m (27ft 4in), length overall rotors turning 9.94m (32ft 7in), fuselage length 7.49m (24ft 7in), height to top of rotor head (std skids) 2.67m (8ft 9in). Main rotor disc area 54.6m^2 (587.5sq ft).

Capacity: Typical seating for five. Alternatively can accommodate two stretchers and medical attendant, plus pilot.

Production: Approximately 4700 Hughes 500s and MD 500s have been built, including large numbers for military customers.

History: The successful Hughes 500/MD 500 series was originally developed in response to a US Army requirement for a light observation helicopter.

Hughes won the US Army observation helicopter contest ahead of Bell and Hiller with its Allison 250 powered OH-6 Cayuse, which first flew in February 1963. By then Hughes was already working on a civil variant, to be marketed as the Hughes 500 (Hughes Model 369). It was offered in basic five and seven seat configurations, and the 500U, later 500C, utility version with a more powerful engine.

From 1976 deliveries were of the 500D, an improved version with a more powerful engine, a T-tail, and new five blade main and optional four blade tail rotors. The 500D was followed by the 500E from 1982 with recontoured nose and various interior improvements including greater head and leg room. The 530F (first delivery January 1984) is a more powerful version optimised for hot and high work.

McDonnell Douglas acquired Hughes Helicopters in January 1984, and from August 1985 the 500E and 530F were built as the MD 500E and MD 530F Lifter. Following the August 1997 Boeing/McDonnell Douglas merger Boeing put the line up for sale. Bell was an early suitor, but its plans were thwarted by the US Federal Trade Commission (FTC) in 1998. Then in January 1999 Boeing announced the sale of the light helicopter lines to MD Helicopters, a newly formed division of Netherlands based RDM Holdings. The sale was finalised in February 1999. In April 2000 MD Helicopters contracted Kaman to build the fuselages for the single engine MDs.

Military variants are marketed under the MD 500 Defender name.

Photo: A Kawasaki built Hughes 500C. (Theo van Loon)

MD Helicopters MD 520N

Country of origin: United States of America

Type: Light utility helicopter

Powerplant: One 280kW (375shp) Rolls-Royce 250-C20R turboshaft driving a five blade main rotor.

Performance: Max cruising speed at S/L 250km/h (135kt). Initial rate of climb 1850ft/min. Service ceiling 14,175ft. Hovering ceiling in ground effect 11,200, out of ground effect 6000ft. Range at S/L 424km (229nm). Endurance at S/L 2hr 24min.

Weights: Empty 742kg (1636lb), max takeoff 1520kg (3350lb), or 1745kg (3850lb) with an external sling load.

Dimensions: Rotor diameter 8.33m (27ft 4in), length overall rotor turning 9.78m (33ft 2in), fuselage length 7.77m (25ft 6in), height with standard skids 2.74m (9ft 0in), height with extended skids 3.01m (9ft 11in). Rotor disc area 54.5m^2 (586.8sq ft).

Capacity: Standard seating for five.

Production: Over 100 MD 520Ns delivered by late 2002.

History: The MD 520N introduced a revolutionary advance in helicopter design as it dispensed with a conventional tail rotor in favour of the Hughes/McDonnell Douglas developed NOTAR (NO TAil Rotor) system.

Development of the revolutionary NOTAR system dates back to late 1975 when Hughes engineers began initial concept development work. In December 1981 Hughes flew an OH-6A fitted with NOTAR for the first time. A more heavily modified prototype demonstrator first flew in March 1986 (by which time McDonnell Douglas had acquired Hughes).

Although the concept, which uses the Coanda effect, took some time to refine, the NOTAR system is simple in theory and works to provide directional control the same way a wing develops lift. Low pressure air is forced through two slots on the right side of the tailboom, causing the downwash from the main rotor to hug the tailboom, producing lift, and thus a measure of directional control. This is augmented by a direct jet thruster and vertical stabilisers.

NOTAR system benefits include far lower external noise (the MD 520N is the quietest certificated helicopter in the world), increased safety due to the lack of a tail rotor, improved handling and performance, reduced vibration and easier maintainability.

McDonnell Douglas originally intended to develop the standard MD 520N alongside the more powerful hot and high optimised MD 530N (both were launched in January 1989 and were based on the conventional MD 500E). The MD 530N was the first to fly, on December 29 1989, the MD 520N first flew on May 1 1990. Development of the MD 530N was suspended when McDonnell Douglas decided that the MD 520N met most customer requirements for the 530N. Certification for the MD 520N was awarded on September 13 1991, and the first was delivered on December 31 that year.

Following the 1997 Boeing/McDonnell Douglas merger, Boeing sold the former MD civil helicopter lines to MD Helicopters in early 1999.

At the 2000 Farnborough Airshow MD Helicopters announced enhancements to the MD 520N including an improved RR 250-C20R+ engine with 3-5% more power for better performance on warm days, and, with changes to the diffuser and fan rigging, increased range.

Photo: An MD 520N. (Paul Sadler)

MD Helicopters MD 600N

Country of origin: United States of America

Type: Eight place light utility helicopter

Powerplant: One 603kW (808shp) Rolls-Royce 250-C47 turboshaft, derated to 447kW (600shp) for takeoff and 395kW (530shp) for max continuous operation driving a six blade main rotor.

Performance: Max cruising speed to 5000ft 248km/h (134kt). Initial rate of climb 1350ft/min. Max operating altitude 20,000ft. Hovering ceiling in ground effect 11,100ft, out of ground effect 6000ft. Max range at 5000ft 707km (382nm) or 633km (342nm) at sea level.

Weights: Empty 952kg (2100lb), max takeoff with internal load 1860kg (4100lb), max takeoff with sling load 2131kg (4700lb).

Dimensions: Rotor diameter 8.38m (27ft 6in), length overall rotor turning 11.79m (35ft 5in), fuselage length 8.99m (29ft 6in), height to top of rotor head 2.65m (8ft 9in), or 2.74m (9ft 0in) with extended skids. Rotor disc area 55.2m² (594.0sq ft)

Capacity: Typical seating for eight.

Production: Deliveries began mid 1997. 45 ordered by US Border Patrol. Approx 70 in service at late 2002.

History: The MD 600N is a stretched eight seat development of the five seat MD 520N helicopter.

McDonnell Douglas Helicopter Systems (MD Helicopters since 1999) first announced it was developing a stretched MD 520N in late 1994, and unveiled the first flying prototype of the new helicopter, at that time designated the MD 630N, at the Heli Expo in Las Vegas in January 1995. This prototype, a modified MD 530F, had made its first flight on November 22 1994. The MD 630N created high levels of interest at the Heli Expo and McDonnell Douglas gave the go-ahead for the production aircraft, redesignated the MD 600N, in March 1995.

The prototype was modified to MD 600N standard with a production standard engine and tail boom and flew in November 1995, followed the next month by the first MD 600N production prototype. Unfortunately this second prototype was destroyed by fire following a forced landing in May 1996, caused by the main rotor contacting the tail boom during extreme control reversal tests.

Thus the third prototype, which first flew on August 9 1996, featured modifications to increase the main rotor-tail boom clearance. Certification was awarded on May 15 1997. Deliveries began in June that year. Further performance improvements were certificated in mid 1998.

McDonnell Douglas stretched the MD 520N fuselage by inserting a plug aft of the cockpit/cabin bulkhead and stretching the NOTAR tail boom. The larger fuselage allows for an extra (middle) row of seats. Other differences compared with the MD 520N include a new six blade main rotor (the MD 520N has a five blade unit) and a more powerful Allison (now Rolls-Royce) 250 turboshaft.

Following the 1997 Boeing/McDonnell Douglas' merger, Boeing sold the former MD civil helicopter lines to Dutch owned MD Helicopters in early 1999.

MD Helicopters developed a yaw stability augmentation system for the MD 600, to reduce pilot workload, which became available as an option from mid 2001.

Photo: A police MD 600N. (Oscar Bernardi)

MD Helicopters MD Explorer

Country of origin: United States of America

Type: Light twin helicopter

Powerplants: Two 469kW (629shp) takeoff rated Pratt & Whitney Canada PW206E turboshafts driving a five blade main rotor.

Performance: Max cruising speed at S/L 248km/h (134kt). Initial rate of climb 2250ft/min. Service ceiling 18,000ft. Hovering ceiling in ground effect 10,400ft (ISA). Max range with standard fuel 543km (293nm). Max endurance 3.2hr.

Weights: Standard empty 1531kg (3375lb), max takeoff 2835kg (6250lb), or 3130kg (6900lb) with external sling load.

Dimensions: Rotor diameter 10.31m (33ft 10in), length overall 11.83m (38ft 10in), fuselage length 9.85m (32ft 4in), height 3.66m (12ft 0in). Main rotor disc area 83.5m² (899.0sq ft).

Capacity: One pilot and passenger on front bucket seats with six passengers in main cabin in club seating arrangement. Max seating for 10 (including pilot). Alternatively can be configured with stretchers and seating for medical attendants.

Production: Approximately 100 delivered by late 2002.

History: The MD Explorer light twin helicopter is the first all new design to incorporate the unique NOTAR (NO TAil Rotor) system.

McDonnell Douglas Helicopters launched the Explorer as the MDX in January 1989. First flight took place on December 18 1992. Full certification for the initial PW206B powered Explorer (unofficially designated MD 900) version was granted in December 1994.

One of the most advanced helicopters in its market segment, the MD Explorer features Boeing's unique NOTAR anti torque system (described in detail under the MD 520N entry), with benefits including increased safety, far lower noise levels and performance and controllability enhancements. (Boeing retains the design rights to the NOTAR technology despite selling the former McDonnell Douglas civil helicopter line to MD Helicopters in early 1999.)

The Explorer also features an advanced bearingless five blade main rotor with composite blades, plus carbonfibre construction tail and fuselage (designed and initially built in Australia, but production was transferred to Turkey).

Initial Explorers were powered by two Pratt & Whitney Canada PW206Bs (the Explorer was the first application for the PW200 series), while plans to offer the Turbomeca Arrius as an option were dropped. In September 1997 a range of improvements were introduced, including PW206E turboshafts with higher single engine inoperative ratings, revised engine air inlets, improved NOTAR inlet design and a more powerful stabiliser control system. Benefits include improved range and endurance and an increased max takeoff weight. This enhanced explorer was unofficially designated the MD 902.

On August 31 1998 the Explorer became the first helicopter to be validated by Europe's JAA JAR Part 27 Category A guidelines, which requires helicopters be capable of safely continuing flight during takeoff or landing on a single engine.

From September 2000 the Explorer has been delivered with the further improved PW207E turboshaft, with improved hot and high and one engine inoperative performance, and a 2948kg (6500lb).

Photo: A Sussex Police Explorer. (Colin Work)

Mil Mi-8, Mi-17 & Mi-171

Country of origin: Russia

Type: Medium lift utility helicopters

Powerplants: Mi-8T – Two 1250kW (1677shp) Klimov (Isotov) TV2-117AG turboshafts driving a five blade main rotor and three blade tail rotor. Mi-171 – Two 1545kW (2070shp) TV3-117VM.

Performance: Mi-8T – Max speed 250km/h (135kt), max cruising speed 225km/h (121kt). Service ceiling 14,765ft. Hovering ceiling in ground effect 5905ft, out of ground effect 2785ft. Range with standard fuel 570km (307nm), with auxiliary fuel 985km (531nm). Mi-171 – Max speed 250km/h (135kt), max cruising speed 230km/h (124kt). Service ceiling 18,700ft. Hovering ceiling out of ground effect 13,055ft. Range with standard fuel 570km (307nm), range with two auxiliary tanks 1065km (575nm).

Weights: Mi-8T – Empty 7149kg (15,760lb), max takeoff (for vertical takeoff) 12,000kg (26,455lb). Mi-171 – Empty equipped 7055kg (15,555lb), max takeoff 13,000kg (28,660lb).

Dimensions: Mi-8T – Main rotor diameter 21.29m (69ft 10in), length overall 25.24m (82ft 10in), fuselage length 18.17m (59ft 8in), height 5.54m (18ft 2in). Main rotor disc area 356.0m² (3932sq ft). Mi-171 – Same except for length overall 25.35m (83ft 2in), fuselage length 18.42m (60ft 6in).

Capacity: Flightcrew of two, with provision for flight engineer. Primarily used for freight transport, internal and/or with external sling loads. Can carry up to 32 passengers in Mi-8, or 24 in Mi-8T. Mi-8 Salon executive version seats 11 passengers. As air ambulance can accommodate 12 stretchers.

Production: Over 12,000 Mi-8s, Mi-17s and Mi-171s built, but majority for military service.

History: Built in greater numbers than any other Russian helicopter, the Mi-8/Mi-17/Mi-171 series (NATO codename 'Hip') was designed primarily as a military transport, but is also in widespread civil use.

The Mi-8 design work began in May 1960. First flight of the prototype (powered by a single Soloviev turboshaft driving a four blade main rotor) occurred in June 1961, while a production standard Mi-8 flew in August 1962 and production began shortly afterwards. Versions of the Mi-8 built for civil use have square windows and include the Mi-8 passenger version, Mi-8T utility transport, Mi-8TM passenger transport with weather radar and Mi-8 Salon executive transport.

Production of the Mi-8 ceased in favour of the re-engined Mi-17, which was first publicly revealed to the west at the 1981 Paris Airshow. The Mi-17 introduced TV3 turboshafts and the tail rotor was relocated to the port side of the tailboom. Civil versions include the base Mi-17P (with square windows), and the Mi-171 and Mi-17M, which both feature more powerful TV3-117VM turboshafts, and are built by Ulan-Ude Aviation and Kazan Helicopters respectively.

The Kazan/Mil Mi-17KF was designed to gain western certification. It had an EFIS instrument panel with colour displays, rounded 'dolphin' nose with space for radar, and a rear loading ramp in place of the clamshell doors. The program was cancelled but the changes are also incorporated on the Kazan Mi-172.

Photo: Kazan's Mi-172 demonstrator. (Gerard Williamson)

Mil Mi-26

Country of origin: Russia

Type: Ultra heavy lift utility helicopter

Powerplants: Two 7457kW (10,000shp) ZMKB Progress (Lotarev) D-136 turboshafts driving eight blade main and five blade tail rotors.

Performance: Max speed 295km/h (160kt), typical cruising speed 255km/h (137kt). Service ceiling 15,100ft. Hovering ceiling in ground effect 14,765ft. Range with max internal fuel at max takeoff weight with reserves 800km (432nm), range with four auxiliary fuel tanks 1920km (1036nm).

Weights: Empty 28,200kg (62,170lb), normal takeoff 49,600kg (109,350lb), max takeoff 56,000kg (123,450lb).

Dimensions: Main rotor diameter 32.00m (105ft 0in), tail rotor diameter 7.61m (25ft 0in), length overall rotors turning 40.03m (131ft 4in), fuselage length 35.91m (117ft 10in), height to top of rotor head 8.15m (26ft 9in), height tail rotor turning 11.60m (38ft 1in). Main rotor disc area 804.3m² (8657sq ft), tail rotor disc area 45.5m² (489.5sq ft).

Capacity: Flightcrew of four comprising two pilots, flight engineer and navigator, plus loadmaster. Four seat passenger compartment behind flightdeck. Main cabin typically accommodates freight (max payload 20 tonnes/44,090lb), but can seat 63 passengers at four abreast. Firefighting version can carry 7500 litres (1650Imp gal/1980US gal) of fire retardant. Medical version equipped with operating theatre and accommodation for stretchers and medical attendants.

Production: Approximately 300 built, mostly for military use.

History: Mil's Mi-26 is the largest helicopter in the world by a significant margin. It has a maximum takeoff weight greater than that of the Fokker 100, and more than twice that of the Boeing Chinook, and a freight hold similar in size to that in the L-100 Hercules.

Development of the Mi-26 began in the early 1970s and resulted in a first flight on December 14 1977. Although mainly in military use, the original design requirement stated that the helicopter would be for civil use, and that it should have a maximum takeoff weight one and a half times that of any previous helicopter. Preproduction machines were built from 1980, production machines sometime after that. Mi-26s became operational with the Soviet military in 1983.

The Mi-26 is notable for its eight blade main rotor, powerful 7457kW (10,000shp) D-136 turboshaft engines and massive size. Several civil versions have been developed or proposed. These include the basic freighter Mi-26T, Mi-26MS medevac version, Mi-26P airliner version with seating for 63 passengers at four abreast, Mi-26TM flying crane with fuselage side mounted gondola for a pilot/sling load supervisor to oversee sling load operations, Mi-26TM firefighter which can carry 15,000 litres internally or 17,260 litres in an underslung bucket (one was delivered to the Moscow fire brigade in 1999) and Mi-26TZ fuel tanker.

The improved Mi-26M remains under development and will feature new 10,700kW (14,350shp) class ZMKB Progress D-127 turboshafts, better hot and high performance, increased maximum payload, composite main rotor blades, improved aerodynamics and EFIS flightdeck.

Photo: An Mi-26 at Orebro, Sweden. (Lars Wahlstrom)

Mooney M-20A to M-20F

Country of origin: United States of America

Type: Four seat high performance light aircraft

Powerplant: M-20C – One 135kW (180hp) Lycoming O-360-A1D flat four piston engine driving a two blade constant speed prop. M-20E – One 150kW (200hp) Lycoming IO-360-A1A fuel injected flat four.

Performance: M-20C – Max speed 288km/h (156kt), max cruising speed 272km/h (147kt), economical cruising speed 236km/h (127kt). Initial rate of climb 800ft/min. Service ceiling 17,200ft. Range with reserves 1464km (790nm). M-20E – Max speed 317km/h (171kt), max cruising speed 301km/h (163kt), economical cruising speed 270km/h (146kt). Initial rate of climb 1120ft/min. Service ceiling 19,500ft. Max range with no reserves 1648km (890nm).

Weights: M-20C – Empty 692kg (1525lb), max takeoff 1168kg (2575lb). M-20E – Empty 714kg (1575lb), max takeoff 1168kg (2575lb).

Dimensions: M-20C/E – Wing span 10.67m (35ft 0in), length 7.06m (23ft 2in), height 2.54m (8ft 4in). Wing area 15.5m² (167.0sq ft).

Capacity: Standard seating for four.

Production: Total M-20 production 10,282. 6188 M-20 to M-20Gs built, including 201 M-20, 501 M-201A, 223 M-20B, 2187 M-20Cs, 161 M-20D, 1478 M-20E, 1247 M-20F and 190 M-20G.

History: Mooney's first design was the 1948 wooden single seat M-18 Mite, but work was soon underway on the much larger M-20 four seater with metal and wood construction and fabric covering.

This M-20 first flew on August 10 1953. Powered by a 105kW (145hp) six cylinder Continental O-300 flat six engine, the M-20 also had retractable undercarriage and introduced the distinctive forward swept tail. Mooney placed it into production soon after with a 110kW (150hp) Lycoming O-320, and a prolific family followed.

These included the 700 plus M-20As with a 135kW (180hp) O-360, and the similarly powered M-20C Mark 21. Very successful with 400 built in its first year, the Mark 21 featured an all metal structure and higher takeoff weight. A lower spec fixed undercarriage version, the M-20D Master, was also offered. The subsequent M-20E Super 21 first flew in July 1963 and featured a more powerful fuel injected 150kW (200hp) IO-360 engine, combining the M-20E's clean aerodynamics and the more powerful engine to give a claimed top speed of 317km/h (171kt). From the mid 1960s all models gained a small fin fillet and a larger squared off rear cabin window.

The M-20F Executive 21 of 1965 was based on the M-20E Super 21 and had a 25cm (10in) fuselage stretch and an extra cabin window on each side, new cabin fittings and extra fuel. In 1967 the range was renamed, the M-20C becoming the Ranger, the M-20F continued as the Executive, the M-20E was discontinued for a time until reappearing as the Chaparral, and a new model, the M-20G Statesman (with the Executive's fuselage and a 135kW/180hp engine) appeared (although only 190 were built).

For a time from 1970 Mooney was known as the Aerostar Aircraft Corporation, and the Ranger became the Aerostar 200, the Chaparral the 201 and Executive the 220. Aerostar ceased production in early 1972, and it was not until 1973 that revised models were built under the Mooney banner (described separately).

Photo: A Mooney M-20C Mark 21. (Keith Myers)

Mooney M-20J to M20S

Country of origin: United States of America

Type: High performance four seat light aircraft

Powerplant: Eagle – One 182kW (244hp) Teledyne Continental IO-550-G fuel injected flat six driving a two blade c/s prop. Bravo – One 200kW (270hp) Textron Lycoming TIO-540-AF1B turbocharged and fuel injected flat six piston engine driving a three blade c/s prop.

Performance: Eagle – Cruising speed 324km/h (175kt). Service ceiling 18,500ft. Range at econ cruising speed 2242km (1210nm). Bravo – Cruising speed at 25,000ft 407km/h (220kt). Initial rate of climb 1230ft/min. Ceiling 25,000ft. Range max fuel 1945km (1050nm).

Weights: Eagle – Basic empty 995kg (2194lb), max takeoff 1451kg (3200lb). Bravo – Empty 1029kg (2268lb), max takeoff 1527kg (3368lb).

Dimensions: Eagle/Bravo – Wing span 11.00m (36ft 1in), length 8.15m (26ft 9in), height 2.54m (8ft 4in). Wing area 16.3m² (175.0sq ft).

Capacity: Standard seating for four.

Production: 2132 M-20J, 1263 M-20K, 41 M20L, 316 M20M, 279 M20R, and 62 M20S built by 2001. Production resumed mid 2002.

History: Mooney's new owners, the Republic Steel Company, placed the M-20 line back into production in late 1973.

The Ranger, Chaparral and Executive, were returned to production, but design efforts centred around the M-20F Executive. The first model developed was the M-20J 201, with a theoretical top speed of 323km/h (175kt), or 201mph. The 201 entered production in 1976, replacing the Executive. The Ranger remained in production until 1979.

Models included the M-20K 231 from late 1978, powered by a turbocharged six cylinder Continental TSIO-360, and the 201LM (Lean Machine) from 1986 with only basic options. The 201 evolved into the M-20J 205 with rounded cabin windows and redesigned wingtips, slightly increasing top speed. A Special Edition 'SE' luxury options package was also offered. The M-20K 252TSE (Turbo Special Edition) was a development of the 231 with a top speed of 405km/h (220kt), or 252mph, and combined the 205's airframe mods with a 155kW (210hp) turbocharged Continental TSIO-360. The Porsche PFM 3200 powered M-20L was built between 1987 and 1991.

The top of the line Bravo – formerly the M20M TLS (Turbo Lycoming Sabre) – was introduced in 1989. It features a slightly stretched fuselage, a turbocharged and intercooled Lycoming TIO-540 and three blade prop. The Bravo name was adopted in 1996.

The Allegro – formerly the M20J MSE 205 – development is powered by a 150kW (200hp) Textron Lycoming IO-360-A3B6D.

The M20R Ovation was introduced in 1994 and was based on the Bravo but is powered by a 210kW (280hp) Continental IO-550G flat six. The Ovation2 was introduced in late 1999 and features a two blade prop which is more efficient than the three blade unit it replaced.

In 1997 Mooney introduced the short lived 370km/h (200kt) cruise M20K Encore which was powered by a turbocharged TSIO-360.

Deliveries of the new entry level M20S Eagle, which combines the extended length fuselage with a 182kW (244hp) Continental IO-550, began in 1999. It effectively replaced the Allegro in the Mooney line-up.

Mooney was acquired by AASI in March 2002 after a period of bankruptcy protection and suspended aircraft production.

Photo: A Mooney Ovation.

Mitsubishi MU-2

Country of origin: Japan

Type: Twin turboprop utility transport

Powerplants: MU-2B – Two 430kW (575shp) Garrett AiResearch TPE331-25A turboprops driving three blade constant speed propellers. Marquise – Two 535kW (715shp) Garrett TPE331-10-501Ms driving four blade constant speed propellers.

Performance: MU-2B – Max cruising speed 500km/h (270kt), economical cruising speed 440km/h (237kt). Initial rate of climb 2220ft/min. Max range with reserves 1930km (1040nm). Marquise – Max cruising speed 571km/h (308kt), economical cruising speed 547km/h (295kt). Service ceiling 29,750ft. Range with max fuel and reserves 2585km (1395nm).

Weights: MU-2B – Empty 2422kg (5340lb), max takeoff 4050kg (8930lb). Marquise – Empty equipped 3470kg (7650lb), max takeoff 5250kg (11,575lb).

Dimensions: MU-2B – Wing span 11.94m (39ft 2in), length 10.13m (33ft 3in), height 3.94m (12ft 11in). Wing area 16.5m² (178sq ft). Marquise – Same except for length 12.01m (39ft 5in), height 4.17m (13ft 8in).

Capacity: Flightcrew of one or two. Short fuselage models had typical seating for seven in main cabin, longer fuselage models up to 11. Many aircraft in various corporate configurations, or used as freighters.

Production: Over 800 built. Production comprised three MU-2As, 34 MU-2Bs, four military MU-2Ds, 18 MU-2Ds, 16 military SAR MU-2Es, 95 MU-2Fs, 46 MU-2Gs, 108 MU-2Js, 83 MU-2Ks, 36 MU-2Ls, 27 MU-2Ms, 36 MU-2Ns, 31 MU-2Ps, 130 plus Marquise and 60 plus Solitaires. Over 480 were in use as corporate aircraft in 2002.

History: The MU-2 was one of postwar Japan's most successful commercial aircraft types.

Development of the MU-2, Mitsubishi's first indigenous postwar aircraft design, began in the late 1950s. Designed as a light twin turboprop transport suitable for a variety of civil and military roles, the MU-2 first flew on September 14 1963. This first MU-2 and the handful of MU-2As built were powered by Turbomeca Astazou turboprops, all other models from the MU-2B onwards had Garrett TPE331s.

The MU-2 lineup can be divided up into two basic types, the standard fuselage and stretched fuselage models. The MU-2B, E, F, K, M, P and Solitaire feature the short fuselage, the others, including the Marquise, the stretched fuselage. The first stretched fuselage MU-2G flew on January 10 1969.

The MU-2 was progressively improved and upgraded throughout its production life. Notable changes include improved and more powerful TPE331 engines, and four blade propellers from the N and P models.

Mitsubishi established a production facility for MU-2s in San Angelo, Texas in the USA in 1967 to build MU-2s for the North American and world markets. The San Angelo Mitsubishi International facility became the sole source of MU-2 production until 1986 when the line finally closed.

Today almost 500 MU-2s are in use as corporate transports (mainly in the USA), while many have been converted as freighters.

Photo: A short fuselage MU-2K. (Rob Finlayson)

NAMC YS-11

Country of origin: Japan

Type: Twin turboprop regional airliner

Powerplants: YS-11A-200 – Two 2280kW (3060shp) Rolls-Royce Dart 542-10K turboprops driving four blade propellers.

Performance: -200 – Max cruising speed 470km/h (253kt), economical cruising speed 452km/h (244kt). Range with max payload and no reserves 1090km (590nm), range with max fuel and no reserves 3215km (1736nm).

Weights: -200 – Operating empty 15,419kg (33,993lb), max takeoff 24,500kg (54,010lb).

Dimensions: Wing span 32.00m (105ft 0in), length 26.30m (86ft 4in), height 8.98m (29ft 6in). Wing area 94.8m² (1020.4sq ft).

Capacity: Flightcrew of two. Typical single class seating in main cabin for 60 at four abreast and 86cm (34in) pitch. The combi YS-11A-300 accommodates freight in the forward portion of the main cabin with seating for 46 behind that.

Production: 182 YS-11s built comprising two prototypes, 48 series 100s, 83 Series 200s, 31 series 300s, eight series 400s, two series 500s and eight series 600s. Production total includes 23 for Japanese military. 46 remained in service at late 2002.

History: The only Japanese airliner to enter production since WW2, the YS-11 achieved a degree of success in its domestic market and in North America.

The YS-11 was a product of the Nihon Aircraft Manufacturing Company (or NAMC), a consortium of Fuji, Kawasaki, Mitsubishi, Nippi, Shin Meiwa (now Shin Maywa) and Showa. NAMC was formed on June 1 1959 to design and develop a short to medium range airliner, with particular attention being paid to meeting the specific operating requirements of the Japanese domestic airlines.

NAMC selected the Rolls-Royce Dart over the Allison 501 to power the new airliner. Fuji was given responsibility for the tail unit, Kawasaki the wings and engine nacelles, Mitsubishi the forward fuselage and final assembly, Nippi the ailerons and flaps, Shin Meiwa the rear fuselage and Showa the light alloy honeycomb structural components.

The YS-11 first flew on August 30 1962 (a second prototype flew that December), and was awarded Japanese certification in August 1964. By that time the first production aircraft were under construction, and the type entered service with Toa Airways (later JAS) in April 1965. Initial production was of the YS-11-100, the follow up YS-11A-200 (first flight November 1967) was designed for export markets and featured an increased max takeoff weight. The YS-11A-300 was a combi passenger/freight model, while the YS-11A-400 was a pure freighter with a forward freight door.

The YS-11A-500, -600 and -700 were equivalent to the -200, -300 and -400, but with a 500kg (1100lb) greater max takeoff weight. Production ceased in February 1974.

By late 2002 almost 50 YS-11s remained in commercial service. The largest operators were the Philippines' Aboitiz Air (8), Air Nippon (5) and Japan Air Commuter – now part of Japan Airlines – (12).

Photo: An Air Philippines YS-11-100. The YS-11 employed the most powerful version of the Dart to go into operation. (Rob Finlayson)

Noorduyn Norseman

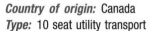

Country of origin: Canada

Type: 10 seat utility transport

Powerplant: Norseman V – One 450kW (600hp) Pratt & Whitney R1340-AN-1 Wasp nine cylinder radial piston engine driving a three blade propeller.

Performance: V – Normal cruising speed 238km/h (128kt). Time to climb to 5000ft 6.5min, time to climb to 15,000ft 28.5min. Service ceiling 17,000ft. Range at 75% power cruising speed with max fuel 1850km (998nm).

Weights: V – Empty 2007kg (4420lb), loaded 3360kg (7400lb).

Dimensions: V – Wing span 15.75m (51ft 8in), length 9.85m (32ft 4in), height 3.12m (10ft 3in).

Capacity: V – Pilot and up to nine passengers on bench seats. Often configured for freight.

Production: Norseman production ran from the late 1930s through until 1946 with Noorduyn, and then with Canadian Car and Foundry until 1959, by which time 904 had been built by both manufacturers. Approximately 20 remain in use in Canada, while one or two may be flying in other countries.

History: The rugged Norseman bush aircraft first flew in the mid 1930s, and so its long in service record equals that of the legendary Douglas DC-3.

The Norseman was designed by Robert Noorduyn, who was born in Holland and later worked for several prominent aircraft companies in England and the USA, including Armstrong Whitworth, British Aerial Transport Sopwith, Fokker (in the USA where he worked on the F.VII/3m), Bellanca and Pitcairn. In 1934 Noorduyn formed Noorduyn Aircraft Ltd (Noorduyn Aviation from 1938). Later in 1934 Noorduyn began work on the Norseman, resulting in the first flight of the float equipped prototype Norseman I from the St Laurence River on November 14 1935.

The Norseman I was powered by a 315kW (420hp) Wright Whirlwind, featured spruce wing spars and a metal tubing fuselage frame with fabric covering. It was the first Canadian aircraft with flaps.

Further development resulted in the heavier Norseman II and the 335kW (450hp) P&W Wasp Junior powered Norseman III. The 415kW (550hp) Norseman IV was the subject of significant Royal Canadian Air Force and civil orders in 1938.

The USA's entry into WW2 in late 1941 saw the US Army Air Force take delivery of 746 Norsemans in C-64A, UC-64A and C-64B variants. These aircraft operated in many theatres and were often equipped with floats or skis. The Norseman V is the civil equivalent of the C-64A.

With the aircraft no longer needed for war, Noorduyn production ceased in 1945 and its Cartierville plant was taken over by Canadair. However through to 1959 Canadian Car and Foundry built small numbers of Norseman Vs for civil customers.

After the war many ex military Norsemans found gainful use with civil operators, and currently about 20 are still airworthy in Canada.

Photo: A surprising number of Norsemans remain in commercial use, primarily in Canada. This float equipped Norseman V is pictured in service with Huron Air of Armstrong, Ontario. (Rodney Kozar)

North American/Ryan Navion

Country of origin: United States of America

Type: High performance four/five seat light aircraft

Powerplant: Super 260 – One 195kW (260hp) Lycoming GO-435-C2 flat six piston engine driving a two blade propeller. Model H – One 215kW (285hp) Continental IO-520-B fuel injected flat six piston engine driving a two blade constant speed McCauley prop.

Performance: Super 260 – Max speed 280km/h (151kt). Model H – Max speed 307km/h (166kt), max cruising speed at 75% power 298km/h (161kt). Initial rate of climb 1300ft/min. Service ceiling 21,500ft. Range with max fuel 2560km (1397nm).

Weights: Super 260 – Max takeoff 1293kg (2850lb). Model H – Empty 882kg (1945lb), max takeoff 1504kg (3315lb).

Dimensions: Super 260 – Wing span 10.19m (33ft 5in), length 8.38m (27ft 6in). Model H – Wing span 10.59m (34ft 9in), length 8.38m (27ft 6in), height 2.54m (8ft 4in). Wing area 17.1m² (184.3sq ft).

Capacity: Usually four, five in Rangemaster.

Production: Approx 2500 built, incl 1109 by North American (inc L-19s), 1240 by Ryan (incl L-19s), and 140 NAC Rangemasters.

History: The Navion was designed in the late 1940s and built by four different companies through until the mid 1970s.

The company responsible for the original Navion was North American Aviation (famous for its WW2 P-51 Mustang fighter). The end of WW2 saw massive military contracts cancelled en masse and so North American designed the original four seat NA-145 to diversify out of military production. The NA-145 Navion was powered by a 140kW (185hp) Continental and North American built more than 1100 in 1946 and 1947. North American also built a number of L-17 observation aircraft based on the Navion for the US military.

Production and development of the Navion then transferred to Ryan. The standard Ryan production model was the Navion 205 or Navion A, which differed from the NA-145 in that it was powered by a 155kW (205hp) Continental E-185. More than 100 were built between 1948 and 1950. Ryan also built a few hundred Navion Super 260s or Navion Bs between 1950 and 1951 (when Ryan ceased Navion production). These were powered by a 195kW (260hp) Lycoming GO-435. In addition Ryan also built almost 200 L-17s (some saw service in Korea).

The basic Navion design resurfaced in 1960 when the Navion Aircraft Company developed a five seater called the Rangemaster. The Rangemaster was powered by the same 195kW (260hp) Lycoming engine as the Navion Super 260, but instead of the rear sliding canopy of earlier Navions, the Rangemaster had a reprofiled, more streamlined five seat cabin. Later production Rangemasters had a smaller tail.

The Rangemaster was last built by the Navion Rangemaster Aircraft Corporation between 1974 and 1976 in improved G and H form.

Camair in the USA also converted a small number of Navions of various models to twin engine configuration, the first flew in 1953.

Navion Aircraft purchased the manufacturing rights to the Navion in 1995 with the intention of returning an improved version of the Rangemaster to production. Changes would have included a reprofiled nose and new avionics.

Photo: The five seat Navion Rangemaster. (Colin Work)

OMF OMF-160 Symphony

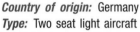

Country of origin: Germany

Type: Two seat light aircraft

Powerplant: One 120kW (160hp) Textron Lycoming O-360-D2A flat four piston engine driving a two blade fixed pitch MT-186R-140-3D propeller.

Performance: Cruising speed at 75% power 243km/h (131kt), stall speed flaps extended 89km/h (48kt). Initial rate of climb 1200ft/min. Certificated service ceiling 16,400ft. Range with max fuel approx 926km (500nm).

Weights: Empty 650kg (1450lb), max takeoff 975kg (2150lb). Useful load 325kg (700lb).

Dimensions: Wing span 10.67m (35ft 0in), length 6.96m (22ft 10in), height 2.82m (9ft 3in). Wing area 11.9m² (128.4sq ft).

Capacity: Seating for two side-by-side.

Production: Approximately 50 built by late 2002. OMF plans a 300 unit a year production rate. Price $US120,000.

History: The OMF-160 Symphony two seat light aircraft is a certificated evolution of the GlaStar kitplane developed by Stoddard Hamilton but now offered by the New GlaStar company.

The GlaStar kit was developed by Arlington Aircraft Developments and first flew on November 24 1999, and Stoddard-Hamilton began deliveries of kits from the following year. The GlaStar quickly proved to be very popular. Compared to a Cessna 172 it offers more cabin space, despite only being a two seater, can lift a similar load, flies faster and farther, and has much lower running costs.

The high wing two seater is available in tricycle and taildragger forms, with the kit (minus engine) initially costing around $US20,000. Design features included a glass fibre fuselage (with a steel tube frame), an LS(1)-0413 (formerly GA(W)-2) aerofoil wing which can be folded back for towing, and a 93kW (125hp) Teledyne Continental IO-240 engine.

German based OMF (Ostmechlenburgische Flugzeubau) was established in May 1998 and set about developing the GlaStar for certification and factory production as the OMF-160 Symphony under an agreement with Arlington Aircraft Developments. The first prototype OMF-160, essentially little changed from the GlaStar kit, flew in May 1999. Two further prototypes incorporated changes to reflect the production standard OMF-160.

Certification to JAR 23 was awarded on August 29 2000, US FAR Part 23 certification followed on April 9 2001. Deliveries began that November.

Compared to the GlaStar the OMF-160 incorporated a number of changes, with a more powerful 120kW (160hp) Textron Lycoming O-320 engine and redesigned wing and undercarriage (spring steel leaf). The constant chord aluminium construction wing is braced and can be folded to reduce storage space. The two occupants sit on crashworthy (tested to 26g forward, 19g vertical) leather covered seats. The wingtips, tailplane strakes, wheel fairings and fin fillet are made from composites.

OMF intends that the Symphony forms the basis of a family of aircraft, with three and four seat and diesel powered derivatives planned.

Photo: A Symphony in Chile. (Alvaro Romero)

Pacific Aerospace CT-4 Airtrainer

Country of origin: New Zealand

Type: Two/three seat basic trainer

Powerplant: CT-4A – One 155kW (210hp) Teledyne Continental IO-360-D fuel injected flat six piston engine driving a two blade constant speed propeller. CT-4E – One 224kW (300hp) Textron Lycoming AEIO-540-L1B5 driving a three blade prop.

Performance: CT-4A – Max speed 285km/h (155kt), cruising speed 240km/h (130kt), long range cruising speed 235km/h (127kt). Initial rate of climb 1345ft/min. Range at long range cruising speed 1300km (700nm). CT-4E – Max speed at s/l 302km/h (163kt), cruising speed at 8500ft 282km/h (152kt). Initial rate of climb 1830ft/min. Service ceiling 18,200ft. Range at s/l with max fuel at 75% power, no reserves 963km (520nm).

Weights: CT-4A – Empty 690kg (1520lb), max takeoff 1090kg (2400lb) or 1203kg (2650lb). CT-4E – Empty equipped 807kg (1780lb), max takeoff 1179kg (2600lb).

Dimensions: CT-4A – Wing span 7.92m (26ft 0in), length 7.06m (23ft 2in), height 2.59m (8ft 6in). Wing area 12.0m² (129.0sq ft). CT-4E – Same except length 7.16m (23ft 6in).

Capacity: Normally two seats side by side, with space for optional third seat or baggage behind.

Production: 78 CT-4As and 38 CT-4Bs built mainly for military orders. Many (30+) ex RAAF CT-4As are now flying in civil hands mainly in Australia, some in New Zealand and the USA. Approx 30 CT-4Es built.

History: The CT-4 Airtrainer was primarily designed as a military trainer, but is also in limited civilian use.

The CT-4 was developed from the Australian Victa Airtourer series (described separately). Victa had developed the four place Aircruiser (first flight in mid 1966) based on the Airtourer, but development work ceased and instead the production rights for the Aircruiser were purchased by Aero Engine Services Ltd (or AESL) of New Zealand in 1969, which already had the rights to the Airtourer series.

AESL made a number of changes to the basic Aircruiser design, including adding a new clamshell canopy, structural strengthening for aerobatic work, and stick controls, making it suitable for military basic training. The first such CT-4A Airtrainer flew on February 23 1972. Primary customers were the Australian, New Zealand and Thai air forces. Production by NZAI (New Zealand Aircraft Industries), as AESL had become, continued until 1977.

In 1990 Pacific Aerospace Corporation (the successor to NZAI) resumed production of the improved CT-4B against an order from the BAe/Ansett Flying College (now BAE Systems Flight Training) in Tamworth, Australia, providing the impetus for further developments.

A turboprop Allison 250 powered CT-4C flew on January 21 1991, and a retractable undercarriage version, the CT-4CR was proposed. Development of the 225kW (300hp) IO-540 powered CT-4E was aimed for the US Air Force's Enhanced Flight Screening competition. Thirty CT-4Es have been built, including 13 for the Royal New Zealand Air Force to replace CT-4As (10 of which were refurbished and sold to BAE Systems Flight Training in Australia).

Photo: A CT-4E. (Peter Clark)

PAC Fletcher FU-24, Cresco & 750XL

Piaggio P.166

Country of origin: New Zealand

Type: Agricultural aircraft

Powerplant: FU-24-954 – One 300kW (400hp) Textron Lycoming IO-720-A1A or -A1B fuel injected flat eight piston engine driving a three blade constant speed Hartzell propeller. Cresco 08-750 – One 560kW (750shp) Pratt & Whitney Canada PT6A-34AG turboprop.

Performance: FU-24-954 – Max speed 233km/h (126kt), max cruising speed 209km/h (113kt), typical operating speed range 165 to 210km/h (90 to 115kt). Initial rate of climb 805ft/min. Service ceiling 16,000ft. Range with max payload and reserves 709km (383nm). 08-750 – Max speed 291km/h (157kt), max cruising speed at 75% power 261km/h (141kt). Initial rate of climb 1657ft/min. Service ceiling 26,000ft. Range with std fuel, no reserves 726km (392nm).

Weights: FU-24-954 – Empty equipped 1188kg (2620lb), max takeoff 2465kg (5430lb). 08-850 – Empty equipped 1315kg (2900lb), normal max takeoff 2925kg (6450lb), ag (restricted) category max takeoff 3742kg (8250lb).

Dimensions: FU-24-954 – Wing span 12.81m (42ft 0in), length 9.70m (31ft 10in), height 2.84m (9ft 4in). Wing area 27.3m² (294.0sq ft). 08-750 – Same except for length 11.07m (36ft 4in), height 3.63m (11ft 11in).

Capacity: Typical arrangement seats pilot and passenger, and chemical hopper (capacity 1210 litres in FU-24-954, 1770 litres in Cresco). Can also be configured for freight work, or can seat six in rear compartment (earlier models can seat five or six passengers).

Production: Almost 300 FU-24s built in the USA and New Zealand (70 in US, balance in NZ) since 1955. Approx 30 Crescos built.

History: Fletcher in the USA originally developed the FU-24 largely for agwork in New Zealand.

The FU-24 flew for the first time in June 1954, and production and deliveries began during 1955, following certification on July 22. Seventy 195kW (260hp) Continental IO-470-D powered FU-24s and slightly larger FU-24As were built in the USA before Fletcher ceased production in 1964, and Air Parts (now Pacific Aerospace) of New Zealand acquired the production rights.

Initial New Zealand production was of two models, one powered by a 215kW (285hp) Continental, the other a 225kW (300hp) unit. The subsequent FU-24-950 was powered by a 300kW (400hp) eight cylinder Lycoming IO-720, and was followed up by the similarly powered FU-24-954 from 1979.

Like many ag aircraft, the Fletcher was a natural candidate for conversion to turboprop power. The resulting Cresco first flew on February 28 1979 powered by a 450kW (600shp) Avco Lycoming (now Textron Lycoming) LTP 101. Nine such aircraft were built, while a tenth was fitted with a 560kW (750shp) PT6A-34AG.

Although PAC announced it would cease aircraft manufacture in 1994, PAC's new owners placed the Cresco back into production. Initial production was of the LTP 101 powered Cresco 08-600, now the focus is on the PT6A powered Cresco 08-750 or Cresco 750.

In 2000 PAC began work on the Cresco based 750XL, optimised for carrying skydivers with an enlarged fuselage. It first flew on September 5 2001 and can accommodate 17 skydivers.

Photo: The 750XL prototype. (Peter Clark)

Country of origin: Italy

Type: Commuter airliner and utility transport

Powerplants: P.166 – Two 255kW (340hp) Lycoming GSO-480-B1C6 geared and supercharged flat six piston engines driving three blade constant speed propellers. P.166DL3SEM – Two 450kW (600shp) AlliedSignal LTP 101-700 turboprops.

Performance: P.166 – Max speed 357km/h (193kt), max cruising speed 333km/h (180kt), economical cruising speed 280km/h (151kt). Initial rate of climb 1240ft/min. Service ceiling 25,000ft. Max range 1930km (1040nm). P.166-DL3SEM – Max speed 400km/h (215kt). Range with max payload 1390km (750nm), range with max fuel 2130km (1150nm).

Weights: P.166 – Empty 2350kg (5180lb), max takeoff 3680kg (8115lb). P.166-DL3SEM – Empty equipped 2688kg (5926lb), max takeoff 4300kg (9480lb).

Dimensions: P.166 – Wing span (without tip tanks) 14.25m (46ft 9in), length 11.61m (38ft 1in), height 5.00m (16ft 5in). Wing area 26.6m² (286sq ft). P.166-DL3SEM – Same except for wing span over tip tanks 14.69m (48ft 3in), length (including chin mounted radar) 11.88m (39ft 0in).

Capacity: Flightcrew of one or two and standard seating for eight or nine in main cabin in airliner configuration. Max seating for 12 in P.166C. Executive configuration seats five or six with toilet and bar. Air ambulance can carry two stretchers and two medical attendants.

Production: Approximately 145 P.166s of all models built. New production aircraft built on demand.

History: The Piaggio P.166 has been built in only small numbers but has been used in a wide variety of utility missions.

Intended for civil use when designed in the late 1950s, the P.166 features a large cabin which has been put to use in a variety of civil, military and quasi military roles, while its gull wing with tip tanks and pusher engines configuration like that on from the P.136 amphibian, ensures it is easily identified.

The prototype P.166 first flew on November 16 1957, and deliveries of the initial P.166 production model took place from April 1959. Just 23 were built before production switched to the P.166B Portofino, which featured more powerful 285kW (380hp) engines and an increased max takeoff weight of 3800kg (8377lb). Five Portofinos were built, while several earlier P.166s were converted to that standard with the more powerful engines.

The P.166C was introduced in 1964 and featured a larger cabin and 3950kg (8708lb) max takeoff weight. It could seat 12 passengers but only two were built.

The turboprop LTP 101 powered P.166.DL3 first flew in 1976 and was certificated in 1978. Alitalia has taken delivery of several for use as crew trainers, but most have been for the Italian government and military. Production of the radar and FLIR equipped P.166-DL3SEM continued into the 1990s for the Italian coast guard and today it remains available on demand. The 459kW (615shp) PT6A-121 powered P.166-DP1 first flew in May 1999 – eight were ordered by Italian customs and coast guard authorities.

Photo: An Australian registered P.166. (Bill Lines)

Piaggio P.180 Avanti

Country of origin: Italy

Type: Twin turboprop executive transport

Powerplants: Two 634kW (850shp) Pratt & Whitney Canada PT6A-66 turboprops driving five blade constant speed Hartzell propellers.

Performance: Max speed 732km/h (395kt), max cruising speed at 39,000ft 644km/h (348kt). Initial rate of climb 2950ft/min. Service ceiling 41,000ft. Range at 39,000ft with IFR reserves 2795km (1509nm).

Weights: Empty equipped 3400kg (7500lb), max takeoff 5240kg (11,550lb).

Dimensions: Wing span 14.03m (46ft 1in), length 14.41m (47ft 4in), height 3.98m (12ft 1in). Wing area 16.0m^2 (172.2sq ft).

Capacity: Flightcrew of one or two (certificated for single pilot operation). Max seating in main cabin for nine in high density airliner configuration. Standard seating for seven in individual seats. Executive/VIP seating for five.

Production: 30 Avantis built by early 1995, production resumed late 1998. Total production over 50.

History: The innovative Avanti was designed to combine jet like performance and with turboprop operating costs

The Avanti program launch was in 1981. Gates Learjet participated in Avanti development from 1983 and would have built the Avanti's forward fuselage, but withdrew from the project in January 1986. Piaggio assumed total control of the program, and all tooling and three forward fuselages for what would have been the Learjet P.180 were transferred to Italy.

The first of two P.180 prototypes first flew on September 23 1986, the second flew in May 1987. Italian certification was granted in March 1990, the first production Avanti flew that May and the first customer delivery took place in September 1990.

The Avanti features three flying surfaces – the canard foreplane, wing and tail. This arrangement not only offers the benefits of the canard, but meant the wing could be positioned in the rear of the fuselage, so that it doesn't intrude on interior cabin space. The small natural laminar flow wing was designed by the Ohio State University. The pusher engine configuration was chosen to reduce cabin noise.

Composites are used in a number of areas, including the tail, engine nacelles, canards, outboard wing flaps, landing gear doors and the tail cone, but generally, unlike the Beech Starship, most construction is conventional. A two multifunction display (plus weather radar display) Rockwell Collins EFIS glass flightdeck is standard, a five screen suite has been offered as an option.

Twice Piaggio has increased the P.180's maximum weight, thus improving its payload range.

Avanti production ceased in 1995 when Piaggio was placed under administration. Under new ownership the company was resurrected in November 1998 and Avanti production resumed.

The Italian air force is the Avanti's biggest operator, while other noted owners are Formula 1 car racer Ralf Schumacher and sports car manufacturer and Formula 1 team operator Ferrari.

Photo: A US registered Avanti. (Keith Gaskell)

Pilatus PC-6 Porter & Turbo Porter

Country of origin: Switzerland

Type: STOL utility transport

Powerplant: PC-6-H2 – One 255kW (340hp) Lycoming GSO-480-B1A6 geared and supercharged six cylinder piston engine driving a three blade constant speed propeller. PC-6/B2-H4 – One 410kW (550shp) flat rated Pratt & Whitney Canada PT6A-27 turboprop.

Performance: PC-6-H2 – Max speed 233km/h (126kt), max cruising speed 216km/h (117kt), economical cruising speed 190km/h (103kt). Initial rate of climb 550ft/min. Service ceiling 17,400ft. Max range with no reserves 1500km (810nm). PC-6/B2-H4 (Utility version) – Economical cruising speed 213km/h (115kt). Initial rate of climb 940ft/min. Max operating ceiling 25,000ft. Range with max payload at econ cruising speed and no reserves 730km (395nm), with max internal fuel 925km (500nm), with external fuel 1610km (870nm).

Weights: PC-6-H2 – Empty 1250kg (2755lb), max takeoff 2200kg (4850lb). PC-6/B2-H4 – Empty 1130kg (2491lb), max takeoff 2800kg (6173lb), max takeoff with skis 2600kg (5732lb).

Dimensions: PC-6-H2 – Wing span 15.14m (49ft 8in), length 10.20m (33ft 6in), height tail down 3.20m (10ft 6in). Wing area 28.8m^2 (310sq ft). PC-6/B2-H4 – Wing span 15.87m (52ft 1in), length 10.90m (35ft 9in), height 3.20m (10ft 6in). Wing area 30.2m^2 (324.5sq ft).

Capacity: Pilot and passenger on flightdeck, with standard seating for six in main cabin. Max seating for 11 including pilot. Alternative layouts include two stretchers and three medical attendants, or 10 skydivers. Some equipped for agricultural spraying.

Production: 522 Porters of all versions built, including 92 under licence in the USA and 45 piston powered Porters.

History: The Pilatus Porter and Turbo Porter STOL utilities are renowned for their exceptional STOL performance and low speed handling and have sold strongly on the strength of their performance.

The high wing taildragger Porter was designed to perform a range of utility roles, and first flew on May 4 1959. The first production aircraft built were delivered from 1960 and were powered by a six cylinder GSO-480 piston engine, but it was not long after that a turboprop powered development flew.

The first PC-6/A Turbo Porter flew in May 1961, powered by a 390kW (523shp) Turbomeca Astazou II turboprop. The majority of PC-6s are PC-6/Bs, powered by the Pratt & Whitney Canada PT6A. PC-6/Cs were powered by a 310kW (575shp) AiResearch TPE331, and were first delivered in 1965.

Smaller numbers of piston powered Porters have been built in parallel with Turbo Porters with Lycoming GSO-480s and IGO-540s.

The PC-6/B was first delivered from 1964. Initial models were powered by the 410kW (550shp) PT6A-6 or -20. The PC-6/B2-H2 first flew in 1970 and introduced the PT6A-27 and an increased maximum takeoff weight.

The final Porter production model was the PC-6/B2-H4 which was introduced in 1985. It features a further increase in max takeoff weight, larger dorsal fin fillet, revised wingtips, strengthened airframe structure and improved undercarriage. The H-4's improvements can be retrofitted to the H-2. Production ceased in 2000.

Photo: A floatplane Turbo Porter. (Keith Myers)

Pilatus PC-12

Country of origin: Switzerland

Type: Corporate, utility and regional airliner turboprop

Powerplant: One 895kW (1200shp) takeoff rated Pratt & Whitney Canada PT6A-67B turboprop driving a four blade constant speed Hartzell propeller.

Performance: Max cruising speed at 25,000ft 500km/h (270kt), economical cruising speed 430km/h (232kt). Initial rate of climb 1680ft/min. Max operating altitude 30,000ft. Max range at economical cruising speed with VFR reserves 4187km (2260nm). Range at max cruising speed with IFR reserves 2965km (1600nm).

Weights: PC-12 – Standard empty 2600kg (5732lb), executive configuration empty 2903kg (6400lb), combi empty 2536kg (5591lb), max takeoff 4500kg (9920lb).

Dimensions: Wing span 16.23m (52ft 3in), length 14.40m (47ft 3in), height 4.27m (14ft 0in). Wing area 25.8m² (277.8sq ft).

Capacity: Flightcrew of one or two pilots (certificated for single pilot). Seating for nine in main cabin in regional airliner configuration. Corporate/executive transport configurations typically seat six in main cabin. Combi passenger/freight version seats four passengers in main cabin plus freight pallet.

Production: The 300th PC-12 was delivered in late 2001.

History: The PC-12 is a King Air class and size turboprop aimed at the corporate transport and regional airliner markets. It is the latest in a line of single engined PT6 powered Pilatus products.

Pilatus announced it was developing the PC-12 at the NBAA's annual convention in October 1989. First flight of the first of two prototypes occurred on May 31 1991. Certification was originally planned for mid 1993, but after a redesign of the wings with the addition of winglets to ensure performance guarantees were met, Swiss certification was awarded on March 30 1994 and US FAA FAR Part 23 approval followed on July 15 1994.

Compared to the King Air 200 twin, its major competitor, the PC-12's most significant design feature (apart from it being a more modern design) is its use of a single PT6A-67B turboshaft. Internally the PC-12's cabin is also longer (by 6cm/2.4in) and wider (by 15cm/6in) than the King Air 200's, and the same height. The cockpit features EFIS displays and the PC-12 is certificated for single pilot operation, while each PC-12 built features a standard cargo door in the rear fuselage. Weather radar is an option but has been fitted to all production aircraft thus far. From 1997 the increased 4.5 tonne MTOW has been standard. New, smaller winglets were introduced in 1998.

The PC-12 is offered in standard nine seat airliner form, in a four passenger seat/freight combi version and as a six place corporate transport. A pure freighter model has also been considered. The PC-12 Eagle is a military special missions platform.

Most PC-12s built thus far have been corporate transports, but important regulatory changes in Australia, Brazil, Canada and the USA in the late 1990s cleared single engine turboprops for IFR RPT operations in those nations. This opened up new markets for the PC-12 as a regional airliner, replacing older King Airs and elderly piston twins such as the Navajo Chieftain and Cessna 400 series.

Photo: A PC-12. (Les Bushell)

Piper Cub

Country of origin: United States of America

Type: Two seat light aircraft

Powerplant: J-3C-65 – One 50kW (65hp) Continental A-65-1 flat four piston engine driving a two blade fixed pitch propeller. PA-12 – One 75kW (100hp) Lycoming O-235 flat four.

Performance: J-3C-65 – Max speed 148km/h (80kt), typical cruising speed 132km/h (71kt). Initial rate of climb 450ft/min. Service ceiling 12,000ft. Range 402km (217nm). PA-12 – Max speed 183km/h (99kt), normal cruising speed 170km/h (90kt). Service ceiling 12,600ft. Range 580km (313nm).

Weights: J-3C-65 – Empty 290kg (640lb), max takeoff 500kg (1100lb). PA-12 – Empty 430kg (950lb), max takeoff 795kg (1750lb).

Dimensions: Wing span 10.75m (35ft 3in), length 6.79m (22ft 3in), height 2.03m (6ft 8in). Wing area 16.6m² (178.5sq ft). PA-12 – Wing span 10.83m (35ft 6in), length 6.74m (22ft 1in), height 2.08m (6ft 10in). Wing area 16.7m² (179.3sq ft).

Capacity: Typical seating for two in tandem in the Cub, Cub Coupe and Cub Special, three in the Cub Cruiser and Super Cruiser, and four in the Family Cruiser.

Production: Production includes 5795 prewar J-3s, 8252 postwar J-3C-65s, 1248 J-4 Cub Coupes, over 1410 J-5 Cub Cruisers, more than 430 PA-11 Cub Specials, 3761 PA-12 Super Cruisers and 521 PA-14 Family Cruisers. Wartime construction of 5687 L-4s.

History: The simple and economical Cub is one of the most well loved light aircraft of all time, and helped make flying an affordable pastime for thousands of pilots in the years surrounding World War 2.

The Piper Cub began life as the Taylor E-2 Tiger Kitten, which was powered by a tiny 15kW (20hp) Brownbach engine. The Tiger Kitten was grossly underpowered and the Taylor Brothers' Airplane Company went bankrupt before a more powerful engine could be found. Businessman William Piper, who had made large profits from the oil industry, purchased a majority holding in the Taylor company in 1931 for $US1000. The company continued building derivatives of the E-2 under the Taylor banner through the 1930s. The first aircraft to be called Cub was the E-2 powered by a Continental A-40. Small numbers were built from 1931.

In 1937 Piper adopted his own name for the company, and the first J-3 Cubs were built. The J-3 was an improved J-2, resulting from a redesign of the three cylinder radial powered H-2 by Walter Janouneay. The affordable J-3 Cub became a runaway sales success and several thousand were sold before the USA's entry into WW2 saw all J-3 production built for the US Army as the L-4. Prewar Piper also built the J-4 Cub Coupe with side by side seating and the three seat J-5 Cub Cruiser.

Postwar Piper reverted to civilian production with the J-3 later becoming the PA-11 Cub Special. Late build PA-11s were powered by a 65kW (90hp) Continental C-90 and had increased range. The PA-12 Super Cruiser has seating for three and a more powerful Lycoming O-235 engine, while the four seat PA-14 Family Cruiser formed the basis for the Super Cub.

Photo: This German registered J-3C Cub was originally built as an L-4A for the USAAF. (Peter Vercruijsse)

Piper PA-18 Super Cub

Country of origin: United States of America

Type: Two seat utility light aircraft

Powerplant: PA-18-95 – One 65kW (90hp) Continental C-90-12F or -8F flat four piston engine driving a two blade fixed pitch propeller. PA-18-150 – One 110kW (150hp) Lycoming O-320.

Performance: PA-18-95 – Max speed 180km/h (97kt), max cruising speed 161km/h (87kt). Initial rate of climb 710ft/min. Service ceiling 15,750ft. Max range with no reserves 580km (313nm). PA-18-150 – Max speed 210km/h (113kt), max cruising speed 185km/h (100kt), economical cruising speed 170km/h (90kt). Initial rate of climb 960ft/min. Service ceiling 19,000ft. Range at max cruising speed and no reserves 740km (400nm).

Weights: PA-18-95 – Empty 367kg (910lb), max takeoff 680kg (1500lb). PA-18-150 – Empty 429kg (946lb), max takeoff 794kg (1750lb).

Dimensions: PA-18-95 – Wing span 10.73m (35ft 3in), length 6.83m (22ft 5in), height 2.02m (6ft 9in). Wing area 16.6m² (178.5sq ft). PA-18-150 – Same except for length 6.88m (22ft 7in).

Capacity: Typical seating for two in tandem.

Production: Almost 7500 Super Cubs (including 1700 military) built until 1981 when production originally ceased. Piper production for WTA between 1982 and 1988 totalled 250. Piper production between 1988 and 1994 approximately 100.

History: The Super Cub is one of Piper's most successful and long lived aircraft programs, with production spanning over four decades.

The PA-18 Super Cub was the ultimate development of Piper's original aircraft, the J-3 Cub (described separately). The four seat development of the Cub, the PA-14 Cub Cruiser, was the basis for the Super Cub, but the later differed in having seating for two in tandem (as on the Cub), all metal wings and, in its initial form, a 65kW (90hp) Continental C-90 in the PA-18-90 or a 80kW (108hp) Lycoming O-235 engine in the PA-18-105. The Super Cub flew for the first time in 1949, and certification was awarded on November 18 that year. The first production Super Cubs were delivered from late 1949, the type replacing the PA-11 Cub Special on Piper's production lines.

The 100kW (135hp) Lycoming O-290 powered PA-18-135 appeared in 1952, while the definitive 110kW (150hp) Lycoming O-320 powered PA-18-150 was certificated on October 1 1954 and delivered from the following year.

The Super Cub remained in production with Piper through until 1981, when almost 7500 had been built over an uninterrupted 32 year production run. Piper continued building Super Cubs on behalf of Texas based WTA who held the manufacturing and marketing rights from 1981 until 1988. In 1988 Piper resumed marketing responsibility for the Super Cub and continued low rate production. Financial troubles meant that Super Cub production ceased in 1992, before resuming once more the following year. Finally in late 1994 Piper announced that the Super Cub would not form part of its model line for 1995 and that it would cease production after the last of 24 on order for distributor Muncie Aviation were completed.

Photo: A US registered PA-18-150 Super Cub. (Keith Myers)

Piper PA-20 Pacer & PA-22 Tri-Pacer & Colt

Country of origin: United States of America

Type: Two and four seat light aircraft

Powerplant: PA-22-108 Colt – One 80kW (108hp) Lycoming O-235-C1B flat four piston engine driving a two blade fixed pitch propeller. PA-22-160 Tri-Pacer – One 119kW (160hp) Lycoming O-320-B2A.

Performance: PA-22-108 – Max speed 193km/h (104kt), max cruising speed 173km/h (93kt). Initial rate of climb 610ft/min. Service ceiling 12,000ft. Max range with no reserves 1110km (600nm). PA-22-160 – Max speed 227km/h (123kt), max cruising speed 216km/h (117kt). Initial rate of climb 800ft/min. Service ceiling 16,500ft. Range with standard fuel and no reserves 862km (465nm), with optional fuel 1054km (569nm).

Weights: PA-22-108 – Empty 447kg (985lb), max takeoff 748kg (1650lb). PA-22-160 – Empty 503kg (1110lb), max takeoff 907kg (2000lb).

Dimensions: PA-22-108 – Wing span 9.14m (30ft 0in), length 6.10m (20ft 0in), height 1.91m (6ft 3in). Wing area 13.66m² (147sq ft). PA-22-160 – Wing span 8.92m (29ft 3in), length 6.28m (20ft 7in), height 2.53m (8ft 4in). Wing area 13.7m² (147.5sq ft).

Capacity: Pacer and Tri-Pacers (including Caribbean) typically seat four, while the Colt seats two side by side. Seaplane versions of the Tri-Pacer could seat three.

Production: Total PA-22 production of 9495 comprising 7688 Tri-Pacers and 1827 Colts, while 1699 PA-20 Pacers were built.

History: The Pacer and Tri-Pacer designs were Piper's volume selling four seaters from 1949 through to the introduction of the Comanche and Cherokee in the early 1960s, while the Colt was a two seat training derivative of the Tri-Pacer.

The original tail dragger PA-20 Pacer was introduced in 1949 alongside the two seat Super Cub, and was powered by a 85kW (115hp) Continental engine. Improvements were made in 1950, including a larger tail, while a 93kW (125hp) variant was added. From 1952 to 1954 when production ceased the Pacer was offered in 93kW (125hp) and 100kW (135hp) variants.

The tricycle undercarriage Tri-Pacer (with the same engine options) initially augmented the Pacer in production from 1950 until Pacer production ceased in 1954. The Tri-Pacer gained a 110kW (150hp) engine and a higher takeoff weight from 1955, and a 120kW (160hp) O-320 from 1957. From 1958 Piper offered a lower spec, less expensive version of the Tri-Pacer as the PA-22-150 Caribbean.

The two seat Colt was derived from the Tri-Pacer but had a less powerful 85kW (108hp) engine, lower maximum takeoff weight, no rear cabin windows, the removal of a rear door and less fuel capacity, but otherwise the two airframes were identical. Piper introduced the Colt to its lineup in late 1960, and the type remained in production for just over two years until the two seat Cherokee could be introduced. Colt production ceased in 1963 after almost 2000 had been built.

The Tri-Pacer and Colt were Piper's only high wing tricycle undercarriage aircraft, and the last in production to feature metal tubing and fabric covering construction.

Photo: A UK registered PA-22-160 Tri-Pacer. (Peter Vercruijsse)

Piper PA-23 Apache & Aztec

Country of origin: United States of America

Type: Four seat light twins

Powerplant: PA-23-235 Apache – Two 175kW (235hp) Lycoming O-540-B1A5 flat six piston engines driving two blade constant speed Hartzell propellers. PA-23-250T Aztec F – Two 185kW (250hp) turbocharged and fuel injected Lycoming TIO-540-C1As.

Performance: PA-23-235 – Max speed 325km/h (176kt), max cruising speed 307km/h (166kt). Initial rate of climb 1450ft/min. Service ceiling 17,200ft. Max range with no reserves 1907km (1030nm). PA-23-250T – Max speed 408km/h (220kt), max cruising speed 390km/h (211kt), economical cruising speed 335km/h (181kt). Initial rate of climb 1470ft/min. Service ceiling 24,000ft. Range at max cruising speed 1797km (970nm), at economical cruising speed 2309km (1246nm).

Weights: PA-23-235 – Empty 1241kg (2735lb), MTOW 2177kg (4800lb). PA-23-250T – Empty 1508kg (3323lb), MTOW 2360kg (5200lb).

Dimensions: PA-23-235 – Wing span 11.32m (37ft 2in), length 8.41m (27ft 7in). Wing area 19.2m² (207sq ft). PA-23-250T – Wing span 11.39m (37ft 4in), length 9.53m (31ft 3in), height 3.08m (10ft 1in). Wing area 19.2m² (207sq ft).

Capacity: Apache standard seating for four. Aztec As seat five, later Aztecs seat six.

Production: Almost 7000 PA-23s built, comprising 2047 Apaches and 4929 Aztecs, including a small number of military variants.

History: The origins of the Apache (one of the first widely available GA twins and Piper's first 'Indian') and the larger and more powerful Aztec lie in the early postwar Twin Stinson design.

Piper acquired the assets of Consolidated Vultee's Stinson Aircraft division in 1948, inheriting a design study for a new four place light twin. Piper left the design dormant for a few years until 1952 when it built a prototype aircraft, designated 23-01, based on the Stinson design. The low wing four seat twin was powered by 93kW (125hp) Lycoming engines, had fabric covering, fixed undercarriage and a twin fin tail design.

Unsatisfactory flight trials led Piper to substantially redesign the 23-01, introducing more powerful 110kW (150hp) engines, metal construction, retractable undercarriage and a conventional tail unit. Designated the PA-23 Apache, the redesigned twin flew for the first time on March 2 1952. Production deliveries began in March 1954.

Apache A, B, C, D and E subvariants of the initial PA-23-150 were built before production switched to the more powerful PA-23-160 Apache F in late 1958. Subsequent Apache developments were the Apache G and H with a third cabin window, and the Apache 235, a lower powered development of the Aztec A introduced in 1962.

The Aztec is an enlarged and more powerful development of the Apache powered by two six cylinder 185kW (250hp) O-540s, and Aztec As were first delivered from early 1960. The Aztec B introduced a longer nose and seating for six, the Aztec C fuel injected engines, the optional Aztec C Turbo was turbocharged, while the Aztec D, E and F and corresponding turbo models introduced detail changes.

Production ceased in 1982.

Photo: A New Zealand registered Aztec. (Rob Finlayson)

Piper PA-24 Comanche

Country of origin: United States of America

Type: Four seat high performance light aircraft

Powerplant: PA-24-250 – One 185kW (250hp) Lycoming O-540-A1A5 flat six driving a constant speed propeller. PA-24-400 – One 300kW (400hp) Lycoming IO-720-A1A flat eight driving a three blade c/s prop. PA-24-260 Turbo C – One 200kW (260hp) turbocharged and fuel injected IO-540-R1A5 flat six driving a two blade c/s prop.

Performance: PA-24-250 – Max speed 306km/h (165kt), max cruising speed 291km/h (157kt). Initial rate of climb 1350ft/min. Service ceiling 20,000ft. Max range with optional fuel 2665km (1440nm). PA-24-400 – Max speed 360km/h (194kt), max cruising speed 343km/h (185kt). Initial rate of climb 1600ft/min. Service ceiling 19,500ft. Range with standard fuel 2012km (1086nm), with optional fuel 2478km (1338nm). PA-24-260 Turbo C – Max speed 390km/h (210kt), max cruising speed 318km/h (172kt). Initial rate of climb 1320ft/min. Operating ceiling 25,000ft. Max range 2052km (1108nm), with optional fuel 2398km (1295nm).

Weights: PA-24-250 – Empty 767kg (1690lb), max TO 1315kg (2900lb). PA-24-400 – Empty 957kg (2110lb), max TO 1633kg (3600lb). PA-24-260 Turbo C – Empty 860kg (1894lb), max takeoff 1450kg (3200lb).

Dimensions: PA-24-250 – Wing span 10.97m (36ft 0in), length 7.59m (24ft 11in), height 2.29m (7ft 6in). Wing area 16.5m² (178sq ft). PA-28-400 – Wing span 10.97m (36ft 0in), length 7.84m (25ft 8in), height 2.39m (7ft 10in). Wing area 16.5m² (178sq ft). PA-24-260 Turbo C – Wing span 10.97m (36ft 0in), length 7.62m (25ft 0in), height 2.29m (7ft 6in). Wing area 16.5m² (178sq ft).

Capacity: Standard seating for four, Comanche B and C could have optional fifth and sixth seats.

Production: Total PA-24 production 4856, including 1143 180s, 2537 250s, 1028 260s and 260 Ts, and 148 400s.

History: Piper's PA-24 Comanche was a high performance retractable undercarriage single designed to challenge the established Beech Bonanza.

Piper's first low wing single engine design, the Comanche featured retractable tricycle undercarriage, swept back tail, flying tail or 'stabilator' horizontal tail surfaces, laminar flow wing and all metal construction, a stark contrast to Piper's earlier high wing fabric covered designs. The Comanche first flew on May 24 1956 and was delivered to customers from late 1957 in PA-24-180 form.

Since then through to the cessation of production in June 1972 (due to flooding of Piper's Lock Haven plant), a number of progressively higher performance variants were released. These included 1958's 185kW (250hp) PA-24-250 and the 300kW (400hp) PA-24-400.

Just 148 400s were built, despite Piper claiming it to be the fastest production four seat single available at the time. Its massive eight cylinder IO-720 engine consumed fuel at a prodigious rate, so it was expensive to operate, and there were problems with cooling the rear cylinders. Today however it has something of a mini cult status.

Following the PA-24-400 was the PA-24-260 from 1964, with a 195kW (260hp) O-540 or IO-540, and finally the Rajay turbocharger fitted PA-24-260 Turbo C, available from 1970.

Photo: Initial Comanches were PA-24-180s and -250s. (Gary Gentle)

Piper PA-25 Pawnee & PA-36 Pawnee Brave

Country of origin: United States of America

Type: Agricultural aircraft

Powerplant: PA-25-235 – One 175kW (235hp) Lycoming O-540-B2B5 flat six piston engine driving a two blade fixed pitch McCauley propeller. PA-36-375 – One 280kW (375hp) Lycoming IO-720-DICD fuel injected flat eight driving a three blade constant speed Hartzell prop.

Performance: PA-25-235 – Max speed 188km/h (102kt), cruising speed 170km/h (91kt), typical spraying speed 145km/h (78kt). Initial rate of climb 630ft/min. Service ceiling 13,000ft. PA-36-325 – Max speed 216km/h (116kt), cruising speed 210km/h (113kt), spraying speed range 161 to 193km/h (87 to 104kt). Initial rate of climb 550ft/min. Service ceiling 15,000ft. Range 772km (417nm).

Weights: PA-25-235 – Empty 585kg (1288lb), max takeoff 1317kg (2900lb). PA-36-375 – Empty 1162kg (2560lb), max takeoff 2180kg (4800lb).

Dimensions: PA-25-235 – Wing span 11.02m (36ft 2in), length 7.55m (24ft 9in), height 2.19m (7ft 2in). Wing area 17.0m² (183sq ft). PA-36-375 – Wing span 11.82m (38ft 10in), length 8.39m (27ft 6in), height 2.29m (7ft 6in). Wing area 21.0m² (225.65sq ft).

Capacity: Seating for pilot only, but can be fitted with an optional jump seat. PA-25-235 – Hopper capacity 568 litres (150US gal/125Imp gal), or 545kg (1200lb). PA-36-375 – Hopper capacity 1041 litres (275US gal/229Imp gal), or 1000kg (2200lb).

Production: Total PA-25 Pawnee production 5015. PA-36 Pawnee Brave production ceased in 1982.

History: The Piper Pawnee was one of the first single seat light aircraft to be specifically designed and built for agricultural spraying and dusting. It was also one of the most successful, with several thousand built.

The PA-25 Pawnee was originally designed by Fred Weick as the Ag-3, and flew in prototype form in 1957. The design was originally powered by a 110kW (150hp) Lycoming O-320, the fuselage structure was designed to absorb impact forces in a crash, the high cockpit had excellent all round vision, the braced wing was fitted with spray bars, and a jump seat could be fitted in the hopper.

Initial production was of the 110kW (150hp) powered Pawnee, which was delivered from August 1959. The Pawnee was replaced by the 175kW (235hp) powered Pawnee B with an enlarged hopper, the Pawnee C followed with oleo type shock absorbers, while the ultimate Pawnee model, the Pawnee D, had a 195kW (260hp) O-540. Production ceased in 1982.

The PA-36 Pawnee Brave meanwhile was a much larger new design, although of the same overall configuration to the Pawnee. The result of Piper research on Pawnee operations, the Pawnee Brave (originally the Pawnee II) was available from 1971. Initial production was of the 210kW (285hp) Continental O-285 Tiara powered PA-36-285. The 225kW (300hp) Lycoming IO-540 powered Brave 300, 280kW (375hp) IO-720 powered Brave 375, and 300kW (400hp) IO-720 powered Brave 400 followed.

Pawnee Brave production ceased in 1982.

Photo: A PA-25-235 Pawnee B. (David Fraser)

Piper PA-28 Cherokee Series

Country of origin: United States of America

Type: Two and four seat light aircraft

Powerplant: PA-28-161 Warrior II – One 110kW (160hp) Lycoming O-320-A2B flat four piston engine driving a two blade fixed pitch propeller. PA-28-181 Archer III – One 135kW (180hp) Textron Lycoming O-360-A4M flat four.

Performance: PA-28-161 – Max speed 235km/h (127kt), max cruising speed 233km/h (126kt), long range cruising speed 195km/h (105kt). Initial rate of climb 644ft/min. Service ceiling 11,000ft. Max range with reserves 1185km (637nm). PA-28-181 – Max speed 246km/h (133kt), normal cruising speed 237km/h (128kt). Initial rate of climb 692ft/min. Service ceiling 14,100ft. Range with reserves at 75% power 822km (444nm), at 55% power 966km (522nm).

Weights: PA-28-161 – Empty 613kg (1352lb), MTOW 1105kg (2440lb). PA-28-181 – Empty equipped 766kg (1689lb), MTOW 1155kg (2550lb).

Dimensions: PA-28-161 – Wing span 10.67m (35ft 0in), length overall 7.25m (23ft 10in), height 2.22m (7ft 4in). Wing area 15.8m² (170sq ft). PA-28-181 – Same except length 7.32m.

Capacity: Seating for four, two in some dedicated trainer versions.

Production: Over 30,000 fixed undercarriage PA-28 Cherokee series built, including approximately 10,100 PA-28-140s, 10,400 PA-28-180s & -181s, 5000 PA-28-151 & -161s, and 2800 PA-28-235 & 236s.

History: The initial PA-28-150 and PA-28-160 Cherokees were introduced in 1961 as replacements for Piper's PA-22 Tri-Pacer and Colt.

Unlike the PA-22 series the new PA-28 was a low wing design with metal construction. The prototype Cherokee was powered by a 120kW (160hp) engine, and flew for the first time on January 14 1960. Production aircraft were powered by either 110kW (150hp) or 120kW (160hp) engines and were delivered from early 1961.

From 1962 a 135kW (180hp) version was added to the lineup. The 175kW (235hp) flat six Lycoming O-540 powered Cherokee 235 was introduced in 1963, while the two seat trainer optimised Colt replacement PA-28-140 entered the marketplace in 1964. With these models the basic PA-28 lineup was in place (the retractable PA-28R and larger PA-32 are described separately).

Subsequent variants include the Cherokee B and Cherokee C, the 180D, 235C, 140 Flite Liner two seat trainer PA-28-140, 180F, 235E, PA-28-180 Cherokee Challenger and PA-28-235 Cherokee Charger, the PA-28-180 Cherokee Archer and PA-28-235 Cherokee Pathfinder, PA-28-151 Cherokee Warrior which introduced the new tapered wing that would become a feature of subsequent PA-28s, PA-28-181 Cherokee Archer II and PA-28-236 Dakota (the Cherokee prefix was later dropped for the Archer II and Warrior), the PA-28-161 Warrior II, PA-28-236T Turbo Dakota and PA-28-161 Cadet.

Small numbers of Warriors, Dakotas and Archers were built in the early 1990s. The Archer III was introduced in 1994, and features a new, streamlined cowling. 1999 models gained new paint, improved interior and a new avionics package. The PA-28-161 Warrior III features a new instrument panel and was introduced in late 1994. Since 1995 Piper has had new owners, and the brand has enjoyed a strong resurgence.

Photo: Piper has built over 500 Archer IIIs since 1995. (Gary Gentle)

Piper PA-28R Cherokee Arrow

Country of origin: United States of America

Type: Four seat light aircraft

Powerplant: PA-28R-180 – One 135kW (180hp) Lycoming IO-360-B1E fuel injected flat four piston engine driving a two blade constant speed Hartzell propeller. PA-28R-201T – One 150kW (200hp) Continental TSIO-360-FB turbocharged and fuel injected flat six.

Performance: PA-28R-180 – Max speed 274km/h (148kt), typical cruising speed 260km/h (140kt), long range cruising speed 230km/h (124kt). Initial rate of climb 875ft/min. Service ceiling 15,000ft. Range at economical cruising speed 1600km (865nm). PA-28R-201T – Max speed 330km/h (178kt), max cruising speed 320km/h (172kt), long range cruising speed 284km/h (153kt). Initial rate of climb 940ft/min. Range with reserves 1667km (900nm).

Weights: PA-28R-180 – Empty 626kg (1380lb), max takeoff 1134kg (2500lb). PA-28R-201T – Empty 786kg (1732lb), max takeoff 1315kg (2900lb).

Dimensions: PA-28R-180 – Wing span 9.14m (30ft 0in), length 7.38m (24ft 3in), height 2.44m (8ft 0in). Wing area 14.2m^2 (160sq ft). PA-28R-201T – Wing span 10.80m (35ft 5in), length 8.33m (27ft 3in), height 2.52m (8ft 3in). Wing area 15.9m^2 (170sq ft).

Capacity: Typical seating for four.

Production: Approx 6000 PA-28Rs built, incl 81 PA-28R-180Bs, 1664 PA-28R-200s and -201s, and 1291 PA-28R-201Ts and PA-28RT-201Ts.

History: The PA-28R began life as a retractable undercarriage variant of the PA-28 Cherokee.

The original PA-28-180R Cherokee Arrow was a development of the PA-28-180 Cherokee D with electro-hydraulically operated retractable undercarriage (with a self lowering system that safeguarded against the pilot failing to do so, automatically lowering when airspeed reached 170km/h/91kt and a certain engine manifold pressure), a fuel injected version of the PA-28-180's O-360, a constant speed propeller and an increased max takeoff weight.

Production switched to the PA-28R-180 and more powerful 150kW (200hp) IO-360-C1C powered PA-28R-200 Cherokee Arrow II. Changes included the same 12.7cm (5in) stretched fuselage introduced on the Cherokee Challenger and Cherokee Charger, with greater rear legroom and baggage capacity, plus larger horizontal tail and dorsal fin fillet.

The PA-28R-201 Arrow III first flew in September 1975, and was introduced from 1976. The major change (also introduced on the fixed undercarriage PA-28s at that time) was a new wing with longer tapered span, while the maximum takeoff weight was increased. The turbocharged PA-28R-201T was also offered.

The PA-28RT-201 and -201T Arrow IV introduced a new all moving T-tail. Production of the Arrow IV stoped in 1982, resumed again in 1989, but ceased once more in 1992. Instead Piper returned the conventional tailed Arrow III back into production. Very small numbers were built in the early 1990s while Piper was under bankruptcy protection. Since the emergence of New Piper Inc in 1995 the Arrow III has been part of the expanded Piper line-up, although only small numbers have been built.

Photo: The T-tailed Arrow IV. (Theo van Loon)

Piper PA-32 Cherokee Six, Lance & Saratoga

Country of origin: United States of America

Type: Six seat high performance light aircraft

Powerplant: PA-32RT-300 Lance II – One 225kW (300hp) Lycoming IO-540-K1G5 fuel injected flat six piston engine driving a two blade c/s prop. PA-32-301T Saratoga II TC – One 225kW (300hp) turbocharged Textron Lycoming TIO-540-AH1A driving a three blade c/s prop.

Performance: PA-32RT-300 – Max speed 306km/h (165kt), max cruising speed 293km/h (158kt), long range cruising speed 258km/h (139kt). Initial rate of climb 1000ft/min. Service ceiling 14,600ft. Max range with reserves 1600km (865nm). PA-32-301T – Max speed 346km/h (187kt), cruising speed at 10,000ft 324km/h (175kt), at 15,000ft 343km/h (185kt). Max certificated ceiling 20,000ft. Range at long range cruise power and 10,000ft 1756km (948nm).

Weights: PA-32RT-300 – Empty 912kg (2011lb), max takeoff 1633kg (3600lb). PA-32R-301T – Empty equipped 1118kg (2465lb), max takeoff 1633kg (3600lb).

Dimensions: PA-32RT-300 – Wing span 9.99m (32ft 10in), length 8.44m (27ft 9in), height 2.90m (9ft 6in). Wing area 16.2m^2 (174.5sq ft). PA-32T-301T – Wing span 11.02m (36ft 2in), length 8.23m (27ft 0in), height 2.59m (8ft 6in). Wing area 16.6m^2 (178.3sq ft).

Capacity: Seating for six, some with an optional seventh seat.

Production: Approximately 7200 PA-32s of all versions have been built, including over 250 Saratoga II HPs/TCs since 1993.

History: The PA-32 series began life as the Cherokee Six, a significantly modified six seat development of the PA-28 Cherokee series.

While similar in configuration to the Cherokee, the Cherokee Six differed in a number of major areas. Two of the big differences were implied in its name, a six cylinder O-540 or IO-540 powerplant, and the six seat configuration. While the wing was based on the Cherokee's, the fuselage was substantially larger, with strengthened undercarriage and a larger tail.

The Cherokee Six first flew on December 6 1963, while deliveries of production PA-32-260s began from mid 1965. Development led to a range of improved models, starting with the 225kW (300hp) fuel injected IO-540 powered Cherokee Six-300 (PA-32-300). Production of the -260 and -300 ended in the late 1970s, but in the meantime they had been joined by the Cherokee Lance. The Cherokee Lance, or just Lance from mid 1977 with the introduction of the improved Lance II, was a retractable undercarriage development. The Lance II and turbocharged PA-32R-300T Turbo Lance also introduced a T-tail and remained in production to late 1979.

The Lance II and Cherokee Six were replaced by the Saratoga. Available in fixed or retractable undercarriage form, with standard or turbocharged powerplants, the major change was the new increased span tapered wing.

Production of the Saratoga ceased in 1985, but Piper reintroduced the Saratoga II HP in 1993 with aerodynamic improvements and a revised instrument panel and interior. The turbocharged Saratoga II TC was introduced in 1997. 1999 models introduced new Garmin and S-TEC avionics. A five seat interior with a entertainment/workstation console (similar to that in the Seneca V) is optional.

Photo: A PA-32R-301T Saratoga SP. (Gerard Frawley)

Piper PA-30 & PA-39 Twin Comanche

Country of origin: United States of America

Type: Six seat light twin

Powerplants: PA-30-160 – Two 120kW (160hp) Lycoming IO-320-B1A fuel injected flat four piston engines driving two blade constant speed Hartzell propellers. PA-39T – Two 120kW (160hp) counter rotating Lycoming IO-320-C1As.

Performance: PA-30-160 – Max speed 330km/h (178kt), max cruising speed 312km/h (168kt), long range cruising speed 267km/h (144kt). Initial rate of climb 1460ft/min. Service ceiling 18,600ft. Max range with no reserves and standard fuel 1795km (970nm), or with tip tanks 2190km (1182nm). PA-39T – Max speed 376km/h (203kt), max cruising speed 357km/h (193kt), economical cruising speed 327km/h (177kt). Initial rate of climb 1460ft/min. Service ceiling 25,000ft. Range at max cruising speed 2373km (1282nm), range at economical cruising speed 2582km (1395nm).

Weights: PA-30-160 – Empty 1002kg (2210lb), max takeoff 1633kg (3600lb), or 1690kg (3725lb) with tip tanks. PA-30-160 – Empty 1097kg (2416lb), max ramp 1690kg (3725lb).

Dimensions: Wing span 10.97m (36ft 0in) or 11.22m (36ft 10in) with tip tanks, length 7.67m (25ft 2in), height 2.49m (8ft 2in). Wing area 16.5m² (178sq ft).

Capacity: Typical seating for four, including pilot in Twin Comanche. Up to six including pilot in Twin Comanche B.

Production: Total Twin Comanche production was 2156, comprising 2001 PA-30s and 155 PA-39s.

History: As its name implies, the Twin Comanche is a twin engine development of the PA-24 Comanche. When in production, it was Piper's premier four/six place light twin, replacing the Apache 235 and positioned beneath the larger and more powerful Aztec.

The Twin Comanche was originally proposed as early as 1956, when the single engine Comanche was undergoing initial development, however the project was delayed while Piper worked on the Comanche and the Aztec twin. So it was not until 1962 that a Comanche was converted to a twin configuration with two 120kW (160hp) IO-320s (originally two 110kW/150hp engines were planned), with first flight on November 7 1962. First flight of a production Twin Comanche was in May 1963, with first deliveries later that year.

The Twin Comanche differed little from its single engine brethren other than changes associated with its twin engine layout, and it quickly proved to be very popular. Improvements to the PA-30 resulted in the introduction of the Twin Comanche B in 1965, which featured a stretched fuselage allowing seating for up to six, as on the equivalent Comanche B single, while turbocharged engines and wingtip tanks were offered as options.

From 1970 the Twin Comanche C featured a slightly higher cruising speed and interior improvements, while the PA-39 Twin Comanche C/R was fitted with counter rotating engines.

Production of the Twin Comanche ceased in 1972 – by which time only the PA-39 was available – due to the flooding of Piper's Lock Haven factory.

Photo: The Twin Comanche B, C and C/R had optional seating for six. This is a PA-39 C/R. (Gerard Frawley)

Piper PA-34 Seneca

Country of origin: United States of America

Type: Six place light twin

Powerplants: PA-34-200 – Two 150kW (200hp) Lycoming IO-360-A1A fuel injected flat fours driving two blade c/s props. Seneca V – Two 165kW (220hp) Teledyne Continental L/TSIO-360-RB turbocharged, intercooled fuel injected counter rotating flat sixes driving two blade Hartzell or optional three blade McCauley c/s props.

Performance: PA-34-200 – Max speed 314km/h (170kt), max cruising speed 300km/h (160kt), long range cruising speed 267km/h (144kt). Initial rate of climb 1360ft/min. Service ceiling 19,400ft. Max range with no reserves 1818km (982nm). Seneca V – Max speed 379km/h (205kt), max cruising speed at 10,000ft 341km/h (184kt), at 18,500ft 367km/h (198kt), normal cruising speed at 10,000ft 322km/h (174kt), at 16,500ft 352km/h (190kt). Initial rate of climb 1550ft/min. Max certificated altitude 25,000ft. Max range with reserves at 10,000ft 1295km (700nm), at 18,500ft 1222km (660nm).

Weights: PA-34-200 – Empty 1190kg (2623lb), MTOW 1905kg (4200lb). Seneca V – Empty equipped 1532kg (3377lb), MTOW 2155kg (4750lb).

Dimensions: PA-34-200 – Wing span 11.85m (38ft 11in), length 8.69m (28ft 6in), height 3.02m (9ft 11in). Wing area 19.2m² (206.5sq ft). Seneca V – Same except length 8.72m (28ft 8in). Wing area 19.4m² (208.7sq ft).

Capacity: Seating for six in all but Seneca V which seats five.

Production: Approx 4750 Senecas built by Piper (incl approx 250 Vs), plus approx 20 Seneca IIs licence built in Poland by PZL Mielec as the M-20 Mewa, and over 870 in Brazil by Neiva as the EMB-810.

History: The most successful six place light twin since its introduction, the Seneca is a twin engine development of the Cherokee Six.

Seneca development began when Piper flew a converted trimotor Cherokee Six, designated PA-32-3M, fitted with two additional 85kW (115hp) Lycomings O-235 on either wing. The subsequent twin engine prototype PA-34 Seneca first flew with two 135kW (180hp) Lycomings, while the definitive standard third Seneca prototype first flew in October 1969 with fuel injected 150kW (200hp) IO-360s. Production deliveries of the initial PA-34-200 model began in late 1971.

Handling and performance criticisms were addressed from the 1974 model year with the PA-34-200T Seneca II which introduced changes to the flight controls and, more importantly, two turbocharged Continental TSIO-360-Es. Piper originally planned that the follow-on Seneca III would feature a T-tail, but these plans were dropped and the main changes introduced were counter rotating 165kW (220hp) TSIO-360s and a revised interior and instrument panel. Introduced in 1981, the Seneca III was replaced by New Piper's improved Seneca IV in 1994 with aerodynamic refinements, axisymmetric engine inlets and a revised interior.

The current Seneca V was introduced in January 1997. It features intercooled turbocharged L/TSIO-360-RB engines which maintain rated power to 19,500ft, and seating for five, with a standard entertainment/executive workstation with extendable worktable and optional phone/fax. A sixth seat in place of the workstation is optional.

Photo: The Seneca V. (Piper)

Piper PA-31 Navajo

Piper PA-31 Mojave, Chieftain & T-1040

Country of origin: United States of America

Type: Six/eight seat corporate transport and commuter airliner

Powerplants: PA-31-310 – Two 230kW (310hp) Lycoming TIO-540-A turbocharged and fuel injected flat six piston engines driving three blade constant speed propellers. PA-31P – Two 317kW (425hp) Lycoming TIGO-541-E1A geared, turbocharged and fuel injected engines.

Performance: PA-31-310 – Max speed 420km/h (227kt), max cruising speed 404km/h (218kt), long range cruising speed 273km/h (147kt). Initial rate of climb 1445ft/min. Service ceiling 27,300ft. Range with reserves 2398km (1295nm). PA-31P – Max speed 451km/h (244kt), max cruising speed 428km/h (231kt), long range cruising speed 306km/h (165kt). Initial rate of climb 1740ft/min. Operational ceiling 29,000ft. Range with reserves 2150km (1160nm).

Weights: PA-31-310 – Empty equipped 1843kg (4062lb), max takeoff 2950kg (6500lb). PA-31P – Empty equipped 2380kg (5250lb), max takeoff 3540kg (7800lb).

Dimensions: PA-31-310 – Wing span 12.40m (40ft 8in), length 9.94m (32ft 8in), height 3.97m (13ft 0in). Wing area 21.3m² (229sq ft). PA-31P – Same except for length 10.52m (34ft 6in), height 4.04m (13ft 3in).

Capacity: Configured to seat six (including pilot) in standard and executive layouts, and eight in commuter layout.

Production: Total PA-31 Navajo production of 2044, including 259 Pressurised Navajo PA-31Ps.

History: The highly successful Navajo six/eight seat cabin class twin has been adapted and operated in a number of commuter, charter, air taxi, light freight and executive transport roles, and has spawned a series of developments.

The PA-31 was developed at the request of company founder William T Piper, and the program for a new larger twin was given the project name Inca. The first prototype PA-31 first flew on September 30 1964 and was Piper's largest aircraft to be built to that time.

Deliveries began in the first half of 1967, with two basic models offered, the 225kW (300hp) IO-540-M powered PA-31-300 Navajo, and the PA-31-310 Turbo Navajo, with turbocharged 230kW (310hp) TIO-540 engines and a higher max takeoff weight. Both featured Piper's distinctive Tiger Shark engine nacelles with optional nacelle lockers. The improved Turbo Navajo B was released in late 1971 (the normally aspirated PA-31-300 was dropped at the same time). The Navajo C and the Navajo C/R, which had more powerful 242kW (325hp) TIO-540-F counter rotating engines, appeared in 1974.

The pressurised Navajo PA-31P was aimed at the corporate aircraft market and had three windows per side of the cabin, geared, turbocharged and fuel injected TIGO-541-E1A engines, a higher takeoff weight and strengthened structure and undercarriage, optional extra fuel, a lengthened nose, and most importantly a cabin pressurisation system. The PA-31P first flew in March 1968, first deliveries took place from 1970, and it remained in production until 1984.

Meanwhile production of the PA-31-310 had ceased in 1983. Further developments of the Navajo, including the Chieftain, Mojave and Cheyenne, are described separately.

Photo: A PA-31-310 Navajo on approach to land. (Les Bushell)

Country of origin: United States of America

Type: Eight/10 seat corporate transport and commuter airliner

Powerplants: PA-31P-350 Mojave – Two 260kW (350hp) Lycoming TIO-540-V2AD turbocharged and fuel injected flat six piston engines driving three blade constant speed Hartzell propellers. PA-31-350 Chieftain – Two 260kW (350hp) Lycoming TIO-540-J2BD turbocharged and fuel injected flat sixes.

Performance: PA-31P-350 – Max speed 447km/h (241kt), max cruising speed 435km/h (235kt), long range cruising speed 361km/h (195kt). Initial rate of climb 1220ft/min. Service ceiling 30,400ft. Max range with reserves 2260km (1220nm). PA-31-350 – Max speed 428km/h (231kt), max cruising speed 320km/h (173kt), long range cruising speed 254km/h (137kt). Initial rate of climb 1120ft/min. Operational ceiling 24,000ft. Max range with reserves and standard fuel 1760km (950nm), with optional fuel 2390km (1290nm).

Weights: PA-31P-350 – Empty equipped 2495kg (5500lb), max takeoff 3265kg (7200lb). PA-31-350 – Empty equipped 1988kg (4383lb), max takeoff 3175kg (7000lb).

Dimensions: PA-31P-350 – Wing span 13.56m (44ft 6in), length 10.52m (34ft 6in), height 3.96m (13ft 0in). Wing area 22.0m² (237sq ft). PA-31-350 – Wing span 12.40m (40ft 8in), length 10.55m (34ft 8in), height 3.96m (13ft 0in). Wing area 21.3m² (229sq ft).

Capacity: Standard seating in Mojave for seven, including one pilot and passenger, or two pilots on flightdeck, with seating for five behind them. Chieftain has max seating for 10.

Production: Mojave production approx 50. 1825 Chieftains built.

History: The PA-31P-350 Mojave was the last pressurised version of the PA-31 series to be built, the PA-31-350 Chieftain was a stretched Navajo, and the T-1040 was a turboprop powered airliner development.

The stretched Navajo Chieftain (originally dubbed the Navajo II) first appeared in 1973, after Piper began design work in 1971 (delays were caused by the destruction of the second prototype and early production aircraft due to flooding at Piper's Lock Haven plant in June 1972). Changes over the basic Navajo were many, including a 61cm (2ft) fuselage stretch, six side cabin windows, larger doors (an extra crew door was optional), and more powerful and counter rotating 260kW (350hp) TIO-540 engines. From the 1980 model year the PA-31-350 became known simply as the Chieftain. Production continued until October 1984.

Small numbers were also built of the airline optimised T-1020 (based on the Chieftain but 'hardened' for airline operations) and Pratt & Whitney Canada PT6A powered T-1040 (PA-31T-3). The latter combined the Chieftain's fuselage with the Cheyenne I's PT6A-11 engines, nose and tail, the Cheyenne IIXL's wings and landing gear, and the Cheyenne III's nacelles and baggage lockers.

The Mojave was a development of the PA-31P, and its airframe was essentially similar to the turboprop powered PA-31T Cheyenne I's. Changes included less powerful 260kW (350hp) counter rotating IO-540-V2As, a lower cabin pressure differential, and longer span wings. Mojaves were built between 1983 and 1986.

Photo: A New Zealand registered Piper T-1040. (Les Bushell)

Piper PA-31T Cheyenne

Country of origin: United States of America

Type: Twin turboprop corporate transports

Powerplants: PA-31T Cheyenne – Two 460kW (620shp) Pratt & Whitney Canada PT6A-28 turboprops driving three blade constant speed Hartzell propellers. PA-31T2-620 Cheyenne IIXL – Two 560kW (750shp) PT6A-135s.

Performance: PA-31T – Max speed and max cruising speed 516km/h (280kt), economical cruising speed 452km/h (244kt). Initial rate of climb 2800ft/min. Service ceiling 29,000ft. Range at max cruising speed 1555km (840nm). PA-31T2-620 – Max speed 510km/h (275kt), max cruising speed 500km/h (270kt), economical cruising speed 385km/h (208kt). Service ceiling 32,400ft. Range at max cruising speed 2608km (1408nm), at economical cruising speed with max fuel 2740km (1478nm).

Weights: PA-31T – Empty equipped 2260kg (4983lb), max takeoff 4082kg (9000lb). PA-31T2-620 – Empty equipped 2580kg (5680lb), max takeoff 4335kg (9540lb).

Dimensions: PA-31T – Wing span 13.01m (42ft 8in), length 10.57m (34ft 8in), height 3.89m (12ft 9in). Wing area 21.3m² (229sq ft). PA-31T2-620 – Same except for length 11.18m (36ft 8in).

Capacity: Cheyenne II, I, IA, and IIXL typically seat six, including pilot, or optionally eight.

Production: Total PA-31T Cheyenne production of approximately 825, comprising 526 Cheyenne IIs, 215 Cheyenne I & IIAs and 82 Cheyenne IIXLs. At late 2002 over 700 PA-31Ts were in corporate use.

History: The Piper Cheyenne family of turboprop corporate aircraft is based on the Navajo and Chieftain piston twins

Work on a turboprop version of the Pressurised Navajo dates back to the mid 1960s, although the first Cheyenne was not delivered until mid 1974. The Cheyenne prototype first flew on August 29 1969, but Piper had to redesign the flight controls to handle the increased loads on the airframe due to the higher speeds. Production deliveries were further delayed due to flooding at Piper's Lock Haven plant in June 1972.

Certification had been granted on May 3 1972, while the first production aircraft (powered by 462kW/620shp PT6A-28s) first flew on October 22 1973.

Piper introduced the lower powered (373kW/500shp PT6A-11s) and less expensive Cheyenne I in 1978, and renamed the original Cheyenne the Cheyenne II. Refinements to the Cheyenne I made in 1983, including more powerful engines, revised cowlings and interior, resulted in the Cheyenne IA.

Meanwhile the stretched Cheyenne IIXL had been introduced in 1979. Compared with the standard length Cheyennes, the IIXL was 61cm (2ft) longer, featured an extra cabin window on the left side, 180kg (400lb) increased max takeoff weight and 560kW (750shp) PT6A-135s.

An improved IIXLA was planned, but did not enter production.

The further stretched and T-tail PA-42 Cheyenne III was also introduced in 1978, and is described separately.

Photo: A Chilean registered PA-31T Cheyenne I at Santiago. (Alvaro Romero)

Piper PA-42 Cheyenne III, IIIA & 400LS

Country of origin: United States of America

Type: Twin turboprop corporate transports

Powerplants: PA-42-720 Cheyenne III – Two 535kW (720shp) Pratt & Whitney Canada PT6A-41 turboprops driving three blade constant speed Hartzell propellers. PA-42-1000 Cheyenne 400LS – Two 1225kW (1645shp) derated to 745kW (1000shp) Garrett TPE331-14A/Bs driving four blade Hartzell props.

Performance: PA-42-720 – Max speed 537km/h (290kt), max cruising speed 461km/h (250kt), economical cruising speed 413km/h (223kt). Initial rate of climb 2235ft/min. Service ceiling 33,000ft. Range at max cruising speed 3100km (1675nm). PA-42-1000 – Max speed 650km/h (351kt), max cruising speed 594km/h (320kt), economical cruising speed 506km/h (273kt). Initial rate of climb 3242ft/min. Range at max cruising speed 3015km (1630nm), range at economical cruising speed 3500km (1890nm).

Weights: PA-42-720 – Empty 2900kg (6389lb), max ramp weight 5125kg (11,285lb). PA-42-1000 – Empty 3412kg (7522lb), max takeoff 5466kg (12,050lb).

Dimensions: PA-42-720 – Wing span (over tip tanks) 14.53m (47ft 8in), length 13.23m (43ft 5in), height 4.50m (14ft 9in). Wing area 27.2m² (293.0sq ft). PA-42-1000 – Same except for height 5.18m (17ft 0in).

Capacity: One or two pilots on flightdeck, with main cabin seating for between six and nine passengers. Typical seating for six in main cabin in corporate configuration.

Production: PA-42 Cheyenne production totals approximately 185 aircraft, of which approximately 145 were Cheyenne IIIs and IIIAs. At late 2002 182 PA-42s were in use.

History: The PA-42 Cheyenne series are larger developments of the earlier PA-31T Cheyennes (in turn themselves turboprop developments of the PA-31 Navajo), and were aimed directly at Beech's successful King Air twin turboprop series.

The PA-42 Cheyenne III was announced in September 1977. The first production Cheyenne III first flew on May 18 1979 and FAA certification was granted in early 1980. Compared with the Cheyenne II the PA-42 was about 1m (3ft) longer, was powered by 537kW (720shp) PT6A-41 turboshafts and introduced a T-tail, the most obvious external difference between the PA-31T and PA-42. Deliveries of production Cheyenne IIIs began on June 30 1980.

Development and improvement of the III led to the PA-42-720 Cheyenne IIIA, with PT6A-61 engines, a higher service ceiling and revised systems and interior.

The higher powered and significantly faster PA-42-1000 is basically similar to the PA-42-720 except for its far more powerful 745kW (1000hp) Garrett TPE331 turboprops driving four blade propellers. Piper's largest and fastest production aircraft to date, the PA-42-1000 was initially called the Cheyenne IV, before becoming known as the Cheyenne 400LS, and then simply the Cheyenne 400. The Cheyenne IV first flew on Feburary 23 1983 and was delivered from late 1984. Both the Cheyenne IIIA and 400 were available on special order through to the early 1990s.

Photo: A Garrett powered PA-42-1000. (Rob Finlayson)

Piper PA-38 Tomahawk

Country of origin: United States of America

Type: Two seat light aircraft and basic trainer

Powerplant: One 85kW (112hp) Avco Lycoming O-235-L2A or -L2C flat four piston engine driving a two blade fixed pitch Sensenich propeller.

Performance: Max speed 202km/h (109kt), max cruising speed 200km/h (108kt), normal cruising speed 185km/h (100kt). Initial rate of climb 718ft/min. Service ceiling 13,000ft. Max range with reserves 867km (468nm).

Weights: Empty 512kg (1128lb), max takeoff 757kg (1670lb).

Dimensions: Wing span 10.36m (34ft 0in), length 7.04m (23ft 1in), height 2.77m (9ft 1in). Wing area 11.6m^2 (124.7sq ft).

Capacity: Seating for two side by side.

Production: 2497 Tomahawks were built between 1978 and 1983.

History: The Piper PA-38 Tomahawk (nicknamed Tommy for short) was the first all new two seat trainer built by one of the USA's big three GA manufacturers in almost three decades when it was introduced.

The PA-38-112 Tomahawk was designed as a relatively inexpensive to acquire and operate two seat trainer to tackle the firmly established definitive basic trainer in the 1970s, the Cessna 150 and 152, and to take over the spot in Piper's model range then occupied by two seat variants of the PA-28 Cherokee series.

Design input for the Tomahawk came from a questionnaire Piper distributed randomly to 10,000 flight instructors during the mid 1970s. With their responses in mind (ideal characteristics included night lighting, dual toe brakes, a fuel selector accessible to both student and instructor, low noise levels, position lights and the ability to spin), Piper developed the PA-38. The resulting aircraft featured a T-tail and NASA Whitcomb GA(W)-1 design low set wing of constant chord and thickness (also featured on the competing but less successful Beech Skipper), a cabin wider than the Cherokee's (and thus much wider than the Cessna 150/152's) with 360° vision and a Lycoming O-235 powerplant. Many parts, such as the main undercarriage wheels and elevators, were interchangeable.

Piper announced it was developing the Tomahawk during late 1977 and first deliveries were made in early 1978. Despite an initial mixed reaction to the new trainer from the flying public, the Tomahawk was an instant sales success with over 1000 built in the first year of production alone. In service the Tomahawk proved to be economical to operate, but the aircraft was dogged by quality control problems (some 19 Airworthiness Directives were issued by the FAA in the PA-38's first four years) and unpredictable stalling characteristics, resulting in a number of stall/spin accidents.

Flow strips were added to the wing on late production Tomahawk Is to improve the much criticised stall characteristics, while a number of other problems, including the poor quality control, were addressed in the improved Tomahawk II, which was introduced for the 1981 model year. Enhancements included improved sound proofing, windscreen defrosting, door latching and nose wheel design.

Piper ceased production of the Tomahawk during 1983.

Photo: The Tomahawk features a NASA Whitcomb GA(W)-1 constant chord and thickness wing, T-tail and car style door. (Paul Sadler)

Piper PA-44 Seminole

Country of origin: United States of America

Type: Four seat light twin

Powerplants: PA-44-180 – Two 135kW (180hp) Lycoming O-360-E1AD flat four piston engines driving two or optionally three blade constant speed Hartzell propellers. PA-44-180T – Two 135kW (180hp) Lycoming TO-360-E1A6D turbocharged flat fours driving two blade constant speed props.

Performance: PA-44-180 – Max speed 311km/h (168kt), max cruising speed 309km/h (167kt), long range cruising speed 280km/h (151kt). Initial rate of climb 1200ft/min. Service ceiling 17,100ft. Range with reserves 1630km (880nm). PA-44-180T – Max speed 363km/h (196kt), max cruising speed 343km/h (185kt), long range cruising speed 293km/h (158kt). Initial rate of climb 1290ft/min. Range with reserves 1520km (820nm).

Weights: PA-44-180 – Empty 1070kg (2360lb), max takeoff 1723kg (3800lb). PA-44-180T – Empty 1116kg (2461lb), max takeoff 1780kg (3925lb).

Dimensions: Wing span 11.77m (38ft 8in), length 8.41m (27ft 7in), height 2.59m (8ft 6in). Wing area 17.1m^2 (183.8sq ft).

Capacity: Typical seating for four.

Production: Total Seminole production through to 1990 of 469, including 87 Turbo Seminoles. Approx 100 PA-44-180s built by New Piper since 1995.

History: The PA-44 Seminole was developed during the heyday of the GA industry in the mid to late 1970s but fell victim to the depressed market from the early 1980s plus the growing reliability and popularity of high performance big singles. As a result it has been built in only fairly modest numbers.

A contemporary of the Gulfstream GA-7 Cougar and Beechcraft Duchess, the Seminole was conceived in part as a Twin Comanche replacement, aimed at the self flying businessperson and the twin engine training market. Developed from the mid 1970s, the Seminole is based on the PA-28R Arrow series, with the Arrow's single engine replaced by two counter rotating 135kW (180hp) Lycoming O-360s, plus a new T-tail and semi tapered wings. The prototype first flew in May 1976. Production machines, designated PA-44-180, were delivered from May 1978.

The turbocharged PA-44-180T was introduced from 1980. Aside from turbocharged TO-360s, the Turbo Seminole introduced prop de-icing and an oxygen system. Just 87 PA-44-180Ts were built when Piper ceased production for the first time in late 1981. Piper reopened the Seminole line in 1988, with 30 non turbocharged PA-44s built before once more suspending production in 1990, due to its parlous financial position at the time.

Once again the PA-28-180 Seminole is back in production, with manufacture restarting in 1995, although sales have been relatively modest. Piper currently offers two avionics packages for the Seminole, a standard fit and an Advanced Training Group package.

Interestingly the PA-44 is the only T-tail Piper currently in production, even though in the late 1970s most Piper aircraft had been modified to feature a T-tail.

Photo: A new production PA-44-180. (Piper)

Piper PA-46 Malibu & Malibu Mirage

Country of origin: United States of America

Type: Six seat high performance light aircraft

Powerplant: PA-46-310P – One 230kW (310hp) Continental TSIO-520-BE turbocharged and fuel injected flat six piston engine driving a two blade constant speed Hartzell propeller. PA-46-350P – One 260kW (350hp) Textron Lycoming TIO-540-AE2A.

Performance: PA-46-310P – Max speed 434km/h (234kt), max cruising speed 398km/h (215kt), long range cruising speed 363km/h (196kt). Initial rate of climb 1170ft/min. Service ceiling 25,000ft. Max range at long range cruising speed and altitude with reserves 2880km (1555nm). PA-46-350P – Max speed at mid cruise weight 407kt (220kt), cruising speed 394kt (213kt). Service ceiling 25,000ft. Range with max fuel and reserves at normal cruising speed and optimum altitude 1953km (1055nm).

Weights: PA-46-310P – Empty 1066kg (2350lb), max takeoff 1860kg (4100lb). PA-46-350P – Empty equipped 1397kg (3080lb), max takeoff 1968kg (4340lb).

Dimensions: PA-46-310P – Wing span 13.11m (43ft 0in), length 8.66m (28ft 5in), height 3.44m (11ft 4in). Wing area 16.3m² (175sq ft). PA-46-350P – Same except for length 8.81m (28ft 11in).

Capacity: Typical seating for pilot and five passengers.

Production: More than 900 PA-46s delivered, comprising 404 PA-46-310Ps and over 512 PA-46-350Ps.

History: According to Piper the all new Piper Malibu was the first pressurised cabin class piston single. It promised to be one of the first of a new generation of light aircraft introduced from the early 1980s before recession and oppressive liability laws in the USA strangled GA production. Nevertheless, the PA-46 has sold relatively strongly.

Piper announced the Malibu in November 1982. Designed with the aid of CAD/CAM (Computer Aided Design/Computer Aided Manufacture), the prototype first flew in 1980. Certification was awarded in September 1983, with deliveries that November.

The production PA-46-310P features the specially developed turbocharged 230kW (310hp) Continental TSIO-520, a high aspect ratio wing, a relatively roomy cabin with club seating for four behind the pilot, a rear airstair style door, IFR avionics as standard, and cabin pressurisation.

The improved PA-46-350P Malibu Mirage replaced the -310P Malibu in production from October 1988. The major change introduced on the Malibu Mirage was the more powerful 260kW (350hp) Textron Lycoming TIO-540-AE2A, while other changes included a new electrical system and revised interior.

New Piper has made a number of minor improvements to the Malibu Mirage, including to the brakes, autopilot and air-conditioning. In 1999 the Mirages gained the strengthened wing of the turboprop Malibu Meridian development, allowing an 18kg (40lb) increase in max takeoff weight. The Mirage is also offered with conventional and EFIS avionics packages.

Production ceased temporarily in 2001 to allow Piper to concentrate on introducing the Meridean to production.

Photo: A PA-46-350P Malibu Mirage. (Bob Grimstead)

Piper PA-46-500TP Malibu Meridian

Country of origin: United States of America

Type: Six seat corporate turboprop

Powerplant: One 373kW (500shp) takeoff rated Pratt & Whitney Canada PT6A-42A turboprop driving a four blade constant speed Hartzell propeller.

Performance: Max cruising speed at 30,000ft and mid cruise weight 485km/h (262kt). Initial rate of climb 1739ft/min. Certificated altitude 30,000ft. Range at max cruising speed at 30,000ft with reserves 1885km (1018nm). Endurance 4hr 22min.

Weights: Standard equipped 1471kg (3243lb), max takeoff 2312kg (5092lb).

Dimensions: Wing span 13.11m (43ft 0in), length 9.02m (29ft 7in), height 3.45m (11ft 4in). Wing area 17.0m² (183.0sq ft).

Capacity: Typical seating for pilot and five passengers. Pilot and four passengers with optional entertainment/refreshment console with drinks cooler, storage and VCR and flat panel monitor.

Production: First production aircraft handed over November 2000. Approx 150 in use by late 2002.

History: The Malibu Meridian is a high performance turboprop development of the popular Malibu Mirage and is the first major aircraft program from New Piper Aircraft Inc.

New Piper announced development of the Meridian at the 1997 NBAA convention. An aerodynamic conforming prototype was rolled out at Piper's Vero Beach, Florida facilities on August 13 1998 and flew for the first time on August 21 that year. Three further Meridian prototypes entered the flight test program during 1999. Certification was awarded on September 27 2000, with the first customer delivery on November 7 2000.

The Meridian's most obvious feature compared with the Malibu is its Pratt & Whitney Canada PT6A-42A turboprop. The -42A has a thermodynamic rating of 901kW (1029shp) but on the Meridian is derated to 373kW (500shp) for takeoff. This allows the engine to maintain max power through to the aircraft's 30,000ft ceiling, giving a 485km/h (262kt) cruising speed.

Major sections of the Meridian's fuselage are common with the Malibu's, but the turboprop features a number of significant changes, including a stainless steel firewall, chord lengthening wing root gloves which increase wing area to ensure a relatively low stall speed, increased area horizontal tail and rudder, and increased fuel capacity.

The Meridian also has a completely new instrument panel. Standard equipment includes a three axis S-TEC 550 autopilot which is coupled to the dual 13cm (5in) colour LCD Garmin GNS 530 integrated GPS displays (incorporating IFR GPS and VOR/ILS receiver with glidescope), and a Meggitt Engine Instrument Display System comprising dual LCDs presenting engine information (such as torque, temps and pressures, propeller RPM, outside air temperature and fuel level at destination and time to destination calculations).

An optional Electronic Flight Display System (EFDS) presents flight information on four Meggitt colour LCDs (two per side), comprising dual primary flight displays and dual navigation displays. Conventional flight instrumentation is standard.

Photo: One of three Meridian certification flight test aircraft. (Piper)

Piper (Ted Smith) Aerostar

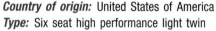

Country of origin: United States of America

Type: Six seat high performance light twin

Powerplants: 600A – Two 215kW (290hp) Lycoming IO-540-K1J5 fuel injected flat six piston engines driving three blade constant speed Hartzell propellers. PA-60-700P – Two 260kW (350hp) turbocharged and counter rotating TIO-540-U2As.

Performance: 600A – Max speed 418km/h (226kt), long range cruising speed 357km/h (193kt). Initial rate of climb 1800ft/min. Service ceiling 21,200ft. Max range with reserves 2225km (1200nm). PA-60-700P – Max speed 490km/h (264kt), max cruising speed 484km/h (261kt), economical cruising speed 390km/h (211kt). Initial rate of climb 1755ft/min. Service ceiling 25,000ft. Range at max cruising speed 1250km (675nm), at economical cruising speed with max fuel 2150km (1160nm).

Weights: 600A – Empty 1695kg (3757lb), max takeoff 2495kg (5500lb). PA-60-700P – Empty 1940kg (4275lb), MTOW 2864kg (6315lb).

Dimensions: 600A – Wing span 10.41m (34ft 2in), length 10.61m (34ft 10in), height 3.89m (12ft 1in). Wing area 15.8m² (170sq ft). PA-60-700P – Same except for wing span 11.18m (36ft 8in). Wing area 16.6m² (178.2sq ft).

Capacity: Typical seating for six.

Production: 1010 Aerostars built, including 519 by Piper.

History: The Aerostar – which in its higher powered forms can lay claim to being the fastest piston twin GA aircraft built – was designed by Ted Smith, who was also responsible for the Aero Commander twins.

Smith's original intention in designing the Aerostar was to develop a family of single and piston twins, twin turboprop and even twin jet powered versions of the same basic aircraft. However the Aerostar appeared in piston twin form only. Smith began design work on the Aerostar in late 1964, with a prototype making its first flight two years later in November 1966.

The prototype was powered by 120kW (160hp) Lycoming IO-320s, but the Aerostar was placed into production from 1968 as the Aerostar 600 with 215kW (290hp) IO-540s. The turbocharged Aerostar 601 followed the 600 into production shortly afterwards, while the turbocharged and pressurised 601P went into production in 1972. By this time Butler Aviation had acquired the production rights of the Aerostar in 1970, producing a small number as Butler Aerostars. Smith bought the line back again in 1972, and his new company, Ted R Smith and Associates, resumed Aerostar manufacture, including of the improved 601B with the same span wings as on the 601P, until Piper acquired the Aerostar line in March 1978.

Piper continued production of the 600A, 601B and 601P at Ted Smith's Santa Maria plant, and introduced the 602P with low compression TIO-540-AA1A5 engines.

When Piper transferred production to its new Vero Beach, Florida factory in early 1982, only the 602P was in production, and this was redesignated the PA-60-602P. The PA-60-700P was the last Aerostar version, and just 25 were built. The 700P, in production between 1983 and 1985, has more powerful engines, a higher max takeoff weight and optional extra fuel capacity.

Photo: A Piper built PA-60-602P Aerostar. (Rob Finlayson)

PZL M-18 Dromader

Country of origin: Poland

Type: Ag spraying and firefighter aircraft

Powerplant: One 745kW (1000hp) PZL Kalisz (Shvetsov) ASz-62IR supercharged nine cylinder radial piston engine driving a four blade constant speed propeller.

Performance: M-18 & M-18A (with ag equipment) – Max cruising speed 237km/h (128kt), typical operating speed range 170 to 190km/h (90 to 103kt). Initial rate of climb 1115ft/min. Service ceiling 21,235ft. Max range with no reserves with max fuel and no ag equipment 970km (520nm). M-18A (without ag equipment) – Max speed 256km/h (138kt), cruising speed 205km/h (110kt), typical operating speed 230km/h (124kt). Initial rate of climb 1360ft/min. Service ceiling 21,235ft. Max range with no reserves with max fuel and no ag equipment 970km (520nm).

Weights: M-18A – Empty 2690kg (5930lb), max takeoff 4700kg (10,360lb) but restricted to 4200kg (9230lb) under FAR Pt 23.

Dimensions: M-18A – Wing span 17.70m (58ft 1in), length 9.47m (31ft 3in), height over tail 3.70m (12ft 2in). Wing area 40.0m² (430.5sq ft).

Capacity: M-18 seats pilot only, M-18A has second seat for a ground loader or mechanic behind the pilot, M-18AS and BS have a second cockpit with instrumentation for an instructor. M-18B hopper capacity of 2500 litres (550Imp gal/660US gal) of liquid or 2200kg (4850lb) of dry chemicals.

Production: By 2002 over 715 Dromaders built, most for export. M-18 single seater production ceased in 1984 after 230 built.

History: The M-18 Dromader agricultural aircraft has been one of Poland's most successful aircraft exports.

PZL Swidnik designed the Dromader in collaboration with Rockwell International in the US during the mid 1970s. From the outset the aim was to certificate the aircraft to western standards. The first prototype of the basic single seat M-18 flew on August 27 1976, a second prototype flew that October. Poland awarded certification for the Dromader during September 1978, series production began in 1979.

The basic Dromader design was conventional, with power supplied by a nine cylinder radial engine, while the outer wing panels were based on those on the Rockwell Thrush Commander.

The basic single seat M-18 was in production for five years until 1984 when it was replaced by the two seat M-18A. The two seat M-18A was developed to allow the carriage of either a mechanic or chemical loader to austere fields. In the meantime PZL Mielec had developed a firebombing derivative which first flew in 1978. The M-18AS trainer has a second cockpit for flight instruction. Since 1996 the M-18B, with a 5300kg (11,684lb) max takeoff weight, has been the standard production model. The M-18BS is a two seat trainer based on the M-18B. The M-18C with 895kW (1200hp) Kalisz K-9 engine flew in 1995 but has not entered production.

In the USA, Melex (part owned by PZL Mielec) developed a PT6A turboprop development dubbed the T45 Turbine Dromader. The Turbine Dromader first flew during 1985 and the US FAA issued it a Supplementary Type Certificate in April 1986. Others have been converted with TPE331s.

Photo: An M-18A Dromader fire bombing. (Theo van Loon)

PZL Swidnik (Mil) Mi-2 & Kania

Countries of origin: Poland & Russia

Type: Light twin utility helicopter

Powerplants: Mi-2 – Two 300kW (400shp) Isotov designed Polish built GTD-350 turboshafts driving a three blade main rotor and two blade tail rotor. Kania – Two 315kW (720shp) Allison 250-C20B turboshafts driving a three blade main and two blade tail rotor.

Performance: Mi-2 – Max cruising speed 200km/h (108kt), long range cruising speed 190km/h (102kt). Max rate of climb 885ft/min. Service ceiling 13,125ft. Hovering ceiling in ground effect 6560ft. Range with max payload and reserves 170km (91nm), range with max fuel 440km (237nm), range with optional fuel 580km (313nm). Kania – Max cruising speed 215km/h (116kt), economical cruising speed 190km/h (102kt). Initial rate of climb 1722ft/min. Service ceiling 13,120ft. Hovering ceiling out of ground effect 4510ft. Range with max fuel and reserves 435km (234nm), with auxiliary fuel and reserves 800km (432nm). Endurance with auxiliary fuel 4hr.

Weights: Mi-2 – Empty equipped 2402kg (5295lb) in passenger version, or 2372kg (5229lb) in transport version; max takeoff 3550kg (7826lb). Kania – Basic empty 2000kg (4410lb), max takeoff 3550kg (7826lb).

Dimensions: Mi-2 – Main rotor diameter 14.50m (47ft 7in), length overall 17.48m (57ft 4in), fuselage length 11.94m (39ft 2in), height (no tail rotor) 2.70m (8ft 10in). Main rotor disc area 166.4m² (1791.1sq ft). Kania – Same except for fuselage length 12.03m (39ft 6in).

Capacity: Mi-2 – Two pilots or one pilot and passenger on flight-deck, main cabin seating for seven. Ambulance configurations can accommodate four stretchers and one medical attendant or two stretchers and two attendants. Kania – Pilot and eight passengers in passenger configuration, pilot and five passengers in corporate configuration. Two stretchers, one seated patient and two medical attendants in ambulance configuration. Ag version capacity 1000kg (2205lb) of chemicals.

Production: More than 5500 mainly military Mi-2s built. 15 Kanias built, last delivered in 1997.

History: Poland's most successful helicopter was originally developed in Russia by Mil, and in its Allison powered Kania (Kitty Hawk) version has been granted US certification.

Mil originally designed the light utility Mi-2 in Russia during the early 1960s, resulting in a first flight in September 1961. In January 1964 an agreement between the USSR and Poland transferred development and production, which commenced in 1965. The Mi-2 evolved since that time and remained in low rate production into the 1990s. The main civil variant is simply designated Mi-2, while Swidnik also developed a diverse number of military variants.

The Kania (Kitty Hawk) is an upgrade of the basic Mi-2, with Allison 250-C20B turboshafts, western avionics, and composite main and tail rotor blades. It also holds US FAR Pt 29 certification. Developed in cooperation with Allison, the Kania first flew on June 3 1979, and US certification was granted in February 1986. The Kania has never entered full scale production but was also offered as an upgrade for existing Mi-2s.

Photo: A Hungarian registered Mi-2. (Viktor László)

PZL Swidnik W-3 Sokol

Countries of origin: Poland

Type: Mid size twin utility helicopter

Powerplants: Two 670kW (900shp) takeoff rated WSK-PZL Rzeszów PZL-10W turboshafts driving a four blade main rotor and three blade tail rotor.

Performance: W-3A – Max cruising speed 243km/h (131kt). Initial rate of climb 2008ft/min. Hovering ceiling (at max takeoff weight) out of ground effect 6220ft. Service ceiling 19,680ft. Max range with reserves 745km (402nm), with auxiliary fuel and reserves 1290km (696nm), with max payload and no reserves 200km (108nm).

Weights: W-3A – Basic operating empty 3850kg (8488lb), max takeoff 6400kg (14,110lb).

Dimensions: Main rotor diameter 15.70m (51ft 6in), length overall rotors turning 18.79m (61ft 8in), fuselage length 14.21m (46ft 8in), height overall 5.14m (16ft 10in), height to top of rotor mast 4.20m (13ft 10in). Main rotor disc area 193.6m² (2034sq ft).

Capacity: Two pilots or pilot and flight engineer or passenger on flightdeck. Main cabin seating for 12 in passenger configuration, or three medical attendants and eight rescued survivors in SAR Anaconda version, or four stretchers and medical attendant in ambulance configuration, one stretcher and medical attendants in critical care EMS version, or five/six passengers in executive configuration. Can carry a 2100kg (4630lb) sling load.

Production: Approximately 150 Sokols of all models have been built, including against Polish military orders.

History: The W-3 Sokol (Falcon) was the first helicopter to be fully designed and built in Poland.

The Sokol made its first flight on November 16 1979, and has since been certificated in Poland, Russia, the US, South Korea and Germany. Following a fairly protracted development program, low rate production of the Sokol commenced during 1985. Initial sales of the general purpose Sokol were within Poland and in the Eastern Bloc, before the collapse of communism allowed PZL Swidnik to broaden its sales base. To do this PZL Swidnik developed the improved W-3A Sokol aimed at achieving western certification. Certification to US FAR Pt 29 standards was granted in May 1993, while German certification was granted in December that year.

The Sokol is of conventional design and construction, with two PZL-10W turboshafts. (These are based on the Russian designed TVD-10B turboprops that power the Polish built An-28). Composites are used in the tail and main rotor blades.

The Sokol is offered in a number of variants and is capable of performing a range of helicopter missions, including passenger transport, VIP, cargo, EMS, medevac, firefighting and search and rescue (the W-3 RM Anaconda).

An upgraded version of the Sokol has been under development, but little recent progress appears to have been made. The SW-5 (a provisional designation) would have twin FADEC equipped 745kW (1000shp) Pratt & Whitney Canada PT6B-67B turboshafts, Thales supplied avionics, a simplified rotor head and greater use of composites.

Photo: A German police W-3A Sokol. (Grzegorz Holdanowicz)

PZL Swidnik SW-4

Country of origin: Poland

Type: Light utility helicopter

Powerplants: One 335kW (450shp) (283kW/380shp max continuous rated) Rolls-Royce 250-C20R/2 turboshaft driving a three blade main rotor and two blade tail rotor. Option of one 460kW (615shp) Pratt & Whitney Canada PW200/9 turboshaft.

Performance: RR 250 engine – Max speed 232km/h (125kt), normal cruising speed 200km/h (108kt). Initial rate of climb 1973ft/min. Service ceiling 17,820ft. Max range with standard fuel and no reserves 860km (464nm). Endurance 5hr 8min.

Weights: RR 250 engine – Empty 850kg (1874lb), max takeoff (internal load) 1600kg (3527lb), max takeoff with sling load 1800kg (3968lb).

Dimensions: Main rotor disc diameter 9.00m (29ft 6in), length overall rotors turning 10.55m (34ft 8in), fuselage length including tailskid 9.08m (29ft 9in), height overall 3.05m (10ft 10in). Main rotor disc area 63.6m² (684.8sq ft).

Capacity: Standard seating for four or five (including pilot). In medevac configuration accommodation for one stretcher patient and two medical attendants. Max sling load 750kg (1655lb).

Production: First production aircraft due to fly in 2003. 47 under order for the Polish air force.

History: The origins of PZL Swidnik's SW-4 five seat light utility helicopter date back to the early 1980s.

Swidnik began development of a new four/five place light utility helicopter in 1981. This original SW-4 was to have been powered by a 300kW (400shp) PZL Rzeszow GTD-350 turboshaft and was built in mock-up form. It would have had a top speed of 240km/h (130kt) and a max range with auxiliary fuel of 900km (485nm).

The collapse of the Iron Curtain allowed Swidnik to substantially redesign the SW-4, based around the Rolls-Royce 250 turboshaft. Aside from the powerplant, design changes included a more streamlined fuselage and revised tail and tailboom.

The first prototype, a non flying ground test aircraft, was rolled out in December 1994. Two flying prototypes have been built, the first of which was completed in 1996 and first flew on October 26 that year. The second flew in early 2001. In 2002 PZL Swidnik was continuing to work towards certification, with the first of a batch of five production aircraft due to fly in 2003.

PZL Swidnik aims to attain US FAA FAR Part 27 certification for the SW-4. The program was delayed somewhat when PZL Swidnik decided to redesign the rotor head, enlarge the horizontal stabiliser and improve the hydraulic system. The helicopter features Bendix King avionics, including an optional IFR instrument package.

PZL Swidnik has expressed interest in developing a Pratt & Whitney Canada PW200 powered variant. A twin engine model has also been considered to allow the helicopter to meet new European regulations which restrict single engine helicopter operations under some conditions.

The SW-4 is expected to be able to fulfil a range of utility missions ranging from executive transport to medevac and police roles.

Photo: The non flying SW-4 prototype. (PZL Swidnik)

PZL Warszawa-Okecie PZL-104 Wilga

Country of origin: Poland

Type: Four seat light utility aircraft

Powerplant: 35A – One 195kW (260hp) PZL AI-14RA nine cylinder radial piston engine driving a two blade c/s prop. 2000 – One 225kW (300hp) Textron Lycoming IO-540 flat six driving a three blade constant speed prop.

Performance: 35A – Max speed 194km/h (105kt), cruising speed at 75% power 157km/h (85kt). Initial rate of climb 905ft/min. Service ceiling 13,250ft. Range with max fuel and reserves 510km (275nm). 2000 – Cruising speed at 75% power 190km/h (103kt). Max range 1500km (810nm).

Weights: 35A – Empty equipped 870kg (1918lb), max takeoff 1300kg (2866lb). 2000 – Empty 900kg (1984lb), max takeoff 1400kg (3086lb).

Dimensions: 35A/2000 – Wing span 11.12m (36ft 6in), length 8.10m (26ft 7in), height 2.96m (9ft 9in). Wing area 15.5m² (166.8sq ft).

Capacity: Typical seating for four including pilot. Rear two seats can be replaced with fuel tank. Ambulance configuration accommodates two stretchers and medical attendants.

Production: More than 965 Wilgas built since the mid 1960s. Approx 10 Wilga 2000s built, first delivery in 1998.

History: The rugged STOL PZL-104 Wilga has been one of Poland's most successful light aircraft exports.

Poland's Light Aircraft Science and Production Centre in Warsaw began development of the Wilga in the early 1960s as a replacement for the general purpose Czechoslovak L-60 Brigadyr utility. The prototype Wilga 1 was powered by a 135kW (180hp) Narkiewicz WN-6B radial and first flew on April 24 1962. A redesign of the basic aircraft followed, and a modified Wilga 2 with a new fuselage and tail and a 145kW (195hp) WN-6RB engine flew in August 1963. That December the 170kW (225hp) Continental O-470 powered Wilga C or (Wilga 32) flew and Lipnur Gelatnik later built 39 in Indonesia.

Poland's first production Wilgas were the 3A four seat utility and 3S ambulance which introduced the 195kW (260hp) Ivchenko designed AI-14 radial. Soon after PZL reconfigured the Wilga's cabin and landing gear, resulting in the definitive production version, the Wilga 35. The prototype Wilga 35 first flew on July 28 1967.

The Wilga 35 remains in production essentially unchanged, and several variants have been offered, while the Wilga 80 is identical to the 35 other than its further rear positioned carburettor air intake. The Wilga 35A and 80A are designed for flying club operations and are fitted with a hook for glider towing, the 35H and 80H are float equipped, the 35P is usually fitted with four seats, the 35R and 80R are agricultural aircraft fitted with a 270kg (595lb) under fuselage chemical hopper and spray bars, and the 35P is an ambulance variant capable of carrying two stretchers.

The PZL-104M Wilga 2000 is an improved development aimed at western customers. It is powered by a 225kW (300hp) Textron Lycoming Continental IO-540 flat six in a reprofiled nose, and features Honeywell avionics and extra fuel. First flight was on August 21 1996, while FAA certification was awarded in 1997, with first delivery (to the Polish border guards) the following year.

Photo: A Polish border guards Wilga 2000. (Sebastian Zacharias)

PZL Warszawa-Okecie Koliber

Country of origin: Poland

Type: Four seat light aircraft

Powerplant: 160A – One 120kW (160hp) Textron Lycoming O-320-D2A flat four piston engine driving a two blade fixed pitch Sensenich propeller. 235A – One 175kW (235hp) Textron Lycoming O-540-B4B5 flat six driving a two blade McCauley or three blade Hartzell constant speed prop.

Performance: 160A – Max speed 220km/h (119kt), cruising speed at 75% power 194km/h (105kt). Service ceiling 11,475ft. Max range at 75% power 919km (496nm), at 65% power 960km (518nm). 235A – Max speed 260km/h (140kt), cruising speed at 75% power 248km/h (134kt). Service ceiling 14,755ft. Max range at 75% power 734km (396nm), at 65% power 958km (517nm).

Weights: 160A – Empty 607kg (1337lb), max takeoff 950kg (2094lb). 235A – Empty 705kg (1553lb), max takeoff 1150kg (2533lb).

Dimensions: 160A & 235A – Wing span 9.75m (32ft 0in), length 7.37m (24ft 2in), height 2.80m (9ft 2in). Wing area 12.7m² (136.5sq ft).

Capacity: Typical seating for four.

Production: Total Franklin powered Series I, II and III production approximately 40 units. Approx 85 Lycoming powered Kolibers built.

History: The Koliber (Hummingbird) is a licence built development of the Socata Rallye.

The Rallye was still in production when PZL Warszawa-Okecie acquired a licence to build and develop the Rallye 100ST in Poland. The prototype Koliber was powered by a 87kW (116hp) PZL-F (Franklin) four cylinder engine (Poland had earlier purchased the design and production rights to Franklin engines) and flew on April 18 1978.

Initial production Kolibers featured the 86kW (116hp) engine, later aircraft a more powerful 95kW (125hp) Franklin engine. Franklin powered versions of the Koliber were the Series I, the initial production model, with 10 built and first flight occurring in May 1979; the Series II developed for Polish aero clubs which was capable of limited aerobatics (25 built); and the improved Series III (45 built). Franklin powered Koliber production ceased in 1988.

The Textron Lycoming O-320 powered Koliber 150 first flew in September 1988. The 150A (Koliber II in the USA) was developed for export and was granted US FAR Part 23 certification in early 1994. According to the type's US and Asia Pacific distributor, this was the first time that a four place fixed undercarriage light aircraft had been fully certificated in the USA in over a decade. The first Koliber 150A delivery was made to a US customer in mid 1994, while Koliber 150s have been delivered to a number of European countries.

The PZL-111 Koliber 235A is a more powerful, higher performance development of the Koliber 150A, powered by a 175kW (235hp) Textron Lycoming O-540. It first flew on September 14 1995 and was awarded Polish certification in December 1996. No production aircraft have been built.

The current production model is the 120kW (160hp) O-320-D2A powered Koliber 160A which was introduced in 1998, replacing the Koliber 150/150A in production. The first two Koliber 160As were delivered to the UK PZL distributor in late 1999.

Photo: A Koliber 150A. (Paul Sadler)

Raytheon Beechcraft Bonanza

Country of origin: United States of America

Type: Four to six seat high performance light aircraft

Powerplant: C33 – One 170kW (225hp) Continental fuel injected IO-470-K flat six driving a two blade constant speed propeller. A36 – One 225kW (300hp) Teledyne Continental IO-550-B engine driving a three blade constant speed McCauley propeller. B36TC – One 225kW (300hp) turbocharged Teledyne Continental TIO-520-UB engine.

Performance: C33 – Max speed 312km/h (168kt), max cruising speed 298km/h (161kt), long range cruising speed 248km/h (134kt). Initial rate of climb 930ft/min. Range with standard fuel and no reserves 957km (515nm), with optional tanks 1818km (980nm). A36 – Max speed 340km/h (184kt), max cruising speed 326km/h (176kt). Initial rate of climb 1208ft/min. Range with 45 minute reserves 1694km (914nm). B36TC – Max speed 394km/h (213kt), high speed cruise 370km/h (200kt). Initial rate of climb 1053ft/min. Range with 45 minute reserves 2022km (1092nm).

Weights: C33 – Empty 807kg (1780lb), max takeoff 1383kg (3050lb). A36 – Empty 1040kg (2295lb), max takeoff 1665kg (3650lb). B36TC – Empty 1104kg (2433lb), max takeoff 1746kg (3850lb).

Dimensions: C33 – Wing span 10.00m (32ft 10in), length 7.77m (25ft 6in), height 2.51m (8ft 3in). Wing area 16.5m² (177.6sq ft). A36 – Wing span 8.38m (27ft 6in), length 8.13m (26ft 8in), height 2.62m (8ft 7in). Wing area 16.8m² (181sq ft). B36TC – Same as for A36.

Capacity: All Model 33s seat four with some models having an optional fifth seat, all Model 36s seat six.

Production: 3352 Model 33s built through to 1996. Approx 3400 normally aspirated Model 36s/A36s built with production continuing. Approx 700 turbocharged models built.

History: Conceived in the late 1950s as a lower cost derivative of the V-tail Bonanza, the conventional tail Bonanza remains in production today.

Compared with the equivalent Model 35, the first model 33 Debonair introduced a conventional three surface tail, a less powerful engine and a more austere interior fit. It first flew on September 14 1959 and was included in Beech's model range the following year.

The subsequent A33 and B33 Debonairs offered a small number of changes, while the C33 introduced a third cabin window and restyled interior. The Debonair was dropped from the range in 1967, by which time the C33A had been released, an aircraft very similar in performance and trim level to the V-tail Bonanzas, and the name Bonanza was adopted for this model range as well. Development of the 33 continued with the E33 and 155kW (285hp) E33A, the aerobatic E33C, the economy G33 and the F33, available in 155kW (285hp) A and aerobatic C models. The F33A remained in production until 1996.

The larger six seat Model 36 was first released in 1968, featuring a stretched cabin, 155kW (285hp) engine and greater takeoff weights. This aircraft remains in production today as the A36. The four seat A36AT (Airline Trainer)'s IO-500 is limited to 216kW (290hp).

The turbocharged 225kW (300hp) A36TC first appeared in 1979, production switched to the current B36TC in 1981.

Photo: An A36. (Raytheon)

Raytheon Beechcraft Baron

Country of origin: United States of America

Type: Four or six place business & utility twin

Powerplants: B55 – Two 140kW (260hp) Continental IO-470-L fuel injected horizontally opposed flat six piston engines driving two blade constant speed propellers. 58 (current production) – Two 225kW (300hp) Teledyne Continental IO-550-C Raytheon Special Edition engines driving three blade constant speed Hartzell props.

Performance: B55 – Max speed 373km/h (201kt), max cruising speed 348km/h (188kt), long range cruising speed 320km/h (173kt). Initial rate of climb 1693ft/min. Range with reserves 1836km (990nm). 58 – Max speed 386km/h (208kt), max cruising speed 376km/h (203kt), cruising speed 356km/h (192kt), economical cruising speed 300km/h (162kt). Initial rate of climb 1735ft/min. Range with reserves 2432km (1313nm).

Weights: B55 – Empty 1468kg (3236lb), max takeoff 2313kg (5100lb). 58 – Empty 1633kg (3600lb), max takeoff 2495kg (5500lb).

Dimensions: B55 – Wing span 11.53m (37ft 10in), length 8.53m (28ft 0in), height 2.92m (9ft 7in). Wing area 18.5m² (199.2sq ft). 58 – Wing span 11.53m (37ft 10in), length 9.09m (29ft 10in), height 2.97m (9ft 9in). Wing area 18.5m² (199.2sq ft).

Capacity: Models 55 and 56 has standard seating for four, with some models offering an optional fifth seat. Model 58 has optional fifth and sixth seats, with optional club seating arrangement.

Production: More than 2600 of all variants built by late 2002. 2000th Model 58 delivered in July 2001.

History: The successful and long running Baron line is widely regarded as the most successful of its class, and has comfortably outlasted its main rivals from Piper and Cessna.

Development of the Baron began in the late 1950s. The first to fly, the Model 95-55 on February 29 1960, was essentially a re-engined development of the Model 95 Travel Air (Beech's first light twin, which first flew in August 1956). As a result the Baron can lay claim to Bonanza and T-34 Mentor lineage, as the Travel Air combined the fuselage of the former with the tail of the latter, plus twin engines, a new wing and other new features. Some 720 Travel Airs were built from the late 1950s to the late 1960s.

The first Barons were delivered during early 1961, although these early production examples were soon followed off the line in 1962 by the improved A55. The subsequent B55 of 1965 remained in production until 1982, during which time it was continually refined. During the B55's model life other variants entered production, these included the more powerful C55, D55 and E55. In the meantime the turbocharged Baron 56TC appeared in 1967 and the A56TC in 1970, although these were produced only in limited numbers.

The IO-550 powered Model 58 is a stretched version of the 55, and first entered production in 1970. It remains in production today, having evolved somewhat in production during that time. Versions include the pressurised 58P and the turbocharged 58TC, both powered by 240kW (325hp) Teledyne Continental TSIO-520s.

Current production (under the Raytheon Aircraft Company banner) runs at around 45 per year.

Photo: A Baron 58 modified with winglets. (Lance Higgerson)

Raytheon Beechcraft King Air 90 & 100

Country of origin: United States of America

Type: Twin turboprop corporate and utility transport

Powerplants: 90 – Two 373kW (500shp) Pratt & Whitney Canada PT6A-6 turboprops driving three blade c/s Hartzell propellers. B100 – Two 533kW (715shp) Garrett TPE331-6-252Bs driving three blade props. C90B – Two 410kW (550shp) PT6A-21s driving four blade props.

Performance: 90 – Max speed 450km/h (243kt), max cruising speed 435km/h (235kt). Initial rate of climb 1900ft/min. Range with reserves 2520km (1360nm). B100 – Max speed 491km/h (265kt). Initial rate of climb 2140ft/min. Range at max cruising speed 2343km (1264nm), at economical cruising speed 2455km (1325nm). C90B – Max cruising speed 457km/h (247kt). Range at economical cruising speed at 24,000ft 2375km (1282nm).

Weights: 90 – Empty equipped 2412kg (5318lb), max takeoff 4218kg (9300lb). B100 – Empty equipped 3212kg (7092lb), max takeoff 5352kg (11,800lb). C90B – Empty 3040kg (6702lb), max takeoff 4580kg (10,100lb).

Dimensions: 90 – Wing span 13.98m (45ft 11in), length 10.82m (35ft 6in), height 4.47m (14ft 8in). Wing area 25.9m² (279.7sq ft). B100 – Wing span 14.00m (45ft 11in), length 12.17m (39ft 11in), height 4.70m (15ft 5in). Wing area 26.0m² (279.7sq ft). C90B – Wing span 15.32m (50ft 3in), length 10.82m (35ft 6in), height 4.34m (14ft 3in). Wing area 27.3m² (293.9sq ft).

Capacity: 90 – Typical seating for six, max seating for eight. 100 – Six to eight in corporate configuration, or max seating for 13.

Production: Approx 1925 of all variants of the King Air 90 family built (including 226 military orders). Approx 350 King Air 100s built.

History: The Model 90 King Air was the first model in the largest and most successful family of corporate turboprop twins yet built.

The King Air began as a turboprop development of the Queen Air designed to meet a US Army requirement for a staff/utility transport. A prototype PT6 powered Queen Air Model 65-80 (later 65-90T) began test flying in 1963 and the type was subsequently ordered by the US Army in unpressurised form as the U-21A.

The civil equivalent, the model 90 King Air, introduced pressurisation and first flew on January 20 1964. Deliveries of production civil aircraft began in late 1964.

Subsequent models include the A90 and B90 with PT6A-20 engines; the C90 with PT6A-21s; the E90 with more powerful PT6A-34Bs; and the F90 with the T-tail of the 200 (described separately), four blade props and other mods. The less expensive 90SE Special Edition was released during 1994, but is no longer offered. The current C90B has been in production since 1991.

The C90B Jaguar Special Edition was announced in January 1998 and features the Jaguar car company's green and gold colours and a Connolly leather interior with walnut and boxwood cabinets.

The King Air 100 series was announced in May 1969. Compared with the 90 series it was 1.27m (4ft 2in) longer, allowing greater seating capacity, and featured a reduced wing span and larger rudder. The A100 is a military version, while the B100 is powered by 535kW (715shp) Garrett TFE331s. Production of the 100 ceased in 1984.

Photo: A US registered King Air 90. (Steve Allsopp)

Raytheon Beechcraft King Air 200

Country of origin: United States of America

Type: Twin turboprop corporate, passenger & utility transport

Powerplants: 200 – Two 635kW (850shp) Pratt & Whitney Canada PT6A-41 turboprops driving three blade constant speed propellers. B200 – Two 635kW (850shp) P&WC PT6A-42s.

Performance: 200 – Max speed 536km/h (289kt), max cruising speed 515km/h (278kt). Initial rate of climb 2450ft/min. Range with reserves at max cruising speed 3254km (1757nm), at econ cruising speed 3495km (1887nm). B200 – Max speed 541km/h (292kt), max cruising speed at 27,000ft 531km/h (287kt), econ cruising speed at 27,000ft 411km/h (222kt). Initial rate of climb 2450ft/min. Range at max cruising speed at 18,000ft 2142km (1157nm), with max fuel at econ cruising speed at 31,000ft 3442km (1859nm).

Weights: 200 – Empty 3318kg (7315lb), max takeoff 5670kg (12,500lb). B200 – Empty 3716kg (8192lb), MTOW 5670kg (12,500lb).

Dimensions: Wing span 16.61m (54ft 6in), length 13.36m (43ft 10in), height 4.52m (14ft 10in). Wing area 28.2m² (303.0sq ft).

Capacity: Flightcrew of one or two. Accommodation for a maximum of 13 passengers in main cabin, plus a further passenger beside the pilot on flightdeck. Typical corporate seating layout for six in main cabin.

Production: Over 1900 King Air 200s have been delivered to civil and commercial buyers, while 397 have been delivered to military forces. Current production rate approx 50 per annum.

History: The King Air 200 is the most popular member of the King Air family, and was introduced with new features including the distinctive T-tail, more powerful engines, greater wing span and area, increased cabin pressurisation, greater fuel capacity and higher operating weights.

Beech began design work on the Super King Air 200 in October 1970, resulting in the type's first flight on October 27 1972. Certificated in mid December 1973, the King Air 200 went on to be the most successful aircraft in its class, eclipsing such rivals as the Cessna Conquest and Piper Cheyenne. Today the King Air 200 is the only one of the three in production.

The improved B200 entered production in May 1980, this version features more efficient PT6A-42 engines, increased zero fuel max weight and increased cabin pressurisation. Subvariants include the B200C with a 1.32m x 1.32m (4ft 4in x 4ft 4in) cargo door, the B200T with removable tip tanks, and the B200CT with tip tanks and cargo door (four built). The Special Edition B200SE was certificated in October 1995 and introduced an EFIS avionics suite. It is no longer available but current production B200s feature a Collins Pro-Line II EFIS suite as standard, while a three screen suite is optional.

Various special mission King Air 200s and B200s have been built, including for navaid calibration, maritime patrol and resource exploration. In addition several hundred Super King Airs have been built for the US military under the designation C-12. C-12s perform a range of missions from electronic surveillance to VIP transport.

In 1996 Raytheon dropped the 'Super' prefix from the King Air name.

Photo: A B200 King Air. (Rob Finlayson)

Raytheon Beechcraft King Air 300 & 350

Country of origin: United States of America

Type: Twin turboprop corporate and utility aircraft

Powerplants: Two 783kW (1050shp) Pratt & Whitney Canada PT6A-60A turboprops driving four blade Hartzell propellers.

Performance: 300 – Max cruising speed 583km/h (315kt), economical cruising speed 568km/h (307kt). Initial rate of climb 2844ft/min. Range with max fuel and reserves 3630km (1960nm). 350 – Max speed 584km/h (315kt), max cruising speed 576km/h (311kt), typical cruising speed at 24,000ft 558km/h (301kt). Initial rate of climb 2731ft/min. Range at max cruising power and 18,000ft 1911km (1032nm), at max range power and 35,000ft 3357km (1813nm).

Weights: 300 – Empty 3850kg (8490lb), max takeoff 6350kg (14,000lb). 350 – Empty 4132kg (9110lb), max takeoff 6804kg (15,000lb).

Dimensions: 300 & 300LW – Wing span 16.61m (54ft 6in), length 13.36m (43ft 10in), height 4.37m (14ft 4in). Wing area 28.2m² (303sq ft). 350 – Wing span 17.65m (57ft 11in), length 14.22m (46ft 8in), height 4.37m (14ft 4in). Wing area 28.8m² (310.0sq ft).

Capacity: 300 – One or two pilots on flightdeck, with standard layout for six passengers in main cabin. Alternative high density seating for 15 (including pilot). 350 – Typical passenger seating for eight in main cabin, optional seating for an extra two, plus one in toilet compartment and one on flightdeck next to the pilot, making a total of 13.

Production: 219 King Air 300s were built when production ended in 1991. Production of the 300LW ceased in 1994 after 35 had been built. Over 350 King Air 350s delivered.

History: The King Air 300 is an updated version of the successful B200 series, and was itself replaced by the further improved King Air 350, the latest model in this long running and very successful line of corporate and utility transports.

Work on an improved development of the successful King Air B200 began in August 1981, the 14 month design effort resulting in the first flight of the new 300 model in October the following year. Improvements over the B200 were numerous, with the main change being the installation of more powerful PT6A-60A turboprops in place of the -42s of the earlier model. Other changes included reprofiled and more aerodynamically clean engine cowls and exhausts and extended wing leading edges, plus minor internal changes. Both empty and max takeoff weights were also increased.

The max weight was reduced for the 300LW or 'Light Weight', intended to minimise weight based airways user fees, particularly in Europe. The 300AT was an airline pilot trainer.

The King Air 300 has been replaced by the 350, its major improvements being a stretched fuselage lengthened by 86cm (2ft 10in) and winglets. The latest member of the King Air family, it had its first flight in 1988, and has been in production since late 1989. The King Air 350C features a built-in airstair and a 132 x 132cm (52 x 52in) freight door. The 350 is also available in a range of special missions and military variants. The 350 is available with three or five screen Collins EFIS avionics suites.

The 'Super' prefix was dropped from the King Air name in 1996.

Photo: A King Air 350. (Raytheon)

Raytheon Beechcraft 1900

Country of origin: United States of America

Type: Regional airliner and corporate transport

Powerplants: 1900C – Two 820kW (1100shp) Pratt & Whitney Canada PT6A-65B turboprops driving four blade constant speed Hartzell propellers. 1900D – Two 954kW (1279shp) P&WC PT6A-67D turboprops.

Performance: 1900C – Max cruising speed 495km/h (267kt). Range with 10 pax at long range cruising speed with reserves 2907km (1570nm). 1900D – Max cruising speed 533km/h (288kt). Range with 10 pax and reserves at long range cruising speed 2776km (1498nm).

Weights: 1900C – Empty 4327kg (9540lb), max takeoff 7530kg (16,600lb). 1900D – Typical empty 4831kg (10,650lb), max takeoff 7688kg (16,950lb).

Dimensions: 1900C – Wing span 16.60m (54ft 6in), length 17.63m (57ft 10in), height 4.54m (14ft 11in). Wing area 28.2m² (303sq ft). 1900D – Wing span (over winglets) 17.67m (58ft 0in), length 17.63m (57ft 10in), height 4.72m (15ft 6in). Wing area 28.8m² (310.0sq ft).

Capacity: Flightcrew of two. Standard passenger accommodation for 19 at two abreast. Executive and corporate shuttle configurations range for between 10 to 18, depending on customer requirements.

Production: 207 civil Beech 1900Cs were built when production ended. Approx 465 1900Ds delivered by late 2002.

History: The Beech 1900 19 seat commuter was chosen along with the smaller 1300, both developments of the King Air 200, and the C99 for Beech's re-entry into the regional airliner market in 1979.

The most obvious change from the King Air 200 to the 1900C is the substantially lengthened fuselage (17.63m/57ft 10in compared to 13.34m/43ft 9in). Other changes include more powerful engines, a modified tail with tailets, and stabilons on the lower rear fuselage.

Development of the 1900 commenced in 1979, with first flight on September 3 1982. US FAA certification was awarded in November 1983, prior to the 1900C's service entry in February the following year. The first Exec-Liner corporate transport version was delivered in mid 1985.

During the course of 1900C production a wet wing was introduced, increasing fuel capacity by 927 litres (204Imp gal/245US gal), while military transport, maritime patrol and electronic surveillance versions were offered.

Beech announced the enlarged 1900D at the annual US Regional Airlines Association meeting in 1989, with the prototype, a converted 1900C, first flying on March 1 1990. Production switched to the improved model in 1991, with first deliveries (to Mesa Air) that November. The main change introduced on the 1900D was the substantially deeper fuselage with stand-up headroom. In addition it also introduced larger passenger and freight doors and windows, twin ventral strakes and auxiliary horizontal fixed tails, while more powerful engines and winglets improve hot and high performance. The cockpit features a four screen Rockwell Collins EFIS suite. A corporate shuttle version is also offered.

Production had effectively come to a halt in late 2002.

Photo: A Beech 1900C freighter. (Rob Finlayson)

Raytheon Beechjet 400

Country of origin: United States of America

Type: Light corporate jet

Powerplants: Two 13.9kN (2965lb) takeoff rated Pratt & Whitney Canada JT15D-5 turbofans.

Performance: 400 – Max speed 837km/h (452kt), cruising speed 748km/h (404kt). Range with four pax, max fuel and reserves 3572km (1929nm). 400A – Max speed 867km/h (468kt), typical cruising speed 834km/h (450kt), long range cruising speed 726km/h (392kt). Initial rate of climb 3770ft/min. Service ceiling 43,450ft. Range with max fuel and reserves cruising at 796km/h (430kt) 2915km (1574nm), at 746km/h (403kt) 3098km (1673nm).

Weights: 400 – Basic empty 4225kg (9315lb), max takeoff 7158kg (15,780lb). 400A – Operating empty (including crew) 4921kg (10850lb), max takeoff 7303kg (16,100lb).

Dimensions: Wing span 13.25m (43ft 6in), length 14.75m (48ft 5in), height 4.24m (13ft 11in). Wing area 22.4m² (241.4sq ft).

Capacity: Flightcrew of one or two pilots, with standard passenger arrangement in main cabin for six with an entertainment/executive console, or seven without (plus provision for an eighth passenger in toilet compartment with seat belt installed).

Production: Total Beechjet 400 production 64 (62 still in service in 2002). 600th 400A delivered in late 2002, total includes 180 built for the US Air Force as T-1A Jayhawk tanker/transport trainers.

History: The Raytheon Beechjet traces its origins back to the Mitsubishi Diamond 2 bizjet, which Beechcraft acquired the design and production rights to in the mid 1980s.

The original Mitsubishi MU-300 Diamond 1 first flew in August 1978, powered by two 11.1kN (2500lb) P&WC JT15D-4 turbofans. The subsequent Diamond 2 flew on June 20 1984, with the first production aircraft flying in January 1985. Only 11 Diamond 2s were built before Beech purchased the design and production rights, resulting in the Model 400 Beechjet.

Beech re-engined the Diamond 2 with P&WC JT15D-5 turbofans, developed a new interior, and incorporated a number of other minor refinements. Deliveries of the Beechjet began in June 1986, with low rate production continuing until that model was replaced by the Model 400A, which was delivered from November 1990.

The new 400A incorporated a number of improvements over its predecessor. A higher max takeoff weight and greater operating ceiling improved performance, while repositioning the rear fuselage fuel tank increased cabin volume. The flightdeck features Collins Pro Line 4 EFIS with three colour displays – two primary flight displays (PFDs) and a multifunction display (MFD) with a second MFD optional.

Following customer feedback Raytheon developed a new luxury standard interior for the Beechjet which was introduced in 1996.

The Beechjet 400A also serves as the basis for the military T-1 Jayhawk tanker and transport aircrew trainer – 180 were delivered between 1992 and 1997. The Japan Air Self Defence Force has also taken delivery of 10 T-400 aircrew trainers (Beechjet 400Ts).

In late 2002 Raytheon introduced a 90kg (200lb) gross weight increase to 7400kg (16,300lb), retrofitable to existing aircraft.

Photo: A Beechjet 400A. (Raytheon)

Raytheon Beechcraft Premier I

Country of origin: United States of America

Type: Light corporate jet

Powerplants: Two 10.2kN (2300lb) Williams-Rolls FJ44-2A turbofans.

Performance: Max speed 835km/h (451kt). Max certificated operating altitude 41,000ft. Takeoff length at MTOW at S/L less than 915m (3000ft). Max range at long range cruising speed with pilot, four passengers and IFR reserves 2468km (1430nm).

Weights: Basic operating including single pilot 3627kg (7996lb), max takeoff 5670kg (12,400lb).

Dimensions: Wing span 13.56m (44ft 6in), length 14.02m (46ft 0in), height 4.67m (15ft 4in). Wing area 23.0m² (247.0sq ft).

Capacity: One or two pilots on flightdeck (is certificated for single pilot). Main cabin seats six in standard configuration with four seats in a club arrangement and two seats behind them. Toilet in rear fuselage. Baggage compartments in nose and tail.

Production: Approx 70 delivered by late 2002.

History: The Premier I is the first new product of Raytheon Aircraft (following Raytheon's September 1994 merger of its Beech and Hawker subsidiaries). It is an all new entry level corporate jet which competes head on with Cessna's highly successful CJ1.

Beech began design work on the Premier I in early 1994 under the designation PD374 (later PD390). Raytheon authorised development go-ahead in early 1995, and initial details of the new jet were released in mid 1995. Raytheon publicly launched the Premier I at the National Business Aviation Association convention in Las Vegas in September 1995, where a full size cabin mock-up was on display.

Construction of the first Premier I began in late 1996 and rollout was on August 19 1998, followed by first flight on December 22 that year. Four Premier Is were used in the flight test program, leading to certification on March 23 2001 (over two years later than originally scheduled). Deliveries began in the third quarter of 2001.

The Premier I was designed using CATIA computer aided design. Features include its composite carbonfibre/epoxy honeycomb fuselage, swept metal construction wings, T-tail and two Williams-Rolls FJ44 turbofans.

The composite fuselage has a number of benefits. Advanced production techniques (using computer controlled automated fibre placement machines) means a Premier I fuselage can be constructed in one week, whereas a conventional airframe would require one to two weeks to complete. The composite construction also allows greater (approx 13%) internal cabin space compared with a conventional construction fuselage of the same external dimensions (it lacks internal frames), while weight is 20% lower than otherwise would be the case.

The Premier I will be certificated for single pilot operations. The flightdeck features the new Collins Pro Line 21 EFIS avionics suite with two 20 x 25cm (8 x 10in) flat panel LCDs (one a primary flight display, the other a multifunction display).

Raytheon has studied stretched Premier II and Premier III developments. At the 2002 NBAA convention Raytheon announced the Premier I would be marketed under the Beechcraft brand.

Photo: A German registered Premier I. (Egon Johansen)

Raytheon Hawker 800 & BAe 125-700

Countries of origin: United Kingdom and USA

Type: Mid size corporate jet

Powerplants: 700 – Two 16.6kN (3700lb) Garrett TFE731-3-RH turbofans. 800XP – Two 20.7kN (4660lb) Honeywell TFE731-5BR-1Hs.

Performance: 700 – Max cruising speed 808km/h (436kt), economical cruising speed 723km/h (390kt). Service ceiling 41,000ft. Range with max fuel, payload and IFR reserves 4725km (2550nm). 800XP – Max speed and max cruising speed 845km/h (456kt), econ cruising speed 740km/h (400kt). Max initial rate of climb 3100ft/min. Max certificated altitude 43,000ft. Range with max payload 4222km (2280nm), range with max fuel and VFR reserves 5472km (2955nm).

Weights: 700 – Empty 5825kg (12,845lb), MTOW 11,567kg (25,500lb). 800XP – Basic empty 7380kg (16,270lb), MTOW 12,700kg (28,000lb).

Dimensions: 700 – Wing span 14.33m (47ft 0in), length 15.46m (50ft 9in), height 5.36m (17ft 7in). Wing area 32.8m² (353.0sq ft). 800XP – Wing span 15.66m (51ft 5in), length 15.60m (51ft 2in), height 5.36m (17ft 7in). Wing area 34.8m² (374.0sq ft).

Capacity: Flightcrew of two. Typical seating for eight passengers in corporate layout, or max seating for 14.

Production: 215 125-700s and 275 Hawker 800s built. Approx 300 Hawker 800XPs built. 1000th 125 series aircraft (including military versions) delivered October 1998.

History: The 125-700 and Hawker 800 are the most recent versions of the world's longest running corporate jet production program.

The 125-700 and Hawker 800 are direct developments of the DH.125 (later the HS.125), which first flew in August 1962. This aircraft was developed into a number of variants through to the HS.125-600, all of which are powered by the Rolls-Royce Viper turbojet and are described separately under Hawker Siddeley.

The introduction of the BAe 125-700 in 1976 brought with it significant performance and fuel economy benefits as the -700 incorporated Garrett TFE731 turbofans. The 125-700 first flew on June 19 1976, and remained in production until it was replaced by the 125-800 in 1984.

The 125-800 first flew on May 26 1983 and it introduced a number of improvements. Aerodynamic changes included a reprofiled nose and windscreen, extended fin leading edge, and greater span wing which decreased drag and increased lift and fuel capacity. Range was boosted further by a larger ventral fuel tank. More powerful TFE731s improved field performance, while a redesigned interior made more efficient use of the space available. The 800 was also the first corporate jet to feature an EFIS cockpit. The 800A was specifically aimed at the US market, the 800B for non US markets.

The 125-800 became the Hawker 800 from mid 1993 when Raytheon purchased BAe's Corporate Jets division. Production was transferred to Wichita in the USA (the first US built 800 flew on November 5 1996, the last UK built 800 on April 29 1997).

Current production is of the 800XP (Extended Performance) which was certificated in 1995 and has improved engines for better climb and cruise performance. A new interior was introduced in 1998. Rockwell Collins' Pro-Line 21 avionics suite is now standard.

Photo: A Chinese registered Hawker 800. (Rob Finlayson)

Raytheon (BAe) Hawker 1000

Countries of origin: United Kingdom and USA

Type: Mid size corporate jet

Powerplants: Two 23.1kN (5200lb) Pratt & Whitney Canada PW305 turbofans.

Performance: Max cruising speed 867km/h (468kt), economical cruising speed 745km/h (402kt). Service ceiling 43,000ft. Range with max payload 5750km (3105nm), range with max fuel and NBAA VFR reserves 6205km (3350nm).

Weights: Empty 7810kg (17,220lb), max takeoff 14,060kg (31,000lb).

Dimensions: Wing span 15.66m (51ft 4in), length 16.42m (53ft 10in), height 5.21m (17ft 1in). Wing area 34.8m² (374.0sq ft).

Capacity: Flightcrew of two. Standard main cabin seating for eight comprising club seating for four at the front of the cabin, a three seat couch and a single seat. Max seating for 15.

Production: Production ceased after 52 built, almost all are in service in North America.

History: The Hawker 1000 was the largest member of the DH/HS/BAe 125/Hawker 800 series of corporate jets.

The Hawker 1000 was based on the smaller Hawker 800, and until 1997 the two types were in production side by side in the famous de Havilland plant in Hatfield in England. The 1000 differs from the 800 in a number of respects however and features a stretched fuselage. The 1000 is identifiable via its seven main cabin windows per side, whereas the 800 has six, and the 0.84m (2ft 9in) stretch (achieved by small fuselage plugs in front of and behind the wing) allowing an increase in max seating to 15. However as it is optimised for long range work, the typical Hawker 1000 configuration seats one less than the smaller Hawker 800.

Other important changes include Pratt & Whitney Canada PW305 turbofans (in place of the AlliedSignal TFE731s on the Hawker 800), extra fuel in the extended forward wing fairing, new lightweight systems, revised and more efficient cabin interior with increased headroom, EFIS glass cockpit and certification to the latest US FAR and European JAR requirements.

British Aerospace launched the BAe 1000 program in October 1989. The first BAe 1000 development aircraft first flew on June 16 1990, with a second following on November 26 that year. These two were followed by the first production aircraft which participated in an 800 hour flight test development program, culminating in UK certification being granted on October 21 1991 (FAA certification followed on October 31 1991). The first production aircraft was delivered in December 1991.

As is the case with the BAe 125-800, the BAe 1000 became the Hawker 1000 from mid 1993 when Raytheon purchased British Aerospace's Corporate Jets division. However, the 1000 never enjoyed the popularity of the 800 and production ceased in 1997 with the delivery of the 52nd aircraft.

The 1000's largest customer was the Net Jets fractional ownership scheme which has 17 in service (including 13 of the last 14 built).

Photo: The Hawker 1000 is recognisable by its stretched fuselage and larger engine nacelles. (Raytheon)

Raytheon Hawker Horizon

Country of origin: United States of America

Type: Super mid size corporate jet

Powerplants: Two 28.9kN (6500lb) Pratt & Whitney Canada PW308A turbofans.

Performance: Max operating speed Mach 0.84 or 896km/h (484kt). Certificated ceiling 45,000ft. Max range 6300km (3400nm), range at Mach 0.82 with six passengers and IFR reserves 5745km (3100nm).

Weights: Basic operating (incl pilots) 9494kg (20,930lb), max takeoff 16,330kg (36,000lb).

Dimensions: Wing span 18.82m (61ft 9in), length 21.08m (69ft 2in), height 5.97m (19ft 7in). Wing area 49.3m² (531.0sq ft).

Capacity: Flightcrew of two. Typical main cabin layout will seat eight, with a toilet in the aft fuselage.

Production: Certification and first deliveries planned for 2003.

History: Raytheon's Hawker Horizon is an all new 'super mid size' corporate jet.

Design work on what became the Horizon was already underway when Raytheon Corporate Jets and Beech merged in early 1995 to form Raytheon Aircraft. The new design, initially labelled PD376 and later Horizon 1000, was one of three projects the new Raytheon Aircraft was working on, along with what became the Premier I. Raytheon worked closely with potential customers during design definition.

Raytheon formally announced the Hawker Horizon immediately prior to the National Business Aviation Association's annual convention in November 1996. The originally planned first flight date of late 1999 slipped (in part due to delays with the Premier I) to August 11 2001, with US FAA certification scheduled for early 2003.

One of Raytheon's design philosophies in developing the Horizon is to combine the earlier Hawkers' popular characteristics with advanced technologies. Experienced Hawker designers formed the core of the Horizon's design team and the aircraft has been designed to look and feel like a Hawker.

Compared to the Hawker 1000 the Horizon has a wider, slightly longer fuselage with a flat floor and stand up headroom and a two tonne heavier max takeoff weight. The Horizon features an all composite fuselage manufactured using the automated fibre placement technology developed for the Premier I. Raytheon says the composite fuselage saves weight and increases cabin volume. The empennage features an aluminium sub structure and carbonfibre skin.

Power is from two digitally controlled Pratt & Whitney Canada PW308A turbofans. P&WC is a risk sharing partner in the program, as is avionics integrator Honeywell (the Horizon will feature Honeywell's Primus Epic avionics suite with five flat panel colour LCDs and cursor control devices – comprising touchpad, joystick, light pen, trackball and soft keys).

The Horizon's new metal construction supercritical 30° sweep, aft loaded wing is built by Fuji Heavy Industries of Japan, another risk sharing partner, and passes beneath the fuselage. Other suppliers/partners include Messier-Dowty (landing gear), Sundstrand, Vickers and Honeywell (APU and environmental control system).

Photo: The Horizon features a composite fuselage. (Andy Hutchings)

Republic RC-3 Seabee

Country of origin: United States of America

Type: Four seat amphibious light aircraft

Powerplant: One 160kW (215hp) Franklin 6A8-215-B8F six cylinder inline piston engine driving a two blade propeller.

Performance: Max speed 193km/h (104kt), max cruising speed 166km/h (90kt). Initial rate of climb 700ft/min. Service ceiling 12,000ft. Range 900km (485nm).

Weights: Empty 885kg (1950lb), max takeoff 1360kg (3000lb).

Dimensions: Wing span 11.48m (37ft 8in), length 8.51m (27ft 11in), height 2.92m (9ft 7in). Wing area 18.2m² (196sq ft).

Capacity: Typical seating for four.

Production: 1060 built between 1946 and 1947.

History: The Republic Seabee was a product of the same company that built the legendary World War 2 P-47 Thunderbolt fighter, and was one of the few amphibious light aircraft to be built in large numbers.

The Seabee was conceived during the latter stages of World War 2 when Republic began to look beyond its massive wartime contracts to projects for peacetime production. The original concept was one that was quite popular during the 1940s – to provide a four seat light aircraft that would cost little more to purchase and operate than a family car. To an extent Republic succeeded in its aims, more than 1000 Seabees were built in just one year of production.

The original prototype Seabee was designated the RC-1 (Republic Commercial design number one) and first appeared during 1944. The RC-1 was a three seat design powered by a 130kW (175hp) six cylinder Franklin 6ALG-365 piston engine. First flown during November 1944, the conventional all metal construction RC-1 for a time was dubbed the Thunderbolt Amphibian.

A comprehensive testing and development program ensued, during which the RC-1 was punishingly tested. One test that illustrated that the RC-1 encompassed Republic aircraft's legendary abilities to absorb punishment involved intentionally making a wheels-up landing on a concrete runway. The RC-1 passed this test without incident, the only damage being a small metal shaving from the keel.

While the RC-1's structural integrity was beyond dispute, Republic nevertheless decided to redesign the RC-1, mainly to significantly reduce production and acquisition costs. What resulted was the RC-3 Seabee, a four seater powered by a 160kW (215hp) Franklin 6A8-215-B8F piston engine. Aside from the increased seating capacity, the Seabee differed from the RC-1 in being lighter, built with far fewer components (450 compared with 1800 in the RC-1), required 25% less tooling to manufacture and, most importantly, cost half of what the RC-1 would have.

Seabee production began in mid 1946, but lasted only until October 1947, when ironically Republic decided to concentrate on its once more lucrative military business (with the development of the F-84 jet fighter), despite healthy Seabee sales.

The decision to cease Seabee production also terminated development plans for twin engined and landplane developments.

Photo: This photograph shows to good effect the Seabee's hull, outrigger floats and undercarriage. (Gordon Reid)

Robin DR 400 & DR 500

Country of origin: France

Type: Four/five seat light aircraft

Powerplant: DR 400/120 – One 84kW (112hp) (Textron) Lycoming O-235-L2A flat four piston engine driving a two blade fixed pitch prop. DR 400/180 – One 135kW (180hp) Textron Lycoming O-360-A.

Performance: DR 400/120 – Max speed 241km/h (130kt), max cruising speed 215km/h (116kt). Initial rate of climb 600ft/min. Service ceiling 12,000ft. Range with standard fuel and no reserves at max cruising speed 860km (465nm). DR 400/180 – Max speed 278km/h (150kt), max cruising speed 260km/h (140kt), econ cruising speed 245km/h (132kt). Initial rate of climb 825ft/min. Service ceiling 15,475ft. Range at econ cruising speed 1450km (783nm).

Weights: DR 400/120 – Empty equipped 535kg (1180lb), max takeoff 900kg (1985lb). DR 400/180 – Empty equipped 600kg (1320lb), max takeoff 1100kg (2425lb).

Dimensions: Wing span 8.72m (28ft 7in), length 6.96m (22ft 10in), height 2.23m (7ft 3in). Wing area 13.6m² (146.4sq ft).

Capacity: Most DR 400 models typically seat four.

Production: Over 1850 DR 400s. Over 40 DR 500s built.

History: The Robin DR 400 series of light aircraft owes its origins to the Jodel series of wooden construction light aircraft.

Avions Pierre Robin was formed by Pierre Robin and the principal designer of Jodel Aircraft, Jean Delemontez, in October 1957 as Centre Est Aeronautique. The company's initial production was of developments of the basic Jodel series of tail draggers, and it was these aircraft that evolved into the DR 400 series. Initial production was of the DR 100 and the DR 1050/1051, while the DR 220, DR 221 and DR 250 featured the Jodel's basic wing with a four seat fuselage. The final links between the Jodels and the DR 400 were the DR 253 and DR 300 series, tricycle developments of the DR 220 series.

First flight of the DR 400 occurred during June 1972, both a DR 400/125 and a DR 400/180 taking flight that month.

Since that time a number of developments have been offered. The least powerful version is the DR 400/120, and it remains available today as the DR 400/120 Dauphin 2+2. Powered by an 84kW (112hp) O-235, the DR 400/120 is really a two seater, although it can seat two children on a rear bench seat. The DR 400/125i has a 93kW (125hp) fuel injected IO-240 and was revealed in 1995. The DR 400/140 Dauphin is powered by a 120kW (160hp) O-320 and is a full four seater. The four seat DR 400/160 Chevalier meanwhile also features a 120kW (160hp) Lycoming O-320 and seats four. It first flew in June 1972. With a different prop, more fuel capacity and slightly different wing it became the DR 400/160 Major from 1980.

The four/five seat DR 400/180 Regent and DR 400 Remo 180R are powered by the 135kW (180hp) (Textron) Lycoming O-360, the Remo being optimised for glider towing. Also optimised for glider tug work is the DR 400/200R Remo 200, the most powerful DR 400 model (powered by a 150kW/200hp IO-360, driving a constant speed prop).

The DR 500i President was unveiled at the 1997 Paris Airshow as the DR 400/200i. It features a 150kW (200hp) IO-360 driving a constant speed prop and widened and taller cabin. Deliveries began in 1998.

Photo: The DR 500i President. (Bob Grimstead)

Robin HR 200 & R 2000 Alpha

Robin R 3000

Country of origin: France

Type: Two seat aerobatic light aircraft

Powerplant: HR 200 Club – One 80kW (108hp) Lycoming O-235-C2A flat four piston engine driving a two blade fixed pitch propeller. R 2160 Alpha Sport – One 120kW (160hp) Lycoming O-320-D.

Performance: HR 200 – Max speed 230km/h (124kt), max cruising speed 215km/h (116kt). Initial rate of climb 670ft/min. Service ceiling 13,000ft. Range with max fuel 1078km (582nm). 2160 – Max speed 257km/h (138kt), max cruising speed 242km/h (130kt), cruising speed 234km/h (126kt). Initial rate of climb 1025ft/min. Service ceiling 15,000ft. Range with max fuel 795km (430nm).

Weights: HR 200 – Empty 500kg (1100lb), max takeoff 760kg (1670lb). 2160 – Empty 550kg (1213lb), max takeoff 800kg (1765lb).

Dimensions: HR 200 – Wing span 8.40m (27ft 7in), length 6.68m (21ft 11in), height 2.18m (7ft 2in). Wing area 12.6m² (135.6sq ft). 2160 – Wing span 8.33m (27ft 4in), length 7.10m (23ft 4in), height 2.13m (7ft 0in). Wing area 13.0m² (140.0sq ft).

Capacity: Seating for two side by side.

Production: Approx 160 200s and 130 R 2000s built.

History: This series of two seat aerobatic aircraft was designed during the 1970s for flying school use, and has been developed in two major variants, both of which are back in production.

The HR 200 was the second all metal aircraft designed for Robin by Christophe Heintz. It first flew on July 19 1971 powered by an 80kW (108hp) O-235, the first production aircraft flew in April 1973.

Three initial versions were built, the 80kW (108hp) powered Club or HR 200/100, the more powerful Acrobin 125 or HR 200/125 (with a 95kW/125hp O-235) and the Acrobin 160 or HR 200/160 (with a 120kW/160hp IO-320). The HR 200 remained in production until the late 1970s, and is once again on offer. Robin has now recommenced production of the HR 200/120B, powered by an 88kW (118hp) Textron Lycoming O-235-L2A and a new instrument panel. The HR 200/160 is powered by the 120kW (160hp) O-320 and was introduced in 1999.

The R 2000 Alpha series meanwhile was a redevelopment of the HR 200. The HR 200's basic fuselage was retained, but changes included an all new wing and enlarged rudder and vertical tail to improve spinning characteristics. The prototype R 2000 was powered by a 135kW (160hp) IO-320 and flew for the first time on January 15 1976. Deliveries of production aircraft began in 1977.

Three developments of the R 2000 series were built, the R 2100, the R 2112 and R 2160 Alpha Sport, with the main differences between the three being the powerplant fitted. The R 2100 is powered by an 80kW (108hp) O-235, the R 2112 has an 84kW (112hp) O-235, and the R 2160 has a 120kW (160hp) O-320.

Of the three, the R 2160 Alpha Sport has been the most popular. Production of the R 2000 series (by Robin factories in France and Canada) originally ceased in 1983, however Robin restarted production of the R 2160 in 1994. Current production is of the R 2160 D and the R 2160i with a fuel injected AEIO-320.

In 2001 Robin unveiled the HR 200/120B based R 2120 Alpha, which features the R 2160's horizontal tail.

Photo: An R 2160 Alpha Sport. (Peter Clark)

Country of origin: France

Type: Two/four seat light aircraft

Powerplant: R 3000/100 – One 87kW (116hp) Lycoming O-235 flat four piston engine driving a two blade fixed pitch propeller. R 3000/160 – One 135kW (180hp) Textron Lycoming O-320-D2A flat four.

Performance: R 3000/100 – Max speed 230km/h (124kt), max cruising speed 210km/h (113kt), normal cruising speed 200km/h (108kt). Initial rate of climb 590ft/min. Service ceiling 13,000ft. Range with standard fuel and no reserves 1120km (605nm), with optional fuel 1420km (767nm). R 3000/160 – Max speed 270km/h (146kt), max cruising speed 255km/h (138kt), economical cruising speed at 65% power 238km/h (128kt). Initial rate of climb 875ft/min. Service ceiling 15,000ft. Range with standard fuel at 75% power cruising speed 1490km (804nm), at 65% power cruising speed 1610km (868nm).

Weights: R 3000/100 – Empty 580kg (1280lb), max takeoff 900kg (1985lb). R 3000/160 – Empty 650kg (1433lb), max takeoff 1150kg (2535lb).

Dimensions: Wing span 9.81m (32ft 2in), length 7.51m (24ft 8in), height 2.66m (8ft 9in). Wing area 14.5m² (155.8sq ft).

Capacity: Seating for two in R 3000/100, three in R 3000/120 and four in R 2000/140 and R 3000/160.

Production: 76 R 3000 delivereds, the last in 1996.

History: Robin began development of the R 3000 in the late 1970s as part of a model range modernisation drive.

Robin originally proposed offering a wide range of R 3000 models, although only a few saw production. Models that were proposed but never saw the light of day include the R 3180S with a turbocharged engine and retractable undercarriage; the fixed gear, but turbocharged R 3180T; the R 3180GT1 and R 3180GT2 with a larger cabin (the GT1 would have been turbocharged, the GT2 turbocharged with retractable gear); and the R 3140T with a solid cabin roof.

A 1981 agreement saw Aerospatiale, GA manufacturer Socata's parent, become responsible for R 3000 marketing between 1983 and 1987, which meant that Robin concentrated on lower power models so as to not compete with Socata's TB range (described separately), and plans for the higher performance models were dropped.

The metal construction R 3000 features a Jodel based wing and forward sliding cockpit canopy and an aerodynamically efficient airframe, and is distinguishable by its T-tail. The first R 3000 model to fly was the R 3140, its first flight occurred on December 8 1980, a second prototype flew in June 1981 and introduced the definitive tapered wings. Production aircraft were delivered from 1985.

The R 3140, later the R 3000/140, was joined in production by the two seat 87kW (116hp) O-235 powered R 3000/100; the three seat R 3120; R 3000/120 (R3120); four seat 105kW (140hp) powered R 3000/140; and the 135kW (180hp) R 3000/180R glider tug.

The last two models built were R 3000/140 and R 3000/160, a development of the R 3000/120 (which went out of production in 1988) with a 119kW (160hp) O-360-D2A.

No R 3000s have been built since 1996.

Photo: A Robin R 3000/120.

Robinson R22

Country of origin: United States of America

Type: Two seat light helicopter

Powerplant: R22 – One 93kW (124hp) Lycoming O-320-A2B flat four piston engine driving two blade main and tail rotors. R22 Beta II – One 98kW (131hp) derated Textron Lycoming O-360-B2C.

Performance: R22 – Max speed 180km/h (97kt), 75% power cruising speed 174km/h (94kt), economical cruising speed 153km/h (82kt). Initial rate of climb 1200ft/min. Service ceiling 14,000ft. Hovering ceiling in ground effect 6500ft. Range with max payload and no reserves 385km (207nm). R22 Beta II – Max speed 180km/h (97kt), 70% power cruising speed 177km/h (96kt), economical cruising speed 153km/h (82kt). Hovering ceiling in ground effect 9400ft. Range with max payload, normal fuel and no reserves over 320km (173nm), with max payload, maximum fuel and no reserves over 482km (260nm). Endurance 3hr 20min.

Weights: R22 – Empty 361kg (796lb), max takeoff 590kg (1300lb). R22 Beta II – Empty 388kg (855lb), max takeoff 620kg (1370lb).

Dimensions: Main rotor diameter 7.67m (25ft 2in), length overall rotors turning 8.76m (28ft 9in), fuselage length 6.30m (20ft 8in), height overall 2.72m (8ft 11in). Main rotor disc area 46.2m² (497.4sq ft).

Capacity: Typical seating for two, side by side. R22 Agricultural is fitted with a 150 litre (33Imp gal/40US gal) capacity chemical tank and spray booms.

Production: Approx 3400 R22s of all versions have been built (including some against military orders) by late 2002.

History: The Robinson R22 has been the world's most popular light helicopter since its introduction in the late 1970s.

The R22 was designed by the founder of the Robinson Helicopter Company, Frank Robinson. He conceived the R22 to be an efficient, cheap to acquire, reliable and economical to operate multi purpose two seat light helicopter.

Design work on the R22 began in the 1970s, and an 85kW (115hp) Lycoming O-235 powered prototype first flew on August 28 1975. Certification of the R22 was delayed somewhat to March 1979 due to the loss of the prototype. Despite this setback the R22 was an overnight success, and several hundred had been ordered by the time the first were delivered from October 1979.

A number of variants and developments of the R22 have been offered. These include the improved R22 Alpha introduced in 1983, and the more powerful R22 Beta from 1985. The R22 Mariner is equipped with floats; the R22 Police version is fitted with special communications gear, a searchlight, siren and loudspeaker; the R22 Agricultural is fitted with tanks and booms for agricultural spraying; while the R22 IFR is fitted with IFR instrumentation for helicopter IFR flight training.

The latest R22 model is the R22 Beta II, powered by a 120kW (160hp) O-360 derated to 98kW (131hp) for takeoff for improved hot and high performance (as takeoff power can be maintained up to 7500ft). The Beta II was introduced into production in 1995 and was certificated in early 1996. It is also offered in IFR, Police, Agricultural and Mariner versions.

Photo: A French registered R22. (Peter Vercruijsse)

Robinson R44

Country of origin: United States of America

Type: Four seat light helicopter

Powerplant: R44 – One 195kW (260hp) Textron Lycoming O-540 flat six piston engine derated to 165kW (225hp) for takeoff and 153kW (205hp) for continuous operation driving a two blade main rotor and two blade tail rotor.

Performance: R44 – Cruising speed at 75% power 209km/h (113kt). Initial rate of climb 1000ft/min. Service ceiling 14,000ft. Hovering ceiling in ground effect 6400ft, out of ground effect 5100ft. Max range with no reserves approx 645km (350nm).

Weights: R44 – Standard empty 635kg (1400lb), max takeoff 1090kg (2400lb).

Dimensions: R44 – Main rotor diameter 10.06m (33ft 0in), length overall rotors turning 11.76m (38ft 7in), height 3.28m (10ft 9in). Main rotor disc area 79.5m² (855.3sq ft).

Capacity: R44 – Typical seating for four.

Production: Over 1310 R44s have been delivered since production began in late 1992.

History: Robinson's R44 light four place piston helicopter has proven a great success, and is the world's best selling helicopter.

While bearing a resemblance to the two place R22, the R44 is much larger and is almost as long as the turbine powered Bell JetRanger. Robinson's aim in developing the R44 was to provide a relatively fast (205 to 215km/h [110 to 115kt] cruising speed) and useful four seat light helicopter that had performance close to that of turbine powered aircraft, yet with an acquisition cost of just a third of turbines and significantly lower maintenance costs.

Robinson Helicopter Company president and founder Frank Robinson first began design work on a light four seat piston engined helicopter during 1986. First flight occurred on March 31 1990, US FAA certification was awarded on December 10 1992.

The R44 uses the same simple design, construction and operating philosophies behind the smaller two place R22. A 194kW (260hp) Textron Lycoming O-540 flat six (derated to 165kW/225hp for takeoff) drives two blade main and tail rotors, while other features include an electronic throttle governor, rotor brake and automatic clutch.

Until mid 2000 the standard R44 model was the R44 Astro. Variants included the float equipped R44 Clipper (certificated in July 1996); the R44 Police law enforcement machine with IR sensor or television camera mounted in a gyrostabilised nose turret, video monitor, a searchlight and bulged door windows (certificated in July 1997); IFR certificated R44 IFR; and the R44 Newscopter which can carry a TV camera in a nose turret.

From mid 2000 Robinson delivered the R44 Raven with a hydraulic flight control system. It was offered in the same special mission forms as the Astro was.

The latest model is the R44 Raven II, delivered from November 2002. It features a 183kW (245hp) Five minute rated fuel injected IO-540, allowing a 45kg (100lb) increase in max takeoff weight and increased hovering heights, while redesigned rotor blades reducing noise and improving lifting capability at altitude.

Photo: An R44 Raven II. (Robinson)

Country of origin: United States of America

Type: Four seat light aircraft

Powerplant: Darter – One 110kW (150hp) Lycoming O-320-A flat four piston engine driving a two blade fixed pitch propeller. Lark – One 135kW (180hp) O-360-A2F.

Performance: Darter – Max speed 214km/h (115kt), max cruising speed 206km/h (111kt). Initial rate of climb 785ft/min. Service ceiling 11,000ft. Range at max cruising speed 820km (443nm). Lark – Max speed 222km/h (120kt), max cruising speed 212km/h (114kt). Initial rate of climb 750ft/min. Service ceiling 13,000ft. Range at max cruising speed 845km (456nm).

Weights: Darter – Empty 580kg (1280lb), max takeoff 1020kg (2250lb). Lark – Empty 658kg (1450lb), max takeoff 1110kg (2450lb).

Dimensions: Darter – Wing span 10.67m (35ft 0in), length 6.86m (22ft 6in), height 2.84m (9ft 4in). Wing area 16.8m² (181sq ft). Lark – Same except for length 7.59m (24ft 11in), height 3.07m (10ft 1in).

Capacity: Typical seating for four.

Production: Approximately 200 Model 100s/Darter Commanders and 250 Lark Commanders built.

History: Aero Commander developed the high wing four seat 100 series in an effort to expand its product range.

The Aero Commander 100 began life as a three seat design from Volaircraft of Aliquippa, Pennsylvania. The basic design was known as the Volaire 10 and first flew during 1960. Features included a high wing, 360° all round visibility and metal construction. A handful of production aircraft, the 1035 powered by a 100kW (135hp) O-290-D and the four seat 110kW (150hp) O-320 powered 1050, were built before Aero Commander purchased the design and manufacturing rights for both in 1965.

Aero Commander only made a small number of changes before the 1035 and 1050 were placed into production as the Aero Commander 100A and 100 respectively in the second half of 1965. In 1966 Aero Commander incorporated a small number of changes including revised windscreen and rear cabin window designs.

By the time the first major changes to the basic design were introduced, Aero Commander had been taken over by North American Rockwell in 1967, and the aircraft was renamed the Model 100/150 Darter Commander. Darter production continued into 1969.

North American Rockwell also introduced the improved 100/180 Lark Commander in 1967 (FAA Type Approval was awarded on September 26 that year). Changes included a more powerful 135kW (180hp) O-360-A2F engine, a swept back fin, reprofiled cowling and 91kg (200lb) increase in max takeoff weight. The aerodynamic changes gave the Lark Commander a sleeker appearance, and the more powerful engine boosted performance. However Rockwell dumped Lark production in 1971, as it had been outsold and was out performed by the less powerful Piper Cherokee and Cessna 172.

Rockwell sold design and production rights for both the Darter (which had been out of production since 1969) and the Lark to Phoenix Aircraft in 1971, but the latter company did not undertake production.

Photo: An Aero Commander 100. (Lance Higgerson)

Country of origin: United States of America

Type: Four seat high performance light aircraft

Powerplant: 112B – One 140kW (200hp) Lycoming IO-360-C1D6 fuel injected flat four piston engine driving a two blade constant speed propeller. 114 – One 195kW (260hp) Lycoming IO-540-T4A5D fuel injected flat six driving a three blade constant speed prop.

Performance: 112B – Max speed 277km/h (150kt), max cruising speed 251km/h (135kt), long range cruising speed 222km/h (120kt). Initial rate of climb 880ft/min. Service ceiling 15,200ft. Max range with reserves 1085km (585nm), or 1647km (890nm) with optional fuel. 114 – Max speed 307km/h (166kt), max cruising speed 290km/h (157kt), long range cruising 254km/h (137kt). Initial rate of climb 1088ft/min. Service ceiling 17,400ft. Max range with reserves 1355km (730nm).

Weights: 112B – Empty 804kg (1773lb), max takeoff 1270kg (2800lb). 114 – Empty 885kg (1885lb), max takeoff 1425kg (3140lb).

Dimensions: Wing span 10.85m (35ft 8in), length 7.63m (25ft 1in), height 2.57m (8ft 5in). Wing area 15.2m² (164sq ft). 114 – Same except wing span 9.98m (32ft 9in). Wing area 14.1m² (152.0sq ft).

Capacity: Typical seating for four.

Production: Production of the 112 and 114 series ceased in 1979.

History: The Rockwell Commander 112 and 114 are high performance, retractable undercarriage light aircraft.

Rockwell's General Aviation Division began development of the original Commander 111 and 112 during the late 1960s, and announced its new range in late 1970. Both models featured conventional construction and a low wing configuration, while the 111 had fixed undercarriage and the 112 had retractable gear. The prototype 112 first flew on December 4 1970, and was powered by a 135kW (180hp) Lycoming O-360, while a prototype 111 first flew late in 1971. The loss of the 112 prototype during flight testing due to the structural failure of the tail unit delayed certification and production of both models until a fix was found. Deliveries of production aircraft took place from late 1972.

Production 111s were powered by 135kW (180hp) O-360s, production 112s were powered by more powerful 150kW (200hp) IO-360s. Only a few 111s were built before Rockwell decided to concentrate on the higher performance retractable gear 112. The updated 112A appeared in 1974 with a higher max takeoff weight, improved cabin ventilation and detail refinements, while the turbocharged 156kW (210hp) TO-360 powered 112TC was introduced in 1976. It also featured a longer span wing and increased takeoff weight.

The 114, which is basically a 112 with a more powerful 194kW (260hp) six cylinder IO-540, was also introduced in 1976. The 114 remained in production basically unchanged until 1979, by which stage it had been named the Gran Turismo Commander. Meanwhile the improved 112B had appeared in 1977, featuring the increased max takeoff weight and the extended wingtips introduced on the 112TC. By that stage the 112TC was designated the 112TC-A, later it became known as the Alpine Commander.

The Commander Aircraft Company began building the 114 based improved 114B and 114TC in 1992, these are described separately.

Photo: A Commander 112TC-A. (Gary Gentle)

Rockwell (Aero) Commander 500/560/680

Country of origin: United States of America

Type: Utility and corporate transports

Powerplants: 685 – Two 325kW (435hp) Lycoming GTSIO-520-F geared, turbocharged and fuel injected flat six piston engines driving three blade constant speed propellers. Rockwell 500S – Two 215kW (290hp) Lycoming IO-540-E1B5.

Performance: 685 – Max speed 449km/h (242kt) at 20,000ft, max cruising speed 412km/h (222kt), long range cruising speed 281km/h (152kt). Initial rate of climb 1490ft/min. Operational ceiling 25,000ft. Max range at 20,000ft with reserves 2125km (1147nm), with optional fuel 2858km (1543nm). 500S – Max speed 346km/h (187kt), max cruising speed 326km/h (176kt), long range cruise 298km/h (161kt). Initial rate of climb 1340ft/min. Service ceiling 19,400ft. Max range with reserves 1915km (1035nm).

Weights: 685 – Empty 2742kg (6046lb), max takeoff 4082kg (9000lb). 500S – Empty 2102kg (4635lb), max TO 3060kg (6750lb).

Dimensions: 685 – Wing span 13.43m (44ft 1in), length 13.10m (43ft 0in), height 4.56m (15ft 0in). Wing area 22.5m^2 (242.5sq ft). 500S – Wing span 14.95m (49ft 1in), length 11.22m (36ft 10in), height 4.56m (15ft 0in). Wing area 23.7m^2 (255.0sq ft).

Capacity: Seating in standard length Commanders for five to seven, including pilot. Stretched Grand Commander seats up to 11.

Production: Total includes 150 520s; 182 560As; 70 560Es; 254 680 Supers; 41 680Es and 13 720s.

History: The origins of this prolific series of twins lies with two ex Douglas employees (one of whom was Ted Smith) who formed the Aero Design and Engineering Corporation in December 1944 after failing to interest their employer in a design they were working on.

Their original design was the six to seven seat L-3805, which first flew on April 23 1948. This aircraft formed the basis for the first Aero Commander production model, the 520, which seated five to seven people and was powered by two 195kW (260hp) Lycoming GO-435s. Production began in late 1951.

About 150 Aero Commander 520s were built through to 1954. Subsequent development led to the more powerful 560 series (1954) with geared engines, the 680 series (1955) with supercharged engines, and the direct drive normally aspirated 500 series (1958). Variants include the 560A which introduced the 25cm (10in) stretched fuselage that became the standard short fuselage length, the 560E which introduced the definitive wing span, the 720 Alti-Cruiser pressurised development of the 680, and the later pressurised 680PF.

The 560 and 680 were joined by the stretched 680FL Grand Commander from 1962. The 500 was introduced to production in 1958 and was originally intended as a low cost model.

In 1967 North American Rockwell took over Aero Commander and the Grand Commander became the Courser Commander and the 500 became the Shrike Commander (gaining its distinctive pointed nose at the same time). The Shrike Commander was the last Commander to remain in production, manufacture ending in 1980.

The final piston powered model was the Rockwell 685 Commander, which was a piston powered Turbo Commander.

Photo: A Shrike Commander. (Robert Wiseman)

Rockwell Turbo Commander

Country of origin: United States of America

Type: Twin turboprop utility and corporate transports

Powerplants: 690A – Two 520kW (700shp) Garrett AiResearch TPE331-5-251K turboprops driving three blade constant speed propellers. Jetprop 1000 – Two 730kW (980shp) Garrett TPE331-10-501Ks flat rated to 610kW (820shp).

Performance: 690A – Max speed 528km/h (285kt), econ cruising speed 465km/h (251kt). Initial rate of climb 2850ft/min. Range with max payload and reserves 1370km (740nm). 1000 – Max speed 571km/h (308kt), econ cruising speed 474km/h (256kt). Initial rate of climb 2802ft/min. Max certificated altitude 35,000ft. Range with max payload and reserves 2430km (1311nm), with max fuel and reserves 3855km (2080nm).

Weights: 690A – Empty 2778kg (6126lb), loaded 4650kg (10,250lb). 1000 – Empty equipped 3307kg (7289lb), max TO 5080kg (11,200lb).

Dimensions: 690A – Wing span 14.22m (46ft 8in), length 13.52m (44ft 5in), height 4.56m (15ft 0in). Wing area 24.7m^2 (266sq ft). 1000 – Wing span 15.89m (52ft 2in), length 13.10m (43ft 0in), height 4.55m (15ft 0in). Wing area 26.0m^2 (279.4sq ft).

Capacity: Pilot and passenger or copilot on flightdeck. Main cabin seating for six to eight. Jetprop 1000 can seat 10 in main cabin.

Production: Approximate production of 1075 includes Gulfstream production of 122 Jetprop 840s, 42 Jetprop 900s, 84 Jetprop 980s and 108 Jetprop 1000s. Over 900 were in corporate use in 2002.

History: The turboprop powered developments of the Aero Commander family of light twins enjoyed a two decade long production run, and were built by three companies before production ceased.

The original Turboprop Commander was based on the 680FLP, and first flew on December 31 1964, but instead of piston engines power was supplied by 450kW (605shp) Garrett AiResearch TPE331 turboprops. This initial Turbo Commander model was designated the 680T and entered production in 1965.

Progressively improved developments of the basic Turbo Commander appeared, including the 680V, which introduced an increased maximum takeoff weight, and the 680W with improved engines. Following North American Rockwell's takeover of Aero Commander and the introduction of the further improved Model 681, the name Hawk Commander was adopted for a time, but it was dropped from 1971 with the release of the 681B.

By the time of the introduction of the 681B, Rockwell was already flight testing the upgraded Turbo Commander 690, which first flew on March 3 1968 and was certificated in July 1971. Rockwell introduced the improved 690A soon after.

In 1979 Rockwell flew the Jetprop Commander 840 and 980, developments of the 690 powered by 625kW (840shp) Garrett TPE331-5 and 730kW (980shp) TPE331-10 turboprops respectively. These went into production with Gulfstream, who had purchased Rockwell's GA lines in 1979. The Jetprop 1000 introduced a revised interior that made better use of the available space and with the 980's engines. The Jetprop 900 combined the revised interior with the 840's engines. Production ceased in 1985.

Photo: A Rockwell Turbo Commander 690A. (Richard Hall)

Rockwell (Ayres) Thrush Commander

Country of origin: United States of America

Type: Agricultural aircraft

Powerplant: Thrush Commander-600 – One 450kW (600hp) Pratt & Whitney R-1340 Wasp nine cylinder piston radial engine driving a two blade propeller. S2R-R1820/510 – One 895kW (1200shp) R-1820 Cyclone radial driving a three blade prop.

Performance: 600 – Max speed 225km/h (122kt), max cruising speed at 70% power 200km/h (108kt), typical working speed range 170 to 185km/h (91 to 100kt). Initial rate of climb 900ft/min. Service ceiling 15,000ft. Ferry range with max fuel at 70% power 648km (350nm). S2R-R1820/510 – Max speed 256km/h (138kt), cruising speed 249km/h (135kt), working speed 161-241km/h (87-130kt). Initial rate of climb 2033ft/min. Ferry range 1078km (582nm).

Weights: 600 – Empty equipped 1678kg (3700lb), max takeoff (agricultural category) 2720kg (6000lb). S2R-R1820/510 – Empty equipped 2263kg (4990lb), typical operating 4536kg (10,000lb).

Dimensions: 600 – Wing span 13.51m (44ft 4in), length 8.95m (29ft 5in), height 2.79m (9ft 2in). Wing area 30.3m² (326.6sq ft). S2R-R1820/510 – Same except wing span 13.54m (44ft 5in), height 9.60m (31ft 6in). Wing area 30.3m² (326.6sq ft).

Capacity: Pilot only, second seat optional.

Production: Over 1650 piston powered Thrushes built.

History: The original Snow S-2 was designed by Leland Snow, who incorporated his knowledge as an experienced ag pilot into the S-2's design.

The Snow S-2 prototype flew for the first time in 1956 and production deliveries began in 1958. S-2 variants differed in engine options, which included the 165kW (220hp) Continental W-670 powered S-2A, the S-2B and S-2C with a Pratt & Whitney R-985, and the R-1340-AN-1 powered S-2C-600.

Aero Commander acquired the design and production rights to the S-2 series in 1965 and built the improved S-2D Ag Commander. The S-2 changed hands once more in 1967 when North American Rockwell (later Rockwell) acquired Aero Commander, continuing the series as the Thrush Commander. Rockwell built the Thrush in two basic models, the basic Thrush Commander-600 with a 450kW (600hp) R-1340 and 1514 litre (400US gal) chemical hopper and the Thrush Commander-800 with a 595kW (800hp) Wright R-1820 Cyclone and larger 1930 litre (510US gal) hopper.

Design and production rights changed hands a final time in 1977 when Ayres (who had previously carried out turboprop conversions to Thrush Commanders) acquired the rights to the Thrush Commander -600 and -800 and their production facilities from Rockwell.

Ayres continued to build the Thrush Commander-600, variously named the Thrush-600, S2R-R1340 Thrush and S2R-600. For a time Ayres also offered a Polish PZL-3 Pezetel radial powered version, the Pezetel Thrush. In the early 1980s Ayres re-introduced the Thrush Commander-800 to production as the Bull Thrush S2R-R1820, which at the time it claimed to be the most powerful agricultural aircraft in production.

Ayres ceased production of the piston Thrushes in the mid 1990s.

Photo: A Rockwell Thrush Commander. (Keith Myers)

Rockwell Sabreliner

Country of origin: United States of America

Type: Mid size corporate jet

Powerplants: 40 – Two 14.7kN (3300lb) Pratt & Whitney JT12A-8 turbojets. 75A – Two 20.2kN (4500lb) General Electric CF700-2D-2s.

Performance: 40 – Max cruising speed 810km/h (440kt), econ cruising speed 743km/h (400kt). Max rate of climb 4700ft/min. Service ceiling 45,000ft. Range with max fuel, four passengers and reserves 3240km (1750nm). 75A – Max cruising speed 906km/h (490kt), econ cruising speed 772km/h (417kt). Service ceiling 45,000ft. Max range with max fuel, four passengers and reserves 3174km (1713nm).

Weights: 40 – Empty equipped 5102kg (11,250lb), max takeoff 9150kg (20,172lb). 75A – Empty equipped 5990kg (13,200lb), max takeoff 10,435kg (23,000lb).

Dimensions: 40 – Wing span 13.61m (44ft 8in), length 14.30m (46ft 11in), height 4.88m (16ft 0in). Wing area 31.8m² (342.1sq ft). 75A – Wing span 13.61m (44ft 8in), length 14.38m (47ft 2in), height 5.26m (17ft 3in). Wing area 31.8m² (342.1sq ft).

Capacity: Flightcrew of two. Main cabin seats up to 10 in high density layout. Various other seating arrangements possible.

Production: Over 600 civil Sabreliners built, plus 200 T-39s. Almost 380 in use in late 2002 including 33 T-39s in civil use and 126 Sabreliner 60s.

History: The Sabreliner was successfully developed for both military and civil use.

North American Aviation began work on the Sabreliner as a private venture but it was formally launched in August 1956 in response to the US Air Force's UTX (Utility Trainer Experimental) requirement for a utility jet aircraft capable of performing transport and combat readiness training missions. A civil configured prototype (designated NA264) first flew on September 16 1958 powered by General Electric YJ85 turbojets. Soon after the USAF ordered the Sabreliner into production, and it and the US Navy went on to order several Pratt & Whitney JT12 turbojet powered versions, including the T-39A pilot proficiency and support transport and the T-39B/D radar trainer.

The first civil aircraft, the NA265-40, was equivalent to the T-39A and was certificated in April 1963. The Series 40 followed from June 1966 and featured a higher cruising speed and greater internal cabin space. The Series 60 was stretched by 97cm (3ft 2in) and is identifiable by its five, rather than three, cabin windows per side. The Series 60A introduced aerodynamic changes over the 60. The Sabreliner 75 meanwhile is based on the 60 and 60A, but has a deeper fuselage with greater headroom.

Turbofan power was introduced to the Sabreliner family in 1973 (by which time North American had become part of Rockwell International) with the introduction of the General Electric CF700 turbofan powered 75A. The 75A also introduced aerodynamic, cabin, equipment and systems improvements. The Series 65A meanwhile is similar to the 60A and 75 but is powered by Garrett AiResearch TFE731-3-1D turbofans. It was delivered from December 1979. Sabreliner production ceased in 1981.

Photo: The TFE731 powered Sabreliner 65. (Theo van Loon)

Saab 340

Country of origin: Sweden

Type: Twin turboprop regional airliner

Powerplants: 340A – Two 1295kW (1735shp) General Electric CT7-5A2 turboprops driving four blade constant speed Dowty or Hamilton Standard props. 340B – Two 1305kW (1750shp) CT7-9Bs.

Performance: 340A – Max cruising speed 515km/h (278kt), economical cruising speed 484km/h (260kt). Range with max payload 1455km (785nm), range with max fuel 3975km (2145nm). 340B – Max cruising speed 523km/h (282kt), long range cruising speed 467km/h (252kt). Range with 35 passengers at max cruising speed 1490km (805nm), at long range cruising speed 1735km (935nm).

Weights: 340A – Operating empty 7810kg (17,215lb), max takeoff 12,370kg (27,275lb). 340B – Operating empty 8140kg (17,945lb), max takeoff 13,155kg (29,000lb).

Dimensions: Wing span 21.44m (70ft 4in), length 19.73m (64ft 9in), height 6.97m (22ft 11in). Wing area 41.8m² (450.0sq ft).

Capacity: Flightcrew of two. Main cabin seats up to 37, or typically 33 to 35 with a galley at three abreast and 76cm (30in) pitch. Combi seats 19 passengers and 1500kg (3310lb) of cargo.

Production: 458 Saab 340s built to 1998. 340A production ended in September 1989 with 159 built. At late 2002 445 were in airline service, with a further three used as corporate transports.

History: The Saab 340 was a popular regional airliner that helped to pioneer the 30 seat turboprop class.

In 1979 Saab-Scania of Sweden and Fairchild in the USA reached an agreement to conduct joint feasibility and development studies on a 30 to 40 seat commuter airliner. The resulting SF340 design was launched in September 1980 with the aim of capturing 25 to 30% of its market. Within the 65/35 Saab-Fairchild partnership split Saab was responsible for the fuselage, fin and final assembly, while Fairchild was responsible for the wings, engine nacelles and empennage. The two companies selected the General Electric CT7 (a commercial development of the T700 turboshaft which powers Sikorsky's S-70 series of military helicopters) to power the new airliner.

The first of three SF340 prototypes first flew on January 25 1983, while the first production aircraft flew in early March 1984. US and European certification was awarded that June. From November 1 1985 Saab assumed overall responsibility for the SF340 following Fairchild's decision to drop out of the program. Saab initially retained the SF340 designation but later changed it to 340A.

The first improved development of the Saab 340 was the 340B. More powerful engines improved hot and high performance, while other changes included a greater span tailplane, a higher max takeoff weight and better range. Deliveries began in September 1989.

The last development of the 340 was the 340B Plus, which introduced changes developed for the larger Saab 2000, including an improved cabin interior, plus optional extended wingtips. The first 340B Plus was delivered in March 1994. Production wound up in 1998.

Saab has developed a bulk freighter conversion of the 340A, with a 4000kg payload, using the existing rear door. The first conversion flew in 2002.

Photo: A Regional Express Saab 340B. (Gerard Williamson)

Saab 2000

Country of origin: Sweden

Type: 50 seat twin turboprop regional airliner

Powerplants: Two 3096kW (4152shp) Allison AE 2100A turboprops driving six blade constant speed Dowty propellers.

Performance: Max cruising speed 682km/h (368kt) at 25,000ft, long range cruising speed 594km/h (321kt). Initial rate of climb 2250ft/min. Service ceiling 31,000ft. High speed range with 50 passengers and reserves 2185km (1180nm), range at long range cruising speed 2868km (1549nm).

Weights: Operating empty 13,800kg (30,423lb), max takeoff 22,800kg (50,2650lb).

Dimensions: Wing span 24.76m (81ft 3in), length 27.28m (89ft 6in), height 7.73m (25ft 4in). Wing area 55.7m² (600.0sq ft).

Capacity: Flightcrew of two. Normal passenger accommodation for 50 at three abreast and 81cm (32in) pitch. Max seating for 58 at three abreast and 76cm (30in) pitch, with repositioned galley and wardrobe.

Production: 63 Saab 2000s built to 1998. In 2002 58 were in airline service with three used as corporate transports.

History: The Saab 2000 was a stretched 50 seat, faster development of the successful 340.

The Saab 2000 has a cruise speed of over 665km/h (360kt), making it one of the fastest turboprop airliners. Saab marketing said it combines near jet speeds, including near jet climb and descent rates, with turboprop economy. Saab launched development of the 2000 in mid December 1988 with a launch order from Crossair (now Swiss) for 25 (plus a further 25 on option) following definition and design studies.

The initial Saab 2000 development plan would have seen the 2000 in service in the second half of 1993, but delays pushed this back until the second half of 1994. The Saab 2000's first flight took place on March 26 1992, and European and US certification was granted in March and April 1994 respectively. Service entry with Crossair occurred a few months later.

While retaining the same cross section as the Saab 340, the 2000 is 7.55m (24ft 9in) longer (seating 15 more passengers), while the same wing section was retained but the 2000's wing span is 15% greater than the 340's, and the engines are positioned further outboard.

The 2000 was the first civil application of the Allison (now Rolls-Royce) AE 2100 turboshaft (derived from the military T406 developed for the V-22 Osprey tiltrotor). They are equipped with FADEC and drive slow turning six blade props. The flightdeck features a Collins Pro Line 4 EFIS avionics suite with six colour CRT displays. Cabin noise is reduced by an active noise control system comprising 72 microphones and 36 speakers which generate anti phase noise.

Several European aerospace firms participated in the Saab 2000 manufacturing program including CASA, which designed and built the wing, Westland, which manufactured the rear fuselage, and Valmet of Finland, which built the tail.

Lack of sales and profitibility forced Saab to cease 340 and 2000 production, with the lines winding up in 1998. The last 2000 was delivered to Crossair in April 1999.

Photo: A Swiss Saab 2000. (Rob Finlayson)

Schweizer/Hughes 300 (& 269)

Schweizer 330 & 333

Country of origin: United States of America

Type: Light utility helicopter

Powerplant: 300C – One 142kW (190hp) Textron Lycoming HIO-360-D1A fuel injected flat four derated from 168kW (225hp) driving a three blade main rotor and two blade tail rotor.

Performance: 300C – Max cruising speed 159km/h (86kt), max range cruising speed 124km/h (67kt). Initial rate of climb 750ft/min. Hovering ceiling in ground effect 10,800ft, out of ground effect 8600ft. Service ceiling 10,200ft. Range with max normal fuel and no reserves 386km (208nm). Max endurance 3hr 48min.

Weights: 300C – Empty 499kg (1100lb), max takeoff 930kg (2050lb), or 975kg (2150lb) with an external sling load.

Dimensions: Main rotor diameter 8.18m (26ft 10in), length overall 9.40m (30ft 10in), fuselage length 6.80m (22ft 0in), height to top of rotor head 2.66m (8ft 9in). Main rotor disc area 52.5m² (565.5sq ft).

Capacity: Typical seating for three on a bench seat in 300 or two in 269. Many aircraft equipped for agricultural spraying and fitted with chemical hoppers and spray booms. Can lift a 475kg (1050lb) payload in an external sling load.

Production: Total 269/TH-58/300 production over 3500 aircraft, of which 2800 were built by Hughes. Total includes military production.

History: The Hughes/Schweizer 300 is one of the most successful piston powered helicopters built, with over three and a half thousand produced by the two manufacturers over four decades.

Development of this versatile utility helicopter dates back to the mid 1950s when Hughes flew the two seat Model 269 for the first time in October 1956. The 269 sparked US Army interest and it ordered five as the YHO-2HU for evaluation in the scout and observation roles. Deliveries of the commercial equivalent Model 269A began in 1961.

The 269A program received a huge boost when Hughes won a US Army contract for a light helicopter primary trainer. In all, 792 were built as the TH-55A Osage and more than 60,000 US Army helicopter pilots learnt to fly in the type.

Hughes followed the two seat 269A with the slightly larger three seat 269B, which it marketed as the Hughes 300, which first flew in 1964. The 300 was followed from 1969 by the improved 300C, with a more powerful 140kW (190hp) Lycoming HIO-360 engine and increased diameter main rotor, giving an increase in payload of 45%, plus performance improvements. The 300C (or 269C) flew in August 1969.

Since 1983 the 300C has been built by Schweizer in the USA. Schweizer built the 300C initially under licence for Hughes, and then acquired all rights to the helicopter in 1986. Under Schweizer's stewardship more than 250 minor improvements were made to the 300C, but the basic design has been left unchanged. Schweizer also offers a version optimised for police work. Named the Sky Knight, it is available with options such as a search light and infrared sensors. For military pilot training the 300C is marketed as the TH-300C.

The 300CB trainer powered by a HO-360-C1A was delivered from late 1995. In March 2002 it was replaced by the 300CBi with a 135kW (180hp) fuel injected HIO-360, a new main rotor driveshaft and hub, and new AES system.

Photo: A Hughes 300. (Lance Higgerson)

Country of origin: United States of America

Type: Light utility helicopters

Powerplant: 333 – One 315kW (420shp) Rolls-Royce 250-C20W turboprop rated at 175kW (235shp) driving a three blade main rotor and two blade tail rotor.

Performance: 333 – Normal cruising speed 194km/h (105kt), economical cruising speed 174km/h (94kt). Max initial rate of climb 1380ft/min. Hovering ceiling at MTOW in ground effect 8700ft, out of ground effect 5100ft. Max range with no reserves 590km (319nm), endurance 4hr 10min.

Weights: 333 – Empty 549kg (1210lb), max takeoff 1156kg (2550lb).

Dimensions: 333 – Main rotor diameter 8.38m (27ft 6in), length overall rotors turning 9.50m (31ft 2in), height overall 3.35m (11ft 0in). Main rotor disc area 55.2m² (594.2sq ft).

Capacity: Typical seating for three, optional seating for four.

Production: 330 deliveries began in mid 1993. 333 deliveries began mid 2000. Approx 45 built.

History: The Schweizer 330 and 333 are turbine developments of the Hughes/Schweizer 300 series of two/three seat light piston engine helicopters.

Schweize acquired the production and manufacturing rights to the Hughes 300, which it had been building under licence since 1983, from McDonnell Douglas in November 1986. In 1987 Schweizer announced it was developing an improved turbine powered version, the 330.

The Schweizer 330 uses the dynamic components, rotors, controls and systems of the 300C, combined with a Rolls-Royce (previously Allison) 250-C20 turboshaft. The engine was derated to just 165kW (220hp), giving the 330 excellent hot and high performance. For example the powerplant will reach its max rated power output right up to 18,000ft. Other changes compared with the piston 300C include an essentially all new fuselage, new vertical tail surfaces and a new tail fairing.

The first 330 (a converted 300C) first flew on June 14 1988. FAA certification was awarded in September 1992 and first deliveries took place from mid 1993.

The improved 330SP was announced in May 1997. Compared to the basic 330 it features a larger main rotor hub, increased chord main blades and raised skids. These mods can be retrofitted to 330s.

To enhance its appeal as a trainer the 330 was offered with a third set of flight controls, allowing the carriage of two students and an instructor on training flights.

Schweizer announced the further improved 333 at Heli-Expo in February 2000. Improvements include upgraded dynamic system components, new rotor blades and standard high ground clearance skids. It has a 30% greater useful load than the 330SP. Deliveries began in mid 2000 (to the San Antonio Police Department).

The 333 in much modified form serves as the basis of the Northrop Grumman RQ-8A Fire Scout VTOL UAV (unmanned Aerial Vehicle) demonstrator built for the US Navy.

Photo: The 333, announced in early 2000. (Schweizer)

Scottish Aviation Twin Pioneer

Country of origin: United Kingdom

Type: Utility transport

Powerplants: Series 3 – Two 475kW (640hp) Alvis Leonides 531 seven cylinder radial piston engines driving three blade constant speed propellers.

Performance: Series 3 – Max cruising speed 257km/h (140kt), economical cruising speed 210km/h (114kt). Initial rate of climb 1370ft/min. Service ceiling 18,000ft. Max range at economical cruising speed 1287km (695nm), range with 1590kg (3500lb) payload 322km (175nm).

Weights: Series 3 – Empty 4630kg (10,200lb), max takeoff 6628kg (14,600lb).

Dimensions: Series 3 – Wing span 23.33m (76ft 6in), length 13.80m (45ft 3in), height 3.74m (12ft 3in). Wing area 62.3m² (670.0sq ft).

Capacity: Flightcrew of two. Main cabin seats 16 in passenger configuration, or can hold 1540kg (3400lb) of freight. Has also been used as a platform for aerial photography.

Production: Total Twin Pioneer production of 91, including 32 CC.1s and seven CC.2s for Britain's Royal Air Force and others for the Royal Malayan Air Force. Production ceased in 1964.

History: The Scottish Aviation Twin Pioneer utility transport saw limited commercial and military service, mainly in the UK and some Commonwealth countries.

Despite its name, the Twin Pioneer is an all new aircraft compared with the Scottish Aviation Pioneer. The original Pioneer was a high wing single engined five seat light aircraft powered by an Alvis radial piston engine which was built in small numbers for the Royal Air Force for liaison duties.

The Twin Pioneer is also powered by Alvis radials and features a high wing, but is much larger, capable of seating up to 16 passengers in the main cabin. Designed for both civil and military applications, the Twin Pioneer was also one of the few postwar aircraft to feature a high wing and tailwheel undercarriage, while its triple vertical tail arrangement makes it easily recognisable.

The prototype Twin Pioneer first flew on June 25 1955, and the first production examples were delivered from April 28 1956. By mid 1964, when production ceased, 94 of three different models had been built. The Royal Air Force in Britain was the largest customer, taking delivery of 39 Twin Pioneers.

The RAF used its Twin Pioneers for a variety of transport and liaison roles, and they could carry 13 troops, or 11 paratroops, or six stretchers and five sitting casualties or medical attendants. Another military operator was Malaya/Malaysia.

The initial Twin Pioneer production model was the Series 1, powered by two 410kW (550hp) Alvis Leonides 514/8 radials. The Series 2 was powered by Pratt & Whitney R-1340 radials. Final production was of the Series 3 (described above), powered by 475kW (640hp) Leonides 531/8 radials.

In 2002 only a handful of Twin Pioneers remained in service, including two Series 3s registered in Australia.

Photo: A Twin Pioneer used for tourist operations in Australia. (Peter Easton)

SIAI-Marchetti S.205 & S.208

Country of origin: Italy

Type: Four seat light aircraft

Powerplant: S.205-20 – One 150kW (200hp) Lycoming IO-360-A1B6D fuel injected flat four piston engine driving a two blade constant speed propeller. S.208 – One 185kW (260hp) Lycoming O-540-E4A5 flat six.

Performance: S.205-20 – Max speed 270km/h (146kt), max cruising speed 250km/h (136kt), normal cruising speed 243km/h (131kt). Initial rate of climb 826ft/min. Service ceiling 15,575ft. Range 1260km (680nm). S.208 – Max speed 320km/h (173kt), max cruising speed 300km/h (162kt). Initial rate of climb 985ft/min. Service ceiling 17,725ft. Range with tip tanks 1800km (970nm).

Weights: S.205-20 – Empty 760kg (1677lb), max takeoff 1300kg (2865lb). S.208 – Empty 827kg (1823lb), max takeoff 1500kg (3307lb).

Dimensions: S.205-20 – Wing span 10.86m (35ft 8in), length 8.00m (26ft 3in), height 2.89m (9ft 6in). Wing area 16.1m² (173sq ft). Same except span over tip tanks 11.23m (36ft 10in), length 8.09m (26ft 7in).

Capacity: Typical seating for four in S.205, up to five in S.208.

Production: Approx 620 S.205s, including 62 S.220 Velas assembled by Waco in the USA. Approx 120 S.208s built, including 40 for the Italian air force.

History: SIAI-Marchetti designed this series of four seat light aircraft to re-enter the GA market.

When SIAI-Marchetti began work on the four seat S.205, the company intended to develop a series of aircraft with various powerplant and other options, such as retractable undercarriage and constant speed propellers. To this end the company was relatively successful, with several hundred S.205s and larger S.208s built, with most sold to European customers.

The first of three S.205 prototypes flew during 1965. This initial aircraft was powered by a 135kW (180hp) Lycoming O-360 and featured fixed undercarriage. In production it became the S.205-18/F (18 for 180hp, F for fixed undercarriage). The first production S.205-18/F flew in February 1966 and with deliveries from later that year.

The lineup was expanded to include the 150kW (200hp) fuel injected IO-360 powered and higher max takeoff weight S.205-20/F, and the retractable undercarriage S.205-18/R and S.205-20/R. The most powerful member of the S.205 family was the S.205-22/R. This aircraft was powered by a 165kW (220hp) Franklin 6A-350-C1 flat six and was also assembled in the USA by Waco as the S.220 Vela.

Production of the S.205 initially ceased in 1975, although SIAI-Marchetti returned it to production as the improved S.205AC from 1977 until 1980 to meet an order for 140 for the Italian aero club.

The S.208 is based on the S.205 but has a larger cabin with seating for five. First flown on May 22 1967, it is powered by a 195kW (260hp) Lycoming O-540 and has retractable undercarriage, a third cabin window per side, optional tip tanks and strengthened structure. Deliveries commenced in 1968, and 44 S.208Ms were built for the Italian air force for liaison and training work.

Production ceased in 1975 and then resumed in 1977 alongside the S.205AC until finally winding up again in 1980.

Photo: A S.205-18/F. (Mike McHugh)

Shorts Skyvan & Skyliner

Country of origin: United Kingdom

Type: STOL utility transport and regional airliner

Powerplants: Srs 3 – Two 535kW (715shp) Garrett TPE331-2-201A turboprops driving three blade Hartzell propellers.

Performance: Srs 3 – Max cruising speed 324km/h (175kt), normal cruising speed 311km/h (168kt), economical cruising speed 278km/h (150kt). Initial rate of climb 1640ft/min. Service ceiling 22,500ft. Range at long range cruising speed with reserves 1115km (600nm), range in typical freighter configuration with a 1815kg (4000lb) payload and reserves at economical cruising speed 300km (162nm).

Weights: Srs 3 – Basic operating 3331kg (7344lb) for Skyvan or 4055kg (8940lb) for Skyliner, max takeoff 5670kg (12,500lb).

Dimensions: Srs 3 – Wing span 19.79m (64ft 11in), length 12.21m (40ft 1in), or 12.60m (41ft 4in) with weather radar, height 4.60m (15ft 1in). Wing area 35.1m² (378sq ft).

Capacity: Flightcrew of one or two. Seating for up to 19 passengers at three abreast in Skyliner, or nine passengers in executive configuration.

Production: 150 Skyvans and Skyliners built between the mid 1960s and 1986, almost all of which were Series 3s (including almost 60 military Series 3Ms).

History: The boxy and rugged Shorts Skyvan and Skyliner date back to the postwar Miles Aerovan project.

In 1958 Short Brothers (or Shorts) acquired the design rights to the HDM.106 Caravan, a development of Miles' HDM.105, an Aerovan fitted with the very high aspect ratio Hurel Dubois designed wing. Shorts thoroughly revised the Caravan design, resulting in the SC.7 Skyvan, featuring a box-like 1.98m x 1.98m (6ft 6in x 6ft 6in) square fuselage (allowing seating for 19 or freight), a rear loading freight ramp, and a reduced span version of the Hurel Dubois wing. Prototype construction began in 1960 but the Series 1 prototype, powered by two Continental 291kW (390hp) GTSIO-520 piston engines, did not fly until January 17 1963 due to problems with the Belfast transport.

Unlike the prototype, initial production SC.7s were powered by 545kW (730shp) Turbomeca Astazou XII turboprops. The original piston powered Series 1 prototype was the first Astazou powered Skyvan to fly (with 390kW/520shp Astazou IIs), in October 1963. The re-engined prototype was designated the Series 1A, while early Astazou powered production aircraft were designated Series 2. The first Series 2 flew in October 1965.

Early on in the SC.7's production run Shorts decided to switch the powerplant choice to 535kW (715shp) Garrett TPE331-201s, resulting in the definitive Series 3 (first flight December 15 1967). Many Series 2 Skyvans were also converted to Garrett power.

The basic Series 3 and the higher takeoff weight Series 3A can perform a number of utility missions including passenger transport, ambulance, aerial survey and freight work, and are called Skyvans. The Skyliner airliner features an improved level of interior equipment and furnishing, while military Skyvans are designated Series 3M and 3M-200 with a higher max takeoff weight.

Low rate production continued to January 1986.

Photo: A Skyvan 3M. (Lance Higgerson)

Shorts 330

Country of origin: United Kingdom

Type: Regional airliner and utility freighter

Powerplants: 330-100 – Two 875kW (1173shp) Pratt & Whitney Canada PT6A-45 turboprops driving five blade constant speed Hartzell propellers. 330-200 – Two 893kW (1198shp) PT6A-45Rs.

Performance: 330-100 – Max cruising speed 356km/h (192kt), long range cruising speed 296km/h (160kt). Initial rate of climb 1200ft/min. Range with 30 passengers and reserves 590km (320nm). 330-200 – Max cruising speed 352km/h (190kt), long range cruising speed 294km/h (159kt). Range with max payload 660km (473nm), range with max fuel and no reserves 1695km (915nm).

Weights: 330-100 – Empty equipped in airliner configuration 6577kg (14,500lb), max takeoff 10,160kg (22,400lb). 330-200 – Operating empty 6697kg (14,764lb), max takeoff 10,387kg (22,900lb).

Dimensions: Wing span 22.76m (74ft 8in), length 17.69m (58ft 1in), height 4.95m (16ft 3in). Wing area 42.1m² (453.0sq ft).

Capacity: Flightcrew of two. Typical passenger accommodation for 30 at three abreast and 76cm (30in) pitch in 10 rows of seats. In combi freight/passenger configuration the 330 houses freight in the front of the cabin and 18 passengers in the rear.

Production: 330 production wound up in September 1992 after 136 had been built, including military C-23 Sherpas and 330UTs. Approximately 64 were in airline service at late 2002.

History: The Shorts 330 (sometimes called the 'Shed') was developed to be a straightforward and reliable 30 seat regional airliner.

The Shorts 330 is a stretched development of the SC.7 Skyvan, and was originally designated SD3-30. The 330 retained the Skyvan's overall configuration, including the slab sided fuselage cross section, supercritical, braced, above fuselage mounted wing design (lengthened by 2.97m/9ft 9in) and twin tails. Compared with the Skyvan the fuselage is stretched by 3.78m (12ft 5in), allowing seating for over 10 more passengers. Power is from two Pratt & Whitney PT6A turboprops driving five blade props, while a pointed nose and retractable undercarriage were added. More than 60% greater fuel capacity boosts range significantly over the Skyvan.

Following project go-ahead for the SD3-30 in May 1973 an engineering prototype of the 330 first flew on August 22 1974. A production prototype flew on July 8 1975. The first true production aircraft followed that December. The 330 entered airline service with Time Air of Canada in August 1976.

Initial Shorts 330s were powered by PT6A-45As and -45Bs and are known as 330s or 330-100s. The definitive 330-200 (announced at the 1981 Paris Airshow) features more powerful PT6A-45Rs and a number of detail improvements, while items previously available as options were made standard equipment.

Various freighter versions of the 330 have been developed, including the Sherpa with a rear loading ramp (in service with the US Air Force and Army as the C-23), and the military 330UTT.

The last civil 330, a UTT for the Quebec provincial government, was delivered in June 1991, the last 330 of any model, a C-23B for the USAF, was delivered in September 1992.

Photo: A Fijian registered 330-200. (Francis Nickelson)

Shorts 360

Country of origin: United Kingdom

Type: 36 seat regional airliner

Powerplants: 360 – Two 990kW (1327shp) Pratt & Whitney Canada PT6A-65R turboprops driving five blade c/s Hartzell props. 360-300 – Two 1062kW (1424shp) PT6A-67Rs driving six blade props.

Performance: 360 – Max cruising speed 390km/h (210kt). Range at max cruising speed with 36 passengers 426km (230nm), range with max fuel 1055km (570nm). 360-300 – Typical cruising speed 400km/h (216kt). Initial rate of climb 952ft/min. Range with 36 passengers and reserves at typical cruising speed 745km (402nm), with 31 passengers and reserves at 337km/h (182kt) cruising speed 1178km (636nm).

Weights: 360 – Operating empty 7530kg (16,600lb), max takeoff 11,657kg (25,700lb). 360-300 – Typical operating empty 7870kg (17,350lb), max takeoff 12,292kg (27,100lb).

Dimensions: Wing span 22.80m (74ft 10in), length 21.58m (70ft 10in), height 7.27m (23ft 10in). Wing area 42.2m² (454.0sq ft).

Capacity: Flightcrew of two. Typical passenger seating for 36 at three abreast and 76cm (30in) pitch in 12 seat rows. Optional seating for 39 in a high density configuration. Freighter 360-300F can house up to five standard LD3 containers or pallets.

Production: Last 360 completed in 1991 after 164 had been built. Approx 138 were in airline service in late 2002.

History: The Shorts 360 is a stretched, larger capacity and improved 36 seat development of the Shorts 330.

The relative success of the rugged Shorts 330 and deregulation in the US which allowed commuter airlines to fly aircraft with more than 30 seats prompted the Northern Ireland based manufacturer to develop a stretched derivative. Shorts announced it was developing the 360 in mid 1980, and a prototype 360 first flew on June 1 1981.

The first production 360 flew in August 1982 and certification was awarded on September 3 that year. The 360 entered service with Suburban Airlines in the US in November 1982.

The two Shorts airliners are very close in overall dimensions and size, but the later 360 is easily identified by its new conventional tail unit mounted on a revised rear fuselage. The 360 is also 91cm (3ft) longer than the 330, allowing two more seat rows and six extra passengers to be carried, while the extra length reduces drag. Power is supplied by two Pratt & Whitney Canada PT6A-65Rs, and the 360's wing span is slightly greater. Otherwise the 330 and 360 share a high degree of commonality (both are unpressurised).

Shorts marketed a number of 360 developments, the first of which was the 360 Advanced with 1062kW (1424shp) PT6A-65ARs. The 360 Advanced was introduced in late 1985, but was soon followed by the further improved 360-300, which entered service in March 1987. The 360-300 introduced advanced six blade propellers, more powerful PT6A-67R engines giving a higher cruise speed and improved hot and high performance, plus other aerodynamic improvements. The 360-300 was also built in 360-300F freighter form.

Shorts 360 production wound up in 1989 but the last 360 was not assembled and flown until 1991.

Photo: A Sunshine Express 360-300. (Rob Finlayson)

Sikorsky S-55

Country of origin: United States of America

Type: Mid size utility helicopter

Powerplant: S-55C – One 520kW (700hp) Pratt & Whitney R-1340-3 nine cylinder radial piston engine driving a three blade main rotor and two blade tail rotor. S-55T – One 625kW (840shp) Garrett AiResearch TSE331-3U-303 turboshaft derated to 485kW (650shp).

Performance: S-55C – Max speed 163km/h (88kt), cruising speed 137km/h (74kt). Initial rate of climb 700ft/min. Hovering ceiling in ground effect 2000ft. Service ceiling 10,500ft. Range 645km (350nm). S-55T – Max speed 183km/h (99kt), cruising speed 157km/h (85kt). Initial rate of climb 1200ft/min. Hovering ceiling out of ground effect 6700ft. Range with reserves 595km (320nm).

Weights: S-55C – Empty 2245kg (4950lb), MTOW 3265kg (7200lb). S-55T – Empty equipped 2132kg (4700lb), MTOW 3265kg (7200lb).

Dimensions: Main rotor diameter 16.16m (53ft 0in), fuselage length 12.87m (42ft 3in), height 4.06m (13ft 4in).

Capacity: Flightcrew of two. Typical seating in main cabin for eight to 12 passengers.

Production: Total Sikorsky S-55 production of 1281 aircraft, most for military service with US forces, 44 built under licence in Japan and 400 as Westland Whirlwinds. Approx 40 S-55T conversions.

History: Like many Sikorsky helicopters, the S-55 started out as a military helicopter for the US armed forces that was later adapted for commercial service.

Sikorsky developed the S-55 in response to a US military requirement for a large general purpose helicopter. The US Defense Department awarded Sikorsky a contract to develop such a helicopter in 1948, and the first prototype flew on November 10 1949. As the H-19 Chickasaw the S-55 saw widespread US military service. Civil certification for the commercial S-55 series was first awarded on March 25 1952.

The initial civil variant was the S-55, powered by a 450kW (600hp) Pratt & Whitney Wasp radial piston engine. Later civil variants include the S-55A which introduced a 520kW (700hp) Wright R-1300 radial piston engine, while the S-55C had a P&W R-1340 engine and the repositioned tail boom of the S-55A.

Westland in the UK licence built 400 S-55s as the Whirlwind for mainly military but also commercial use. Early Whirlwinds were similar to the S-55 save for their Alvis Leonides radial engine, later developments were powered by a 785kW (1050shp) Rolls-Royce Bristol Gnome H.1000 turboshaft. S-55 licence manufacture was also undertaken in Japan and France.

In January 1971 Aviation Specialties was awarded a type certificate for its turboprop powered conversion of the S-55, dubbed the S-55T. Aviation Specialties formed the Helitec Corp to market and convert S-55s, and approximately 40 were fitted with a Garrett AiResearch TSE331 turboshaft. The conversion reduced the S-55's empty weight by approximately 410kg (900lb).

Photo: A Papillon Grand Canyon Helicopters S-55T at Las Vegas. A feature of the S-55 is its nose mounted engine, with the driveshaft to the main rotor passing over the main cabin and behind the flightdeck. (Oscar Bernardi)

Sikorsky S-58

Country of origin: United States of America

Type: Mid size utility helicopter

Powerplant: S-58 – One 1140kW (1525hp) Wright R-1820-84 radial piston engine driving four blade main and tail rotors. S-58T – One 1340kW (1800shp) Pratt & Whitney Canada PT6T-3 Twin Pac turboshaft (two PT6s linked through a combining transmission) or one 1400kW (1875shp) PT6T-6.

Performance: S-58 – Max speed 198km/h (107kt), max cruising speed 158km/h (85kt). Initial rate of climb 1100ft/min. Hovering ceiling out of ground effect 2400ft. Range with max fuel and reserves 450km (243nm). S-58T (with PT6T-6s) – Max speed 222km/h (120kt), cruising speed 158km/h (85kt). Hovering ceiling out of ground effect 6500ft. Range with reserves 480km (260nm).

Weights: S-58 – Empty equipped 3461kg (7630lb), MTOW 5895kg (13,000lb). S-58T – Empty 3355kg (7400lb), MTOW 5895kg (13,000lb).

Dimensions: S-58 – Main rotor diameter 17.07m (56ft 0in), length overall rotors turning 17.27m (56ft 8in), fuselage length 14.25m (46ft 9in), height 4.36m (14ft 4in). Main rotor disc area 228.5m² (2460sq ft). S-58T – Same except for fuselage length 14.41m (47ft 3in).

Capacity: Flightcrew of two. Main cabin seats between 10 and 16 passengers or freight. Can also carry external sling loads.

Production: 1821 S-58s built mainly for military but also civil use between 1954 and 1970.

History: The Sikorsky S-58 was one of the most successful piston powered mid size helicopters built.

Sikorsky developed the S-58 in response to a US Navy requirement for an anti submarine warfare helicopter. Design features included a single Wright R-1820 radial piston engine mounted in the nose (with a driveshaft passing over the cabin and beneath the cockpit), a voluminous fuselage, and a raised flightdeck. As the XHSS-1 the S-58 first flew on March 8 1954.

Hundreds of S-58s were built to serve with the US Navy in anti submarine warfare roles as the SH-34G and SH-34J Seabat, and in utility roles with the US Marines as the UH-34D Seahorse. The US Army operated large numbers as the CH-34 Choctaw while many other allied countries operated the S-58 in military service.

In the UK Westland licence built the Wessex Rolls-Royce Gnome turboshaft powered development, some of which saw civil service.

Smaller numbers of piston powered S-58s saw civil service with most delivered to customers within the USA. The S-58 offered a very large fuselage and good lifting capability, but its piston engine made it expensive to operate.

In 1970 Sikorsky announced it was developing a turboprop conversion package for the S-58. Turboprop powered S-58s are designated the S-58T and were initially powered by a 1340kW (1800shp) Pratt & Whitney PT6T-3 Twin-Pac, later aircraft a 1400kW (1875shp) PT6T-6. The first S-58T conversion flew on August 19 1970. Sikorsky set up a production line to convert customer S-58s, offered kits for S-58 operators to perform the conversion themselves, and purchased used S-58s, converted them to turbine power and offered them for resale. Small numbers remain in commercial service.

Photo: An S-58T. (Paul Merritt)

Sikorsky S-61L & S-61N

Country of origin: United States of America

Type: Medium lift utility helicopter

Powerplants: S-61N Mk II – Two 1120kW (1500shp) General Electric CT58-140-1 or 140-2 turboshafts driving five blade main and tail rotors.

Performance: S-61N Mk II – Economical cruising speed 222km/h (120kt). Service ceiling 12,500ft. Hovering ceiling out of ground effect 8700ft. Range with max fuel and reserves 833km (450nm).

Weights: S-61N Mk II – Empty 5595kg (12,336lb), max takeoff 8620kg (19,000lb). S-61L Mk II – Empty 5,308kg (11,701lb).

Dimensions: Main rotor diameter 18.90m (62ft 0in), length overall rotors turning 22.20m (72ft 10in), fuselage length 17.96m (58ft 11in), height 5.32m (17ft 6in). Main rotor disc area 280.5m² (3019.0sq ft).

Capacity: Flightcrew of two. Main cabin seating for up to 26 in early production aircraft and 30 in later production aircraft. Payloader can lift a 4990kg (11,000lb) external sling load.

Production: Production ceased in 1979 when 116 S-61Ns and S-61Ls had been delivered.

History: The Sikorsky S-61N and S-61L are based on the SH-3/S-61A/B Sea King series originally developed in the late 1950s. They are widely used as oil rig support helicopters.

In September 1957 the US Navy awarded Sikorsky a development contract to produce what became the Sea King, an amphibious anti submarine warfare helicopter capable of detecting and attacking submarines. The prototype first flew on March 11 1959, while deliveries of production Sea Kings took place from September 1961. Power for initial production aircraft was supplied by two 930kW (1250shp) General Electric T58-GE-8B turboshafts.

Development of a civil version was undertaken almost concurrently, with the commercial S-61L making its first flight on November 2 1961 (certification was awarded on November 2 1961). While based on the Sea King, the S-61L is 1.27m (4ft 3in) longer, allowing it to carry a substantial payload of freight or passengers. Power for initial production S-61Ls was supplied by two 1005kW (1350shp) GE CT58-140 turboshafts, the civil equivalent of the T58. Other changes include a modified rotor head and stabiliser. Unlike the Sea King, the S-61L features a modified landing gear without float stabilisers.

The S-61N, which first flew on August 7 1962, retains the floats, making it suitable for overwater operations, particularly for oil rig support. Both the S-61L and S-61N were subsequently updated to Mk II standard with improvements including more powerful CT58-110 engines giving better hot and high performance, vibration damping and other detail refinements.

A third civil development of the S-61 series to be offered was the Payloader, stripped down and optimised for aerial crane work. The Payloader features the fixed undercarriage of the S-61L, but with an empty weight almost 900kg (2000lb) less than the standard S-61N.

S-61 production ceased in 1979.

The Helipro S-61 Shortsky is a shortened (1.6m/50in) conversion of the S-61N and L, designed to increase single engine performance and external payload. The conversion first flew in February 1996.

Photo: A Bristow S-61N. (Keith Gaskell)

Country of origin: United States of America

Type: Heavylift utility helicopter

Powerplants: S-64E – Two 3355kW (4500shp) takeoff rated 2983kW (4000shp) max cont rated Pratt & Whitney JFTD12-4A turboshafts driving a six blade main rotor and four blade tail rotor.

Performance: S-64E – Max speed at sea level 203km/h (109kt), max cruising speed 169km/h (91kt). Initial rate of climb 1330ft/min. Service ceiling 9000ft. Hovering ceiling out of ground effect 6900ft. Range with max fuel and reserves 370km (200nm).

Weights: S-64E – Empty 8724kg (19,234lb), max takeoff 19,050kg (42,000lb).

Dimensions: Main rotor diameter 21.95m (72ft 0in), length overall rotors turning 26.97m (88ft 6in), fuselage length 21.41m (70ft 3in), height to top of rotor hub 5.67m (18ft 7in). Main rotor disc area 378.1m² (4070sq ft).

Capacity: Flightcrew of two, can carry an observer in rearwards facing seat in cabin. S-64E external load limit 9072kg (20,000lb), S-64F external load limit 11,350kg (25,000lb).

Production: Sikorsky built 101 CH-54s. Erickson Air-crane has re-built 14 S-64Es and Fs.

History: The Sikorsky S-64 heavylift helicopter has been adapted by Oregon based Erickson Air-Crane for use in a number of utility missions including firefighting and aerial crane work.

Sikorsky developed the S-64 Skycrane as a heavy lift aerial crane for the US Army in the early 1960s. A key feature of the Skycrane was its ability to lift 20,000lb (or 9072kg) loads, either in the form of external sling loads, or in purpose designed pods carried under the backbone like fuselage. The first S-64A first flew on May 9 1962, the US Army ordered an initial six in 1963 as the CH-54A Tahre. The improved CH-54B, which was first delivered in 1969, could lift 11,350kg (25,000lb).

Sikorsky launched the FAA certificated civil S-64E Skycrane in 1969. Erickson Air-Crane purchased its first S-64E in January 1972 for use for logging and other aerial crane tasks.

In 1992 Erickson purchased the S-64's type certificate from Sikorksy, becoming the world authority for the type, which it named the Aircrane. Erickson has rebuilt Aircranes from ex US Army Skycranes, manufactures spare parts, and can even build new S-64s from scratch. Erickson also certificated the improved 11,350kg (25,000lb) capacity S-64F (based on the CH-54B and with twin main undercarriage wheels) and developed the Helitanker waterbomber kit.

The S-64F Helitanker can lift 9000 litres of water in a single load, which its experienced crews can drop with great accuracy. The Helitanker can refill its tanks in as little as 45 seconds, so if nearby water sources are available, an S-64 can drop up to 114,000 litres of water in an hour.

Erickson runs a rolling preventative maintenance program for the Aircranes which has extended the S-64's mean time between over-hauls to 2000 hours, up from as little as 200 hours in military service. Erickson's pilots also tend to be highly experienced.

Photo: An S-64F Helitanker. (Paul Sadler)

Country of origin: United States of America

Type: Mid size corporate & utility helicopter

Powerplants: S-76 Mk II – Two 485kW (650shp) takeoff rated Allison 250-C30S turboshafts driving four blade main and tail rotors. S-76C+ – Two 638kW (856shp) takeoff rated Turbomeca Arriel 2S1s.

Performance: S-76 Mk II – Max cruising speed 287km/h (155kt), long range cruising speed 232km/h (125kt). Initial rate of climb 1350ft/min. Service ceiling 15,000ft. Range with 12 passengers, standard fuel and reserves 748km (404nm), with eight passengers, auxiliary fuel and reserves 1112km (600nm). S-76C+ – Max speed 287km/h (155kt), cruising speed 269km/h (145kt). Initial rate of climb 1625ft/min. Hovering ceiling out of ground effect 1800ft. Range at 259km/h (140kt) with reserves 713km (385nm).

Weights: S-76 Mk II – Empty (standard equipment) 2540kg (5600lb), max takeoff 4672kg (10,300lb). S-76C+ – Empty (executive configuration) 3691kg (8138lb), max takeoff 5307kg (11,700lb).

Dimensions: Main rotor diameter 13.41m (44ft 0in), length overall 16.00m (52ft 6in), fuselage length 13.22m (43ft 4in), height overall 4.41m (14ft 6in). Main rotor disc area 141.3m² (1520.5sq ft).

Capacity: Flightcrew of two. Max seating for 12 or 13 passengers at 79cm (31in) pitch in oil rig support aircraft. VIP configurations offered in six or eight passenger seat form. EMS configured aircraft accommodate one or two stretchers and four medical attendants.

Production: S-76 production includes 284 S-76As, 101 S-76Bs, 17 S-76A+, 43 S-76Cs and approx 70 S-76C+s. Over 70 S-76As converted to S-76A+ standard. 500th S-76 registered in May 1999.

History: Sikorsky's S-76 is a popular mid size corporate and oil rig support helicopter.

Sikorsky began development work on the S-76 (for a time named Spirit) in the mid 1970s and used technologies and experience gained from the military S-70 Black Hawk program. The resulting S-76A was powered by two Allison 250-C30S turboshafts and could seat 12. First flight was on March 13 1977 and FAA certification was awarded in November 1978.

The first improved model was the S-76 Mark II (introduced in March 1982) with more powerful Allison engines and 40 detail refinements. The S-76B is powered by two Pratt & Whitney Canada PT6B-36s (the 101st and last B was due to be delivered in December 1998), while the S-76C is powered by two Turbomeca Arriel 1S1 engines. The S-76A+ designation covers undelivered S-76As subsequently fitted and delivered with Arriel engines, and S-76As converted to Arriel power.

Current production is of the S-76C+ with 18% more powerful FADEC equipped Arriel 2S1 engines. Certification of the C+ was awarded in mid 1996. Forthcoming improvements include composite blades, a quiet tail rotor with curved blades, an active noise and vibration control system, and an advanced health and usage monitoring system. A three LCD screen integrated instrument display system (IIDS) for engine and rotor information is now standard, supplementing the four screen Honeywell EFIS suite.

Photo: An S-76A+. (Greg Wood)

Sikorsky S-92 Helibus

Country of origin: United States of America

Type: Medium to heavy lift airliner and utility helicopter

Powerplants: S-92A – Two 1790kW (2400shp) takeoff rated General Electric CT7-8 turboshafts driving four blade main and tail rotors.

Performance: S-92A – Max cruising speed 280km/h (151kt), economical cruising speed 252km/h (136kt). Hovering ceiling out of ground effect 5500ft. Range with 19 passengers and reserves 870km (470nm), with internal auxiliary fuel 1240km (670nm).

Weights: S-92A – Empty 7030kg (15,500lb), max takeoff 11,430kg (25,200lb), max takeoff with sling load 12,020kg (26,500lb).

Dimensions: Main rotor diameter 17.71m (56ft 4in), length overall rotors turning 20.88m (68ft 6in), fuselage length 17.25m (56ft 7in), height overall 5.41m (17ft 9in). Main rotor disc area 231.6m² (2492.4sq ft).

Capacity: Flightcrew of two. Accommodation in main cabin for 19 passengers or up to three standard LD3 containers.

Production: First deliveries planned for 2004. Approx 15 on order.

History: The S-92A Helibus is a new medium/heavy lift helicopter Sikorsky is developing with a number of international partners.

Development of the S-92 was first announced in 1992 when Sikorsky unveiled a mockup of the new helicopter. However in 1993 Sikorsky postponed launching the S-92 due to the international helicopter market downturn and instead began searching for international risk sharing partners. By 1995 Sikorsky had formed its Team S-92 grouping and formally launched the S-92 at that year's Paris Airshow.

Sikorsky has built five prototype S-92s, four of which are flying aircraft. The first is a civil S-92A, which first flew on December 23 1998. The international utility/military S-92IU development has been dropped with the S-92A filling civil and military roles. S-92A certification to FAR/JAR Pt 29 was awarded on December 12 2002 with first deliveries scheduled for the first quarter of 2004.

As originally envisaged the S-92 was to combine upgraded dynamic system components of the H-60/S-70 series with a larger cabin. However the S-92 is essentially an all new helicopter, with larger, composite construction, swept, tapered and anhedral tipped main rotor blades, new tail rotor, and a new four stage transmission based on the three stage S-70 unit. In mid 2000 Sikorsky announced further design changes including a lengthened cabin, reduced height tail and relocated horizontal stabiliser.

Some 40% of the aircraft is of composite construction. The S-92's main cabin is wider and longer than the S-70's and features a rear ramp, while the cockpit features Rockwell Collins' Pro Line 21 EFIS system with four colour liquid crystal displays, with a fifth optional. Power is from two FADEC equipped GE CT7-8D turboshafts. Rolls-Royce Turbomeca RTM322s could be a future alternative engine.

Team S-92 members include risk sharing partners Mitsubishi Heavy Industries (7.5%, responsible for the main cabin), Gamesa of Spain (7% – cabin interior and transmission housing) and China's Jingdezhen Helicopter Group/CATIC (2% – tail pylon and tailplane), while Taiwan's AIDC (6.5% – flightdeck) and Embraer (4% – sponsons and fuel system) are fixed price suppliers/partners.

Photo: The S-92 in flight. (Sikorsky)

Sino Swearingen SJ30-2

Country of origin: United States of America

Type: Light corporate jet

Powerplants: Two 10.2kN (2300lb) Williams Rolls FJ44-2A turbofans.

Performance: High speed cruise Mach 0.80+, long range cruising speed Mach 0.78 or 828km/h (447kt). Max certificated altitude 49,000ft. Takeoff balanced field length 1217m (3993ft). Range with one pilot and three passengers and NBAA IFR reserves at Mach 0.78 4635km (2500nm).

Weights: Empty equipped 3493kg (7700lb), operating empty 3629kg (8000lb), max takeoff 6123kg (13,500lb).

Dimensions: Wing span 12.90m (42ft 4in), length 14.26m (46ft 10in), height 4.34m (14ft 3in). Wing area 17.7m² (190.7sq ft).

Capacity: Typically pilot and passenger (or copilot) on flightdeck (will be certificated for single pilot operation). Typical main cabin seating for five with four in a club arrangement and fifth seat opposite main cabin door.

Production: First deliveries scheduled for early 2003.

History: The promising but oft delayed Sino Swearingen SJ30-2 is a high performance seven place entry level corporate jet.

The SJ30 concept was for an advanced technology and relatively high performance, yet low cost entry level corporate jet. It will compete against the Cessna CJ1 and Raytheon Premier I.

Development work dates back to the SA-30 Fanjet which was announced in October 1986. Swearingen Engineering and Technology, under the leadership of Ed Swearingen (designer of the Metro and Merlin turboprops), began to design and develop the SA-30 for Gulfstream. Gulfstream planned to market the aircraft as the SA-30 Gulfjet, however it withdrew from the program in September 1989. Instead the Jaffe Group took Gulfstream's place. Construction of a prototype began in San Antonio, Texas, but in 1990 the Jaffe Group also withdrew from the then SJ30 program.

The first SJ30 prototype first flew on February 13 1991 and development progressed slowly until the 1994 announcement that Swearingen would form a joint venture with Taiwanese investors to create Sino Swearingen to build the SJ30 at a new factory in Martinsburg, West Virginia.

Sino Swearingen decided to enlarge the basic SJ30, resulting in the 1.32m (4ft 4in) stretched, increased wing span SJ30-2. The SJ30 prototype was modified to represent the SJ30-2 and flew in this configuration in November 1996. The definitive, more powerful FJ44-2A turbofans were installed on this aircraft in September 1997. Three new build production representative prototypes are being built. The first of these flew on November 30 2000, the second was due to fly in late 2002, the third in early 2003.

Features of the SJ30-2 include a Honeywell Primus Epic avionics suite with three 20 x 25cm (8 x 10in) colour, flat panel LCDs and IC-615 integrated avionics computer, a 32° swept wing, increased fuel capacity compared with the basic SJ30 design, a Mach 0.80+ cruise speed and a 4635km (2500nm) range.

Photo: The first production representative SJ30-2 prototype in company with a Hawker Hunter chaseplane.

Socata (Morane-Saulnier) Rallye

Country of origin: France

Type: Series of two/four seat light aircraft

Powerplant: MS 880B – One 75kW (100hp) Continental O-200-A flat four piston engine driving a two blade c/s prop. 235 GT – One 175kW (235hp) Lycoming O-540-B4B5 flat six, three blade c/s prop.

Performance: MS 880B – Max speed 195km/h (105kt), max cruising speed 174km/h (94kt). Initial rate of climb 540ft/min. Service ceiling 10,500ft. Max range 853km (460nm). 235 GT – Max speed 275km/h (150kt), max cruising speed 245km/h (132kt), normal cruising speed 231km/h (125kt). Initial rate of climb 980ft/min. Service ceiling 14,750ft. Max range with reserves 1090km (590nm).

Weights: MS 880B – Empty 450kg (990lb), max takeoff 770kg (1695lb). 235 GT – Empty 695kg (1530lb), max TO 1200kg (2645lb).

Dimensions: MS 880B – Wing span 9.61m (31ft 6in), length 6.97m (22ft 11in), height 2.69m (8ft 10in). Wing area 12.3m² (132sq ft). 235 GT – Wing span 9.74m (31ft 11in), length 7.25m (23ft 10in), height 3.67m (9ft 2in). Wing area 12.8m² (137.3sq ft).

Capacity: Seating for three adults or two adults and two children in MS 880B Rallye-Club/Rallye 100, Rallye 125 and the MS 886 Super Rallye/Rallye 150T. All other variants seat four adults.

Production: More than 3500 built.

History: The prolific Rallye family is Europe's most successful light aircraft series.

Morane Saulnier designed the Rallye in response to a late 1950s French government competition. The resulting Rallye first flew on June 10 1959. This first MS 880A prototype was powered by a 67kW (90hp) Continental C90 flat four engine.

Sud Aviation (who took over the Rallye after Morane Saulnier collapsed in the mid 1960s) and then Socata developed a wide range of Rallye models. The main two/three seat production version was the 75kW (100hp) Continental O-200 powered MS 880B Rallye-Club. Other Rallye-Clubs inlcude the 78kW (105hp) Potez powered MS 881 and 85kW (115hp) Lycoming O-235 powered MS 883. A more powerful Rallye-Club development was the 110kW (145hp) Continental O-300 flat six powered Super Rallye (later the Rallye 150 S, then 150 ST and later still the Garnament with 115kW/155hp O-320).

The first true four seater was the MS 890 Rallye Commodore (deliveries began in 1964), which differed from the Super Rallye in having a higher max takeoff weight and strengthened structure. Developments included the 110kW (150hp) Lycoming O-320 powered MS 892 Commodore 150 (later the Rallye 150 GT), the 135kW (180hp) O-360 powered MS 893 Commodore 180 (later the Rallye 180 GT and then the Gaillard), the 165kW (220hp) Franklin 6A-350 powered MS 894 Rallye Minerva (later the Rallye 220 GT and sold in the US as the Waco Minerva); and 175kW (235hp) O-540 powered Rallye 235 GT (later the Gabier).

Improvements led to the Rallye-Club based Rallye 100S with two seats and 100ST with three seats; both replaced by the Rallye 100 ST Galopin with a 82kW (110hp) O-235; the Rallye 125 2+2 seater; the glider towing 180 T Galerien; and the tail dragger Gaucho ag sprayer. French production ceased in 1983.

Photo: A MS-893A Rallye Commodore 180. (Peter Vercruijsse)

Socata GY-80 Horizon & ST10 Diplomate

Country of origin: France

Type: Four seat light aircraft

Powerplant: GY-80-160 – One 120kW (160hp) Lycoming O-320-D flat four piston engine driving a two blade fixed pitch or optional constant speed propeller. ST10 – One 150kW (200hp) Lycoming IO-360-C fuel injected flat four driving a two blade fixed pitch or optional constant speed propeller.

Performance: GY-80-160 – Max speed 240km/h (130kt), cruising speed 234km/h (126kt). Initial rate of climb 690ft/min. Service ceiling 13,940ft. Range with max fuel 950km (515nm). ST10 – Max speed 280km/h (151kt), cruising speed 265km/h (143kt). Initial rate of climb 1005ft/min. Service ceiling 16,400ft. Range with four people on board 1385km (745nm).

Weights: GY-80-160 – Empty 620kg (1365lb), max takeoff 1100kg (2425lb). ST10 – Empty 723kg (1594lb), max takeoff 1220kg (2690lb).

Dimensions: GY-80-160 – Wing span 9.70m (31ft 10in), length 6.64m (21ft 10in), height 2.60m (8ft 6in). Wing area 13.0m² (139.9sq ft). ST10 – Same except length 7.26m (22ft 10in), height 2.88m (9ft 6in).

Capacity: Typical seating for four.

Production: Approximately 260 GY-80 Horizons of all models and 55 ST10 Diplomates were built. Production ceased in 1974.

History: The Horizon and Diplomate are rretractable undercarriage four seaters which were built in relatively modest numbers.

The initial GY-80 Horizon began life as a privately developed design penned by Yves Gardan, who had also been responsible for a number of other postwar light aircraft designs. Gardan built a prototype which flew on July 21 1960. Two years later, Sud Aviation (now Aerospatiale) acquired the design and production rights for the GY-80 and placed the type into production. Sud Aviation built three preproduction development aircraft before placing the GY-80 into series production in late 1963.

A key aspect to the GY-80 was its simple design and method of construction. The GY-80 was of conventional construction, featuring retractable tricycle undercarriage, Frise slotted ailerons and Fowler flaps (the flaps, ailerons and horizontal tail pieces were interchangeable to reduce maintenance costs). The Horizon was built using car assembly techniques, with just 11 production jigs.

Three versions of the Horizon were built, differing in powerplant and fuel tankage. These were the 110kW (150hp) Lycoming O-320-A powered GY-80-150, the 120kW (160hp) O-320-D powered GY-80-160, and the 135kW (180hp) Lycoming O-360-A powered GY-80-180. These were built firstly by Sud Aviation, and then by its newly established light aircraft division Socata from 1966.

Socata flew an improved development of the GY-80, initially called the Super Horizon 200, on November 7 1967. This new development featured a stretched cabin and a more powerful 150kW (200hp) fuel injected Lycoming IO-360-C. In production between 1969 and 1974, the Super Horizon was renamed Provence, and then the ST10 Diplomate, the latter becoming the type's definitive name.

Photo: A GY-80-160D Horizon. (Jim Thorn)

Sud Caravelle

Country of origin: France

Type: Short range airliner

Powerplants: Caravelle 10B – Two 64.4kN (14,500lb) Pratt & Whitney JT8D-9 turbofans. Earlier Caravelle versions (Mk I, IA, III and VI) were powered by two 48.9 to 56.0kN (11,000 to 12,600lb) thrust class Rolls-Royce RA.29 Avon turbojets.

Performance: Caravelle 10B – Max cruising speed 825km/h (445kt). Range with max payload 2650km (1450nm), range with max fuel 3640km (1965nm).

Weights: 10B – Operating empty 30,055kg (66,260lb), max takeoff 56,000kg (123,460lb). Earlier series Avon powered versions max takeoff weights range from 46,000kg (101,413lb) for the Mk III to 50,000kg (110,230lb) for the Mk VI-R.

Dimensions: Caravelle 10B – Wing span 34.30m (112ft 6in), length 33.01m (108ft 3.5in), height 8.72m (28ft 7in). Wing area 146.7m² (1579sq ft). Caravelle Mks I, IA, III and VI same except for length 32.01m (105ft 0in). Caravelle 12 featured 3.21m (10ft 7in) fuselage stretch over the Caravelle 10.

Capacity: Caravelle 10 – Flightcrew of two pilots and one flight engineer. Max passengers 100 at five abreast in a high density layout. Typical accommodation for 91 passengers in a mixed class arrangement. Maximum payload 9100kg (20,600lb).

Production: 282 production Caravelles built between 1958 and 1972. Eight remained in commercial service in late 2002.

History: The Caravelle was the first jet airliner to enter production in continental Europe and pioneered the rear mounted engine layout.

The Caravelle was designed in response to a French Secretariat General of Commercial and Civil Aviation requirement for a 1600 to 2000km (865 to 1080nm) range airliner (allowing operations between France and its North African dependants) with a 6000 to 7000kg (2725 to 3180lb) payload at a speed of 620km/h (335kt). SNCASE (Societe Nationale de Constructions Aeronautiques de Sud-Est, later Sud Aviation, and subsequently merged into Aerospatiale) responded with a trijet design designated the X120, with three rear mounted SNECMA Atar turbojets. This design then matured to feature two rear mounted Rolls-Royce Avons.

The French government ordered two flying and two static prototypes of the twinjet in 1953, resulting in the type's first flight on May 27 1955. Entry into service of the SE 210 Caravelle I with Air France was on May 12 1959 on the Paris/Rome/Istanbul route.

The Caravelle III featured 50.7kN (11,400lb) Avon RA.29 Mk 527s (one Caravelle III was powered by General Electric CJ805-23C turbofans, but production never eventuated), The 54.3kN (12,200lb) Avon RA.2 Mk 531 powered VI-N and the VI-R with a modified windscreen and thrust reversers followed.

The Caravelle 10R (first delivery July 1965) introduced more fuel efficient Pratt & Whitney JT8D turbofans, while the 11R was a convertible passenger/freighter based on the 10R. The ultimate Caravelle model was the 3.20m (10ft 6in) stretched Caravelle 12. It could seat up to 128 single class passengers. Caravelle 10s and 12s are often called Super Caravelles.

Photo: A Caravelle 10. (Gianfranco Beting)

Sukhoi Su-26, Su-29 & Su-31

Country of origin: Russia

Type: Single and two seat aerobatic light aircraft

Powerplant: Su-29 – One 265kW (255hp) VOKBM M-14PT nine cylinder radial piston engine driving a constant speed three blade propeller. Su-31T – One 294kW (394hp) M-14PF.

Performance: Su-29 – Max speed 325km/h (175kt). Initial rate of climb 3150ft/min. Service ceiling 13,120ft. Range with max fuel 1200km (648nm). Su-31T – Max speed 330km/h (178kt). Initial rate of climb 4725ft/min. Service ceiling 13,125ft. Range with internal fuel 290km (155nm), max ferry range up to 1200km (648nm).

Weights: Su-29 – Empty 735kg (1620lb), MTOW 1204kg (2654lb). Su-31T – Empty equipped 670kg (1480lb), MTOW 968kg (2134lb).

Dimensions: Su-26M – Wing span 8.20m (26ft 11in), length 7.29m (23ft 11in), height 2.89m (9ft 6in). Wing area 12.2m² (127.0sq ft). Su-31T – Wing span 7.80m (25ft 7in), length 6.90m (22ft 8in), height 2.76m (9ft 1in). Wing area 11.8m² (127.0sq ft).

Capacity: Accommodation for pilot only in Su-26, Su-26M, Su-31T and Su-31U. Seating for two in tandem in Su-29.

Production: Over 170 Su-29s, Su-26s and Su-31s built.

History: Sukhoi's highly regarded aerobatic aircraft have won numerous international aerobatic events.

Sukhoi is perhaps better known as one of the two pre-eminent Russian high performance combat aircraft designers, but it turned its attention to design a single seat aircraft for unlimited aerobatics competitions in the early 1980s. The prototype of the single seat Su-26, the first of the series, first flew in June 1984, and remarkably competed in the World Aerobatic Championships held in Hungary only two months later.

Features introduced on the initial Su-26 include the Vedneyev, now VOKBM, M-14 nine cylinder piston radial engine, which is highly regarded for its simplicity, power to weight ratio, fuel economy and low oil consumption. The airframe itself is extremely strong, capable of withstanding +11 and -9g, while the wing's aerofoil section is symmetrical and attached to the airframe at zero incidence and dihedral for similar positive and negative angle of attack flight characteristics.

Modifications to the Su-26 including a squared off vertical tail and less glass led to the Su-26M, which participated in the 1986 World Aerobatic Championships in the UK. The Su-26MX is an export version. Su-26 production ceased in 1996.

The two seat, dual control Su-29 first flew during 1991. Differences include the second seat, greater span wing and increased length. The Su-29M has an improved M-14 based M-9F engine (with 309kW/414hp) and lightened structure. The Su-29AR for the Argentine air force has some western equipment.

The ultimate development is the Su-31, which first flew in June 1992 as the Su-29T. The Su-31 is a single seater based on the Su-29 but with a more powerful engine. The basic version is the Su-31T, the Su-31X is for export and the Su-31U would have retractable undercarriage, the Su-31M2 has an M-9F engine and lightened structure. Production began in 1994.

Photo: An Su-31. (Daryl Williams)

Sukhoi S-80

Country of origin: Russia

Type: Twin turboprop utility transport

Powerplant: Prototype – Two 1305kW (1750shp) General Electric CT7-9B turboprops driving four blade propellers. Production aircraft will have Russian assembled CT7s built by NPO Saturn.

Performance: Max cruising speed 470km/h (254kt). Max certificated altitude 24,900ft. Takeoff run 555m (1820ft). Range with 30 passengers 1400km (755nm), range with 1950kg (4300lb) payload 2450km (1322nm).

Weights: Max takeoff 13,500kg (29,762lb). Max payload 3300kg (7275lb).

Dimensions: Wing span 23.17m (76ft 0in), length 18.26m (59ft 11in), height 5.52m (18ft 1in). Wing area 44.0m^2 (473.6sq ft).

Capacity: Two pilots. Prototype can seat 26 passengers, or 10 stretcher patients, or nine, 12 or 16 passengers in a corporate configuration. Production aircraft can seat 32 passengers. Freighter configuration has a row of passenger seats behind pilots.

Production: Prototype due to be joined by four production representative aircraft (including two for static testing) under construction with KnAAPO in 2002. Approx 30 on order.

History: Sukhoi's S-80 transport is being developed to replace a range of regional airliners and utility transports.

The S-80 has endured a prolonged gestation. It was first conceived in 1989 as a replacement for An-24s, An-28s, Yak-40s and L-410s. A model of the S-80 was displayed at the 1989 Paris Airshow but the project was suspended following the collapse of the Soviet Union. The project was resurrected in 1992, but like many Russian aircraft programs of late, progress has been slow due to funding problems. Prototype construction was underway by 1993, but this aircraft did not make its first flight until September 2001.

Originally the S-80 was to be powered by Rybinsk TVD-500 turboprops, but under a 1995 agreement with General Electric it has CT7s (which also power the Saab 340). Production aircraft would be powered by CT7s assembled in Russia by NPO Saturn (formerly Rybinsk). Any military aircraft would likely feature 1860kW (2495shp) Klimov TV-117s.

S-80 design features include its high mounted wing and twin boom tail configuration, rear loading ramp, wide track undercarriage which retract into the engine nacelles/tail booms, a high aspect ration wing with winglets, and small stub wings which join the top of the rear fuselage with the tail booms. The S-80 is made largely from aluminium but features some composites. The cockpit features Rockwell Collins' Pro Line 21 EFIS suite with five colour displays.

Compared to the prototype, four airframes under final assembly with manufacturer KnAAPO feature 1.4m (4.6ft) stretched fuselages, allowing seating for 32. Two of these airframes will be used for static testing, while the first of the flying aircraft is due to be completed by the end of 2003.

The S-80 is due to be certificated to Russian, European JAA and US FAA standards.

Photo: The S-80 made its public debut in August 2001. (S Zacharias)

Taylorcraft

Country of origin: United States of America

Type: Two seat light aircraft

Powerplant: BC-12D – One 50kW (65hp) Continental A-65 flat four piston engine driving a two blade fixed pitch propeller. F-21 – One 88kW (118hp) Avco Lycoming O-235-L2C flat four.

Performance: BC-12D – Max speed 177km/h (96kt), cruising speed 153km/h (83kt). Initial rate of climb 600ft/min. Service ceiling 17,000ft. Max range 805km (435nm). F-21 – Max cruising speed at 75% power 196km/h (106kt). Initial rate of climb 875ft/min. Service ceiling 18,000ft. Range with max fuel 645km (347nm).

Weights: BC-12D – Empty 304kg (670lb), max takeoff 522kg (1150lb). F-21 – Empty 450kg (990lb), max takeoff 680kg (1500lb).

Dimensions: BC-12D – Wing span 10.98m (36ft 0in), length 6.71m (22ft 0in), height 2.03m (6ft 8in). Wing area 17.1m^2 (183.5sq ft). F-21 – Wing span 10.98m (36ft 0in), length 6.78m (22ft 3in), height 1.98m (6ft 6in). Wing area 17.1m^2 (183.5sq ft).

Capacity: Seating for two, except four in the Model 15 Tourist.

Production: Taylorcraft production includes 100 prewar Model As, 1800 military L-2s, more than 2800 postwar BC-12Ds, and more than 120 F-19 Sportsmans.

History: The Taylorcraft series of two seaters has a very chequered production history.

The original Taylor Brother's Airplane Company was responsible for the Piper Cub design, and William T Piper purchased the company and its designs in 1931 when it ran into financial difficulties. Gilbert Taylor stayed on as president with the company under Piper's ownership (the Taylor name was initially retained) until 1935 when he resigned to establish his own company, this time named Taylorcraft.

Taylorcraft's first aircraft was similar to the Piper Cub except that it seated two side by side and was powered by a 30kW (40hp) Continental engine. Prewar it was built in A, B, D and D Tandem Trainer forms, the latter seating two in tandem.

The Tandem Trainer formed the basis for the wartime L-2, nicknamed Grasshopper. More than 1600 were built during World War 2 for the US Army Air Force.

Postwar Taylorcraft resumed production of the B-12 as the BC-12D. Almost 3000 BC-12Ds were built before the company encountered financial troubles and the firm was bought out by Gilbert Taylor in March 1947. The new Taylorcraft Inc then built the two seat Ace, Traveller, De Luxe and Sportsman; the four seat Tourist, Ranch Wagon, Topper agricultural aircraft and float equipped Seabird and Zephyr.

Once more Taylorcraft ceased trading, and did not reform until 1968 when it was set up to support existing aircraft. In 1973 this company began building the Continental O-200 powered F-19 Sportsman 100, and from 1983 the Lycoming O-235 powered F-21, which were based on the prewar Model B, but production ceased in 1986. Then in January 1990 Taylorcraft flew the improved Textron Lycoming O-235-L2C powered F-22, small numbers of which were built before production ceased for the final time in October 1992.

Photo: A BC-12D. (Peter Vercruijsse)

Technoavia SM-92 & SMG-92 Finist

Country of origin: Russia

Type: STOL utility transport

Powerplant: SM-92 – One 265kW (355hp) VOKBM M-14Kh nine cylinder radial piston engine driving a three blade variable pitch Mühlbauer MTV-3 propeller. SMG-92 – One 400kW (536shp) Walter M 601D-2 turboshaft driving a three blade prop.

Performance: SM-92 – Max level speed 260km/h (140kt), max cruising speed 200km/h (108kt), economical cruising speed 170km/h (92kt). Stalling speed with full flap 100km/h (54kt). Range with max fuel 1200km (647nm). Endurance with max fuel 7hr 30min. SMG-92 – Max speed 295km/h (159kt). Initial rate of climb 1500ft/min. Max operating altitude 19,500ft. Max range with optional fuel 600km (324nm).

Weights: SM-92 – Operating empty 1500kg (3307lb), max takeoff 2350kg (5180lb). SMG-92 – Empty 1450kg (3197lb), max takeoff 2700kg (5952lb)

Dimensions: SM-92 – Wing span 14.60m (47ft 11in), length 9.30m (30ft 6in), height 3.08m (10ft 1in). Wing area 20.5m² (220.7sq ft). SMG-92 – Same except length 9.93m (32ft 7in).

Capacity: SM-92 – One pilot and one passenger on flightdeck. Seating for six passengers in main cabin arranged in pairs. Alternatively can accommodate six parachutists, or 600kg (1320lb) of freight. SMG-92 – Up to 10 parachutists or seven passengers

Production: Production aircraft built at the Smolensk Aircraft Factory. Approximately 15 Finists and 2 Turbo Finists built by 2002.

History: The Technoavia Finist is a STOL utility transport similar in concept to the venerable DHC-2 Beaver.

The Finist (named after a magical Russian bird) was the first product of the Technoavia Design Bureau. Technoavia was established in 1991 by Slava Kondratiev, a renowned Russian designer responsible for the world beating Sukhoi Su-26, Su-29 and Su-31 series of aerobatic aircraft. Kondratiev provided finance for the new company by purchasing the rights and placing into limited production the four seat Yak-18T light aircraft (described separately).

The high wing Finist features the M-14P radial, a high aspect ratio (10.5) wing with Fowler flaps and Frise ailerons, a large main cabin door on the left side and faired steel main landing gear units.

The prototype Finist first flew on December 28 1993, while production deliveries began in January 1995. Russian certification to AP-23 standard (equivalent to the US FAR Part 23) was awarded in 1998. So far US certification has not been sought.

Technoavia has studied further developments of the basic aircraft, primarily a Pratt & Whitney Canada PT6 turbine powered model. However the first turbine powered Finist is the Hungarian financed SMG-92 Turbo Finist, powered by a Walter M 601D-2 turboshaft. The first, a new build aircraft, first flew on November 7 2000. A Hungarian type certificate was awarded late that year. The first aircraft was delivered to a UK skydiving operation in early 2001, while a second Turbo Finist, a converted Finist, flew in 2001 and flies in Germany.

The armed SM-92P was ordered by the Russian border guards. Up to 300 were required but production has not been undertaken.

Photo: The second Finist built, in Australia. (Lance Higgerson)

Tupolev Tu-134

Country of origin: Russia

Type: Short range airliner

Powerplants: Tu-134 – Two 64.5kN (14,490lb) Soloviev D-30 turbofans. Tu-134A – Two 66.7kN (14,990lb) Soloviev D-30 Series IIs.

Performance: Tu-134 – Max cruising speed 900km/h (485kt), economical cruising speed 750km/h (405kt). Normal operating ceiling 39,730ft. Range with 7000kg (15,420lb) payload and reserves 2400km (1295nm), with 3000kg (6600lb) payload 3500km (1890nm). Tu-134A – Max cruising speed 900km/h (485kt), economical cruising speed 750km/h (405kt). Range with 5000kg (11,025lb) payload and reserves 3020km (1630nm).

Weights: Tu-134 – Operating empty 27,500kg (60,627lb), max takeoff 44,500kg (98,105lb). Tu-134A – Operating empty 29,050kg (64,045lb), max takeoff 47,000kg (103,600lb).

Dimensions: Tu-134 – Wing span 29.00m (95ft 2in), length 34.35m (112ft 8in), height 9.02m (29ft 7in). Wing area 127.3m² (1370.3sq ft). Tu-134A – Same except length 37.05m (121ft 7in), height 9.14m (30ft 0in).

Capacity: Flightcrew of three, comprising two pilots and a navigator. Tu-134 seats 72 in a single class. Tu-134A seats up to 84 passengers in a single class at four abreast, or 12 first class and 54 economy class at four abreast in a two class arrangement. Tu-134B-3 can seat up to 96 in a single class.

Production: Production estimated at over 700, most for Aeroflot, but approximately 170 exported to various east European airlines and other Soviet client states. Approx 305 in service in late 2002.

History: For many years the Tupolev Tu-134 was the standard short haul jet airliner in the Soviet Union and eastern Europe.

The Tupolev design bureau was responsible for the Soviet Union's first jet powered airliner, the Tu-104 (which was based on the Tu-16 'Badger' bomber), and the Tu-104's smaller brother, the Tu-124. Both of these short range jetliners suffered from a number of performance shortfalls however, thus prompting development of the Tu-134.

The initial Tu-134 design was based fairly closely on the Tu-124, and for a time was designated the Tu-124A. However Tupolev decided to reconfigure the aircraft to feature rear fuselage mounted engines and a T-tail, resulting in the new designation.

Six development Tu-134s were built, with the first flying on July 29 1963. Production began in 1964 although it was not until September 1967 that Aeroflot launched full commercial services.

Initial production was of the standard fuselage length Tu-134, while the stretched Tu-134A entered Aeroflot service in the second half of 1970. The Tu-134A differed from the Tu-134 in having a 2.10m (6ft 11in) fuselage stretch, a reprofiled nose (many without glazing and with weather radar), more powerful D-30 engines and an APU, and seated up to 76 in a single class.

Other versions created by conversion are the Tu-134B with a forward facing position for the third crew member between and behind the pilots, the Tu-134B-1 which has a revised interior to seat up to 90 passengers without a galley, and the Tu-134B-3 which can seat 96 with full galley and toilet facilities retained.

Photo: A Tu-134B-3. (Toni Marimon)

Tupolev Tu-154

Country of origin: Russia

Type: Medium range airliner

Powerplants: Tu-154 – Three 93.2kN (20,950lb) Kuznetsov NK-8-2 turbofans. Tu-154M – Three 103.6kN (23,380lb) Aviadvigatel (Soloviev) D-30KU-154-II turbofans.

Performance: Tu-154 – Max cruising speed 975km/h (527kt), economical cruising speed 900km/h (486kt), long range cruising speed 850km/h (460kt). Range with max payload and reserves 3460km (1870nm), range with max fuel and 13,650kg (31,100lb) payload 5280km (2850nm). Tu-154M – Max cruising speed 950km/h (513kt). Range with max payload 3700km (1997nm), range with max fuel and 5450kg (12,015lb) payload 6600km (3563nm).

Weights: Tu-154 – Operating empty 43,500kg (95,900lb), max takeoff 90,000kg (198,415lb). Tu-154M – Basic operating empty 55,300kg (121,915lb), max takeoff 100,000kg (220,460lb).

Dimensions: Wing span 37.55m (123ft 3in), length 47.90m (157ft 2in), height 11.40m (37ft 5in). Wing area 201.5m² (2168.4sq ft).

Capacity: Flightcrew of three or four. Single class seating for 158 to 164 at six abreast, or 167 in a high density layout for Tu-154; Tu-154M seats up to 180 at six abreast and 75cm (29.5in) seat pitch.

Production: Approx 900 Tu-154s of all models built, including approx 320 Tu-154Ms. About 490 were in service in late 2002.

History: Tupolev's Tu-154 trijet remains the standard medium range airliner within many states of the former Soviet Union and is still in widespread use.

The Tu-154 was developed to replace the turbojet powered Tupolev Tu-104, plus the An-10 and Il-18 turboprops. Design criteria in replacing these three relatively diverse aircraft included the ability to operate from gravel or packed earth airfields, to be able to fly at high altitudes above most Soviet Union air traffic, and good field performance. To meet these aims the initial Tu-154 design featured three Kuznetsov (now KKBM) NK-8 turbofans (which also powered the larger, longer range Il-62) giving a relatively good thrust to weight ratio, double bogey main undercarriage units which retract into wing pods, and a rear engine T-tail configuration.

The Tu-154 first flew on October 4 1968. The first production example was delivered to Aeroflot in early 1971, although regular commercial service did not begin until February 1972.

Three Kuznetsov powered variants of the Tu-154 were built, the initial Tu-154, the improved Tu-154A with more powerful engines and a higher max takeoff weight, and the Tu-154B with a further increased max takeoff weight. Tu-154C is a freighter version of the Tu-154B.

The Tu-154M with far more economical, quieter and reliable Soloviev (now Aviadvigatel) turbofans first flew in 1982. Production continued until 1996, with several unfinished airframes in storage now unlikely to be delivered. A handful of converted Tu-154M-100s have modernised interiors and new Russian avionics.

The proposed Tu-154M2 with two PS-90A turbofans was not built while a re-engining program with CFM56s has also been studied.

Engine manufacturer NPO Saturn offers a Stage 3 hushkit for the Tu-154M, and is developing a Stage 4 hushkit.

Photo: A Slovak Airlines Tu-154M. (Rob Finlayson)

Tupolev Tu-204, Tu-214, Tu-224 & Tu-234

Country of origin: Russia

Type: Medium range airliner

Powerplants: Tu-204 – Two 158.3kN (35,580lb) Aviadvigatel PS-90A turbofans. Tu-204-220 – Two 191.7kN (43,100lb) Rolls-Royce RB211-535E4 or -535F5 turbofans.

Performance: Tu-204 – Cruising speed 810km/h to 850km/h (437 to 460kt). Range with max payload 2430km (1312nm), with design payload 3400km (1835nm). Tu-204-220 – Speeds same. Range with max payload 4600km (2483m).

Weights: Tu-204 – Operating empty 58,300kg (128,530lb), max takeoff 94,600kg (208,550lb). Tu-204-220 – Operating empty 59,000kg (130,070lb), max takeoff 110,750kg (244,155lb).

Dimensions: Tu-204 – Wing span 41.80m (137ft 2in), length 46.10m (151ft 3in), height 13.90m (45ft 7in). Wing area 182.4m² (1963.4sq ft).

Capacity: Flightcrew of two, although original Aeroflot requirement specified a flight engineer. Tu-204-200 seats up to 212 six abreast at 82cm (32in) pitch, or two class seating for 30 business class at 96cm (38in) pitch at six abreast and 154 economy at 81cm (32in) pitch and six abreast. Tu-224/-234 seats 166 in a single class.

Production: 15 Tu-204s in airline service in 2002.

History: The Tupolev Tu-204 is a medium range narrowbody twinjet.

Tupolev began development of the Tu-204 to meet an Aeroflot requirement for a replacement for the medium range Tu-154 trijet. This all new twin featured a supercritical wing, while engine designer Soloviev (now Aviadvigatel) specifically developed the PS-90 turbofan. Other Tu-204 design features include fly-by-wire and a six screen EFIS flightdeck. First flight was on January 2 1989.

The Tu-204 is offered in a number of models. The base model is the Tu-204, while the Tu-204-100 and -200 have higher max takeoff weights, more fuel and greater range. The Tu-204C and Tu-204-100C are freighters with a forward main deck freight door. Kazan builds the Tu-214 (first delivered May 2001), the Tu-214C³ combi convertible development, and the Tu-214C freighter.

Tupolev was keen to develop a westernised Tu-204 to broaden the type's market appeal, resulting in the Rolls-Royce RB211-535 powered Tu-204-120, which first flew on August 14 1992. All but the first five feature Honeywell's VIA 2000 EFIS avionics.

Rolls-Royce powered variants include the Tu-204-120C freighter, -122 with Rockwell Collins avionics (none built), increased weight -220 and equivalent cargo -220C, and the -222 with Collins avionics. Air Cairo of Egypt became the launch operator when it took delivery of a Tu-204-120 and -120C in November 1998.

Tupolev is also developing a shortened development of the Tu-204, in the form of the 166 seat RB211-535E4 powered Tu-224 and the 158kN (35,580lb) PS-90P powered Tu-234 (and Tu-234C freighter). The Tu-234 prototype (converted from the Tu-204 prototype) was publicly displayed at the 1995 Moscow Airshow. Lack of funding has delayed first flight.

Other proposed developments include a Pratt & Whitney PW2240 powered model, the 250 seat stretched Tu-204-400, a business jet and a maritime patrol platform.

Photo: A Tu-204-120C freighter. (Charles Falk)

Tupolev Tu-334

Country of origin: Russia

Type: Short to medium range airliner

Powerplants: Tu-334-100 – Two 73.6kN (16,535lb) ZMKB Progress D-436T1 turbofans. Tu-334-200 – Two 80.5kN (18,100lb) D-436T2s or Rolls-Royce BR715-55s.

Performance: Tu-334-100 – Typical cruising speeds at 35,000ft 800 to 820km/h (430 to 442kt). Range with max payload passengers 2000km (1080nm). Tu-334-200 – Range with max payload 2200km (1187nm).

Weights: Tu-334-100 – Empty 30,050kg (66,250lb), max takeoff 46,100kg (101,630lb). Tu-334-200 – Empty 34,375kg (75,785lb), max takeoff 54,800kg (120,815lb).

Dimensions: Tu-334-100 – Wing span 29.77m (97ft 8in), length 31.26m (102ft 7in), height 9.38m (30ft 9in). Wing area 83.2m² (895.8sq ft). Tu-334-200 – Wing span 32.61m (107ft 0in), length 35.16m (115ft 5in). Wing area 100.0m² (1076.4sq ft).

Capacity: Tu-334-100 – Flightcrew of two or three. Seats 102 in a single class arrangement at six abreast, or 72 in two classes (12 first and 60 economy class). Tu-334-200 – 126 single class passengers.

Production: 42 on order. Production aircraft would be built at RSK MiG, Aviacor and Aviant (in the Ukraine).

History: The Tupolev Tu-334 100 seat jet is being developed as a replacement for the ageing Tu-134.

Development of a replacement for the Tu-134 has been underway since the late 1980s, but it was not until August 1995 at the Moscow Airshow that the first prototype was displayed publicly. This aircraft made its first flight on December 8 1999.

The Tu-334 is based on the much larger Tu-204 twinjet with Tupolev using as many Tu-204 features in the new design as practical to reduce development time and costs. Examples of this include an identical flightdeck and a shortened Tu-204 fuselage. In addition the Tu-334's wing is based on the Tu-204's, although the latter's is a significantly larger unit.

Apart from commonality with the Tu-204, other notable Tu-334 design features are the rear fuselage mounted Progress D-436 turbofans, T-tail and fly-by-wire flight controls.

The Tu-334 is being developed in a number of versions. The first is the basic Tu-334-100, while the Tu-334-120D is planned to be powered by Rolls-Royce BR715 turbofans. The Tu-354-200 (alternatively Tu-354) is a stretched, 35m (115ft) long, 110 to 126 seater (in a single class). Apart from the fuselage stretch, changes will include more powerful D436T2 or BR715-55 turbofans, an increased span wing and four wheel main undercarriage units. The similar Tu-334-220 has BR715-55s and a further increased MTOW. The Tu-334-200C would be a Combi variant of the -200.

The Tu-334-100D will be a longer range Tu-334-100 featuring the -100's standard length fuselage but with more powerful engines, increased fuel capacity, a higher max takeoff weight and the increased span wings of the Tu-334-200. Tupolev has also studied the Tu-334C, which would be a freighter and even the cyrogenic fuelled Tu-336.

Funding problems have slowed development, but work continues.

Photo: The prototype Tu-334-100. (Paul Merritt)

Transavia Airtruk & Skyfarmer

Country of origin: Australia

Type: Agricultural aircraft

Powerplant: PL12-U – One 225kW (300hp) Continental IO-520-D fuel injected flat six piston engine driving a two blade constant speed McCauley propeller. T-300A – One 225kW (300hp) Textron Lycoming IO-540 fuel injected flat six driving a three blade constant speed Hartzell prop.

Performance: PL12-U – Max cruising speed 188km/h (102kt). Initial rate of climb 800ft/min. Service ceiling 10,500ft. Range with max payload 1205km (650nm), with max fuel 1295km (700nm). T-300A – Max speed 196km/h (106kt), max cruising speed (75% power) 188km/h (102kt). Initial rate of climb 515ft/min. Service ceiling 12,500ft.

Weights: PL12-U – Empty 830kg (1830lb), max takeoff 1723kg (3800lb). T-300A – Typical empty 955kg (2100lb), max takeoff (ag category) 1925kg (4244lb).

Dimensions: PL12-U – Wing span 12.15m (39ft 11in), length 6.35m (20ft 10in), height 2.79m (9ft 2in). Wing area 23.5m² (252.7sq ft). T-300A – Wing span 11.98m (39ft 4in), length 6.35m (20ft 10in), height 2.79m (9ft 2in). Wing area (including lower stub wing) 24.5m² (264.0sq ft).

Capacity: Single pilot in all versions. PL12, T-300 and T-400 – Seats for two passengers and fitted with a chemical hopper. PL12-U seats five with no hopper.

Production: Over 120 built, incl 18 assembled in New Zealand.

History: The Airtruk and Skyfarmer owe their origins to New Zealand's first commercial aircraft, the Waitomo Airtruck.

The original Waitomo Airtruck was designed by Luigi Pellarini in the mid 1950s, and used a number of components from the WW2 North American T-6 Texan/Harvard piston engine military advanced trainer. These parts included main undercarriage wheels and assembly, fuel tanks and the 410kW (550hp) Pratt & Whitney R-1340 radial piston engine. The Airtruck also featured a fairly tall and squat fuselage that accommodated a pilot, two passengers and a chemical hopper, tricycle undercarriage, a high mounted wing and boom mounted twin tails. The unusual twin tail configuration was adopted as it solved the problem of chemicals contaminating the rear fuselage, while it also allowed easier loading of the chemical hopper. The Airtruck first flew on August 2 1960.

The Airtruck was not built in New Zealand, and instead was further developed in Australia by Transavia as the PL12 Airtruk. The Airtruk differed from the Airtruck in having a flat six Continental engine and additional lower stub wings. It was delivered from December 1966.

The PL12-U utility seats five and has the chemical tank deleted. It was delivered from 1971. The T-300 and T-300A Skyfarmers are improved developments of the PL12 with a Textron Lycoming IO-540 engine; the T-300 first flew in July 1971, the T-300A, which introduced aerodynamic improvements, first flew in 1981. The final development was the 300kW (400hp) flat eight IO-720 powered T-400, four were delivered to China. Production ceased in 1993.

Photo: An Airtruk. (Lance Higgerson)

Vickers Viscount

Country of origin: United Kingdom

Type: Turboprop airliner and freighter

Powerplants: V.700D – Four 1297kW (1740ehp) Rolls-Royce Dart 510 turboprops driving four blade constant speed propellers. V.810 – Four 1485kW (1990ehp) Dart 525s.

Performance: V.700D – Max cruising speed 537km/h (290kt), economical cruising speed 521km/h (282kt). Service ceiling 25,500ft. Range with max payload and no reserves 2140km (1157nm), range with max fuel and 43 passengers 2768km (1496nm). V.810 – Max cruising speed 587km/h (318kt), economical cruising speed 565km/h (305kt). Range with 64 passengers 2780km (1500nm), range with max fuel 2832km (1530nm).

Weights: V.700D – Basic empty 17,200kg (37,918lb), max takeoff 29,257kg (64,500lb). V.810 – Operating empty 19,959kg (43,200lb), max takeoff 32,866kg (72,500lb).

Dimensions: V.700 – Wing span 28.56m (93ft 9in), length with radar 24.94m (81ft 10in), height 8.16m (26ft 9in). Wing area 89.5m² (963sq ft). V.800 – Same except for length 26.11m (85ft 8in).

Capacity: Flightcrew of two or three. V.700 – Typical layouts included 40 passengers at four abreast, or between 47 to 63 at five abreast. V.800 – Typical seating for 65 at five abreast and 97cm (38in) pitch.

Production: Total Viscount orders reached 438, plus development aircraft. Approx 3 Viscounts in service in late 2002, all in Africa.

History: Vicker's trailblazing Viscount was the first turboprop airliner to enter service.

The Viscount was one of the results of the UK's wartime Brabazon Committee, which was set up to define requirements for British postwar commercial aircraft. Discussions between the committee and Vickers designers in late 1944, who had already been working on the VC1 Viking airliner development of the Wellington bomber, resulted in what was eventually to become the Viscount. The committee's requirement was for a 24 seat, 1000 mile (1600km/868nm) range airliner, and by the end of 1945 Vickers had selected the Rolls-Royce Dart turboprop engine that was then under development to power the new aircraft.

In March 1946 the British government placed a contract with Vickers to build two prototypes of its design (called Viceroy), one powered by Darts, the other by Armstrong Siddeley Mamba turboprops. By the time of the Dart powered prototype's first flight on July 16 1948 the design had grown to seat 34. Airline indifference to the 34 seat Viscount and the availability of more powerful Dart variants however led Vickers to stretch the design to seat 40. This development was designated the Type 700, and first flew on April 19 1950.

Airline interest in the Viscount 700 was much stronger, and after receiving certification on April 17 1953 it entered service with BEA the following day. The Viscount was the subject of numerous large orders including from North America, its smoothness, good operating economics and pressurisation contributing to its success.

Capitalising on the 700's success Vickers developed the stretched 800 with seating for up to 69, while the final Viscount development was the 810 with more powerful engines and higher weights.

Photo: A Viscount 800 in South Africa. (Keith Gaskell)

Victa Airtourer

Country of origin: Australia

Type: Two seat light aircraft

Powerplant: 115 – One 85kW (115hp) Lycoming O-235 flat four piston engine driving a two blade fixed pitch propeller. T4 – One 110kW (150hp) Lycoming O-320.

Performance: 115 – Max speed 228km/h (123kt), max cruising speed 210km/h (113kt), long range cruising speed 177km/h (96kt). Initial rate of climb 900ft/min. Service ceiling 14,000ft. Max range with no reserves 1140km (617nm). T4 – Max speed 241km/h (130kt), max cruising speed 225km/h (122kt), long range cruising speed 198km/h (107kt). Initial rate of climb 1100ft/min. Service ceiling 15,500ft. Max range with no reserves 1005km (543nm).

Weights: 115 – Empty 490kg (1080lb), max takeoff 750kg (1650lb). T4 – Empty 528kg (1165lb), max takeoff 793kg (1750lb).

Dimensions: Wing span 7.92m (26ft 0in), length 6.55m (21ft 6in), height 2.13m (7ft 0in). Wing area 11.2m² (120sq ft).

Capacity: Seating for two, side by side.

Production: 170 Victa built 100s and 115s, AESL production of 94.

History: The popular Airtourer was designed by Australian Dr Henry Millicer (chief aerodynamicist of Australia's Government Aircraft Factory) in response to a Royal Aero Club (in the UK) sponsored Light Aircraft Design competition.

Millicer's design won the competition, and the Ultra Light Aircraft Association of Australia formed the Air Tourer Group to build a 50kW (65hp) Continental powered wooden prototype, which first flew on March 31 1959.

The wooden prototype aroused the interest of Victa (an Australian company more known for its lawnmowers), who in 1960 decided to develop the design and produce it as the Airtourer. Victa's first all metal prototype of the Airtourer was powered by a 75kW (100hp) Continental, and first flew on December 12 1961. The first production Airtourer 100 flew in June 1962, and type approval was awarded the following month. The more powerful Airtourer 115 flew for the first time in September 1962.

Victa built 170 production Airtourers before its inability to compete against cheap American imports (which were aided by a favourable exchange rate) which were swamping the Australian market forced production to end. Plans to build the four seat Aircruiser development were dropped.

However New Zealand's AESL (Aero Engine Services Ltd) purchased the Airtourer design and production rights in early 1967. AESL (later NZAI and now PAC) built the Airtourer 115, the more powerful 110kW (150hp) model Airtourer 150, and constant speed prop fitted Super 150. Later the 115 became the T2, the 150 the T4 and the Super 150 the T5. The T3 was powered by a 95kW (130hp) RR Continental O-240, while the T6 was a militarised version based on the T5 built for New Zealand. NZAI production ceased in 1974.

In December 1997 Australia's Millicer Aircraft Industries purchased the Airtourer's production rights and it planned to deliver new build M10-140 and M10-160 AirTourers from 1999. However the venture was wound up in 2000.

Photo: A Victa Airtourer 115. (Craig Murray)

VulcanAir (Partenavia) P.68

Country of origin: Italy

Type: Six/seven seat light twin

Powerplants: P.68B – Two 150kW (200hp) Lycoming IO-360-A1B fuel injected flat four piston engines driving two blade constant speed propellers. P.68TC – Two 155kW (210hp) turbocharged Textron Lycoming TIO-360-C1A6Ds.

Performance: P.68B – Max speed 322km/h (174kt), max cruising speed 306km/h (165kt), economical cruising speed 295km/h (160kt). Initial rate of climb 1600ft/min. Service ceiling 20,000ft. Range at economical cruising speed 1700km (920nm). P.68TC – Max speed 352km/h (190kt), max cruising speed 324km/h (175kt), economical cruising speed 278km/h (150kt). Initial rate of climb 1550ft/min. Service ceiling 27,000ft. Range with max payload 555km (300nm), range with max fuel 1924km (1040nm).

Weights: P.68B – Empty 1200kg (2645lb), max takeoff 1960kg (4321lb). P.68TC – Empty equipped 1300kg (2866lb), max takeoff 1990kg (4387lb).

Dimensions: P.68B – Wing span 12.00m (39ft 5in), length 9.35m (30ft 8in), height 3.40m (11ft 2in). Wing area 18.6m² (200.0sq ft). P.68TC – Same except for length 9.55m (31ft 4in).

Capacity: Standard seating arrangement for seven, comprising one pilot and six passengers, or two pilots and five passengers.

Production: 403 P.68s through to 1994, incl 13 preproduction P.68As and 150 P.68B Victors. VulcanAir production began in 1998.

History: Partenavia designed the P.68 as an efficient multirole twin capable of performing a number of utility roles.

The P.68 Victor first flew on May 25 1970 and it soon demonstrated performance similar to that of aircraft in its class (such as the Seneca) which had retractable undercarriage. The high wing design also incorporated a large degree of glass fibre reinforced plastic construction in non load bearing areas. Thirteen preproduction P.68As were built between 1971 and 1973 before the improved production standard P.68B, with a longer cabin, increased takeoff weight and redesigned instrument panel, was delivered from 1974. A retractable undercarriage variant, the P.68R, was tested over 1976/77 but did not enter production.

The P.68C replaced the B in 1979 and introduced a longer nose to house weather radar and more avionics, extra fuel, revised cabin interior and redesigned wheel fairings. The turbocharged TC was introduced in 1980 and features two turbocharged 157kW (210hp) TIO-360s. Observer versions of both the P.68B and P.68C have been built, these featuring a clear nose section for improved visibility.

A turboprop development, the AT.68TP-300 Spartacus, first flew in 1978, and led to the larger AP.68TP Viator, which is in Italian government service.

Partenavia ceased production in 1994 following its bankruptcy. The company's assets were purchased by Santo de Fe in 1997 and he renamed the company VulcanAir in 1998. VulcanAir resumed P.68 production in 1998 and deliveries began in November 1999. Models offered are the P.68C and P.68C-TC (both also offered in Observer form).

Photo: A P.68B used for surf patrol. (Glenn Alderton)

VulcanAir VF 600W Mission

Country of origin: Italy

Type: Single turboprop utility transport

Powerplants: One 580kW (777shp) Walter M601F-11 turboprop driving a five blade constant speed Avia V 510 propeller.

Performance: Max cruising speed 342km/h (185kt), long range cruising speed at 65% power approx 258km/h (139kt). Takeoff run over a 50ft obstacle 615m (2020ft). Range at max cruising speed with 11 passengers 1615km (872nm), with max payload 352km (190nm). Range at economical cruising speed with 11 passengers 1688km (911nm), max range at economical cruising speed 1895km (1022nm).

Weights: Max takeoff 3900kg (8598lb).

Dimensions: Wing span 15.50m (50ft 10in), length 13.12m (43ft 1in), height 4.55m (15ft 0in).

Capacity: Standard seating for pilot and 11 passengers. Alternatively can carry six 80 x 120cm (31.5 x 47.2in) pallets. Max payload 1600kg (3525lb).

Production: Deliveries of production aircraft planned for 2005.

History: VulcanAir's new VF 600W Mission single engine turboprop is a development of the SF 600 Cangaru and is aimed squarely at Cessna's very successful Caravan.

The Cangaru (Kangaroo) utility twin was designed by Stelio Frati and first flew on December 30 1978, with the General Avia built F.600 prototype powered by 260kW (350hp) Lycoming TIO-540 piston engines. The SIAI-Marchetti turboprop powered Allison 250 ST 600TP development was certificated in Italy in 1987. However just nine production aircraft were built before SIAI-Marchetti was sold to Aermacchi in 1997 and the Canguro program was transferred to VulcanAir. VulcanAir continues to promote the Cangaru but it has yet to attract serious sales interest.

Naples based VulcanAir launched the VF 600W single development in 1999. Construction of the first prototype began in May 2001, it was rolled out on July 16 2002 and was due to make its first flight before the end of that year. Certification is planned for late 2004, with deliveries following in 2005.

The VF 600W retains the Cangaru's square sided constant section fuselage with a modified wing with improved aerodynamics (particularly new wingtips which will reduce drag). The wings and fuselage are made from aluminium alloy and composites. But the heart of the VF 600W is its Czech Walter M601F turboprop, which is significantly cheaper than the ubiquitous Pratt & Whitney Canada PT6. The M601 (which also powers the Let L 410/420 regional airliner) drives a five blade Avia prop (with shortened blades to reduce noise). Another change is single main undercarriage wheels (instead of twin units on the SF 600). Conventional flight instruments will be standard, with a glass cockpit optional.

VulcanAir says the VF 600W will match the performance of the Caravan, but will sell for significantly less and have 50% lower operating costs.

A more expensive VF 600W with a PT6 could be offered later, as could a floatplane version.

Photo: The VF 600W Mission prototype.

Weatherly 201, 620 & 620TP

Country of origin: United States of America

Type: Agricultural aircraft

Powerplants: 201C – One 335kW (450hp) Pratt & Whitney R-985 nine cylinder radial piston engine driving a two blade constant speed Hartzell propeller. 620 – Same except for a three blade constant speed prop. 620TP – One 375kW (500shp) Pratt & Whitney Canada PT6A-11AG turboprop.

Performance: 201C – Typical cruising speed 170km/h (91kt). Initial rate of climb 960ft/min. 620 – Endurance 2hr 30min. 620TP – Endurance 2hr 0min.

Weights: Empty 1157kg (2550lb), max takeoff restricted category 2177kg (4800lb). 620 – Empty 1270kg (2800lb), max takeoff restricted category 2495kg (5500lb), design takeoff 1815kg (4000lb). 620TP – Empty 1135kg (2500lb), max takeoff restricted category 2450kg (5400lb), design takeoff 1815kg (4000lb).

Dimensions: 201C – Wing span 11.89m (39ft 0in), length 8.29m (27ft 3in), height 2.48m (8ft 2in). Wing area 23.3m^2 (251.5sq ft). 620 & 620TP – Wing span 12.50m (41ft 0in), or 14.33m (47ft 0in) with optional wingtip guide vanes.

Capacity: Pilot only in all models. Hopper capacity in 201C is 1022 litres (270US gal/225Imp gal); hopper capacity in 620 is 1268 litres (335US gal/280Imp gal); hopper capacity in 620TP is 1287 litres (340US gal/283Imp gal).

Production: Weatherlys in production between 1967 and 1982. The three model types were built in relatively small numbers (including more than 100 Model 201s).

History: The Weatherly 201 and 620 agricultural aircraft were built in relatively small numbers between the late 1960s and early 1980s.

The Weatherly 201 and its successors date back to the Weatherly WM-62C agricultural aircraft built between January 1961 and late 1965 (19 were made). The WM-62s were conversions of the basic Fairchild M-62 airframe, fitted with a chemical hopper, spray booms and either a Wright W670 or Pratt & Whitney R-985 radial engine.

Weatherly used its experience in designing and converting the WM-62s in developing its own agricultural aircraft design. The resulting Model 201 was a larger and of conventional ag aircraft configuration, with a low wing, a Pratt & Whitney R-985 radial, integral chemical hopper and spray booms and an enclosed cockpit for the pilot. The initial production 201 was certificated in 1967, the improved 201C was granted its type certificate in 1975. A unique feature was the use of wingtip vanes which were developed to increase the effective swath width, while reducing the amount of chemicals lost from the spraying swath (they could be folded back beneath the wings for hangar storage).

The Model 620 replaced the 201C in production from 1980. The 620 featured a longer span wing with optional wingtip vanes and a larger chemical hopper, but the same R-985 engine.

The Pratt & Whitney Canada PT6A-11AG turboprop powered 620TP joined the 620 in production in 1980, and featured a longer nose and a slightly larger chemical hopper. Production of the 620 and 620TP ceased in 1982.

Photo: A Weatherly 620B fitted with the wingtip vanes. (Bill Lines)

Xian Y7 & MA-60

Country of origin: China (Ukraine)

Type: Regional airliners and freighters

Powerplants: Y7-100 – Two 2080kW (2790shp) Wongan WJ5A I turboprops. MA-60 – Two 2050kW (2750shp) Pratt & Whitney Canada PW127J turboshafts driving four blade Hamilton Standard props.

Performance: Y7-100 – Max cruising speed 476km/h (257kt). Range with 52 pax 910km (491nm). MA-60 – Max cruising speed at 18,000ft 450km/h (243kt). Max operating altitude 25,000ft. Range at 20,000ft with max payload 1600km (864nm), range with max fuel 2450km (1322nm).

Weights: Y7-100 – Operating empty 14,900kg (32,850lb), max takeoff 21,800kg (48,060lb). MA-60 – Operating empty 13,700kg (30,203lb), max takeoff 21,800kg (48,060lb).

Dimensions: Y7-100 – Wing span 29.64m (97ft 3in), length 23.71m (77ft 10in), height 8.55m (28ft 1in). Wing area 75.0m^2 (807sq ft). MA-60 – Wing span 29.20m (95ft 10in), length 24.71m (81ft 1in), height 8.85m (29ft 1in). Wing area 75.0m^2 (807.1sq ft).

Capacity: Y7-100 – Flightcrew of two pilots and flight engineer, plus optional radio operator. Seating for up to 50 at four abreast. MA-60 – Flightcrew of two pilots and flight engineer. Standard seating for 56 at four abreast and 78cm (31in) pitch.

Production: Over 105 Y7s built. MA-60 entered service in August 2000. Xian hopes to sell over 200.

History: Xian's Y7 is a development of the Antonov An-24 turboprop freighter and airliner. The MA-60 is the ultimate development of the An-24/Y7 line, with western engines and avionics.

China began reverse engineering the An-24 in 1966, with the first of three Y7 prototypes first flying in December 1970. However Chinese certification was not awarded until 1980 and production did not begin until 1984. Compared to the An-24 the Y7 has a slightly wider fuselage and larger wing, plus Chinese Dongan WJ5A engines. Sixteen initial production Y7s were built.

The improved Y7-100, developed with the technical assistance of HAECO in Hong Kong during the 1980s, incorporates a revised passenger interior and flightdeck, wingtip winglets, and an all new 52 seat passenger interior.

The Y7-200A features 2050kW (2750shp) Pratt & Whitney Canada PW127C turboprops and Collins EFIS avionics. If flew in December 1993 and was certificated in 1998, but has been superseded by the MA-60. The Y7-200B has Collins avionics but Chinese engines. The hot and high Y7E flew in 1994. The Y7H and Y7H-500 are military and freighter versions of the An-26, with only three known to be built.

The ultimate development is the stretched, Pratt & Whitney Canada PW127J powered 56 to 60 seat MA-60, which was publicly unveiled at the 2000 Zhuhai Airshow. It features Collins avionics, a new cabin interior and a Honeywell APU.

When the MA-60 made its public debut at the November 2000 Airshow China it had already entered service with Wuhan Airlines. State owned Shenzen Financial Leasing plans to acquire 60.

The MA-40 is a proposed shortened, hot and high version, the MA-MPA a possible maritime patrol variant.

Photo: The Xian MA-60. (Ian Moy)

Yakovlev Yak-18T

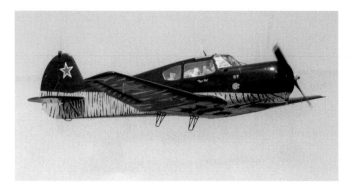

Country of origin: Russia

Type: Four seat light aircraft

Powerplant: One 265kW (355hp) Vedneyev/VOKBM M-14P nine cylinder radial piston engine driving a two blade variable pitch metal prop.

Performance: Max speed 295km/h (159kt), max cruising speed 250km/h (135kt), economical cruising speed 210km/h (113kt). Initial rate of climb 985ft/min. Service ceiling 18,120ft. Range with four people, max fuel and reserves 580km (313nm).

Weights: Empty 1217kg (2683lb), max takeoff (with four people) 1650kg (3637lb).

Dimensions: Wing span 11.16m (36ft 7in), length 8.39m (27ft 7in), height 3.40m (11ft 2in). Wing area 18.8m² (202.4sq ft).

Capacity: Typical seating for four with rear bench seat removable. New production aircraft seat six.

Production: Estimated Yak-18T production of 200. Production initially ceased in 1989, but resumed by the Smolensk Aircraft Factory in 1993 since when approx 80 built.

History: The rugged Yak-18T has its basis in the Yak-18 series of two seat military trainers and was one of the very few four seat light aircraft to be built in the Soviet Union during the Cold War years.

The Yak-18 first flew in 1946 and went on to be built in massive numbers (including more than 8000 for the Soviet air force which used it as its standard military basic trainer for many decades). Most production was of the Yak-18A. Several single seat models were built for competition aerobatics, including the Yak-18P, Yak-18PM and Yak-18PS. Many have since appeared in the west.

The four seat Yak-18T was the last production model, and the most extensively modified. Compared with the single and two seat Yak-18 models, the Yak-18T introduced a much enlarged cabin with seating for four, tricycle undercarriage (single seat Yak-18PMs had tricycle undercarriage also), plus the 265kW (355hp) Vedneyev (now VOKBM) M-14 nine cylinder radial engine.

First flight occurred in mid 1967 and the Yak-18T was then subsequently placed into series production in Smolensk. The Yak-18T went on to become the standard basic trainer with Aeroflot flight schools, while small numbers also entered service with the Soviet air force as liaison and communications aircraft. After approximately 200 were built, mainly for Aeroflot, production ceased in the late 1980s.

In 1993 the Smolensk Aircraft Factory placed the -18T back into production against a number of new contracts, including 20 for the Philippines air force. Several Yak-18Ts have also found their way into the west. Recent improvements include a two piece windscreen, increased fuel capacity and seating for six (with leather seats), improvements originally developed for the Technoavia SM-94 development which would have had further improvements. The small number of SM-94s that were built are basically standard Yak-18Ts.

Compared with western four seat light aircraft, the Yak-18T is much larger, heavier and less economic to operate with a far more powerful engine, although it was never intended for private pilot operation. It has an aerobatic capability, while its handling is described as docile.

Photo: A Yak-18T. (Paul Merritt)

Yakovlev Yak-40

Country of origin: Russia

Type: Regional jet airliner

Powerplants: Yak-40 – Three 14.7kN (3300lb) Ivchenko AI-25 turbofans. Yak-40V – Three 17.2kN (3858lb) AI-25Ts.

Performance: Yak-40 – Max cruising speed 550km/h (297kt), econ cruising speed 470km/h (254kt). Range with max payload of 32 passengers 1450km (780nm), range with max fuel 1800km (970nm).

Weights: Yak-40 – Operating empty 9400kg (20,725lb), max takeoff 16,000kg (35,275lb). Yak-40V – Max takeoff 16,500kg (36,375lb).

Dimensions: Wing span 25.00m (82ft 0in), length 20.36m (66ft 10in), height 6.50m (21ft 4in). Wing area 70.0m² (735.5sq ft).

Capacity: Flightcrew of two. Typical passenger seating arrangement for 27 at three abreast and 78cm (30in) pitch. Max seating for 32 at four abreast. Some fitted with corporate interiors.

Production: Estimated total Yak-40 production is 1000, of which approximately 750 were built for Aeroflot. Approximately 440 in airline service in late 2002. Others used as corporate transports.

History: The Yak-40 was the first jet powered airliner in its class in service in large numbers anywhere in the world, preceding the ERJ 135 and 328JET by three decades.

Design of the Yak-40 resulted from a mid 1960s Aeroflot requirement for a replacement for the thousands of Lisunov Li-2s (Soviet built DC-3s), Ilyushin Il-12s and Il-14s then in service. Aeroflot attached great significance to the Yak-40 program, as the aircraft was intended to operate regional services that accounted for 50% of Aeroflot's passenger traffic.

A S Yakovlev (after whom the design bureau is named) led the Yak-40 design team, and the program's existence was revealed on October 21 1966, when the prototype first flew. The type went into production in 1967 and entered service with Aeroflot in September 1968. Production continued until 1978, with around 1000 built.

The Yak-40's most noticeable design feature is its trijet configuration, with three specially developed Ivchenko AI-25 two shaft turbofans. The three jet engine layout was chosen for increased redundancy (and hence better one engine out performance, allowing good short field performance) – operating economics was a lesser priority. The unswept, high aspect ratio wing is also designed for good field performance. An APU and a ventral airstair in the rear fuselage allow autonomous operation at remote airfields.

The Yak-40 remained basically unchanged during its production life, with the only variant to enter production being the Yak-40V, an export model with a higher max takeoff weight and more powerful engines. In addition a number of developments were proposed, including the 40 seat stretched Yak-40M.

In the early 1980s US company ICX Aviation planned to build the type in the USA with western avionics and three more efficient Garrett TFE731 turbofans. In 1991 the Yak-40TL twin engine conversion was also proposed. The main difference would have been the replacement of the Yak-40's three engines with two Lycoming LF 507s.

The Smolensk plant offers an upgrade which increases fuel capacity, taking range to 2500km (4630nm).

Photo: A Yak-40 of Samara Airlines. (Leonid Faerberg)

Yakovlev Yak-42

Country of origin: Russia

Type: Short range airliner

Powerplants: Three 63.7kN (14,330lb) ZMKB Progress (Lotarev) D-36 turbofans.

Performance: Yak-42 – Max cruising speed 810km/h (437kt), economical cruising speed 750km/h (405kt). Range with max payload and reserves 1380nm (745nm), with 120 passengers 1900km (1025nm), with 104 passengers 2300km (1240nm), with max fuel and 42 passengers 4100km (2215nm). Yak-42D – Range with 120 passengers 2200km (1185nm).

Weights: Yak-42 – Empty equipped with 104 seats 34,500kg (76,058lb), with 120 seats 34,515kg (76,092lb); max takeoff 57,000kg (125,660lb). Yak-42D – Max takeoff 57,500kg (126,765lb).

Dimensions: Wing span 34.88m (114ft 5in), length 36.38m (119ft 4in), height 9.83m (32ft 3in). Wing area 150.0m² (1614.6sq ft).

Capacity: Flightcrew of two pilots, with provision for a flight engineer. High density single class seating for 120 at six abreast. Two class seating for eight at four abreast and 96 economy class at six abreast.

Production: More than 180 built, last delivery 1999. Approx 145 were in commercial service in 2002.

History: The Yak-42 trijet was developed as a replacement for Tupolev's Tu-134 twinjet and Antonov's An-24 turboprop.

The Yak-42 is an all new design, although, like the smaller Yak-40, it features a three engine configuration for increased redundancy and good short field performance. A moderately swept wing was a compromise between the need for good field performance and high speed cruise capabilities. An integral airstair, APU and double main undercarriage are all incorporated into the Yak-42 design for austere airfield operations. The Lotarev turbofan meanwhile was one of the USSR's first true turbofans.

The first of three prototypes flew on March 7 1975. Development flying revealed the need for increased wing sweep back, and the change of wing sweep angle and suspected development problems with the new three shaft turbofans delayed service entry to late 1980.

Most production was of the basic Yak-42. The Yak-42D with increased range was introduced in 1989.

The Yak-42D-100 development had a four screen Honeywell EFIS cockpit and Stage 3 noise level compliance, among other improvements. One was displayed at the 1993 Paris Salon (as the Yak-142). One version that could enter production is the Yak-42A, based on the D but with more fuel, new Russian avionics and some of the improvements developed for the Yak-42D-100.

The Yak-242 was an all new design study with the Yak-42's cross section, two PS-90A turbofans and seating for up to 180.

The Yak-42-200 was announced in 1997, it would feature a 6.03m (19ft 10in) stretch, increasing all economy class seating to 150. Max takeoff weight would be 65,000kg (143,300lb). The Yak-42T is a freighter design study.

At the 2000 Singapore Airshow, Swiss company Airline Partners launched the CityStar 100 which would have featured western avionics and a new interior, both fitted in Switzerland.

Photo: A Russian registered Yak-42. (Tim Dath)

Yakovlev Yak-55 & Yak-54

Country of origin: Russia

Type: Aerobatic aircraft

Powerplants: Yak-55M – One 265kW (355hp) VOKBM M-14P nine cylinder radial piston driving a two blade variable pitch propeller. Yak-54 – Same except three blade prop.

Performance: Yak-55M – Max speed 360km/h (194kt). Initial rate of climb 3050ft/min. Rate of roll 345°/sec. G limits +9/-6. Yak-54 – Never exceed speed 450km/h (243kt). Initial rate of climb 2950ft/min. Rate of roll 345°/sec. Ferry range 700km (377nm). G limits +9/-7.

Weights: Yak-55M – Max takeoff 840kg (1852lb). Yak-54 – Max takeoff 990kg (2182lb).

Dimensions: Yak-55M – Wing span 8.10m (26ft 7in), length 7.00m (23ft 0in), height 2.80m (9ft 2in). Wing area 12.8m² (137.8sq ft). Yak-54 – Wing span 8.16m (26ft 9in), length 6.91m (22ft 8in). Wing area 12.9m² (138.8sq ft).

Capacity: Yak-55M – Pilot only. Yak-54 – Seating for two in tandem.

Production: 120 Yak-55s built for the DOSAAF paramilitary training organisation through to 1991. Over 100 Yak-55Ms built, many exported included to the US. Approx 15 Yak-54s have been built.

History: Yakovlev's Yak-55, Yak-55M and Yak-54 are competition standard aerobatic aircraft, all powered by Russia's ubiquitous M-14 radial piston engine.

The Yak-55 made an unexpected public debut at the 11th World Aerobatics Championships being held in Spitzerberg, Austria in August 1982. At the time it was thought the new Yakovlev was an evolution of the Yak-18/Yak-50 series. However, despite featuring a common powerplant, the Vedneyev (now VOKBM) M-14P radial, the Yak-55 was an all new, smaller aircraft, featuring all metal construction, with a mid mounted wing, seating for the pilot only and tailwheel undercarriage.

However inflight structural failures necessitated a complete redesign of the basic aircraft including a new wing, the Yak-55 appearing in its new form at the 1984 World Aerobatic Championships. Through to 1991 some 120 Yak-55s were built, primarily for the Soviet paramilitary training organisation DOSAAF, four of these were later exported to the United States.

In 1991 production began of the improved Yak-55M, which introduced further improvements. About 60 were believed to be built for DOSAAF, but many of these were subsequently sold, with a number making their way to the US. In all about 100 were built to early 1996, many of which were for export.

The Yak-54 two seater is essentially an all new aircraft compared with the Yak-55M, but again is powered by the M-14P. Like the Yak-55M, the 54's mid mounted wing is symmetrical with no angle of incidence, dihedral or anhedral.

The Yak-54 first flew on December 24 1993, with production beginning at Saratov in 1995, since which time approximately 15 built, with many of these exported to the USA. Two variants of the Yak-54 have been proposed, the retractable undercarriage Yak-56 trainer and the single seat Yak-57.

Photo: Compared with the similar Su-26 series, the Yak-54 features a mid, rather than low, mounted wing. (Sebastian Zacharias)

Zlin Trener & Akrobat

Zlin Z 42, Z 43, Z 142, Z 242 & Z 143

Country of origin: Czech Republic

Type: One and two seat aerobatic and training light aircraft

Powerplant: Z 226 – One 120kW (160hp) Walter Minor 6-III inverted inline six cylinder piston engine driving a two blade fixed pitch propeller. Z 526F – One 135kW (180hp) Avia M 137 A inverted inline six driving a two blade constant speed propeller.

Performance: Z 226 – Max speed 220km/h (120kt), normal cruising speed 195km/h (105kt). Initial rate of climb 950ft/min. Service ceiling 17,390ft. Range 485km (260nm). Z 526F – Max speed 244km/h (132kt), normal cruising speed 210km/h (113kt). Initial rate of climb 1180ft/min. Service ceiling 17,060ft. Range with standard fuel 475km (256nm), range with wingtip tanks 837km (452nm).

Weights: Z 226 – Empty 570kg (1257lb), max takeoff 820kg (1808lb). Z 526F – Empty 665kg (1465lb), max takeoff 975kg (2150lb).

Dimensions: Z 226 – Wing span 10.29m (33ft 9in), length 7.80m (25ft 7in), height 2.06m (6ft 9in). Wing area 14.9m^2 (160.4sq ft). Z 526F – Wing span 10.60m (34ft 9in), length 8.00m (26ft 3in), height 2.06m (6ft 9in). Wing area 15.5m^2 (166.3sq ft).

Capacity: Seating for two in Z 26, Z 126, Z 226, Z 326, Z 526 and Z 726. Pilot only in Z 226A, 326A, 526A, Z 526AF and Z 526AFS.

Production: More than 1400 of all variants built, many against military and government flying school orders.

History: The renowned Zlin two seat Trener trainers and single seat Akrobat aerobatic aircraft were very succesful, winning numerous world aerobatic championship titles during the 1960s.

The original Z 26 Trener was designed in response to a Czechoslovak government requirement for a two seat basic trainer for flying school and military use. The Z 26 was powered by a 78kW (105hp) Walter Minor 4-III inline four cylinder engine, featured wooden construction and fixed, taildragger undercarriage. The prototype first flew in 1947 and 16 production Z 26s were built before it was replaced from 1953 by the metal construction Z 126.

Development over a three decade production run resulted in numerous further improved variants. In 1952 Zlin introduced the Z 226 Trener-6 which featured a more powerful 120kW (160hp) six cylinder Walter Minor 6-III engine. The Z 226 was also built in single seat Z 226A Akrobat, glider tug Z 226B and Z 226T trainer forms.

The similar Z 326 Trener-Master and single seat Z 326A Akrobat introduced retractable undercarriage, a feature that became standard on all subsequent models. Deliveries began in 1959. The Z 526 differed in that the pilot flew the aircraft from the rear, rather than the front seat, with optional tip tanks and a constant speed prop. The Z 526F introduced in 1968 had a 135kW (180hp) Avia M 137A engine. The otherwise similar Z 526L differed in being powered by a 150kW (200hp) Lycoming AIO-360 flat four and was intended for export.

Single seat Z 526s were the Z 526A, Z 526AS, and Z 526AFS.

The Z 526 AFM was built between 1981 and 1984 and was powered by a 155kW (210hp) Avia M337 engine, had tip tanks and the Z 526AFS's lengthened fuselage.

Final development was the Z 726 series, the Z 726 Universal had reduced span wing, the Z 726K a 155kW (210hp) Avia M 337 engine.

Photo: A Z 226 Trener-6. (Sebastian Zacharias)

Country of origin: Czech Republic

Type: Two/four seat light aircraft

Powerplant: Z 43 – One 155kW (210hp) Avia M 337 six cylinder inline inverted piston engine driving a two blade propeller. Z 242 L – One 150kW (200hp) Textron Lycoming AEIO-360-A1B6 flat four driving a three blade c/s prop. Z 143 – One 175kW (235hp) Textron Lycoming O-540-J3A5 flat six driving a three blade variable pitch Mühlbauer prop.

Performance: Z 43 – Max speed 235km/h (127kt), cruising speed 210km/h (113kt). Initial rate of climb 690ft/min. Range with max fuel 1100km (595nm). Z 242 L – Max speed 236km/h (127kt), max cruising speed 214km/h (114kt). Initial rate of climb 1102ft/min. Range with max fuel 1056km (570nm). Z 143 – Max speed 265km/h (143kt), max cruising speed at 75% power 235km/h (127kt), econ cruising speed at 60% power 216km/h (226kt). Initial rate of climb 1457ft/min. Range at 65% power 1335km (720nm).

Weights: Z 43 – Empty 730kg (1609lb), max TO 1350kg (2976lb). Z 242 L – Basic empty 730kg (1609lb), max TO 1090kg (2403lb). Z 143 – Empty equipped 830kg (1830lb), max TO 1350kg (2976lb).

Dimensions: Z 43 – Wing span 9.76m (32ft 0in), length 7.75m (25ft 5in), height 2.91m (9ft 7in). Wing area 14.5m^2 (156.1sq ft). Z 242 L – Wing span 9.34m (30ft 8in), length 6.94m (24ft 9in), height 2.95m (9ft 8in). Z 143 – Wing span 10.14m (33ft 3in), length 7.58m (24ft 11in), height 2.91m (9ft 7in). Wing area 14.8m^2 (159.1sq ft).

Capacity: Seating for two in tandem in Z 42, Z 142 and Z 242, seating for four in Z 43 and Z 143.

Production: Total production includes more than 350 142s, approx 100 Z 242 Ls and 45 Z 143s, including military orders.

History: This series of two seat trainers and four seat light aircraft was initially developed to replacement for the successful Zlin Trener.

The initial Z 42 was developed during the mid 1960s and seats two side by side. It flew for the first time on October 17 1967. The improved Z 42M meanwhile introduced a constant speed propeller and the larger tail developed for the Z 43 four seater, and replaced the Z 42 in production in 1974.

Development of the two seat line continued with the further improved Z 142, which first flew on December 29 1979. Changes included a larger cockpit canopy and faired undercarriage. The Z 142 remained in production in Z 142C form to the mid 1990s. The latest two seater of this family to be developed is the 150kW (200hp) Textron Lycoming AEIO-360 flat four powered Z 242 L. Changes aside from the engine include a three blade constant speed prop and revised engine cowling profile. First flight was on February 14 1990.

Development of the four seat models, the Z 43 and Z 143, has followed that of the two seaters. The Z 43 appeared a year after the Z 42, first flying on December 10 1968. The Z 42 and Z 43 share the same basic airframe, but differ in that the Z 43 features a larger and wider cabin with seating for four, and a more powerful engine.

The current Z 143 L first flew on April 24 1992, and is similar in structure to the Z 242, but has a larger cabin with seating for four and a more powerful Textron Lycoming O-540 flat six.

Photo: A Zlin Z 242 L. (Lance Higgerson)

The 2003/2004 World Airline Guide

A fleet list of every airline in the world operating jet airliners, compiled by Gordon Reid.

ABAKAN AVIA – ABG
Kantegir Hotel, Abakan 662608, Russia.
Il-76x5.

ACES COLOMBIA – VX/AES
Calle 10 Sur, No 50C-75, Medellin, Colombia.
727-200x4, A320-200x8, ATR 42-500x6, ATR 42-300x5, DHC-6-300x5.

ADC AIRLINES – ADK
PMB 21751, Ikeja, Nigeria.
737-200x2.

ADRIA AIRWAYS – JP/ADR
Kuzmiceva 7, SLO-61001 Ljubljana, Slovenia.
A320-200x3, CRJ200x4.

AEGEAN CRONUS AIRLINES – A3/AEE
572 Vouliagmenis Avenue, Athens GR-164 51, Greece.
737-400x3, 737-300x4, RJ100x6, ATR 72-200x3.

AER LINGUS – EI/EIN
PO Box 180, Dublin Airport, County Dublin, Ireland.
A330-300x3, A330-200x3, A321-200x6, A320-200x4, 737-400x5, 737-500x8, 146-300x8, Fokker 50x4.
On order: A320-200x2, A319-100x4.

AER TURAS – ATT
Corballis Park, Dublin Airport, County Dublin, Ireland.
DC-8-63Fx2.

AERIS – SH/AIS
BP 44, F-31702 Blagnac Cedex, France.
767-300x1, 737-300x5.

AERO ASIA INTERNATIONAL – E4/RSO
47-E/1, Block 6, Pechs, Karachi 75400, Pakistan.
Yak-42Dx4, 737-200x1, RomBac 111-500x4.

AEROBRATSK – BRP
Bratsk Airport, Bratsk 665711, Russia.
Tu-154Mx2, Tu-154Bx1, Yak-40x7.

AEROCALIFORNIA – JR/SER
Calle Hidalgo, Esquina con Serdan 316, La Paz 23000, Mexico.
DC-9-30x11, DC-9-10x11.

AEROCARIBE – QA/CBE
Paseo de Montejo 500-B, Merida 97000, Mexico.
DC-9-30x6, FH-227Dx1, J32EPx6.

AERO-CHARTER UKRAINE – DW/UCR
23 Klimenko Street, Kiev 03110, Ukraine.
An-74x1, Yak-40x4.

AERO CONTINENTE CHILE – C7/NTI
Marchant Pereyra 381, Santiago, Chile.
767-200x2, 737-200x2.

AEROFLOT-DON – D9/DNV
Prospekt Sholokhova 272, Rostov-na-Donu 344009, Russia.
Tu-154Mx2, Tu-154Bx8, Tu-134Ax5, An-12x3, Yak-40x1.

AEROFLOT-RUSSIAN AIRLINES – SU/AFL
Sheremetyevo Airport, Moscow 103340, Russia.
777-200x2, 767-300x4, 737-400x10, DC-10-40Fx2, Il-96-300x6, Il-86x16, Il-76TDx12, Il-62Mx9, A310-300x11, Tu-154Mx22, Tu-154Bx1, Tu-134Ax 16.
On order: A320/A319x20

AEROFREIGHT AIRLINES – FRT
Ul. Verkhnyaya Maslovka 20, Moscow 125083. Russia.
Il-62Mx1, Tu-204x1, An-12x7.

AEROKUZBASS – NKZ
Novokuznetsk Airport, Novokuznetsk 654007, Russia.
Tu-154Mx3, Tu-154Bx2, An-24x1.

AEROLINEAS ARGENTINAS – AR/ARG
Bouchard 547, Buenos Aires 1106, Argentina.
747-200x7, 737-200x28, A340-200x4, MD-88x5, MD-83x1.
On order: A340-600x6

AEROLINEAS BALEARES – DF/ABH
C/Moll Vell 1-1, E-07013 Palma de Mallorca, Spain.
717-200x4.

AEROLINEAS INTERNACIONALES – N2/LNT
Blvd Vincente Guerrero 46, Cuernavaca 62270, Mexico.
727-200x6, 727-100x2.

AERO LLOYD – YP/AEF
Lessingstr. 7-9, D-61440 Oberursel, Germany.
A321-200x11, A320-200x8.

AEROLYOzN – 4Q/AEY
BP-138, F-69125 Lyon-Exupery, France.
DC-10-30x3.

AEROMAR-LINEAS AEREAS DOMINICANAS – BQ/ROM
Avenue Winston Churchill 71, Santo Domingo, Dominican Republic.
767-300x1.

AEROMEXICO – AM/AMX
Paseo de la Reforma 445, Mexico City 06500, Mexico.
767-300x1, 767-200x4, 757-200x8, MD-88x10, MD-87x10, MD-83x9, MD-82x12, DC-9-30x15.
On order: 737-700x15.

AEROMEXPRESS – QO/MPX
Avenue Texcoco, Mexico City 15620, Mexico.
727-200Fx1.

AEROPOSTAL – VH/LAV
Torre Polar Oeste, Los Caobos, Caracas 1051, Venezuela.
727-200x5, DC-9-51x12, DC-9-30x7, DC-9-20x3.

AERO RENT – NRO
Kaloshin pereulok 2/24, Moscow 121002, Russia.
Tu-134Ax2.

AEROREPUBLICA – P5/RPB
Carrera 10a No 27-51, Oficina 303, Bogota, Colombia.
MD-81x2, DC-9-30x8.

AEROSTARS – ASE
Domededovo Airport, Moscow 142045, Russia.
Il-76TDx9, An-12x1.

AEROSUR – 5L
Casilla Correo 3104, Santa Cruz de la Sierra, Bolivia.
727-200x2, 727-100x1.

AEROSUCRE – KRE
Eldorado Airport, Bogota, Colombia.
727-200Fx1, 727-100Fx3, 737-200Fx1, Caravellex2.

AEROSVIT AIRLINES – VV/AEW
Bulvar Shevchenko 58A, Kiev 01032, Ukraine.
737-300x1, 737-500x2, 737-200x1.

AEROTRANS – ATG
Taraz Airport, Taraz 484020, Kazakstan.
Tu-154Bx1.

AEROTRANS AIRLINES – 6F/PFO
PO Box 61008, Paphos CY-8130, Cyprus.
Rombac 111-500x2.

AEROUNION – TNO
Questzacoatal 113, Mexico City 06500, Mexico.
A300B4-200Fx1.

AFRICAN AIRLINES INTERNATIONAL – AIK
PO Box 19202, Nairobi, Kenya.
707-320Cx1.

AFRICAN EXPRESS AIRWAYS – AXK
PO Box 19202, Nairobi, Kenya.
727-200x1, DC-9-32x2.

AFRICAN INTERNATIONAL AIRWAYS – AIN
Newton Road, Crawley, West Sussex RH10 2TU, UK.
DC-8-62Fx1, DC-8-54Fx2.

AFRICA ONE – Y2
14 Upper Fitzwillam Street, Dublin 2, Ireland.
DC-10-30x1, DC-9-50x1.

AFRIQIYAH AIRWAYS – 8U/AAW
PO Box 83428, Tripoli, Libya.
737-400x2.

AIGLE AZUR – AAF
46 Place de la Siene, F-94573 Rungis Cedex, France.
737-300x1, 737-200x2.

AIR ADRIATIC – AHR
Riva 8, Rijeka HR-51000, Croatia.
MD-82x1, MD-81x1, Fokker 50x1.

AIR ALGERIE – AH/DAH
BP 130, Dar-El-Beida DZ-16000, Algeria.
767-300x3, 727-200x10, 737-800x7, 737-400x1, 737-600x3, 737-200x14, A310-200x2, L-382Gx2, F27-400Mx7.
On order: 737-600x2

AIR ALM – LM/ALM
Aeropuerto Hato, Curacoa, Netherlands Antilles.
MD-82x3.

An Aerolineas MD-88. (Rob Finlayson)

An Air Europa 737-300. (Rob Finlayson)

AIR ASIA – AK/AXM
SAAS Airport, Suban 47200, Malaysia.
737-300x4.

AIR ATLANTA ICELAND – CC/ABD
PO Box 80, IS-270 Mosfellssbaer, Iceland.
747-300x5, 747-200x10, 747-200Fx2, 747-100x1,
767-200x3.

AIR AUSTRAL – UU/REU
BP-611, F-97472 St Denis Cedex, Reunion.
737-300x2, 737-500x1, ATR 72-200x1.

AIR BALTIC – BT/BTI
Riga Airport, Riga LV-153, Latvia.
RJ70x3, Fokker 50x3.

AIR-BERLIN – AB/BER
Saatwinkler Damm 42-43, D-13627 Berlin, Germany.
737-800x25, 737-400x5.
On order: 737-800x2.

AIRBORNE EXPRESS – GB/ABX
145 Hunter Drive, Wilmington, Ohio 45177, USA.
DC-8-63Fx17, DC-8-62Fx6, DC-8-61Fx11, DC-9-
41Fx29, DC-9-30Fx43, DC-9-15Fx2, 767-200Fx19.

AIR BOSNA – JA/BON
Kasindolska 136, Sarajevo BA-71000, Bosnia-
Herzegovina.
MD-82x1, Yak-42Dx1.
On order: A319-100x2.

AIR BOTNIA – KF/KFB
FIN-05131, Vantaa, Finland.
RJ85x5, Saab 2000x5.

AIR BOTSWANA – BP/BOT
PO Box 92, Gaborone, Botswana.
146-100x1, ATR42-500x3.

AIR BURKINA –2J/VBW
01 BP 1459, Ouagadougou, Burkina Faso.
F28-4000x1, F28-2000x1.

AIR CAIRO – CCE
Export Centre, Cairo International Airport, Cairo,
Egypt.
Tu-204x3, Tu-204Fx3.

AIRCALIN – SB/ACI
8 Rue Frederic-Surleu, Noumea, New Caledonie.
A330-200x1, 737-300x1, DHC-6-300x1.
On order: A330-200x1.

AIR CANADA – AC/ACA
PO Box 14000, Montreal, Quebec H4Y 1H4,
Canada.
747-400x7, 747-200x3, 767-300x33, 767-200x23,
737-200x40, A340-300x11, A330-300x8, A321-
200x12, A320-200x50, A319-100x46, DC-9-32x23,
CRJ100x25.
On order: A340-600x3, A340-500x2, A319-100x2.

AIR CANADA JAZZ – QK/ARN
310 Goudey Drive, Halifax International Airport, Nova
Scotia B2T 1E4, Canada.
146-200x10, F28-1000x27, CRJ200x9, Dash 8-
300x26, Dash 8-100x62, Beech 1900Dx5.

AIR CARAIBES – TX/FWI
Immeuble Caducee, F-97139 Les Abymes,
Guadeloupe.
ERJ 145x2, ATR 72-200x3, ATR 42-500x2, Dornier
228-200x9, Cessna 208Bx6.
On order: Embraer 170x2.

AIR CHINA – CA/CCA
Capital International Airport, 100621 Beijing, China.
747-400x12, 747-200Fx4, 777-200x10, 767-300x4,
767-200x6, 737-800x11, 737-700x2, 737-300x19,
A340-300x3, 146-100x4, Y7-100Cx4.
On order: 737-700x4, A318-100x8.

AIR CONTRACTORS – AG/ABR
The Plaza, New Street, Swords, County Dublin, Ireland.
A300B4-200Fx5, A300B4-100Fx3, 727-200Fx6,
L-382Gx2.

AIR CORDIAL – ORC
Broadfreight Terminal Bldg, Manchester Airport M90
5PZ, UK.
A300B4-200x2.

AIR DO – HD/ADO
Oak Sapporo Bldg, Chuo-ku, Sapporo, Hokkaido
060-0001, Japan.
767-300x2.

AIR DOLOMITI – EN/DLA
Via A.Tambarin 36, I-34077 Ronchi dei Legionari, Italy.
CRJ200x5, ATR 72-500x6, ATR 42-500x10.
On order: CRJ200x1, ATR 72-500x2.

AIR EUROPA – UX/AEA
Apartado Correos PO Box 132, Poligono Son
Noguera, E-07620 Baleares, Spain.
767-300x3, 757-200x6, 737-800x14, 737-400x5,
737-300x3.

AIR EUROPE – PE/AEL
Via Carlo Noe'3, I-21013 Gallarate, Italy.
777-200x2, 767-300x1.

AIR FRANCE – AF/AFR
45 rue de Paris, F95747 Roisey-CDG, France.
747-400x13, 747-400Fx3, 747-300x2, 747-200x12,
747-200Fx11, 777-200x25, 767-300x5, 737-300x9,
737-500x27, A340-300x22, A330-200x8, A310-
300x2, A321-200x12, A321-100x5, A320-200x50,
A320-100x13, A319-100x39, Concordex5.
On order: A380-800x10, A330-300x6, A330-200x4,
A321-200x4, A319-100x2, A318-100x14, 747-
400Fx2, 777-300ERx10, 777-300x3.

AIRFREIGHT EXPRESS – AFX
611 Sipson Road, West Drayton, Middlesex UB7
OJD, UK.
747-200Fx2.

AIR GABON –GN/AGN
BP 2206, Libreville, Gabon.

747-200x1, 767-200x1, 727-200x1, 737-400x1,
737-300x1, 737-200x2, F28-2000x2.

AIR GEMINI – GLL
Avenida 4 de Fevereiro 32, Luanda, Angola.
727-100Fx5.

AIR GREAT WALL – CGW
32 Nanliu Road, Taigucheng, 315040 Ningbo, China.
737-200x3.

AIR GREENLAND – GL/GRL
PO Box 1012, DK-3900 Nuuk, Greenland.
757-200x1, Dash 7-100x6, DHC-6-300x2, S-61Nx3.

AIR GUINEE – GIB
BP 12, Conakry, Guinea.
737-200x1, Y7-100x1, Dash 7-100x1.

AIR HOLLAND – HLN
PO Box 75116, NL-1117 Schipol, Netherlands.
757-200x2.

AIR HONG KONG – LD/AHK
Unit 3601-08, Tower 1, Millenium City, 338 Kwun
Tong Road, Kowloon, Hong Kong.
747-200Fx3.

AIR INDIA – AI/AIC
Air-India Bldg, Nariman Point, Mumbai 400021, India.
747-400x6, 747-300x2, 747-200x4, A300B4-200x3,
A310-300x10.

AIR IVOIRE – VU/VUN
BP 7782, Abidjan 01, Ivory Coast.
F28-4000x3.

AIR JAMAICA – JM/AJM
Norman Manley International Airport, Kingston,
Jamaica.
A340-300x3, A310-300x4, A321-200x3, A320-200x10,
MD-83x2.

AIR JET – V6/AIJ
BP 10297, F-95700 Roissy CDG, France.
146-200QCx2, Saab 2000x1.

AIR KAZAKSTAN – 9Y/KZK
14 Ogareva Str, Almaty 480079, Kazakstan.
Il-86x6, Il-76TDx3, A310-300x2, 767-200x1,
737-200x5, Tu-154Mx2, Tu-154Bx7, Tu-134Ax2,
Yak-42Dx1, An-24x24.

AIR KHARKOV – KHV
Ul. Sumskaya 104, Kharkov 310031, Ukraine.
Tu-134Ax9, An-26x3.

AIR KORYO – JS/KOR
Sunan District, Pyongyang, North Korea.
Il-76MDx3, Il-62Mx4, Il-18x2, Tu-154Bx4, Tu-
134Bx2, An-24x5.

AIR LEONE – RLL
8 Walpole Street, Freetown, Sierra Leone.
Il-76TDx2, DC-9-32x3, BAC 111-500x3.

AIR LIB – IJ/LIB
BP 854, F-94551 Orly Airport, France.
A340-300x4, DC-10-30x11, MD-83x14, MD-82x4.

AIRLINES 400 – VAZ
Vnokuva Airport, Moscow 103027, Russia.
Il-76TDx2, Tu-154Mx3.

AIRLINK ZIMBABWE – FEM
PO Box 5687, Harare, Zimbabwe.
ERJ 135x1, J41x1.

AIR LITTORAL – FU/LIT
417 rue Samuel Morse, F-34961 Montpellier,
France.
Fokker 100x1, Fokker 70x5, CRJ100x17, ATR
42-500x13.

AIR LUXOR – LK/LXR
Luxor Plaza, Avenue da Republica 101, P-1050-190,
Lisbon, Portugal.
L-1011-500x2, A320-200x5.

AIR MACAU – NX/AMU
PO Box 1810, Macau.
A321-200x1, A321-100x4, A320-200x3, A319-100x2.
On order: A319-100x3.

AIR MADAGASCAR – MD/MDG
BP 437, Antananarivo 101, Madagascar.
767-300x1, 737-300x1, 737-200x2, ATR 42-300x3, DHC-6-300x3.

AIR MALAWI – QM/AML
PO Box 84, Blantyre, Malawi.
737-300x1, ATR 42-300x1.

AIR MALTA – KM/AMC
Luqa LQA 05, Malta.
A320-200x4, 737-300x7, 737-200x2.
On order: A320-200x5, A319-100x7.

AIRMARK INDONESIA
Halim Airport, Jakarta 13610, Indonesia.
737-200x1.

AIR MAURITANIE – MR/MRT
BP 41, Nouakchott 174, Mauritania.
737-200x1, Fokker F28-4000x2.

AIR MAURITIUS – MK/MAU
5 President John Kennedy St, Port Louis, Mauritius.
A340-300x5, A319-100x2, 767-200x2, ATR 72-500x1, ATR 42-500x2, ATR 42-300x1.

AIR MEDITERRANEE – BIE
Tarbes Airport, F-65290 Juillan, France.
737-500x1, 737-200x5, 737-200Fx2.

AIR MEMPHIS – MHS
4 Ahmed Lofty Street, Heliopolos, Egypt.
707-320Cx3, DC-9-30x1.

AIR MOLDOVA – 9U/MLD
Chisinau Airport, MD-2026 Chisinau, Moldova.
Tu-134Ax8, An-26x1, An-24x5, ERJ 145x1, EMB-120ERx1, Yak-40x1.

AIR MOLDOVA INTERNATIONAL – RM/MLV
Chisinau Airport, MD-2026 Chisinau, Moldova.
Yak-42Dx2, ERJ 145x2.

AIR NACOIA – ANL
Rua Comandante Che Guevara, Luanda, Angola.
707-320Cx1, 727-200Fx1.

AIR NAMIBIA-NATIONAL AIRLINES OF THE REPUBLIC – SW/NMB
PO Box 731, Windhoek 9000, Namibia.
747-400x1, 737-200x1, F28-3000x2, CN-235x2.

AIR NAURU – ON/RON
PO Box 40, Yaren District, Nauru.
737-400x1.

AIR NEW ZEALAND – NZ/ANZ
Private Bag 92007, Auckland 1020, New Zealand.
747-400x8, 767-300x9, 767-200x4, 737-300x15.
On order: A320-200x15.

AIR NIPPON – EL/ANK
3-5-10 Hanedakuko, Ota-ku, Tokyo 100-0013, Japan.
737-400x2, 737-500x24, YS-11x6, Dash 8-300x4, DHC-6-300x2.

AIR NIUGINI – PX/ANG
PO Box 7186, Boroko, Papua New Guinea.
767-300x1, F28-4000x6, F28-1000x3, Dash 8-200x1.

AIR NOSTRUM – YW/ANS
Calle Francisco Valldecabres 31, E-46940 Valencia, Spain.
CRJ200x16, ATR 72-500x5, Fokker 50x18, Dash 8-300x15
On order: CRJ200x5, Dash 8-300x13.

AIR ONE – AP/ADH
Via Sardegna 14, I-00187 Rome, Italy.
737-400x12, 737-300x6, 737-200x3.

AIR PACIFIC – FJ/FJI
PO Box 9266, Nadi Airport, Fiji.
747-200x1, 767-300x1, 737-800x2, 737-700x1.
On order: 747-400x2.

AIR PHILIPPINES – 2P/GAP
Andrews Avenue, Pasay City, Metro Manila 1300, Philippines.
737-300x2, 737-200x8.

AIR PLUS COMET – A7/MPD
Edificio Air Plus, Calle Bahia de Pollensa 21-23, E-28042 Madrid, Spain.
A310-300x6.

AIRQUARIUS AIR CHARTER – SSN
PO Box 733, Lanseria 1748, South Africa.
F28-4000x3, BAe 748x2.

AIR SAHARA – S2
28 Barakhamba Road, New Delhi 110001, India.
737-800x2, 737-400x4, 737-700x3, 737-200x1.

AIR SENEGAL INTERNATIONAL – V7/SNG
BP 29127, Dakar, Senegal.
737-700x1, 737-200x1, Dash 8-300x1.

AIR SEYCHELLES – HM/SEY
PO Box 386, Victoria Mahe, Seychelles.
767-300x2, 737-700x1, DHC-6-300x3.

AIR SINAI – 4D/ASD
12 Kasr el Nil Street, Cairo, Egypt.
737-500x1.

AIRSTAN – JSC
Ul. Z Sultana 12, Kazan 420022, Russia.
Il-76TDx3, An-26x1.

AIR TAHITI NUI – TN/THT
BP 1673, F-98713, Papeete, Tahiti.
A340-300x2, A340-200x1.
On order: A340-300x3.

AIR TANZANIA – TC/ATC
PO Box 543, Dar-es-Salaam, Tanzania.
737-300x1, 737-200x2, F27-600x1, Dornier 228-200x1.

AIR TOGO – YT/TGA
BP 20393, Lome, Togo.
A300B4-100x1.

AIRTRAN AIRWAYS – FL/TRS
9955 Airtran Boulevard, Orlando, Florida 32827-5330, USA.
717-200x40, DC-9-32x31, 737-200x2.
On order: 717-200x42.

AIR TRANSAT – TS/TSC
11600 Cargo Road, Mirabel International Airport, Quebec J7N 1G9, Canada.
A330-300x1, A330-200x3, A310-300x6, L-1011-500x6, L-1011-100x5, 757-200x4.

AIR TRANSPORT INTERNATIONAL – 8C/ATN
2800 Cantrell Rd, Little Rock, Arkansas 72202, USA.
DC-8-71Fx11, DC-8-63Fx3, DC-8-62Fx5.

AIR UKRAINE – 6U/UKR
Prospekt Peremogy 14, Kiev 252135, Ukraine.
Il-62Mx3, Tu-154Mx2, Tu-154Bx7, Tu-134Ax5.

AIR UNIVERSAL
PO Box 19151, Amman, Jordan.
L-1011-250x1, L-1011-100x1.

AIR VALLEE – DO/RVL
Localita Airport, I-11020, Saint-Christophe, Italy.
328JETx3.

AIR VANUATU – NF/AVN
PO Box 148, Port Vila, Vanuatu.
737-300x1.

AIR WISCONSIN – ZW/AWI
6390 W Challenger Drive, Appleton, Wisconsin 54914-9120, USA.
146-300x5, 146-200x12, 146-100x1, CRJ200x39, Dornier 328x20.
On order: CRJ200x21.

AIRWORK (NZ) – PST
PO Box 72516, Papakura 1733, New Zealand.
737-200Cx1, F27-500x3, Metro 23x2, Metro IIIx4.

AIRWORLD – SPZ
PO Box 4970, Kempton Park 1620, South Africa.
727-200Fx2, BAe 748x1.

AIRZENA GEORGIAN AIRLINES – A9/TGZ
40 Shartava Street, Tbilisi 380060, Georgia.
737-500x2.

AIR ZIMBABWE – UM/AZW
PO Box AP1, Harare Airport, Zimbabwe.
767-200x2, 737-300x3, 146-200x1.

AIR 2000 – DP/AMM
Jetset House, Church Road, Crawley, West Sussex RH11 0PQ, UK.
767-300x3, 757-200x16, A321-200x6, A320-200x6.
On order: 757-200x4.

AJT AIR INTERNATIONAL – E9/TRJ
Ul. Saidovaya-Kudrinskaya 25, Moscow 103001, Russia.
Il-86x4, Tu-154Mx1.

ALANIA – OST
Beslan Airport, Vladikavkaz 363028, Russia.
Tu-134Ax3.

ALASKA AIRLINES – AS/ASA
PO Box 68900, Seattle, Washington 98168, USA.
737-900x11, 737-400x40, 737-700x17, 737-200x9, MD-83x28, MD-82x4.
On order: 737-700x2.

ALBANIAN AIRLINES – LV/LBC
Rruga-Mine Peza 2, Tirana, Albania.
Tu-134Ax1, 146-200x1.

ALBARKA AIR SERVICES – NBK
8 Udu Street, Abuja, Nigeria.
727-200x1, BAC 111-500x3, BAC 111-400x1, BAe 748x1.

Aircalin took delivery of its first A330-200 in December 2002. (Airbus)

ALFA AIRLINES – H7/LFA
Fatih Cad 21, Gunesli-Istanbul TR-34540, Turkey.
A300-600Rx3, A300B4-100x1.

ALISEA AIRLINES
Reykjavik Airport, Reykjavik, Iceland
737-300x1.

ALITALIA EXPRESS – XM/SMX
Centro Direzionale, I-00148, Rome, Italy.
ERJ 145x8, ATR 72-200x7, ATR 42-300x6.

ALITALIA – AZ/AZA
Centro Direzionale, I-00148, Rome, Italy.
747-200x7, 777-200x4, 767-300x11, MD-11x8,
MD-82x89, A321-100x23, A320-200x6.
On order: 777-200x2, A319-100x12.

ALL CANADA EXPRESS – CNX
50 Burnhamthorpe Road West, Mississauga, Ontario
L5B 3C2, Canada.
727-200Fx10, 727-100Fx1.

ALL NIPPON AIRWAYS – NH/ANA
3-5-10 Hanedakuko, Tokyo 144-0041, Japan.
747-400x23, 747-200x2, 747-100SRx9, 777-300x5,
777-200x19, 767-300x51, 767-200x10, A321-
100x7, A320-200x25.
On order: 777-300ERx6, 777-300x10, 767-300x9,
A320-200x3.

ALLEGIANT AIR – G4/AAY
4955 East Anderson, Fresno, California 93727, USA.
MD-87x2, DC-9-20x1.

ALLEGRO AIR – LL/GRO
Avenida Cuba, Cancun 77500, Mexico.
727-200x8, MD-83x2.

ALLIANCE AIR – CD/LLR
IGI Airport, New Delhi 110037, India.
737-200x11.

ALLIANCE AIRLINES - QQ
PO Box 1126, Eagle Farm, Qld 4009, Australia.
Fokker 100x2, EMB-120ERx2.
On order: Fokker 100x2.

ALLIANCE AVIA – NZP
Glinihchevsky pereulok 3, Moscow 103808, Russia.
Tu-134Ax1, An-74x3.

ALOHA AIRLINES – AQ/AAH
PO Box 30028, Honolulu, Hawaii 96820-0028, USA.
737-700x7, 737-200x18.

ALPI EAGLES – E8/ELG
Via Mattei i/c, I-30020, Marcon, Italy.
Fokker 100x8.

ALROSA – DRU
Mirny Airport, Mirny 678170, Russia.
Il-76TDx4, Tu-154Mx4, Tu-134Bx2, An-26x4,
An-24x9, An-38x2.

ALROSA-AVIA – LRO
Zhukovsky Airport, Moscow 140160, Russia.
Tu-134Ax2.

AMC AVIATION – AMV
5 El Nasr Street, El Nozha El Guedida, Cairo, Egypt.
A300B4-200x1, MD-90x1, 737-200x1.

AMERICA WEST AIRLINES – HP/AWE
4000 East Sky Harbor Blvd, Phoenix, Arizona 85034,
USA.
757-200x13, 737-300x39, 737-200x12, A320-
200x49, A319-100x33,
On order: A320-200x5, A318-100x15.

AMERICAN AIRLINES – AA/AAL
PO Box 619616, DFW International Airport, Texas
75261-9616, USA.
777-200x43, 767-300x57, 767-200x21, 757-200x150,
727-200x42, 737-800x77, MD-11x3, DC-10-30x2,
DC-10-10x8, MD-83x33, MD-82x228, A300-600x33,
Fokker 100x74.

On order: 777-200x4, 767-300x9, 737-800x41.

AMERICAN EAGLE AIRLINES – MQ/EGF
PO Box 612527, DFW International Airport, Texas
75261-2527, USA.
CRJ700x9, ERJ 145x56, ERJ 140x50, ERJ 135x40,
ATR 72-500x12, ATR 72-200x30, ATR 42-300x28,
Saab 340Bx101.
On order: CRJ700x16, ERJ 140x90.

AMERICAN FALCON – WK/AFB
Avenida Santa Fe 1730, Bueno Aires 1060, Argentina.
737-200x2, F28-1000x1.

AMERIJET INTERNATIONAL – M6/AJT
2800 St Andrews Avenue, Ft Lauderdale, Florida
33316, USA.
727-200Fx6.

AMERISTAR AIR CARGO – AJI
PO Box 700548, Dallas, Texas 75370-0548, USA.
737-200Fx2.

ANATOLIA – NTL
Florya Caddesi, Florya-Istanbul TR-34810, Turkey.
A300B4-200x2, 737-400x2.

ANGOLA AIR CHARTER – AGO
CP 3010, Luanda, Angola.
Il-76Tx3, 727-100Fx3, 737-200x1.

ANTINEA AIRLINES – HO/DJA
33 Blvd. Said Hamdine, Algiers DZ-16000, Algeria.
737-200x1.

ANTONOV AIRLINES – ADB
Ul. Tupoleva 1, Kiev 252062, Ukraine.
An-225x1, An-124x7, An-22x1, An-12x3, An-74x1,
An-32x2, An-26x1.

ARAM AIR – IRW
PO Box 8248, Sharjah, United Arab Emirates.
Il-76TDx3.

ARGENTINA – MJ/LPR
Ave Santa Fe 1970, Buenos Aires 1123, Argentina.
737-700x8, 737-200x6.
On order: 737-700x4.

ARIA AIR – IRX
PO Box 40893, Dubai, United Arab Emirates.
Tu-154Mx2, Yak-40x3.

ARIANA AFGHAN AIRLINES – FG/AFG
PO Box 76, Kabul, Afghanistan.
727-200x1, An-24RVx1.
On order: A310-300x3.

ARKHANGELSK AIRLINES – 5N/AUL
Talagi Airport, Arkhangelsk 163053, Russia.
Tu-154Bx5, Tu-134Ax7, An-26x10, An-24x4.

ARKIA ISRAELI AIRLINES – IZ/AIZ
PO Box 39301, Dov Airport, Tel Aviv 61392, Israel.
757-300x2, 757-200x2, ATR 72-500x4, Dash 7x4.

ARMAVIA – RNV
Machtols Avenue 15, 375002 Yerevan, Armenia.
Tu-134Ax1, A320-200x1.

ARMENIAN AIRLINES – R3/RME
Zvartnots Airport, 375042 Yerevan, Armenia.
Il-86x2, A310-200x2, A320-200x1, Tu-154Bx6,
Tu-134Ax6, An-12x1, An-32x1, An-24x3, Yak-40x4.

ASA-AFRICAN SAFARI AIRWAYS – QSC
PO Box 81443, Mombasa, Kenya.
A310-300x1.

ASA-ATLANTIC SOUTHEAST AIRLINES – EV/CAA
100 Hartsfield Central Parkway, Altanta, Georgia
30354-1356, USA.
CRJ700x17, CRJ200x79, CRJ100x3, ATR 72-
200x19,
Embraer EMB-120x43.
On order: CRJ700x13, CRJ200x3.

ASERCA AIRLINES – R7/OCA
Avda Bolivar Norte, Valencia, Venezuela.
737-200x3, DC-9-30x10, DC-9-15x2.

ASIANA AIRLINES – OZ/AAR
47 Ose-Dong, Seoul, South Korea.
747-400x8, 747-400Fx5, 777-200x4, 767-300x14,
737-400x22, 737-500x3, A321-200x9, A321-100x2.
On order: 747-400Fx2, 777-300x1, 777-200x5,
A330-300x3, A330-200x3, A321-200x6.

ASTAIR – SUW
2-01 Smolensky pereulok ʃ, Moscow 121099, Russia.
Yak-42x3.

ASTRAKHAN AIRLINES – OB/ASZ
Narimanova Airport, Astrakhan 414023, Russia.
Tu-134Ax5, An-24x3.

ASTRAEUS
London Gatwick Airport, UK
737-700x1.

ATA-AMERICAN TRANSAIR – TZ/AMT
PO Box 51609, Indianapolis, Indiana 46251-0609,
USA.
L-1011-500x5, L-1011-100x3, L-1011-50x10,
757-300x10, 757-200x16, 727-200x19, 737-800x31.
On order: 757-300x2, 737-800x9.

ATI AIRCOMPANY – TII
Ul. Yanvarskogo vosstania 17/2, Kiev 252015,
Ukraine.
Il-76x11, An-26Bx1.

ATLANT-HUNGARY AIRLINES – ATU
Visegrad 18/b, H-1132, Budapest, Hungary.
Il-76x3.

ATLANT-SOYUZ AIRLINES – 3G/AYZ
Ul. Novy Arbat 11/1, Moscow 121019, Russia.
Il-96-300x1, Il-86x2, Il-76TDx17.

ATLANTIC AIRWAYS – RC/FLI
Vagar Airport, FO-380 Soervagur, Faroe Islands.
146-200x2.

ATLANTIC COAST AIRLINES – DH/BLR
45200 Business Court, Dulles, Virginia 20166, USA.
CRJ200x71, 328JETx42, J41x31.
On order: CRJ200x25, 328JETx20.

An Aloha 737-700. (Boeing)

ATLAS AIR – 5Y/GTI
2000 Westchester Avenue, Purchase, New York 10577-2543, USA.
747-400Fx16, 747-300Fx3, 747-200Fx22.

ATLAS AIR – IRH
PO Box 19395-6768, Tehran, Iran.
Il-76TDx3.

ATLAS INTERNATIONAL – OGE
Zumrutova Mahallesi Sinanoglu, Antalya, TR-07790, Turkey.
757-200x3.

ATRAN-AVIATRANS CARGO AIRLINES – V8/VAS
Domodedovo Airport, Moscow 142015, Russia.
Il-76x5, An-12x7, An-26x2.

ATRUVERA – AUV
Ul. Basseinaya 33, St Petersburg 196070, Russia.
Il-76TDx5.

ATYRAU AIRWAYS – AAW
PO Box 50, Atyrau Airport, Atyrau 465050, Kazakstan.
Tu-154Bx1, Tu-134Ax4.

AUSTRALIAN AIR EXPRESS – XM/XME
PO Box 1324L, Melbourne, Victoria 3001, Australia.
727-200Fx6, 727-100Fx1, 146-300QTx2, 146-100QCx1, BAe 748x2, Fairchild Expediterx3.

AUSTRALIAN AIRLINES – AO/AUZ
Qantas Centre, 203 Coward Street, Mascot, NSW 2020, Australia.
767-300x4.

AUSTRIAN AIRLINES – OS/AUA
Postfach 50, A-1107 Wien, Austria.
A340-300x2, A340-200x2, A330-200x4, A321-200x3, A321-100x3, A320-200x8, MD-87x4, MD-83x2, MD-82x3, Fokker 70x6.
On order: A320-200x6

AUSTRAL – AU/AUT
Bouchard 547, Bueno Aires 1106, Argentina.
MD-83x2, MD-81x2, DC-9-30x2, 737-200x9.

AVENSA – VE/AVE
Avenue Rio Caura, Caracas 101, Venezuela.
DC-10-30x3, 727-200x3, 727-100x3, 737-200x2.

AVIACOM ZITOTRANS – AZS
Ul. Dobrolyubova 8a, Ekaterinberg 620014, Russia.
Il-76x4.

AVIACSA – 6A/CHP
Hangar 13, Col Aviacion General, Mexico City 15520, Mexico.
727-200x12, 737-200x6, DC-9-15x3.

AVIANCA – AV/AVA
Avenida Eldorado No 93-30, Bogota, Colombia.
767-300x2, 767-200x4, 757-200x5, MD-83x15, Fokker 50x10.

AVIANDINA – SJ
Jorge Chavez International Airport, Lima, Peru.
727-200x3, 737-200x2.

AVIAEKSPRESSKRUIZ – BKS
Leningradsky prospect 37, Moscow 125836, Russia.
Tu-154Mx3, Yak-40x6.

AVIAENERGO – 7U/ERG
Tverskaya-Tamskaya 16/23, Moscow 125047, Russia.
Il-76TDx1, Il-62Mx2, Tu-154Mx2, Tu-134Ax1.

AVIAST – VVA
Ul. Utkina 44, Moscow 105275, Russia.
Il-76x7, An-12x3, Yak-40x1.

AVIASTAR AIRLINES – FUE
Prospekt Leninskogo Komsomola 38, Ulyanovsk 432067, Russia.
Il-76x1, Tu-204x1, An-12x2, An-26x2, Yak-40x3.

AVIATECA GUATEMALA – GU/GUG

Azurra operates RJ85s and RJ70s (pictured) on behalf of Alitalia. (Rob Finlayson)

Avenida Hincapie 12-22, Guatemala City 01013, Guatemala.
737-200x5.

AVIOGENEX – AGX
Vladimira Popovica 8, Belgrade YU-11070, Yugoslavia.
727-200x3, 737-200x1.

AVIOIMPEX – M4/AXX
PO Box 544, Skopje MK-1000, Macedonia.
MD-81x1, DC-9-33x1.

AXIS AIRWAYS – AXY
BP 90, F-13728 Marignac, France.
737-300x1, 737-200x1.

AZAL AZERBAIJAN AIRLINES – J2/AHY
Bina Airport, Baku 370109, Azerbaijan.
757-200x2, 727-200x2, Tu-154Mx4, Tu-154Bx1, Tu-134Ax8,
Yak-40x5.

AZAL CARGO – AHC
Bina Airport, Baku 370109, Azerbaijan.
Il-76x5, An-12x1, An-32x1, An-26x2.

AZTECA AIRLINES – ZE/LCD
Zona de Hangares 27C, Col. Aviacion General, Mexico City 15620, Mexico.
737-700x2, 737-300x2.

AZZA TRANSPORT – AZZ
PO Box 11586, Kartoum, Sudan.
Il-76TDx2, 707-320Cx2, An-12x1, An-26x1, Y8F-100x1, DHC-5x1.

AZOV-AVIA AIRCOMPANY – AZV
Voenny gorodok, Melitopol 332307, Ukraine.
Il-76TDx1.

AZZURRAAIR – ZS/AZI
Via Paleocapa 3D, I-24122, Bergamo, Italy.
737-700x7, RJ85x3, RJ70x4.

BAHAMASAIR – UP/BHS
PO Box N-4881, Nassau, Bahamas.
737-200x2, Dash 8-300x5.

BAIKAL AIRLINES – BKL
Ul. Shiryamova 8, Irkutsk 664009, Russia.
Il-76TDx2, Tu-154Mx4, Tu-154Bx4, An-26x4, An-24RVx8

BALI AIR – BLN
PO Box 2965, Jakarta 10720, Indonesia.
737-200x2, F28-4000x1, BAe 748x4.

BALKAN BULGARIAN AIRLINES – LZ/LAZ
Sofia Airport, Sofia BG-1540, Bulgaria.
Tu-154Mx4, 737-300x2, An-12x4, An-24x3.

BANGKOK AIR – PG/BKP
60 Queen Sirikit, Klongtoey, Bangkok 10110, Thailand.
717-200x2, ATR 72-500x3, ATR 72-200x7.
On order: 717-200x2, ATR 72-500x3.

BASHKIRIAN AIRLINES – V9/BTC
Airport, Ufa 450056, Russia.

Tu-145Mx10, Tu-134Ax3, An-74x3, An-24RVx1.

BATAVIA AIR
Jl. Salam 4, Jakarta 11540, Indonesia.
737-700x2, 737-200x1.

BAX GLOBAL – 8W
1 Aircargo Parkway East, Swanton, Ohio 43558, USA.
DC-8-71Fx11, DC-8-63Fx4, DC-8-62Fx1, 727-200Fx4.

BAYU INDONESIA AIR – BYU
Jalan Bikatamsu 29E, Medan 20151, Indonesia.
737-200x1.

BELAIR AIRLINES – BHP
Postfach 90, CH-8058 Zurich Airport, Switzerland.
757-200x2.

BELAVIA – B2/BRU
Ul.Nemiga 14, 220004 Minsk, Belarus.
Tu-154Mx5, Tu-154Bx4, Tu-134Ax7, An-24x2, Yak-40x3.

BELLVIEW AIRLINES – B3/BLV
PO Box 6571, Marina-Lagos, Nigeria.
737-200x1, DC-9-32x2.

BETA-BRASILIAN EXPRESS – BSI
Guarulhos Airport, CEP-07141-970, Sao Paulo, Brazil.
707-320Cx4.

BIMAN BANGLADESH AIRLINES – BG/BBC
Balaka Bhaban, Dhaka 1229, Bangladesh.
DC-10-30x6, A310-300x4, F28-4000x3, ATPx2.

BLAGOVESHCHENSK AIRLINES
Ul. Gorkogo 175A, Blagoveshchensk 675016, Russia.
Tu-154Mx4, Yak-40x3.

BLUEBIRD CARGO – BF/BBD
PO Box 515, Keflavik Airport IS-232, Iceland
737-300Fx1.

BLUE DART AVIATION
88/89 Old International Terminal, Meenambakkam Airport, Chennai 600027, India.
737-200x3.

BLUE PANORAMA AIRLINES – BV/BPA
Via Corona Boreale 86, I00187, Rome, Italy.
767-300x2, 737-400x4.

BMI BRITISH MIDLAND – BD/BMA
Donington Hall, Castle Donington, Derby DE74 2SB, UK.
A330-200x4, A321-200x11, A320-200x10, 737-400x1, 737-300x5, 737-500x8, Fokker 100x6, Fokker 70x1.
On order: A320-200x2.

BMI REGIONAL – WW/GNT
Aberdeen Airport, Dyce, Aberdeenshire AB21 7EU, UK.
ERJ 145x11, ERJ 135x4.

BOSPHORUS EUROPEAN AIRWAYS
Mehmet Akif Caddeesi 2, Sirinevier-Istanbul TR-34510, Turkey.
A300B4-100x3.

BOTIR-AVIA –B8/BTR

Cathay Pacific's first A340-600 gets airborne. (Airbus)

14 Suyumbaev Street, 720021 Bishkek, Kyrgyzstan.
Il-76x3, Yak-40x1.

BOURAQ INDONESIA AIRLINES – BO/BOU
PO Box 2965, Jakarta 10720, Indonesia.
737-200x6.

BRA-TRANSPORTES AEREOS – BRB
Av. Ipiranga 318, CEP-01046-010 Sao Paulo, Brazil.
737-300x3.

BRAATHENS – BU/BRA
Postboks 55, NO-1330 Fornebu, Norway.
737-400x5, 737-700x13, 737-500x15.

BRIT AIR – DB/BZH
BP 156, F-29204Morlaix, France.
Fokker 100x7, CRJ700x9, CRJ100x20, ATR
72-200x2, ATR 42-300x6.
On order: CRJ700x3.

BRITANNIA AIRWAYS – BY/BAL
Luton Airport, Luton, Bedfordshire LU2 9ND, UK.
767-300x10, 767-200x4, 757-200x19.

BRITANNIA AIRWAYS AB – 6B/BLX
PO Box 611, S-194 26 Upplands-Vasby, Sweden.
737-800x8.

BRITISH AIRWAYS – BA/BAW
PO Box 365, Harmondsworth, Middlesex UB7
0GB, UK.
747-400x57, 747-200x8, 777-200x40, 767-300x21,
757-200x29, 737-400x31, 737-300x11, 737-500x10,
Concordex7, A320-200x15, A320-100x5,
A319-100x34, RJ100x16, ATR 72-200x5.
On order: A321-200x4, A320-200x11, A319-100x5.

BRITISH AIRWAYS CITIEXPRESS – BRY
Worle Parkway, Weston-Super-Mare, Avon BS22
6WA, UK.
ERJ 145x7, Dash 8-300x15.

**BRITISH AIRWAYS CITIEXPRESS (Isle of Man) –
TH/BRT**
Ronaldsway Airport, Ballasalla IM9 2JE, Isle of
Man, UK.
146-300x1, 146-200x3, 146-100x1, ATPx 13,
J41x 13, ERJ 145x23.

BRITISH EUROPEAN – BE/BEE
Exeter Airport, Exeter, Devon EX5 2BD, UK.
146-300x6, 146-200x8, 146-100x2, CRJ200x4,
Dash 8-400x4, Dash 8-300x6, Dash 8-200x3.

BRITISH MEDITERRANEAN AIRWAYS – KJ/LAJ
Cirrus House, Bedfont Lane, Staines, Middlesex
TW19 7NL, UK.
A321-200x2, A320-200x4.

BRUSSELS AIRLINES – SN/DAT
Airport Building 117, B-1820 Melsboek, Belgium.
A330-300x3, RJ100x12, RJ85x14, 146-200x6.

BUKOVYNA – BKV
Ul. Chkalova 30, Chernovtsy 274009, Ukraine.
Tu-134Ax2.

BULGARIAN AIR CHARTER – BUC
Julie Curie Street 20, Sofia BG-1113, Bulgaria.
Tu-154Mx4.

BUZZ – UK
Endeavour House, Stansted Airport, Stansted, Essex
CM24 1RS, UK.
737-300x2, 146-300x8.
On order: 737-600x6.

BWIA-WEST INDIES AIRWAYS – BW/BWA
Administration Bldg, Piarco International Airport,
Trinidad & Tobago.
A340-300x2, L-1011-500x4, 737-800x6, MD-83x3,
Dash 8-300x3.

CAL CARGO AIR LINES – 5C/ICL
11 Galgalei Haplada Street, Herzeliya 46722, Israel.
747-200Fx2.

CAMEROON AIRLINES – UY/UYC
BP 4092, Douala, Cameroon.
737-300x1, 767-300x1, 767-200x1, 757-200x2,
757-200Fx1, 737-200x1, CRJ700x1, CRJ200x1,
CRJ100x1, BAe 748x1.

CANADIAN NORTH – 5T/ANX
300-5201 50th Avenue, Yellowknife, Northern Terri-
tories X1A 3S9, Canada.
737-200x4, F28-1000x3.

CAPITAL CARGO INTL AIRLINES – PT/CCI
6200 Hazeltine National Drive, Orlando, Florida
32822, USA.
727-200Fx12.

CARGOLUX AIRLINES INTERNATIONAL – CV/CLX
Luxembourg Airport, Luxembourg L-2990, GD Luxembourg.
747-400Fx12.

CARGO PLUS AVIATION – 8L/CGP
PO Box 5581, Dubai, United Arab Emirates.
707-320Cx1, DC-8-55Fx2.

CASINO EXPRESS – CXP
976 Mountain City Highway, Elko, Nevada 89801-
2728, USA.
737-200x4.

CASPIAN AIRLINES – CPN
Enghlab Avenue, Kalege Cross, Tehran 15336, Iran.
Tu-154Mx3, Yak-42Dx1.

CATHAY PACIFIC AIRWAYS – CX/CPA
8 Scenic Road, Hong Kong International Airport,
Lantau, Hong Kong.
747-400x20, 747-400Fx5, 747-200Fx4, 777-300x7,
777-200x5, A340-600x1. A340-300x15, A330-
300x20.
On order: A340-600x2, A330-300x3.

CAYMAN AIRWAYS – KX/CAY
PO Box 1101, Georgetown, Grand Cayman, Cayman
Islands.
737-200x3.

CCM AIRLINES – XK/CCM
BP 505, F-20186 Ajaccio, France.
Fokker 100x4, ATR 72-200x2, ATR 72-100x4.

CEBU PACIFIC AIR – 5J/CEB
Pioneer Street, Mandaluyong City, Metro Manila,
Philippines.
757-200x2, DC-9-30x13.

CENTRE-AVIA – J7/CVC
Ul. Sovetskaya 19, Bykova 140150, Russia.
Yak-42Dx7, An-24RVx1.

CENTURION AIR CARGO – WE/CWC
1800 NW 89th Place, Maiami, Florida 33172, USA.
DC-10-40Fx3.

CHABAHAB AIR – IRU
15 Sattari Street, Mirdamad Blvd, Tehran 19689, Iran.
Il-76TDx2.

CHAMPION AIR – MG/CCP
8009 34th Avenue South, Bloomington, Minnesota
55425-1674, USA.
727-200x12.

CHANCHANGI AIRLINES – 3U/NCH
PO Box 679, Kaduna, Nigeria.
727-200x3, BAC 111-500x2.

CHANNEL EXPRESS – LS/EXS
Bournemouth International Airport, Christchurch,
Dorset BH23 6SE, UK.
A300B4-200Fx3, 737-300x6, L-188Fx1, F27-600Fx2,
F27-500Fx6.

CHAUTAUQUA AIRLINES – RP/CHQ
2500 South High School Road, Indianapolis, Indiana
46241-4943, USA.
ERJ 145x38, ERJ 140x10, Saab 340Ax17.
On order: ERJ 145x7, ERJ 140x5, ERJ 135x15.

CHEBOKSARY AIR ENTERPRISE – CBK
Cheboksary Airport, Cheboksary 428021, Russia.
Tu-134Ax4, An-24x3.

CHERNOMOR-AVIA – CMK
Sochi Airport, Sochi 354355, Russia.
Tu-154Bx3, Tu-134Ax3.

CHINA AIRLINES – CI/CAL
131 Nanking East Road, Taipei 104, Taiwan.
747-400x13, 747-400Fx12, 747-200Fx5, 737-
800x11, MD-11x1, A340-300x5, A300-600Rx12,
A300B4-200x4.
On order: 747-400Fx3, 737-800x2, A340-300x2.

CHINA EASTERN AIRLINES – MU/CES
2550 Hongqiao Road, Hongqiao International Airport, 200335 Shanghai, China.
MD-11x3, MD-11Fx3, MD-90x9, MD-82x3, A340-
300x5, A300-600x10, A320-200x20, A319-100x9,
737-700x2, 737-300x7, Y7-100Cx4.
On order: A340-600x5, A320-200x20, A319-100x1,
737-700x2.

CHINA NORTHERN AIRLINES – CJ/CBF
Taoxian International Airport, 110043 Shenyang,
China.
A300-600Rx6, A321-200x4, MD-90x13, MD-82x24,
Y7-100x10
On order: A321-200x6.

CHINA SOUTHERN AIRLINES – CZ/CSN
Baiyun Intl Airport, 510405 Guangzhou, China.
747-400Fx2, 777-200x9, 757-200x18, 737-800x5,
737-300x25, 737-500x12, A320-200x20.
On order: 777-200x1, 737-800x15, A319-100x4.

CHINA SOUTHWEST AIRLINES – SZ/CXN
Shunangliu International Airport, 610202 Chengdu,
China.
A340-300x3, 757-200x13, 737-800x5, 737-600x3,
737-300x15.
On order: Tu-204-100x3, 737-800x1, 737-600x3.

CHINA UNITED AIRLINES – CUA
14 Xisanhuan Naniu, Fengtai District, 100073 Beijing, China.
Il-76x20, Tu-154Mx16, 737-300x8.

CHINA XINHUA AIRLINES – XW/CXH
1 Jingsong Nanlu, Chaoyang District, 100021 Beijing, China.
737-400x3, 737-300x6.

CHINA XINJIANG AIRLINES – XO/CXJ
Diwobao International Airport, 830016, Urumqi, China.
Il-86x3, 757-200x9, 737-700x4, 737-300x2, ATR 72-500x5.

CHINA YUNNAN AIRLINES – 3Q/CYH
Wujiabao Airport, 650200 Kunming, China.
767-300x3, 737-700x4, 737-300x13, CRJ200x8.

CHITAAVIA – CHF
Chita-Kadala Airport, Chita 672018, Russia.
Tu-154Mx2, Tu-154Bx2.

CHROME AIR SERVICES – CHO
PO Box 71898, Victoria Island, Lagos, Nigeria.
BAC 111-500x1, BAC 111-400x1.

CIMBER AIR – QI/CIM
Lufthavnsvej 2, DK-6400 Soenderborg, Denmark.
CRJ200x2, ATR 72-500x3, ATR42-500x3, ATR 42-300x7.

CITYJET – WX/BCY
The Atrium, Level 5, Terminal Building, Dublin Airport, Ireland.
146-200x11.

CIRRUS AIRLINES – C9/RUS
Flughafen, D-66131 Saarbrucken, Germany.
ERJ 145x1, Dash 8-300x1, Dash 8-100x3, Dornier 328-100x2.

CNAC-ZHEJIANG AIRLINES – F6/CAG
No 78 Shiqiao Road, 310004, Hangzhou, China.
A320-200x5, A319-100x3.

COMAIR – MN/CAW
PO Box 7015, Bonaero Park 1622, South Africa.
727-200x4, 737-400x3, 737-200x11.

COMAIR AIRLINES – OH/COM
PO Box 75021, Cincinnati, Ohio 45275, USA.
CRJ-700x8, CRJ200x36, CRJ100x89, EMB-120x19.
On order: CRJ700x19, CRJ200x30.

CONCORS – COS
PO Box 63, Riga LV-1029, Latvia.
Yak-42Dx3, Il-18x1.

CONDOR – DE/CFG
Postfach 1164, D-65440 Kelsterbach, Germany.
767-300x9, 757-300x13, 757-200x16.

CONDOR BERLIN – CIB
Flughafen Schonefeld, D-12521 Berlin, Germany.
A320-200x12.

CONTINENTAL AIRLINES – CO/COA
1600 Smith Street, Houston, Texas 77002, USA.
777-200x18, 767-400x15, 767-200x10, 757-300x11, 757-200x41, 737-900x15, 737-800x92, 737-700x36, 737-300x65, 737-500x66, DC-10-30x20, MD-83x4, MD-82x50, MD-81x3.
On order: 767-400x1, 757-300x4, 737-800x23, 737-700x15.

CONTINENTAL EXPRESS – BTA
PO Box 4607, Houston, Texas 77002, USA.
ERJ145x139, ERJ135x39, EMB120x18, ATR 420-300x31.
On order: ERJ145x82, ERJ135x11.

CONTINENTAL AIRWAYS – PC/PVV
Hotel Complex Sheremetyevo 2, Moscow 103340, Russia.
Il-86x2, Tu-154Mx2.

CONTRACT AIR CARGO – TSU
6860 South Service Drive, Waterford, Michigan 48327-1652, USA.
727-100x1, Convair 5800x3, Convair 580x9.

COPA AIRLINES – CM/CMP
Apartado Postal 1572, Panama 1, Republic of Panama.
737-700x12, 737-200x10.
On order: 737-800x2, 737-700x4.

CORSAIR – SS/CRL
Avenue Charles Lindbergh 2, F-94636 Rungis Cedex, France.
747-300x4, 747-200x2, 747-100x1, 747SPx1, 737-400x2, 737-300x4, A330-200x2.

CRIMEA AIR – OR/CRF
Tsentrainy Airport, Simferopol 333009, Ukraine.
Yak-42x1, An-24x5.

CROATIA AIRLINES – OU/CTN
Savska 41, Zagreb HR-10000, Croatia.
A320-200x3, A319-100x4, BAe 146-200x1, ATR 42-300x3.

CSA CZECH AIRLINES – OK/CSA
Ruzyne Airport, CZ-160 08 Prague 8, Czech Republic.
A310-300x2, 737-400x10, 737-500x10, ATR 72-200x4, ATR 42-300x3, ATR 42-400x2.
On order: 728JETx8.

CUBANA – CU/CUB
Calle 23 No 64, Vedado, Havana 10400, Cuba.
Il-62Mx4, Il-76Fx1, Yak-42Dx4, An-24RVx7, F27-600x2, ATR 42-500x1.

CUSTOM AIR TRANSPORT – CTT
4160 Ravenswood Road, Fort Lauderdale, Florida 33312, USA.
727-200Fx4, 727-100Fx1.

CYGNUS AIR – RGN
Aguetol 7, E-28042 Madrid, Spain.
DC-862Fx2.

CYPRUS AIRWAYS – CY/CYP
PO Box 21903, Nicosia CY-1514, Cyprus.
A330-200x1, A310-200x4, A320-200x10, A319-100x2.
On order: A330-200x1.

DAALLO AIRLINES – D3/DAO
PO Box 21297, Dubai, United Arab Emirates.
Tu-154Mx1, An24x2.

DAGHESTAN AIRLINES – DAG
Makhachkala Airport, Makhachkala 367016, Russia.
Tu-154Mx3, Tu-134Bx2, An-24x2.

DALAVIA – H8/KHB
Khabarovsk Airport, Khabarovsk 680012, Russia.
Il-62Mx10, Tu-214x2, Tu-154Mx1, Tu-154Bx12, An-26x9, An-24x17.

DASAB AIRLINES
Plot 1059, Adekotumbo, Abuja, Nigeria.
727-200x1.

DAS AIR CARGO – WD/DSR
Brighton Road, Crawley, Sussex RH11 9BP, UK.
DC-10-30Fx4, 707-320Cx1.

DELSEY AIRLINES – IV
Luchthavenlei 1/56, B-2100 Deurne, Belgium.
A330-200x3.

DELTA AIRLINES – DL/DAL
PO Box 20707, Atlanta, Georgia 30320, USA.
777-200x8, 767-400x21, 767-300x87, 767-200x15, 757-200x121, 727-200x32, 737-800x71, 737-300x26, 737-200x52, MD-11x15, MD-90x16, MD-88x125.
On order: 777-200x4, 737-800x61.

DEUTSCHE BA – DI BAG
Postfach 23 16 24, D-85325 Munich, Germany.
737-300x16.

DHL AERO EXPRESS – D5/DAE
Apartado Aereo 11491, Panama City 6, Republic of Panama.
727-200Fx3.

DHL AIR – DHK
AMI Cargo West, East Midlands Airport, Derby DE74 2TR, UK.
757-200Fx22.
On order: 757-200Fx6.

DHL AIRWAYS – ER/DHL
PO Box 75122, Cincinnati, Ohio 45275, USA.
A300B4-200Fx6, DC-8-73Fx7, 727-200Fx16, 727-100Fx10.

DINAR – D7/RDN
Carlos Pellegrini 675, Bueno Aires 1009, Argentina.
MD-81x1, DC-9-40x4, DC-9-30x2, 737-200x1.

DNEPR AIR – Z6/UDN
Dnepropetrovsk Airport, Dnepropetrovsk 49042, Ukraine.
Yak-42Dx7, Yak-40x5, An-26x1.

DOBROLET AIRLINES – G2/DOB
Bolshoi Savvinsky pereulok 9, Moscow 121019, Russia.
Il-76Tx4.

DOMODEDOVO AIRLINES – E3/DMO
Domodedovo Airport, Domdedovo 142045, Russia.
Il-96-300x3, Il-76TDx4, Il-62Mx16.

DONBASS AIR LINES – UDD
Donetsk Airport, Donetsk 83021, Ukraine.
Tu-154Mx1.

DONBASS-EASTERN UKRAINE AIRLINES – 7D/UDC
Donetsk Airport, Donetsk 83021, Ukraine.
Yak-42x10, An-24x7.

A China Southwest 757-200. (Rob Finlayson)

Eva Air MD-11F. (Rob Finlayson)

DRAGONAIR – KA/HDA
Dragonair House, 11 Tung Fai Road, Hong Kong International Airport, Lantau, Hong Kong.
747-300Fx3, A330-300x9, A321-200x4, A320-200x8.
On order: A321-200x2, A320-200x3.

DRUK AIR/ROYAL BHUTAN AIRLINES – KB/DRK
Nemizampa, Paro, Bhutan.
146-100x2.

DUTCHBIRD – 5D/DBR
PO Box 75798, NL-1118, Schipol, Netherlands.
757-200x3.

EAS AIRLINES – EXW
PO Box 2051, Ikeja-Lagos, Nigeria.
BAC 111-500x5.

EASTERN AIRWAYS – T3/EZE
Schipol House, Humberside International Airport, Humberside DN39 6YH, UK.
ERJ 135x1, J41x1, J32x9, J31x1.

EASTLINE AIRLINES – P7/ESL
Domodedovo Airport, Domodedovo 142015, Russia.
Il-86x2, Il-76x12, Il-62x1, Tu-154Mx3, Tu-154Bx1, Tu-134Ax1, An-12x1, Yak-42Dx5.

EASYJET AIRLINE –U2/EZY
Easyland, Luton Airport, Bedfordshire Lu2 9LS, UK.
737-700x18, 737-300x41.
On order: 737-700x14, A319-100x125.

EASYJET SWITZERLAND - EZS
Route de l'Aeroport 5, CH-1215 Geneva, Switzerland.
737-300x4.

EAT-EUROPEAN AIR TRANSPORT – QY/BCS
Building 4-5, Brussels National Airport, Zaventem B-1930, Belgium.
A300B4-200Fx9, 757-200Fx6, 727-200Fx9, 727-100Fx4.

ECUATO GUINEANA DE AVIACION – EGA
Apartado 665, Malabo, Qquatorial Guinea.
ERJ 145x1, An-24x1.

EDELWEISS AIR – 8R/EDW
Postfach, CH-8058 Zurich Airport, Switzerland.
A330-200x1, A320-200x3.

EGYPT AIR – MS/MSR
Cairo International Airport, Heliopolis, Egypt.
747-300x2, 777-200x5, 707-320Cx1, 737-500x5, A340-200x3, A300-600Rx7, A300-200Fx2, A321-200x4, A320-200x7
On order: A340-600x2, A318-100x5.

EL AL ISRAEL AIRLINES – LY/ELY
PO Box 41, Ben Gurion International Airport 70100, Israel.
747-400x4, 747-200x4, 747-200Fx3, 777-200x4, 767-200x6, 757-200x6, 737-800x3, 737-700x2.

ELECTRA AIRLINES – ELD
Gounari Street 187, Glyfada GR-166 74, Greece.
DC-10-30Fx1, DC-10-10x2.

ELF AIR – EFR
Zhukovsky Airport, Zhukovsky 140185, Russia.
Il-76x3, Il-18x2, Tu-134Ax1.

EMIRATES – EK/UAE
PO Box 686, Dubai, United Arab Emirates.
A330-200x23, A300-600x1, 777-300x9, 777-200x9
On order: A380-800x20, A380-800Fx2, A340-500x6, A330-200x5, 777-300x3.

ENCOR – H6/ENK
Chelyabinsk Airport, Chelyabinsk 454133, Russia.
Tu-154Mx5, Tu-154Bx1, Tu-134Ax3, Yak-42Dx7.

ESTAFETA CARGA AEREA – E7/ESF
Carretera 57, San Luis Potosi 78430, Mexico.
737-200Fx3.

ESTONIAN AIR – OV/ELL
Lennujaama 13, EE-11101 Tallinn, Estonia.
737-500x2, Fokker 50x2.

ETHIOPIAN AIRLINES – ET/ETH
PO Box 1755, Addis Ababa, Ethiopia.
767-300x3, 767-200x2, 757-200x4, 757-200Fx1, 737-200x2, L-382Gx2, Fokker 50x5, ATR 42-300x2, DHC-6-300x3.

EURALAIR – RN/EUL
Le Bourget Airport, F-93350 Le Bourget, France.
737-800x5.

EURASIA AIR COMPANY – UH/EUS
Ul. D Ulyanova 6, Moscow 117292, Russia.
Il-86x1, Tu-154Bx1, An-12x2, Yak-40x2.

EUROATLANTIC AIRWAYS – MM/MMZ
Rua das Sesmarias 3, Quinta da Beloura, Estrada de Albarraque, P-2710-444 Sintra, Portugal.
L-1011-500x1, 737-300x2.

EUROCYPRIA AIRLINES – UI/ECA
PO Box 40970, Larnaca CY-6308, USA.
A320-200x4.
On order: 737-800x4.

EUROFLY – GJ/EEZ
Via 24 Maggio 6, I-20099 Sesto San Giovanni, Italy.
A330-200x3, A320-200x5, 767-300x1, MD-83x2.

Emirates' growing fleet includes 777s and A330s, with A380s on order. (Paul Merritt)

EUROPE AIRPOST – FPO
BP 10454, F-95708 Charles de Gaulle Airport, France.
A300B4-100Fx3, 737-300Fx15, 737-200Fx3, ATR 72-200Fx4.

EUROPEAN AIR CHARTER – EAC/EAL
European House, Bournemouth International Airport, Dorset BH23 6EA, UK.
747-200x3, 737-200x8.

EUROWINGS – EW/EWG
Flughaffenstrasse 100, D-90411 Nuremberg, Germany.
BAe 146-300x4, BAe 146-200x6, CRJ200x16, CRJ100x2, ATR 72-500x6, ATR 72-200x10, ATR 42-500x10, ATR 42-300Fx2.

EVA AIR – BR/EVA
EVA Air Building, 376 Hsin-nan Road, Luchu, Taoyuan Hsien 338, Taiwan.
747-400x15, 747-400Fx3, 767-300z4, 767-200x4, MD-11x 3, MD-11Fx9, MD-90x1.
On order: 777-300ERx4, 777-200x3, A330-200x8.

EVERGREEN INTERNATIONAL AIRLINES – EZ/EIA
3850 Three Mile Lane, McMinnville, Oregon 97128-9409, USA.
747-200Fx5, 747-100Fx6, DC-9-33Fx5, DC-9-15Fx2.

EXCEL AIRWAYS – JN/XLA
Mitre Court, Crawley, West Sussex RH10 2NJ, UK.
767-200x3, 737-800x8.

EXPRESS AIRLINES – 9E/FLG
1689 Nonconnah Boulevard, Memphis, Tennessee 38132-2111, USA.
CRJ200x40, Saab 340Bx11, Saab 340Ax13.
On order: CRJ200x14.

EXPRESS.NET AIRLINES – XNA
101 Aviation Drive, North Naples, Florida 34104, USA.
A300B4-200Fx9, 727-200Fx1, 727-100Fx2.

EXPRESS ONE INTERNATIONAL – EO/LHN
1420 Viceroy Drive, Dallas, Texas 75235-2008, USA.
727-200Fx19, 727-100Fx2.

FALCON AIR – IH/FCN
PO Box 36, S-230 32 Malmo-Sturup, Sweden.
737-300x3.

FALCON AIR EXPRESS – F2/FAO
9500 NW 41st Street, Miami, Florida 33178, USA.
727-200Fx8.

FAR EASTERN AIR TRANSPORT – EF/FEA
Tun Hwa North Road, FAT Building, Taipei 10592, Taiwan.
757-200x7, DC-9-83x5, DC-9-82x4.

FARNAIR NETHERLANDS – FRN
PO Box 12110, NL-3004 Rotterdam, Netherlands.
A300B4-100Fx3, F27-500Fx6.

FEDEX EXPRESS – FX/FDX
PO Box 727, Memphis, Tennessee 38194-2424, USA.
MD-11Fx42, DC-10-30Fx26, DC-10-10Fx93, A300-600Fx43, A310-300Fx2, A310-200Fx49, 727-200Fx95, 727-100Fx52, F27-600Fx 8, F27-500Fx24, Cessna 208Bx250.
On order: A380-800Fx10.

FINE AIR – FB/FBF
PO Box 523726, Miami, Florida 33152, USA.
L-1011-200Fx4, DC-8-63Fx3, DC-8-62Fx6, DC-8-61Fx2,
DC-8-54Fx5, DC-8-51Fx3.

FINNAIR – AY/FIN
PO Box 15, FIN-01053 Finnair Vantaa, Finland.
MD-11x4, MD-83x10, MD-82x6, DC-9-51x10, A300B4-200x2, A321-200x3, A320-200x7, A319-100x6, ATR 72-200x9, Saab 340A/Bx2.
On order: A320-200x5, A319-100x3.

FIRST AIR – 7F/FAB
3257 Carp Road, Carp, Ontario K0A 1L0, Canada.
727-200Fx4, 727-100x2, 737-200x3, L-382Gx1, Dash 7-100x1, DHC-6-300x5, BAe 748x8, ATR 42-300x4, Beech 99x1.

FIRST INTERNATIONAL AIRWAYS
Airport Terminal, B-8400 Ostend, Belgium.
707-320Cx3.

FISCHER AIR – 8F/FFR
PO Box 15, Ruzyne Airport, Prague 6, Czech Republic.
737-300x3.

FLIGHTLINE – B5/FLT
Viscount House, Southend Airport, Southend-on-Sea, Essex SS2 6YF, UK.
146-300x3, 146-200x7.

FLORIDA WEST INTERNATIONAL AIRWAYS – RF/FWL
PO Box 025752, Miami, Florida 33102-5752, USA.
767-300Fx1, DC-8-71Fx1.

FLY – 4H/FLB
Rua Evaristo da Veiga 47, CEP-20031-040 Rio de Janeiro, Brazil.
727-200x3.

FREEBIRD AIRLINES – FHY
Yesilkoy Caddesi 9-A, Florya-Islanbul TR-34810, Turkey.
MD-83x3.

FREEDOM AIR INTERNATIONAL – FOM
PO Box 109-698 Newmarket, Auckland, New Zealand.
737-300x3.

FREEDOM AIR SERVICES – FFF
3 Dallaji Road, Kaduna, Nigeria.
727-200x2.

FRONTIER AIRLINES – F9/FFT
PO Box 39177, Denver, Colorado 80239, USA.
A319-100x16, 737-300x17, 737-200x7.
On order: A319-100x10, A318-100x6.

FUTURA INTERNATIONAL AIRWAYS – FH/FUA
Gran Via Asima 17, Poligon Son Castello, E-07009 Palma de Mallorca, Spain.
737-800x6, 737-400x7.

GABON EXPRESS – GBE
BP 13893, Libreville, Gabon.
Caravelle 11Rx1, BAe 748 Andoverx2, BAe 748x1.

GALAIRCERVIS – GLS
Ul. Lopatinskogo 85, Grabovets 82400, Ukraine.
Il-76TDx1.

GAMBIA INTERNATIONAL AIRLINES – GC/GNR
Banjul International Airport, PMB, Banjul, Gambia.
F28-3000x1.

GAMBIA NEW MILLENIOUM AIR – NML
State House, Banjul, Gambia.
Il-62Mx1.

GANDALF AIRLINES – G7/GNF
Via Aeroporto 13, I-24050 Orio al Serio, Italy.
328JETx7, Dornier 328x3.

GARUDA INDONESIA – GA/GIA
Medan Merdeka Selatan 13, Jakarta 10110, Indonesia.
747-400x3, 747-200x4, 737-400x14, 737-300x6, 737-500x5, F28-4000x2, F28-3000x3.
On order: 777-200x6, 737-700x18.

GAZPROMAVIA – GZP
Ul. Nametkina 16, Moscow 117884, Russia.
Il-76x4, Tu-154Mx4, Tu-134Ax2, Yak-42Dx6, Yak-40Kx4, An-74x12,

GB AIRWAYS – GT/GBL
The Beehive, Beehive Ring Road, Gatwick Airport, West Sussex RH6 0LA, UK.
A321-200x2, A320-200x5, 737-400x1, 737-300x4.
On order: A321-200x1, A320-200x2.

GEMINI AIR CARGO – GR/GCO

Part of the Finnair fleet at the airline's Helsinki home. (Rob Finlayson)

44965 Aviation Drive, Dulles, Virginia 20166, USA.
MD-11Fx4, DC-10-30Fx12.

GEORGIAN AIRLINES – 6R/GEG
Tbilisi Airport, Tbilisi 380058, Georgia.
Tu-154Bx2, Tu-134Ax2, Yak-40x3.

GERMAN WINGS – 4U/GWI
Flugplatz 21, D-44319 Dortmund, Germany.
A320-200x1, A319-100x5.
On order: A319-100x1.

GERMANIA – ST/GMI
Flughafen Tegel, D-13405 Berlin, Germany.
737-700x10, 737-300x2.

GHANA AIRWAYS – GH/GHA
PO Box 1636, Accra, Ghana.
DC-10-30x3, DC-9-51x2.

GOL TRANSPORTES AEREOS – G3/GLO
Av. Dom Jaime de Barros Camara 300, CEP-09895-400, Sao Paulo, Brazil.
737-800x3, 737-700x14.

GOMELAVIA – YD/GOM
Gomel Airport, 246011 Gomel, Belarus.
Tu-154Bx1, An-24x6.

GROMOV AIR – GAI
Gromova, Zhukovsky 140182, Russia.
Tu-154Mx1, Tu-134Ax7, An-12x3, An-24x1.

GST AERO – BMK
Str. Zheltoksan 115, Almaty 480079, Kazakstan.
Il-76TDx1, An-12Bx1.

GULF AIR – GF/GFA
PO Box 138, Manama, Bahrain.
A340-300x5, A330-200x6, A320-200x12, 767-300x9.

HAINAN AIRLINES – HU/CHH
HNA Development Bldg, 20 Haixiu Dadao, 570206 Haikou, China.
767-300x3, 737-800x10, 737-400x7, 737-300x5, 328JETx19.
On order: 737-800x3.

HAMBURG INTERNATIONAL – HHI
Obenhauptstrasse 3, D-2235, Hamburg, Germany.
737-700x3.

HAPAG-LLOYD – HF/HLF
Postfach 42 02 40, D-30662 Hannover, Germany.
A310-300x2, A310-200x4, 737-800x30, 737-400x2, 737-500x1.

HAWAIIAN AIRLINES – HA/HAL
PO Box 30008, Honolulu, Hawaii 96820, USA.
DC-10-30x3, DC-10-10x7, DC-9-51x15, 767-300x7, 717-200x13.
On order: 767-300x5.

HBA-HEWA BORA AIRWAYS – EO/ALX
BP 12847, Kinshasa 1, Republic of Congo.
L-1011-250x1, 707-320Cx2, 727-200x2, 727-100x1, 737-200x1.

HELIOS AIRWAYS – ZU/HCY
Nietsche Street 22, Larnaca CY-6028, Cyprus.
737-800x2.

HEMUS AIR – DU/HMS
Sofia Airport, Sofia BG-1540, Bulgaria.
Tu-154Mx6, Tu-134x5, Yak-40x7.

HMY AIRWAYS - HQ
Vancouver, Canada
757-200x2.

HOLA AIRLINES
Malorca, Spain
737-300x2

HORIZON AIR – QX/QXE
PO Box 48309, Seattle, Washington 98148, USA.
CRJ700x12, F28-4000x18, Dash 8-400x15, Dash 8-200x28, Dash 8-100x8.
On order: CRJ700x18.

HUK HUNGARIAN-UKRAINIAN AIRLINES – HUK
Pf.198, H-1675 Budapest, Hungary.
Il-76x2

HUNAIR HUNGARIAN AIRLINES – HUV
Pf.196, H-1675 Budapest, Hungary.
Il-76x1.

HYDRO AIR – HYC
PO Box 868, Silverton 0127, South Africa.
747-200Fx1.

IBERIA – IB/IBE
Calle Velazquez 130, E-28006, Madrid, Spain.
747-300x3, 747-200x6, 737-200x1, 757-200x18, A340-300x18, A321-200x9, A320-200x57, A319-100x4, MD-88x13, MD-87x24.
On order: A340-600x3, A340-300x1, A321-200x6, A320-200x13.

IBERWORLD AIRLINES – TY/IWD
Gran via Asima 23, Poligono son Castello, E-07009 Palma de Mallorca, Spain.
A330-200x1, A310-300x1, A320-200x10.

ICC AIR CARGO – CIC
3220 Orlando Drive, Mississauga, Ontario L4V 1R5, Canada
A300B4-203Fx5.

ICELANDAIR – FI/ICE
Reykjavik Airport, Reykjavik IS-101, Iceland.
757-300x1, 757-200x9, 757-200Fx1, 737-400x1, 737-300Fx1.
On order: 757-300x1.

JetBlue – the successful two class, low cost New York based airline. (Ron Finlayson)

ILAVIA AIRLINES – ILV
PO Box 100, Moscow 125438, Russia.
Il-76x2, Yak-40x1.

IMAIR – IK/ITX
115 Hasi Aslanov Street, Baku 370000, Azerbaijan.
Tu-154Mx2.

INDIAN AIRLINES – IC/IAC
Airlines House, 113 Gurdware Rakabganj Road,
New Delhi 110000, India.
A300B4-200x4, A300B2-100x6, A320-200x34,
737-200x11, Dornier 228-200x3.

INDONESIAN AIRLINES – IAA
Management Building, Soekarna Hatta International
Airport, Jakarta 19110, Indonesia.
737-300x2.

INTENSIVE AIR – IM/XRA
PO Box 91212, Auckland Park 2006, South Africa.
F28-4000x3, BAe 748x3.

INTER – ICT
Avenida Eldorado, Bogota, Colombia.
DC-9-15x6, Dash 8-300x1.

INTER AIR – INX
Caglayan Mah, Barinaklar-Antalya TR-07100, Turkey.
737-800x2.
On order: 737-800x1.

INTERAIR SOUTH AFRICA – D6/ILN
Private Bag 8, PO Johannesburg International Airport 1627, South Africa.
707-320Cx1, 727-100x1, 737-200x2.

INVERSIA – INV
Riga Airport, LV-1053 Riga, Latvia.
Il-76x2.

IRAN AIR – IR/IRA
Mehradad Airport, Tehran 13185-775, Iran
747-200x1, 747-200Fx1, 747-100x1, 747SPx4,
707-320x3, 707-320Cx1, 727-200x4, 727-100x2,
737-200x4, A300-600x2, A300-200x4, A310-300x1,
A310-200x6, Fokker 100x5.

IRAN AIR TOURS – B9/IRB
191 Motahari Avenue, Tehran 15879, Iran.
Tu-154Mx9.

IRAN ASSEMAN AIRLINES – EP/IRC
PO Box 13145-1476, Tehran, Iran.
727-200x4, F28-4000x4, F28-1000x2, ATR
72-500x1, ATR 72-200x4.

IRAQI AIRWAYS – IA/IAW
Saddam International Airport, Baghdad, Iraq.
747-200x1, 747SPx2, 707-320Cx2, 727-200x6,
Il-76x1, An-26x1.

IRON DRAGONFLY – IDF
PO Box 652, Kazan 420044, Russia.
Il-76x1, Il-62Mx1, Tu-154Bx2.

IRS AERO – LDF
Leningradsky prospekt 37/1, Moscow 125836, Russia.

Tu-154Mx1, Tu-154Bx1, Il-18x3.

IRS AIRLINES
Murtala Mohammed Airport, Ikeja, Nigeria.
727-200x2.

IRTYSH-AVIA – IT/IRT
Kamenogorsk Airport, Ust-Kamenogorsk 492009,
Kazakstan.
Yak-42Dx5, Yak-40x13.

ISLANDSFLUG – HH/ICB
Reykjavik Airport, Reykjavik IS-101, Iceland.
A300-600Rx1, A300-600Fx1, A310-300Fx1,
737-300x4, 737-200Fx1, ATR 42-300x2, Dornier
228-200x3.

ISRAIR – 6H/ISR
PO Box 26444, Tel Aviv 63806, Israel.
757-200x1, ATR 42-300x4.

ITEK AIR – IKA
Chui Avenue 128/10, 720001, Bishkek, Kyrgyzstan.
Tu-154Bx1, Tu-134Ax1.

IZHAVIA – IZA
Izhevsk Airport, Izhevsk 426015, Russia.
Yak-42Dx1, Tu-134Ax2, An-26x2, An-24x2.

J-AIR - JL
10-2 Kannonshinmachi, Hiroshima 733-0036, Japan.
CRJ200x5, J32x2.

JAL EXPRESS – JC/JEX
4-11 Higashi-Shinagawa, Tokyo 140-8637, Japan.
737-400x5

JALWAYS – JO/JAZ
4-11 Higashi-Shinagawa, Tokyo 140-8637, Japan.
747-300x1, DC-10-40x4.

JAPAN AIRLINES – JL/JAL
4-11 Higashi-Shinagawa, Tokyo 140-8637, Japan.
747-400x45, 747-300x13, 747-200x8, 747-200Fx11,
747-100x4, 777-300x5, 777-200x8, 767-300x23,
767-200x3, 737-400x6, MD-11x10, DC-10-40x12.
On order: 747-400Fx2, 777-300ERx8, 777-200x13.

JAPAN AIR SYSTEM – JD/JAS
JAS M1 Building, 5-1 Hanedakuko, Tokyo
1440041, Japan.
777-200x7, A300-600Rx22, A300B4-300x9,
A300B4-200x8, MD-90x16, MD-81x18, MD-87x8,
YS-11Ax12.

JAPAN ASIA AIRWAYS – EG/JAA
Yurakucho Denki Bldg, Yurakucho, Tokyo 100-0006,
Japan.
747-300x1, 747-200x4, 747-100x1, 767-300x3,
DC-10-40x4.

JAPAN TRANSOCEAN AIR – NU/JTA
Yamashita Cho 3-24, Okinawa 900-0027, Japan.
737-400x15, 737-200x3.

JAT YUGOSLAV AIRLINES – JU/JAT
Bulevar Umetnosti 16, Belgrade YU-11070, Yugoslavia.
DC-10-30x1, DC-9-32x9, 727-200x8, 737-300x9,

A319-100x2, ATR 72-200x3.
On order: A319-100x6

JET AIRWAYS – 9W/JAI
Andheri-Kurla Road, Mumbai 400059, India.
737-800x15, 737-400x9, 737-700x11, ATR 72-500x8.
On order: 737-800x2.

JETBLUE AIRWAYS – B6/JBU
80-02 Kew Gardens Road, Kew Gardens, New York
11415-3600, USA.
A320-200x29.
On order: A320-200x47.

JET LINE INTERNATIONAL – MJL
31 August Str, MD-2008 Chisinau, Moldova.
Il-76Tx1.

JMC AIRLINES – MT/JMC
Commonwealth House, Chicago Avenue, Manches-
ter Airport M90 3FL, UK.
A330-200x2, A320-200x10, 757-300x2, 757-200x15.

KABO AIR – QNK
PO Box 3439, Kano, Nigeria.
747-200x4, 737-100x3, 727-200x2, BAC 111-400x6,
BAC 111-200x2.

KALININGRAD AIR – KLN
Khrabrova Airport, Kaliningrad 238315, Russia.
Tu-154Mx2, Tu-134Ax9.

KAMPUCHEA AIRLINES – KMP
106th Street, Phnom Penh 12202, Cambodia.
L-1011x6.

KAPO – KAO
Letny otryad, Kazan 420036, Russia.
Il-62Mx2, Tu-214x1, An-12x1, An-26x1, Yak-40x1.

KARAT – V2/AKT
Prospekt Vernadskogo 37/2, Moscow 117415,
Russia.
Tu-154Bx2, Tu-134Ax4, Yak-42Dx4, Yak-40Kx2,
An-24x2.

KARTHAGO AIRLINES – 5R/KAJ
Immeuble Marhabia, Tunix Cedex 1008, Tunisia.
737-300x2.

KARTIKA AIRLINES – KAE
Jl. Medan Merdeka, Jakarta 10110, Indonesia.
737-200x2.

KAZAIR WEST – KAW
Atyrau Airport, Atyrau 465050, Kazakstan.
Tu-134Ax1.

KELOWNA FLIGHTCRAFT – KW/KFA
5655 Airport Way, Kelowna, British Columbia VIV
1S1, Canada.
727-200Fx12, 727-100Fx7, Convair 5800x1, Convair
580x16.

KENYA AIRWAYS – KQ/KQA
PO Box 19002, Nairobi, Kenya.
767-300x5, 737-700x3, 737-300x4, 737-200x2,
A310-300x1.
On order: 777-200x3, 737-700x1.

KHAKASIA AIRLINES
Abakan Airport, Abakan 662608, Russia.
Tu-154M.

KHALIFA AIRWAYS – K6/KZW
Lot 5, Base Equipee, Dar-el-Beida DZ-16000, Algeria.
A340-300x2, A330-300x2, A310-300x7,
A320-200x1, A319-100x3, 737-800x2, 737-400x2,
ATR 72-500x13, ATR 42-300x4.

KHORS AIRCOMPANY – X9/KHO
Bulvar Lesi Ukrainki 34, Kiev 01133, Ukraine.
Il-76TDx1, DC-9-51x1, An-12x3.

KIROV AIR ENTERPRISE – KTA
Kirov Airport, Kirov 610009, Russia.
Tu-134Ax3, An-26x5, An-24x5.

KISH AIR – IRK
PO Box 80271, Dubai, United Arab Emirates.
Tu-154Mx4, Yak-42Dx1, Yak-40x2, Fokker 50x1.

KITTY HAWK AIR CARGO – KR/KHA
PO Box 612787, DFW International Airport, Texas 75261, USA.
727-200Fx38.

KLM-ROYAL DUTCH AIRLINES – KL/KLM
PO Box 7700, NL-1117 Schipol-Oost, Netherlands.
747-400x22, 747-300x3, 747-200x7, 747-200Fx2, 767-300x12, 737-900x4, 737-800x13, 737-400x14, 737-300x15, MD-11x10.
On order: 747-400x2, 747-400Fx3, 777-200x10, A330-200x6.

KLM CITYHOPPER – WA/KLC
Postbus 7700, NL-1117 Schipol-Oost, Netherlands.
Fokker 70x20, Fokker 50x13,

KLM EXEL – XT/AXL
PO Box 300, NL-6190 Maastricht-Aachen Airport, Netherlands.
ERJ 145x3, EMB-120x3, ATR 72-200x1, ATR 42-300x7.

KLM UK – UK/UKA
Endeavour House, Stansted Airport, Esseex CM24 1RS, UK.
Fokker 100x15, Fokker 50x9, ATR 72-200x5.

KMV – KV/MVD
Minerainye Vody Airport, Minerainy Vody 357205, Russia.
Tu-204x2, Tu-154Mx3, Tu-154Bx12, Tu-134A5.

KOLAVIA – 7K/KGL
Kogalym Airport, Kogalym 626481, Russia.
Tu-154Mx5, Tu-154Bx2, Tu-134Ax6.

KOMIITERAVIA – 8J/KMV
Ul. Sovetskaya 69, Syktyvkar 167610, Russia.
Tu-134Ax21, An-24x7, Yak-40x2.

KOREAN AIRLINES – KE/KAL
1370 Gonghang-dong, Seoul, South Korea.
747-400x27, 747-400Fx9, 747-300x1, 747-300Fx1, 747-200x1, 747-200Fx7, 777-300x4, 777-200x8, 737-900x7, 737-800x15, MD-11Fx4, MD-83x2, MD-82x2, A330-300x15, A330-200x3, A300-600x16, A300F4-200x2, Fokker 100x10.
On order: 747-400Fx1, 737-900x9, A330-300x1.

KOSMOS AIRLINES – KSM
Borovskoe shosse 1, Moscow 103027, Russia.
Il-76x1, Tu-134Ax3, An-12x2.

KRAS AIR – 7B/KJC
Krasnoyarsk Airport, Krasnoyarsk 663020, Russia.
Il-86x4, Il-76x9, Il-62x3, Tu-204x3, Tu-154Mx13, Tu-154Bx7, Tu-134A3, Yak 40x2.

KTHY – YK/KYV
Bedreddin Demirel Avenue, Yenisehir-Lefkosa, North Cyprus.
A310-200x2, 727-200x4, 737-800x3.

KUBAN AIRLINES – GW/KIL
Krasnodar Airport, Krasnodar 350912, Russia.
Tu-154Bx2, Yak-42x11, An-24x1.

KUWAIT AIRWAYS – KU/KAC
PO Box 394, Safat 13004, Kuwait.
747-200x2, 777-200x2, A340-300x4, A300-600Rx5, A300C4-600x1, A310-300x4, A320-200x3.

KYRGYZ INTERNATIONAL AIRLINES
Bishkek, Kyrgyzstan.
A300-600x2.

KYRGYZSTAN AIRLINES – R8/KGA
Manus Airport, 720062 Bishkek, Kyrgyzstan.
Il-76x1, Tu-154Mx2, Tu-154Bx11, Tu-134Ax6, An-26x1, Yak-40x21.

LAB AIRLINES – LB/LLB

A Korean 777-300 at Seoul's new Incheon Airport. (Rob Finlayson)

Casilla Correo 132, Cochabamba, Bolivia.
A310-300x1, 727-200x4, 727-100x3, 737-200x2, F27-200x1.

LAC-LIGNES AERIENNES CONGOLAISES – 6V/LCG
BP 204, Kinshasa 1, Republic of Congo.
DC-8-54Fx1, 737-200x1.

LACSA COSTA RICA – LR/LRC
Apartado 1531-1000, San Jose, Costa Rica.
A320-200x7, 737-200x5.

LAER – 2L
Caputo S/No, Parana 3100, Argentina.
F28-1000x1, ATR 42-300x2, J32x3.

LAKER AIRWAYS – 7Z/LBH
1170 Lee Wagener Blvd, Fort Lauderdale, Florida 33315, USA.
727-200x2.

LAM – TM/LAM
PO Box 2060, Maputo, Mozambique.
767-200x1, 737-200x3, Fokker 100x1, Beech 1900Cx1.

LAN CHILE – LA/LAN
Estado 10, Piso 21, Casilla 147-D, Santiago, Chile.
A340-300x6, A320-200x12, 737-200x22.
On order: A340-300x1, A320-200x13.

LAN CHILE CARGO – UC/LCO
Avda. Americo Vespucio 901, Renca, Santiago, Chile.
767-300Fx6, 737-200Fx1, DC-8-71Fx4.

LANPERU - LP/LPE
Avenue Jose Pardo 513, Lima 18, Peru.
A320-200x2.

LASER – LER
Avda. Francisco de Miranda Torre, Caracas, Venezuela,
DC-9-32x2, DC-9-14x1.

LAT CHARTER – 6Y/LTC
Riga Airport, Riga LV-1053, Latvia.
Yak-42Dx2, Tu-134Bx2.

LATPASS AIRLINES – QJ/LTP
Riga Airport, Riga LV-1053, Latvia.
Tu-154Bx1.

LAUDA AIR – NG/LDA
Postfach 56, A-1300 Vienna Airport, Austria.
777-200x3, 767-300x7, 737-800x4, 737-700x2, 737-400x2, 737-600x2, 737-300x2, CRJ100x4.
On order: 777-200x1.

LIBYAN ARAB AIR CARGO – LCR
PO Box 48697, Tripoli, Libya.
An-124x1, An-26Bx5, Il-76x19, L-382E/Gx4.

LIBYAN ARAB AIRLINES – LN/LAA
PO Box 2555, Tripoli, Libya.
A300-600Rx2, A310-200x2, 707-320Cx1, 727-200x7, F28-4000x5, F27-600x12, F27-500x2, F27-400x1, DHC-6-300x13.

LINEAS AEREAS SURAMERICANAS – LAU

Eldorado Airport, Bogota, Colombia.
727-100Fx5, Caravellex2, DC-9-15Fx2.

LION AIRLINES – JT/LNI
Gedung Jaya, Jakarta 13047, Indonesia.
A310-300x2, MD-82x1, Yak-42Dx4, 737-200x1.

LIPETSK AIR ENTERPRISE – LIP
Lipetsk Airport, Lipetsk 398000, Russia.
Yak-42Dx2, Yak-40x8.

LITHUANIAN AIRLINES – TE/LIL
A Gustaicio 4, Vilnius Airport LI-2038, Lithuania.
737-300x1, 737-200x2, Saab 2000x2, Saab 340Bx1.

LOT POLISH AIRLINES – LO/LOT
Ul. 17 Stycznia 39, Warsaw PL-00-906, Poland.
767-300x3, 767-200x2, 737-400x7, 737-300x2, 737-500x10, ERJ 145x15.
On order: 737-800x2.

LOTUS AIR – TAS
Kamal Hassan Ali Street, Heliopolis, Egypt.
A320-200x4.
On order: A320-200x2.

LTE INTERNATIONAL AIRWAYS – XO/LTE
Calle del Ter 27, Poligono de Son Fuster, E-07009 Palma de Mallorca, Spain.
757-200x3, A320-200x1.
On order: A320-200x4.

LTU INTERNATIONAL AIRWAYS – LT/LTU
Halle 8, Flughafen, D-40474 Dusseldorf, Germany.
A330-300x5, A330-200x7, A321-200x1, A320-200x10.
On order: A321-200x2, A320-200x2.

LUFTHANSA – LH/DLH
Postfach 63 03 00, D-22313, Hamburg, Germany.
747-400x30, 747-200x5, 737-300x43, 737-500x30, A340-300x28, A340-200x6, A300-600x14, A310-300x6, A321-200x6, A321-100x20, A320-200x36, A319-100x20.
On order: A380-800x15, A340-600x10, A340-300x6, A330-300x10.

LUFTHANSA CARGO – LH/GEC
Postfach 1244, D-65441 Kelsterbach, Germany.
747-200Fx3, MD-11Fx14.

LUFTHANSA CITYLINE – CL/CLH
Heinrich Steinmann Strasse, D-51147 Cologne, Germany.
RJ85x18, CRJ700x11, CRJ200x10, CRJ100x33, Fokker 50x11.
On order: CRJ700x9.

LUGANSK AVIATION ENTERPRISE – LHS
Lugansk Airport, Lugansk 348039, Ukraine.
Tu-154Bx3, An-24RVx5.

LUXAIR – LG/LGL
BP 2203, Luxembourg L-2987, GD Luxembourg.
737-400x2, 737-500x3, Fokker 50x3, ERJ 145x8.

LVIV AIRLINES – 5V/UKW
Lviv Airport, Lviv 79000, Ukraine.

Il-76MDx3, Il-18x1, Yak-42x7, An-12BKx2, An-24Bx7.

MACEDONIAN AIRLINES – MCS
154 Syngrou Avenue, Athens GR-176 71, Greece.
737-400x3.

MAERSK AIR – VB/MSK
Maersk Air House, 2245-49 Coventry Road, Birmingham B26 3NG, UK.
737-500x3, CRJ700x5, CRJ200x6.

MAERSK AIR – DM/DAN
Copenhagen Airport South, DK-2791 Dragoer, Denmark.
737-700x10, 737-500x10, CRJ200x4.

MAGADAN AIRLINES – H5/MVL
Sokol Airport, Magadan 685018, Russia.
Il-62Mx1, Tu-154Mx5, Tu-154Bx5.

MAGNICHARTERS – GMT
La Barca 1128, Monterrey 64020, Mexico.
737-200x4.

MAHAN AIR – W5/IRM
PO Box 14515-411, Tehran, Iran.
A300B4-200x1, A300B4-100x2, A310-300x3, Tu-154Mx2, Yak-40x1.

MAHFFOZ AVIATION – M2/MZS
PO Box 6664, Jeddah 21452, Saudi Arabia.
707-320x1, 707-320Cx1, 727-200x5.

MALAYSIA AIRLINES – MH/MAS
Jalan Sultan Ismail, Bangunan MAS, Kuala Lumpar 50250, Malaysia.
747-400x19, 747-300Fx1, 747-200Fx2, 777-200x15, 737-400x39, A330-300x9, Fokker 50x10, DHC-6-300x6.
On order: 747-400x2, 777-200x2,

MALEV HUNGARIAN AIRLINES – MA/MAH
Pf.122, H-1637 Budapest, Hungary.
767-200x2, 737-400x6, 737-300x7, 737-500x2, Fokker 70x6, CRJ200x2.
On order: 737-800x3, 737-700x7, 737-600x6, CRJ200x2.

MALMO AVIATION - TF/SCW
Po Box 37, S-201 20 Malmo, Sweden.
RJ100x9, 146-200x2.

MANDALA AIRLINES – RI/MDL
PO Box 3706, Jakarta 1140, Indonesia.
737-400x1, 737-200x12.

MANDARIN AIRLINES – AE/MDA
135 Min Sheng East Road, Taipei, Taiwan.
737-800x3, Fokker 100x2, Fokker 50x7, Dornier 228-200x3.

MARTINAIR – MP/MPH
PO Box 7507, NL-1118 Schipol, Netherlands.
747-200x1, 747-200Fx1, 767-300x6, 757-200x1, MD-11x4, MD-11Fx2.

MAS AIR – MY/MAA
Hangar 9, Aviacion General, Mexico City 15620, Mexico.
767-300x1, DC-8-71Fx3.

MAT-MACEDONIAN AIRLINES – IN/MAK
Vasil Glavinov 3, Skopje MK-1000, Macedonia.
737-300x2.

MD AIRLINES – W3/MDI
Hamraborg 12, Kopavogur IS-200, Iceland.
MD-83x2.

MEDITERRANEAN AIR SERVICE – DR
Rue 101 Immeuble Astree, Tunis 2045, Tunisia.
737-200Fx1.

MERIDIAN AIR – MMM
Vnukovo Airport, Moscow 103027, Russia.
Tu-134Ax2.

MERIDIANA – IG/ISS
Aeroporto Costo Smeralda, I-07026 Olbia, Italy.
MD-83x8, MD-82x9, 146-200x4.

MERPATI – MZ/MNA
Kotak Pos 1323, Jakarta 10720, Indonesia.
737-200x7, Fokker 100x3, F28-4000x8, F27-500x9, CN-235x9, NC-212x7, DHC-6-300x6.

MESA AIRLINES – YV/ASH
410 Nth 44th Street, Phoenix, Arizona 85008, USA.
CRJ700x4, CRJ200x32, ERJ 145x36, Dash 8-200x12, Beech 1900Dx57.
On order: CRJ900x20, CRJ700x16.

MESABA AIRLINES – XJ/MES
7501 26th Avenue South, Minneapolis, Minnesota 55450, USA.
RJ85x36, Saab 340Bx50, Saab 340Ax20.

MEXICANA – MX/MXA
Xola 535, Mexico City 03100, Mexico.
757-200x8, 727-200x20, A320-200x24, A319-100x4, Fokker 100x12.
On order: A320-200x8.

MIAMI AIR –GL/BSK
PO Box 660880, Miami Springs, Florida 33266-0880, USA.
727-200x5, 727-200Fx4, 737-800x2.

MIAT-MONGOLIAN AIRLINES – OM/MGL
PO Box 45, Ulaanbaatar 210734, Mongolia.
A310-300x1, 727-200x2, 737-800x1, An-26x3, An-24x10.

MIDDLE EAST AIRLINES – ME/MEA
PO Box 206, Beirut, Lebanon.
A300-600x1, A310-200x3, A321-200x2, A320-200x3, 707-320Cx4.
On order: A330-200x3, A321-200x6.

MIDWEST AIRLINES – MY/MWA
61 El Oruba Street, Heliopolis, Egypt.
A310-300x2, A320-200x2.

MIDWEST EXPRESS AIRLINES – YX/MEP
6744 South Howell Avenue, Oak Creek, Wisconsin 53154-1474, USA.

A Mexicana 757 in a retro scheme. (Sam Chui)

MD-88x2, MD-82x3, MD-81x8, DC-9-30x16, DC-9-15x8.
On order: 717-200x25.

MILLION AIR CHARTER
PO Box 6119, Rivonia 2128, South Africa.
727-100x1, DC-9-32x4.

MISTRAL AIR – MSA
Aeroporto Ciampino Ovest, I-00040 Rome, Italy.
146-200QTx2.

MK AIRLINES – 7G/MKA
Hartfield, East Sussex TN7 4DL, UK.
747-200Fx2, DC-8-63Fx2, DC-8-62Fx3, DC-8-55Fx4.

MNG AIRLINES – MB/MNB
Cemal Ulusoy Ceddesi, Yenibosna-Istanbul TR-34620, Turkey.
A300C4-200x2, A300B4-200x1, A300B4-200Fx1, A300F4-200x2, 737-400x2.

MOLDAVIAN AIRLINES – 2M/MDV
Chisinau Airport, MD-2026 Chisinau, Moldova.
Tu-134Ax1, Saab 340Bx3.

MONARCH AIRLINES – ZB/MON
Luton Airport, Luton, Bedfordshire LU2 9NU, UK.
A330-200x2, A300-600x4, A321-200x5, A320-200x3, 757-200x7.
On order: A321-200x3.

MONTENEGRO AIRLINES – YM/MGX
Ul. Beogradska 10, Podgorica YU-81000, Yugoslavia.
Fokker 100x2.

MORNINGSTAR AIR EXPRESS – MAL
PO Box 14, Edmonton, Alberta T5G 0W6, Canada.
727-100Fx4, Cessna 208Bx6.

MYANMA AIRWAYS – UB/UBA
104 Kanna Road, Yangon, Myanmar.
F28-4000x4, F28-1000x1, F27-600x5, F27-400x1, F27-100x1.

MYANMAR AIRWAYS INTERNATIONAL – 8M
339 Bogyoke Aung San Road, Yangon, Myanmar.
737-300x1.

MYTRAVEL AIRWAYS – VZ/MYT
Parkway Business Centre, 300 Princess Road, Manchester M14 7Qu, UK.
DC-10-30x1, DC-10-10x3, A330-300x3, A330-200x4, A321-200x4, A320-200x23.
On order: A321-200x4.

NATIONAL JET SYSTEMS – NC/NJS
28 James Schofield Drive, Adelaide Airport, SA 5950, Australia.
146-300x2, 146-300QTx2, 146-200x9, 146-100x7, 146-100QCx1, Avro RJ70x1, Dash 8-300x1, Dash 8-200x7, Dash 8-100x4, Reims F406x3, Commander 500Sx1, BN-2B-20x6.

NATIONWIDE AIRLINES – CE/NTW
PO Box 422, Lanseria 1748, South Africa.
727-200x1, 727-100x1, 727-100Fx1, 737-200x7, BAC 111-500x6, BAC 111-400x5.

NEOS – NO
68 via dell Chiesa, I-21019 Sommo Lombardo, Italy.
737-800x2.

NIGERIA AIRWAYS – WT/NGA
PMB 21024, Ikeja, Nigeria.
747-200x1, 737-200x2, DC-10-30x1, A310-200x1.

NIPPON CARGO AIRLINES – KZ/NCA
Shin-kasumigaseki, Chiyoda-shi, Tokyo 100-0013, Japan.
747-200Fx10, 747SR-100Fx1.

NIZHNY NOVGOROD AIRLINES – NGL
Nizhny Novgorod Airport, Nizhny Novgorod 603056, Russia.
Tu-154Bx7, Tu-134Ax5, An-245.

NORDESTE – JH/NES

Avenida Tancredo Neves 1672, CEP-41820-020, Bahia, Brazil.
737-500x4, Fokker 50x4, EMB-120x3.

NORDIC AIRLINK – 7I/NDC
Flyplats, S-904 22 Umea, Sweden.
MD-82x2, MD-81x1, Saab 340Bx1.

NORFOLK JET EXPRESS - ST
PO Box 2206, Brisbane, Queensland 4001, Australia.
737-400x1.

NORTH AMERICAN AIRLINES – NA/NAO
Bldg 75, JFK International Airport, Jamaica, New York 11430, USA.
767-300x1, 757-200x4, 737-800x1.

NORTHERN AIR CARGO – NC/NAC
3900 West International Airport Road, Anchorage, Alaska 99502-1097, USA.
727-100Fx3, DC-6x12.

NORTHWEST AIRLINES – NW/NWA
5101 Northwest Drive, International Airport, St Paul, Minnesota 55111-3034, USA.
747-400x16, 747-300Fx2, 747-200x21, 747-200Fx12, 757-300x4, 757-200x56, 727-200x34, DC-10-30x23, DC-10-40x13, MD-82x7, DC-9-50x35, DC-9-40x12, DC-9-30x114, DC-9-10x9, A320-200x76, A319-100x46, RJ85x36, CRJ200x40.
On order: 757-300x12, A330-300x36, A320-200x8, A319-100x32, CRJ200x14.

NORWEGIAN AIR SHUTTLE
Oslo, Norway.
737-300x2, 737-500x1.

NOUVELAIR – BJ/LBT
Zone Touristique Dkhila, Monastir 5065, Tunisia.
A320-200x3, MD-83x3, MD-82x1.

NOVAIR – NVR
Sveavagen 155, S-113 46 Stockholm, Sweden.
A330-200x2, 737-800x3.

ODESSA AIRLINES – 5K/ODS
Central Airport, Odessa 65054, Ukraine.
Tu-154Bx3, An-140x2, Yak-40x5.

OKADA AIR – OKJ
17B Sapele Road, Benin City, Nigeria.
BAC 111-500x2, BAC 111-400x8, BAC 111-300x4, BAC 111-200x2.

OLYMPIC AIRWAYS – OA/OAL
96-100 Syngrou Avenue, Athens GR-117 41, Greece.
747-200x4, 737-400x13, 737-300x1, 737-200x11, A340-300x4, A300-600Rx3.

OLYMPIC AVIATION – OLY
Posidonos Avenue 69, Athens GR-174 56, Greece.
717-200x3, ATR 72-200x7, ATR 42-300x4, Dornier 228-200x6.

OMAN AIR – WY/OMA
PO Box 58, CPO, Seeb Intl Airport 111, Oman.
737-800x1, 737-700x3, 737-400x1, ATR 42-500x4.
On order: 737-700x1.

OMNI AIR INTERNATIONAL – OY/OAE
PO Box 582527, Tulsa, Oklahoma 74158, USA.
DC-10-30x3, DC-10-10x2.

OMSKAVIA – N3/OMS
Aviatsionnaya 143, Omsk 644103, Russia.
Tu-154Mx10, An-24x2.

ONUR AIR – 8Q/OHY
Senik Mah, Florya-Islanbul Tr-34810, Turkey.
A300B2-200x1, A300B4-200x2, A300B4-100x2, A321-100x2, MD-88x5.

ORENBURG AIRLINES – R2/ORB
Orenburg-Tsentrainy Airport, Orenburg 460049, Russia.
Tu-154Mx1, Tu-154Bx4, Tu-134Ax4, An-24Bx5, Yak-40x3.

A Pulkovo Tu-154. (Sam Chui)

ORIENT THAI AIRLINES – OX/OEA
138/70 17th Floor, Jewellery Center, Siphaya, Bangkok 10500, Thailand.
747-200x1, 747-100x1.

ORIENTAL AIRLINES – OAC
14 Simbat Abiola Road, Ikeja-Lagos, Nigeria.
BAC 111-500x2.

PACE AIRLINES – PCE
PO Box 525, Winston Salem, North Carolina 27102-0525, USA.
727-200x1, 737-400x1, 737-300x6, 737-200x4.

PACIFIC AIRLINES – BL/PIC
112 Hong Ha Street, Ho Chi Minh City, Vietnam.

PAKISTAN INTERNATIONAL AIRLINES – PK/PIA
PIA Building, Quaid-e-Azam International Airport, Karachi 75200, Pakistan.
747-300x5, 747-200x2, 737-300x6, A300B4-200x8, A310-300x6, F27-200x10, F27-400x1.
On order: 777-300ERx3.

PALESTINIAN AIRLINES – PF/PNW
PO Box 4043, Gaza City, Palestine.
727-200x1, Fokker 50x2, Dash 8-300x2.
On order: CRJ200x2.

PAN AIR
Edificio TNT, 2 Planta, Aeropuert de Barajas, E-28042, Madrid, Spain.
A300B4-200Fx1, A300B4-100Fx1, 146-200QTx6.

PANAIR – PIT
Aeroporto Ciampino Ovest, I-00040, Rome, Italy.
737-400x1, 737-300x1.

PAN AM – PN/PAA
14 Aviation Avenue, Portsmouth, New Hampshire 03801, USA
727-200x30.

PANAVIA – PVI
Apartado 8140030, Panama City, Republic of Panama.
727-100Fx1.

PANNON AIRLINES – PHP
Viztorony Street 20, H-1193 Budapest, Hungary.
Tu-154Mx1.

PAYAM AVIATION SERVICES – IRP

3 Topchhi Street, Tehran 16765-3166, Iran.
Il-76TDx2, EMB-110x5.

PB AIR – 9Q/PBA
101 Samsen Road, Bangkok 10300, Thailand.
F28-4000x3.

PEGASUS AIRLINES – PGT
Istasyon Caddesi 24, Yesilyurt-Istanbul TR-34800, Turkey.
737-800x14, 737-400x8.

PELITA AIR – 6D/PAS
Jalan Abdul Muis 52-56A, Jakarta 10160, Indonesia.
Fokker 100x3, F28-4000x4, RJ85x1, Dash 7-100x5, NC-212x8.

PERM AIRLINES – PGP
Bolshoe Savino Airport, Perm 614078, Russia.
Tu-154Bx2, Tu-134Ax5, An-26x3, An-24Bx3.

PGA PORTUGALIA AIRLINES – NI/PGA
Aeroporta de Lisboa, Rua C, Edificio 70, P-1749-078, Lisbon, Portugal.
Fokker 100x6, ERJ 145x8.

PHAROH AIRLINES – PHR
30 Ammar Ibn Yasser Street, Heliopolis, Egypt.
737-200x1.

PHILIPPINE AIRLINES – PR/PAL
Legaspi Street, Makati City 1229, Philippines.
747-400x4, 747-200x3, 737-400x3, 737-300x7, A340-300x4, A330-300x8, A320-200x3.

PHOENIX AVIATION – PHG
PO Box 7801, Sharjah Airport, United Arab Emirates.
Il-76x3, Il-18x10, 737-200x1, Yak-40x2.

PHUKET AIRLINES – 9R/VAP
1168/1 25th Floor, Lumpini Tower Bldg, Sathorn, Bangkok 10120, Thailand.
737-200x2.

PLANET AIRWAYS – PLZ
1050 Lee Wagener Blvd, Fort Lauderdale, Florida 33315-3500, USA.
727-200x5, 727-100x1.

PLUNA – PU/PUA
Puntas de Santiago 1604, Montevideo, Uruguay.
767-300x1, 737-300x1, 737-200x3.

Philippine Airlines operates four 747-400s. (John Adlard)

Qantas became an Airbus operator in December 2002. (Jason Milligan)

POLAR AIR CARGO – PO/PAC
100 Oceangate, Long Beach, California 90802, USA.
747-400Fx5, 747-200Fx6, 747-100Fx10.

POLET FLIGHT – POT
Ul. Sofi Perovskoi 37A, Voronezh 394035, Russia.
An-124x7.

POLYNESIAN AIRLINES – PH/PAO
PO Box 599, Apia, Samoa.
737-800x2, DHC-6-300x2.

PRESIDENT AIRLINES – TO/PSD
50 Norodom Boulevard, Phnom Penh 12206, Cambodia.
F28-1000x1, F27-100x1, An-12x2, An-26x1, An-24x1.

PRIMAIR – PMM
Orekhovy bulvar 8, Moscow 115582, Russia.
Tu-134Ax2.

PULKOVA AVIATION ENTERPRISE – FV/PLK
Ul. Pilotov 18/4, St Petersburg 196210, Russia.
Il-86x9, Tu-154Mx15, Tu-154Bx9, Tu-134Ax11.

QANTAS AIRWAYS – QF/QFA
Qantas Centre, 203 Coward Street, Mascot, NSW 2020, Australia.
747-400ERx3, 747-400x24, 747-300x6, 767-300x25, 767-200x7, 737-800x15, 737-400x22, 737-300x16, A330-200x2.
On order: 747-400ERx3, 737-800x8, A380-800x12, A330-300x6, A330-200x5.

QANTASLINK/AIRLINK – QF/QFA
203 Coward Street, Mascot, NSW 2020, Australia.
146-300x2, 146-200x9, 146-100x6.

QANTASLINK/IMPULSE AIRLINES – QF/QFA
Flight Facilites Terminal, Sydney Airport, NSW 2020, Australia.
717-200x14.

QANTAS/JETCONNECT – QF/QFA
Auckland, New Zealand
737-300x5.

QATAR AIRWAYS – QR/QTR
PO Box 22550, Doha, Qatar.
A330-200x4, A300-600x7, A320-200x9.
On order: A380-800x2, A330-200x1, A320-200x4.

QESHM AIRLINES – IRQ
3 Khaled Eslambolid Avenue, Tehran 15117, Iran.
Il-76TDx2, Yak-40x2.

QUEST CARGO INTERNATIONAL
PO Box 660880, Miami, Florida 33266-0880, USA.
727-200Fx4.

RAF-AVIA – MTL
2a Jura Alunana Street, Riga LV-1010, Latvia.
An-74Kx1, An-26x5.

REGIONAIR – RGA
50 Cuscaden Road, Singapore 249724, Republic of Singapore.
A300-600Rx1, A310-300x1, A321-100x2, 737-300x1.

REGIONAL – YS/RAE
Nantes Airport, F-44345 Bouguenais Cedex, France.
Fokker 100x3, ERJ 145x27, ERJ 135x17, EMB-120x19, Saab 2000x8, Beech 1900Dx14.

REGIONAL AIR – QP
PO Box 30357, Nairobi, Kenya.
737-200x1.

REGIONAL AIR LINES – FN/RGL
BP 12518, Aeroport Mohammed V, Casablanca 20050, Morocco.
ERJ 135x2, Beech 1900Dx4.
On order: ERJ 135x3.

RELIANT AIRLINES – RLT
PO Box 827, Willow Run Airport, Ypsilanti, Michigan 48198-0899, USA.
DC-9-15Fx4, Falcon 20C/Dx12.

RHEINTALFLUG – WE/RTL
Bahnhofstrasse 10, Bregenz A-6900, Austria.
ERJ 145x3.

RIO SUL – SL/RSL
Av. Rio Branco 85, CEP-20040-004 Rio de Janeiro, Brazil.
737-700x1, 737-300x4, 737-500x14, ERJ 145x15, EMB-120x5.

ROMAVIA – WQ/RMV
B-dul Dimitrie Cantemir, Bucharest, Romania.
707-320Cx1, Rombac 111-500x4, Il-18x2.

ROYAL AIR MAROC – AT/RAM
Aeroport Anfa, Casablanca, Morocco.
747-400x1, 767-300x2, 757-200x2, 737-800x6, 737-400x7, 737-700x5, 737-500x6, 737-200x6, ATR 42-300x2.
On order: A321-200x4, 737-800x10.

ROYAL BRUNEI AIRLINES – BI/RBA
PO Box 737, Bander Seri Begawan BB1907, Brunei.
767-300x8, 757-200x2.
On order: A319-100x2

ROYAL JORDANIAN
PO Box 302, Amman 11193, Jordan.
A340-200x3, A300-600Rx2, A310-300x9, A310-200x2, A320-200x5, 707-320x2.

ROYAL NEPAL AIRLINES – RA/RNA
PO Box 401, Kathmandu, Nepal.
757-200x3, BAe 748x1, DHC-6-300x7.

ROYAL TONGAN AIRLINES – WR/HRH
Private Bag 9, Nuku'alofa, Tonga.
757-200x1, Shorts 360-200x1, DHC-6-300x1.

RUSAIR – CGI
Leningradsky Prospekt 37A, Moscow 125167, Russia.
Tu-134Ax3.

RUTACA AIRLINES – RUC
Ciudad Bolivar Airport, Venezuela.
737-200x1.

RWANDA AIRLINES – RUA
BP 3246, Kigali, Rwanda.
BAC 111-200x1, L 410UVPx1.

RYAN INTERNATIONAL AIRLINES – RYN
266 North Main, Wichita, Kansas 67202, USA.
DC-10-10x2, 727-200Fx11, 727-100Fx4, 737-400x1, 737-200x2.

RYANAIR – FR/RYR
Dublin Airport, County Dublin, Ireland.
737-800x30, 737-200x21.
On order: 737-800x98.

SAFAIR – FA/SFR
PO Box 938, Kempton Park 1620, South Africa.
A300B4-200Fx5, 727-200Fx8, 727-100Fx1, 737-400x3, 737-200x21, 737-200Fx2, L-382Gx8, MD-82x5, MD-81x2, ATR 72-500x3.

SAFIRAN AIRLINES – SFN
PO Box 15855-389, Tehran, Iran.
Il-76TDx1.

SAHA AIR – IRZ
PO Box 13865-164, Tehran, Iran.
747-200Fx3, 747-100Fx1, 707-320x5, F27-600x2, F27-400x1.

SAKHAAVIA – K7
Ul. Gagarina 10, Yakutsk 677014, Russia.
Il-76x2, Tu-154Mx4, Tu-154Bx3, An-12x2, An-26x1, An-24x2, Yak-40x4.

SAM – MM/SAM
Avda Eldorado No 93-30, Bogota, Colombia.
MD-83x2, Fokker 50x4.

SAMARA AIRLINES – E5/BRZ
Samara Airport, Samara 443901, Russia.
Il-76TDx3, Tu-154Mx9, Tu-154Bx3, Tu-134Ax8, Yak-42Dx2, Yak-40x3.

SARAVIA – 6W/SOV
Ul. Zhukovskogo 25, Saratov 410010, Russia.
Yak-42Dx11, An-24x1.

SAS SCANDINAVIAN AIRLINES – SK/SAS
Fack, S-195 87 Stockholm-Bromma, Sweden.
A340-300x9, A321-200x8, 767-300x10, 737-800x18, 737-700x6, 737-600x30, MD-90x8, MD-87x15,

Regional operates a fleet of aircraft for Air France, including ERJ 135s. (Embraer)

MD-83x2, MD-82x32, MD-81x15.
On order: A340-300x2, A321-200x4, 737-800x4.

SAT AIRLINES – HZ/SHU
Ul. Gorkogo 50A, Yuzhno-Sakhalinsk 693023, Russia.
Il-62Mx1, An-26Bx3, An-24RVx6.

SATA INTERNATIONAL – S4/RZO
Parque 4, Aeroporta de Lisboa, P-1700, Lisbon,
Portugal.
A310-300x2, 737-400x2, 737-300x1.

SAUDI ARABIAN AIRLINES – SV/SVA
PO Box 620, Jeddah 21231, Saudi Arabia.
747-400x5, 747-300x9, 747-200Fx1, 747-100x7,
747SPx1, 777-200x23, 737-200x10, MD-11Fx4,
MD-90x29, A300-600x11.

SAVANNAH AIRLINES – SNI
PO Box 55, Kano, Nigeria.
BAC 111-500x2.

SAYAKHAT – W7/SAH
Bogenbay Batyra Street 124, Almaty 480091,
Kazakstan.
Il-76TDx4, Tu-154Mx6.

SEMEIAVIA – SMK
Semipalatinsk Airport, Semipalatinsk 490035,
Kazakstan.
Yak-40Kx3.

SERVIVENSA – VC/SVV
Av. Rio Caura, Caracas 101, Venezuela.
727-200x3, 727-100x1, 737-200x1, DC-3x5.

SHANDONG AIRLINES – SC/CDG
International Business Division, 18 Dongwailhuan
Road, 250107 Jinan, China.
737-300x8, CRJ200x10, Saab 340Bx4.
On order: CRJ700x2.

SHANGHAI AIRLINES – FM/CSH
212 Jiangning Road, 200041 Shanghai, China.
767-300x4, 757-200x7, 737-800x6, 737-700x7,
CRJ200x3
On order: 737-700x3.

SHANEEN AIR INTERNATIONAL – NL/SAI
157-B Clifton Road, Clifton, Karachi, Pakistan.
Tu-154Bx3, Yak-42Dx2.

SHANS AIR – SNF
Leningradsky prospekt 17, Moscow 125040, Russia.
Tu-134Ax3.

SHENZHEN AIRLINES – ZH/CSZ
Baoan International Airport, 518128 Shenzhen,
China.
737-700x8, 737-300x6.

SHOROUK AIR – 7Q/SHK
PO Box 2684 Horreia, Heliopolis, Egypt.
A320-200x4.

SIBAVIATRANS –5M/SIB
Ul. Vzietnaya 5a, Krasnoyarsk 660077, Russia.
Tu-154Bx1, Tu-134Ax5, An-74x1, An-32x1,
An-24RVx5, Yak-40x3.

SIBIR AIRLINES – S7/SBI
Tolmachevo Airport, Ob-4 633104, Russia.
Il-86x13, Tu-204x2, Tu-154Mx22, Tu-154Bx11, An-
26x1.

SICHUAN AIRLINES – CSC
Sichuan Airlines Hotel, Sunaglu International Air-
port, 610202 Chendu, China.
A321-200x2, A320-200x5, MA-60x5, Y7-100Cx 5,
ERJ 145x5.

SIERRA PACIFIC AIRLINES – SI/SPA
7700 North Business Park Drive, Tucson, Arizona
85743-9622, USA.
737-200x2.

SILKAIR – MI/SLK
PO Box 104, Changi Airport, Singapore 918144,

Republic of Singapore.
A320-200x5, A319-100x4.
On order: A320-200x1.

SINGAPORE AIRLINES – SQ/SIA
PO Box 501, Singapore 918101, Rep of Singapore.
747-400x41, 777-300x8, 777-200x34, A340-300x5,
A310-300x16.
On order: A380-800x10, 777-200x16, A340-500x5,
A340-300x6.

SINGAPORE AIRLINES CARGO – SQ/SQC
PO Box 501, Singapore 918101, Rep of Singapore.
747-400x11.
On order: 747-400Fx6.

SIRIUS AERO – CIG
Blagoveshchensky pereulok 3, Moscow 103001,
Russia.
Tu-134Ax6.

SKY AIRLINE – H2/SKU
Nuble 179, Santiago, Chile.
737-200x2.

SKY AIRLINES – SHY
Caglayan Mah, Barinaklar-Antalya TR-07104, Turkey.
737-800x1, 737-400x2.

SKY AVIATION – FZE
PO Box 7867, Sharjah, United Arab Emirates.
747-200x2, 747SPx1, 707-320Cx3, 727-200x3.

SKYMASTER AIRLINES – SKC
Estrada Torquatro Tapajos 6464, CEP-69075-000
Manaus, Brazil.
707-320Cx3.

SKYMARK AIRLINES – BC/SKY
World Trade Center Bldg, 2-4-1 Hamamtsu-Cho, Tokyo 105-6103, Japan.
767-300x3.

SKYNET AIRLINES – SI
Ballycasey Court, Shannon, County Clare, Ireland.
737-400x2.

SKYSERVICE AIRLINES – 6J/SSV
9785 Ryan Avenue, Dorval, Quebec H9P 1A2, Canada.
A330-300x3, A320-200x15, A319-100x1, 727-200x1.

SKYWAY AIRLINES – AL/SYX
1190 West Rawson Avenue, Oak Creek, Wisconsin
53154-1453, USA.
328JETx12, Beech 1900Dx15.
On order: ERJ 140x20.

SKYWAY ENTERPRISES – SKZ
3031 West Patrick Road, Kissimee, Florida 34741,
USA.
DC-9-15Fx1, Shorts 360-200Fx15.

SKYWAYS EXPRESS – JZ/SKX
ERJ 145x4, Fokker 50x13, Saab 340Ax6.

SKYWEST AIRLINES – XR
PO Box 176, Cloverdale, WA 6985, Australia.
Fokker 100x1, Fokker 50x5.

SKYWEST AIRLINES – OO/SKW
444 South River Road, St George, Utah 84790,
USA.
CRJ200x71, CRJ100x10, EMB-120x90.
On order: CRJ200x35.

SLOVAK AIRLINES – 6Q/SLL
Trnavska cesta 56, SK-821 01 Bratislava, Slovakia.
Tu-154Mx3.

SOBELAIR – Q7/SLR
Brussels National Airport, Building 45, B-1932
Zaventem, Belgium.
767-300x2, 737-400x4, 737-300x2.

SOSOLISO AIRLINES – OSL
Enugu Airport, Enugu, Nigeria.
DC-9-32x1.

SOUTH AFRICAN AIRLINK – 4Z/LNK
PO Box 7529, Bonaero Park 1622, South Africa.
ERJ 135x6, J41x16.
On order: ERJ 135x24

SOUTH AFRICAN AIRWAYS – SA/SAA
Private Bag X13, Johannesburg International Airport
1627, South Africa.
747-400x8, 747-300x6, 747-200x5, 747SPx3,
767-200x2, 737-800x21, 737-200x22, A340-600x3.
On order: A340-600x6, A340-300x6, A320-200x15,
A319-100x11.

SOUTH AFRICAN EXPRESS AIRWAYS – YB/EXY
PO Box 101, Johannesburg International Airport
1627, South Africa.
CRJ200x6, Dash 8-300x7.

SOUTH AIRLINES – YG/OTL
85 Kanatnaya Street, Odessa 65012, Ukraine.
Tu-134Ax2.

SOUTHEAST AIRLINES – SNK
12552 Belcher Road, Largo, Florida 33773-3014, USA.
MD-88x2, MD-82x2, DC-9-30x8.

SOUTHERN AIR – 9S/SOO
PO Box 32485, Columbus, Ohio 43232, USA.
747-200Fx1.

SOUTHERN WINDS AIRLINES
Avda Colon 544, Cordoba, Argentina.
767-300x2, CRJ200x2, CRJ100x4, Dash 8-100x6.

SOUTHWEST AIRLINES – WN/SWA
PO Box 36611, Dallas, Texas 75235-1611, USA.

*SAS flies no fewer than 30 Boeing 737-600s, making it the largest operator of the smallest
member of the 737 NG family. (Rob Finlayson)*

Florida based Southeast Airlines oeprates four MD-80s. (Rob Finlayson)

737-700x131, 737-300x194, 737-500x25, 737-200x32.
On order: 737-700x107.

SPANAIR – JK/JKK
Aeropuerto de Palma de Mallorca, Palma de Mallorca, Spain.
767-300x2, A321-200x4, A320-200x7, MD-83x24, MD-82x10, MD-87x3.
On order: A321-200x1, A320-200x4.

SPIRIT AIRLINES – NK/NKS
2800 Executive Way, Mirimar, Florida 33025, USA.
MD-87x1, MD-83x3, MD-82x15, MD-81x6, DC-9-40x2, DC-9-30x4.

SRILANKAN AIRLINES – UL/ALK
Echelon Square, Colombo 01, Sri Lanka.
A340-300x3, A330-4, A320-200x1.

STAR AIR – SRR
Copenhagen Airport South, DK-2791 Dragoer, Denmark.
757-200Fx1, 727-100Fx8.

STAR AIR – 5H/STQ
PO Box 4724, Jakarta 10610, Indonesia.
737-200x5.

STAR AIRLINES – 2R/SEU
Immeuble Horizon, 10 Allee Bienvenue, F93885 Noisy-le-Grande, France.
A330-200x1, A320-200x6.
On order: A330-200x1.

STERLING EUROPEAN AIRLINES – NB/SNB
Copenhagen Airport South, DK-2791 Dragoer, Denmark.
737-800x6.

SUDAN AIRWAYS – SD/SUD
PO Box 2619, Khartoum, Sudan.
A300-600Rx2, A300-200x1, 707-320Cx3, 737-200x1, F27-600x1.

SUN COUNTRY AIRLINES – SY/SCX
2520 Pilot Knob Road, Mendota Heights, Minnesota 55120, USA.
737-800x6, 737-700x1.

SUNAIR – AQ
PO Box 736, Lanseria 1748, South Africa.
DC-9-32x3.

SUNEXPRESS – XQ/SXS
PO Box 28, Antalya TR-07100, Turkey.
737-800x4, 737-700x2.

SUN WORLD INTERNATIONAL AIRLINES – SM/SWI
PO Box 75030, Cincinnati, Ohio 45275-5030, USA.
727-200x2.

SURINAM AIRWAYS – PY/SLM
PO Box 2029, Paramaribo, Surinam.
DC-9-50x1, DHC-6-300x2.

SWIFTAIR – SWT
Ing. Torres Quevedo 14, Polygono Fin de Semana, E-28022 Madrid, Spain.

727-200Fx6, Convair 580Fx9, EMB-120Fx5, Metro IIIx2, MetroIIx1, Fairchild Merlin IVAx1.

SWISS – LX/CRX
Postfach, CH-4002, Basle, Switzerland.
MD-11x14, MD-83x10, MD-82x1, A330-200x13, A321-100x8, A320-200x12, A319-100x7, RJ100x15, RJ85x4, Saab 2000x29, Saab 340Bx12, ERJ 145x25.
On order: A340-300x13, Embraer 190x30, Embraer 170x30.

SYRIANAIR – RB/SYR
PO Box 417, Damascus, Syria.
747SPx2, 727-200x6, Il-76Mx4, Tu-154Mx3, Tu-134Bx6, A320-200x6, An-26x6, An-24x1, Yak-40x6.

TAAG-ANGOLA AIRLINES – DT/DTA
CP 3010, Luanda, Angola.
747-300x2, 737-200x5.

TACA INTERNATIONAL AIRLINES – TA/TAI
Edificio Caribe, San Salvador, El Salvador.
767-200x1, 737-200x10, A320-200x28, A319-100x10.
On order: A320-200x13

TACA PERU – TPU
Avenida Comandante Espinar 331, Lima 18, Peru.
A320-200x1, A319-100x4.

TACV-CABO VERDE AIRLINES – VR/TCV
CP 1, Praia, Ilha do Santiago, Cape Verde Islands.
757-200x1, ATR 42-300x3, DHC-6-300x1.

TAJIKISTAN AIRLINES – 7J/TZK
Ul.Titova 32/1, 734006 Dushanbe, Tajikistan.
Tu-154Mx4, Tu-154Bx6, Tu-134Ax6, An-26x2, An-24x6, Yak-40x11.

TAM – JJ/TAM
Rua Gal. Pantaleo Telles 210, CEP-04355-040 Sao Paulo, Brazil.
A330-200x13, A320-200x29, A319-100x12, Fokker 100x50, Cessna 208Bx24, Cessna 208Ax2.
On order: A320-200x9, A319-100x2,

TAME – EQ/TAE
Avenida Amazonas 1354, PO Box 17-07-8736, Quito, Ecuador.
727-200x5, 727-100x2, F28-4000x2, BAe 748x2.

TAMPA – QT/TPA
Carrera 76 No 34A-61, Medellin, Colombia.
DC-8-71Fx3.

TANS – TJ/ELV
Avenida Arequipa 5200, Lima 18, Peru.
737-200x4, F28-1000x1.

TAP AIR PORTUGAL - TP/TAP
Apartado 50194, P-1704-801 Lisboa Codex, Portugal.
A340-300x4, A310-300x5, A321-200x3, A320-200x8, A319-100x16.

TAPO-AVIA – TPR
Ul. M Hasanovol 34, Tashkent 700016, Uzbekistan.
Il-76TDx4, An-12x2.

TARAZ WINGS – TWC
Taraz Airport, Taraz 484020, Kazakstan.
Yak-40x7.

TAROM – RO/ROT
Sos. Bucuresti-Ploiesti, Bucharest, Romania.
A310-300x2, 707-320Cx1, 737-700x2, 737-300x7, ATR 42-500x7.
On order: 737-800x4, 737-700x2.

TATARSTAN AIR – U9/KAZ
Kazan Airport, Kazan 420017, Russia.
Tu-154Mx2, Tu-154Bx3, Tu-134Ax3, Yak-42Dx8, Yak-40Kx1, An-26x1, An-24RVx4.

TCB-TRANSPORTES CHARTER DO BRASIL – TCJ
Rua Jaguara 707, CEP-30050-001 Sao Paulo, Brazil.
DC-8-63Fx2, DC-8-54Fx1, DC-8-52Fx1.

TEHRAN AIRWAYS – THR
Isfahan Airport, Iran.
Yak-42D x2.

TESIS – UZ/TIS
Ul. Profsoyuznaya 93a, Moscow 117858, Russia.
Il-76TDx9, Tu-154Bx2.

THAI AIRWAYS INTERNATIONAL – TG/THA
89 Vibhavadi Rangsit Super Highway, PO Box 1075 GOP, Bangkok 10900, Thailand.
747-400x16, 747-300x2, 777-300x6, 777-200x8, 737-400x10, MD-11x4, A330-300x12, A300-600x21, ATR 72-200x2.

Swiss – the reborn Crossair and Swissair – came to life on January 31 2002. (Ron Finlayson)

THOMAS COOK AIRLINES BELGIUM – FQ/TCW
Park Station, Woluwelaan 150B, B-1831 Ddiegem, Belgium.
A320-200x5.

TIKAL JETS AIRLINES – WU/TKC
Avenida Hincapie 18 Calle, Guatemala City 01013, Guatemala.
BAe 111-401x2, L 410UVPx3.

TITAN AERO – RTT
Ul. Krasnoarmeiskaya 11, Moscow 125167, Russia.
Il-76TDx2, Il-18x1.

TITAN AIRWAYS – AWC
Enterprise House, London Stansted Airport, Essex CM24 1QW, UK.
737-300x1, 146-200QCx3, ATR 42-300x2.

TMA CARGO – TL/TMA
PO Box 30, Beirut International Airport, Beirut 1001, Lebanon.
A310-300x1, 707-320Cx6.

TNT AIRWAYS – 3V/TAY
Rue de l'Aeroport, B-4460 Grace-Hollogne, Belgium.
747-400Fx1, A300B4-200Fx4, 146-300QTx8, 146-200QTx3.

TOP AIR – TOP
Ataturk Havalimani, Sefakoy-Istanbul TR-34640, Turkey.
727-200x3.

TOTAL – TTL
Rua Boa Ventura 2312, CEP-32170-310 Belo Horizonte, Brazil.
727-200Fx2, ATR 42-300x5, EMB-120x1, EMB-110x1.

TRADEWINDS AIRLINES – WI/TDX
PO Box 35327, Greensboro, North Carolina 27425-5327, USA.
L-1011Fx1, A300B4-200Fx7.

TRANSAERO AIRLINES – UN/TSO
Smolensky perenlok ∫, Moscow 121089, Russia.
Il-86x1, 737-700x2, 737-200x4.

TRANSAFRIK INTERNATIONAL – TFK
CP 2839, Luanda, Angola.
727-200Fx1, 727-100Fx8, L-382Gx12.

TRANS AIR BENIN – TNB
BP 0985, Cotonou 01, Benin.
727-200x1, L 410x2.

TRANS AIR CONGO – Q8/TSG
BP 4450, Point Noire, Brazzaville, Congo.
727-200x1, 727-100x2, An-12BPx1, An-24x3, Beech 1900Dx1.

TRANS ARABIAN AIR TRANSPORT – TRT
PO Box 1461, Khartoum, Sudan.
707-320Cx1, An-12x1.

TRANSASIA AIRWAYS – GE/TNA
139 Cheng Chou Road, Taipei, Taiwan.
A321-100x6, A320-200x3, ATR72-500x8, ATR 72-200x4.

TRANS ATTICO – ETC
PO Box 7953, Sharjah, United Arab Emirates.
Il-76TDx2, An-12Bx2, An-26Bx1.

TRANSAUSTRALIAN AIR EXPRESS
PO Box 159, Sanctuary Cove, Qld, Australia.
727-200Fx6, 727-100Fx1.

TRANS AVIA EXPORT CARGO AIRLINES – AL/TXC
Ul.Zakharova 44, 220034 Minsk, Belarus.
Il-76x24.

TRANSAVIA AIRLINES – HV/TRA
PO Box 7777, NL-1118, Schipol Airport Centre, Netherlands.
757-200x4, 737-800x16, 737-700x1, 737-300x3.
On order: 737-700x7.

TRANSBRASIL – TR/TBA

Tunisair flies seven 737-600s. (Rob Finlayson)

Rua General Pantaleao Telles 40, CEP-04355-040 Sao Paulo, Brazil.
767-300x1, 767-200x3, 737-400x4.

TRANSJET AIRWAYS – SWL
Djupdalsvagen 25, S-192 65 Sollentuna, Sweden.
747-200x1, 747-100x1, MD-83x6.

TRANSMERIDIAN AIRLINES – T9/TRZ
680 Thornton Way, Lithia Springs, Georgia 30122, USA.
757-200x2, 727-200x5.

TRANSMILE AIR SERVICES – TH/TSE
Transmile Centre, SAAS Airport, Subang 47200, Malaysia.
727-200Fx2, 737-200x6.

TRANS SAHARA AIR – SBJ
PO Box 215, Kano, Nigeria.
727-200x1.

TRANS STATE AIRLINES – 9N/LOF
9275 Genaire Drive, St Louis, Missouri 63134-1912, USA.
ERJ 145x12, ERJ 140x10, ATR 72-200x3, ATR 42-300x5, J41x25, J32x7.

TRANSTEL – TTG
BP 10032, Lome, Togo.
DC-9-32x1, Viscount 800x2.

TRAVEL SERVICE AIRLINES – QS/TVS
PO Box 119, CZ-160 Prague 6, Czech Republic.
737-800x4, 737-400x2.

TRAVEL SERVICE HUNGARY – TVL
Oktober 6, H-1051 Budapest, Hungary.
737-400x1.

TRETYAKOVA AIR TRANSPORT – TKO
Box 7, Vastryakovo 142791, Russia.
Il-62Mx3, Il-18x2, Tu-134x1.

TSELINA – TZL
Astana Airport, Astana 473026, Kazakstan.
Tu-154Mx1, An-24x3.

TULPAR AVIATION COMPANY – TUL
Prospekt Pobody 15, Kazan 420138, Russia.
Yak-42Dx6, Yak-40Kx4.

TUNINTER – UG/TUI
10 rue de l'Artisant, Tunis 2035, Tunisia.
737-200x1, ATR 72-200x2, ATR 42-300x1.

TUNISAIR – TU/TAR
Boulevard 7 Novembre, Carthage, Tunis 2035, Tunisia.
A300-600Rx3, A320-200x12, A319-100x2, 737-700x1, 737-600x7, 737-500x4, 737-200x4.

TURAN AIR – 3T/URN
Mardanov Brothers Street 102, Baku 370022, Azerbaijan.

Tu-154Mx2, Tu-154Bx2.

TURKISH AIRLINES – TK/THY
Genel Yonetim Binsai, Yesilkoy-Istanbul TR-34830, Turkey.
A340-300x7, A310-300x7, 727-200Fx1, 737-800x26, 737-400x16, 737-500x2, RJ100x9, RJ70x3.

TURKMENISTAN AIRLINES – T5/TUA
Chary Nurimova Street 3A, 744000 Ashkhabad, Turkmenistan.
Il-76x4, 757-200x4, 737-300x3, 717-200x3, Tu-154Bx1, Yak-42Dx2, Yak-40x5, An-26x2, An-24x3.

TYROLEAN AIRWAYS – VO/TYR
Postfach 98, Innsbruck A-6026, Austria.
Fokker 70x6, CRJ200x12, Dash 8-400x6, Dash 8-300x14
On order: CRJ200x3, Dash 8-400x2.

TYROLEAN JET SERVICE – TJS
Postfach 101, Innsbruck A-6026, Austria.
328JETx2.

TYUMEN AIRLINES – 7M/TYM
Roshchino Airport, Tyumen 625033, Russia.
Il-76x5, Tu-154Bx7, Tu-134Ax9, An-12x1, An-24Bx6, Yak-40Kx1.

TYUMENAVIATRANS – P2/TMN
Piekhanovo Airport, Surgut 628422, Russia.
Tu-154Mx8, Tu-154Bx3, Tu-134Ax4.

UKRAINE INTERNATIONAL AIRLINES – PS/AUI
Prospekt Peremogy 14, Kiev 01135, Ukraine.
737-300x3, 737-500x3, 737-200x2.
On order: 737-700x1.

UKRAINIAN CARGO AIRLINES – UCA
Melnikova Street 24, Kiev 04050, Ukraine.
Il-78x2, Il-76x20, Tu-154Bx1, An-12x2, An-26x1.

UM AIR – UF/UKM
22 Pavlovskaia Str, Kiev 01135, Ukraine.
Yak-42Dx1, Tu-134Ax2.

UNI AIR – B7/UIA
100 Chang-An East Road, Taipei 104, Taiwan.
MD-90x13, Dash 8-300x12, Dash 8-200x1, Dornier 228-200x3.

UNITED AIRLINES – UA/UAL
PO Box 66100, Chicago, Illinois 60666-0100, USA.
747-400x44, 747-200x5, 777-200x60, 767-300x37, 767-200x22, 757-200x97, 727-200x70, 737-300x101, 737-500x57, 737-200x21, A320-200x97, A319-100x55.
On order: 777-200x1, A320-200x20, A319-100x23.

UNIVERSAL AIRLINES – UW/UVG
142 Regent Street, Georgetown, Guyana.
767-300x1.

UPS AIRLINES – 5X/UPS
1400 North Hurstbourne Parkway, Louisville, Kentucky

A winglet equipped Virgin Blue 737-700 gets airborne. (Paul Sadler)

40223, USA.
747-200Fx9, 747-100Fx12, 767-300Fx32,
757-200Fx75, 727-200Fx8, 727-100Fx51, MD-11Fx6,
DC-8-73Fx26, DC-8-71Fx23, A300F4-600Fx7.
On order: MD-11Fx7, A300F4-600Fx45.

URAL AIRLINES – U6/SVR
Ul. Sputnikov 6, Ekaterinburg 620910, Russia.
Il-86x3, Tu-154Mx2, Tu-154Bx13, An-24x3.

US AIRWAYS – US/USA
2345 Crystal Drive, Arlington, Virginia 22227-0001, USA.
A330-300x9, A321-200x33, A320-200x24, A319-
100x66, 767-200x11, 757-200x34, 737-400x54,
737-300x85, 737-200x51, MD-82x10, MD-81x14,
Fokker 100x40.
On order: A330-300x1, A321-200x8, A320-200x21,
A319-100x3.

USA JET AIRLINES – JUS
2068 East Street, Willow Run Airport, Belleville,
Michigan 48111-1278, USA.
DC-9-30Fx4, DC-9-15Fx8, Falcon 20Cx13.

USA 3000 – U5/GWY
335 Bishop Hollow Road, Newton Square, Pennsylvania 19073, USA.
A320-200x5.

UZBEKISTAN AIRWAYS – HY/UZB
Movarounnakhr kucasi 41, Tashkent 700060,
Uzbekistan.
Il-86x10, Il-76TDx15, Il-62Mx8, Il-114x2, 767-300x4,
757-200x3, A310-300x3, Tu-154Mx3, Tu-154Bx14,
RJ85x3, An-12x2, An-24x11, Yak-40x12.

VARIG – RG/VRG
Av. Almirante Silvio de Noronha 365, CEP-20021-
010 Rio de Janeiro, Brazil.
777-200x2, 767-300x6, 767-200x6, 737-800x2,
737-700x5, 737-400x4, 737-300x32, 737-200x7.
On order: 777-200x4, 767-300x6, 737-800x10,
737-700x4.

VARIG LOG – 4V/VLO
Rua Leopoldo de Bulhoes 40, CEP-04022-020 Sao
Paulo, Brazil.
DC-10-30Fx3, 727-200Fx2, 727-100Fx4.

VASO AIRLINES – VSO
Ul. Tsiolkovskogo 27, Voronezh 394029, Russia.
Il-86x2, An-12BPx1, An-24RVx1.

VASP – VP/VSP
Aeroporto de Congonhas, CEP-04626-910, Sao

Paulo, Brazil.
A300B2-200x3, 727-200x3, 737-300x4,
737-200x22.

VENESCAR INTERNACIONAL – V4/VEC
Seccion Venscar, Maiquetia 1161, Venezuela.
727-100Fx2, ATR 42-300Fx3.

VIA BULGARIAN AIRWAYS – VL/VIM
54 GM Dimitrov Boulevard, Sofia BG-1125, Bulgaria.
Tu-154Mx5.

VIETNAM AIRLINES – VN/HVN
200 Nguyen Son Road, Hanoi 1000, Vietnam.
767-300x6, A321-100x2, A320-200x10, Fokker
70x2, ATR 72-500x5, ATR 72-200x6.
On order: 777-200x6.

VIRGIN ATLANTIC – VS/VIR
Crawley Business Quarter, Crawley, West Sussex
RH10 2NU, UK.
A340-600x2, A340-300x10, 747-400x13, 747-200x6.
On order: A380-800x6, A340-600x8.

VIRGIN BLUE AIRLINES – DJ/VOZ
PO Box 1034, Spring Hill, Qld 4004, Australia.
737-800x10, 737-700x17, 737-400x1, 737-300x1.
On order: 737-800x4.

VIRGIN EXPRESS – TV/VEX
Building 116, B-1820 Melsbroek Airport, Belgium.
737-400x7, 737-300x7.

VLADIVOSTOK AIR – XF/VLK
Ul. Portovaya 41, Artem 692811, Russia.
Il-76x3, Tu-154Mx4, Tu-154Bx3, Yak-40x11.

VOLARE AIRCOMPANY – VRE
Ul. Svyatoshinskaya 2, Kiev 03115, Ukraine.
Il-76x5, An-12x6.

VOLARE AIRLINES – VA/VLE
Corso Garibaldi 186, I-36016 Tiene, Italy.
A330-200x4, A321-200x2, A320-200x17.
On order: A330-200x1.

VOLGA AVIAEXPRESS – WLG
Volgograd Airport, Volgograd 400036, Russia.
Yak-42Dx3, Tu-134Ax2.

VOLGA-DNEPR AIRLINES – VI/VDA
Ul. Karbysheva 14, Ulyanovsk 432072, Russia.
An-124x10, Il-76TDx1, Yak-40x5.

VORONEZHAVIA – VRN
Vornezh Airport, Voronezh 394025, Russia.
Tu-134Ax8, An-24RVx3.

WALTAIR
Kinshasa, Republic of Congo.
Caravelle 10Bx1, Caravelle 11Rx1, Andoverx1.

WDL AVIATION – WDL
Postfach 98 02 67, D-51130 Cologne, Germany.
146-200x3, BA 146-100x1, F27-600Fx13, F27-400Fx2.

WESTJET – WS/WJA
5055 11th Street NE, Calgary, Alberta T2E 8N4,
Canada.
737-800x2, 737-700x12, 737-200x23.
On order: 737-700x26.

WETRAFA AIRLIFT
Ndjiili Airport, Kinshasa, Republic of Congo.
727-100x1, DC-9-32x1.

WHITE EAGLE AVIATION – WEA
17 Stycznia 47, Warsaw PL-02-146, Poland.
737-800x1, 737-400x1, ATR 42-300x1, L 410UVPx7.

WORLD AIRWAYS – WO/WOA
101 World Drive, Peachtree City, Georgia 30269, USA.
MD-11Fx7, MD-11Fx1, DC-10-30x3, DC-10-30Fx4.

WUHAN AIRLINES – CWU
435 Jianshe Dadao, 430030 Wuhan, China.
737-800x2, 737-300x6, MA-60x3, Y7-100Cx 6.

XIAMEN AIRLINES – MF-CXA
Gaoqi International Airport, 361009 Xiamen, China.
757-200Cx 6, 737-700x6, 737-300x4, 737-500x6,
737-200x2.
On order: 757-200Xx1, 737-700x4.

YAKUTSK AIRLINES – KUT
Ul. Gagarina 8, Yakutsk 677014, Russia.
Tu-154Mx2, An-24RVx1.

YAMAL AIRLINES – YL/LLM
Ul. Aviatsionnaya 27, Salekhard 626603, Russia.
Tu-154Mx1, Tu-154Bx1, Tu-134Ax8, An-74x3, An-
24RVx2, Yak-40x6.

YEMENIA – IY/IYE
PO Box 1183, Sana'a, Republic of Yemen.
Il-76x2, A310-300x4, 727-200x5, 737-800x3,
737-200x3, L-382Cx2,
Dash 7x3, DHC-6-300x3.

YER-AVIA – ERV
Busand Street 1/3, 375010 Yerevan, Armenia.
Il-76Mx2.

YES – YSS
Rotunda Nuno Rodrigues, P-2685-223 Portela LRS,
Portugal.
L-1011-500x2.

YUZHNAYA AIRCOMPANY – UGN
Ul. Baizakova 316/40, Almaty 480000, Kazakstan.
Tu-154Bx2, An-24x1.

ZANTOP INTERNATIONAL AIRLINES – ZAN
840 Willow Run Airport, Ypsilanti, Michigan 48196-
0840, USA.
DC-8-54Fx2, L-188Fx13, Convair 640Fx5.

ZHONGYUAN AIRLINES – CYN
Xinzheng International Airport, 451161 Zhengzhou,
China.
737-300x2, Y7-100Cx2.

ZIP AIR – 3J
Calgary, Canada.
737-200x6.

Civil Aircraft Index